BRITANNICA JUNIOR
ENCYCLOPÆDIA

For Boys and Girls

14
TUV

Prepared under the supervision of the editors of ENCYCLOPÆDIA BRITANNICA

William Benton, *Publisher*

ENCYCLOPÆDIA BRITANNICA, INC.

Chicago   London   Toronto   Geneva   Sydney   Tokyo   Manila

Library of Congress Catalog Card Number: 70-157519
International Standard Book Number: 0-85229-164-7

KEY TO PRONUNCIATION

It is of especial importance that an encyclopaedia for children give the pronunciation where the boy or girl might go astray. In all such instances the pronunciation in BRITANNICA JUNIOR ENCYCLOPÆDIA is clearly marked. The accent is shown by the mark (′). The sounds for the different letters, when not self-evident, are as follows:

ā as in *pale*
ã as in *care*
ă as in *bat*
ä as in *farm*
ȧ as in *task*
a̤ as in *ball*
ē as in *be*
ĕ as in *met*

ẽ as in *her*
ī as in *mice*
ĭ as in *tin*
ō as in *cold*
ŏ as in *not*
ô as in *for*
oi as in *oil*
o͞o as in *loot*

ou as in *out*
ū as in *use*
ŭ as in *run*
ụ as in *pull*
ü as in French *début*, German *über*
g (always hard) as in *gay*
j for *g* as in *gentle*
K for *ch* as in German *Bach* or Scottish *loch*

ṅ (nasal) as in French *bon*
th as in *think*
t̶h̶ as in *thee*
t̨ as in *picture* (Sound varies from *t* to *ch*)
z̨ as in *pleasure* (Sound varies from *z* to *zh*)

Printed in the U.S.A.

THE UNIVERSITY
OF CHICAGO

BRITANNICA JUNIOR ENCYCLOPÆDIA IS PUB-
LISHED WITH THE EDITORIAL ADVICE OF THE
FACULTIES OF THE UNIVERSITY OF CHICAGO
AND THE UNIVERSITY LABORATORY SCHOOLS

Let knowledge grow from more to more and thus be human life enriched

Courtesy, The Sunday Times, London

The age of automation and its television programs have made robots favorite toys. Some of these battery-operated or key-wound mechanical men walk, talk, flash lights, or even throw suction darts. See TELEVISION; TOY.

TABERNACLE (*tăb'ēr năk''l*), according to the Bible, was the portable sanctuary built by the Israelites in the wilderness after their exodus from Egypt. It was used by them for sacrifices and divine worship throughout their 40-year journey through the wilderness.

The Book of Exodus (chapters 25–31; 35–40) describes the tabernacle. The "tent of meeting," or the "tabernacle of the congregation," as it is referred to in the Bible, was of very light construction. It consisted mainly of tapestry curtains and wooden frames overlaid with gold. The curtains were hung over these frames, forming the northern, southern, and western walls. The eastern end was an entrance that led to the interior, which was divided by curtains into two rooms: the outer room, referred to as the "holy place"; and the inner room, referred to as the "most holy place" or "holy of holies."

The entire structure was surrounded by a court that was enclosed by linen curtains. In the court were an altar for burnt offerings and a basin for washing. A number of elaborate furnishings adorned the interior. In the "holy place" were the table holding consecrated breads, the seven-branched candlestick, and the altar of incense. The "most holy place" housed the sacred Ark of the Covenant, which was a chest containing the two tablets of the Ten Commandments. To the Israelites the Ark was a symbol of God's presence and protection.

After the Israelites settled in Canaan, the tabernacle rested first in Shechem and later in Shiloh. In the days of King David a new tabernacle was built for the Ark on Mount Zion in Jerusalem. It was not until the time of King Solomon that a permanent temple was built in Jerusalem to take the place of the tabernacle that had its origin in the days of Moses.

Within the tabernacle reposed the sacred Ark of the Covenant, containing the tablets inscribed with the Ten Commandments.

Brown Brothers

TABLE (*tā'b'l*) **TENNIS** (*tĕn'ĭs*) is an indoor game similar to lawn tennis. It is played on a table with rackets and a small ball. The official table is $2\frac{1}{2}$ feet high, 9 feet long, and 5 feet wide. It is divided in the center by a net six inches high. The plywood rackets, or paddles, are covered by pebbled rubber. The hollow celluloid ball weighs between 37 and 41 grains and has a circumference between $4\frac{1}{2}$ and $4\frac{3}{4}$ inches.

Two (singles) or four (doubles) people may play the game. Play begins when the server, standing behind his end line, strikes the ball with his racket so that it bounces on his side of the net, clears the net, and bounces on his opponent's side of the net. Thereafter, each player must return the ball over the net to his opponent's side. Failure to do so results in a point for the opponent. The ball must be allowed to bounce once before it may be returned. Each player serves for five points. The serve then passes to the opposite side. Game is 21 points, unless the score is tied at 20-all. At 20-all, each serve alternates until one player or side gains a lead of two points, thereby winning the game.

In doubles, the serve must be made from the server's right court to the receiver's right court, and each player on a team must alternate with his partner in striking the ball.

The exact origin of table tennis is not known. It may have been devised in New England or in England in the late 19th century. The game was known as Gossima early in its history and

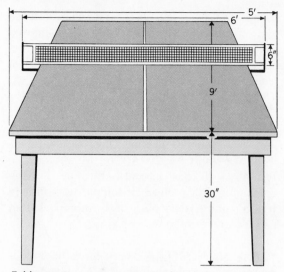

Table tennis, or ping-pong, is played by two or four players on a regulation-sized table. Its measurements are standardized by the International Table Tennis Federation (I.T.T.F.).

was later named ping-pong by the manufacturers of the game's equipment. The game's official name is table tennis.

Championship tournaments are especially popular in Europe and in the Orient. The International Table Tennis Federation (I.T.T.F.) establishes the rules. In the United States the rules are administered by the U.S. Table Tennis Association, which is affiliated with the I.T.T.F.

TABOO (*tă bōō'*) is a term meaning banned, forbidden, or prohibited. The term usually refers to customs, actions, or things.

The concept of taboo is found in many societies, but it is most common in Polynesia. The term is of Polynesian origin and usually is used in reference to primitive Polynesian societies. The English explorer Captain James Cook, sailing the South Pacific in 1771, found the word *tabu* (sometimes *tapu* or *kapu*) widely used among the natives of Tonga (Friendly Islands). His written account of the voyage introduced the word into the English language.

The taboos of Polynesia cover all parts of daily life. They are basically religious. A person, place, thing, or action is usually taboo because it is thought to have some supernatural quality—some sacred, mystical power. This is true especially of the mysterious, strange, or unknown. However, a thing also may be taboo because it is unclean or in some other way harmful. Even in these instances the underlying reason for the taboo is usually religious.

Taboo is enforced by custom, not by written law. When a taboo is violated, the offender need not be punished by his society because it is believed that punishment—such as death, disease, or accident—is automatic. The individual offender or the members of his family may be punished. In some cases violation of a taboo may endanger the entire society, bringing famine or pestilence.

Taboos may be classed in two groups: A person, place, thing, or action may be taboo because of its basic nature or because it has been proclaimed taboo. A priest, ruler, or sacred animal would fall in the first group. Because of their holiness, they are held to be taboo. The taboo may be that they are not to be touched, or in some cases not to be seen. A plot of ground or a particular food declared taboo by a priest or other person of authority are examples of the second group.

A large number and a wide variety of taboos exist. They date from early cultures and are found throughout the world. Taboos are common in other parts of the South Pacific as well as in Polynesia. The Indians of North America also had many taboos affecting daily living. Taboos are common among certain tribes of Africa. In parts of the world, prohibitions are not labeled taboos. Rather, they are linked with superstitions, social customs, or religious rituals. In India the flesh of the cow, a sacred animal, is not to be eaten, and according to the Hindu caste system, some persons are considered untouchable. In Western societies, many of the rituals connected with religion, marriage, and death might be called taboos. These usually differ from the primitive taboos in that they are not always connected with the forbidden. (See SUPERSTITION.)

TACONITE (*tăk'ō nīt*) is an iron-bearing rock found mainly in the Mesabi Range of northern Minnesota. It is composed of magnetite, hematite, quartz, and several silicates. It contains from 25 to 30 per cent iron. Other iron ores

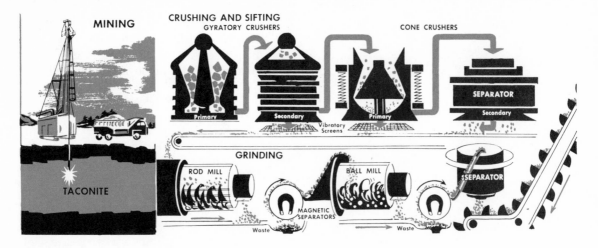

MINING

CRUSHING AND SIFTING
GYRATORY CRUSHERS

CONE CRUSHERS

SEPARATOR
Secondary

Primary

Secondary

Primary

Vibratory Screens

TACONITE

GRINDING

ROD MILL

BALL MILL

SEPARATOR

MAGNETIC SEPARATORS

Waste

Waste

such as magnetite or hematite are much richer in iron. Because of this taconite was not mined while other ores were more easily obtained. When the plentiful supply of other ores began to diminish, methods to extract iron from taconite were sought. Early experiments failed.

Because taconite is one of the hardest substances known to man, the iron could not be separated from the rock by the usual ways of drilling, grinding, and crushing. The particles of iron in taconite are almost microscopic in size and so widely scattered throughout the rock that it was necessary to grind the rock to powder. In powdered form the iron could be separated from the rock by magnetic action. Powdered iron, however, could not be used in the blast furnaces of steel mills, so a method was found to make the powder into pellets or chunks.

The engineering problems also have been solved. Drilling has been speeded up by the development of the jet piercer. This machine works on the principle that intense heat causes hard rock to spall, or chip. The jet piercer is mounted on a chassis. Attached to the front of the chassis is a tall derrick that raises and lowers the cutting unit in the hole that is being drilled. The unit feeds kerosene or light fuel oil and liquid oxygen to a burner, and burning gases shoot out from jets into the hole. Fine streams of water are shot into the burning area, where they instantly turn into steam. The heat from the burning gases causes the hard taconite to flake, and the steam flushes the flakes out of the hole. A hole sizer reams out the hole as the burner works its way down. The hole sizer is a toothed steel casing that fits over the burner. After the holes are made, explosives can be set

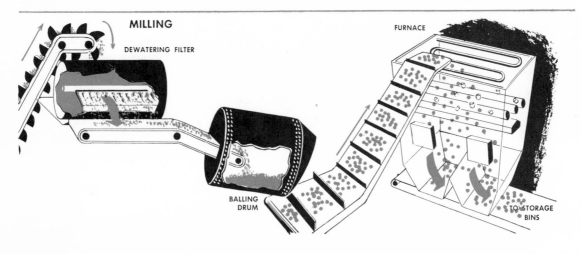

MILLING

DEWATERING FILTER

FURNACE

BALLING DRUM

TO STORAGE BINS

in them so the rock can be blasted into chunks. These chunks are crushed several times until they are small pieces.

In this form the rock is mixed with water and fed into a rod mill, which is a large, rotating cylinder containing steel rods. Rock and water enter one end, and, as the cylinder rotates, the cascading motion of the rods grinds the rock into smaller bits.

Material discharged from the rod mill goes through its first stage of magnetic separation. The partially separated iron mineral is then sent into ball mills, which are like rod mills except they contain steel balls. In the ball mills the material is ground into fine particles. It is then further separated from the nonmagnetic waste material. The iron mineral has much of the water removed and is filtered. After the filtering process the material is in the form of a cake of moist iron concentrate.

By one process the concentrate, mixed with powdered coal, is fed into a balling drum where the material is formed into pellets. These pellets are 64 per cent iron. Before they are shipped to manufacturers they are hardened by baking at high temperatures.

In another process the concentrate is mixed with powdered coke and fed onto a moving grate. There it is sintered, or formed into clinkers by heating without melting. (See IRON AND STEEL; MINING.)

TADZHIK (*ta jik'*) **SOVIET SOCIALIST REPUBLIC, U.S.S.R.,** is one of the southern republics of the Soviet Union. It is bordered by the Uzbek S.S.R. (Soviet Socialist Republic) to the west and northwest, the Kirghiz S.S.R. to the north, China to the east, and Afghanistan

Locator map of the Tadzhik Soviet Socialist Republic.

to the south. The republic has an area of 55,251 square miles. Its traditional name is Tadzhikistan. In 1924 the Soviet government established Tadzhikistan as an autonomous republic within the Uzbek S.S.R. In 1929 the autonomous republic became a soviet socialist republic.

The Tadzhik Republic is a mountainous land. Its eastern half is dominated by the lofty Pamir Mountains. Two of the highest peaks in the U.S.S.R., Communism Peak (24,590 feet) and Lenin Peak (23,405 feet), are located there. The summits of the Pamir Mountains are covered by snowfields and glaciers. One of the glaciers, the Fedchenko, extends nearly 45 miles and is one of the longest mountain glaciers in the world. The climate in the mountains is severe, dry, and extremely cold. Farming is possible only in the sheltered western valleys.

About 53 percent of the republic's inhabitants are Tadzhiks. The Tadzhiks are of Iranian descent and are traditionally Muslim. Agriculture has been their main livelihood for many years. Uzbeks, another agricultural people, make up 23 percent of the population, and Russians account for 13 percent.

Irrigated crops in the valleys include cotton, fruit, and rice. Silk is also important. On mountain slopes grow wheat and barley, and sheep, goats, cattle, and horses are raised.

The republic's industry is concentrated in the cities. These include Dushanbe, the capital and largest city, and Leninabad, the second largest city. The republic has good mineral resources, including lead, zinc, gold, fluorite, arsenic, bismuth, and salts. The most important industries process mineral and agricultural products and produce construction materials and textiles.

The Tadzhik S.S.R. has a population of 2,900,000 (1970).

TAFT (*tăft*), **LORADO** (*lō rä'dō*) (1860–1936), was a sculptor, as well as a lecturer, critic, and teacher of sculpture. He was born in Elmwood, Illinois. He studied at the University of Illinois in Urbana and then at the Ecole des Beaux-Arts in Paris.

When Taft returned to the United States, he went to Chicago, Illinois. There, in addition to creating many splendid pieces of work, he taught modeling at the Art Institute and lectured at The University of Chicago.

Taft's chief contribution to sculpture in the United States was the creation of portrait busts and public monuments. For the Columbian Exposition held in Chicago (1893), he modeled "The Sleep of the Flowers" and "The Awakening of the Flowers." His "Spirit of the Great Lakes" and "The Fountain of Time" are also in Chicago. His Washington Monument is in Seattle, Washington, a Columbus memorial fountain is in Washington, D.C., and the heroic statue "Black Hawk" overlooks the

Century Photos

"Black Hawk," Lorado Taft's monument to the Indians, overlooks the Rock River near Oregon, Illinois.

Rock River, near Oregon, Illinois. His war memorials and public fountains are in parks and squares throughout the country. In most of them the principal figures are expressed with joyous, hopeful spirit.

Among the books by Lorado Taft are his thorough and authoritative *The History of American Sculpture* and *Modern Tendencies in Sculpture.*

TAFT, ROBERT ALPHONSO (1889–1953), a United States senator, was the leader of the conservative wing of the Republican party in mid-20th century. He was often called "Mr. Republican."

Taft was born in Cincinnati, Ohio, on September 8, 1889. His family had a long record of public service. His father, William Howard Taft, was the 27th president of the United States. His grandfather had been in the cabinet of President Ulysses S. Grant.

Taft graduated first in his class from both Yale University and Harvard Law School. Returning to Cincinnati in 1913, he began to practice law. The following year he married Martha Bowers. During the 1920's and 1930's he served in the Ohio legislature.

In 1938 Taft was elected to the United States Senate, and was re-elected in 1944 and 1950. There he became the leader of the Republicans in the Senate and of the conservatives in his party. Taft was against most measures of the Franklin Roosevelt and Harry Truman administrations. He was against huge spending and more government control. He was, however, for public housing, federal aid to education, and a national health bill. An isolationist before World War II, Taft afterward supported a strong navy and air force as the best defense against the Communist threat. But he was against economic and military aid to foreign countries.

Taft sought the Republican presidential nomination several times. In his most important attempts he was defeated by Thomas E. Dewey in 1948, and by Dwight D. Eisenhower in 1952.

Upon Eisenhower's election, Taft became Senate majority leader. He was work-

Wide World

Robert Alphonso Taft.

ing to unite his party in support of the new administration when he died on July 31, 1953. A memorial bell tower to him was erected in Washington, D.C., in 1959.

TAFT, WILLIAM HOWARD (1857–1930), the 27th president of the United States, was the only man to serve as both president and chief justice of the Supreme Court.

A good natured man, Taft weighed more than 300 pounds. Although he seemed lazy at times and liked to put things off, he was honest, intelligent and capable.

William Howard Taft, U.S. President, 1909–1913.

Taft was born in Cincinnati, Ohio, on September 15, 1857. He was the son of Alphonso Taft, a successful lawyer who had been secretary of war and attorney-general in President Ulysses S. Grant's cabinet.

Early Career

Taft was a good student and was always at the top of his classes. He entered Yale University at the age of 17 and graduated second in his class. Returning home he studied law at the Cincinnati Law School and shared the highest honors with another student. He graduated from law school in 1880 and was admitted to the practice of law. However, he did not open a law office but worked as a newspaper reporter for the Cincinnati *Commercial*. The next year he was appointed assistant prosecuting attorney of Hamilton County. He was to hold various public offices most of the next 32 years. In 1882 he became a collector of internal revenue. Although he did a good job, he wanted to make law his career. He resigned in 1883 and opened a law office in partnership with

one of his father's former associates.

For the next four years Taft practiced law. He also served as assistant county solicitor. In 1886 he married Helen Herron, the daughter of a well known Cincinnati attorney. They had two sons and a daughter. One son, Robert, later became a Senator and Republican party leader. (See TAFT, ROBERT ALPHONSO.) Mrs. Taft was an intelligent woman who worked and planned with the hope that her husband would some day become president. Taft, himself, was not as ambitious and was more interested in a career as a judge. There is little doubt that opportunities to advance in politics came to him because of his wife's ambition and his father's position as a leader in the Republican party.

In 1887 Taft was appointed to fill a vacancy on the Superior Court of Ohio. Two years later he was elected to continue on this court. This was the only time he was elected to public office until he became president.

Federal Service

Taft began his many years of service for the federal government when President Benjamin Harrison appointed him solicitor general of the United States in 1890. He prepared cases for the attorney general and argued many of the government's cases before the Supreme Court. He met many important people, and his work earned him a national reputation.

In 1892 Taft became a judge of the United States Circuit Court of Appeals and moved back to Ohio. For eight years he served as judge and during the last four years he was also a professor and dean at the Cincinnati Law School. These were years when many people were seeking ways to control the power of big business firms and to protect the workingman. There were also several violent strikes. As a judge, Taft had de-

Helen Taft.

clared that employees had the right to form labor unions but in most disputes between business and labor his personal feelings were generally on the side of the employer.

In 1900 President William McKinley appointed Taft president of the Philippine Commission. The United States had recently gained possession of the Philippine Islands as a result of the Spanish-American War. The army controlled the islands, but some Filipinos were in revolt against United States rule. Taft's job was to win the confidence of the people and to replace the military occupation with civilian government. In 1901 he became the first civil governor of the Philippines.

Taft was successful at a difficult task. He believed it would be many years before the Filipinos would be able to govern themselves but he believed that the United States held the islands only to help the native people. He set up local governments and a system of courts, started schools, improved sanitation and made many other public improvements.

When President Theodore Roosevelt offered to appoint him to the Supreme Court Taft refused because he did not feel he could leave the Philippines. In 1904, however, he returned to the United States to become Roosevelt's secretary of war. While holding this office he was sent on many important missions and traveled to many parts of the world. In 1906 when there was trouble in Cuba the United States sent in troops and Taft acted as governor until order was restored. The following year he visited the Panama Canal Zone, Cuba, and Puerto Rico. He reorganized the work of building the Panama Canal.

The Presidency

Taft became well known as an honest, capable public servant. With Roosevelt's support he easily gained the Republican nomination for president, with James S. Sherman nominated for vice-president. Taft was elected over the Democratic candidate, William Jennings Bryan, in 1908.

Taft did not want to be president and he was unhappy in the White House. He was a friendly man but not a politician. His attitude

Brown Brothers

Taft with his family. His son Robert, on the right, later became the Senate majority leader.

toward government was that of a judge who moves slowly and thinks about things carefully. Roosevelt had been a strong and active president who led the public and his party and enjoyed a good fight with Congress. As president, Taft was less willing to use the power of government to bring about social reforms. He had counted on his wife's judgment and advice but a serious illness weakened her health soon after he became president.

Nevertheless, Taft tried to improve the workings of the government and he was able to save money in the cost of operation. Also, his administration is given credit for many changes and improvements. The Department of Commerce and Labor was divided with the new secretary of labor becoming a member of the cabinet. A federal children's bureau was formed in the Department of Labor. The post office added the postal savings system, which gave small depositors the chance to save money without fear of bank failure. Also added was the parcel post service, which carried packages at low rates. The Interstate Commerce Commission was given increased powers by the Mann-Elkins Act (1910) and a law was passed requiring candidates in federal elections to report how much money they had spent in their campaign. New Mexico and Arizona entered the Union in 1912 bringing the number of states to 48. Alaska was given territorial government.

Brown Brothers

President Taft presented Wilbur and Orville Wright with a gold medal honoring their flight at Kitty Hawk.

Two new amendments were proposed by Congress. The 16th, starting the income tax, was approved by the states just before Taft left office. The 17th Amendment, providing for direct election of United States senators, became law a few months later.

Problems at Home

One act which caused Taft to lose much popularity was the Payne-Aldrich Tariff Act. The taxes on imports had been increasing since the War Between the States (1861–1865) and had raised the prices on things purchased by farmers and other consumers. Taft had promised lower tariff rates in his campaign. The Payne-Aldrich Tariff Act, as finally passed, lowered the duties on unimportant items but raised duties on 600 items. Although tariff rates remained high, Taft signed the bill and defended it.

Taft was in favor of the movement to conserve natural resources but many people came to believe that he was against conservation. Lands that Roosevelt had reserved he put up for public sale for he did not believe Roosevelt had the authority to withdraw these lands. At the same time, Taft persuaded Congress to give him the power to reserve valuable mineral deposits. He was the first president to withdraw oil lands from public sale.

Taft's secretary of the interior, Richard Ballin-

ger, was accused of dishonesty in helping private interests get valuable coal lands in Alaska. When an investigating committee of Congress cleared him of these charges, Taft dismissed Gifford Pinchot, chief of the Forest Service, who had accused Ballinger. This angered many Progressives. Pinchot had been appointed by Roosevelt and was a leader in the conservation movement.

Taft favored government regulation of trusts or the big business combinations that prevented competition in many industries. (See TRUST.) His administration actually started more cases against big business corporations than was done under Roosevelt, and Taft was really the greater "trust buster."

The Taft policy in China and Latin America came to be known as "dollar-diplomacy." Under this policy United States businessmen were encouraged to invest in foreign countries. They were to loan money to develop railroads and other projects. These would make a market for United States exports, and also help United States interests and influence.

During Taft's term as president, the people were demanding more reforms like those which Roosevelt had favored. But Taft did not do enough to satisfy the progressive Republicans in Congress. These Progressives revolted against the party leadership, and began to vote with the Democrats on some issues. This combination was responsible for some of the laws passed under the Taft administration. The Progressives did not trust Taft because of his support of the Payne-Aldrich tariff and because of the dismissal of Pinchot.

In 1912 Taft received the Republican nomination but the progressive Republicans withdrew and formed the Progressive party with Theodore Roosevelt as its nominee. (See PROGRESSIVE PARTY.) With the Republican vote split between Taft and Roosevelt the Democratic candidate, Woodrow Wilson, won easily. Taft received fewer votes than either Roosevelt or Wilson, carrying Utah and Vermont.

Taft's United States

While Taft was president, factories were first producing automobiles in large numbers, though

TAFT'S LIFETIME

1857	Taft born.
1861	War Between the States.
1869	Railroad reaches Pacific.
1878	Taft graduates from Yale.
1880	Taft a lawyer.
1887	Taft a judge.
1890	Sherman Anti-Trust Act. Taft solicitor-general.
1892	Taft circuit judge.
1898	War with Spain.
1901	Taft first governor of Philippines.
1903	1st airplane flight.
1904	Taft secretary of war.

PRESIDENCY	
1913	Taft to Yale.
1917	U.S. enters World War.
1921	Taft chief justice.
1929	Great depression.
1930	Taft dies.

Taft's Term of Office (1909–1913)

1909	Payne-Aldrich Tariff Act.
	NAACP founded.
	Peary reaches North Pole.
1910	Postal Savings bank.
	Population tops 91,000,000.
	Boys Scouts founded.
	Mann-Elkins Act.
	Presidential preference. Primary in Oregon.
1911	Revolution in Mexico.
	Amundsen reaches South Pole.
1912	Arizona and New Mexico enter Union.
	Titanic sunk.
	Revolution in China.

the nation had few of the good roads autos needed. The army had its first airplane and people were beginning to talk of air travel. A law required steamships leaving United States ports to carry a wireless radio. When the passenger liner *Titanic* hit an iceberg in 1912, a radio call for help brought aid in time to save some of the passengers.

Scientists were trying to wipe out hookworm, a parasite that infected millions of people. The new plastics industry began with the invention of bakelite. In 1909 Robert Peary reached the North Pole and two years later the Norwegian explorer Roald Amundsen reached the South Pole.

Negroes were beginning to move from South to North. In 1909 the National Association for the Advancement of Colored People (NAACP) was formed to help win equal rights for Negroes. In local and state governments the Progressives were still working for reforms. Many states were giving women the right to vote. Oregon adopted the presidential preference primary which permitted the people to help pick presidential candidates. Massachusetts set a minimum wage for women and children.

Later Years

Taft retired from the presidency to return to Yale University as a professor of law in 1913. In the same year he was elected president of the American Bar Association. He also lectured and wrote many magazine articles.

At the time of World War I, Taft supported Wilson's efforts to keep the United States out of the war. After the United States entered the war, he loyally supported the war effort. He was a joint chairman of the National War Labor Board, which was formed to settle labor disputes.

Taft favored Wilson's plan for a League of Nations. He gave speeches supporting the League but urged certain changes so that the Senate might approve it.

In 1921 President Warren Harding appointed Taft chief justice of the Supreme Court. He was happier in this position than he had ever been in the White House. Taft worked so hard that he finally had to resign because of failing health on February 3, 1930. He died about a month later on March 8.

TAILORBIRD (*tā′lẽr bẽrd′*), a bird of the Old World warbler family found in most of tropical and south temperate Asia. The most common species, the Indian tailorbird, is about five inches long and has a bright olive-green back and tail, reddish-brown head, brownish wings and light underparts.

The tailorbird (about five inches long) fastens leaves together to make its nest.

Their nests are built in the shape of a cone by sewing the edges of leaves together with plant fiber in a running stitch. In areas where cotton fibers are easy to find the stitches are knotted at both ends to stop them from slipping through the leaf. The name tailorbird came from their habit of sewing.

These nests are usually not made higher than three feet from the ground. In India, they may be placed in potted plants found on porches or in bushes close to a house. The nest itself, set inside the sewn leaf, is a rough cup of stringy plant material or hair. Into it three to four eggs are laid. The eggs are reddish or bluish-white usually spotted with reddish-brown. Both male and female share in the work of building the nest and taking care of the young. They feed on ants, mosquitoes, and other small insects.

The birds are usually quite friendly. They like to be with other birds, and often are found in groups in the forest. Because they are not afraid of people, they sometimes live near homes. Their songs are generally loud and cheery.

TAIPEI (*tī bā'*), **TAIWAN,** is the largest city of the island. It is the administrative center of Taiwan (Formosa), as well as the provisional capital of the Republic of China (Nationalist China).

Taipei is an inland city located near the island's northern tip. It is connected by railroad with Keelung (Chilung), a major port city along the island's north coast. The basin within which Taipei lies is rimmed with mountains. This is one of the chief agricultural areas of the island. The lower hillsides are in terraced rice paddies. The higher slopes are forested. The city's climate, like most of the island's climate, is subtropical. Mean annual temperatures are about 59 degrees Fahrenheit for January and about 83 degrees for July. Summer months are the most humid, but rainfall is abundant throughout the year.

Taipei is a planned city. Much of it is laid out in squares rather than the jumble of narrow twisting streets that characterizes many Asian cities. Thousands of pedicabs fill the downtown streets. Government buildings border the central square. The city is the home of National Taiwan University and the Taiwan Provincial Normal University. The industries reflect, in part, the region's agriculture, and they include the processing of tea, camphor, tobacco, and lumber.

Taipei, formerly Taihoku, was founded in 1708 by Chinese immigrants. It became the island's capital during the long period of Japanese occupation. The government of the Republic of China moved to Taipei in 1949. The population is 1,175,000 (1966). (See TAIWAN [FORMOSA], ASIA.)

TAIWAN (*tī wän*) **(FORMOSA)** (*fôr mō'sä*), **ASIA,** is an island in the western Pacific Ocean. It is the seat of the Republic of China (Nationalist China). Taiwan Strait, a channel about 100 miles wide, separates the island from mainland Asia. The island lies between the Philippine Islands on the south and Japan on the north.

The official name,

Pictorial Parade

Pedicabs are a common sight in the streets of Taipei.

Taiwan, as used by the Nationalist Chinese government includes numerous smaller nearby islands, such as Quemoy, Matsu, and the Pescadores. The island is known also as Formosa. This name comes from *Ilha Formos,* an expression used by Portuguese sailors meaning Island Beautiful.

Taiwan is large. High mountains extend north and south through the length of the island. Several peaks rise to more than 10,000 feet. On the east side of the island, the slopes are steep, often rising as cliffs from the sea. The slopes on the west side are not so steep. Along the Taiwan Strait is a flat, fertile coastal plain. Taiwan is part of the high west Pacific chain of volcanic islands. As a result, the island experiences numerous earthquakes every year.

The Tropic of Cancer passes through Taiwan. Except in the high mountains, the climate is subtropical. Average January temperatures in the lowlands range in the 60's, average July temperatures in the 80's. Snow occurs in the mountains, but the lowlands are mainly frost free. Monsoon winds bring rain to Taiwan in summer. The highlands are very humid. Mountain weather stations record more than 200 inches of rain a year. Destructive typhoons occur during late summer.

Forests are one of Taiwan's greatest natural resources. More than half of the island is forested, and forests cover most of the highlands. The type of forest varies with the elevation. Coniferous forests cover the higher slopes, but they are more difficult to reach. Lowland for-

Locator map of Taiwan.

ests include cypress, bamboo, palm, and camphor trees. Natural camphor is an export item of the island.

Taiwan has numerous mineral resources, but none are of world importance. Coal is the chief mineral product, but it is of low quality. Copper, gold, and sulfur occur in varying amounts. The island lacks most of the minerals necessary for heavy manufacturing. The greatest potential source of energy is hydroelectric power. Because there is abundant rainfall, there are many swift-flowing streams that can be used to generate electricity.

The people of Taiwan are mainly Chinese, and the official language is Chinese, or Mandarin. There are other peoples, including small groups of aborigines, who are of Indonesian origin. Each group of people reflects a distinct period of settlement in the history of Taiwan. Malays, Portuguese, Dutch, and Spaniards all lived on the island. Except for the aborigines who inhabit the central mountain sector, most Taiwanese live along the island's western coastal plain.

Taiwan is one of the most densely settled areas of the world. The population is mainly rural, but in recent decades the cities have been growing rapidly. Taipei, the island's largest city, is on the north end. It has been the temporary capital of the Republic of China since 1949. (See TAIPEI.) Keelung (Chilung)

FACTS ABOUT TAIWAN

CAPITAL: Taipei.
AREA: 13,952 square miles (including smaller islands).
POPULATION (1964 estimate): 12,445,000.
HIGHEST POINT: Yu Shan (Sinkao Shan) (12,959 feet).
FORM OF GOVERNMENT: Republic.
CHIEF OF STATE: President.
HEAD OF GOVERNMENT: Premier (president of the Executive Yuan).
POLITICAL DIVISIONS: 18 counties (including Quemoy and Matsu); 6 municipalities (including 1 administration).
CHIEF PRODUCTS: *manufactured,* food products, textiles, chemicals, glass, cement; *agricultural,* rice, sugarcane, sweet potatoes, tea, pineapples, mushrooms.
MONETARY UNIT: New Taiwan dollar; 40.10 New Taiwan dollars equal one U.S. dollar.

Dominis, © 1959 Time Inc.

Taiwan is a land of farmers. Rice, the chief crop, is grown in paddies all over the island. Because of the long growing season, several crops are harvested each year from a single paddy.

and Kaohsiung are the principal ports. Kaohsiung, in the south, is the island's most industrialized city. Other cities include Taichung, Tainan, and Changhua. All are within Taiwan's densely populated western lowland.

The economy of Taiwan is basically agricultural. Most of the people depend upon farming for a livelihood. Many also earn a living in fishing activities. Rice is the leading crop. Sugarcane is the island's chief export. The island is one of the world's largest producers of sugar. Tea still ranks as a leading export item, although its relative importance has declined. Other important crops include sweet potatoes, pineapples, peanuts, mushrooms, tobacco, ramie, hemp, jute, bananas, wheat, soybeans, corn, and various fruits. Taiwan is self-sufficient in most basic foodstuffs.

Japan is responsible for much of Taiwan's industrial development. During the years of Japanese occupation, many products of the island were used to offset shortages in Japan. Today food processing is the island's major industry. This includes sugar refining, rice milling, and mushroom and pineapple canning. Citronella oil, from citronella grass, also is an important agricultural product.

The development of hydroelectric power has encouraged the growth of manufacturing. The textile industry (cotton, wool, rayon, and silk) is expanding. Other factories produce chemical fertilizers, which are needed to replenish the fertility of the island's soil. Glass, leather and rubber goods, electrical equipment, cement, paper, refined metal, and petroleum also are products of Taiwan's industry.

The people, language, and religious characteristics of Taiwan reflect Chinese culture. It has not always been so. The island was known to the Chinese as early as the 7th century. Before the 17th century, different peoples visited and settled Taiwan. Chinese, Portuguese, Spaniards, and Dutch each maintained settlements. Permanent Chinese occupation did not begin until 1661 when refugees of the Ming government fled from the mainland during the Manchu invasion. Eventually all previous settlers except the aborigines were driven away.

The island became a province of China in

Kaohsiung, the industrial center of Taiwan, is a port city in the southern part of the island.

Hedda Morrison, Camera Press-Pix from Publix

1886. It was ceded to Japan by China in 1895 after the Sino (Chinese)-Japanese War. Much of Taiwan's economic and population growth took place during the 50 years of Japanese occupation. The Japanese used Taiwan as a base of operation during World War II. Upon the defeat of the Japanese in 1945, the island was returned to China.

Following the war the Communists gained control of mainland China, and in 1949 the Nationalist government was forced to leave. Led by Chiang Kai-shek, the Nationalists made Taiwan the center of the Republic of China. It is now the only Chinese territory (along with certain smaller islands) controlled by the Nationalist government.

The Nationalists regard Taiwan only as a province of China. They hope eventually to regain control of the mainland. They consider theirs to be the legal government of China. Several Western countries recognize it as such, and it is a member of the United Nations. The Communists, however, consider the government at Peking to be the only legal one and consider Taiwan a province of the People's Republic of China. (See CHIANG KAI-SHEK; CHINA.)

TAIYUAN (*tī'yü än'*), **CHINA,** is an industrial city located in the hilly lands of northern China west of the China Plain. It is the capital of Shansi Province. Surrounding the city is a densely populated agricultural plain of the Fen Ho, a tributary of the Hwang Ho (Yellow River). The leading crops of the plain are the grains wheat and kaoliang, and tobacco, cotton, fruits, and vegetables.

Near Taiyuan are abundant supplies of iron ore and high-grade coal. Since coming under Communist control in 1949, heavy industry has been emphasized at Taiyuan, especially steelmaking. Other industries produce cement, fertilizer, flour, and textiles. The city's educational institutions include Taiyuan Institute of Technology and a medical college.

Taiyuan is an old city, known to exist since the 3rd century, B.C. It was an important defensive stronghold against Mongol invasions and occupied a strategic location between Peking to the northeast and Sian to the southwest. It was visited by Marco Polo in the 13th century. Taiyuan became the capital of Shansi Province during the Ming dynasty (1368–1644). The city was controlled by the Japanese from 1937 to 1945. The population is 1,053,000 (1958 estimate).

TAJ MAHAL (*täj mä häl'*), at Agra, India, is one of the most beautiful buildings in the world. It is the perfect example of Islamic architecture and the costliest tomb in history. It was built by the Mogul emperor Shah Jahan in the 17th century in memory of his favorite wife, Mumtaz Mahal. Taj Mahal, which means "Chosen One of the Palace," is a shortened form of her name.

When Mumtaz Mahal died in 1631, the emperor was heartbroken and even considered giving up his throne. The best architects and artists of India, Turkey, Persia, and Arabia were hired to plan a magnificent tomb for her. Ustad Isa, who was either Persian or Turkish, was chosen to direct the project, begun in 1632. More than 20,000 men worked on the building and grounds over a period of 22 years. The style of the building is Persian and Muslim, because Shah Jahan's ancestors came from Persia (Iran) and brought along their native arts and Islam faith.

At the entrance to the Taj Mahal is a courtyard. A towering red sandstone gateway opens into a beautiful garden of flowering shrubs, cypresses, and marble walks. Lily pools reflect the Taj. In spite of its great size, the Taj is so perfectly proportioned and carved that it seems barely to touch the ground. On terraces at either side stand identical mosques: one a true place of worship, the other a storehouse. From a marble platform 312 feet square, with minarets (towers) at the four corners, the Taj rises 243 feet above garden level. Of white marble, the eight-sided building is decorated with semiprecious stones and religious sayings from the Koran.

On the opposite bank of the Jumna River, Shah Jahan planned to build an exact copy, of black marble, for himself. The two were to be connected with a silver bridge, as a symbol of their love. This project was ended in 1658 when the shah's son imprisoned him in the palace. From then on, until he was buried at his wife's side in the central hall of the Taj, the emperor's chief pleasure lay in gazing across the river at the Taj Mahal. (See Plate 1 in INDIA.)

TALC (tălk) is a fairly common, crystalline mineral made up of magnesium, silicon, oxygen, and hydrogen in chemical combination. It is closely related to mica. (See MICA.) As in mica, the atoms of silicon and oxygen are linked together into sheets. In talc, pairs of the silicon-oxygen sheets are held close together by other atoms of magnesium, oxygen, and hydrogen. Many of talc's properties are a direct result of this arrangement into sheets of atoms. When talc is rubbed, for example, these flake-like sheets easily slide over one another. This makes talc feel greasy, or soapy, to the touch. Talc is one of the softest minerals known; it can be scratched with a fingernail.

Talc is commonly pale green in color, but pure white, gray, yellow, and deep green varieties are also found. All varieties are found in steatite and soapstone, both metamorphic rocks. (See ROCK.) Talc is usually found associated with amphibole, mica, quartz, and calcite.

Talc and talc-bearing rocks have many industrial uses. White talc in powdered form is used in paint, talcum powder, soaps, ceramic wares, and cosmetic creams and rouges. The colored varieties of talc are used in weatherproof cements, such as are used in roofing. Steatite is resistant to most acids. It is cut into blocks to make sinks and tabletops in laboratories and factories. Soapstone has been used for thousands of years to make carvings and vases.

In the United States, major talc deposits occur in several places along the Appalachian Mountains from Vermont to Georgia, and also in the western states of California, Washington, and Texas. Outside the United States large deposits are found in China, France, Italy, Austria, Norway, Germany, and India.

TALLAHASSEE (tăl'ä hăs'ē), **FLORIDA,** is the state capital. It is in the northern part of Florida, about 20 miles north of the Gulf of Mexico.

Surrounding it is a hilly farming region, dotted with lakes and springs. The city's industries process meat, pecans, tobacco, and other agricultural products. Manufacturing includes wood products and naval stores.

In addition to being a commercial center for the surrounding region, Tallahassee is a political and educational center. Florida State University and Florida Agricultural and Mechanical University are located there.

In the winter of 1539–1540, Hernando de Soto and his men found an Indian village where Tallahassee now stands. Florida was alternately controlled by Spain and England for several years. (See FLORIDA.) When it became a U.S. territory, Tallahassee was made the capital (1824). Florida became a state (1845); the city remained the capital.

Before the U.S. Civil War, Tallahassee was a center of social life. After the war, it suffered the troubles of the Reconstruction period, even though it was never taken by Union forces. The city has been growing rapidly since World War II.

The city has a council-manager form of government. The population is 71,897 (1970).

TALLEYRAND-PERIGORD (tăl'ĭ rănd pā'rē gôr), **CHARLES MAURICE DE** (1754–1838), was a French statesman. He was prominent in French and European politics during the French Revolution, the Napoleonic era, and the period that followed.

Talleyrand was born in Paris into a noble family. As a child he suffered an accident which lamed him for life. His limp made a military career impossible, so he entered the priesthood. He had little interest in a religious life and was not a conscientious priest, although he did become Bishop of Autun (1789).

When the French Revolution broke out that same year, Talleyrand was a member of the National Assembly which led the country. He had liberal views and proposed that the bankrupt government take church property in order to finance itself. When the Roman Catholics broke relations with the leaders of the Revolution, Talleyrand was one of the few leading churchmen who left the Church.

Talleyrand became noted for his diplomatic ability, and he served his country in its foreign affairs. When the Revolution turned into the Reign of Terror, however, he fled to England and the United States for a time. When Napoleon seized control of France, Talleyrand was made Foreign Minister. When he saw that Napoleon's ambition was to rule all of Europe and that France as a result would suffer, Talleyrand plotted against him.

When Napoleon was defeated and overthrown in 1814 by a coalition of European powers, Talleyrand was largely responsible for the restoration of the Bourbons as rulers of France. Talleyrand was appointed by King Louis XVIII to represent France in the peace negotiations. It was because of his diplomacy that France did not lose territory it had held before 1792. During the Congress of Vienna in 1815 he succeeded in recovering France's position as a leading European power.

In 1831, although he was 77 years old, Talleyrand again served his country during a crisis. He arranged an agreement between France and Great Britain by which those two countries supported the independence of Belgium. In this action Talleyrand remained true to the liberal principles that had influenced his life. Talleyrand has been much criticized for his lack of personal scruples. He became a rich man while in public office, although this kind of dishonesty was more widely accepted in his day than it is today. Before his death Talleyrand was received back into the Church.

TALMUD (*täl'mŏŏd*) is the body of Jewish law and tradition. It comes from the Hebrew word meaning instruction and is a collection of teachings set down by Jewish scholars.

Tradition says that when Moses received the Ten Commandments from God on Mount Sinai, he also was given another set of laws to be passed on by word of mouth. Tradition also teaches that Moses gave to the Jewish people the Torah, the written law consisting of the first five books of the Old Testament. He also taught them the unwritten or oral law, which was then handed down from generation to generation. The oral law was used to explain the meaning of the written law.

Many hundreds of years later it became necessary to write down the oral law. The explanations had become too numerous for any one person to memorize, and Jewish leaders disagreed about the correct explanation of the law. Then, too, many rabbis, who were the only leaders trained to explain the law, had been killed by the Romans.

The lifelong task of writing down the oral law was accomplished by Rabbi Judah the Prince in Palestine about A.D. 200. The material is arranged in six groups, called orders, and deals with (1) agriculture, (2) the sabbath and festivals, (3) marriage, (4) civil and criminal law, (5) ritual sacrifices, and (6) cleanliness. These orders are subdivided further into 63 tracts, or books. The whole work is called the Mishnah, meaning the second law.

A new series of oral explanations was developed around the Mishnah. Later it was put into written form and called the Gemara. These two parts make up the Talmud. The Mishnah serves as text, and the Gemara serves as a series of comments and notes. Two versions of the Gemara exist. One was compiled in the 4th century by the scholars of Palestine. The other was compiled at the beginning of the 5th century by the scholars of Babylonia. The Mishnah together with the Palestinian Gemara is known as the Palestinian Talmud. The Mishnah with the Babylonian Gemara is known as the Babylonian Talmud.

The Talmud contains two kinds of literature: Halachah, which is the law, and Haggadah, which consists of stories, legends, and sermons that explain the spirit of the law. The complete work is a vast collection that covers all phases of secular and religious life. It is therefore important not only as a study of religion and philosophy but as a history of Middle Eastern civilizations.

Orthodox and Conservative Judaism today accept the authority of the Talmud as divine. Reform Judaism does not believe that the Talmud has absolute binding power. All groups, however, recognize the importance of the Talmud in Jewish history and value its teachings highly.

Tamerlane, the "Prince of Destruction," was a renowned Oriental conqueror. He was an extremely tall man, with a large head, highly colored complexion, and white hair.

TAMERLANE (tăm′ĕr lăn) (1336–1405) was a Mongol Turk and one of the greatest of the Tatar conquerors. He was born in Kesh (now Shahr-i-Sabz), a town about 50 miles south of Samarkand (now in the U.S.S.R.). His father, Taragai, was said to be a chieftain of the Barlas tribe of Turkestan. According to legend, Taragai had a dream in which he saw a young man with a glowing sword whose radiance was so great that it illuminated the whole world. A sheik who interpreted the dream told Taragai that he would have a child who would someday become a world conqueror. When Taragai had a male child, he took him to the sheik, who was in the act of reading the Koran. The sheik was interrupted by his visitor upon reaching the word *Tamurru*, so they named the child Timur, meaning iron.

Entered into service as a warrior at an early age, Timur was wounded by arrows and became permanently crippled. Thereafter he was called Timur the Lame and was later known in Europe as Tamerlane or Tamburlaine. He was illiterate, though conversant with Turkish and Persian dialects, and he was a devoted Muslim. He first entered service under the emir (lord) Kazgan of Transoxiana and later married the emir's granddaughter. After the death of Kazgan, Timur eliminated his brother-in-law Prince Hussein and captured control of Transoxiana. By 1370 he ruled Samarkand.

Central Asia at the time was a frequent battleground of the various remnants of the disintegrated Mongol Empire. Timur's dream was to achieve its unification. From 1373 to the time of his death, he conducted 19 major campaigns, which brought his empire north to the Aral Sea, west to the Black Sea, south to the Indus Valley, and east to China.

Tamerlane achieved great fame by defeating a powerful army of the Great Khan of the Golden Horde and slaying more than 100,000 of his men. His military fame reached its peak when he destroyed the army of the ruler of the Ottoman Empire. Tamerlane inspired great fear by his cruel treatment of those who refused to surrender. In his campaign against the city of Baghdad, for example, Tamerlane laid the city waste, and upon the site he erected 120 pyramids from the skulls of 90,000 of the city's inhabitants. He became known as the "Prince of Destruction."

Although a great conqueror, Tamerlane, unlike his ancestor Genghis Khan, did not introduce new tactics of war. He differed also in being unable to form a stable empire among his nomadic followers. Tamerlane found little loyalty among local chieftains, and at his death the empire crumbled. The most famous account of his conquests is Christopher Marlowe's tragedy *Tamburlaine the Great*.

TAMMANY (tăm′ä nē) **HALL** is the executive committee of the Democratic party in New York County. It was once a powerful political organization that ran New York City.

The name comes from the Sons of St. Tammany, a group that opposed the British in the years before the American Revolution. This group was named after Tammanend, a Delaware Indian chief known for his wisdom and love of freedom.

After the Revolution the society broke up, but in 1789 a new group was formed, called the Society of St. Tammany or Columbian Order. The society wanted more democracy in New York government and opposed the wealthy people then running the city and state government. It supported Thomas Jefferson and Aaron Burr in national politics and De Witt Clinton in local politics. Before long, Tammany Hall, as it had come to be known, was the Democratic party in New York City.

Tammany Hall reached its position of power for several reasons. Before the 1820's, people without property could not vote. Tammany joined such citizens in their fight for the right to vote. When the right was given to all people, Tammany Hall had gained many new supporters. It also won support among many of New York City's immigrants, whom it had helped find jobs and become citizens.

Most important, Tammany officials often controlled many jobs in the city government. These jobs were given to people who could win votes for Tammany candidates. In the years after the Civil War these methods were used in many U.S. cities. Groups like Tammany were called political machines. Often they elected dishonest men to office. At one time, a city council full of Tammany leaders was called "the 40 thieves."

The most powerful and best-known leader was William Marcy Tweed, who ran Tammany Hall in the 1860's. "Boss" Tweed placed his friends in important jobs, and with their help he was able to steal millions of dollars from the city. This group, known as the "Tweed Ring," was finally broken up, and in 1873 Tweed himself was jailed. (See TWEED, WILLIAM MARCY.) For a few years following, a reform group led by Samuel Tilden ran New York, but soon many of the former corrupt leaders of Tammany Hall were back in power.

Tammany controlled the city through most of the period to 1933. It frequently supported honest and able men like Al Smith and Franklin Delano Roosevelt for higher offices. However, it tried to elect its own people to lesser offices. In 1933 a group of reform Democrats and Republicans elected Fiorello H. La Guardia mayor of New York. He did much to reform the city government, and during his 12 years as mayor, Tammany lost power. More and more city jobs required civil service examinations. (See CIVIL SERVICE.)

When the Democrats regained control of New York City in 1945, the Tammany organization was just one of five borough groups. Under Carmine G. De Sapio, Tammany regained some of its influence in the 1950's, but it never regained the power it once had.

TAMPA (tăm'pä), **FLORIDA,** is an important port city. It is located on Florida's west coast, near the mouth of the Hillsborough River on Tampa Bay. The city has a tropical climate. Average daily temperatures range between 80 and 90 degrees Fahrenheit in summer and 60 and 70 degrees in winter.

Spanish explorers discovered Tampa Bay in the early 1500's. Panfilo de Narvaez landed in the harbor in 1528, and Hernando de Soto in 1539. Fort Brooke, the first American settlement, was established in 1823. The population increased as settlers moved to the area for protection during the Seminole Indian wars (1835–1842). During the U.S. Civil War the town was occupied by Federal troops.

With the opening of the Panama Canal in 1914, Tampa became an important port of entry for goods from Central and South America. About two-thirds of Florida's citrus fruit is raised in the vicinity of Tampa, and the city is therefore a leading fruit-processing center. A large percentage of the phosphate mined in the United States comes from nearby mines. Cigar making is one of Tampa's leading industries. Such other materials as cement, boxes, paint, and chemicals are manufactured in the city's many factories.

Tampa's lovely beaches and resorts attract a significant tourist trade. The city is also a favored site for retirement. In addition to the libraries, theaters, and art galleries, the University of Tampa, Florida Christian College, and the University of South Florida are located there.

Tampa has a mayor-council form of city government. The population is 277,767 (1970).

The scarlet tanager (7 to 7½ inches) is bright red with black wings. It lives in the semi-open woods.

TANAGER (*tăn'ä jĕr*) is any bird belonging to the New World family Thraupidae in the order of perching birds. There are more than 200 species, the smallest three inches long, the largest twelve inches. They live mostly in Latin America. Most of the species are brightly colored, some glossy, in greens, reds, oranges, purples, browns, yellows, blues, blacks, and whites. Some species seem to wear all these colors in contrasting patches. The tanagers found in the United States and Canada are in reds, yellows, greens, and blacks. In late summer the colors of all these species change into dull greenish yellow as they lose their old feathers, or molt.

The male scarlet tanager, which nests in the eastern United States and southeastern Canada, is a brilliant scarlet with velvet-black wings and tail. He and the all-red summer tanager are about seven and one-half inches long. The western tanager, an inch shorter, has black wings and tail with a band of black on the upper back; the rest of his plumage is bright yellow except for a red head. The male hepatic tanager, about the same size as the scarlet tanager, is dull red and reddish-brown above and bright red below. The females, like the males in winter, are usually dull yellowish-green and black in color. The summer tanager nests in the central and southeastern United States; the hepatic and western tanagers are found in the western United States.

All four species build rather loosely woven shallow cuplike nests of thin sticks, branches, and twigs, in which are laid two to four whitish eggs, spotted with brown at the bigger end. The songs are varied. The scarlet tanager's main diet is insects, although it does eat some fruit and vegetable matter.

TANANARIVE (*tà'nà'nà'rēv'*), **MALAGASY REPUBLIC,** is the capital and largest city of the country. Its English name is Antananarivo.

The city is located on a ridge in the high central plateau at an altitude of 4,600 feet above sea level. The climate is moderate. The average temperature does not rise above 65 degrees Fahrenheit during any month.

Roads and rail lines connect Tananarive with other Malagasy towns. An international airport is located nearby. The simple industries of the city process agricultural and mineral products. The city is the distribution center for the surrounding rice-growing region. Small factories produce cotton textiles, leather goods, tobacco, soap, cement, bricks, and tiles for local use. There are also handicraft industries that make household articles.

Sidewalk markets are a common sight along the narrow, winding streets of Tananarive.

Tananarive is noted as a beautiful and picturesque city. There are many handsome buildings, including the cathedrals and the government buildings. Tananarive is the home of the University of Madagascar, a technical school, and schools of civil engineering, business, and medicine. The city also has an observatory, research institutes, and hospitals.

Tananarive was founded in the 17th century as the capital of the Merina (Hova) people, who made up one of the main kingdoms of the island. The French captured Tananarive in 1895 and made it the seat of the French colony of Madagascar. When Malagasy became an independent country in 1960, Tananarive remained the capital.

The population is 306,637 (1966 estimate).

TANGIER (*tan jir'*), or **TANGER, MOROCCO,** is a port city on the Atlantic Ocean. It is located in the extreme northwest corner of Africa, in a strategic position near the western end of the Strait of Gibraltar. The city slopes upward from the sea. The land around it is rugged. Summers are hot and dry. The average temperature for August is 76 degrees Fahrenheit. There is about 32 inches of rain each year, most of which falls during the mild winter months.

Because of its location, Tangier has long been of interest to other countries. At different times it has been under the control of the Arabs, Moors, Portuguese, Spanish, and English. In 1923 Great Britain, France, and Spain made an agreement creating an International Zone of the city and surrounding region. As such it was part of the kingdom of the Sultan of Morocco but was governed by a commission of representatives of other countries. Many foreigners established businesses in the city because no restrictions were placed on the trade of the free port and no taxes were levied in the free zone.

Morocco became an independent country in 1956, and four years later the free zone status of Tangier was ended. The city was integrated into the economy of Morocco, and Moroccan trade laws and taxes were put into effect. A serious depression resulted, causing many residents to leave and many businesses to close. More than 40 percent of the city's commercial activity stopped, and employment fell. A free zone was later established in the port.

The industries of Tangier today are minor, consisting mainly of handicrafts, such as leather goods. Fishing is of some importance, but the main industry is the tourist trade. Railroads link the city with other Moroccan cities, and it is served by international airlines.

Tangier is a fascinating city. The Moorish and European architecture, as well as the old and new traditions, presents interesting contrasts. One of the most handsome buildings is the Tangier governor's Moorish palace, which overlooks the Strait of Gibraltar. The city's population is 166,290 (1967 estimate).

Jacques Belin

Tangier at one time was a bustling seaport with no trade restrictions. Since it has become a part of Morocco, the city is more important as a tourist center.

TANK

The famous Sherman tank of World War II was the most widely used of all U.S. tanks.
Courtesy U.S. Army

TANK (tăngk), a motor-driven, armored military vehicle, moves on caterpillar tracks. Tanks carry one powerful gun and several machine guns. Modern tanks combine three of the most important military elements—mobility, firepower, and protection of crewmen. They can travel on good roads at speeds up to 30 miles an hour or move slowly across country, over rough terrain, through underbrush or barbed

or more men. Tanks are equipped with radios so that crewmen can communicate with other tank crews, and with periscopes so that crewmen can see outside the tank without being exposed to enemy fire.

History

Ancient armies used war chariots drawn by horses to scatter their enemies. In the 15th

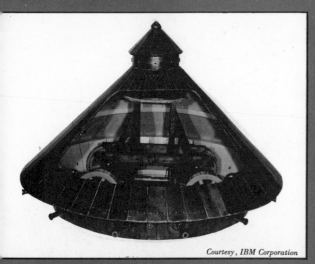
Courtesy, IBM Corporation

Nearly 500 years ago Leonardo da Vinci drew plans for an armored tank. This model has been built from them.

UPI Compix

The British first used tanks in World War I. This 29-ton tank had eight crewmen, two cannon, and machine guns.

wire, and even across shallow streams. Their big guns can attack enemy fortifications or tanks, and their machine guns can be used against enemy troops. Behind their steel walls they carry a crew of at least two men—a driver and a gunner—and the larger tanks carry four

century Leonardo da Vinci conceived the idea of building a covered vehicle capable of moving forward under enemy fire; but the development of the modern tank had to await the appearance of a suitable engine. The steam engine was far too cumbersome for tank use.

Courtesy Canada Department of National Defense

In modern warfare the tank has replaced the cavalry. This 50-ton Canadian Centurion crosses a pontoon bridge.

Courtesy G. B. Jarrett

The Panther tank was one of the most feared during World War II. It was used by German Panzer divisions.

Courtesy U.S. Army

U.S. forces developed the M-5, a small, light tank for use on rough terrain in World War II.

Sovfoto

The U.S.S.R. also developed huge tanks for World War II battles. The Joseph Stalin was the Soviet's largest.

Not until gasoline and diesel engines were invented in the late 19th century did the modern tank become possible. The first step was the building of motor-driven armored cars with mounted machine guns. The next step was to use caterpillar tracks such as those found on farm tractors. Moving on such tracks, these machines could easily cross over trenches and other obstacles.

In World War I (1914–1918), machine guns, rapid-firing rifles, and artillery barrages forced both sides to seek safety in trenches. Trench warfare resulted in a temporary stalemate. Foot soldiers could not advance in the face of enemy fire. It was then that the British Army turned to the kind of armored vehicle proposed by Colonel Ernest D. Swinton. Colonel Swinton is generally called the inventor of the tank. To keep the enemy from learning about the new secret weapons when they were being brought up to the front lines, the British soldiers were told that the strange-looking ve-

hicles were tanks for carrying water. The name stuck and ever since they have been known as "tanks" in both German and English.

In their first attack, at the Battle of the Somme, September 1916, the 30-ton British tanks gained some ground but their success was not great. Many of them broke down or got stuck in the mud before they reached the enemy lines. A year later, at the Battle of Cambrai, tanks were used in larger numbers and were more successful. The French, Germans, and Americans also used tanks before the war ended.

During the years between 1918 and the outbreak of World War II in September 1939, all the leading armies of the world experimented with tanks of improved design. The German Army excelled in this new kind of warfare. It won rapid victories over Poland, Belgium, the Netherlands, and France with its blitzkrieg ("lightning war") methods using both tanks and airplanes in combination. The two best-known

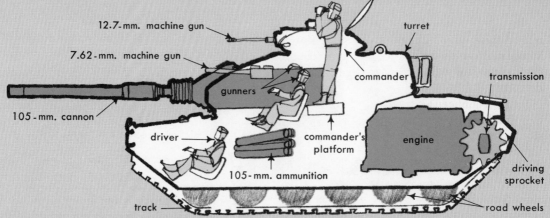

12.7-mm. machine gun

7.62-mm. machine gun

105-mm. cannon

gunners

driver

105-mm. ammunition

commander's platform

turret

commander

transmission

engine

driving sprocket

track

road wheels

The M-60, a modern U.S. tank, carries a crew of four: a driver, two gunners, and a commander. The tank is steered by a wheel that controls the speed of both tracks. When the driver turns the wheel to the left, power to the left track is reduced and the tank turns in that direction. The tank's huge, quick-firing cannon is capable of destroying any tank known.

Photo, Wide World

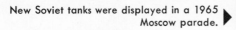
New Soviet tanks were displayed in a 1965 Moscow parade. ▶

German tanks in World War II were the Panther and the Tiger. The 47-ton Panther had thick, sloping armor plate and carried a 75-millimeter (mm.) gun. The 63-ton Tiger mounted the famous German 88-mm. cannon.

The U.S. Army, which had to transport its equipment to distant battlefields, adopted tanks of light and medium weight instead of heavy tanks. The best-known medium tanks, weighing from 30 to 35 tons, were the General Grant (M-3) and the General Sherman (M-4). Both carried 75-mm. guns, though late model Shermans had high-velocity 76-mm. guns. Toward the end of the war a new tank was produced, the 45-ton General Pershing (M-26). It mounted a powerful 90-mm. gun. Some U.S. tanks in World War II were equipped to fire rockets and others carried flame throwers.

When atomic bombs were produced by the United States at the end of World War II, along with rockets and missiles, some military experts thought that tanks would no longer be useful in war. But others argued that tanks would be even more valuable than before. All the leading military countries continued to ex-

periment with improved tanks, and some new models saw action in the Korean War (1950–1953). Experiments were carried on with light tanks that could be transported to the battlefield by airplanes or helicopters. Amphibious tanks were produced that could cross rivers as well as travel on land. The main battle tank of the U.S. Army became the M-60, which was first produced in quantity in 1960. It mounted a new and powerful 105-mm. gun, was powered by a diesel engine, weighed 46 tons, and carried a crew of four men. (See ARMY.)

TANNHAEUSER (tän'hoi zĕr) was a good knight and famous minstrel, or singer, in an old German legend. Today his story is remembered chiefly because it is told in the well-known opera *Tannhaeuser* by the German composer Richard Wagner. (See WAGNER, WILHELM RICHARD.)

One day Tannhaeuser, while riding through the country, came to a mountain called Venusberg (or Hoerselberg). It was thought that Venus, the Frau Hulda of German folklore, had retired there when Christianity came to Europe. Venus supposedly had hidden in an enchanted cave where she still lived with her nymphs and demons.

When Tannhaeuser passed the cave, he saw the goddess. She was so beautiful that he stopped and entered the cave, where he lived for seven years. One day he walked out of the cave to see the outside world, which he had forgotten was so wonderful. He realized, also, that he had forgotten his religion and had become a sinner. Full of regret, he went to Rome to ask the pope for forgiveness. But stern Pope Urban said that Tannhaeuser's guilt was too great and that his old, dry walking stick would become young and grow leaves before God would forgive Tannhaeuser. Sadly, Tannhaeuser went back to Venusberg. Just after he disappeared again into the cave, a messenger arrived from the pope. A miracle had happened. The pope's staff had turned green and begun to sprout leaves. But it was too late—Tannhaeuser never was seen again.

In Wagner's opera the story of Tannhaeuser is a little different. Wagner added another character, Elizabeth. Through her goodness and her pure love for Tannhaeuser, he was persuaded not to go back to Venus.

TANTALUS (*tăn'tă lŭs*) was a great king in Greek mythology. The gods honored him above all others. He was the only human ever to taste the food and drink of the gods, and the gods even went to his palace to attend a banquet.

Tantalus was wicked, however, and prepared a horrible dinner for his guests. He had his own son, Pelops, killed, boiled, and served to the gods. The gods, who knew everything, would not touch the frightful meal. Instead, they decided to punish Tantalus for trying to make cannibals of them. They condemned him to stand forever in a pool in Hades, the underground home of the dead. (See HADES.) He was to suffer forever with a terrible thirst and hunger. Every time he stooped to drink from the pool beneath him, the water would run off into the ground. All around the pool were wonderful fruit trees, whose branches hung low over his head. Whenever he reached up to pick a pear, apple, pomegranate, or fig, however, the branch would pull away beyond his reach.

The gods brought Pelops back to life. A piece of his shoulder had been accidentally eaten, so the gods made him a new shoulder of ivory.

TANZANIA (*tăn zăn'ĭ ä*), **AFRICA,** is a country on the eastern coast of the continent. It includes the small islands of Zanzibar and Pemba, about 25 miles off the coast in the Indian Ocean. The mainland portion of Tanzania was formerly Tanganyika. It is bordered by Kenya, Lake Victoria, and Uganda on the north; by Rwanda, Burundi, Lake Tanganyika, Zambia, Malawi, and Lake Nyasa on the west; and by Mozambique on the south.

A low, narrow coastal plain extends along the coast of mainland Tanzania. On the interior edge of the plain is a steep rise to the plateau that occupies most of the interior of the country. There are several mountainous areas near the edges of the plateau. Mount Kilimanjaro in northern Tanzania is 19,340 feet above sea level, making it the highest mountain of Africa.

The islands and the coastal plain of mainland Tanzania are hot and humid. The rainfall along the coast averages about 45 inches a

Locator map of Tanzania.

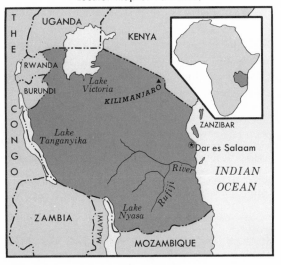

Ylla—Rapho Guillumette

Tanzania has a huge variety and number of wildlife. Most is protected in parks and game reserves, such as Serengeti National Park, near Mount Kilimanjaro (background).

year, and some usually occurs during each month. The interior of Tanzania is drier. The rainfall is unreliable, and serious droughts often occur.

The disease-carrying tsetse fly is widespread in Tanzania. Wild animals are numerous. They include the elephant, giraffe, zebra, hippopotamus, rhinoceros, lion, leopard, and buffalo. The principal mineral resource of Tanzania is diamonds. Rich diamond mines are at Shinyanga and Mwadui.

The population of mainland Tanzania is unevenly distributed. The areas of densest settlement are along the coast of the Indian Ocean and in the far interior near the shores of Lake Victoria. The population includes more than 200 different African tribes, as well as many Asians and some Europeans. Most of the Africans are of the Bantu language group. The

FACTS ABOUT TANZANIA

CAPITAL: Dar es Salaam.

AREA: 361,800 square miles.

POPULATION: 12,231,342 (1967 estimate).

HIGHEST MOUNTAIN PEAK: Mount Kilimanjaro (19,340 feet).

FORM OF GOVERNMENT: Republic.

CHIEF OF STATE and HEAD OF GOVERNMENT: President.

POLITICAL DIVISIONS: Regions.

CHIEF PRODUCTS: *manufactured,* processed food; *agricultural,* sisal, cotton, coffee, cloves, coconuts; *mined,* diamonds.

MONETARY UNIT: East African shilling; 7.12 East African shillings equal one U.S. dollar.

Masai people are one of the African tribes of the mainland. They are cattle-keeping people but rarely eat the meat of their animals. The cattle are kept for milk as well as for social prestige.

Dar es Salaam is the country's capital and largest city. It is also the chief seaport and principal industrial and transportation center. A railroad connects it with the port of Kigoma on Lake Tanganyika and the port of Mwanza on Lake Victoria. Tanga is the second largest city of the country. It is situated on the coast to the north of Dar es Salaam and is also an important port. The chief settlement of the islands is the port city of Zanzibar.

Most of the people of Tanzania earn a living in agriculture. Yams, millet, corn, cassava, and beans are grown for home use. Commercial agriculture is important to the country's economy. Mainland Tanzania is the world's largest producer of sisal, a fiber crop and the country's most valuable export. The two other principal commercial crops of the mainland are cotton and coffee. Zanzibar and Pemba produce cloves and coconuts. Much of the world's supply of cloves comes from these two islands.

Tanzania is believed by some scientists to be the home of man's earliest ancestors. In 1964 British anthropologist Louis S. B. Leakey announced his discovery of the remains of *Homo habilis.* These remains, found at Olduvai Gorge in the northern part of Tanzania, are nearly two million years old.

Although the area may be man's ancestral home, little is known of its early history. Arab traders established settlements on the mainland coast and on Zanzibar and Pemba before the arrival of the Portuguese in the late 15th century. Gradually the Arabs regained control from the Portuguese.

The area came under German influence in 1884 and was made a part of the protectorate of German East Africa in 1891. At the end of World War I, most of the protectorate was mandated to Great Britain by the League of Nations. The area was called Tanganyika at that time. After World War II, Tanganyika was administered by Great Britain as a United Nations Trust Territory. In 1961 Tanganyika became an independent country.

Zanzibar and Pemba were established as a British protectorate in 1890, and in 1963 became the independent country of Zanzibar. In 1964 Zanzibar and Tanganyika formed the United Republic of Tanzania. It is a member of the Commonwealth of Nations. (See ZANZIBAR).

TAOISM (*tou'izm*) is a religion that originated in China in the 4th century B.C. It started as a philosophy of extreme personal freedom based on the teachings of Lao-Tzu. This great teacher probably lived at about the same time as Confucius. It is possible that they may have known one another.

Lao-Tzu wrote a book entitled *Tao Te Ching* (*The Way and Its Power*). This brief work advocated a return to a simple way of life, rejected the influences of the past, and suggested that all government be held to a minimum. It was a practical approach to life that scorned anything likely to direct a person's private beliefs. Lao-Tzu clearly wanted to start no religion.

Lao-Tzu's ideas were directly opposed to the principles of Confucianism. Confucius had advocated an ordered life in which respect for the goodness of man and of ancient customs was more important than the rights of individuals and their freedom of thought. After Lao-Tzu's death his teachings were followed by all those discontented with Confucianism and all those opposed to the ruling government.

From a philosophy, Taoism was gradually changed into a religion. It acquired priests and sorcerers with their myths, superstitions, gods, goddesses, and genies. A mystical church evolved with a supreme pontiff, nuns, a complicated ritual, and a large body of sacred literature. By this time the religion had little in common with Lao-Tzu's original ideas.

Occasionally Taoism was in power at the emperor's court, but more often it was not. It was always a refuge for the unhappy and the discontented. Again and again the rebels who attempted to overthrow the throne came from its ranks or at least based their actions on its principles.

There are remnants of the Taoist church in China today. It is still heavily superstitious. In 1926 the Chinese government took all property from the supreme pontiff. The Communist government, which took over in 1949, is even more unsympathetic because of the group's reputation for political upheaval. The church has made few converts outside of China.

TAPESTRY (*tăp'ĭs trĭ*) is cloth with a design woven into it by an artist or talented craftsman. Most tapestries are used as wall hangings, curtains, or upholstery for furniture.

The picture or design of a tapestry is part of the fabric rather than an embroidery. (See EMBROIDERY.) Tapestries are woven in a special

In high warp weaving, the outline of the design is marked on the parallel, undyed warp threads with crayon (left). A master weaver then uses a spindle to pass the colored, horizontal weft threads through the vertical warp (center). As the tapestry progresses, the finished section is covered to keep it clean, and rolled at the bottom to keep the part being worked on at a convenient height (right).

Photos, Dalmas—Pix from Publix

Tapestry weaving is an old art, indigenous to many of the world's cultures. The Coptic tapestry (left) was done sometime before A.D. 700. The Peruvian one (right) was woven by Inca Indians during the colonial period (1533-1821).

Courtesy (left) Museum of Fine Arts, Boston, (right) The Brooklyn Museum

way. Parallel threads, called the warp, are stretched on a loom. The warp yarns are usually of linen or wool and are undyed. Other threads, called the weft, are passed back and forth at right angles between them. The weft threads are of different colors. Silk, gold, or silver threads may be added for richness and highlights. The weft is pushed together so closely that its pattern covers the warp yarns. A true tapestry weave must be made by hand, while almost all other weaves can be made by machine. (See SPINNING AND WEAVING.)

If the warp threads are stretched vertically on an upright loom, the tapestry is called high warp or *haute-lisse*. If the loom is horizontal the tapestry is called low warp or *basse-lisse*. On both looms the weaver works from the reverse side of the cloth. The pattern, or "cartoon," for the high warp tapestry is mounted behind the weaver. He marks the outline of the design on the warp yarns and weaves in the colored weft to produce the picture. At his side is a tray of bobbins wound with the colored yarns he will use. A mirror on the opposite side of the warp allows him to see the right side of the cloth as he weaves the design. On the low warp tapestry the weaver works with the cartoon beneath the warp yarns.

Tapestry weaving is probably as old as weaving itself. Primitive weavers in many countries are known to have used the tapestry weave to introduce color and pattern into the fabric. Pieces of tapestry weave dating from the 15th century B.C. have been found in Egyptian tombs. Pictures on the walls of the tombs show

how the spinning, dyeing, and weaving of cloth were done. Quite different are examples of tapestry weaving found much later in Upper Egypt. These were made by an early Christian people known as Copts, about A.D. 400 to 700. Their patterns were influenced by Byzantine and Hellenistic design.

Tapestry weaving reached a high state of perfection in China many centuries ago. It was usually of silk in a very fine weave, and was used for costumes as well as for wall hangings. The designs were flowers, birds, and Chinese symbols. The weave, now almost a lost art, was called *k'ssu*. The threads were woven in so that the reverse side showed no loose ends and was as beautiful as the right side.

The Indians of Peru in South America were skilled weavers. In their tombs examples of cloth of tapestry weave have been found. Some of them are 1500 years old. Their designs were rather crude human figures, birds, animals, and fishes.

In Europe in the Middle Ages, much tapestry weaving was done in convents and monasteries. As the demand for tapestries increased, workshops, or "ateliers," were started. France and Flanders (as Belgium, parts of the Netherlands, and northern France were then called) became famous for their tapestry works. The 14th and 15th centuries have been called the "Golden Age" of tapestry. Paris, Arras, Tournai, and Brussels are credited with producing some of the finest tapestries ever created. Arras was often used as another name for tapestry.

In 1422 Paris was taken by King Henry V of

England, and the tapestry art was discouraged. The town of Arras was destroyed by the English in 1435, and the tapestry industry there was ruined. Leadership passed to the Flemish towns of Tournai, Brussels, and Bruges, and Flemish weavers became famous throughout Europe for their skill. They were often lured to other countries, such as Italy, France, Spain, England, and Sweden, where they continued to weave in the Flemish way. Guilds of dyers and of weavers were formed (somewhat like our trade unions). They set high standards; only perfect work would allow a man to be called a master weaver. Tapestries were often signed with the initials or mark of the weaver, or of the town where the weaving was done.

In the 16th century, a change took place in tapestry design. Pope Leo X in 1515 commissioned the Renaissance painter Raphael to produce cartoons for a series called "The Acts of the Apostles." He introduced life-size, three-

"The Unicorn in Captivity," one of the most beautiful tapestries ever woven, is one of a Gothic series entitled "The Hunt of the Unicorn" done in France in about 1515.

Courtesy The Metropolitan Museum of Art, The Cloisters Collection, Gift of John D. Rockefeller, Jr., 1937

Courtesy The Art Institute of Chicago

This 17th-century tapestry represents Meleager bringing the head of the boar to Atalanta.

dimensional figures, with distant landscapes in the background. He also added wide and elaborate borders, often with a series of scenes carrying out a secondary story. To copy these colorful pictures the technique of tapestry weaving had to be changed by the Brussels weavers. Far more colors were needed. The copying of pictures became the method of the weaver.

In the 17th century, King Louis XIV and his minister, J. B. Colbert, established several tapestry works in France. The Gobelins and Savonnerie in Paris, and the ateliers at Beauvais and Aubusson were made Royal factories (1660–1670). In England, James I established the Mortlake factory in 1619 and imported about 50 Flemish weavers. This factory had a few years of prosperity and produced some fine tapestries, but it was abandoned in 1703.

In the 18th century as many as 1,000 shades of color were used in a tapestry. Subjects were often nymphs, shepherdesses, and goddesses in elaborate settings. Borders became wider until the picture might be merely a medallion in the center. Or the border might be a faithful copy of a gilded wooden frame. Tapestries were often fastened flat to the wall instead of hanging freely. Small patterns were used for chairs and sofas. Toward the end of the century interest in tapestries had almost died out. Some 120 fine old pieces were said to have been burned to recover the gold in the threads.

The 19th century saw a revival of interest. Museums and private buyers, beginning to appreciate the older pieces, acquired them for their collections. A real attempt to revive the art was made by William Morris in England. He established a factory in 1881 at Merton Abbey, and many of his designs were by the painter Burne-Jones. This factory is still in existence.

In the 20th century, France has seen a revival of tapestry weaving, spurred by such artists as Jean Lurcat. Modern designs are being used with bright, clear colors. The number of shades is limited to 30 or 40, as in the Gothic tapestries. Designs do not show perspective. The ateliers of the Gobelins are active in weaving the new designs. The Beauvais factory, destroyed in World War II, has a new building at the Gobelins. There are many tapestry weavers at work in the U.S. today. There is also mending and restoring of valuable old tapestries to be done. In art classes in some schools, students are learning the tapestry weave on simple homemade frames.

TAPEWORM (*tāp′wẽrm′*). Tapeworms, or cestodes, belong to the flatworm group. They are intestinal parasites. They live in the digestive tract of another animal, called the host, and are fed by food which the host has partly digested.

The host of the tapeworm is nearly always a backboned animal, such as a fish, a dog, or a man. The parasite has sucking discs on its head, by means of which it attaches itself to the inside of the intestine. It has no sense organs such as eyes or ears. Its muscles are almost useless, and its nervous system is primitive. It has no mouth or digestive tract as it absorbs dissolved food through the walls of its body.

There are many species of tapeworms, ranging in length from about $\frac{1}{25}$ of an inch to 30 feet. They are of many shapes.

They may be unsegmented (or undivided), or composed of a chain of segmentlike parts. These grow one after the other always forming behind the head. Each adult is both male and female.

The eggs often have a hard shell and must pass out of the intestinal tract of the host before the larvae are freed. They usually enter the human body through the eating of undercooked beef, pork, or veal.

Tapeworms can infect many animals. Sometimes they cause heavy losses among poultry and cattle. They injure the host not only by taking from it part of the nourishment of its food, but also by secreting poisonous substances. They do not cause death to man except in rare cases.

The symptoms may be an unusually large or irregular appetite, a run-down condition, and, occasionally, convulsions. The only sure symptom is the presence of parts of the worm or eggs in the feces. Remedies are pomegranate or extract of male fern. The feces are examined until the small, knoblike "head" of the worm is found. If it is not eliminated the worm will grow again.

TAPIOCA (*tăp′i ō′kä*). In the warm countries of the world grows a large shrub from the roots of which tapioca is made. The shrub is called *manioc* or *cassava* in English, but it is sometimes known as *yuca* or *mandioca*. Sometimes the shrub itself is called tapioca.

The storage roots of the manioc plant are about one-third starch and two-thirds water, but they also contain prussic acid, a deadly poison. Much of the poison is in the skin of the root and can be removed by peeling the root. The rest of the poison can be removed by soaking the roots or by cooking them.

Preparation and Use

Usually a great deal of time is needed to get the manioc roots ready for eating. They are first washed and peeled. They may then be put into water in a pot or a stream and left to soak for three or four days. Or they may be grated or pounded into a paste without soaking. The paste can be cooked and eaten, or it can be dried and made into flour.

To make tapioca the grated root is mixed well with very clean water, and then left to stand. The pure starch grains slowly settle to the bottom, and any dirt can be poured off with the water. The starch is then taken out and mixed with clean water again and the process repeated, sometimes four or five times. When the starch is perfectly clean it is spread on a metal plate over a low fire and cooked. It is stirred all the time that it is over the fire. As the starch grains cook they stick together to form irregular little balls.

After the pure starch is cooked it is called tapioca. Most of the tapioca used in the United States and Europe comes from Java, Brazil, and Madagascar.

In the United States and Europe tapioca is used to make puddings or to thicken soups and sauces. In South America and Africa manioc is eaten in the form of a paste or simply as a dry flour.

Pure manioc starch that has not been cooked is known in the United States as tapioca flour. It is used to give a good finish to cotton cloth, and to make fine adhesives, such as are used on postage stamps. It is often mixed with other foods and in the United States is used in such different products as breakfast cereals and fish food.

Tapioca flour and other manioc products also are used as cattle and pig food.

TAPIR (*tā′pẽr*). In prehistoric times tapirs lived in many parts of the Northern Hemisphere. In modern times they have been found in two widely separated areas, America and Asia.

The tapir is one of three members of a group of odd-toed, hoofed mammals, the others being the horse and the rhinoceros. The tapir has four toes on the front feet and three toes on the hind feet. American tapirs are about six feet long and three feet high at the shoulder; the Malay tapir is a little larger. The tapir's body is fat, its legs short, tail tiny, and proboscis, or nose, like a small trunk of an elephant. Tapirs weigh from 400 to 700 pounds and have lived as long as 32 years in captivity.

Tapirs of Central America and tropical South America are light or dark brown with gray on the throat, chest, and cheeks. The South American mountain tapir is almost black. The Malay tapir is black and gray.

Tapirs feed on plants, eating such things as grass, leaves, fallen fruit, and moss in great

The Asiatic tapir (about 3½ feet high) has a broad band of white on back and sides. It lives in forests, usually near water, and uses its snout to bring food to its mouth.

quantities. They feed at night, always keeping on the move, taking a bite here and a bite there. At dawn they drink and then find a patch of dense jungle where they sleep.

The jaguar and the puma of America and the tiger of Asia are their only enemies. Their protection is to run or to escape in the water. If attacked, their heavy hide protects them. On their necks and heads it is from $\frac{1}{2}$ to 1 inch thick.

TAR (*tär*). Tar is a thick, dark-colored, sticky liquid made by distilling coal, wood, bone, or other organic substances. Tars do not dissolve in water and thus are hard to remove from the skin or clothes. They have a lasting odor which may or may not be pleasant, depending on the kind of tar. The odor usually has a burnt or smoky flavor.

When certain organic substances are heated in an oven, vapors and gas are given off, and finally only black, solid char remains in the oven. The heating process is called *destructive distillation*.

The vapors pass through water-cooled tubes which condense them to a liquid. The liquid becomes thicker and more tarry as the oven becomes hotter. The tar part of the liquid separates from the watery portion. The crude tar is usually heated and refined by distilling before use.

Large quantities of wood are destructively distilled to produce charcoal, chemicals, and tars. Usually the wood used is not good for other purposes. But the tars have many uses. Pine tar comes from destructive distillation of old pine stumps and dead trees, such as are found in Florida and other southern states. Pine tar is added to natural rubber and helps to make it a tough, durable material. Pine tar is also added to rope fiber to form *oakum*, a fragrant, woolly material used to calk cracks in boats. Oakum is also used with lead in making the joints in cast-iron sewer pipes used in many homes.

Hardwoods such as maple, birch, and oak are destructively distilled on a large scale. The woods used are forest waste, such as branches, small tree thinnings, and old and crooked trees which are not suitable for lumber. Charcoal is the main product, but the hardwood tar can also be made into many useful products. The crude tar is black, but refined parts may have an amber color or even be water white. Important products from hardwood tar include an oil used in separating a metal ore from impurity and medicines used in cough drops and in veterinary remedies. A refined hardwood tar oil is used indirectly in making a clear, glasslike plastic.

Coal tar is obtained in making coke. It has many uses on roads, in roofing materials, and in preserving wood. Many important chemicals are obtained from coal tar.

TARANTULA (*tä răn′ṭū lä*). In the Middle Ages it was thought that people bitten by a tarantula spider became ill with "tarantism." In this disease, which was superstition, the victim developed a strong desire to dance, and he would continue dancing until he fell down from exhaustion. The dance was called the tarantella. The spider, the disease, and the dance were all named after Taranto, a city in Italy.

The tarantula that was thought to cause tarantism is a single species, *Lycosa tarantula*, that is native to southern Europe. This spider's body is about an inch long and it has spindly legs.

TARANTULA HAS EIGHT EYES ON TOP OF HEAD

The tarantula of North America grows to about two inches in body length. It feeds on large insects and small animals such as frogs, toads, and mice.

It belongs to the family Lycosidae, the wolf spiders, so named because they catch their prey by running after them.

A second type of tarantula includes a whole family, the Theraphosidae, found in the Western Hemisphere. The typical tarantula of this family has a heavy body and is rather hairy. It lives in the southwestern United States, Mexico, and Central America. Its bite, like that of the European tarantula, is harmless to man. Most American tarantulas live in burrows in the ground or under sticks and stones. Another type, the funnel-web tarantula, spins a web.

The bird-eating spiders of South America, sometimes called tarantulas, are closely related to those of the United States. The largest of these, with legs extended, are the size of a man's hand.

TARIFF (*tăr′if*) is the rate, or rates, of duties, levies, or taxes placed upon commerce among countries or other geographic areas. More accurately, the word *tariff* refers to a list or schedule of charges to be collected when certain articles of commerce are imported, or sometimes exported. The charges themselves are usually called customs, or import, duties. All of a country's customs duties makes up its tariff. Today most countries of the world have a customs tariff.

There are several legends about how the word tariff came to be. One of them states that the word comes from Tarifa, the name of an ancient Arab town near the western end of the Mediterranean Sea and at the southern tip of Spain. It is said that because this little seaport was favorably located at the very crossroad of the ocean trade during the Middle Ages, the people who lived there were able to collect fees from passing ships for the privilege of entering or leaving the Mediterranean.

In ancient times, taxes usually were collected by rulers on goods coming into a country and, at times, even on articles moving over the highways within a country. During the Middle Ages feudal lords used such methods as a means of raising revenue for their realm and for adding to their personal fortunes. Rulers of areas through which important trade routes passed were thus able to demand fees for the protection of trade passing over these highways. Levies were sometimes made on goods entering the gates of towns.

Kinds of Tariffs

Import duties in most countries are set up by tariff acts or laws. The tariff schedule includes (1) a list, or classification, of all possible goods which might be imported; and (2) the rates of duty at which each item on the list should be taxed. Some items are dutiable (taxable) and some are free. Countries often permit some imports to enter free of duty when they are important to the national welfare. The items that are not taxable are usually called the free list. Taxable goods are taxed at different rates—for example, rubber at one rate, sugar at another, cotton cloth at still another.

In order to collect duties, countries have established customs offices at their main seaports, border cities, and at airports which serve as ports of entry for planes from other countries. The customs officers inspect all imported goods and decide on the amount of tax to be charged according to the rates provided in the tariff schedule. In the United States, import duties are collected by the Bureau of Customs, which is a part of the Department of the Treasury. It is also the duty of the customs officers, with the help of the Coast Guard and others, to prevent smuggling—that is, to prevent the importation of goods without payment of duty.

A few countries have export tariffs as well as import tariffs. Countries that have export duties are generally those which have little industrial development but which export valuable raw materials. For example, Bolivia imposes an export tax on tin, and Chile imposes one on copper. In the United States, export duties are forbidden by the federal Constitution.

Imports which are taxable may be subject to either specific or ad valorem rates of duty. A specific duty taxes the article according to the unit, or quantity: $1.25 per dozen, per yard, per quart, or per pound. If a specific tax were charged on dolls, the duty would be the same whether the doll was valued at 50 cents or $5. An ad valorem duty is one that is levied as a percentage of the value of the imported article—for example, 25 per cent.

Frequently, compound rates of duty, which include both a specific and an ad valorem rate, are used. A compound rate of duty on shoes would mean that there might be a specific rate of $1.50 per pair, plus 30 per cent ad valorem. After World War II, a number of countries replaced many of their specific duties with those of the ad valorem type.

Purposes of Tariffs

A country may use its tariff—that is, impose import duties—for two purposes: (1) to raise income or revenue, or (2) to protect domestic producers from foreign competition in the home market. If protective duties were not imposed, foreign products might sell at lower prices than the same products produced in the home country. Many of the smaller countries, particularly those with little industrial development, depend heavily on import duties for government revenue. Yet they also may have a few duties which protect certain home industries. Many highly industrialized nations, on the other hand, use their tariffs mainly for protective purposes. If the protective duties succeed in keeping goods from being imported, they bring the government little or no revenue. The United States government, for example, obtains less than 2 per cent of its revenue from import duties. Countries using their tariff to raise revenue seldom have a long free list. But those which use their customs duties chiefly for protection frequently have a long free list. Such a free list includes primarily raw materials and other goods which are not produced at home.

Throughout the 19th century, England was the world's principal low-tariff country. Many of its statesmen and businessmen believed in free trade—that is, little interference with imports. England had developed into a great trading and manufacturing nation. It wished to make the importation of raw materials as cheap as possible so that these materials could be manufactured into goods that could be exported to the rest of the world. By 1860 so many of England's duties had been lowered or completely dropped that it almost reached a condition of free trade. After World War I, however, England adopted many protective duties.

Since 1816 the United States has had a protective tariff. The level of protection, however, has varied from time to time. The Republican party generally has favored a high tariff and the Democratic party a low tariff. Those persons who support a low tariff argue that high rates of duty interfere with trade among nations and, by doing so, interfere with world prosperity as well as with the prosperity of the individual nation itself. They say that protective duties force many persons in the United States to pay unnecessarily high prices for goods, and that in this way the high duties benefit only a small number of persons at the expense of all others.

Under President Woodrow Wilson, the tariff was lowered, and a tariff commission was created to "take the tariff out of politics." Under Presidents Warren G. Harding, Calvin Coolidge, and Herbert Hoover, the tariff was again raised.

Reciprocal Trade Program

After World War I, and again after the depression following 1929, countries began to raise their tariffs. Many had little money to buy the goods of other nations. They were eager to build their own industries and to sell goods abroad, but they wished to buy little from others. Each country wished to keep the home market for its own industries. Tariffs and other methods (quotas, licenses, etc.) were used to control imports. In a way, a tariff war was going on.

In 1934 the United States Congress adopted the Reciprocal Trade Agreements Act, which eventually resulted in the reduction of hundreds of United States import duties. In fact, it brought about a general reduction in the United States tariff. Trade agreements were made with many other countries. These countries reduced their duties in exchange for reductions that the United States made. The Reciprocal Trade Agreements Act was an effort by President Franklin D. Roosevelt's administration to encourage trade among nations and thereby build world prosperity. Congress renewed the Reciprocal Trade Agreements Act from time to time after 1934, and many changes were made in it. In 1962 Congress passed the Trade Expansion Act which continued the trade agreements program.

By World War II the United States had signed reciprocal trade agreements with nearly 30 countries. After the war the Reciprocal Trade Agreements Act led to the adoption of an international program whereby many countries lowered their tariffs and reduced other trade barriers. In 1947 the representatives of 23 countries met at Geneva, Switzerland, and signed the General Agreement on Tariffs and Trade (G.A.T.T.). In this agreement, the G.A.T.T. members agreed to reduce rates of duty on thousands of items that make up more than three-quarters of the world's trade. The members also set up rules of fair play to control their trade with one another. Additional tariff negotiations were held at Annecy, France, in 1949; at Torquay, England, in 1950–1951; and again at Geneva in 1956, 1960–1962, and 1964–1967. In May 1967 an agreement was reached that virtually eliminated the tariff barrier to world trade. More than 70 countries were full members of G.A.T.T. by 1967. Several countries were seeking membership, others had special arrangements, and still others were provisional members.

During the 20 years following World War II, most countries found it desirable to revise their tariffs. Two important reasons for these changes were: (1) the world-wide increase in prices had caused old rates of duty to be out of date; and (2) changes in the kind of trade that a country engaged in often required that new duties be added or old ones be adjusted.

Between 1957 and 1965 groups of countries in several parts of the world joined together to do away with all tariffs between members of the group. This they felt would help to increase trade with one another and make all the member countries more prosperous. The most important tariff group is the European Economic Community (EEC), also called the Common Market. Its six members are Belgium, the Netherlands, Luxembourg, France, Germany, and Italy. Another group formed in Europe is the European Free Trade Association (EFTA). Its seven members are Austria, Denmark, Norway, Portugal, Sweden, Switzerland, and the United Kingdom.

After the formation of the EEC and EFTA free trade groups became popular. Two groups were formed in the Western Hemisphere. Eight countries in South America joined with Mexico to form LAFTA (The Latin American Free Trade Association). Five other countries formed a group usually called the Central American Common Market. Two "common markets" were formed in Africa.

Although there is no satisfactory way of measuring the differences in tariffs between countries, some writers have attempted comparison. In 1961 one impartial source ranked various countries as follows, according to the amount of their tariffs on industrial goods (ranked from high to low): Japan, Austria, the United Kingdom, New Zealand, Canada, the European Economic Community, Australia, United States, Norway, Sweden, Switzerland, and Denmark.

TARKINGTON (tär'king tŭn), **NEWTON** (nū't'n) **BOOTH** (booth) (1869–1946), U.S. novelist, short-story writer, and playwright, is known to young readers mainly as the author of a series of books about a young boy named Penrod. The boy's adventures are contained in three books: *Penrod* (1914), *Penrod and Sam* (1916), and *Penrod Jashber* (1929).

Tarkington was born in Indianapolis, Indiana, and received his education at Phillips Exeter Academy in New Hampshire and at Purdue and Princeton universities.

Tarkington also wrote a number of novels for adults, mainly about life in the Middle West. His first successful novel, *The Gentleman From Indiana* (1899), was a story of a country editor who fought dishonest politicians in his community. His next, *Monsieur Beaucaire* (1900), was a romantic novel about the duke of Orleans, who left France and traveled throughout 18th-century England disguised as a barber.

Booth Tarkington.

Other of Tarkington's stories set in the Midwest were *The Magnificent Ambersons* (1918) and *Alice Adams* (1921); both received Pulitzer prizes. The first of these told the story of three generations of a prominent Indiana family, and was the second part of a trilogy called *Growth*. The first volume of the three-part work was *The Turmoil* (1915) and the final volume was *The Midlander* (1924). *Alice Adams* was a searching character study.

In addition to the books about Penrod, Tarkington wrote a number of other books about young people, including *Seventeen* (1916), *Gentle Julia* (1922), and *Little Orvie* (1934). He also wrote many plays and dramatized several of his novels.

TARPON (tär'pŏn), or *Tarpon atlanticus*, is one of the finest game fish found in the west-

Courtesy Marineland of Florida

The average adult tarpon, a powerful game fish, is about four feet in length, but many get to be seven feet long.

ern Atlantic Ocean. It also is called silver king, silverfish, and savanilla, and is related to the herrings.

Adult tarpon average about 4 feet in length and about 60 pounds in weight. The tarpon's long body is covered with large, silvery scales. These thick scales may exceed two inches in length and are often used by man as decorations. Tarpon have a blue-gray back, bright silver sides, and a long, trailing dorsal fin.

Tarpon are fighters known for their spectacular leaps. They usually are released after they are caught because their meat is too coarse and soft for good eating. The best tarpon fishing is along the Florida and Texas coasts and around Puerto Rico, where the fish breed.

Tarpon spawn in shallow waters over rocky bottoms. The young tarpon migrate up creeks and rivers when they are about two and one-half inches long. Maturity is reached in about three years.

Tarpon feed on crabs, shrimp, pinfish, and especially pigfish. Although they range from Nova Scotia to Brazil, tarpon are rarely caught outside tropical or semitropical waters.

TARTAN (*tär'tän*) is a woolen cloth woven in a pattern of crossbars. These bars are of a specified width and color for each pattern, or sett, of tartan. They are the same in both directions, that is, the warp and the woof.

Tartans are properly associated with the people of Scotland. The various setts of tartan derive their names from the clans. The clan was the ancient form of social organization in the Scottish Highlands. The people living in a district grouped themselves under the leadership of a chief for protection. The title of chief remained in the same family. The chief was selected, however, according to custom, as the most able and suitable member of the ruling family. The name of the chief's family became the name of the clan. Other families belonging to the clan, but not sharing the name, were called septs.

The principal source of clothing for the Highlanders was the wool of sheep that grazed on the hillsides. This wool was colored with native vegetable dyes and was woven into garments. Gradually the different clans began to adopt certain colors and patterns to distinguish themselves. Since these clans frequently waged war on each other, their tartans served as a uniform for the chieftains' followers. Eventually each clan came to have a special tartan and the wearing of it showed the clan membership.

Patterns and Garments

Within the clan itself various setts of tartan were worn. The chief's dress sett was worn only by him and his family. The clan tartan was worn by the other members of the clan.

A tartan was adopted for hunting by those clans whose ordinary tartan was of bright colors. Greens and browns that would blend with the countryside were more suitable in these setts. Sometimes a sept of a clan would devise a tartan of its own. There also were separate mourning setts. The arisaid setts were worn by women. They were usually patterns of their clan tartan, but on a white background.

Other patterns were used outside the clan. District tartans were worn by people of a certain district who did not belong to any clan.

The clergy also adopted a sett. They selected a dark blue pattern for their use. The royal tartan was that adopted by the House of Stuart and worn by the Scottish monarch and his family. It has become the official tartan of the royal family of Great Britain.

Tartan was worn in several ways. Before the 18th century, the Highlander wore the *breacan-*

Drawn for Encyclopædia Britannica, Inc., by George Armstrong

HISTORIC AND MODERN SCOTTISH DRESS

Upper row, left to right: (1) The breacan-feile, an ancient one-piece costume. (2) The arisard, dress of the Highland women of the past. The background of women's tartan was almost always white. (3) A clansman in the army of "Bonnie Prince Charlie" (1745) wearing jacket, waistcoat, and kilt of three different tartans. (4) An 18th-century outfit of tartan doublet and trews (close-fitting pants). (5) A private of the Gordon Highlanders (1798).

Second row, left to right: (6) An officer of the Argyll and Sutherland Highlanders in "Number One Dress." (7) A piper of the Queen's Own Cameron Highlanders in full dress. The kilt and plaid are of the royal tartan. (8) Modern Scottish sports dress. (9) and (10) Evening wear for women and men. The man is wearing the MacLeod dress tartan.

PLATE 2 TARTAN

ROYAL STUART

BLACK WATCH

BUCHANAN

ROB ROY

GORDON (DRESS)

MACLEOD (DRESS)

Tartan samples furnished by Peter C. Martin, Edinburgh

MACDONALD (CLAN)

MACPHERSON (CHIEF, DRESS)

MACINTOSH (CLAN)

DOUGLAS

MACKENZIE

MACLACHLAN

Tartan samples furnished by Peter C. Martin, Edinburgh

PLATE 4 TARTAN

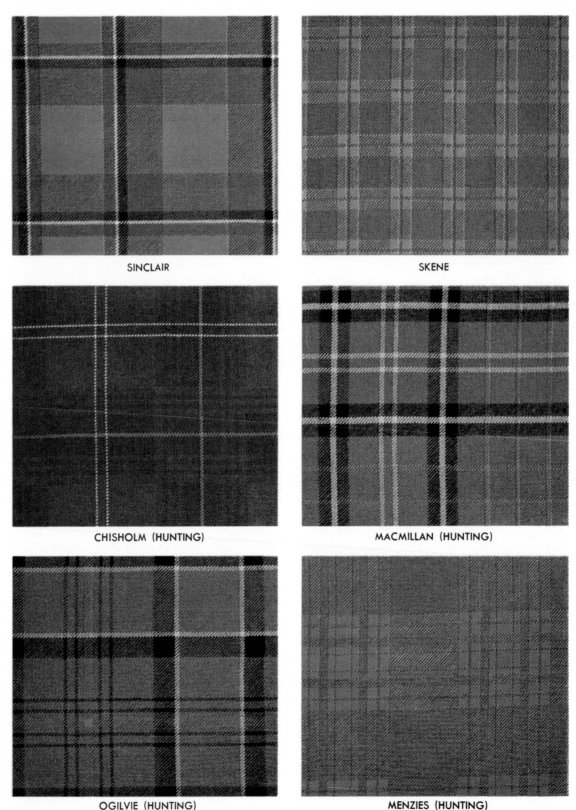

SINCLAIR

SKENE

CHISHOLM (HUNTING)

MACMILLAN (HUNTING)

OGILVIE (HUNTING)

MENZIES (HUNTING)

Tartan samples furnished by Peter C. Martin, Edinburgh

feile, or belted plaid (*plăd*). This was a garment made of tartan about five feet wide and five or six yards long. It was worn with the lower half draped around the waist and secured by a belt. The upper half was draped over the belt, brought around to the back, and fastened at the left shoulder with a pin, or brooch.

Later this garment was cut into two pieces, the lower half becoming the *feile-beag,* or kilt (a short skirt), and the upper part the plaid. Today the word *plaid* (usually pronounced *plăd*) sometimes is used to mean tartan. More correctly, it refers to a garment worn like a shawl. It is wrapped around the body and fastened at the left shoulder.

Tartan also was made into trews, or tartan breeches, which were tight fitting. The sett was displayed diagonally and was usually smaller than for the plaid. Trews were worn by gentlemen on horseback and by Highlanders when traveling in the Lowlands. The pattern also was worn on the diagonal in jackets of tartan. Women dressed in full skirts and shawls of tartan.

Tartans and History

Tartans have played an important role in Scottish history. They have been connected with the clan system and used to identify fighters in battle. Throughout the latter part of the 17th and the early 18th centuries, there were many rebellions by the Scottish Highlanders against the rule of England. This series of rebellions ended with the attempt by "Bonnie Prince Charlie," the grandson of the exiled James II of England, to regain the English throne for the Stuarts. His army of clansmen was at first successful, but the English finally defeated the Highland Army at the Battle of Culloden Moor in 1746. To destroy the Scottish national spirit, the English Parliament then passed laws abolishing the clan system. They prohibited the playing of bagpipes and outlawed the wearing of the kilt or any other garment made of tartan. These harsh laws were not repealed until 1782. In this 36-year period, much of the old Scottish culture was lost, including the setts of many of the tartans.

After 1746 much of the martial tradition of Scotland was carried on by certain regiments of the British Army that were recruited in Scotland. These soldiers were uniformed in tartan kilts and furnished with bagpipe bands. The first and most famous of these regiments was the Black Watch, at one time also known as the 42nd Foot Regiment. It was formed in 1729 as a police unit of the regular army. It adopted an original tartan of a dark green, blue, and black sett from which came the name Black Watch.

In the early 1800's, the kilt and the wearing of tartan came back into fashion. What had in ancient times, however, been the everyday garb of the Highland clansman became the national costume of Highlander and Lowlander alike. It was kept for sporting and ceremonial occasions.

A demand for tartans arose, and manufacturers designed new setts to replace the ancient ones that had been lost. The Black Watch tartan served as a basis for many new setts, with additional lines of white, red, or yellow. Tartan material was exported and became popular all over the world.

Regimental Tartans

The Scottish regiments of the British Army are divided into the Highland and the Lowland brigades. The Highland Brigade wears kilts. The Lowland Brigade wears trews.

The regiments of the Highland Brigade are the Black Watch and the Argyle and Sutherland Highlanders, whose members all wear the Black Watch tartan; the Queen's Own Highlanders, with its MacKenzie tartan; and the Gordon Highlanders, with its Gordon tartan.

The regiments of the Lowland Brigade are the Royal Scots, whose members wear the Hunting Stuart; the Royal Highland Fusiliers, with its MacKenzie tartan; the Cameronians, with its Douglas tartan; and the King's Own Scottish Borderers, with its Leslie tartan.

The pipers of the Black Watch, the Royal Scots, the Royal Highland Fusiliers, and the King's Own Scottish Borderers wear kilts of the Royal Stuart tartan. The pipes and drums unit and the military band of the Queen's Own Highlanders wear kilts of Cameron of Erracht tartan.

TASHKENT (*tăsh kĕnt'*), **U.S.S.R.,** one of the largest cities of the Soviet Union, is the capital of the Uzbek Soviet Socialist Republic. It is in an oasis that is watered by tributaries of the Syr Darya River.

Tashkent is an important industrial center and the chief market center for the rich agricultural region surrounding the city. The region specializes in irrigated cotton, fruit, rice, and some wheat. Tashkent is one of the leading producers of cotton textiles in the Soviet Union. It also manufactures textile-making and cotton-picking machinery.

Other industries in Tashkent are based on the resources of the surrounding region. The city manufactures mining equipment for the mines in the nearby Fergana Valley. Other industries are the processing of flour, wine, canned goods, meat, tobacco, and leather, and the manufacturing of radios, porcelain, and abrasives.

Located at the junction of historic caravan routes, Tashkent has been a trade center for centuries. At one time the city was reached only by camel caravan. Now it is a center of rail, road, and air travel. The city is divided into two sections. The newer, northeast part of the city, built by the Russians in the latter part of the 19th century, is European in nature. The older part reflects earlier, oriental influences.

Tashkent is an important educational center. In the city is a university; a teachers college; colleges of law, medicine, and agriculture; and textile and railroad trade schools. The city also has the Uzbek Academy of Sciences, a historical museum, a museum of arts, a theater of opera and ballet, and several mosques where the many Muslim residents worship.

Tashkent was founded in the 7th century A.D. Until the 11th century it was ruled by Arabs. It was dominated by the Turks until the 14th century when it came under Mongol rule.

In 1865 Tashkent was taken over by the Russians, who made it the capital of their newly acquired territory in Turkestan. In 1930 Tashkent replaced Samarkand as the capital of the Uzbek S.S.R. In recent years the great expansion of cotton-growing in the oases of Soviet Middle Asia has brought growth and prosperity to Tashkent. The population is 1,385,000 (1970).

TASSO (*tăs'ō* or *täs'sō*), **TORQUATO** (*tôr kwä'tō*) (1544–1595), was the greatest Italian poet of the late Renaissance. The *Faerie Queene* of Edmund Spenser and the *Paradise Lost* of John Milton were greatly influenced by his work.

Torquato Tasso.

Tasso was born at Sorrento and was educated by Jesuits at Naples, and at the universities of Padua and Bologna. He wrote sonnets, and then—under the influence of his father, who was also an epic poet of note—wrote *Rinaldo*. This long poem about the peers of Charlemagne was published in 1562.

Tasso made his home at Ferrara, first in the service of Luigi Cardinal d'Este, then of Duke Alfonso II. His great epic *Jerusalem Delivered* was finished in 1575. The subject was the capture of Jerusalem during the First Crusade. Romantic love stories that Tasso worked into the narrative gave his genius full play. The style was full of ornament and metaphor. For nearly a century it set the fashion in poetry all over Europe.

After 1575 Tasso was mentally ill, and from 1579 to 1586 he was confined. He continued writing, however, and in 1594 he was invited to Rome to be crowned in the Capitol as the greatest poet of his day. He died before the delayed ceremony could take place.

TATARS (*tä'tĕrz*) were nomads from central Asia who poured out of their homeland, along with many other nomadic groups, to overrun western Asia and Europe in the 12th and 13th centuries. They not only invaded but settled as far west as Finland, Poland, and Austria. Today their descendants still live in these regions as well as to the south and east—in Rumania, Bulgaria, Crimea (now included in the Ukraine), and other parts of Soviet territory.

Early historians used the term *Tatar,* and occasionally *Tartar,* to describe any and all Mongols who roamed over Asia during those centuries. Even today some writers use the term loosely to designate all Mongols of that time.

From studies of skeletal remains it is now known that the early Tatars were not true Mongols, but a mixed Mongoloid-Caucasoid (white) stock, already formed in central Asia from an ancient, Europeanlike type of man. Many Tatars may be classified racially as Nordic. These early Turkic-speaking peoples brought with them not only their language but the Islam religion. They formed part of the famous Golden Horde who, under Mongol leadership, began their far-reaching conquests in 1237, including the sacking of Moscow. They ruled in western Asia for about 250 years and were a constant threat to Europe.

In the 13th century, Lithuania (now part of the U.S.S.R.) was the first European country to welcome the Tatars within its borders. The government gave them grants of land and certain privileges in return for their services in the army. In Poland many of the greatest military heroes were Tatars. In both countries the Tatars changed their language to that of their adopted country but retained their Islam religion.

In modern times the Tatars are Muslims of the Turko-Tatar stock. As a proper name, *Tatar* is used only to refer to certain Turkic-speaking groups in the Soviet Union.

TATTOOING (tă tōō'ing) is an old and worldwide custom of decorating the surface of the skin with permanent designs or pictures, or by scarring. The word *tattoo* comes from the Polynesian languages of Maori, *ta,* and Tahitian, *tatu.*

Tattooing was done in early times by honored and well-paid specialists who pricked the skin with sharp instruments. A single-pointed needle of shell (clam, tortoise), bone (bird, animal, human, fish), or stone (flint) usually was used. Sometimes the specialist used an instrument made of many needles (from 3 in Hawaii to 60 in Japan) tightly bound along a wooden handle like a comb or bunched together like a

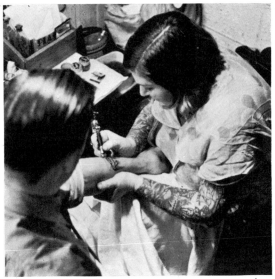

Acme

Ordinarily, a tattoo is made by pricking the skin in dots and lines with a needle, and inserting coloring matter to form a design.

stiff brush. Designs were sketched onto the skin with charcoal mixed with water or oil. The instrument was dipped into a dye, usually red or blue, placed upon the skin, and tapped sharply with a small mallet.

Since tattooing leaves indelible marks, it has served many purposes. Among certain men it was used as a permanent record of personal achievements (warriors in Sumatra were allowed to tattoo a record of slain enemies) or as a symbol of rank shown by the size and position of the pictures. Tattoos have been used to designate the first born son (Marquesas Islands), keepers of tribal pipes (Osage Indians), or royalty (Egyptian mummies), and as a class mark to identify slaves (Hawaii), criminals (Europe), and prisoners (Nazis tattooed numbers on the chests or arms of Jews). Tattoos also have been used as trademarks of professions (carpenters in feudal Japan or sailors of all nationalities), as payments for services (in Polynesia), and as pure decoration (as among the early Britons). The Hupa Indians had marks tattooed on the inside of their left arms to help them measure "shell" money.

Among primitive people, women usually were decorated less than men. The tattooing of a woman usually served as a sign either that she was ready for marriage or that she was already married. Tattooing most frequently was a mark of tribal membership or of beauty, but in Hawaii, tattooed tongues were a sign of mourning.

A single tattooing operation took from a day to three months, depending on the culture and the purpose. Ceremonies, special houses, and rigid taboos, often accompanied the process. In the Marquesas, for example, an untattooed hand could not be used to eat out of the same bowl as a tattooed hand.

Today tattooing still is used for decorative purposes, although it is outlawed in certain areas because of the danger of infection from unclean instruments. Medically, tattooing has been used for blood-type identification and to help conceal unsightly body markings.

TAXATION (*tăks ā'shŭn*) is the collection of money from citizens to pay the costs of government. A government must provide military defense against foreign attack, maintain a police force to protect against crime, and guard the country's welfare. All of these services and others cost money. Taxes are the payments that must be made so that the government can give the necessary services.

Governments through the centuries have used direct and indirect ways of raising money. A direct tax is one that is paid directly to the government. The income tax and property tax are direct taxes. Under the income tax, the government takes a percentage of the taxpayer's income. Under the property tax, the government each year collects an amount based on the value of a taxpayer's property.

An indirect tax is one that is shifted to other people by the person who pays it. The most important indirect taxes are sales and excise taxes and the tariff. Under sales and excise taxes, the government adds a tax to the selling price of goods and services sold to consumers or to business. The tariff, or customs tax, is a tax on goods imported from foreign countries. These indirect taxes are added to the prices of the taxed products and are paid eventually by the consumer.

The United States has three levels of government—local, state, and national. Each needs taxes to support its services. There are about 100,000 local governments in the United States. They include school districts, town and city governments, and county governments.

School districts pay teachers, build and maintain buildings, and provide the services needed by a school system. The school boards usually must present a budget to the public. The budget shows how much the board plans to spend and how much money will be necessary to pay for the services that the school district will provide to the people of the community. State, county, city, town, and village governments also prepare budgets, showing the amounts needed for government services and how the money is to be provided.

Local governments and school districts get most of their money from property taxes. The average homeowner pays several hundred dollars a year in such taxes. The more valuable the properties are, the higher the taxes are. An official called the tax assessor decides how much a piece of property is worth. In most states the property tax is paid only on real estate, that is, on land and buildings. In other states, personal property, such as jewelry and automobiles, also is taxed.

In many small New England towns, the governments still operate as they did in the early days of the American colonies. The citizens meet once a year to decide how much the town will spend. This, in turn, determines how much each family will have to pay in taxes. In voting on what is to be spent, each person helps set the tax rate and has some control over what the tax money will be spent for.

State governments get their money mainly from sales and excise taxes, income taxes, inheritance taxes, and a variety of taxes on business. State governments often provide money to help local governments pay for schools.

Federal Taxes

The federal government uses fewer taxes. More than half of its revenue comes from the individual income tax. (See INCOME TAX.) The second largest source of federal government revenue is the corporation income tax. A new tax law passed in 1964 provided that corporations with large earnings must pay 48 per cent of their profits as taxes.

A third source of federal revenue is the excise tax on tobacco, alcoholic beverages, cars, gasoline, household appliances, luxury articles, theater tickets, telephone service, and many other items. Thus, a watch costing $10 will carry a ten per cent federal excise tax of $1. On each gallon of gasoline bought in 1963 a federal excise tax of four cents was paid in addition to the state gasoline tax.

A similar tax is the tariff paid on imports. This tax is often deliberately set high to protect U.S. manufacturers from foreign competition. A higher tariff will often bring in less money than a low tariff by raising the price on the imported product so high that people no longer will buy it. (See TARIFF.)

There also are other federal taxes on wages and salaries and on the income of people who work for themselves. In 1963 every employed person gave the government $3\frac{5}{8}$ per cent of his wages or salary up to $4,800 to pay for old-age pensions and insurance. Every employer made an equal contribution for each employee. (See SOCIAL SECURITY.)

In addition, the federal government taxes large estates left by people when they die. (See INHERITANCE TAX.)

Taxes in Other Countries

The tax system of Canada is very similar to that of the United States. The provincial governments, however, depend upon money from the national government more than the state governments do in the United States. The national government levies a general sales tax on manufacturers, and most of the provincial governments levy a sales tax on merchants. Because of a greater use of sales taxes, income tax rates are lower in Canada than in the United States.

In Great Britain, the national government gets almost half of the money it needs from the income tax. Excises on luxury goods, tobacco, and alcoholic beverages are very high. The tax on tobacco is about three times the cost of the tobacco itself; the tax on liquor is about twice the cost of the product. Great Britain also

uses a "purchase" tax, which is similar to the general sales tax in the United States. Local governments in Great Britain get their revenues primarily from taxes on property.

The tax system in France is peculiar in that it depends mostly on a "value-added" tax, which is a tax levied at every stage of production. That is, the manufacturer who changes a product and "adds value" to it pays the tax. There is also a "turnover" tax, a form of sales tax paid whenever goods are sold. This is slightly different from the sales tax, which is levied only when a product is sold to the consumer. Local property taxes in France are much less important than they are in the United States or Great Britain. The income tax is used in France, but it has been much less successful there than in other countries.

A country's system of taxation tells much about its economy. Agricultural countries get most of their money from taxes on land, excise taxes, and taxes on exports and imports. On the other hand, highly industrialized countries such as the United States and Great Britain usually get most of their money from income taxes and general sales taxes.

History of Taxation

The governments of the ancient world often depended for revenue upon tribute or direct cash payments from conquered peoples. In most ancient empires the conqueror or the ruling classes paid few if any taxes, though there were land taxes and excise taxes.

Under the feudal governments of the Middle Ages, the average person had to pay dues, tolls, fees, and taxes to support his feudal lord. The farmer had to give the lord part of his harvest, and the merchant or traveler had to pay a toll to use the roads and rivers. A major step toward modern forms of government was taken when the kings of Europe took the power to tax away from the barons and lords. The abolition of tolls on roads and rivers within a country made possible the growth of commerce.

As the feudal lords lost the power to tax, so the kings of most European countries lost that power to representatives of the people. (See PARLIAMENT.) Many revolutions were fought

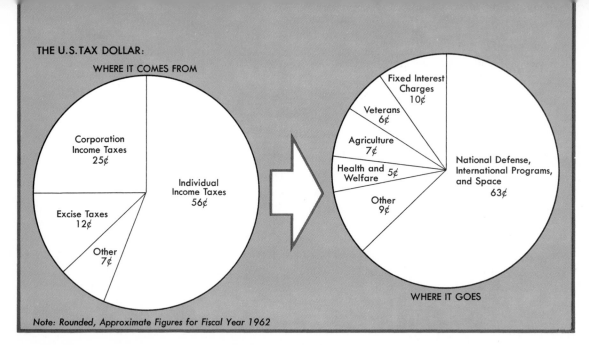

THE U.S. TAX DOLLAR:

WHERE IT COMES FROM

Corporation Income Taxes 25¢

Individual Income Taxes 56¢

Excise Taxes 12¢

Other 7¢

Fixed Interest Charges 10¢

Veterans 6¢

Agriculture 7¢

Health and Welfare 5¢

Other 9¢

National Defense, International Programs, and Space 63¢

WHERE IT GOES

Note: Rounded, Approximate Figures for Fiscal Year 1962

to defend the idea of "no taxation without representation." This was one of the slogans of the American Revolution. Unjust taxation was also one of the causes of the French Revolution.

The leaders of the American Revolution distrusted the British king and opposed his right to levy certain taxes. After their revolt they refused to give the American Continental Congress any taxing powers of its own. The new government under the Articles of Confederation got its money from the state governments. The failure of the states to provide enough money was one of the reasons the Articles did not work. (See ARTICLES OF CONFEDERATION.)

As a result, the Constitution that replaced the Articles gave Congress the right to set and collect taxes. The Constitution also limited these taxing powers. It says that ". . . All Duties, Imposts and Excises shall be uniform throughout the United States . . ." For many years this was taken to mean that the government could not levy an income tax with different rates on different people.

Through most of the 19th century the federal government got the major share of its money from customs duties and from the sale of land. During war periods, however, extra taxes were added. After the Civil War, excise taxes became more important as the government's need for money and the peoples' demand for services increased.

The Income Tax

In 1913 the 16th Amendment gave Congress the power to tax income. The first income tax in 1913 had rates that went from 1 per cent on taxable income of more than $4,000 to 7 per cent on taxable income of more than $500,000. Since that time, the costs of two world wars and the growing cost of government services have increased the nation's need for money. The tremendous increase in federal government expenditures forced the government to increase the rates of the income tax.

State governments began taxing income at about the time of World War I. Wisconsin in 1911 was the first state to levy an income tax. During the 1920's and 1930's many other states followed. By 1962 there were 33 states levying an individual income tax and a corporation income tax.

An important fact about the individual income tax is that it is "progressive." That is, the larger a person's income, the larger his tax rate. The principle of progressive income tax recognizes that a poor family suffers more by giving up ten per cent of its income than a wealthy family that gives up ten per cent. Many other kinds of taxes are called "regressive" taxes. These are taxes in which the burden falls more heavily on the poor than on the rich. The sales tax and many kinds of excise taxes are often called regressive taxes. Though both rich and poor pay the same rate, the poor pay a larger portion of their income.

It is only in modern times that nations have tried to be fair in setting taxes. In earlier times it was the poor who paid almost all the taxes. The general acceptance of the progressive income tax helped to make the tax system more just. All citizens in a democracy have a responsibility to pay something, but those who can afford to pay more are asked to do so.

Taxes and Business

A country's methods of taxing will affect its business and economic growth. It is important to have a tax system that will not discourage hard work and the formation and expansion of business. Heavy taxes may discourage people from setting up new businesses and expanding old ones.

There also may be difficulties in trying to decide what is fair and what is good for the country's economic growth. For example, some persons believe that it would be fair to tax the profits that a person gets from selling his business in the same way that wages are taxed. Others feel that if profits of this sort were taxed, fewer persons would take the risks of investing in businesses.

TAXIDERMY (*tăk'sĭ dẽr mē*) is the art of mounting birds, mammals, fish, and reptiles so that they appear lifelike. One of the oldest examples of the taxidermist's art is a rhinoceros on exhibit in the Royal Museum of Florence, Italy. It is said to have been mounted in the 16th century. For many years taxidermy was referred to as "stuffing animals." A filling material was stuffed into the preserved skin, but even the best of these specimens did not look very lifelike.

About 1900, Carl Akeley, a U.S. naturalist, tried different ways of mounting animals. He wanted them to be in lifelike poses with scenery around them to show how they live in nature. Akeley, an expert sculptor, found the best way was first to make an accurate, life-sized model of the animal. Over this he stretched the hide or skin which had been tanned or preserved. His method was soon adopted by museums

throughout the world. (See AKELEY, CARL.)

The Mounting of Birds

When a bird specimen is collected, an accurate description or color sketch is made of the eyes, bill, feet, and fleshy parts. For most birds only one cut is made for removing the skin from the body. The slit extends from the tip of the breastbone to the tail. Large birds often require more than one opening. The skin is carefully peeled away from the body, leaving only the skull, wing, and leg bones attached to the skin. Then the flesh and muscles on these bones are removed. Care is used not to break or damage the feathers. Powdered borax is dusted on the inside of the skin to preserve it.

Drawings and measurements are taken from the natural body as soon as the skin is removed. These measurements are used to construct an artificial body, which is carved from cork or balsa wood. The neck is made of fine cotton wrapped on a wire that extends through the artificial body into the skull to hold the head in position. The legs and wings are wired, and fine cotton is used to replace the muscles that were cut away. The body is placed in the skin, the legs and wings are wired to it, and the opening is sewed together.

The bird is then set on its base, or perch, and held in place by the wires extending from the feet. The taxidermist shapes and arranges the mounted specimen into a natural and lifelike position. Glass eyes, of the proper size and color, are glued in place. The feathers are held in position with pins and thread. After the bird is dry, the pins and thread are removed. All fleshy parts that have faded are restored with oil paints to match the colors in the original sketch.

The Mounting of Mammals

Small mammals are mounted by a method similar to the method used in mounting birds. The opening cut is made, and the original body is replaced with an artificial one. The animal is then shaped in a true-to-life position and allowed to dry.

The mounting of larger mammals requires experience and a complete knowledge of the new-

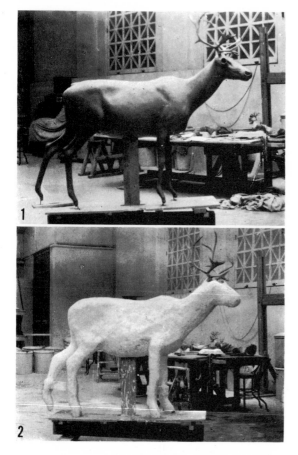

(1) In preparing museum specimens the animal is modeled in clay over the original skeleton. (2) A plaster of Paris mold is made over the clay form. An artificial body is then made inside this mold. (3) The tanned skin of the animal, a caribou, is fitted into place over the artificial body.

Photos, Courtesy Chicago Natural History Museum

est methods of taxidermy. The animals are modeled in clay in about the same way a sculptor models a statue. Measurements are made of different parts of the body and the skin is carefully removed. The opening cut is made down the belly, and others are made on the inner side of each leg. The skin is scraped and salted in order to preserve it. The flesh and muscles are cut away from the animal's skeleton, and all bones are cleaned. The skins of all large mammals are tanned, or leathered, so they will not crack and allow the hair to fall out.

The animal's skeleton is posed in the position desired. Wet modeling clay is then put over the skeleton. The taxidermist, with his knowledge of animal anatomy, models the exact size and shape of the animal's body in clay. Next, a plaster of Paris mold is made over the clay model. This is done one section at a time so that it will come apart after the mold has set. The sections are then removed and several layers of papier-mache, burlap, or wire cloth are laid in each. The sections are then joined and soaked in water. The plaster is broken away from the other layers, leaving a model. Over the model the tanned skin is fitted and fastened in place with a skin paste. Glass eyes are put into position; the antlers or horns, if present, are oiled; the hair is combed and brushed; and the mounted animal is allowed to dry. Oil paints are used to restore faded parts of the skin around the eyes, nostrils, and lips.

The Mounting of Fish and Reptiles

Fish are mounted by making a cast in plaster of Paris. The most important step in fish taxidermy is making accurate color notes of the specimen as soon as it is taken from the water. The delicate colors are soon lost; therefore, color notes are needed when painting the cast to make it look natural.

The fish is placed in a natural pose on a bed of sand, and plaster is poured on and allowed to harden. When the fish has been carefully worked free from its plaster mold, the tail and fins are cut from the specimen, spread out on a board with cardboard and pins, and dried. A plaster separator is painted on the inside of the mold and more plaster is poured in to make the cast. Cast and mold are soaked in water, and the mold then is broken away from the cast, which is an exact duplicate of the fish. When the cast is dry the fins and tail are anchored in position with wires, glass eyes are set in place, and lifelike coloring is applied with oil paints.

The most recent improvements in taxidermy have been in the preparation of reptiles. They are best reproduced in a plastic material instead of a mounted skin. Accurate color notes are made of the reptile as soon as the specimen is caught. The body is then posed, and plaster of Paris is very carefully brushed and poured over the surfaces. Plastic paints are then applied. A backing of several different materials is worked into the mold for strength. As this backing dries it becomes part of the model. After drying, the mold is put into water and the plaster is broken away. The result is a true-to-life reproduction in colored plastic. Glass eyes are added, and the reptile model is adjusted on its base.

TAYLOR (tā′lẽr), **ZACHARY** (zăk′ä rē) (1784–1850), was the 12th president of the United States. He was the second and last member of the Whig party to be elected president. (See WHIG PARTY.) Both he and the first Whig president, William Henry Harrison, died in office.

Taylor was born on November 24, 1784, at Montebello, the family farm in Orange County, Virginia. His parents were Richard and Mary Strother Taylor. His father had been an officer in the Continental Army during the American Revolution. In 1785 the family moved to a farm in Jefferson County, Kentucky. They lived near a fort that soon became the village of Louisville. There Zachary worked on the family farm until 1808, when he was appointed a lieutenant in the U.S. Army. His schooling was brief. He studied for a short time with a tutor that his father had hired.

The future president married Margaret Mackall Smith of Maryland in 1810. They had six children, five girls followed by one boy, Richard, born in 1826. Richard, or "Dick," Taylor served in the Confederate Army during the Civil War and reached the rank of lieutenant

general. The second of Taylor's daughters, Sarah, married lieutenant Jefferson Davis, who later became president of the Confederate States. She died at twenty years of age, however, less than three months after the wedding, and Davis later remarried.

Military Career

Taylor served as a major in the War of 1812 against Great Britain. After the war he continued to advance in rank as he fought in several Indian wars, against England's Indian allies in Illinois and Indiana territories. In 1832 a group of Indians under Chief Black Hawk went on the warpath to protect their hunting rights in Wisconsin and northwestern Illinois. Taylor was with the troops that defeated the Indians and captured Black Hawk. (See BLACK HAWK.) Taylor fought from 1837 to 1840 in Florida Territory in the Seminole War. He was a popular leader, and the men in his command gave him the nickname of "Old Rough and Ready." He was not a great general, but his men had confidence in him and always

Zachary Taylor, U.S. president, 1849–1850.

Brown Brothers

TAYLOR'S LIFETIME

1783	American Revolution ends.
1784	Taylor born.
1803	Louisiana Purchase.
1808	Taylor enters army.
1810	Marries Margaret Mackall Smith.
1812	War with England.
1832	Black Hawk War.
1835	Seminole War.
1846	Mexican War.
1847	Battle of Buena Vista.
	PRESIDENT
1850	Compromise of 1850.

Taylor's Term of Office (1849–1850)

1849	California Gold Rush. California asks statehood.
1850	Clayton-Bulwer Treaty. Southern talk of secession. Compromise discussions. President Taylor dies.

fought hard. His successes against the Indians eventually made him one of the most important generals in the army.

When Texas was annexed in 1845, Taylor was given orders to move into Texas and take up positions near the Rio Grande River on land that the Mexicans claimed. The Mexican War started in 1846 when some U.S. troops were fired on. Taylor quickly won several minor battles and seized the Mexican cities of Matamoros and Monterrey. His most important victory was the Battle of Buena Vista in 1847. Although outnumbered by the Mexicans four to one, Taylor's troops won a decisive victory. (See MEXICAN WAR.)

Elected President

Taylor's victories in the Mexican War made him well known throughout the country and led to his nomination by the Whig party as their candidate for president in 1848. Millard Fillmore was the Whig candidate for vice-president. Taylor won 163 electoral votes to 127 for his Democratic opponent, Lewis Cass.

Like many professional soldiers, Taylor had never voted in a presidential election. As president he had to learn about politics, and often he had to rely on his cabinet to help him with problems he knew nothing about.

Taylor's biggest problem as president involved the lands the United States took over after the Mexican War. Gold was discovered in California in 1848 and by the end of the year more than 80,000 persons moved into the territory. California applied for admission as a free state. Although a slaveowner, President Taylor favored the admission of California, but most southerners did not want another free state in the Union. At that time there were 15 slave states and 15 free states. Slavery was one of many issues dividing North and South. Many southerners were talking about secession, and Henry Clay tried to work out a compromise on many of the issues dividing the North and South. It is probable that Taylor would have refused to sign some of the measures Congress was considering as parts of the compromise, since he insisted that California be admitted without any compromise, but he died during the debates. President Fillmore later signed the bills that made up the "Compromise of 1850." This may have postponed the outbreak of the Civil War by ten years. (See COMPROMISE OF 1850.)

The California Gold Rush caused another problem. People began looking for some way of getting to California that would be quicker and easier than the slow overland trip or the sea voyage around South America. Some thought about a canal across Central America. At that time England was trying to take over part of Central America. After the United States protested, the two countries agreed to the Clayton-Bulwer Treaty of 1850 under which any canal across Central America would be supervised by both countries. Neither country was to extend its control over Central American lands. The canal was not built for more than 50 years, though a railroad across the isthmus of Panama was completed in 1855.

Taylor served as president for less than half of the term for which he had been elected. On July 4, 1850, he laid the cornerstone of the Washington Monument in Washington, D.C. He was taken ill during the ceremonies, which were held on an extremely

Brown Brothers
Margaret Taylor.

hot day. He died on July 9, 1850.

Taylor's United States

During this period the United States was rapidly becoming a large and powerful country. In the years just before Taylor's election, Texas, Oregon, and the Southwest had been added to the nation. The United States stretched from ocean to ocean, and many people thought that it was going to continue to grow. Southerners were especially interested in Cuba because slavery was profitable there, but Taylor refused to start a fight with Spain over that island.

The nation was young and energetic. The population passed 23 million in 1850. Settlers were coming in ever larger numbers from Ireland and Germany. Many Irishmen were forced to leave their homeland because of a serious famine. Some of them took jobs building the railroad network that was beginning to cover the eastern United States. Many Germans flocked to cities like Milwaukee, Wisconsin, and St. Louis, Missouri. As fast as these new people arrived in the East, others moved West. Indian warriors still ruled the plains, but slow wagon trains were carrying more and more settlers to the fertile valleys of Oregon and California. Men were talking about railroads and telegraph lines to the Pacific Coast.

After the discovery of gold in California, many would not wait any longer to go West. They crossed the plains and mountains or went by boat around the tip of South America. New towns appeared overnight. Ships that stopped in California ports often lost their crews, who deserted to look for gold. The village of San Francisco suddenly became a city of shanties and tents, as gold-hungry men from all over the world came to find their fortunes. (See CALIFORNIA.) With a large number of newcomers, there was so much crime that citizens often got together in vigilance committees to punish criminals. Many of these criminals were lynched, or killed, without trial.

Zachary Taylor's time was a great period in American literature, often called the "flowering of New England" because most of the best writers were from New England. In Massa-chusetts a group called the Transcendentalists gathered around Ralph Waldo Emerson. One of them, Henry Thoreau, wrote an essay on "Civil Disobedience," in which he said a man ought to do what he thought right, even though it meant disobeying the laws. Nathaniel Hawthorne published *The Scarlet Letter* in 1850, and Herman Melville was writing *Moby Dick*. Historian Francis Parkman was writing about the Oregon Trail, and William Prescott was writing about Spanish and Latin-American history. Outstanding poets of the period included Henry Wadsworth Longfellow, John Greenleaf Whittier, and James Russell Lowell. The outstanding writer outside New England was a Southern poet and short-story writer, Edgar Allan Poe. (See articles on individual writers.)

TBILISI (*t'pi'li sē*), **U.S.S.R.,** is the capital of the Georgian Soviet Socialist Republic. The city is situated on both banks of the Kura River. The name *Tbilisi* comes from a Georgian term meaning "warm springs." Several warm sulfur springs are located within the city.

The old section of Tbilisi looks like a city of the Middle East. The streets were deliberately laid out in a narrow, crooked pattern in order to prevent invading horsemen from using them. Along these streets are fascinating bazaars where the skilled work of Georgian craftsmen is displayed. The wares include guns, swords, carpets, hand-wrought silver products, and silk textiles. In the old part of the city are several ancient structures, including St. David's Church and the 5th-century Zion Cathedral, seat of the patriarch of the Georgian Orthodox Church.

The newer section, built by the Russians, contrasts sharply in appearance with the old section. In the new part are wide, tree-lined boulevards, public gardens, and modern government buildings. The city has an opera house, a ballet theater, and a museum of arts. Educational institutions include an academy of sciences, a university, an academy of arts, and special teacher-training, technical, and medical colleges.

Tbilisi is a transportation hub for rail and road travel within the Caucasus Mountains. The city is also an industrial center. It has railroad shops; factories that manufacture machinery for making textiles, tea, and wine; woodworking shops; and factories that process tobacco, food products, and wine.

Tbilisi was founded in the 4th century A.D. In the 6th century it became a capital of the region of Iberia, which is now the eastern part of Georgia. In the following centuries it was repeatedly looted and destroyed by Persians, Byzantines, Arabs, Mongols, and Turks. The city was rebuilt each time. The Georgians were not always able to fight off the invaders, but Tbilisi remained the center of Georgian resistance to oppression. Between 1800 and 1867, in a series of annexations, the Russians annexed Georgia, and the city became known by its Russian name, Tiflis. During the 1930's the name was changed back to Tbilisi. Soviet Premier Joseph Stalin, a Georgian, spent several of his early years in Tbilisi, first studying for the priesthood and later entering into early Communist revolutionary activities.

The population of Tbilisi is 889,000 (1970).

TCHAIKOVSKY (*chī kôf'skē*), **PETER** (*pē'tĕr*) **ILICH** (*il'yĕch'*) (1840–1893), Russian composer, was born at Votkinsk. As a child he did not show any great musical talent, though he had piano lessons and loved music. He was sent to the preparatory classes for the School of Jurisprudence in St. Petersburg (now Leningrad). Later he graduated from that school and entered the civil service in the Ministry of Justice. He began studying music seriously at the conservatory in St. Petersburg. Anton Rubinstein, the director of the conservatory, was the source of great inspiration to Tchaikovsky.

Tchaikovsky was strongly influenced by the Italian school of music, and he loved the music of Wolfgang Mozart. Tchaikovsky's music was received with more enthusiasm abroad than it was in Russia, probably because of its artistic individuality. His compositions are filled with warmth and feeling that touch the listener.

During his adult life, Tchaikovsky suffered from an emotional instability that resulted in feelings of sadness and melancholy. In 1877 he entered into a disastrous marriage with Antonina Ivanovna Milyukova. It lasted only a

Peter Ilich Tchaikovsky.

few weeks, and Tchaikovsky was deeply affected by its sad outcome. Perhaps the most important person in his life was Nadezhda Filaretovna von Meck, a wealthy widow from whom he received financial assistance for 13 years but whom he never met. This support solved his financial problems until he gained a reputation and was able to support himself.

In 1891 Tchaikovsky visited the United States and was received with great enthusiasm. Among his most important works are the symphonies four, five, and six (best known as the *Pathetique*); the opera *Eugen Onegin*; the ballets *Swan Lake, The Sleeping Beauty,* and *The Nutcracker;* the Concerto Number 1 for piano; *March Slav; 1812 Overture;* and the overture-fantasy *Romeo and Juliet.*

TEA (*tē*) is the dried leaves of the tea plant (*Camellia sinensis*) or the drink made from such leaves. An afternoon party at which the drink is served may also be called a tea.

Under natural conditions tea plants grow into trees 30 feet high or more. When they are grown on tea plantations, however, they are pruned as shrubs, three to five feet in height, so that the leaves will be easier to pick and so that there will be more tender young leaves. The leaves are evergreen, usually leathery and shiny, and are from one to five inches long. The fragrant, white, and waxy flowers are an inch or more in width.

Tea plants grow in a warm, humid climate. More than a third of the world's tea supply is produced in North India and Pakistan, and the next largest producer is Ceylon. Tea can be grown in the southern United States, but it is less expensive to import it. The climate and soil of Australia are right for growing tea, but the cost of labor is too great. Soviet scientists have developed a tea plant that grows well in their climate, and much of the tea used in the

U.S.S.R. is now raised there.

Next to water, tea is the most universally consumed beverage. It is estimated that in the United Kingdom an average of nearly ten pounds of tea per person is used each year. It also is estimated that 107,000,000 pounds of tea are used each year in the United States. Its use is increasing in other countries, especially in Asia and Africa.

There are many legends about the discovery and early use of tea. The Chinese have enjoyed its mildly stimulating effects for nearly 5,000 years. In about A.D. 1000, bricks of powdered tea were placed in golden boxes by Chinese tea growers and sent to their emperor as tribute. In 1610 a Dutch trader exchanged dried sage for tea and brought the tea from China to Europe. England's first tea was imported in the mid-17th century.

Tea even played a role in the American Revolution. The "Boston Tea Party" took place in 1773. The American colonists liked tea, but they did not like to pay England a tax on it when they had nothing to say about the tax. As a protest against taxation they dumped more than 300 chests of tea into Boston Harbor. After the war, tea was an important item in American commerce. Fast clipper ships were built to speed tea from China to North America and Europe.

Tea plants are grown from seed planted directly in the field or, more often, in a nursery. Plants also are started from cuttings taken from especially fine trees, and by layering, or bending a shoot over into the ground to take root. The plants will begin to bear commercially in the third year and may yield well for 50 or more years. The leaves are picked by hand or cut with scissors. Experiments indicate that machines may be developed for picking, which would greatly reduce the cost of harvesting. The best tea comes from the bud and the first two leaves. It is estimated that it takes 32,000 tea shoots for one pound of tea.

Black, green, and oolong tea come from the same plants but are processed differently. To make black tea, the freshly picked leaves are spread on a shelf to wilt. Then they are put into the rolling machines to remove the juice. The dry leaves are spread on tables where they oxidize, or take up oxygen from the air. This process changes the green leaves to a bright copper color and gives strength and body to the tea. Next they are fired in a hot oven to stop the oxidation, and their final color is blackish. To make green tea, the leaves are softened by steaming or are partially dried in a hot pan. The softened leaves are steamed and rolled until they begin to crisp and then are dried thoroughly. To make oolong tea, the leaves are only partly oxidized. After drying, all three kinds are sifted, graded, and packed for shipment. Almost all tea is blended before it is packed. Blending produces the desired appearance, flavor, aroma, and strength. At least 2,000 blends are possible. Gardenia or jasmine flow-

On East African tea plantations most of the tea picking is done by men. Only the tender tips, usually consisting of two leaves and a leaf bud, are picked and dried for the production of commercial tea.

Courtesy (right) Ceylon Tea Bureau, London

ers, orange rind, and various spices are added to some teas to increase the fragrance. The quality of the tea leaves depends on their tenderness, the altitude at which the tea is grown, the soil, and the weather.

Tea to drink is made from the dried tea leaves. The leaves may be loose, in tea bags, powdered, or pressed into bricks. Much of the tea used in the U.S.S.R., Mongolia, and Tibet is in the brick form. The stimulating effect of tea, as of coffee, comes from the presence of caffeine. Tea also contains tannin and certain essential oils. If tea is boiled or steeped too long, too much tannin will be released, giving the tea a bitter taste. Tea may be served either hot or iced. It is estimated that 2,500,000,000 glasses of iced tea are consumed yearly in the United States.

Not all tea is used as a beverage. In China, Burma, and Siam, tea leaves are sometimes pickled and eaten as a salad; in Tibet, tea is made into a soup. Tablets of compressed tea are used in Manchuria, Mongolia, and parts of Siberia as money.

The leaves of some other plants are used to make such drinks as Labrador tea, Mexican tea, New Jersey tea, alfalfa tea, Oswego tea, and mate. Other parts of plants are used in making such teas as rose hip, sassafras, and camomile. Well-known herb teas are made of catnip, horehound, lemon balm, mint, and sage.

TEAK (*tēk*), or *Tectona grandis*, is one of the most valuable timber trees in the world. It grows in India and Southeast Asia, and may attain a height of 200 feet and a circumference of 20 feet. It bears small, white flowers and large, rough leaves that are used as sandpaper by some people. In Asia its beautiful golden brown wood is used for furniture, houses, bridges, railroad ties, and many other purposes. It is an important export item from that area of the world. The teak tree is so highly valued that extensive teak plantations have been established.

Logging these large trees is an interesting industry because even today much of the work is done by elephants. The animals drag the logs down the slopes to the rivers where they may be floated to the sawmills. Teak wood is so dense that when it is green it will not float. Consequently trees to be cut are girdled so that they will die. This is done by stripping a band of bark and sap wood from around the base of the tree. The tree is left on the stump to dry for about three years before cutting.

The *Merrimac* and the *Monitor*, the first iron-clad warships, ushered in a naval era in which teak played a most vital role. It became the construction wood on which to fasten the armor plate, because it was the only commercial wood that did not cause the iron or steel plates to rust. In addition, the wood was hard, resistant to insects and decay, and stood up well even though exposed to salt water, extreme climatic conditions, and rough usage. Because it did not splinter, it was ideal for decking. It continued to be a major naval timber until the early 1900's. Even today many navies use it for decking, hand rails, and other fittings.

TECUMSEH (*tē kŭm'sĕ*) (1768?–1813) was an Indian leader. The son of a Shawnee chief, he was born near the present site of Springfield, Ohio. As a youth he took part in attacks on settlers who were moving into the Ohio River Valley. Intelligent and a good speaker, he became one of the Indian leaders in their talks with the settlers.

As the Indians were pushed farther west, Tecumseh realized that the tribes had to join together if they were to protect their lands. Some time after 1808, he and his brother, known as the Prophet, built a town in Indiana at the

Elephants serve as trucks for the teak industry in northern Thailand.

OROC

mouth of the Tippecanoe River. There, at the Prophet's Town, liquor was forbidden, and many Indians began to farm the land.

Tecumseh claimed that the United States took Indian lands by unfair treaties. It was his belief that a chief could not sell land without the consent of his people. Many other tribes agreed to work with him in a confederation. As the settlers moved farther and farther west, more tribes joined Tecumseh, until he had followers from Michigan to Florida. The British agreed to give Tecumseh arms and ammunition.

In 1811 Tecumseh went south to organize the southern Indians. While he was gone, William Henry Harrison, governor of Indiana territory, marched with a small army to the Prophet's Town. The Prophet and Tecumseh's army were defeated in the hard-fought Battle of Tippecanoe. (See HARRISON, WILLIAM HENRY.)

When the War of 1812 began, Tecumseh believed that the British would protect the Indians. He joined the British in Canada with a group of Indian braves. (See WAR OF 1812.) As a brigadier general in the British army he took part in the capture of Detroit. Tecumseh would not let the Indians massacre United States prisoners. He was killed in Canada during the Battle of the Thames, a British defeat.

TEETH (*tēth*) are hard, almost rocklike structures firmly fixed in bony sockets in the upper and lower jaw. They are used to bite and chew food and mix it with saliva. Teeth also aid in speech as they help to form certain sounds. Also, well-formed jaws and teeth in proper position help make the face more attractive.

Man has two sets of teeth: a first (primary) or baby set, and a second or permanent set.

In a full set of teeth there are four types and each type has a special duty. The *incisors*, in the center of the mouth, cut or incise food. The *cuspids,* which tear food, are on either side of the incisors at the corners of the mouth. They have long, heavy roots and sharp, pointed crowns. The *bicuspids,* just back of the cuspids, have two points, or cusps, and one or two roots. They tear and crush food. The *molars,* in the back of the mouth, have several cusps and two or three roots. They grind food.

Each tooth has the same two parts: a *root* or roots, which anchors it in the jawbone, and a *crown,* the part that can be seen in the mouth. There are four different materials in a tooth. The *enamel* is hard and shiny, and covers the crown. The *cementum* is a bonelike material that covers the root. The *dentine* is an ivorylike material that forms the bulk or body of the tooth. The *dental pulp* is in a hollow space called the pulp chamber inside the tooth. The dental pulp is made up of tissue that contains nerves, arteries, veins, and lymphatics. These enter the tooth through an opening at or near the root end.

First Teeth

There are 20 teeth in the first set, 10 in each jaw. They begin to form about 30 weeks before birth. In most children the first teeth to appear are the lower incisors. They usually appear when a child is about six months old, but some children cut teeth more slowly than others. Between the 6th and the 30th month, the rest of the primary teeth appear. Most children have all 20 of their first teeth when they are two and one-half or three years old. The primary teeth in each jaw are the four incisors; two cuspids, one on each side of the jaw; and four molars, two on each side of the jaw.

As the permanent teeth develop under the gums in the jawbone, the roots of the first teeth gradually dissolve. When a permanent tooth is formed and ready to erupt (appear), the primary tooth it will replace loosens and comes out.

Permanent Teeth

Twenty-eight of the 32 teeth in the permanent set usually erupt between the 6th and the 14th years. The other four, the third molars or wisdom teeth, erupt between the 17th and 21st years.

The permanent teeth are four incisors, two cuspids, four bicuspids, and six molars in each jaw. The 12 permanent molars do not replace any of the primary teeth. As the jaws become longer, they grow behind the primary teeth. The bicuspids in the permanent set replace molars in the first set.

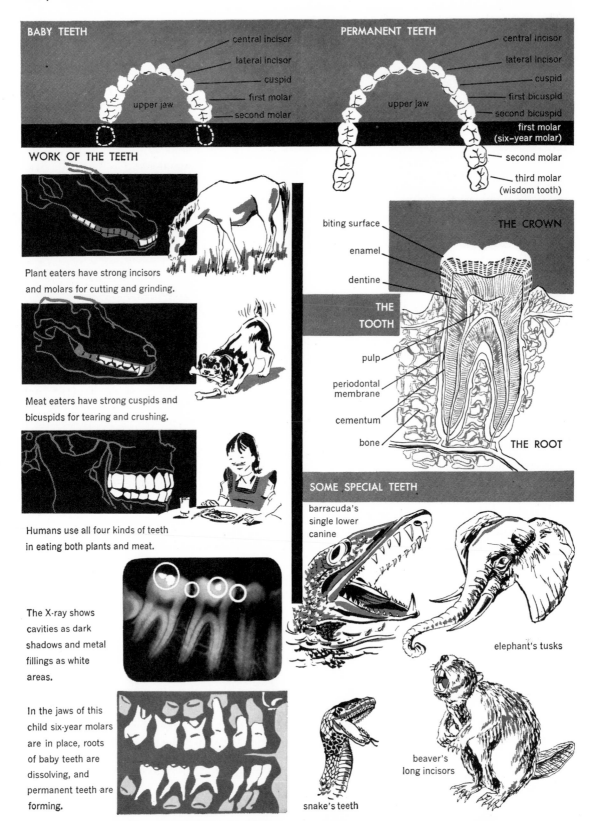

BABY TEETH
- central incisor
- lateral incisor
- cuspid
- first molar
- second molar

upper jaw

PERMANENT TEETH
- central incisor
- lateral incisor
- cuspid
- first bicuspid
- second bicuspid
- first molar (six-year molar)
- second molar
- third molar (wisdom tooth)

upper jaw

WORK OF THE TEETH

Plant eaters have strong incisors and molars for cutting and grinding.

Meat eaters have strong cuspids and bicuspids for tearing and crushing.

Humans use all four kinds of teeth in eating both plants and meat.

The X-ray shows cavities as dark shadows and metal fillings as white areas.

In the jaws of this child six-year molars are in place, roots of baby teeth are dissolving, and permanent teeth are forming.

THE CROWN
- biting surface
- enamel
- dentine

THE TOOTH
- pulp
- periodontal membrane
- cementum
- bone

THE ROOT

SOME SPECIAL TEETH

barracuda's single lower canine

elephant's tusks

beaver's long incisors

snake's teeth

The first molars, which are often called the six-year molars, usually are the first to erupt. They are the largest and among the most important teeth. Their position in the jaw helps determine the shape of the lower part of the face and the position of the other permanent teeth. They come in right behind the primary molars and often are mistakenly thought of as primary teeth.

Tooth Decay

In man, tooth decay is caused by bacteria in the mouth acting on carbohydrates, chiefly sugar. This action produces an acid which can dissolve tooth enamel and so start a cavity. Usually the acid begins to work where there is a scratch or crack in the enamel or where the enamel is hard to clean. As the enamel dissolves a small hole is formed, and decay begins. The hole that is formed is called a cavity.

A dentist must remove the decay and fill the cavity. If he does not do this, the decay will go from the enamel into the dentine and then into the pulp. When the pulp is exposed, infection takes place and the tooth may have to be removed.

Eating fewer sweets and brushing teeth right after eating help to reduce tooth decay. If brushing is not possible, the mouth should be rinsed thoroughly with water.

Research has shown that drinking water containing at least one part per million of fluoride from the time of birth helps children develop teeth that resist decay.

Animal and Fish Teeth

The type of teeth animals have tells about their habits and food. Thus, animals that eat other animals have tearing teeth; rats and other rodents have gnawing teeth, and cattle have grinding teeth. The crowns of the molars are alike in all animals of the same family group.

The largest teeth are the tusks of the male African elephant. They are a kind of incisor that may grow as large as 10 feet and weigh as much as 220 pounds. These tusks are not used in eating but as weapons. The great cutting teeth of a beaver are also a kind of incisor. The tusks of the walrus, wild boar, and wolf are large canines (cuspids). The canine teeth of dogs and cats are sharp and long so that it is easy for them to catch and hold their prey. The teeth of the squirrel are shaped in such a way that they can easily gnaw through the hard shell of a nut. The molar teeth of horses are grinding teeth. Teeth develop so evenly in all horses for the first ten years that it is possible to know just about how old a horse is by his teeth.

The teeth of fish are forms of scales. They usually are set in several rows. The teeth in the back row replace the missing teeth in the front row. Some sharks have cutting teeth for eating fish, while others have blunt teeth for crushing shellfish. The sword of the swordfish is an extension of the upper jawbone and has teeth on it for cutting. When the pike swallows food its teeth lean backward. Then they move upright again. The sturgeon has no teeth. Turtles have horny jaws instead of teeth, and frogs have teeth only in their upper jaws.

The teeth of snakes are set so that they lean inward at an angle. This makes it nearly impossible for their prey to escape. In poisonous snakes, as in the cobra, the poison fangs may always be upright. Or, as in the rattlesnake, they may lie flat in the mouth and be upright only when the jaws open for striking. The teeth of lizards usually are a number of pegs in both jaws. Birds, which once had teeth like those of the reptiles, are now toothless.

TEGUCIGALPA (*tĕ goo sĭ găl'pä*), **HONDURAS,** is the capital and largest city of the country. It is an inland city located on the Choluteca River. Tegucigalpa is in an elevated basin at about 3,200 feet above sea level and is almost completely surrounded by mountain peaks.

Of all the Central American capitals, Tegucigalpa is the only one that is not served by a railroad. Furthermore, it is the only capital not located on the Pan-American Highway. It is linked to it, however, by a paved road 65 miles long. Air transportation has therefore become vital to the city, and it is now an important Central American air-route center.

The city enjoys a mild climate. Average daily temperatures range between 65 and 75 degrees

Fahrenheit. The rainy season lasts from May to November.

The main function of the city is as an administrative center and a place of commerce. Industries are small. At one time, mining of the nearby silver and gold mines was important, but that industry has declined. Agriculture is now the significant industry. Small factories process food and manufacture cigarettes, textiles, leather, furniture, candy, and building materials.

Most of the buildings in Tegucigalpa are only two and three stories high. In recent years, however, new buildings have risen to heights of eight stories. The main buildings include the Presidential Palace, the cathedral, the congressional building, and the national university. The main square is Plaza Morazan, named for Francisco Morazan. (See MORAZAN, FRANCISCO.) The central shopping area is along Avenida Paz Barahona, the main avenue.

Tegucigalpa was founded by the Spanish about 1579 as a gold- and silver-mining center. In the years between 1824 and 1880 it alternated with Comayagua as the capital of Honduras, but since that time has been the permanent capital of the republic.

The population is 134,075 (1961).

TEHERAN (*tĕ'ĕ răn'*) (TEHRAN), **IRAN,** is the capital and largest city of the country. It is also Iran's cultural and industrial center.

Along the crowded, narrow streets of Teheran's bazaars, merchants display the city's many products.

Samy Abboud—Pix from Publix

The city is about 70 miles south of the Caspian Sea on a fertile plain between two mountain ranges. Surrounding Teheran are fields of wheat, sugar beets, fruit, and cotton. To the south of the plain, the mountains rise to heights ranging from 5,000 to 7,000 feet above sea level. To the north, about 10 miles away, the snowy Elburz Mountains rise to peaks of more than 18,000 feet. The altitude of the city itself is 3,810 feet.

Teheran has hot, dry summers, with a July average of 85 degrees Fahrenheit. Winters are cool and brisk, with a January average of 34.

About 25 percent of Iran's industry is in Teheran. Most important among the city's many products are refined copper, ammunition, textiles, sugar, glass, cigarettes, leather goods, and lumber. Railways and roads connect the city with all other important towns and cities in Iran. International airlines connect it with major foreign cities.

After 1925 the government of Shah Riza Khan speeded up the country's modernization program by tearing down the ancient earthen walls surrounding the city. At the center of the city is a large square surrounded by government buildings. To the north and west of it, the modernization program has produced broad, tree-lined avenues with European-style buildings. The marble castle of the shah, the ambassadors' homes, and the homes of Iran's wealthy families are in this modern section. To the south of the square, however, narrow, crooked streets hemmed in by the walls of the houses remain. In this area is the bazaar quarter, where merchants and buyers bargain over rugs, jewelry, pottery, and other products.

Teheran is a center of Muslim culture. It has many mosques, a college of religion, a university, and two museums.

Teheran is believed to have existed in the 9th century A.D. Mongol hordes nearly destroyed it in the early 13th century. It developed slowly and in about 1788 became the capital of Iran under Agha Mohammed Khan.

In recent years Teheran has grown rapidly. The population since 1925 has increased sixfold. The 1966 estimated population was 2,488,-583. (See IRAN.)

TEL AVIV-JAFFA (tĕl ä vēv′ jăf′å), **ISRAEL,** is the largest and most modern city of the country. It is actually two adjoining municipalities, Tel Aviv and Jaffa, that have been combined to form one. It is also called Tel Aviv-Yafo.

Tel Aviv-Jaffa is a port city, situated on the shores of the Mediterranean Sea. Its location provides the mild climate the city enjoys, and, in fact, *Tel Aviv* means "Hill of Spring." Summers are warm and dry, with a July mean temperature of 81 degrees Fahrenheit. Winters are mild, with a January mean temperature of 55 degrees Fahrenheit.

Tel Aviv-Jaffa is Israel's economic center and fastest growing city. It has many of the country's industries. Food processing and textiles are important, as are furniture and leather-goods manufacture, printing, and watchmaking. As the financial center of Israel, Tel Aviv-Jaffa has a stock exchange and is the headquarters for banks and insurance companies. It is served by an international airline, and road and rail communications are excellent. As a port, Tel Aviv-Jaffa is second only to Haifa for handling Israel's imports and exports.

The cultural activities of Israel are centered at Tel Aviv-Jaffa. The city has libraries, an art museum, and Tel Aviv University. The Israel Philharmonic Orchestra has its headquarters there, and the world-famous Habima (the Israel National Theater) is among several other cultural institutions. The city has hundreds of synagogues including the Great Synagogue, the largest in Israel.

Each new group of immigrants that has entered Tel Aviv-Jaffa in the years since its found-

A. L. Goldman – Rapho Guillumette

The theater building of the Habima (the Israel National Theater) was opened in Tel Aviv in 1945.

ing has added a new touch of color, dress, talent, and energy. The city now has an international atmosphere. Many tourists are attracted by the modern hotels; wide, tree-lined streets; neat, white stucco buildings; outdoor cafes; and beautiful beaches.

Jaffa is an ancient city that may have existed in 2000 B.C. It is mentioned in ancient Egyptian writings and in the Old Testament. In the 12th century A.D. it was captured by Crusaders. The Arabs recaptured it, and for several centuries it remained basically an Arabian city.

In 1909 a few of the Jewish families of the city migrated just north of it and founded a small settlement, Tel Aviv. Gradually the settlement grew. The 1921 riots in Jaffa between the Arabs and the Jews caused several thousand Jews to move to Tel Aviv. Later conflicts in eastern Europe and the rise of anti-Semitism in Nazi Germany sent countless numbers of refugees to the city.

During the struggle for Palestine that followed World War II, Tel Aviv was the scene of many battles between the Arabs and Jews. When the state of Israel was proclaimed in 1948, the city became its provisional capital. The government seat was moved to Jerusalem in 1949. (See ISRAEL, STATE OF.)

Tel Aviv-Jaffa is presently a major center for Israeli immigrants. Most of the Arabs have left. The population of Tel Aviv-Jaffa (1961 census) is 386,070.

Tel Aviv's pleasant climate, lovely beaches, and modern hotels attract many tourists to the city.

A. L. Goldman – Rapho Guillumette

HOW TO BUILD A TELEGRAPH

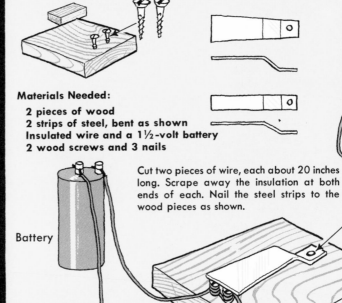

In 1794 the semaphore, above, used wooden signals to send messages. The first electric telegraph message, below, was sent in 1844.

Materials Needed:
2 pieces of wood
2 strips of steel, bent as shown
Insulated wire and a 1½-volt battery
2 wood screws and 3 nails

Battery

Cut two pieces of wire, each about 20 inches long. Scrape away the insulation at both ends of each. Nail the steel strips to the wood pieces as shown.

Receiver

Fasten the end of one wire to the nail that holds the steel strip to the sender.

Sender

About 10 inches from the end, wrap the wire around one screw of the receiver six times, then around the other screw six times. Fasten the free end to one battery terminal. Fasten one end of the second wire to the second terminal, the other to the sender as shown.

TELEGRAPH (*těl'ĭ grăf*) is an apparatus or system for transmitting coded messages from one point to another by means of electric signals. Before electricity was used to send messages, many types of telegraph had been developed. Smoke signals were used by ancient Greeks and American Indians. African tribesmen beat out messages on tom-toms and wooden drums. In France, Napoleon sent messages to his forces by semaphore telegraphy. These devices used movable wooden or metal arms set at angles like railroad signals. None of these systems, however, could communicate farther than one was able to see or hear. It was not until electricity was used that long distance, rapid communication became possible.

As early as 1753 British inventors were experimenting with electric devices to carry messages. In 1800 the Italian physicist Alessandro Volta developed the electric battery, called a voltaic pile. This led to new developments in telegraphy. In the United States, John Coxe in 1816 and Harrison Dyar in 1828 developed devices to send signals over wires by using electric currents from batteries. Dyar operated a

telegraph line eight miles long on Long Island.

In 1820, Hans Christian Oersted of Denmark found that electric impulses transmitted by a wire could be detected magnetically with a compass needle. This led to the first approach to today's telegraphy. In France, Andre Marie Ampere put magnetic needles at the ends of 26 wires so their reaction would signal the 26 letters of the alphabet.

The first practical telegraph system was developed by Samuel F. B. Morse while he was a

INTERNATIONAL MORSE CODE

A ·—	Q ——·—	4 ····—
B —···	R ·—·	5 ·····
C —·—·	S ···	6 —····
D —··	T —	7 ——···
E ·	U ··—	8 ———··
F ··—·	V ···—	9 ————·
G ——·	W ·——	0 —————
H ····	X —··—	
I ··	Y —·——	
J ·———	Z ——··	**COMMA** ·—·—·—
K —·—		
L ·—··		**PERIOD** ··—··—·
M ——	**NUMERALS**	
N —·	1 ·————	**SEMICOLON** —·—·—·
O ———	2 ··———	
P ·——·	3 ···——	**QUESTION** ··——··

The Morse code is a series of dots and dashes that stand for letters, numerals, and other symbols. It was used almost universally until the 1920's. Today, other codes, which are in keeping with electronic systems, have nearly replaced the Morse code.

An exact duplicate, right, of anything written, printed, or drawn can be transmitted from one point to another by facsimile telegraph.

A teleprinter, below, can be connected to an almost unlimited number of locations.

A huge microwave antenna, below right, is part of a coast-to-coast transmission system.

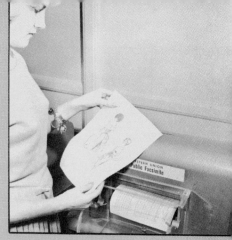

Photos, Courtesy Western Union

The modern telegraph today does things unheard of 50 years ago.

teacher at New York University. (See MORSE, SAMUEL FINLEY BREESE.) Morse exhibited his invention to a skeptical public in 1837 and to the U.S. president and other high officials in Washington, D.C., in 1838. In 1843 Congress appropriated $30,000 to build a line from Washington, D.C., to Baltimore, Maryland.

On May 24, 1844, Morse sent the first historic message over this line—"What hath God wrought!" But, because government officials could not be convinced that the telegraph would ever pay, private capital took over. The Western Union Telegraph Company was formed as the leader in the new field, and the industry was developed successfully in the United States. At about the same time the Electric Telegraph Company was organized in England.

Early Improvements

In 1836 Morse had devised a relay for renewing weakened electric circuits. This aided in sending telegraphed messages over long distances. His first relay weighed 300 pounds.

Today relays weigh less than a pound and have become one of the most important methods of controlling electric circuits. Morse's associate and financial helper, Alfred Vail, constructed the first demonstration instruments. He also simplified Morse's telegraph sending key.

Telegraph operators learned to translate, or read, messages by listening to the clicks of an electromagnet relay. Eventually the operators were able to read and transmit messages with great speed. This improvement helped the Morse system replace all others.

From 1853 to 1872 various inventors worked on duplexing systems—methods of sending one message each way at the same time over the same wire. In 1874, Thomas Edison perfected a system by which two messages could be sent each way at the same time over the same wire. Continued advances permitted more and more messages to be transmitted simultaneously.

Modern Telegraphic Services

Much of today's work handled by the telegraph companies is done with telegraph printers, called teleprinters. The sending operator types out a message on an instrument with a typewriter keyboard, a teletypewriter. An instrument at the receiving end of the wire circuit types the message on a roll of paper.

Some stock tickers, as found in stock and commodity exchanges and brokers' offices, are a special form of the printing telegraph. These tickers report changing prices throughout the working day.

The most modern telegraph equipment does not send separate signals for each letter. Whole messages are transmitted at one time in a fraction of a second. The original typed message is wrapped around a special cylinder, which "sees" the message and transmits it as a "picture."

Many industrial customers use teleprinters, on a leased arrangement, between their large city offices, factories, and warehouses. With such an installation a company can quickly transmit orders, get delivery and shipping dates, and exchange other information between these points.

Another telegraph service is "telegraphing" flowers. In this case, a customer tells his local florist what flowers he wants delivered to an address in another city. The order is telegraphed by the florist to a member of the Florists' Transworld Delivery Association in the distant city. That florist can deliver the flowers a short time after the original order was placed.

An important service of the telegraph companies is the transfer of money by means of telegraph money orders. A person may deposit a sum of money with his local telegraph office, and have that sum delivered to any destination he may choose throughout the world. He is assured that, within a matter of minutes or a few hours, the money, and any message he may send, is in the hands of the recipient. Millions of dollars are sent each year by telegraph money order.

For many years telegraph messages have been sent across the ocean. These are cablegrams. The difficulties encountered in laying a transatlantic cable and how they were overcome is a fascinating story in the history of communication. (See CABLE, ELECTRIC.)

Using modern carrier systems, hundreds of telegrams now can be sent simultaneously over one pair of wires. Numerous pitches or tones are used, each of which carries a stream of messages.

Most significant in recent telegraph advancement is microwave radio beam transmission. (See Electromagnetic Spectrum table in RADIATION.) This was started by Western Union in 1945 to serve New York City and Philadelphia. It is now nationwide. High radio towers spaced 30 to 50 miles apart connect major cities throughout the United States. Transmitting by radio beams makes possible high volume communication at extremely high speeds. It is predicted that super-high-frequency radio beam transmission will eventually eliminate the need for the familiar pole lines between main telegraph centers. (See RADIO: *Directional Sending and Radio Relay.*)

A special telegraph network serving the Civil Aeronautics Administration gathers and sends weather information to about 700 cities in the United States and Canada. Every large newspaper today has teletype machines in its plant to receive up-to-the-minute news dispatches.

A global telegraphic communications network has been installed for the U.S. Air Force. It is the largest private wire system in the world. The system covers hundreds of thousands of miles and serves several hundred Air Force locations.

Telegraph equipment is also used to operate a nuclear-bomb alarm system. It will alert the country's civilian and military leaders in the event of nuclear blast. It operates in locations designated as potential target areas.

Pictures by Telegraph

Facsimile or picture telegraphy is another of the many telegraph services. There are several types. One of the most widely used, Intrafax, sends written or printed matter between several offices. When a person sends a message by Intrafax, he places the message in the Intrafax sender, an electric eye goes over, or "scans," the telegram, and sends an exact picture to the receiving instrument.

The U.S. Weather Bureau and the Strategic Air Command use Intrafax to transmit weather maps nationwide. Railroads and airlines use Intrafax to speed the accurate handling of train and plane reservations. Banks use it to flash facsimiles of signatures between departments and branches for verification.

Another of Western Union's telegraphic data transmission services is Telex. This is a dial-direct, customer-to-customer service. With it, a Telex subscriber can dial directly to any other Telex subscriber in the United States, Canada, or Mexico and carry on direct, two-way printed message and data communication. He may also dial the international Telex center and have similar contact with 87 foreign countries.

Kinds of Telegrams

For the general public, there are three classes of telegrams. Full-rate telegrams are the fastest and usually are delivered minutes after sending. Day letters are used for messages that do not require as much speed. They cost less than full-rate telegrams. Night letters are for messages that may be delivered the following morning. Longer messages can be sent by night letter at less cost than by either of the other two services.

There are two kinds of cablegrams to countries abroad. Full-rate cablegrams are the usual, fast-service, international messages. They may be written in any language that can be expressed in Roman-style letters, or they can be in a secret code. Cable letters are for overnight, overseas service and are used for plain-language messages only.

TELEPHONE (*tĕl′ē fōn*) is an apparatus or system for transmitting voice messages from one point to another by means of electric signals. Robert Hooke, an English physicist, invented a device in 1667 that was later to be called a string telephone. With it, voice or sound waves that caused a diaphragm to vibrate at one end of a string were transmitted over a tight string or wire to another diaphragm at the distant end of the string. The vibrations roughly reproduced the original sound. By 1796 the word "telephone" was applied to megaphones and shortly thereafter to speaking tubes. In the early 1800's telephonic devices that em-

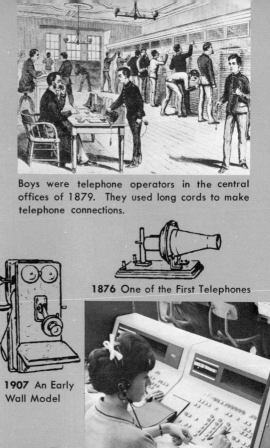

Boys were telephone operators in the central offices of 1879. They used long cords to make telephone connections.

1876 One of the First Telephones

1907 An Early Wall Model

Today most subscribers do their own dialing. Operators are available for assistance.

1913 An Early Home-Intercom Model

1919 One of the First Dial Telephones

Modern telephone equipment includes the Picturephone. Both the caller and the person called can be seen if they wish.

1930 An Early "French" Telephone

Photos, Courtesy American Telephone and Telegraph Company

Years ago overhead telephone wires (above) cluttered cities. Underground cables are now widely used, and microwave towers (right) replace many long-distance telephone wires.

ployed electric current to reproduce musical sounds appeared, but none was capable of transmitting articulate speech.

The first practical electric telephone was thought of in 1874 by Alexander Graham Bell in Boston, Massachusetts. (See BELL, ALEXANDER GRAHAM; GRAY, ELISHA.) He built the first telephone in 1875. It was capable of transmitting recognizable voice sounds. The first complete sentence was transmitted over an improved model a year later. It was from Bell to his assistant, Thomas A. Watson, in a nearby laboratory. The message was: "Mr. Watson, come here; I want you." Many inventors had been working to find a way to transmit sounds. Although Bell was the first to patent his invention in the U.S., Elisha Gray had patented a device similar to Bell's in England in 1874. He applied for a U.S. patent just after Bell did. After a long series of lawsuits, the U.S. Supreme Court recognized Bell as the inventor of the electromagnetic transmitter and receiver. He was issued a patent on March 7, 1876.

By 1878 the first commercial central office for switching telephone calls was in operation in New Haven, Connecticut. A telephone exchange with seven or eight telephones operated in London, England, in the following year. Improved versions of the telephone transmitter were invented by Emile Berliner, Thomas A. Edison, and Francis Blake. A method of manufacturing hard-drawn copper wire was developed by Thomas B. Doolittle of Connecticut. This was most important in improving the transmission of voice currents over long-distance lines.

John J. Carty, chief engineer of the American Telephone and Telegraph Company from 1907 to 1919, was responsible for the first two-wire telephone circuit that is still used today. He also developed the "phantom circuit," by which three telephone conversations can be transmitted at the same time over two pairs of wires.

In 1889, Almon B. Strowger invented an automatic telephone switching device. The Strowger switch made it possible to select and signal one out of a group of many telephones. Calls no longer had to be completed by an operator. In 1892 the world's first commercial automatic telephone exchange was installed in La Porte, Indiana.

The Telephone Instrument

In all, there are 475 parts in one of the modern telephones. To understand its operation, however, it is necessary to understand only a few of the parts. Both the transmitter and receiver are transducers, or devices capable of changing one form of energy into another (in this case, sound waves and electromagnetic waves).

Principal parts of the main type of transmitter are a diaphragm and a dome. The diaphragm is a circular piece of thin aluminum. It is set in the mouthpiece and vibrates when struck by

Transmission by microwave follows straight lines (above) from tower to tower. The towers cannot be spaced too far apart because the earth is curved. Many towers, therefore, are required for long-distance transmission.

sound waves from a voice. The gold-plated dome is at the center of the diaphragm. It projects into a chamber of carbon granules.

An electric current flows through the transmitter when the telephone handpiece is lifted. As one speaks directly into the transmitter, the sound waves strike against the diaphragm, which moves back and forth reproducing the pattern of vibrations produced by the sound waves of the voice. These vibrations, in turn, cause the diaphragm dome to vibrate against the carbon granules. This causes the density of the electric current passing through the granules to vary in a pattern similar to that originally produced by the sound waves. In this pattern, the electric current moves out onto the telephone circuit. The receiver then converts this specially created electric current into sound.

Principal parts of a receiver are an aluminum diaphragm, with an outer ring of magnetic iron; an electromagnet consisting of a ring of soft metal with a coil of wire wound around it; and a cup-shaped permanent magnet. The latter surrounds the diaphragm and the electromagnet.

The permanent magnet provides a steady pull on the inner edge of the diaphragm's outer ring, or armature. Between the ring and the pole piece of the magnet extends a small space around the inner edge of the armature. A steady magnetic force flows across this gap, pulling on the inner edge of the armature.

When the varying electric currents from the transmitter of the calling telephone flow into the coil of the receiver, the coil forms an electromagnet that aids or opposes the permanent magnet. Magnetic force within the receiver is alternately increased or decreased, depending on the direction in which the current is flowing. This variation in magnetic pull causes the flexible armature to move in and out with the ring at the same rate. This, in turn, causes the air to vibrate at the same rate. The voice heard in the telephone receiver is the vibrating air.

Making a Telephone Call

To complete a telephone call, a telephone line must be connected with the line of another telephone. This is done in a central office, where the lines of all telephones in the area terminate. In a small or medium-sized community, one central office is enough. In a large city, it is necessary to have many central offices connected by trunk lines.

For many years all telephone connections were made by operators working at switchboards in the central offices. Operators wore telephone headsets for speaking to callers and to other operators. Connections were made by inserting metal plugs at the end of flexible wire cords into sockets, or jacks. The subscriber's telephone was connected to these jacks.

Practically all calls made now are through dial switching equipment. Telephone companies, however, still employ many operators to handle a variety of special types of calls. These include special assistance calls, information

Transmission between two widely spaced towers is impossible. The beam of microwaves (below) goes off into space.

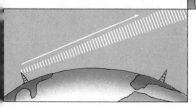

A satellite (above and right) forms a link between two widely spaced towers. It takes the place of an extremely tall tower. The satellite is, in a sense, a "tower in the sky."

calls, calls to and from automobiles and trucks, ship-to-shore calls, and some long-distance calls.

Transmission Systems

Wire continues to be an important means for providing circuits over which most telephone messages are transmitted. Instead of wires strung singly, most wires are now encased together in cables. A cable consists of bundles of insulated pairs of wires. It is covered with a protective shield of lead or a tough synthetic. The wires are thus protected from rain, ice, and wind. Some cables contain more than 2,000 pairs of wires. Some cable is placed on poles, but most is placed in underground conduits. Cables are also run under lakes, in river beds, and on ocean floors. A telephone cable was laid under the English Channel between England and France in 1891.

Beginning in 1927, circuits for overseas telephone calls were provided by short-wave radio. To improve this service, cables were laid across the ocean bottoms. The first of these was laid in 1956, linking North America and Great Britain. Since then, additional cables have been laid in the Atlantic, the Pacific, the Gulf of Mexico, and the Caribbean Sea.

Coaxial cables multiply the number of conversations that can be transmitted over the same circuit at the same time. A coaxial cable consists of a number (usually 8, 12, or 20) of copper tubes, each about the diameter of a fountain pen. In each tube is a copper wire held in place by disks. The coaxial system carries electric waves on a wide frequency band. This band can be split hundreds of times to provide a corresponding number of voice pathways.

Telephone conversations, television programs, and telegrams are also transmitted over microwave relay systems. Today this is becoming a principal method of sending long-distance calls. (See Telegraph: *Modern Telegraphic Services.*)

Telephoning Via Satellite

The most dramatic use of microwave radio has been with communications satellites. The first experimental operations began in 1962. They have been used for transoceanic transmission of telephone messages, television programs, facsimile and telemetry signals, photographs, and data. (See Space Exploration.)

When the satellite attains its outer space

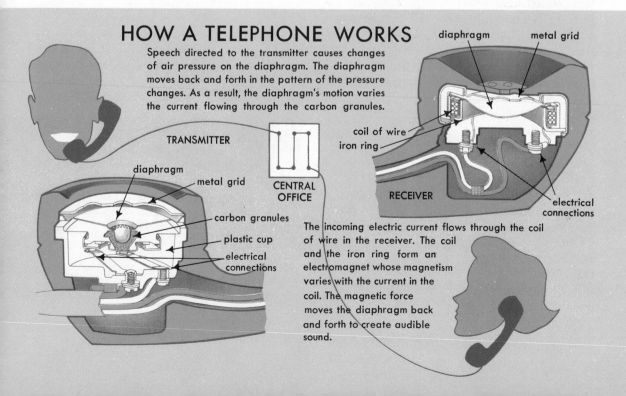

HOW A TELEPHONE WORKS

Speech directed to the transmitter causes changes of air pressure on the diaphragm. The diaphragm moves back and forth in the pattern of the pressure changes. As a result, the diaphragm's motion varies the current flowing through the carbon granules.

TRANSMITTER

CENTRAL OFFICE

RECEIVER

diaphragm
metal grid
coil of wire
iron ring
electrical connections

diaphragm
metal grid
carbon granules
plastic cup
electrical connections

The incoming electric current flows through the coil of wire in the receiver. The coil and the iron ring form an electromagnet whose magnetism varies with the current in the coil. The magnetic force moves the diaphragm back and forth to create audible sound.

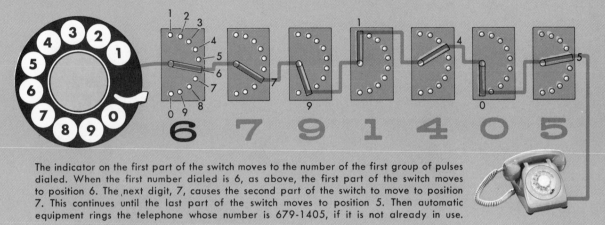

Each number dialed on the telephone produces a certain number of electrical pulses. When 3 is dialed, 3 pulses are produced; when 5 is dialed, 5 are produced. The digit 0 produces 10 pulses. The pulses are transferred to one of the many switches in the telephone central office.

The indicator on the first part of the switch moves to the number of the first group of pulses dialed. When the first number dialed is 6, as above, the first part of the switch moves to position 6. The next digit, 7, causes the second part of the switch to move to position 7. This continues until the last part of the switch moves to position 5. Then automatic equipment rings the telephone whose number is 679-1405, if it is not already in use.

Photo, Courtesy Automatic Electric Company

orbit, it receives microwave signals that have been accurately aimed at it from ground stations. A transmitter within the satellite then beams the signals to the selected overseas ground station. Names of the early communications satellites were Telstar (I and II), Relay (I and II), and Syncom (I, II, and III).

Telephone Companies

The United States has always been the largest user of telephone service in the world. It has about 98,000,000 telephones. Telephone service is furnished almost entirely by private companies in the United States, although in many countries they are operated by government agencies. About 85 percent of all telephone service in the United States is operated by the Bell System. It consists of the American Telephone and Telegraph Company and its operating, manufacturing, and research affiliates.

Other service in the United States is provided by 2,500 independent telephone companies. The largest of these is the General Telephone and Electronics Corporation. The telephone systems of all companies are interconnected.

Telephone service rapidly has become worldwide for the U.S. telephone user. He can place long-distance calls to all but 2 percent of all the telephones in the world. By 1964 there were approximately six million telephone messages annually between the United States and overseas points. This total is increasing by 15 percent each year.

TELESCOPE (*těl'ě skōp*). A telescope is an instrument which makes distant objects appear closer. It is used in looking at distant objects on earth and in studying the stars and other heavenly bodies. (See ASTRONOMY.)

A telescope works by gathering light sent from an object—more light than the naked eye can gather—and focusing it to a tiny, sharp point. This point is then magnified to an image which seems very large and close to the observer. There are two main types of telescopes, *refracting* and *reflecting*. The refractor uses a lens and the reflector uses a mirror to gather light. In a refractor the observer looks directly at the object; in a reflector he looks at its reflection in a mirror. In both kinds of telescopes, objects are seen upside down. Another lens may be added to the eyepiece to turn the image right side up, but this is not necessary for studying stars.

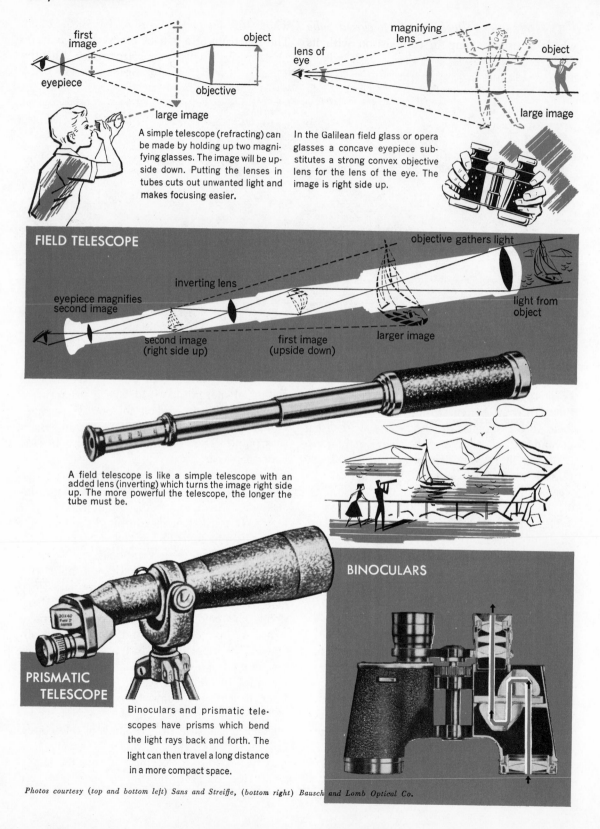

first image

object

eyepiece

objective

large image

magnifying lens

lens of eye

object

large image

A simple telescope (refracting) can be made by holding up two magnifying glasses. The image will be upside down. Putting the lenses in tubes cuts out unwanted light and makes focusing easier.

In the Galilean field glass or opera glasses a concave eyepiece substitutes a strong convex objective lens for the lens of the eye. The image is right side up.

FIELD TELESCOPE

objective gathers light

inverting lens

eyepiece magnifies second image

second image (right side up)

first image (upside down)

larger image

light from object

A field telescope is like a simple telescope with an added lens (inverting) which turns the image right side up. The more powerful the telescope, the longer the tube must be.

PRISMATIC TELESCOPE

BINOCULARS

Binoculars and prismatic telescopes have prisms which bend the light rays back and forth. The light can then travel a long distance in a more compact space.

Photos courtesy (top and bottom left) Sans and Streiffe, (bottom right) Bausch and Lomb Optical Co.

The refracting telescope has a closed *tube* which is usually long in comparison with its diameter. In the top of the tube is the *object glass*, made of two or more lenses, through which passes the light from the object observed. This light is *refracted* (bent) by the lenses to a bright, sharp focus at the lower end of the tube, where the eyepiece is located. The eyepiece then acts like an ordinary magnifying glass and enlarges this bright image. The observer can look at an object through the eyepiece with his own eye, or he may attach a camera to the telescope to record the object on a photographic plate. (See LENS; LIGHT.)

The reflecting telescope needs only one lens in the eyepiece. Its tube is usually a skeleton framework, open at the top. At the lower end of the tube is a mirror made of glass coated with silver or aluminum and shaped like a large, shallow dish. Light from a star or other distant object is gathered by this mirror and *reflected* to a bright, sharp focus. A smaller mirror at this focal point sends the image to an eyepiece or camera placed at the side of the tube. A large reflecting telescope may be used for looking at objects, but its greatest value is for photography.

The telescope *mounting* holds the tube in position so that it can be rotated and pointed toward the object to be observed. Mountings are designed to go with the telescope tube to be held.

Some telescopes are planned for special kinds of work. The *coronagraph* is used for studying the corona and prominences of the sun on any clear day, without waiting for a total eclipse. The sun towers at Mount Wilson Observatory, near Pasadena, California, 60 and 150 feet high, are telescopes used only for observing the sun. With the *transit telescope* correct time is obtained from the stars.

Used in connection with regular telescopes are such instruments as the photoelectric cell, or "electric eye," for measuring the brightness of the light of the stars, and the thermocouple for measuring their heat.

Two other instruments used with the telescope are the camera and the spectroscope. With the spectroscope, the light from a heavenly body may be examined, and its spectrum, which this instrument forms, may be studied. The spectrum of a star or other object may be photographed with the spectrograph. With the camera a permanent record may be made which can be studied by the astronomer at his leisure or shared with other astronomers. By means of photographs much more can be recorded. (See SPECTRUM AND SPECTROSCOPE.)

History

In 1608 a Dutch spectacle maker, Hans Lippershey, was at work one day in his shop in Middelburg, Holland. By chance he picked up two lenses. Holding them together, he looked through them at the weather vane on the steeple of a nearby church. The cock on the weather vane looked as large as life. Accidentally, Lippershey had found the way to make a telescope. It then became a simple matter to place two lenses, one convex (thicker at the center) and the other concave (thinner at the center), in a tube of lead or paper. With this instrument distant objects were magnified and made to look nearer and clearer.

A German astronomer named Simon Marius succeeded in getting an instrument from Holland. In Italy Galileo Galilei made his own, to which he gave the name of telescope. Marius and Galileo both had the idea of using their telescopes to study the sky. At almost the same time both of them saw four of the satellites of Jupiter, which have since been called the Galilean satellites. During the next few years Galileo proved the value of the telescope by his discoveries of the mountains on the moon, the phases of Venus, the spots on the sun, and many faint stars that cannot be seen with the unaided eye. All Galileo's observations were made with little telescopes with tubes not more than three or four feet long and lenses less than two inches in diameter. These instruments were refracting telescopes.

Astronomers tried grinding larger lenses and making longer tubes. In 1656 Christian Huygens, a Dutch scientist, made a telescope 23 feet long, with which he could see Saturn's rings. Later he made an instrument 122 feet long, with a lens six inches in diameter, and others 170 and 210 feet in length. But the

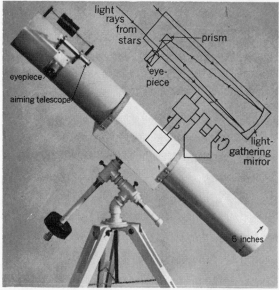

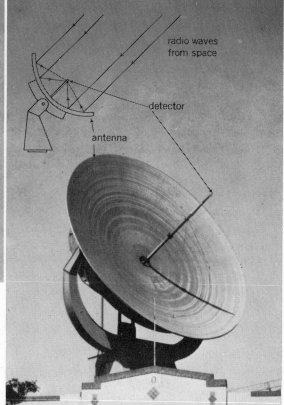

Courtesy (left) Mr. and Mrs. Paul Lind, (right) U.S. Navy.

Above: A six-inch reflecting telescope built by a student. The curved mirror focuses the image on the prism which reflects it to the eyepiece. Right: The Naval Research Laboratory's 50-foot radio telescope at Washington, D.C. The antenna reflects many very weak radio waves to one point, the detector.

larger lenses were not satisfactory for they made everything look blurred.

In 1663 James Gregory, a Scots mathematician, worked out a scheme for a reflecting telescope. In 1668 Isaac Newton actually made one. In 1671 he made a second reflector, which may still be seen in London. Including its mounting, this telescope is only 15 inches high. The tube is a little over six inches long, and the metal mirror in its lower end is two inches in diameter. These little instruments made by Newton were the first successful reflecting telescopes.

The most recent development in telescopes is the *radio telescope*. In the 1930's radio signals from outer space were detected but could not be related to any particular objects in the sky. At first this seemed unimportant to astronomy, but in 1948 *radio interferometers* were built. These were made of two bowl-shaped radio antennas several hundred yards apart connected to the same receiver. Radio waves com-

ing in at an angle from outer space reached one aerial a little before the other. This produced interference. As the "telescope" swept the sky, radio noise became stronger or weaker, and the size of the object sending the waves could be determined. As larger and better radio telescopes were built, the paths of satellites and meteors, the atmosphere of planets, parts of the Milky Way blurred by dust clouds, and great clouds of hydrogen in our own Galaxy and others have been studied. The largest radio telescope in operation is a 250-foot bowl at Jodrell Bank, England.

Well-Known Telescopes

The two largest refracting telescopes are the 36-inch instrument at Lick Observatory of the University of California, located on Mount Hamilton, California, and the 40-inch telescope of the Yerkes Observatory of The University of Chicago, located at Lake Geneva, Wisconsin. The tube of the Yerkes Observatory refractor is 63 feet long. With this instrument the building of refractors seems to have reached its limit. Since its completion in 1897, no equally large refracting telescope has been built.

Both refracting and reflecting telescopes are valuable for different kinds of astronomical observations. However, because reflectors are easier to build and are required for studying nebulae and faint and distant stars, all the large telescopes made in recent years are reflecting telescopes.

Including the 200-inch Hale telescope installed on Palomar Mountain, California, in 1947, there are about 30 reflectors with mirrors 36 inches or larger in observatories throughout the world. Among these are the 82-inch reflector at the McDonald Observatory of the University of Texas and The University of Chicago, at Fort Davis, Texas, the 100-inch Hooker telescope of the Mount Wilson Observatory and the 120-inch reflector at the Lick Observatory.

The Hale telescope was built by the California Institute of Technology. This reflector is housed in an observatory on Palomar Mountain, about 90 miles southeast of Pasadena, California. The dome is 135 feet high and 137 feet in diameter. The whole telescope, with the

The Jodrell Bank radio telescope in Cheshire, England, is 250 feet in diameter.

Courtesy British Information Services

mirror, weighs nearly 500 tons. The tube is about 55 feet long and can be moved to point at different parts of the sky. The 200-inch mirror, with four times the light-gathering power of the 100-inch telescope on Mount Wilson, is at the lower end of the tube.

In making the 200-inch telescope, the most difficult part was casting and finishing the single piece of Pyrex glass that forms the mirror. First, a huge disk of glass, 17 feet in diameter, was cast at Corning, New York. This disk was allowed to cool slowly for a year to keep flaws from forming. Then the glass was packed upright on a specially equipped flatcar and taken by a special train to Pasadena, arriving in April 1936. Except for a long interruption during World War II, the work of grinding, polishing, and testing the glass to within two-millionths of an inch of perfection went on steadily from 1936 to 1947.

The glass has a concave surface and somewhat resembles a shallow dish 200 inches across and 4 inches deep in the center. It has been coated with aluminum to give it a reflecting surface, so that it really is a mirror.

The glass was taken to Palomar Mountain to be placed in the telescope tube in 1947, and it was dedicated to George Ellery Hale in June 1948.

The Hale telescope is not used for all kinds of astronomical observations but only for those that cannot be made with smaller telescopes. (See OBSERVATORY.)

Other Uses of Telescopes

Refracting telescopes are used by thousands of people for bird watching, nature study, hunting, and target shooting. They have lenses which make the object appear right-side up. They may be focused without moving the telescope or losing sight of the object.

Magnification, the enlargement of the observed object, is important. The number of times an object is magnified depends on the eyepiece used. These are made in different strengths, or powers. A 20-power eyepiece magnifies 20 times or 20×.

The eyepiece selected depends on what the telescope is being used to see. For instance, to identify wild birds, the telescope should magnify 20 or 30 times. When lightweight, portable telescopes are used for looking at the stars, a 60-power eyepiece is best. The telescope can be put on an ordinary camera tripod with a movable head and set up on the lawn or roof, or in an open country field. Without a telescope, the human eye can see about 6,000 stars. With a 60-power eyepiece, 900,000 stars are visible.

The binoculars used as field glasses or opera glasses are actually a pair of telescopes of lower magnifying strength. Gun sights and many of the instruments used by defense forces are other kinds of telescopes. They all serve the purpose of making an object appear larger, clearer, and nearer.

TELEVISION (*těl'ě vĭzh'ŭn*) is an electronic system of "seeing at a distance." It is a method of transmitting (sending) pictures of events as they happen, or of transmitting motion pictures from film or "videotape" recordings. At the same time that the pictures are broadcast, the sounds heard at the scene or the sounds recorded with the pictures are sent along by radio.

Very few people knew much about television until the 1930's, when the first regular television broadcasts began in some cities of the United States and Europe. World War II delayed somewhat the development of "TV," as it came to be called. By 1948, however, the number of television sets annually manufactured in the United States passed the million mark. In 1968 more than 56 million American homes (about 95 percent of all homes) had television sets.

History of Television

The chain of events leading to television began in 1818, when a Swedish chemist named Jons Jakob Berzelius discovered the chemical element *selenium*. Later it was found that the amount of electrical current selenium would carry depended on the amount of light which struck it. This property in conducting materials is called "photoelectricity."

In 1875, this discovery led a United States inventor, G. R. Carey, to make the first crude television system, using photoelectric cells.

(See PHOTOELECTRICITY.)

Carey constructed a bank of photoelectric cells with many of them side by side. Each cell was connected by a wire to a corresponding electric light bulb in a bank, or panel. As a scene or object was focused through a lens onto the bank of photoelectric cells, each cell would control the amount of electricity it would pass on to its corresponding light bulb. Crude outlines of the object that was projected on the photoelectric cells would then show in the lights on the bank of bulbs.

Carey's apparatus needed a great number of wires, photoelectric cells, and light bulbs. The amount of detail or clarity with which the original picture could be reproduced was quite limited. As this was in the days before radio, wires had to connect the picture-taking end and the receiving end.

In an effort to simplify Carey's apparatus, Paul Nipkow in 1884 invented what is known as the scanning disk. It is a round, flat disk with holes arranged in spiral fashion on its surface; that is, the first hole is placed fairly close to the center of the disk, and the others are spaced progressively closer to the edge.

Operation of the scanning-disk television system was as follows: At the sending end, a scanning disk was placed between the object to be televised and a photoelectric cell. The disk was whirled around by a motor, causing strips of the object to be exposed to the photoelectric cell through the holes in the disk. The current which the photoelectric cell gave off then corresponded to the amount of light reflected from the object through each hole in the disk. This changing current was transmitted by wires to an electric light bulb. A second scanning disk was placed between the light bulb and the person observing the picture. Both the sending and receiving disks revolved at the same speed and exposed corresponding holes at the same time.

As the disks whirled, a person watching at the receiver would see, through the holes in the disk, a series of lines of light, varying in brightness according to the lights and shadows making up the picture at the sending end. Because the eye has *retentivity* (the ability to keep impressions for short periods of time), the person saw a picture of the original object.

The Nipkow scanning disk simplified the television system. Only one photoelectric cell and one lamp were needed. However, the pictures still were not very clear, mostly because of the limited number of holes that could be punched into a disk and the speed at which the disk could be rotated.

Additions and improvements came fast in the 20th century. The first practical transmissions over wires were accomplished in 1923 by Baird in England and Jenkins in the United States. Vladimir Zworykin and Philo Farnsworth both made great advances in developing devices to serve as television cameras. In the 1920's Zworykin invented the *iconoscope* and in 1928 Farnsworth developed a tube known as the *image dissector*. Through 1935 either one or the other was used in television cameras as the light-sensitive device to pick up the television pictures. Later the dissector was used largely in industrial television, and the iconoscope was limited to film work.

The photoelectric cells in the iconoscope are microscopic in size, and are on a plate called a mosaic. This mosaic is about three inches by four inches and contains thousands of tiny photoelectric cells, each insulated from the others. Magnified it would look something like the thousands of squares on graph paper. When a light image made up of blacks, grays, and whites is focused upon this mosaic plate, each cell takes on an electrical charge. The size of the charge depends on the amount of light (white) striking it. To change these electrical charges back into light energy to make a picture, it is necessary to scan all the charges and make them form a new light image at some distant receiving point.

In the neck of the iconoscope a stream of electrons (tiny electric charges) is shot onto the mosaic plate, and is made to scan the plate by magnetic or other means. The "electron eye" moves from left to right and from top to bottom, just as a person's eye reads a printed page. The stream of electrons reaches each photoelectric cell and releases the charges stored in it in definite scanning order. This continuous stream of differing electric charges is amplified (made stronger) and passed on to a radio transmitter.

Unlike the iconoscope, which is a storage device, the image dissector projects the picture onto a light-sensitive surface. From this surface, electrons are released in proportion to the strength of the light, thus forming an electron image. These electrons, which are moving slowly, are speeded up by a voltage between the light-sensitive screen and a coating on the far end of the tube. The amplified charges are passed on to a transmitter.

The Image Orthicon and the Kinescope

By 1945 both of these camera pickup tubes had been replaced by the *image orthicon*. The image orthicon is more sensitive to light than either the iconoscope or dissector.

In the image orthicon the camera lens focuses a picture on a light-sensitive plate of glass. This plate throws off electrons, many in bright areas and few in dark areas of the picture. The electrons are collected on a target

A television studio. The control room is in the background.

Courtesy CBS Television Network

where they displace other electrons to form a positively charged image of the picture. The released electrons are carried away by a fine wire mesh. The electron scanning beam from the cathode sweeps back and forth in 525 lines across the back of the target and covers the entire surface 30 times a second. Where there is a shortage of electrons (a bright area) on the target, the scanning beam must leave some electrons behind. Thus the return beam is modulated (sometimes weak, sometimes strong) according to the charge image on the target. This varying impulse is amplified and transmitted.

Courtesy American Telephone & Telegraph Company

A microwave relay station. Such stations are used to transmit long-distance telephone conversations as well as television programs.

Television processes are much like those in sound radio broadcasting, in which variations in sound are picked up by the microphone and changed into electrical variations. As in sound broadcasting, the impulses sent from the television transmitter are picked up by a receiving antenna and fed to a television receiver.

In the receiver, in place of the mechanical Nipkow disk, modern television sets use a cathode-ray tube known as a *kinescope*, or picture tube. (See ELECTRONICS.) On this tube the picture is shown by using exactly the same scanning principle used in the television camera.

In the neck of the picture tube is an electron gun which scans the screen with the modulated electron beam sent out by the television transmitter. The screen is coated with phosphor which gives off light when it is hit by the electron beam. Again the screen is swept in 525 lines 30 times a second. This time, because the scanning beam varies in strength, the light given off by the screen also varies and a picture is formed exactly like the one in the camera pickup tube. Because the eye holds the moving spot of light for an instant, the viewer seems to see a continuous picture.

Early television home receivers had picture tubes measuring 7 to 12 inches diagonally. Today, most sets have 18- to 21-inch picture tubes, and a few measure as much as 30 inches. For use in large auditoriums and motion-picture theaters, television equipment has been developed that projects a huge picture.

Transmitting the Picture

By 1965, television pictures had been transmitted from as far away as the moon. In the earth's atmosphere, however, the distance a television broadcasting station can transmit its pictures is a little beyond the horizon as seen from the transmitting antenna. This is because television waves must be broadcast at a frequency much higher than frequencies used in radio broadcasting. "Frequency" refers to the number of waves sent out per given unit of time. The waves on a given frequency are received by sets whose circuits are tuned to that frequency. (See RADIO.)

Sending a television picture with an image orthicon, or camera tube.

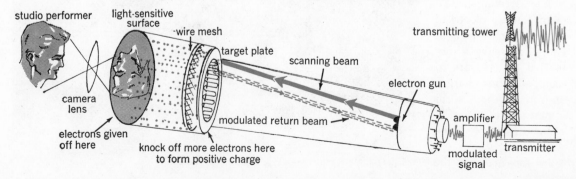

studio performer

light-sensitive surface

wire mesh

target plate

scanning beam

transmitting tower

electron gun

camera lens

amplifier

electrons given off here

modulated return beam

knock off more electrons here to form positive charge

modulated signal

transmitter

The Very High Frequency (VHF) television waves travel in nearly straight lines, and do not follow the curve of the earth. The higher the television transmitting antenna and the receiving antenna are placed, therefore, the greater the distance at which television can be received. In New York City several television stations share an antenna on top of the Empire State Building. Their pictures can be received more than 50 miles away. A transmitter with an antenna placed 100 feet high can send a picture about 12 or 15 miles.

In order to send programs over long distances and make them available to many stations, television chains or networks have grown up. Either of two methods may be used to connect television transmitters in various cities: coaxial cable or microwave relay stations.

A coaxial cable is a small, hollow wire placed inside a larger, hollow wire and suspended by spacers in such a way that the insulating material between the wires is mostly air. Hollow wires are used because high-frequency currents tend to travel only on the surface of a conductor, and placing one wire inside another reduces loss by radiation.

The microwave relay station consists of a television receiver and a television transmitter. The antennas are placed on top of towers spaced at distances which permit a clear path from tower to tower.

The choice of these two methods depends on the country to be crossed. Where there are mountains or large bodies of water, the microwave relay system is preferred. In level areas, or where the network must pass through cities, the coaxial cable is ordinarily more efficient and easier to maintain.

In 1946 New York City and Washington, D.C., were connected by a coaxial cable. From this service grew three networks that now link all major cities in the United States by coaxial cable and microwave relays.

Coaxial cables strung from antennas hundreds of feet high are also used to transmit television programs directly to the home. This community antenna television system, or CATV, is used in areas that are too far from television stations to obtain satisfactory reception using individual home antennas.

Stations not linked to a network are not always limited to local programs. They may also telecast motion pictures or video tape recordings. Videotape simultaneously records audio and visual signals by methods similar to those used in tape-recording sound. Kinescope recordings (filming of a "live" program directly from the kinescope) are of poor quality and by the 1960's were largely replaced by tape. (See RECORDING.) The average station not connected with a network uses most of its time for programs on film and videotape and the rest for local "live" programs.

Growth of Commercial Television

A few stations in the United States experimented with television in the late 1920's and the 1930's. The Federal Communications Commission, which regulates broadcasting, authorized commercial television (using television for advertising) in 1941. One year later ten commercial stations were operating, but because of material shortages during World War II, few receiving sets were in use.

In 1945 the Federal Communications Com-

Receiving a television picture with a kinescope.

receiver antenna

phosphor-coated screen

modulated scanning beam

electron gun

amplifier

modulated signal

focusing and guiding devices

The screen has 525 lines. The electron gun scans every other line, then makes another trip to scan the remaining lines, completely scanning the screen 30 times a second.

first trip

second trip

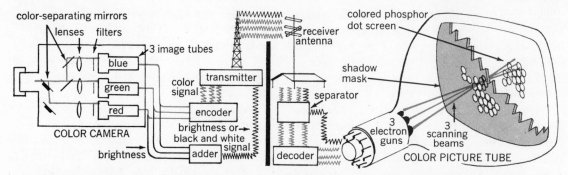

color-separating mirrors

lenses filters

3 image tubes

blue

green

red

COLOR CAMERA

brightness

color signal

transmitter

encoder

brightness or black and white signal

adder

receiver antenna

separator

decoder

colored phosphor dot screen

shadow mask

3 electron guns

3 scanning beams

COLOR PICTURE TUBE

How color television is transmitted and received. Black and white sets receive only the brightness signal.

mission set aside 13 VHF channels between 44 and 216 megacycles for commercial television; and by 1952, 108 television stations were operating in the United States. It was believed that more channels would be needed. After careful study, the Commission reduced the VHF channels to 12, added seventy UHF (Ultra High Frequency) channels between 470 and 890 megacycles, and made certain rules on the power and separation of stations. Some of the UHF channels were set aside for noncommercial or educational use. This made it possible to have about 2,200 television stations in the United States.

In 1969 the number of television stations operating in the United States had increased to 641. Japan had about 1,400, while the other two leading countries, Canada and Australia, had about 70 and 43, respectively.

All television programs fall into two main classes. Some are "live" programs, in which action and sound are broadcast at the instant they are picked up by television cameras and microphones. Others are prerecorded programs, prepared in advance of broadcast time.

In subject, television presents nearly every form of entertainment and education, including drama, music, religious services, and lessons in many fields. With equipment which may be carried away from the studios in trucks, television also broadcasts many civic and athletic events, spot news, and interesting events of all kinds. (When portable equipment is used in this way, pictures and sound may be relayed to the main transmitter for rebroadcast, or they may be recorded for a later broadcast time.)

Two types of commercial television that were developed in the early 1950's were still only in limited use in the late 1960's. These were systems of subscription television by which a television set owner could pay for certain programs, such as first-run motion pictures, Broadway shows, and sports events, which would not be broadcast over the regular channels. These systems generally operate by sending out a scrambled picture and supplying an unscrambling and key signal, either by wire or through the air, upon the payment of money. Another form of presenting events to the public for the payment of money is called "theater television." Theaters show their audiences special events, such as sporting events, not shown to the home television audience.

Color Television

Color television was first demonstrated in 1928, but it was not until 1945 that the Federal Communications Commission allotted certain UHF frequencies for color experimentation. Among several methods then developed, the most successful was the "field sequential" system, which used rotating disks with red, green, and blue filters. On the camera, these filters viewed the corresponding colors in a scene separately and transmitted them one after the other. On the receiver, a similar rotating filter disk was placed before the screen, and the eye added the three colors together to make a color picture.

This system was not "compatible," which means that the picture could not be received well in black and white through ordinary receivers. It was authorized by the Federal

Communications Commission in 1950. The National Television Systems Committee, representing the television industry, encouraged the development of a better color method, which was found in the "simultaneous" system. This system was authorized by the Federal Communications Commission in 1953. Within a decade, most stations in the United States were equipped for this type of transmission. By 1968 about 13 million color television sets were in use in the United States.

In simultaneous color television, the camera uses three image orthicon tubes. Each tube has a filter (red, green, or blue) and picks up only the corresponding color from the scene. Impulses from the tubes are transmitted simultaneously to receiving sets.

In black and white sets, these impulses form a regular black and white picture. In color sets, however, the picture tube has three electron guns (cathodes) instead of the one found in black and white sets. One gun works from the red impulses, the next from the green, and the third from the blue impulses. Streams of electrons thrown to the other end of the tube strike red, blue, and green phosphor dots on a plate. These dots glow in response to the electrons striking them from each cathode; and the result, seen on the outer surface of the tube, is blended by the eye into a color picture.

Other Uses of Television

Although television was developed for broadcasting entertainment and education, many important uses have been found that have nothing to do with broadcasting. In these services, television is used on a "closed circuit" system, which means that the picture is taken from the camera to the receiving set by coaxial cable and is not transmitted to homes.

In industrial plants, for example, television cameras are used to watch processes in places where it would be difficult or even dangerous for a human to be present. Sometimes cameras are mounted to give a view of furnace flames, so explosions or extra smoke may be avoided. In steel plants, rolling-mill operators may examine hot steel plates by television. Cameras serve as eyes for men handling radioactive ma-

terials by mechanical arms from behind a shield; television checks the tests of rocket motors; and television cameras have even gone far down into the ocean to inspect sunken ships.

In education, closed-circuit television makes it easy for a whole class to see everything a teacher demonstrates. Any number of students may look through a microscope at the same time when television does the "looking" for them, and a whole roomful of young doctors may get a close-up view of a delicate operation when a television camera watches the surgeon's hands and a microphone carries his description of the techniques he is using.

Among other applications, television is used to give a bank cashier a quick means of comparing the signature on a check with the records in another part of the building, to locate railroad cars in freight yards, and to help scientists study the ocean depths. Satellites carry television cameras far into space to observe the earth and flash back weather conditions. Cameras mounted on space vehicles have gone to the moon and to Mars, revealing features hitherto concealed from even the most powerful of Earth telescopes.

Television, described as "a window on the world," has become a window with a view of almost everything in the universe.

Recording a television lesson in history which will later be broadcast from an airplane to classrooms in several states.

Courtesy WTTW-Channel 11

Following Gessler's orders, William Tell shot an apple off his son's head. If the arrow had hit his son, Tell planned to shoot Gessler.

TELL (*tĕl*), **WILLIAM,** is the national hero of Switzerland. According to legend, he was a strong and skillful hunter who lived in the 14th century. At that time Switzerland was under the rule of Austria. The freedom-loving Swiss hated the Austrians—especially Gessler, the Austrian governor. Gessler had set up a cap on a pole in the center of the village of Altdorf. He ordered the Swiss to bow down before it as a sign of obedience. William Tell refused to do so. The angry Gessler ordered Tell to shoot an apple from his son's head 150 paces away; otherwise, Gessler said, Tell would be killed.

Tell took out two arrows. He put one in his belt, then shot the other through the apple. His son was saved. Tell told Gessler that the second arrow would have pierced Gessler's heart if the first had killed his son.

Gessler put Tell in a boat to take him to a prison across a lake. Suddenly a violent storm came up. The Austrians, who could not control the boat, unfastened Tell's chains. He steered to shore. Grabbing his bow, he jumped out and ran into the woods, where he hid. Gessler and his men escaped from the storm. When Gessler walked by Tell's hiding place, Tell shot him.

The death of Gessler inspired the Swiss to fight against their Austrian rulers. The war, which lasted almost 200 years, brought freedom.

Although the story of William Tell is probably not true, it does show Switzerland's desire for freedom. In 1804 a German poet, Johann Friedrich Schiller, wrote a play about William Tell. In 1829 an Italian composer, Gioachino Rossini, told the story as an opera.

TELLER (*tĕl'ĕr*), **EDWARD** (1908–   ), is a Hungarian-born U.S. physicist, known as the "Father of the Hydrogen Bomb." He was born in Budapest, and studied at the Institute of Technology, Karlsruhe, the University of Munich, and the University of Leipzig, all in Germany. After receiving his doctor's degree in 1930, he worked at universities in Leipzig  and Göttingen, Germany; Copenhagen, Denmark; and London, England. In 1935 he moved to the United States as a professor of physics at George Washington University, Washington, D.C. He later taught at Columbia University in New York City.

In 1941 he became a U.S. citizen, and from 1942 to 1946 he devoted his attention to the development of nuclear energy in the Manhattan Engineer District (as the atomic bomb project was called). For a time he taught at The University of Chicago, then became assistant director of the Los Alamos Scientific Laboratory in New Mexico. Since 1952 he has been engaged in research on peaceful applications of nuclear energy at the University of California at Berkeley.

Edward Teller.

Teller is the author or co-author of several books, including *The Legacy of Hiroshima*, *The Structure of Matter*, and *Our Nuclear Future*. He has received both the Albert Einstein and the Enrico Fermi awards.

TEMPLARS (*tĕm'plĕrz*), **KNIGHTS,** was one of three great military-religious orders founded during the Crusades. The others were the Hospitallers and the Teutonic Knights.

In 1099, during the First Crusade, the

Christians captured Jerusalem from the Muslims and established the kingdom of Jerusalem. In the following years, thousands of pilgrims flocked to the Holy Land. A group of French knights, led by Hugues de Payns of Burgundy, in 1119, organized a religious order. Baldwin II, king of Jerusalem, gave them the part of his palace that was next to the supposed site of Solomon's Temple. Thus, they became known as the Poor Knights of Christ and of the Temple of Solomon, or simply as Knights Templars.

In 1128 the church council of Troyes (France) approved the rules of the order. The head of the order was the grand master. Brethren were admitted either for life or for a term of years. Married men were admitted if they bequeathed half of their property to the order. Priests who attached themselves to the order owed obedience to the grand master and to the pope. The Templars wore white robes with the Crusaders' red cross on their breasts.

When Jerusalem fell to the Muslims in 1187, hundreds of Templars died in battle. The Christians launched the Third Crusade in an attempt to regain control of the Holy Land. They succeeded in capturing Acre, and this city became the new center of the Templars. Nearby, the order built its famous Castle Pilgrim. In 1291, Acre fell again to the Muslims, thus ending Christian power in the Holy Land. The grand master was slain during the siege of the town, and the surviving Templars withdrew to Cyprus, where they established a new center.

By this time the Knights Templars had become extremely influential. Groups of Templars were established in nearly every kingdom of the Christian world. The Templars also had become bankers, and their Paris Temple was the banking center of the Christian world.

In the late 13th century, Philip IV, king of France, found himself in financial trouble. He had long wanted to curb the power of the Templars, and he saw that by eliminating the order he could take over its riches and solve his financial problems. In 1307 he ordered all Templars in France arrested on charges of immorality, sorcery, and heresy. In 1312 the pope abolished the order.

Two years later, the last grand master, Jacques de Molay, was brought to the Cathedral of Notre Dame in Paris. There he was to repeat publicly the confession he had been forced to make years earlier and to receive a sentence of life-long imprisonment. Instead, he withdrew his confession and proclaimed the innocence of the Templars before a crowd of thousands. Philip ordered him to be burned at the stake, and the Knights Templars, who for two centuries had beaten back the Muslims, passed out of history. (See also CRUSADES; HOSPITALLERS; TEUTONIC KNIGHTS.)

TENNESSEE (tĕn′ĕ sē′), UNITED STATES, is
a state in the east central part of the country. It extends from the Appalachian Mountains on the east to the Mississippi River on the west. Tennessee is bordered by eight states. On the north are Kentucky and Virginia, on the south, Mississippi, Alabama, and Georgia, on the west, Arkansas and Missouri, and on the east, North Carolina.

The Cherokee Indians gave the name "Tennessee" to one of their main villages and to the river that now bears the name. Later the entire area was called Tennessee.

This very narrow state has three natural land regions. The eastern part of the state is the Appalachian Highland region, the central part the Hill region, the west the Lowland region.

The Tennessee River winds through the eastern part of the state, and also crosses the western part. The great changes in the river and valley made by the Tennessee Valley Authority (TVA) demonstrate how natural resources can be used to improve the standard of living. (See TENNESSEE VALLEY AUTHORITY.)

The leading mineral and water-power resources are in the east, making it the leading industrial section of the state. Cotton raising, commerce on the Mississippi River, and recreation are important in the west.

Tennessee has a mild climate. There is enough rainfall and sunshine to grow many kinds of crops including cotton, corn, tobacco, and wheat. Almost half of the land is wooded.

In addition to smaller animals, bears and wild deer are found in the state. Fish are plentiful in the streams and lakes.

Courtesy Paul A. Moore, Tennessee Conservation Department

The Appalachian Range stretches across eastern Tennessee.

Until recently, Tennessee was mainly an agricultural state. But manufacturing is now more important in terms of cash value. The principal industries are chemicals, textiles, food products, clothing, printing and publishing, lumbering, and metal works.

Landscape

From a height of more than 6,000 feet above sea level in the east, the land of Tennessee slopes westward to less than 200 feet at the western border.

The Appalachian Highland region is also called East Tennessee. Along the North Carolina border rise the Great Smoky and Unaka mountains. The Smokies were given this name because of the soft haze that hangs over the peaks. In these mountains is the highest elevation in Tennessee, Clingmans Dome (6,642 feet).

Westward from these high peaks the land dips into a broad valley known as the Great Appalachian Valley. The valley follows the entire length of the great Appalachian Mountain chain which extends from Canada to Alabama. Beyond the valley the land rises into the Cumberland Plateau, a rolling upland with an average elevation of 1,800 feet. (See APPALACHIAN MOUNTAINS.)

The Hill region is also known as Middle Tennessee. It is an area of rolling land which drops slightly in the center to the Central Basin. The Basin is an area of lower elevation than the surrounding hills. In the central portion of the Basin is Nashville.

The Lowland is the flat region of the state known as West Tennessee. It descends gently from the Hill region westward until it drops suddenly over the bluffs above the Mississippi River flood plain. The flood plain is low, bottom land containing many swamps and ponds. Memphis is on the far southern part of this plain. Through the eastern portion of the Lowland flows the lower Tennessee River. In the northwest is Reelfoot Lake, the largest natural lake in the state. It is made up of over 20 miles of swamp and open water. The lake was formed by an earthquake in 1811.

Tennessee has a good water supply from rivers, lakes and reservoirs (man-made lakes). These also provide transportation and power. The state is crossed twice by the Tennessee River as it loops through the state. The Cumberland River forms a network of water courses in the northern portion of the state, and the Mississippi River flows along the western boundary.

With the building of many dams by the TVA, the Tennessee River became the most completely controlled river in the world. The reservoirs formed by these dams and by those on the Cumberland River are known as the "Great Lakes of the South." Among the largest of these are Kentucky Lake (partly in Kentucky), Norris Lake, Cherokee Reservoir, Center Hill Reservoir, and Dale Hollow Reservoir. The reservoirs on the Tennessee River form a broad inland waterway which extends from East Tennessee to the Ohio River.

Much of the original forest of Tennessee is gone, but almost one-half of the land is in timber or woodland. Hardwoods, including oak, hickory, yellow poplar, beech, elm, and gum, are the main forest trees. Cedar trees are found throughout the state, especially in Middle Tennessee. The forests support an important lumber and wood products industry.

Climate

The climate of Tennessee is mild. Except in the mountains, the summers are hot and the winters mild. The average annual temperature is 59 degrees Fahrenheit. Most of the state has a frost-free growing season ranging from 180 to 220 days.

The average annual rainfall is about 47 inches with January and March the rainiest months. Outside the mountain area of the east, snows are rare and seldom remain for longer than a few days.

Animal Life

Most of the original large game animals have vanished, except in national and state parks, and game reservations. Smaller game, the fox, raccoon, opossum, squirrel, rabbit, ground hog, and skunk, are found throughout the state. Muskrat and mink are trapped along creek and river beds. The lakes and streams are rich in bass, crappie, trout, bream, and catfish. There is a hunting season on wild game and birds, but fishing is a year-round activity. One of the most interesting sports of the state is the wild-boar hunt of East Tennessee.

Two of the North American flyways (air routes) for migratory birds pass through Tennessee. One follows the Mississippi River Valley, the other the Great Appalachian Valley. Reelfoot Lake forms a natural, year-round home for waterfowl.

Resources

In addition to the forest and water resources, the state has many mineral resources. The most important mineral, coal, is mined in the Cumberland Plateau of the Appalachian Highland region. These deposits are a part of the Appalachian coal belt which extends from Pennsylvania to Alabama. The large amounts of limestone found in the state are used in making cement. The phosphate rock of Middle Tennessee is used for fertilizers. Other important minerals are clay, zinc, and copper.

The People

The earliest Indians in the area were the Mound Builders. The reason for their disap-

Average Daily Temperature

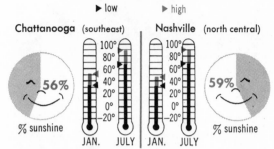

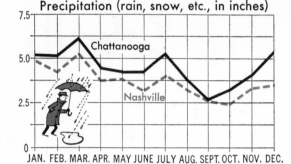

pearance is unknown, but remainders of their civilization are still found. (See MOUND BUILDERS.)

The first English settlers to cross the Appalachian Mountains into what is now Tennessee found the Cherokees living in the eastern part of the state. The lands of West Tennessee were occupied by the Chickasaw Indians. Middle Tennessee was the hunting ground of these two tribes. A third tribe, the Creek Indians, lived in the south. Today about 650 Indians live in the state.

Tennessee was on the main route between French Canada and Louisiana. French traders and trappers explored the Cumberland and Tennessee Rivers, but they made no settlements in what is now Tennessee.

The land of the western part of the state was settled largely by migration from the Middle Atlantic colonies of North Carolina, Virginia, and Pennsylvania. These settlers crossed the mountains and moved into the Great Appalachian Valley. Because land in the middle and western parts of Tennessee was better for agriculture, many settlers continued to move westward.

Many families remained behind in small com-

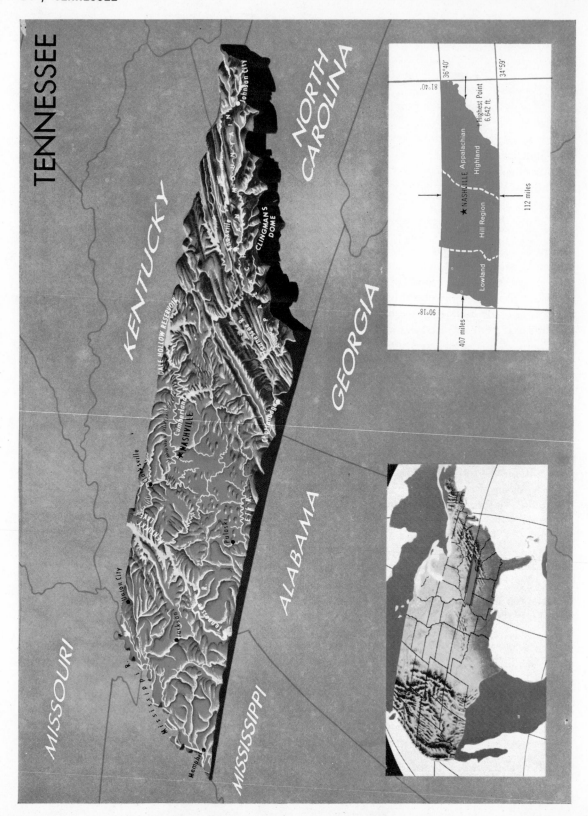

TENNESSEE

MISSOURI

KENTUCKY

NORTH CAROLINA

GEORGIA

ALABAMA

MISSISSIPPI

Johnson City

CLINGMAN'S DOME

DALE HOLLOW RESERVOIR

NASHVILLE

Cumberland

Clarksville

Union City

Jackson

Memphis

Pulaski

Mississippi R.

81°40'

36°40'

34°59'

+Highest Point
6,642 ft

NASHVILLE
★

Appalachian
Highland

Hill Region

Lowland

112 miles

407 miles

90°18'

Nickname: "Volunteer State"
Capital: Nashville
Motto: "Agriculture and Commerce"
Date admitted to the Union: June 1, 1796
Order of admission as state: 16th
Song: "When It's Iris Time in Tennessee"

Iris   Tulip Poplar   Mockingbird

Physical

AREA: 42,244 square miles, including 878 square miles of water; 1.2 percent of total United States; 34th state in size.

POPULATION (1970): 3,924,164; 2.0 percent of total United States; 17th state in population; 92.9 persons per square mile; 58.7 percent urban, 41.3 percent rural.

MOUNTAIN RANGES: Great Smoky, Unicoi, Unaka, Bald, Iron.

CHIEF MOUNTAIN PEAKS (height in feet): Clingmans Dome (6,642); Guyot (6,621); Le Conte (6,593).

LARGEST LAKES: Chickamauga, Douglas, Kentucky, Cherokee.

MOST IMPORTANT RIVERS: Tennessee, Mississippi, Cumberland.

NATIONAL PARK: Great Smoky Mountains National Park, 516,626 acres in Tennessee and North Carolina (239,768 acres in Tennessee; established 1934).

STATE PARKS: Total of 21 including Big Ridge, Chickasaw, Cumberland Mountain, Fall Creek Falls, Harrison Bay, Montgomery Bell, Natchez Trace, Paris Landing, Shelby Forest.

ADDITIONAL PLACES OF INTEREST: Lookout Mountain, Cherokee National Forest; Norris Dam; Dunbar Cave, near St. Bethlehem; The Parthenon, Nashville; Casey Jones Home, Jackson; Cedars of Lebanon Forest; Shiloh Battlefield; Meriwether Lewis Monument, Hohenwald; Birthplace of Davy Crockett, Greeneville.

Transportation and Communication

RAILROADS: 3,398 miles of track; first railroad, La Grange to Memphis, 1842.

ROADS: Total, 77,495 miles; surfaced, 75,448 miles.

MOTOR VEHICLES: Total, 1,971,160; automobiles, 1,583,187; trucks and buses, 387,973.

AIRPORTS: Total, 105; private, 43.

NEWSPAPERS: 33 dailies; 122 weeklies; 14 Sunday; first newspaper, Knoxville Gazette, Rogersville, 1791.

RADIO STATIONS: 198; first station, WNOX, Knoxville, 1921.

TELEVISION STATIONS: 20; first station, WNCT, Memphis, 1948.

TELEPHONES: Total, 1,845,900; residence, 1,369,200; business, 476,700.

POST OFFICES: 610.

People

CHIEF CITIES: Memphis (623,530); Nashville (447,877); Knoxville (174,587); Chattanooga (119,082).

NATIONAL BACKGROUNDS: 99.6 percent native-born; 0.4 percent foreign-born.

CHURCH MEMBERSHIP: Of the total state population, 40.1 percent are church members: 95.8 percent Protestant (including Southern Baptist, 49.8 percent; Methodist, 27.1 percent; Presbyterian, 8.2 percent; Disciples of Christ, 2.8 percent; Episcopal, 2.0 percent), 3.2 percent Catholic, and 1.0 percent Jewish.

LEADING UNIVERSITIES AND COLLEGES: University of Tennessee, Knoxville; Memphis State University, Memphis; East Tennessee State University, Johnson City; Vanderbilt University, Nashville; Tennessee Agricultural and Industrial State University, Nashville.

MUSEUMS: American Museum of Atomic Energy, Oak Ridge; Hermitage Association, Hermitage, home of Andrew Jackson; Chucalissa Indian Museum, Memphis, archaeology; Children's Museum, Nashville, natural history; Brooks Memorial Art Gallery, Memphis.

SPECIAL SCHOOLS: Tennessee School for the Deaf, Knoxville; Tennessee School for the Blind, Donelson; Clover Bottom Home (for mentally handicapped), Donelson; Greene Valley Home (for mentally handicapped), Greeneville.

CORRECTIONAL AND PENAL INSTITUTIONS: State Penitentiary, Nashville; Brushy Mountain Penitentiary, Petros; State Farm, Fort Pillow; Vocational Schools for Girls, Tullahoma and Nashville; Vocational Training Schools for Boys, Jordonia and Pikeville.

Government

NUMBER OF U.S. SENATORS: 2.

NUMBER OF U.S. REPRESENTATIVES: 8.

NUMBER OF STATE SENATORS: 33. TERM: 4 years.

NUMBER OF STATE REPRESENTATIVES: 99. TERM: 2 years.

STATE LEGISLATURE CONVENES: January, odd-numbered years.

SESSION LIMIT: Regular, 90 days with pay; extra, 30 days with pay.

CONSTITUTION ADOPTED: 1870.

GOVERNOR'S TERM: 4 years. He may not succeed himself.

NUMBER OF COUNTIES: 95.

VOTING QUALIFICATIONS: Legal voting age; residence in state 1 year, in county 3 months.

STATE HOLIDAYS: Including Robert E. Lee's Birthday, January 19; Andrew Jackson's Birthday, March 15; Good Friday; Confederate Memorial Day, June 3; Nathan Forrest's Birthday, July 13.

ANNUAL STATE EVENTS: Cotton Carnival, Memphis, May; Rhododendron Festival, Roan Mountain, June; Southern Highlands Handicraft, Gatlinburg, July; State Fair, Nashville, September.

Historic Events

1540—Hernando De Soto reaches Tennessee area.

1682—Rene La Salle establishes fort near present site of Memphis; claims entire Mississippi River Valley for France.

1763—French and Indian War ends; Tennessee becomes British.

1769—William Bean is first white settler in Tennessee region.

1779—Tennessee area becomes part of North Carolina.

1784—State of Franklin is organized; ends four years later.

1796—Tennessee becomes 16th state; capital at Knoxville.

1843—Nashville becomes state capital.

1861—Tennessee secedes from Union; Tennessee is scene of major battles in the American Civil War.

1865—Ku Klux Klan starts at Pulaski.

1866—Tennessee is readmitted to Union.

1933—Tennessee Valley Authority is established by Congress.

1942—Atomic Power Installation opens at Oak Ridge.

1953—State constitution is amended for first time.

1966—Legislature approves reapportionment.

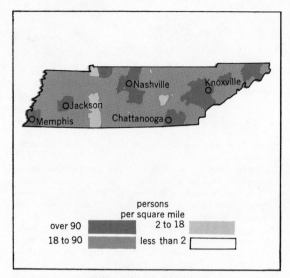

persons per square mile

over 90 — 2 to 18

18 to 90 — less than 2

Where the people live.

industrial city in the center of East Tennessee. Chattanooga is Tennessee's fourth largest city. Oak Ridge, one of the state's newest cities, was built during World War II to produce atomic energy. It is a center for research in the peaceful uses of atomic materials.

How the People Make a Living

During the 19th and part of the 20th centuries, agriculture was the leading occupation of Tennessee. Recently manufacturing has grown rapidly to become the most important source of wealth. But agriculture continues to be important. About 14 percent of the working people are in agriculture. Manufacturing employs about twice as many people. Mining, lumbering, and the tourist trade are other important industries.

Agriculture. With a mild climate, plenty of water, and rich agricultural lands, many kinds of crops can be grown in Tennessee. The four most important crops are cotton, corn, tobacco, and hay. Soybeans, oats, barley, and other grains rank high, but they are important as livestock feed rather than as cash crops. Cotton and tobacco are the main cash crops. Truck gardens and fruit orchards are found throughout the state. Strawberries, Tennessee's most valuable truck crop, are grown widely.

Livestock raising is one of the major occupations of the state. The value of livestock is greater than that of crops. The bluegrass region of Middle Tennessee has become the leading cattle-producing and dairying area of the state. Livestock production is carried on also in the upland and mountainous areas which are better

munities in the valleys of East Tennessee. They lived in log cabins and had little contact with others. Until the 20th century they continued to live in the rugged, primitive manner of their forefathers.

When these small centers were about to disappear, steps were taken to preserve their early-American way of life. Today, in home and shop, the descendants of pioneer settlers carry on a profitable business selling their handicraft and demonstrating their skills to visitors.

There are only eight cities in Tennessee with populations of 25,000 or more. About 41 percent of the people live in small rural towns. There has been a shift in recent years to the city because of the rapid growth of industry.

Negroes make up about one-sixth of the population and live mainly in the larger cities and in the cotton-producing sections. A very small percentage of the population is foreign-born.

Memphis, largest city in the state, is an inland port on the Mississippi River. The leading industries are manufacture and shipment of cotton and lumber products. (See MEMPHIS.)

On the Cumberland River is Nashville, the capital of Tennessee and the center of a wholesale and retail trade. It is the second largest city in the state. The leading industries are chemicals, leather goods, and publishing. (See NASHVILLE.)

Knoxville, the third largest city, is a thriving

Sources of income.

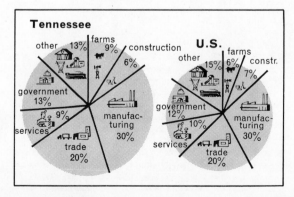

Tennessee

other 13% — farms 9% — construction 6%

government 13%

services 9%

trade 20%

manufacturing 30%

U.S.

other 15% — farms 6% — constr. 7%

government 12%

services 10%

trade 20%

manufacturing 30%

suited to pasture lands than to crops. Cattle, hogs, and sheep are widespread throughout the state.

Horse raising has always been a particular source of pride to Tennesseans. Horse racing was a favorite sport of frontier life. A plantation horse, called the Tennessee Walking Horse because of its easy gait, was developed in the early days. When the automobile and the tractor appeared, this breed lost much of its value as a plantation horse. In recent years there has been new interest throughout Middle Tennessee in raising saddle horses. The Tennessee Walker has once again become important, but now as an attraction at horse shows.

Manufacturing. The rapid growth of manufacturing has been due largely to the TVA. This broad system of dams and steam plants supplies power for almost the entire state. It has attracted many industries, such as the atomic power installation at Oak Ridge. The most heavily industrialized region of the state is the Great Appalachian Valley of East Tennessee where Knoxville, Chattanooga, Oak Ridge, and the tri-cities of Kingsport, Johnson City, and Bristol are located.

Chemical manufacturing employs more people and brings more money to the state than any other industry. Large chemical factories at Chattanooga, Nashville, Memphis, Old Hickory, and Kingsport turn out such products as synthetic fibers, industrial chemicals, drugs and medicines, plastics and cotton seed products.

Textiles, wearing apparel, and the food products industries also are very important. Nashville has several large plants producing rayon, hosiery, and other articles of clothing. Flour and feed milling is done in Nashville. Food products are processed in Knoxville, as well as in Bristol and Johnson City. Meat packing plants are in Memphis and Nashville.

Metal products are produced in the industrial centers of the state. Chattanooga is the center of heavy industry. This industry produces farm machinery and such other iron and steel products as stoves, pumps, and tools.

The forests of Tennessee support the important lumbering and wood products industry. Paper products, publishing and printing, furni-

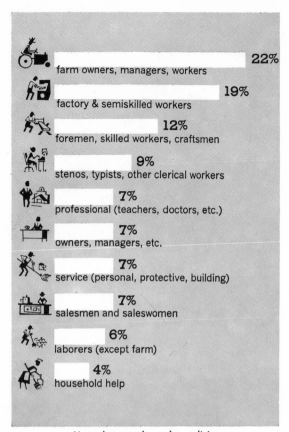

farm owners, managers, workers	22%
factory & semiskilled workers	19%
foremen, skilled workers, craftsmen	12%
stenos, typists, other clerical workers	9%
professional (teachers, doctors, etc.)	7%
owners, managers, etc.	7%
service (personal, protective, building)	7%
salesmen and saleswomen	7%
laborers (except farm)	6%
household help	4%

How the people make a living.

ture and hard-wood flooring manufacture employ a large number of the people. Johnson City is the center of hard-wood flooring production.

Minerals also provide materials for industry. Large deposits of clay are used in the ceramics industry. Tennessee ranks second in the nation as a producer of marble. This industry is centered at Knoxville. Sandstone from the Cumberland Plateau is important in construction work. Glass products are made in Chattanooga. Large aluminum plants operate in Alcoa.

In Oak Ridge are atomic plants and a nuclear research center controlled by the Atomic Energy Commission. Materials are prepared for use in atomic weapons, and research is conducted to find peaceful uses of atomic energy.

Another important way the people of Tennessee make a living is by serving tourists. Gatlinburg in East Tennessee is one of several resort areas. Many people are also attracted

TENNESSEE

LAND USE

FOREST 48%

BUILT-ON 5%

WASTELAND 6%

PASTURE & GRAZING LAND 7%

CROPLAND 34%

VALUE OF PRODUCTS
(FIGURES IN $ MILLIONS)

FARMING
COTTON 79
DAIRY PRODUCTS 77
CATTLE 74
TOBACCO 73
HOGS 53

MINING
COAL 31
STONE 24

MANUFACTURING
CHEMICALS 559
FOOD 241
TEXTILES 154
PRIMARY METALS 144
METAL PRODUCTS 135
PULP, PAPER, & PROD. 114
CLOTHING 108
TRANSPORTATION EQUIP. 87

Map cities and features

Bristol
Johnson City
Kingsport
Cherokee Reservoir
Douglas Reservoir
KNOXVILLE
Norris Dam
Oak Ridge
CLINCH R.
Cleveland
Chattanooga
TENNESSEE R.
Watts Bar Reservoir
Watts Bar Dam
Chickamauga Reservoir
Chickamauga Dam
Dale Hollow Reservoir
CUMBERLAND R.
NASHVILLE
Clarksville
DUCK R.
Kentucky Res.
TENNESSEE R.
Pickwick Dam
Pickwick Reservoir
Pickwick Landing
Jackson
Dyersburg
MEMPHIS
MISSISSIPPI R.

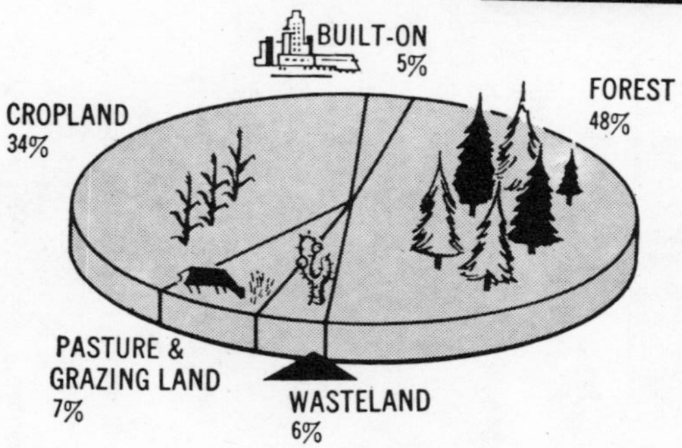

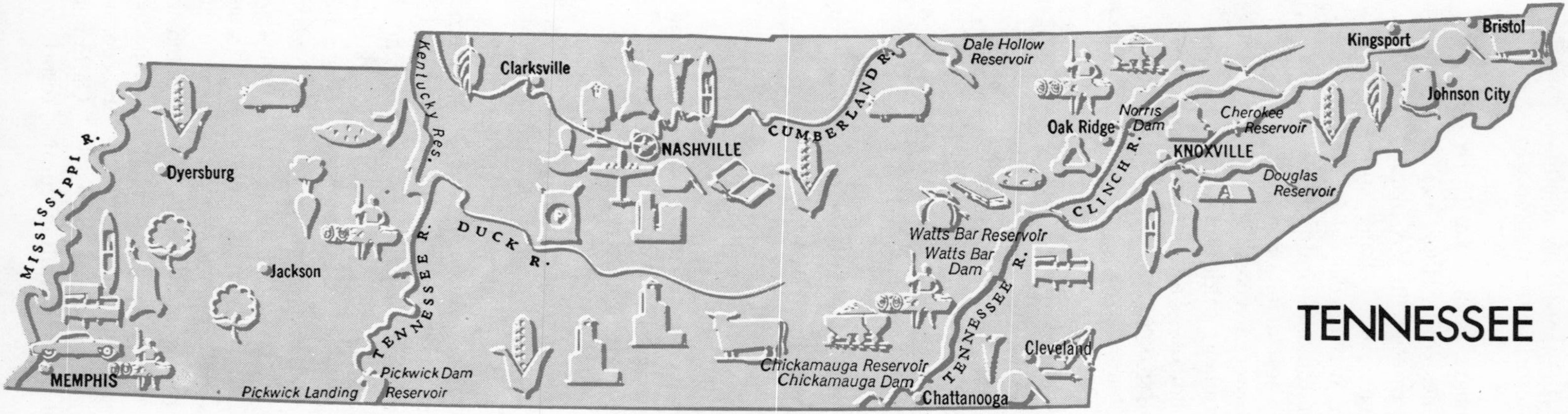

KEY TO SYMBOLS

COTTON
MILLING
PRINTING & PUBLISHING
DRUGS & CHEMICALS
COAL
COPPER ORE
GRAIN
STONE
PHOSPHATE
CLOTHING MFG.
POTATOES
TOBACCO
RAYON
ALUMINUM
AIRCRAFT
CATTLE
FURNITURE
TRUCK CROPS
AUTOMOTIVE EQUIPMENT
ATOMIC PROJECT
CEMENT
SWEET POTATOES
TEXTILES
TANNING
LUMBERING
MARBLE
CORN
METAL PRODUCTS
HOGS
MEAT PACKING
PEACHES

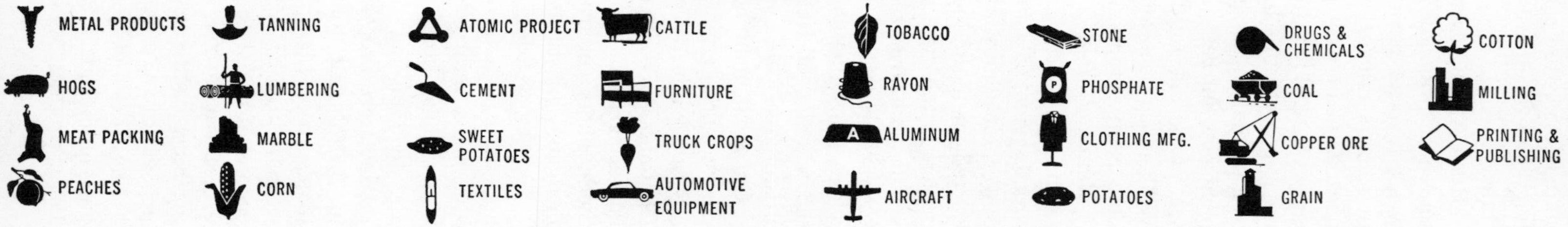

to the "Great Lakes" of Middle Tennessee and to the state and national parks throughout the state.

Transportation

Almost every spot in Tennessee is near river transportation. Three great rivers, the Cumberland, Mississippi, and Tennessee, and their tributaries cross the state. They provide about 30,000 miles of rivers and streams.

Land transportation in the early days was difficult because of the mountain barriers and the slowness of horse-drawn vehicles. Thus even in the early days much of the shipping of goods and products was on the water ways. Now the Tennessee River alone is deep enough for boats and barges to travel the 650 miles from Knoxville, in the eastern mountains, to Paducah, Kentucky, on the Ohio River. Along this route, and on the Cumberland and Mississippi rivers, barges carry products to and from the markets of the state.

Part of the Natchez Trace, an Indian trail, cuts through the state. Before the invention of the steamboat this early road was a very important connection between Nashville and Natchez, Mississippi. The Trace is now being rebuilt as a modern scenic highway.

Tennessee has a network of modern roads and many miles of railroad track. Its central position also places it on major air routes crossing the country.

Government

The powers of the state government are divided into three branches: the executive, legislative, and judicial. The legislative branch is made up of a Senate and a House of Representatives. The members of the legislature are elected from counties and districts divided according to population. The governor heads the executive branch. The state Supreme Court, the highest court, is made up of five judges. Three are elected from the major divisions of East, Middle, and West Tennessee; the remaining two from the state as a whole.

Education

There were no public schools in Tennessee

Courtesy Tennessee Valley Authority

Beef cattle in a rich Tennessee pasture.

before 1854. But in that year Governor Andrew Johnson, who later became president of the United States, persuaded the legislature to levy a tax for the support of public education. The state is now rapidly replacing its one- and two-room rural schools with modern schools served by school buses.

In addition to the University of Tennessee in Knoxville, and the Tennessee Agricultural and Industrial State University in Nashville, the state operates two colleges in each of the three geographic divisions of the state. Vanderbilt

Tobacco is one of the state's most important crops.

Courtesy Tennessee Conservation Department

Courtesy United States Forest Service

Both hardwood and softwood are used in this pulp mill.

University, a privately supported school, is in Nashville.

The progress made in education in recent years has been made possible by the growing wealth of the state. All children under 17 years of age are required to attend school.

The State Museum in Nashville presents the history of the state through a collection of relics which begin with the prehistoric animals. The State Library and Archives Building, also in Nashville, contains the written records of the state. It is a research center used by scholars and historians.

Health and Welfare

Tennessee established a State Board of Health in 1877. The terrible yellow fever epidemic of 1878 brought about a state-wide fight against disease. In 1879 authority was given to the Board to fight the spread of cholera, yellow fever, and smallpox. Since that time the State Board has been replaced by the Department of Health which supervises the entire field of public health, with the co-operation of counties and cities. Tennessee has a modern program for the care of the aged, disabled, and mentally ill and for child welfare.

Tennessee has shared with other states the federal government's program to improve health conditions. The program includes distribution of surplus agricultural products as well as slum-clearance projects. An outstanding example of slum clearance carried on in Tennessee is the removal of the slums around the state capitol building in Nashville.

Recreation

Tennessee has many recreational attractions. More visitors go to Great Smoky Mountains National Park in East Tennessee than to any other park in the United States. Other features are Clingmans Dome, Lookout Mountain at Chattanooga, and Roan Mountain with its well-known purple rhododendron.

In addition to several state parks, Reelfoot Lake and the "Great Lakes" have fishing, boating, and picnic areas. Many of the parks have cabins and camping sites.

Tennessee has numerous historical attractions. Among these are the "Hermitage," home of Andrew Jackson, Natchez Trace State Park, and the battlefields of the War Between the States. Of special interest is the exact copy of the Parthenon of Athens, Greece, which has been built in Nashville's Centennial Park.

History

Although Tennessee had no permanent white settlements until the Revolutionary War period (1775–1781), it was not an unknown land. As

Tennessee is a leading marble-producing state.

Courtesy Tennessee Conservation Department

early as 1540 Hernando De Soto, the Spanish explorer, touched the southern portion of Tennessee and reached the Mississippi River. More than a century passed before there is record of another white man entering the area. Then in 1673 James Needham scouted the territory. The same year Jacques Marquette, the French missionary and explorer, camped along the western border. Another Frenchman, Rene La Salle, established a fort near the present city of Memphis in 1682.

Early in the 18th century French Canadians traded and trapped along the Mississippi River and its tributaries. They built a trading post on the Cumberland River where Nashville now stands. This was called "French Lick."

Neither the Spanish nor the French helped much in the colonization of the Tennessee area. Adventurous traders and explorers from the English colonies crossed the mountains by foot and traded with the Cherokee Indians. But it was not until the land east of the Appalachian Mountains had been claimed by the English, and the soils of older lands worn out, that the eastern colonists began to think of moving west of the mountains.

In 1769 William Bean built a log cabin at the headwaters of the Tennessee River to become the first permanent white settler in Tennessee. Hundreds of others followed. In 1772 they formed the Watauga Association, the first free government west of the Allegheny Mountains. In 1776 the settlers chose to become a part of North Carolina. In 1777 the entire Tennessee area of settlement became Washington County of North Carolina. This was the first place to be named for George Washington.

Other frontiersmen, attracted by reports of rich river-bottom land on which grazed herds of buffalo (bison), elk, and deer, continued to move westward into Middle Tennessee. In 1779 James Robertson, leading a group of men, crossed through Cumberland Gap to French Lick on the Cumberland River. He returned to Watauga and arranged to take settlers to the area to build a fort on the bluffs of the Cumberland.

On Christmas Day, 1779, Robertson and his men returned to the Cumberland area. Three

Courtesy Tennessee Conservation Department

Memphis, center of the state's cotton area, holds a yearly Cotton Carnival.

months later, after a journey of great hardship and courage, a small fleet carrying women and children also arrived at the site. They had made the journey down the Tennessee River and up the Cumberland under the command of Colonel John Donelson. The settlement was later named Nashborough, for the Revolutionary War hero, General Francis Nash.

The little settlement was a part of North Carolina, but the settlers drew up their own form of government. This Cumberland Compact was signed by 256 men and remained in effect until 1783 when North Carolina included the area in the newly-formed Davidson County.

The settlers began to copy the ways of life which they had left behind them in Virginia, North Carolina, and Pennsylvania. Today there still can be seen in Middle Tennessee a number of homes built by the original settlers.

At first the frontier settlements were so busy fighting off Indian attacks that they gave little thought to the American Revolution. However, when word came that a British officer, Major Patrick Ferguson, was threatening to attack, they crossed the mountains and met him at King's Mountain. After defeating the British, the settlers returned to their homes and continued their work of pushing the frontier westward.

In 1784 the eastern settlements, feeling that

Courtesy Atomic Energy Commission

The Atomic Energy Commission's Oak Ridge plant makes uranium products.

North Carolina did little to protect them from the Indians and cared little for their interests, declared themselves free from North Carolina. They organized themselves into the State of Franklin and adopted a constitution. The Cumberland settlements of Middle Tennessee did not co-operate. In a few years the new state collapsed and the territory once again became a part of North Carolina.

In 1789 North Carolina turned the land which is now Tennessee over to the United States.

Norris Dam on the Clinch River is the oldest dam in the TVA network.

Courtesy Tennessee Conservation Department

The following year President Washington appointed William Blount as governor of the territory. By 1796 the population had reached the required amount for statehood. The same year Tennessee became the 16th state of the Union. John Sevier, one of the original leaders of the Watauga Association, was elected the first governor.

The early history of Tennessee as a state was largely the story of Indian wars, land disputes, and law enforcement. By 1800 Andrew Jackson had become an important political figure. Soon the state was divided by disputes over loyalty to Andrew Jackson or to John Sevier. Sevier, governor six times, ran the state. But Jackson gained nation-wide fame by defeating the Creek Indians at Horseshoe Bend (1814), and the British at the Battle of New Orleans (1815). He replaced Sevier as the state's hero. During this period Tennessee lost much of its frontier character and became an agricultural state. (See JACKSON, ANDREW.)

Jackson was elected president of the United States in 1828 and again in 1832. During this period, Tennessee was important in national affairs. While Jackson was president, many Tennesseans migrated to Texas. Among them were David Crockett, hero of the Alamo, and Sam Houston, first president of the Texas Republic.

In 1845, while Tennessee's James K. Polk was president of the United States, the Mexican War began. The people of the state volunteered in such numbers that since that time Tennessee has been known as the Volunteer State. (See POLK, JAMES KNOX.)

Bitter sectional differences split Tennessee when the War Between the States started in 1861. In June the people of West and Middle Tennessee voted to withdraw from the Union and support the Confederacy. These sections contained many plantations, on which slaves did the work as in the South. But East Tennessee chose to remain a part of the Union. The East with its more rugged land was made up chiefly of small farms on which slave labor was not profitable. This difference of political views has carried over into present-day politics. East Tennessee usually votes Republican while the Middle and West divisions vote Democratic.

Andrew Johnson, United States senator from East Tennessee at the time, kept his seat in the Senate. Later he became military governor of Tennessee and afterwards was elected vice-president. When Abraham Lincoln was assassinated Johnson became president of the United States. (See JOHNSON, ANDREW.)

Next to Virginia, Tennessee was the chief battleground of the war. (See WAR BETWEEN THE STATES, THE.) In 1866 Tennessee was the first of the seceding states to return to the Union, but much bitterness remained. In December 1865 the Ku Klux Klan was organized at Pulaski, Tennessee. Recovery from the war was slow. The 50 years following the war were spent restoring the fertility of the farms, rebuilding the wrecked railroads and roads, and repaying the state war debt.

After World War I progress was rapid. Under the leadership of Governor Austin Peay the state government was reorganized. Many new roads were built. Later governors continued the building of highways and of farm-to-market roads. Public education received more and more of the tax dollar until, under the governorship of Jim McCord in 1947, a new sales tax raised more money for public education.

The political bitterness that followed the United States Civil War has disappeared and the state again plays an important part in national politics. Cordell Hull represented Tennessee in the United States Senate for many years. He later became Secretary of State under Franklin D. Roosevelt during the difficult years before and during World War II. More recently Senator Estes Kefauver became nationally known as a vice-presidential candidate. Howard H. Baker, Jr., elected by popular vote in 1966, became Tennessee's first Republican U.S. senator.

TENNESSEE VALLEY (văl′ē) AUTHORITY

(ạ thŏr′ĭ tē) was formed in 1933, the first year of President Franklin D. Roosevelt's administration. It was to be a planned program of conservation and development for an entire river valley, which included parts of seven states.

The ideas expressed in the act were not new.

Their history was a long one. In the early 1900's Gifford Pinchot, a great conservationist, and others joined with President Theodore Roosevelt to save the nation's natural resources. They thought that a whole river from its source to the sea should be developed "for all of the uses of the water and benefits to be derived from their control." (See CONSERVATION.)

Muscle Shoals

During World War I the federal government built two nitrate factories in northern Alabama along a stretch of the Tennessee River known as Muscle Shoals. There, the water was very shallow and there were many rapids. Wilson Dam was built nearby to furnish electricity.

In the years that followed, there were debates in Congress to decide the use of the almost idle Muscle Shoals properties. Congress had passed two bills that planned for government operation of the plants and for development of the Tennessee River Basin. Presidents Calvin Coolidge and Herbert Hoover vetoed the bills.

When Franklin Roosevelt became president, Senator George Norris of Nebraska again led the fight for the project in Congress. He hoped that this act would help one area of the country that was hard hit by the Great Depression of the 1930's. The bill passed and the Muscle Shoals properties were turned over to the Tennessee Valley Authority (TVA).

TVA's Goals

The TVA is an agency of the federal government. It had no new powers, but it made use of old powers in two new ways. First, it was to develop all the natural resources of the entire valley. Before this time the many different tasks had been given to separate departments. Second, TVA set up headquarters in the valley, not in Washington. It made its decisions in co-operation with the people of the area, and the local and state governments.

Three main purposes of the TVA have been flood control, navigation, and generation of electric power. In addition, TVA was to restore fertility to misused and worn out land; bring back the forests to full usefulness; encourage

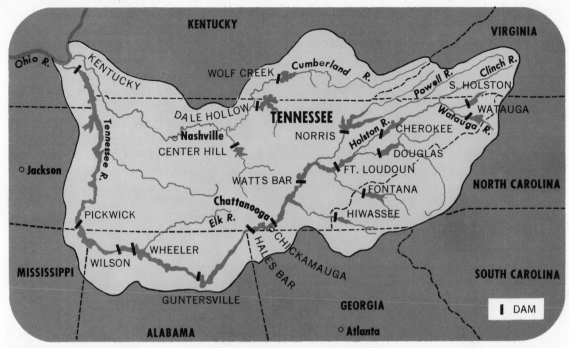

Location map of TVA area and major dams.

industrial development; and provide recreational areas. It also helped with national defense needs.

The Tennessee River Basin covers about 39,-000 square miles. The area rises to more than 6,000 feet above sea level in the Great Smoky Mountains and falls to about 300 feet where the Tennessee joins the Ohio River.

Before TVA, the river had never been developed for navigation, and only a small part of the power in the valley had been used. No effort had been made to control floods, so the river caused damage in the Tennessee Valley and added to floods in the lower Ohio and Mississippi valleys. For these many reasons this valley offered opportunities for intelligent planning and resource development. The TVA, through its three-man Board of Directors, met this challenge.

How TVA Works

The area of the Tennessee and its tributaries has the heaviest rainfall in the United States, except for the Northwest and parts of Hawaii. It averages 51.5 inches a year and is as much as 84 inches in some of the mountains. To

control this water TVA built a system of 19 multiple-purpose and 7 single-purpose dams. In addition there are 6 single-purpose dams owned by the Aluminum Company of America. These dams make the valley almost flood-proof. They also can hold back enough water to keep the crests of Mississippi River floods at Cairo, Illinois, four feet lower.

The multiple-purpose dams control flood waters, and they also form a series of inland lakes, connected by locks. Today there is a 650-mile channel for 9-foot navigation from Knoxville, Tennessee, to Paducah, Kentucky, where the Tennessee flows into the Ohio River. This waterway carries millions of tons of goods each year. The new 100-foot single-lift lock, the highest in the world, completed at Wilson Dam in November 1959, opened the river for even more traffic.

The TVA dams also produce electric power. When TVA began producing electricity, many people criticized it for competing with private industry. However, the government electricity is not supposed to compete with private enterprise. TVA does not sell directly to homes and farms. Rather, it sells power wholesale to 153 city, county, and co-operative systems that sell it to the people. So great was the demand for power that steam plants have been built to add to the capacity of the dams. Today these steam plants produce about three-fourths of the 60 billion kilowatt hours generated each year. About half of this power is used by federal defense agencies, chiefly the Atomic Energy Commission.

Farmers in two-thirds of the United States are co-operating in testing and using fertilizers produced at Muscle Shoals. The TVA also works closely with the state and local government agencies and with the agricultural colleges in the valley and elsewhere. Demonstrations of contour plowing, reforestation of hillsides, and the use of cover crops and fertilizers have increased farm and livestock production and halted erosion. TVA has tried to get other agencies to take over these tasks. Today many demonstrations and most of the seedlings for reforestation are provided by the states, where TVA was once the only source.

The recreational value of the Tennessee Valley is high; 13 state parks and 62 local parks along the reservoirs provide areas for camping and boating. Recreational and commercial fishing have increased. The shores of the waterway are being used by industry. Since 1933 private enterprise has invested more than three-quarters of a billion dollars in 135 water front plants and terminals along the Tennessee.

TVA also has helped in national defense. Power from the dams and steam plants is used by the Munitions Development Center at Muscle Shoals in the production of aluminum, and in atomic energy research at Oak Ridge, Tennessee.

TVA has had great importance inside and outside the valley. Its regional program has been urged for other areas. Its dams and power plants have been praised by many architects and engineers. The purpose of these structures stands inscribed upon each one: "Built for the People of the United States." Whether programs like TVA are the best way to help sections of a country is still being argued. Politically there have been strong arguments on each side.

TENNIEL (těn'yěl), **SIR JOHN** (1820–1914), was an English artist, best known for his illustrations for the book *Alice in Wonderland*.

Tenniel was born in London. As a young man he lost an eye while fencing, but this did not stop him from developing great skill in art. He studied art at the Royal Academy for a short time.

His first pictures were exhibited in 1836. Then his designs for a mural in the Palace of Westminster won a prize and a commission to paint a fresco in the House of Lords. At the same time he learned to draw cartoons, and in 1850 he joined the magazine *Punch* as a cartoonist. His more than 2,300 cartoons of many kinds show his ability, particularly in the field of political cartoons.

Tenniel worked closely with Lewis Carroll to illustrate *Alice's Adventures in Wonderland* and *Through the Looking Glass*. The books have been reprinted many times since the first editions. The artist expressed perfectly Carroll's gentle and unusual humor. His drawings of Alice are still popular even though the styles of illustration have changed since that time. (See CARROLL, LEWIS.)

Tenniel was knighted in 1893 in recognition of his outstanding work as a political cartoonist.

TENNIS (těn'ĭs). Tennis is an active game usually played out of doors. Lawn tennis is one of the few games played world wide by the same set of rules. The game is played on a large flat surface or *court* of grass, clay, gravel, cinder, asphalt, or cement. The court is 78 feet long, 27 feet wide (for two players) or 36 feet (for four); a *net* 3 feet high divides it across the middle. Playing areas are clearly marked by white tape, lime, or paint. Games played by two are called "singles." Games played by four (two on either side) are called "doubles."

The tennis *ball* is made of air-filled rubber covered with felt; it is $2\frac{1}{2}$ inches in diameter. The *racket* has a long handle and an oval "face," tightly strung with gut, silk, or nylon strings; racket frames are usually hickory or ash. The object of the game is to use the

TENNIS

To become a good tennis player one must learn
to grip the racket in the correct way and to master the
forehand and backhand drives and the overhead service.

FOREHAND

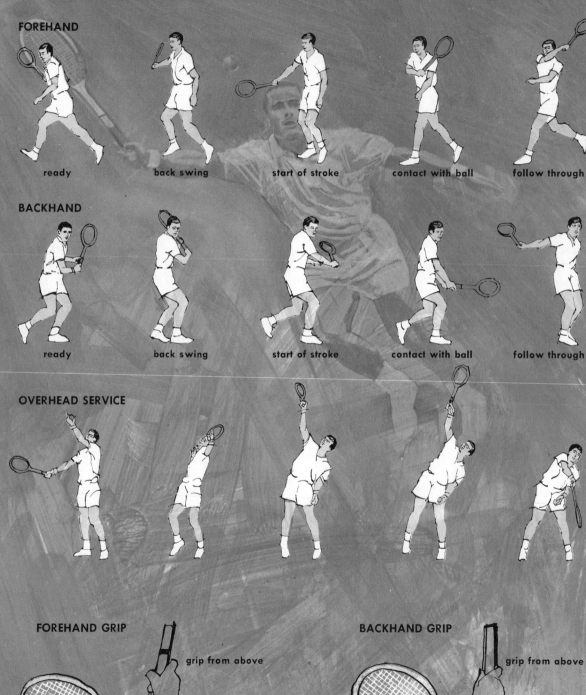

ready   back swing   start of stroke   contact with ball   follow through

BACKHAND

ready   back swing   start of stroke   contact with ball   follow through

OVERHEAD SERVICE

FOREHAND GRIP

grip from above

BACKHAND GRIP

grip from above

racket to hit the ball over the net and into the opponent's court. The ball should be sent over in such a way that the opponent will not be able to return the ball over the net and into the other player's court. The ball must be hit while in the air or on the first bounce.

The game begins with one player making the first stroke, or *service*. He stands behind the right side of the base line and attempts to hit the ball into the receiving court of his opponent. This is the court diagonally opposite the server. He generally uses an overhead stroke and plenty of speed. If his first ball strikes outside the proper receiving court it is called a *fault,* and another ball is served. If this, too, is inaccurately hit it is called a *double fault,* and the server loses the point. If a service is accurate, the receiver tries to hit the ball back on the first bounce. After the service both players may hit the ball into any part of the opposite court, either before it bounces (called a *volley*) or on the first bounce. A player is not permitted to reach the racket over the net or to touch the net with the body. The second point is played the same as the first, except it is served from behind the left side of the base line into the opposite receiving court.

Services during a game are from alternate sides of the center of the base line; players take turns in serving games.

In doubles play all four players alternate in serving and must alternate in receiving the serve.

The score of the server is always called first. If the server wins the first point, the score is 15-love (*love* means *zero*); if he loses it, the score is love-15. Each point counts 15 for the one who wins it, except the third point won by a player is called 40. Thus, the score of a game may run: 15-love, 30-love, 40-love, and game, and the server will have won a love game. When the score is tied, it is 15-all or 30-all, except when it is tied at 40, then it is called *deuce*. The next point after deuce is not game, but *advantage* for the one winning the point. When one player has the advantage and wins the next point, he wins the game. If he loses the point, the score is deuce again. The winning of six games makes a *set*. However, if the players tie at 5-all, play continues until one side is two games ahead of the other. In a match, three out of five sets decide a men's major championship; two out of three a women's championship.

To be a good tennis player it is very important to *grip* the racket in the correct way. Imagine the racket is standing straight up on its edge with the long strings parallel to the ground. The handle is pointed toward you, so

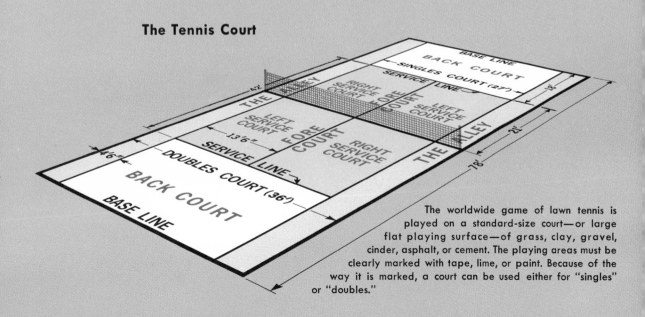

The Tennis Court

The worldwide game of lawn tennis is played on a standard-size court—or large flat playing surface—of grass, clay, gravel, cinder, asphalt, or cement. The playing areas must be clearly marked with tape, lime, or paint. Because of the way it is marked, a court can be used either for "singles" or "doubles."

just reach out and "shake hands" with it. This grip is used in forehand strokes. For backhand strokes the grip is shifted so that the hand is more on top of the handle. The serve, with a backhand grip, can be made with a slicing stroke putting spin on the ball. The right spin causes the ball to bounce at an odd angle and makes the return more difficult. This service, called the "American Twist," is popular with advanced players. Another type of service is the slice service, used most by beginners. The grip for the slice service is halfway between forehand and backhand positions.

The origin of tennis is unknown, but it probably developed from games played for centuries by people in Europe and Asia. They played with a ball which was batted between players, first by hand, then by paddles or rackets. Modern lawn tennis has developed from a game first played in France in the 14th century known as *jeu de paume*. This later came to be known as court tennis. The name tennis is believed to come from the French *Tenez!* which means "Play!"

Court tennis and lawn tennis are very different, although they seem to have closely connected origins. Lawn tennis has become the more popular.

The modern game of lawn tennis was invented by Major Walter C. Wingfield, an officer in the British Army. It was introduced in 1873 in Wales at a lawn party. In 1874 Miss Mary E. Outerbridge of New York saw the game played in Bermuda. She took rackets and balls back to her home and showed her friends how to play the game. About the same time James Dwight and F. R. Sears, Jr., laid out a tennis court at Nahant, Massachusetts. In 1881 the United States Lawn Tennis Association was formed. This association is a member of the International Lawn Tennis Federation, which made the code of rules for amateur tennis.

International competition started in 1900 when Dwight F. Davis of St. Louis, Missouri, offered a large silver bowl to the winning international team. The trophy bears the name of the "International Lawn Tennis Challenge Trophy," but is better known as the "Davis Cup." Countries which have won the Davis Cup are the United States, Australia, England, and France. Each year the Davis Cup holder meets a challenging team that has won the right to compete by winning in international team play. Teams consist of two, three, or four players. There are four "singles" matches and one "doubles" match in Davis Cup play. In 1923 Mrs. George W. Wightman offered a cup (the Wightman Cup) to be played for each year by teams of women representing the United States and England.

The teams that compete for these cups are made up of amateur players. Professional tennis became popular in the 1920's, and attracted many former amateur players and champions.

TENNYSON (tĕn′ĭ s′n) **ALFRED,** Lord (1809–1892), was the most famous and best-loved English poet during the 19th century. When he was 41, he was named Poet Laureate, the highest honor that the British government can give to a poet. This award meant that he was considered the leading British poet of his time. (See Poet Laureate.)

Alfred Tennyson.

Tennyson, the son of a minister, was born in the little village of Somersby, Lincolnshire, England. There were 12 children in the family —all very talented. But even in this unusual family Alfred's ability was outstanding. As a child of five he had already shown poetic talent.

While in their teens, Alfred and two of his brothers, Charles and Frederick, received honors for their poetry. In 1827, when Alfred was only 18, he and Charles published a book called *Poems by Two Brothers.* A year later Alfred and Charles left home to attend Cambridge University. Frederick, who was already a student there, won a prize for one of his poems. In 1829 Alfred also won a prize at the university for his poem "Timbuctoo."

When Tennyson was 21, he published his first volume of poems. His second book was published two years later (1832). "The Lady of Shalott," one of his most famous poems, was included in this second volume. For the next ten years, he continued writing poetry, but he did not publish any more of his work. Perhaps this was because of the death of his dearest friend, Arthur Hallam, in 1833. Tennyson suffered very deeply after Hallam's death, and many of his poems express this great sorrow.

During this ten-year period, Tennyson also worked very hard to improve his poetry. He wrote and rewrote and improved many of his best poems. Finally, in 1842, he published a two-volume collection of these poems. Some of the best known were "Ulysses," "Locksley Hall," and "Break, Break, Break." This collection brought him fame as England's leading poet.

The year 1850 was a very important one for Tennyson. He was named Poet Laureate, and he was married. Also he published one of his most important works, *In Memoriam*, a very long poem written in the memory of his friend Hallam. Because it was written over a period of many years, it shows the changes in Tennyson's feelings about his friend's death.

Like several other poets of his time, Tennyson became very interested in the legends about King Arthur. (See ARTHURIAN LEGENDS.) He wrote a group of 12 poems, called *The Idylls of the King*, telling of King Arthur and his Knights of the Round Table.

When Tennyson was 81, he wrote his famous short poem, "Crossing the Bar." In this poem he asks that there be no weeping when he dies.

Tennyson continued to be admired all his life. In 1884 Queen Victoria honored him still more by making him a lord.

TERMITE (tĕr′mĭt) is the wood-eating insect of the order Isoptera. Because of their resemblance to ants, termites are often incorrectly called white ants. Unlike ants, however, they have thick waists and are usually a whitish color.

About 2,000 species of termites are known. The greatest number live in the rainy, tropical regions around the world. Only two species occur in Europe. About 50 species are found in the United States and southern Canada. They live in every state of the United States, but many are found only in the southern states.

Social Organization

Termites live together in colonies that are organized into groups. Each group has a special task to perform, and each member of a group is adapted to performing his specific task.

There are reproductive male and female termites, as there are with most insects, but there are also two other kinds of termites—soldiers and workers—that cannot reproduce. A reproductive male and reproductive female become the king and queen. They head the colony, and their task is to reproduce termites. A queen can lay several thousand eggs a day. These eggs hatch into nymphs, which look like small workers and soldiers but do not necessarily become workers or soldiers when they mature.

By shedding their skins, the nymphs gradually increase in size until they are full grown. They may grow into males, females, soldiers, or workers. With the exception of the workers, each group seems to prevent the nymphs from becoming one of their own group. Most nymphs, therefore, grow to be workers.

It is thought that the queen gives off a substance from her body. If this is eaten by the other termites in large amounts, it prevents the nymphs from growing into females, or queens. The king seems to do the same and so prevents other kings from developing.

If a king or queen dies, however, a new one may develop in its place. Since the substance is not then present, a few nymphs can grow into a king or queen as the case may be. If a colony gets very large, other queens may appear.

The soldiers protect the colony from its enemies. They do not have wings and are blind, but they are nevertheless able to defend a colony when it is disturbed. Different species have different ways of fighting. Most have long jaws to bite the enemy. Certain tropical termites have small, useless jaws but have a gland in the head that gives off a poisonous gas. Still others have nozzle-shaped heads that throw a sticky, harmful fluid at the enemy.

The workers, which are also wingless and blind, have the job of feeding the colony. They eat wood, and when it is digested, they feed it to the other termites. In the hind intestine of a nymph or a worker is a liquid that is made up of thousands of single-celled animals, or protozoans. The protozoans turn the cellulose of the wood into sugar. The sugar is digested by the worker and fed to the others. These protozoans are found only in termites, and many termites cannot live without them.

At a certain time of the year, just before the rainy season in the tropics, a number of nymphs grow into winged males and females. They leave the nest in swarms to start new colonies. They separate into pairs, and after a short flight they alight. The wings break off at the base. The pairs mate and then burrow into pieces of dry wood or under the bark of dead tree stumps.

In a few weeks, the first eggs are laid. The first nymphs are fed by the young king and queen. They grow into small soldiers and workers. As more and more eggs hatch and the colony grows large, the workers must feed the king, queen, nymphs, and soldiers. Winged males and females do not appear in the new colony for three or four years.

Courtesy Buffalo Society of Natural Sciences

The huge termite queen is tended in her chamber by worker and soldier termites. Her king hovers near her at the left.

Termites have existed for millions of years. The earliest fossil termites belong to the Tertiary period. At that time, termites like those now living became trapped in the sap of trees. The sap hardened into amber and preserved the insects. (See FOSSIL.)

The early termites developed from primitive roaches that ate wood and kept protozoans to help them digest it. These earliest termites had males, females, nymphs, and soldiers but no workers. The nymphs fed the grown termites. The colonies consisted of only a few hundred insects living in burrows made in logs. Such primitive termites are still found in the western and southern United States as well as in the tropics.

Termite Homes

Termites burrow in wood and eat out the wood in which the colony lives, forming rooms. They may line the rooms with excrement to keep the inner air moist. In the tropics many kinds of termites build nests. Some are mounds on the ground that may be 30 feet high and 50 feet across. Others build tree nests of various shapes that are usually about the size of a basketball. These nests protect the colonies from

birds, lizards, spiders, and ants. They also keep the air moist so that the soft bodies of the termites do not dry out.

The nests of some African species have umbrellalike caps to shed the rain. The nests of an Australian species are built in a north-south direction and are about ten feet long. Across the nest, or from east to west, they are about two feet wide. The top is sharp. Due to this placing of the nest in a north-south direction, the nest absorbs heat only in the cool of the mornings and evenings. During the middle of the day there is little surface exposed to the rays of the hot sun.

Termite nest building is an example of working by instinct. In a new colony the nest must be built by the workers born there. They have no way to learn from other termites, yet, they carry out the specialized tasks. When finished, the nest is like the one in the old colony from which the king and queen came.

Destruction by Termites

In the United States, termites fall into three groups: those that burrow under stones; those

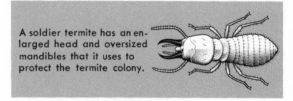

A soldier termite has an enlarged head and oversized mandibles that it uses to protect the termite colony.

Photos, Courtesy G. F. Hill

An Australian species of termite builds its nest in a north-south direction and makes it several feet wide but only a few feet thick so that it absorbs little midday sun.

John H. Gerard

Some termites grow wings when mature and fly from the nest to mate and build new nests. After their short colonizing flight, their wings break off at the base.

that burrow in wood; and those that burrow through the ground until they reach wood. Although termites will eat living wood, they prefer it dead. Because of this, they are a menace to homes. They may eat out the inside of beams, causing the structure supported by the beams to collapse. Sometimes termites burrow into libraries and eat shelves of books.

Because of their soft bodies, most termites cannot stand contact with dry air. They therefore make no holes to the surface. For this reason their presence is not known until the damage is complete.

Termite damage to houses, furniture, and libraries in the United States is estimated at $40 million each year. Although termites are destructive in most places, in the forests they become useful because they clean up dead wood and reduce it to a form that can be used again by other organisms.

Wood can be treated so that termites will not attack it. One method is to soak it with coal tar creosote under pressure so that the creosote reaches the center. When building, care should be taken not to let untreated wood come closer than two feet from the ground. Although moist conditions are necessary for most termites, some dry-wood termites in the southern United States live in drier conditions.

TETANUS (*tĕt′ 'n ŭs*) is a disease caused by an infection. It is also known as lockjaw because the most common symptom is stiffness of the jaw. The infecting germ is the bacillus *Clostridium tetani*. This germ normally is found in soil, where it can live for many years.

Certain small or large wounds may be infected if they come in contact with dirt in which the germs live. In order for the germ to develop, there must be dead tissue in the wound and no opening to the air. This is because the bacillus grows best without light and air.

The bacillus does not do its damage by spreading through the tissues. Instead it settles in the wound and produces a deadly poison, tetanus toxin. This toxin travels through the motor nerves to the spinal cord and brain stem. The motor nerves are affected, causing muscles to contract and become rigid. The toxin also affects the brain and nerves more generally, causing violent convulsions.

The trouble may start as early as 2 days or as late as 85 days after injury. Early symptoms may be stiffness and soreness of the muscles nearest the wound. Stiffness of the jaw usually appears early also. Soon the patient is restless and irritable; has stiffness of the neck, legs, and arms; and goes through convulsions and delirium. If unchecked, the toxin causes death.

All persons who might receive cuts or wounds should be injected with tetanus toxoid. This gives immunity for several years. Booster injections are advisable every two years thereafter. Following an injury, the patient receives an additional booster injection. In the United States, immunization has made tetanus a rare disease. (See also IMMUNITY AND RESISTANCE TO DISEASE.)

The treatment of the person who has not been given immunity can be difficult. For rapid protection, the patient is given large doses of a tetanus antitoxin. When tetanus develops, the patient must be kept in a hospital.

Tetanus has been recognized as a disease for many centuries. It often came from battle wounds and farm injuries. In the 1880's and 1890's German physician Arthur Nicolaier and others proved that it was infectious and discovered the bacillus that causes it.

TEUTONIC (*tū tän′ik*) **KNIGHTS** (*nīts*), or the Order of Teutonic Knights of St. Mary's Hospital at Jerusalem, was one of three great military-religious orders that began during the Crusades. (See CRUSADES.)

It was founded by German crusaders at Acre in Palestine in about 1190, later than the other two orders—the Hospitallers and the Templars. The Teutonic Order was at first connected with a hospital in the Holy Land, where sick and wounded pilgrims and Crusaders were cared for. The order soon became more military than charitable and more active in Germany than in Palestine. In 1228 the bishop of Prussia invited the knights to come to his lands and help fight the pagan Prussians and Lithuanians and convert them to Christianity.

The order thus began to play an important

role in the "drive to the East," the focus of German history from the 12th to the 14th centuries. The knights helped establish the eastern frontier of Germany, spreading German influence by building cities and bringing German peasants to farm the land. In 1229 the knights began the conquest and conversion of the Prussians. Later, the establishment of independence from all authority except the pope gave the order even greater influence. By the early 14th century the order controlled a powerful state

A Teutonic Knight wore a white robe decorated with a black cross. The knight shown here wears German armor of the late 14th century.

stretching along the Baltic coast from the Oder River to present-day Leningrad. The order thus became a governing aristocracy with a thorough system of administration.

The order prospered as long as the interests of the knights remained those of the towns and the Hanseatic League. (See HANSEATIC LEAGUE.) The defeat the knights suffered from the Poles at the Battle of Tannenberg (1410) was the first step in the decline of the order.

Dissatisfied subject peoples were encouraged to seek greater freedom under Polish rule. After years of war with the Polish-Lithuanian state, the order lost much of its territory. The French Revolution deprived the knights of the remaining estates, and in 1809 the order died out altogether. In 1840 the Teutonic Knights was restored as a semireligious order in Austria. (See HOSPITALLERS; TEMPLARS, KNIGHTS.)

TEXAS (*těk'säs*), **UNITED STATES,** is the second largest state in the nation. Its vast area of 267,339 square miles is centered along the southern border of the main part of the United States. Oklahoma borders Texas on the north, Arkansas and Louisiana on the east, the Gulf of Mexico on the southeast, Mexico on the southwest, and New Mexico on the northwest. Large parts of the state boundary lines are rivers and sea coast. The Rio Grande separates Texas from Mexico, the Red River forms most of the boundary between Texas and Oklahoma, and the Sabine River divides Texas from Louisiana for half of that boundary. The coastline along the gulf extends about 370 miles.

Texas got its name from a small tribe of Indians who lived in the eastern part of the state near the Sabine River. These Indians were known as the Tejas (*tā'häs*).

So large an area has many kinds of climate, plant life, and land surface. Rolling plains cover most of the state. The plains are low and flat along the gulf coast, but become much higher in western Texas. In the southwest are mountains that rise to more than 8,000 feet.

Most of the people live in the eastern and southeastern parts of the state. Oil, gas, water, and other natural resources are the reason for much of the rapid population growth along the coastal plain.

Texas is a great agricultural state. But Texas is probably best known for its oil and gas industries, which have brought many other industries to the state. About two-fifths of the nation's oil and natural gas comes from Texas wells.

Landscape

The state has four major land regions—the

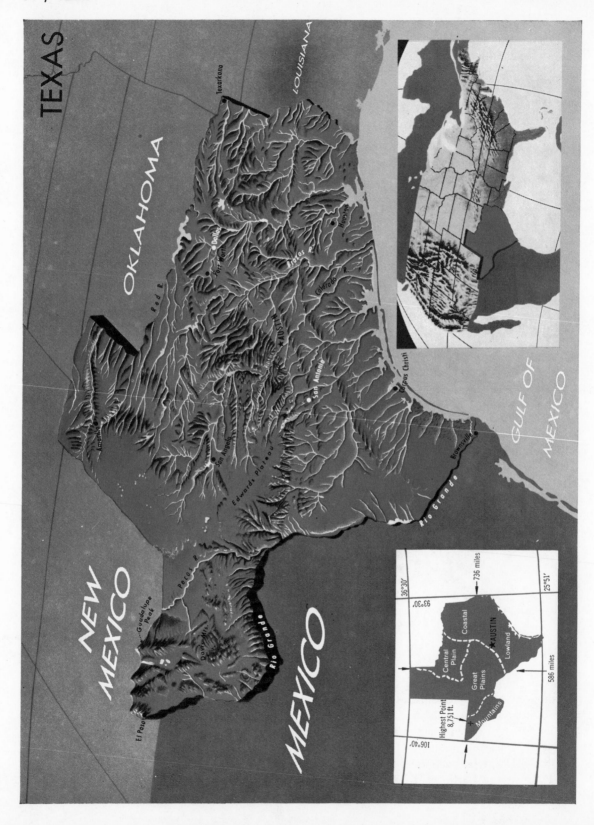

TEXAS

OKLAHOMA

NEW MEXICO

MEXICO

LOUISIANA

GULF OF MEXICO

Red R.

Brazos R.

Colorado R.

Pecos R.

Rio Grande

Edwards Plateau

Guadalupe Peak

Davis Mts.

Amarillo

Dallas

Fort Worth

AUSTIN

San Angelo

San Antonio

Houston

Corpus Christi

Brownsville

Texarkana

El Paso

Rio Grande

106°40'

36°30'

93°30'

25°51'

736 miles

586 miles

Central Plain

Coastal Plain

Great Plains

Lowland

AUSTIN

Mountains

Highest Point 8,751 ft.

Nickname: "Lone Star State"
Capital: Austin
Motto: "Friendship"
Date admitted to the Union: December 29, 1845
Order of admission as state: 28th
Song: "Texas, Our Texas"

Bluebonnet   Pecan   Mockingbird

Physical

AREA: 267,339 square miles, including 4,369 square miles of water; 7.4 per cent of total United States; 2nd state in size.

POPULATION (1970): 11,196,730; 5.5 per cent of total United States; 4th state in population; 41.9 persons per square mile; 79.7 per cent urban, 20.3 per cent rural.

MOUNTAIN RANGES: Guadalupe, Davis, Delaware, Santiago, Quitman, Tierra Vieja, Chisos.

CHIEF MOUNTAIN PEAKS (height in feet): Guadalupe (8,751); El Capitan (8,078); Emory (7,835); Chinati (7,730).

LARGEST LAKES: Kemp, Buchanan, Texoma, Tawakoni.

MOST IMPORTANT RIVERS: Brazos, Colorado, Sabine, Neches, Trinity, Red, Rio Grande, Canadian, Nueces, Pecos.

NATIONAL PARKS AND MONUMENTS: Big Bend, 708,221 acres (1944); Guadalupe Mountains, 82,279 acres (1966); Padre Island National Seashore, 133,918 acres (1962).

STATE PARKS: Total of 61 including Bastrop, Fort Parker, Garner, Huntsville, Inks Lake, Lake Brownwood.

INDIAN RESERVATIONS: Alabama and Coushatta.

ADDITIONAL PLACES OF INTEREST: The Alamo, San Antonio; McDonald Observatory, on Mount Locke; Matagorda Island; San Jacinto Monument, near Houston; King Ranch, Kingsville; Tascosa Ghost Town.

Transportation and Communication

RAILROADS: 14,277 miles of main-line track; first railroad, Harrisburg to Alleyton, 1860.

ROADS: Total, 243,450 miles; surfaced, 177,199 miles.

MOTOR VEHICLES: Total, 6,506,385; automobiles, 5,016,840; trucks and buses, 1,489,545.

AIRPORTS: Total, 960; private, 718.

NEWSPAPERS: 112 dailies; 491 weeklies; 83 Sunday; first newspaper, El Mejicano, Nacogdoches, 1813.

RADIO STATIONS: 398; first station, WRR, Dallas, 1920.

TELEVISION STATIONS: 57; first station, WBAP, Fort Worth, 1948.

TELEPHONES: Total, 5,995,300; residence, 4,251,500; business, 1,743,800.

POST OFFICES: 1,582.

People

CHIEF CITIES: Houston (1,232,802); Dallas (844,401); San Antonio (654,153); Fort Worth (393,476); El Paso (322,261).

NATIONAL BACKGROUNDS: 96.9 per cent native-born; 3.1 per cent foreign-born.

CHURCH MEMBERSHIP: Of the state population, 53.6 per cent are church members: 64.4 per cent Protestant (including Southern Baptist, 33.1 per cent; Methodist, 15.4 per cent; Lutheran, 3.5 per cent; Presbyterian, 3.3 per cent; Disciples of Christ, 3.1 per cent), 33.9 per cent Catholic, and 1.2 per cent Jewish.

LEADING UNIVERSITIES AND COLLEGES: University of Texas, Austin; University of Houston, Houston; Texas Technological College, Lubbock; North Texas State University, Denton; Baylor University, Waco; Texas Agricultural and Mechanical University, College Station; Southern Methodist University, Dallas.

MUSEUMS: McNay Art Institute, San Antonio, modern French paintings; Witte Museum, San Antonio, archaeology; Children's Museum and Planetarium, Fort Worth; Laguna Gloria Museum, Austin, fine arts; Texas Memorial Museum, Austin, history.

SPECIAL SCHOOLS: Texas School for the Deaf, Austin; Texas State School for the Blind, Austin; Texas Blind, Deaf, and Orphan School, Austin; State Schools (for mentally handicapped), Mexia, Denton, Austin, Abilene.

CORRECTIONAL AND PENAL INSTITUTIONS: Texas Department of Correction, Huntsville and 12 other units; State Schools for Girls, Gainesville and Crockett; State School for Boys, Gatesville.

Government

NUMBER OF U.S. SENATORS: 2.

NUMBER OF U.S. REPRESENTATIVES: 24.

NUMBER OF STATE SENATORS: 31. TERM: 4 years.

NUMBER OF STATE REPRESENTATIVES: 150. TERM: 2 years.

STATE LEGISLATURE CONVENES: January, odd-numbered years.

SESSION LIMIT: Regular, 140 days; special, 30 days.

CONSTITUTION ADOPTED: 1876.

GOVERNOR'S TERM: 2 years. He may succeed himself.

NUMBER OF COUNTIES: 254.

VOTING QUALIFICATIONS: Legal voting age; residence in state 1 year, in county and district 6 months.

STATE HOLIDAYS: Including Lee's Birthday, January 19; Texas Independence Day, March 2; San Jacinto Day, April 21; Birthday of Jefferson Davis, June 3.

ANNUAL STATE EVENTS: Cotton Bowl Football Game, Dallas, January 1; Fiesta de San Jacinto, San Antonio, April; Rose Festival, Tyler, October; State Fair, Dallas, October; Sun Carnival, El Paso, December.

Historic Events

1519—Alonso de Pineda sails along coast of Texas region.

1521—Hernan Cortes conquers Mexico including Texas region.

1528—Alvaro Nunez Cabeza de Vaca arrives in Texas region.

1541—Francisco Vasquez de Coronado explores western Texas.

1542—Hernando De Soto explores east Texas.

1685—Rene Robert Cavelier, Sieur de la Salle, claims Texas region for France; builds post at Nacogdoches.

1690—Spanish mission, San Francisco de los Tejas, established.

1718—Spanish found San Antonio.

1821—Mexico declares independence from Spain.

1836—War of Independence; Republic of Texas is formed.

1845—Texas becomes 28th state; capital at Austin.

1846—Mexican War.

1861—Texas secedes from Union during the Civil War.

1870—Texas is readmitted to Union.

1901—Spindletop oil gusher explodes near Beaumont.

1921—Severe storms sweep Texas coast.

1942—Marshall Ford Dam is completed on Colorado River.

1953—Falcon Dam is completed on Rio Grande.

1963—President John F. Kennedy assassinated in Dallas.

Coastal Lowland, Great Plains, Central Plain, and Mountain region. The Coastal Lowland is a broad belt of flat land extending along the coast from the Red River to the Rio Grande. It varies in width from 100 to nearly 300 miles and in elevation from sea level to about 500 feet above sea level.

Extending from the Rio Grande to the Red River is a belt of hills that rise rather sharply from the Coastal Lowland. They run from north of Del Rio to San Antonio, then curve northward and pass near Austin, Waco, and Fort Worth. South of Fort Worth the hills form the boundary between the Great Plains and the Coastal Lowland. North of Fort Worth the hills separate the Central Plain and the Coastal Lowland.

The Great Plains or High Plains region of Texas is shaped much like the letter "L." It extends southward from the Panhandle along the western border and turns eastward. The southeastern part of the region is known as the Edwards Plateau. The Great Plains is a flat grassland rising to about 4,000 feet in elevation. (See GREAT PLAINS.)

The Central Plain region is low, rolling land covering the north-central part of the state. It ranges in elevation from 500 to 800 feet on the east and southeast to a height of about 2,500 feet on the west.

The Mountain region makes up most of the land between the Pecos River and the Rio Grande in western Texas. This area also is known as the Basin and Range region. The Stockton Plateau in the eastern part of the Mountain region rises from 2,000 to 4,000 feet above sea level. In the western part are many short mountain ranges, separated by broad, flat valleys or basins. Among the highest ranges are the Davis, Chisos, and Guadalupe mountains. Guadalupe Peak (over 8,700 feet) is the highest point in the state.

Much of the state's land can be used for farming and ranching. The fertile, black soil of the western part of the Coastal Lowland is especially good. In the Mountain region only the valleys have good soils and generally these need irrigation.

There are more than 500 lakes in Texas, many of which are man-made (reservoirs). They are used for recreation, to store water for cities and factories, and to help prevent rivers from flooding during the rainy season. Some of the larger lakes are Buchanan, Texoma, Whitney Dam, McGee Bend Reservoir, Hamlin, Corpus Christi, Possum Kingdom, Falcon, and San Angelo.

All the rivers of Texas flow into the Gulf of Mexico. From the southwest to the northeast the chief rivers are the Rio Grande and its important tributary the Pecos, the Nueces, Colorado, Brazos, Trinity, Neches, and Sabine. The Red and Canadian Rivers flow to the gulf through the Mississippi River. Because the land is hilly and rain often falls as heavy thunder storms, erosion and flooding have been great problems. However, by building dams and by using conservation measures, both are being controlled. (See CONSERVATION; EROSION.)

In eastern Texas tall pine trees cover much of the land. Farther west the pine trees are replaced by oak, hickory, and other hardwoods. Juniper, commonly called cedar, is found in the central hills. Mesquite is scattered widely over the southern, western, and north-central parts

Average Daily Temperature

▶ low   ▶ high

Corpus Christi (south coast)   Dallas (east central)

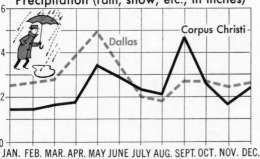

67%   67%

% sunshine   % sunshine

JAN. JULY | JAN. JULY

Precipitation (rain, snow, etc., in inches)

Dallas

Corpus Christi

JAN. FEB. MAR. APR. MAY JUNE JULY AUG. SEPT. OCT. NOV. DEC.

of the state. Except in the mountains, few trees are found in western Texas.

Climate

The great size and different elevations give Texas many climates. The lower Rio Grande Valley is the warmest part of the state. There the average yearly temperature is 74 degrees Fahrenheit. The state's coolest region is the northwestern Panhandle, which has an average annual temperature of 54 degrees.

All parts of the state have some hot periods when the temperature rises above 100 degrees and occasional periods when temperatures drop below freezing (32 degrees). Temperatures as high as 120 degrees and as low as 23 degrees below zero have been recorded.

Rainfall is heaviest in eastern Texas and lightest in the west. Along the Louisiana border the rains are frequent and heavy, averaging more than 50 inches a year in the southeast corner. The far western tip of Texas receives less than 10 inches annually. Precipitation is lightest during the winter months.

The growing season ranges from about 180 days in the northwestern corner of the Panhandle to more than 320 days along the gulf coast.

During the spring Texas is often struck by tornadoes. These violent, circular winds cover small areas, but sometimes do great damage. Texas averages about 27 tornadoes a year, but as many as 164 have been reported in one year. Only Kansas has more tornadoes reported each year. During the summer the Texas coast is often struck by hurricanes which move in from the Gulf of Mexico.

Animal Life

In addition to buffalo (bison), which were nearly all killed during the westward movement of settlers, there are antelope, deer, wolves, wildcats, squirrels, rabbits, foxes, badgers, muskrats, opossums, skunks, bighorn sheep, armadillos, and raccoons in Texas.

Many reptiles are also found in Texas. The poisonous snakes are the copperhead, rattlesnake, water moccasin, and coral snake. There are also harmless snakes, horned toads, lizards, and some alligators.

Corson from A. Devaney, Inc.

Oil wells along the streets of Kilgore, Texas.

Resources

Oil and gas are Texas' most valuable mineral resources. The first producing oil well was drilled in Nacogdoches County in 1859. Since then, oil has been found in about 80 per cent of the counties. It is estimated that Texas contains about half of the known oil and gas reserves in the United States.

Sulfur, magnesium, building stone, cement, carbon black, salt, sand, and gravel are produced in large amounts. Texas also has deposits of iron ore lignite, copper, silver, uranium, lead, graphite, and many other metals.

Of growing importance are the state's forest resources. The most valuable timber lands are in east Texas.

The People

Long before the white man came, Texas was the home of many Indians. In the forests of north and east Texas, a number of tribes made up the Caddo family or confederation. These Indians lived in straw-covered homes and farmed the land around their houses.

In the hills of central Texas lived the Tonkawa tribes. Their homes were made of willow limbs covered with skin, grass, or brushwood. The women did some farming and the men hunted. On the coastal prairies were the Ka-

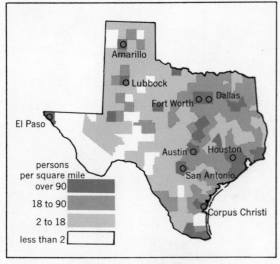

persons
per square mile
over 90
18 to 90
2 to 18
less than 2

Where the people live.

rankawas. These Indians moved often, depending on fish and other water life for food, and living in crudely built skin-covered houses.

The Comanches and Apaches moved into west Texas, hunted wild game, and lived in easily moved skin homes. They were a nomadic or wandering type of people who carried most of their possessions with them as they moved from place to place.

As southern United States was settled, Indians from that region—the Cherokees, Delawares, Osages, Alabamas, Choctaws, and Seminoles—were driven into Texas.

Wars with the white settlers and with other Indians, plus the lack of food, caused many Indians to die or move farther west and north. Others married early Spanish settlers. In 1854 the remaining Indians were settled on the small Alabama and Coushatta reservation near Livingston in east Texas. In 1967 a reservation was created for the Tiguas tribe at El Paso. These two reservations are all that is left of Indian tribal life in Texas. Indian place names like Comanche, Texas, and Wichita remain.

Although what is now Texas was visited by Spanish explorers in the early 1500's, no settlements were made until 1713. Meanwhile, Spanish and French gold hunters, adventurers, and explorers had visited the land. A French settlement failed, and no trace of French influence remained after the break-up of the colony of Nacogdoches in 1687. The French were followed by Spanish soldiers and priests who came in greater numbers and founded the missions around San Antonio.

Colonists from the United States began to arrive in the early 1820's. After Texas became independent of Mexico (1836), a steady flow of immigrants from the United States began moving to and passing through Texas. This was a part of the great westward movement across the continent. (See WESTWARD MOVEMENT.)

After Texas became a state in 1845, the population increased rapidly. The country was being cleared of hostile Indian tribes and the land opened for settlement. French settlements were made in 1844 and 1855. German settlers founded New Braunfels in 1845 and also Fredericksburg, Boerne, and Comfort soon thereafter. Poles, Irishmen, and other Europeans came in large numbers between 1846 and 1860. Later, Canadians, Czechoslovakians, and Italians moved to the state. The people coming to Texas brought their own cultures, customs, and languages. Gradually, there has been a blending of these customs and cultures.

Many people moved to Texas from Mexico. These people are often called Latin-Americans. The Spanish language is spoken by large numbers of these people. Latin-Americans in Texas dress and live quite like their Anglo-American neighbors. Some communities celebrate Mexican holidays and customs. Among the many Texas communities which have Spanish names are San Antonio, Del Rio, and El Paso.

By 1970 the Texas population was more than 11,000,000, with an average of more than 35 persons per square mile. Of this number about 13 per cent were Negro and 16 per cent Latin-American (largely Mexican). Most of the Negro population is in the eastern part of the state. Most of the Latin-American people live in the southern part along the Rio Grande Valley.

About 80 per cent of the people live in cities and towns of 2,500 persons or more. Many of the larger cities are in the Coastal Lowland region.

The building of many new industries during and after World War II has helped bring about a great shift in population from the farms to

Courtesy Texas Highway Department

Dallas' business section and residential districts are located along the Trinity River. The city is an important banking, trade, and light manufacturing center for Texas. It is also one of the centers of the world's petroleum industry.

the cities. Cities grew rapidly between 1960 and 1970. Much of the development was related to nearby oil and gas fields, water and other resources, as well as excellent transportation. Texas, in 1970, had 10 cities with populations greater than 100,000. They were Houston, Dallas, San Antonio, Fort Worth, El Paso, Austin, Corpus Christi, Amarillo, Lubbock, and Beaumont.

Houston, the largest city, is well known as an oil and gas center and for its heavy industry and shipping. Similar but smaller centers are on or near the gulf coast stretching from Port Arthur and Beaumont on the east to Corpus Christi on the south. Dallas, the second largest city, is noted for manufacturing, retailing, and trade. Fort Worth is important as a center for the cattle industry. (See DALLAS; FORT WORTH; HOUSTON.)

San Antonio is a historic center, cattle shipping point, and an army and air force training area. Austin is the state capital.

The great size of the state, its unusual history, and the stories and legends brought about by the cattle and oil industries, have built a feeling of great pride among its people.

How the People Make a Living

Manufacturing and mining are the leading industries in Texas, but farming and ranching are also important ways of making a living.

Agriculture. Nationally Texas is outranked in value of farm crops only by Illinois and California. Texas leads the United States in production of cotton, producing more than 2,850,000 bales annually. This is about one-third of the nation's total production.

Wheat, corn, oats, barley, rye, rice, and grain sorghums also are produced. In addition, vegetables and fruits, such as tomatoes, onions, cabbage, oranges, grapefruit, and lemons, are raised in large quantities. Most of the vegetables are grown in the southern and eastern parts of the state.

Many large ranches raise cattle, sheep, goats, hogs, chickens, turkeys, and other livestock. Ranchers also produce hay and grain as feed for livestock. Cattle raising, one of the oldest industries in Texas, is still important in most of the state. Many of the stories from Texas history and literature are of cattle raising. Most of the livestock raised are beef cattle. Such breeds as Hereford, Shorthorn, Angus, Brahman, and Santa Gertrudis are raised easily on Texas ranches.

For years cotton, which is Texas' basic farm crop, was raised mainly in central and northern Texas. Now it is grown on the irrigated lands of west and south Texas. Cattle raising has

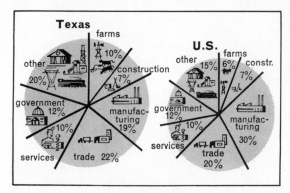

Sources of income.

shifted from west to east Texas.

Most farms are supplied with electricity, and use power tools and modern methods of farming. With the improved farm machinery one farmer can produce many times as much as several farmers could produce 20 years ago. Farm-to-market roads have been paved, and 90 per cent of the farm and ranch lands now are controlled by soil conservation programs. The average farm size is nearly 630 acres.

Mining. Texas produces about 25 per cent of the total mineral output of the United States. It has been the country's most important mineral producer for more than a quarter of a century. Petroleum and natural gas are the chief minerals produced. The total annual value of the state's mineral production is more than four billion dollars.

Texas sometimes pumps more than one billion barrels of crude oil from the earth in a year. Oil has a greater value than all other minerals of Texas put together. Natural gas, taken from many oil fields, is sent by pipeline to major cities and towns in Texas and other states. Production of natural gas is more than five billion cubic feet annually.

Oil and natural gas come from about 40 major producing "fields" with about 200,000 producing wells. Some oil fields, such as Powell and Spindletop in east Texas, opened in the early 1900's and still are producing. More recent discoveries have been in south and west Texas, and beneath the floor of the Gulf of Mexico.

Texas also ranks among the leading states in the production of helium, natural gas liq-

uids, asphalt, graphite, magnesium, sulfur, salt, building stone, cement, bromine, carbon black, and clays. It produces about two-thirds of the nation's helium output.

Asphalt, found in south Texas around Uvalde, is used in road construction. Cement is produced in factories near San Antonio, Houston, Dallas, Fort Worth, Waco, Corpus Christi, and El Paso. There are also large deposits of granite and other building stone. Principal deposits are found in Burnet and Llano counties. Some coal and large amounts of iron ore are found in east Texas near Daingerfield and Houston. Texas is one of the world's great sulfur-producing areas. Sulfur is mined near the gulf coast around Brazosport, and in other widely scattered areas.

Manufacturing. With the development of petroleum and natural gas came an increase in manufacturing. From these fuels comes power for industries. The presence of water, raw

How the people make a living.

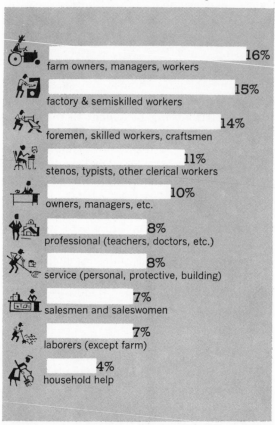

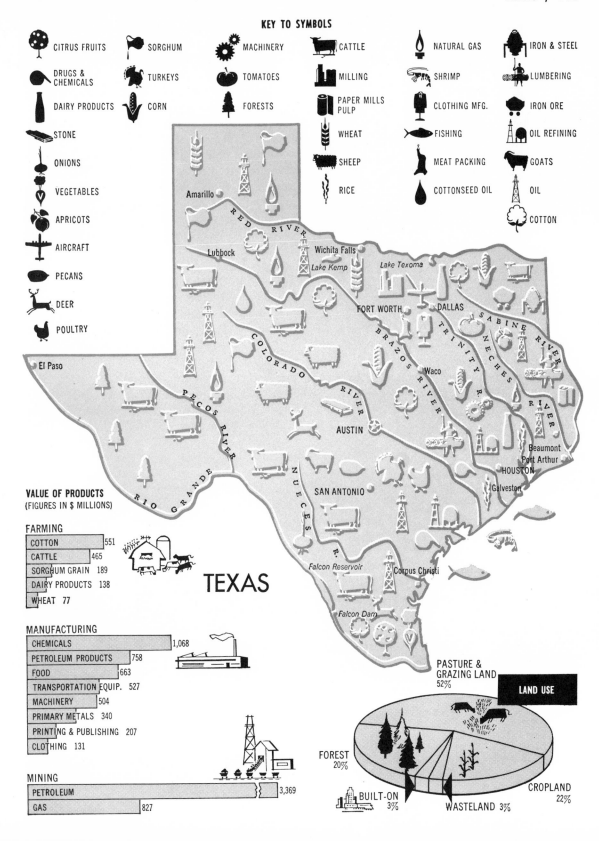

KEY TO SYMBOLS

CITRUS FRUITS
DRUGS & CHEMICALS
DAIRY PRODUCTS
STONE
ONIONS
VEGETABLES
APRICOTS
AIRCRAFT
PECANS
DEER
POULTRY

SORGHUM
TURKEYS
CORN

MACHINERY
TOMATOES
FORESTS

CATTLE
MILLING
PAPER MILLS PULP
WHEAT
SHEEP
RICE

NATURAL GAS
SHRIMP
CLOTHING MFG.
FISHING
MEAT PACKING
COTTONSEED OIL

IRON & STEEL
LUMBERING
IRON ORE
OIL REFINING
GOATS
OIL

COTTON

Amarillo
Lubbock
El Paso

RED RIVER
Wichita Falls
Lake Kemp
Lake Texoma

FORT WORTH
DALLAS
Waco

SABINE RIVER
NECHES
TRINITY R.

COLORADO RIVER
BRAZOS RIVER
PECOS RIVER

AUSTIN
NUECES R.
SAN ANTONIO
RIO GRANDE

Beaumont
Port Arthur
HOUSTON
Galveston

Falcon Reservoir
Corpus Christi
Falcon Dam

TEXAS

VALUE OF PRODUCTS
(FIGURES IN $ MILLIONS)

FARMING

COTTON	551
CATTLE	465
SORGHUM GRAIN	189
DAIRY PRODUCTS	138
WHEAT	77

MANUFACTURING

CHEMICALS	1,068
PETROLEUM PRODUCTS	758
FOOD	663
TRANSPORTATION EQUIP.	527
MACHINERY	504
PRIMARY METALS	340
PRINTING & PUBLISHING	207
CLOTHING	131

MINING

PETROLEUM	3,369
GAS	827

LAND USE

PASTURE & GRAZING LAND 52%
FOREST 20%
BUILT-ON 3%
WASTELAND 3%
CROPLAND 22%

Courtesy Texas Highway Department

Texas grows about one-fourth of the nation's cotton.

materials, and power have been important factors in the state's industrial growth since World War II. The annual value of manufactured products more than doubled between 1947 and 1954. In value of products, Texas ranks among the ten most important manufacturing states.

The chemical industries lead in value, with petroleum refining second. However, the food-producing industries employ the most people, followed by petroleum refining and chemicals.

Texas refineries process about 70 per cent of the state's crude oil production and produce about 30 per cent of the nation's gasoline, 35 per cent of its kerosene, 30 per cent of its fuel oil, 30 per cent of its jet fuel, 30 per cent of its lubricating oils, 20 per cent of its wax, and 15 per cent of its petroleum asphalt.

Most of the chemical industries are near the gulf coast. These industries had their beginning in or around 1940 and now lead the state in value of products. The chemical industries depend upon the state's large supplies of natural resources. Products such as benzene, toluene, xylene, and methane are produced and in turn are used in the manufacture of nylon, orlon, and other synthetics. Some of the nation's leading chemical plants are at Freeport.

Among the food products manufactured are flour, packed meats, dairy products, and frozen and canned foods. Candy and soft drink plants also are important. Meat packing is carried on chiefly in Fort Worth, San Antonio, Houston, El Paso, Dallas, and Amarillo. There are breweries in San Antonio, Houston, Galveston, El Paso, and Shiner.

Textiles, aluminum, clay and glass products, furniture, printing and publishing, transportation equipment, shipbuilding, leather goods, and machinery are other important products of Texas. The state's iron and steel industry is centered at Houston and Daingerfield.

Aircraft plants in the Dallas–Fort Worth area produce a large share of the nation's fighter and training aircraft, as well as propeller and jet aircraft for commercial and military needs. Automobile assembly plants are also in the Dallas–Fort Worth area.

Other Occupations. Commercial fishing off the Texas coast provides a livelihood for a small number of people. Of the commercial catch, menhaden is by far the greatest in value. It is used for oil and fertilizer. Redfish, trout, flounder, drum, and mullet are taken in large numbers. Shrimp, crab, and oysters also are taken and processed along the Texas coast.

The vast timber resources of Texas are used in making paper, lumber and veneer products, turpentine, and as fuel wood. Most of the pro-

A gas plant in eastern Texas.

Courtesy Texas Highway Department

duction is from yellow pine and other soft-woods which are grown chiefly in east Texas. Large paper mills are in the Lufkin and Houston areas.

Tourist attractions in Texas provide employment for people in resorts and historic centers. Annually thousands of tourists visit the gulf coast. Its main attractions are its beaches, fishing, and mild climate. Resort centers on Padre Island, near Brownsville and Corpus Christi, also are important.

Transportation and Communication

The first trails in the Texas region were made by Indians as they searched for food and water. Later when Texas became independent, roads and cattle trails connected the early towns and settlements. Today Texas has more miles of roads than any other state.

Railroads had been built in Texas before the United States Civil War, but construction came to a stop when the war started (1861). It was not until 1881 that the first trans-Texas railroad was completed, connecting Houston, Fort Worth, San Antonio, and El Paso. Railroad lines now connect important cities and link Texas with Mexico and all parts of the United States.

Commercial air transportation in Texas started in 1926. There are now more than a half dozen major airlines serving the state. One of them connects Texas with Mexico and South America.

Texas has 12 deepwater ports including Houston, one of the largest ports in the United States. Houston is connected to the Gulf of Mexico by a 57-mile canal or channel. A canal connects the cities of the Texas coast with Louisiana and Mexico. Most of Texas' shipping is coastal trade with other states.

In addition to publishing dozens of daily and weekly newspapers, Texas has about 400 radio stations and more than 50 television stations.

Government

The state government has three branches—the executive branch, the legislative branch or the Legislature, and the judicial branch. The

Courtesy Houston Chamber of Commerce

The turning basin of the Houston Ship Channel.

governor is head of the executive branch, which includes 30 other elected officers and about 180 officials, boards, and commissions, most of whom are appointed by the governor.

The Legislature has two houses, the Senate and the House of Representatives. The highest court in the judicial branch is the Supreme Court. Other courts include the Court of Criminal Appeals, Court of Civil Appeals, district courts, and the county courts.

Each of the 254 counties is governed by a Commissioner's Court, which is made up of a county judge and four commissioners, all of whom are elected. While the body is called a court, it is not one in a real sense. It serves about as a city commission does in a city. This court approves the budget, sets dates for elections, sets county tax rates, and performs other administrative duties. Among the other elected county officers are the sheriff, superintendent of schools, treasurer, and tax assessor.

Education

Public schools were first provided for by the Constitution of the Republic of Texas. Public lands were set aside for the support of schools, but it was not until 1854 that a public school system was started with funds to support it.

The chief education officer of the state is the

Commissioner of Education, who is appointed by the 21-member State Board of Education. However, control of the schools rests largely with local boards of education.

There are more than 130 junior and senior colleges of which about 50 are state supported. The largest of the state supported institutions is the University of Texas. In addition, there are private colleges, such as Rice University in Houston; municipal universities, such as the University of Houston; and parochial colleges and universities. Texas also supports several schools for the blind and deaf.

Religion, Health, and Welfare

The first missionary work recorded in Texas history was with the Tejas Indian tribe of east Texas. In 1690 the Spanish Captain Juan Ponce de Leon, with Father Damian Massanet, a French Catholic missionary, started the mission of San Francisco de los Tejas near the present town of Crockett. This mission did not last long.

Beginning in 1718 Catholic priests built missions among the Indians near San Antonio. In all, about five missions were built including the famous Alamo. Agriculture, handicrafts, and better health practices were taught by the missionaries.

Protestant faiths were brought to Texas by the Anglo-American settlers from the United

San Jose, one of many missions built by the Spaniards early in the history of Texas.

Courtesy San Antonio Chamber of Commerce

States. Methodist, Baptist, and Presbyterian preachers came to Texas and helped to build churches and schools. Some of Texas' best-known colleges of today were founded by the early missionaries.

In the early history, improving the health of the people was part of the missionaries' work. After 1845, when Texas became a part of the United States, the state established hospitals for its less fortunate people. With the founding of the University of Texas in 1883, the training of physicians became a part of its curriculum; and in 1891 a medical branch was opened in Galveston. Since that time, medical and dental branches have been established in other Texas cities. There are more than 550 hospitals in Texas of which 12 are state owned.

Recreation

Texas attracts thousands of tourists annually. State parks and museums, municipal parks, museums, professional athletic teams, and zoological gardens, as well as the land itself, interest many people.

Big Bend National Park in western Texas, established in 1944, covers about 708,000 acres and contains the Chisos Mountains and the deep canyons of the Rio Grande. Padre Island National Seashore, established in 1962, consists of 80 miles of barrier beach between Corpus Christi and Port Isabel.

Other points of interest are Texas Memorial Museum in Austin, the Texas Hall of State in Dallas, the International Museum in El Paso, San Jacinto Monument in Houston, the Alamo, La Villita, and the Witte Memorial Museum in San Antonio.

Annually, the state and local communities have special fairs of national interest. The State Fair of Texas, held in Dallas during October; the Rose Festival in Tyler, also held in October; and the Sun Carnival in El Paso in December are the most popular.

The State Fair regularly attracts more than 2,500,000 visitors. It is considered the largest agricultural fair and exposition in the United States. The famous Cotton Bowl football game is played in the fair grounds' stadium on New Year's Day each year. Other attractions at the fair grounds include an aquarium, several museums, and a music hall.

History

Probably the first white man to sight the Texas coast was a Spanish sea captain named Alonso de Pineda. In 1519 he was sent by the governor of Jamaica to explore the Gulf of Mexico, in search of a route to India. Two years later Hernan Cortes conquered Mexico for Spain. Texas was included in his conquest.

Alvaro Nunez Cabeza de Vaca in 1528 explored much of the country after he was shipwrecked in the gulf. The tales of fabulous gold supplies brought other Spaniards in search of wealth and fame. Friar Marcos and Francisco Vasquez de Coronado explored the western regions of what is now the state and southwestern United States (1541). Hernando De Soto, another Spaniard, also explored the gulf coastal regions as far as East Texas in 1542.

In 1685 a Frenchman named Rene Robert Cavelier, Sieur de La Salle, explored the Mississippi River and part of Texas. La Salle and his party claimed Texas for France, and built an outpost called Nacogdoches. The Spanish viceroy (governor) of Mexico sent Captain Ponce de Leon to drive the French from Texas. When he arrived the French had already gone.

After 1690 the Spanish began settling Texas and establishing missions. Beginning in 1718 San Antonio was established. By 1819 Spain was having trouble with its Mexican colony. The Mexicans overthrew the Spanish governor in 1821 and declared their independence. Texas was now under Mexican control. Meanwhile, Galveston Island had become a pirate stronghold. Jean Lafitte was perhaps the most famous. The pirates were driven off the island by the United States Navy.

The first attempt to establish an American colony was made in 1821 by Moses Austin. Although he died before his colony was started, his plans were carried out by his son, Stephen F. Austin. (See AUSTIN, STEPHEN FULLER.) Other leaders who brought colonists to Texas were Green DeWitt, Hayden Edwards, David G. Burnet, Benjamin R. Milam, Lorenzo de Savala, Sterling C. Robertson, John McMullen, Patrick

Courtesy American Airlines

Santa Gertrudis cattle were first produced on the King Ranch in Texas by crossing the Shorthorn and the Brahman.

McGloin, and Martin de Leon.

The colonists settled chiefly on the gulf coast between the present cities of Houston and Corpus Christi. By 1835 several towns had been started. They were San Felipe de Austin, Columbia, Brazoria, Gonzales, and Victoria. Older settlements, such as Nacogdoches, San Antonio, and Goliad, continued to grow.

The United States colonists in Texas soon became unhappy with the Mexican government. It started no schools, and would not let the colonists worship as they wished. There were other problems, too. The new Texans disliked Spanish courts, laws, and customs. Trade with the United States was easier than trade with Mexico.

On March 2, 1836, the Texans met at Washington-on-the-Brazos and drafted a Declaration of Independence. The War of Independence followed, with battles fought at the Alamo, in San Antonio, and at Goliad. The Mexican armies won these battles. Colonel William B. Travis and about 186 other Texans were killed in the famous Battle of the Alamo. The colonists now took up the battle cry of "Remember the Alamo. Remember Goliad." Under the leadership of General Sam Houston, they defeated the Mexicans led by General Santa Anna in the battle of San Jacinto on April 21, 1836. (See ALAMO, THE; HOUSTON, SAM.)

After the surrender of the Mexican armies, Texas became an independent republic. It modeled its government on that of the United States. Its first president was General Sam

Houston. The Republic of Texas lasted ten years. During this time the republic adopted a constitution, elected four different presidents, and in 1839 moved the capital to Austin.

On December 29, 1845, Texas was accepted into the Union. Between 1846 and 1848 the United States was at war with Mexico; and Texans again took up arms, as United States citizens this time, against the Mexicans. By the Treaty of Guadalupe Hidalgo, which ended the war, Mexico gave up all claim to Texas. (See MEXICAN WAR.)

In 1849 many settlers in western Texas were killed by the Indians. Since the United States was unable to give protection at this time, Texas appointed Rangers to protect the frontiersmen and enlisted soldiers to assist them. Later the United States built a string of forts across Texas from Fort Worth on the Trinity River to Fort Duncan on the Rio Grande near the present city of Del Rio.

During the United States Civil War (1861–1865), Texas withdrew from the Union and joined the Confederate States. When the Confederacy had been defeated, Texas was once again a part of the United States.

In the years that followed, farming and ranching became important ways of making a living. Cotton became an important agricultural product, and Texas longhorn cattle were raised on the grasslands. Gradually other crops were introduced in the state, and the longhorn was replaced by other breeds of cattle. Between 1865 and 1885 cattle were driven to market on the Old Chisholm Trail to railroad points in Kansas. Stories and songs were written about cattle, the cowboy, and life on the trails. (See TRAILS, U.S. HISTORIC.)

As people moved westward, other troubles developed. Homesteaders began to build homes and cultivate the lands on which ranchers grazed their herds of cattle. Farmers fenced their lands as a protection against destruction of crops by cattle. Cattlemen cut the fences, and a "fence" war raged in south and west Texas. Law and order was established by Texas Rangers and United States soldiers.

In 1900 the first major petroleum field—the Powell field—was discovered near Corsicana.

This was the beginning of a new era in Texas history. The following year a great gusher called Spindletop was discovered in the Beaumont area. This gusher was the first that had great commercial importance. Many other huge fields have been discovered since then.

With such large quantities of mineral fuels (petroleum and natural gas), and shipping routes to other parts of the world through gulf coast ports, industries rapidly developed. Both mining and manufacturing soon passed agriculture in importance.

One of the worst storms to sweep along the gulf coast struck Texas in September 1921. Thirty inches of rain fell within a two-day period and 224 people lost their lives.

During World War II more than 1,250,000 men in all branches of service were trained at bases in Texas. There are now more than 35 military installations, most of which are Air Force bases.

In May 1953 Waco, Texas, was struck by one of the state's most destructive tornadoes. It caused the deaths of 114 people and injured nearly 600 others.

Texas had a population in 1970 of 11,196,730. This was an increase of 16.9 per cent over the 1960 census figure.

TEXTILES (*tĕks′tĭlz*) originally were "woven fabrics," but today the term generally includes fibers and yarns, and the cloth made from them, whether woven, knitted, netted, or felted.

The textile industry is one of the largest industries in the United States, both in the value of its product and in the number of people employed. It includes the preparation of textile fibers for spinning, the spinning of yarn, and the manufacture of yarn into cloth. The manufacture of cloth into clothing, household goods, and industrial products is a large branch of the industry. The making of machinery for textile manufacturing and the designing, transporting, and selling of textiles involve many people.

Today, about 40 per cent of all textiles is made into clothing. A large percentage is used in household furnishings, including draperies, rugs, bedding, towels, and table linens; and another large percentage is used in industrial

Even today, in some areas of the world, the spinning of fibers is done by hand on a spinning wheel—as this housewife from the Valaisan Alps in Switzerland is doing.

The United Cotton Mill in Peking, China, employing 12,000 workers to operate its efficient, modern machinery, is typical of the large plants used by the textile industry today to process natural fibers into thread and then into fabrics.

Courtesy (left) American Cotton Manufacturers Institute, (right) Swiss National Tourist Office; photo, (above) Henri Cartier-Bresson—Magnum

The cotton plant is the world's largest source of natural fibers for textiles. When a cotton boll is ripe, as the one shown here, it is picked, cleaned, ginned, and spun into thread before finally being woven into cloth.

products, including sacks and other containers, tire fabrics, conveyer belts, insulating, and padding.

The Origins of Textiles

The use of textiles goes back to times before written records. Primitive man must first have killed animals for food, and discovered that the skins of these animals could be used as protection against the cold. Some early shepherd probably discovered that fibers from the pelts of his sheep could be twisted into yarns, and these yarns woven to form a firm cloth.

Knowledge of the use of textiles in past ages comes from many sources. Museums have cloths taken from ancient Egyptian and Central American tombs. Paintings and sculptures from these tombs show people spinning, weaving, and dyeing cloth. Pottery has been found with the imprint of woven fabrics in the clay. In many parts of the world today, people still use primitive methods of spinning and weaving.

Wool and flax (a plant from which linen is made) were probably the first fibers to be used

in fabrics. Strands of linen fish nets found in Swiss lake dwellings are thought to be at least 10,000 years old.

Many references to fine linen and to spinning and weaving appear in the Bible. Ancient Greeks and Romans used flax and wool, and the Romans are said to have developed a fine breed of sheep for their wool. This breed is thought to have been the basis for the famous Merino sheep later developed by the Spaniards. Cotton was used less than flax in the ancient world around the Mediterranean Sea. In India and other countries of the Far East and in the Western Hemisphere, however, cotton was known and used.

The Chinese are believed to have cultivated silk since about 2000 B.C. It has always been a precious and luxurious fabric. For many centuries China kept the secret of how silk was made, while the country exported beautiful silks by camel caravan to Persia and the Near East.

Until the 18th century, practically all operations in the manufacture of fabrics were done by hand. In the Middle Ages in Europe skilled craftsmen joined together to form guilds. Weavers, dyers, and finishers each had their own trade guild, patron saint, and guildhall. (See GUILD.)

During the 18th century a series of inventions made it possible to increase the speed of spinning and weaving, and gradually these processes were taken out of homes and put into factories. The whole picture of industrial life was changed. Most of these inventions originated in England, which became the leading textile-manufacturing nation of the world. (See INDUSTRIAL REVOLUTION, THE; SPINNING AND WEAVING.)

Natural Fibers

When most fabrics were spun and woven in homes, the weavers knew the fibers they were using and, indeed, often had raised the sheep and shorn the wool, or raised the flax and prepared the fiber. Even in the early part of the 20th century, the natural fibers of wool, cotton, flax, and silk were the only fibers a buyer was likely to find in fabrics.

Different fibers have different properties, and the fabrics made from them reflect these variations. Each type of fiber, too, has a range in quality so that there are grades from good to poor of a certain fiber. The skill and care used in spinning, weaving, dyeing, and finishing also affect the quality of the finished fabric.

Cotton is a short fiber, varying from $\frac{1}{2}$ to 2 inches; the longer the fiber, or staple, the stronger the yarn made from it can be. Cotton has a natural twist that helps the short fibers to stay together in a yarn when spun. Cotton is strong and durable, can stand fairly high heat and strong soaps and bleaches, absorbs moisture, can be dyed in fast (nonfading) colors, and is fairly inexpensive. It also lends itself to such a variety of materials that it is one of the most versatile fibers. Cotton accounts for about two-thirds of all fibers used in the United States. Cotton, however, is not elastic or resilient, it is dull rather than lustrous, and it is subject to mildew attack. These properties are partially remedied by mercerizing (treating with caustic soda) and by applying other fin-

ishes to the yarn or cloth. (See COTTON.)

Wool fibers generally are from two to eight inches in length. The fiber has a natural crimp (waviness) that helps it to cling in spinning and to form a bulky yarn. Wool is warm, durable, resilient, and elastic, takes dyes readily, and holds a large amount of moisture without feeling damp. It is, however, expensive, subject to attack by moths, and must be dry-cleaned or washed with care. Fine qualities may be very soft; coarser qualities may be wiry and harsh to the touch. Other hair fibers such as cashmere, camel's hair, mohair, and angora rabbit also are used in clothing. (See WOOL.)

Flax fibers are strong, lustrous, and absorbent. They retain their beauty in fabrics throughout their use. Linen is expensive, lacks resilience and elasticity, and is much less versatile than cotton. Most of the flax used in the Western world comes from Ireland and Europe, largely in the form of finished cloth. Other plant fibers, such as jute, hemp, and ramie are used for household and commercial products. (See FLAX; HEMP; JUTE.)

Silk fibers are long, strong, elastic, resilient, and lustrous. They can be dyed many colors, and the fabric made of them has a natural luxurious feel and drape that other fabrics often are made to imitate. The United States imports silk, as fiber or as finished cloth, from Japan and, in lesser quantities, from Italy and France. (See SILK.)

Man-Made Fibers

As long ago as the 17th century, chemists attempted to produce an artificial silk fiber. Success in developing the first man-made fiber is credited to a Frenchman, Count Hilaire de Chardonnet. Dresses made from his fiber were exhibited at the Paris Exposition in 1889. Soon other processes were developed in Germany and in England. In 1910 the English firm of Courtauld's, Ltd., established a plant in Pennsylvania for the manufacture of "artificial silk." In 1924 the name "rayon" was adopted for these artificial silk fibers. In the same year the production of á similar fiber, cellulose acetate, was started. Since both rayon and acetate are made from the fibrous cellulose of wood pulp

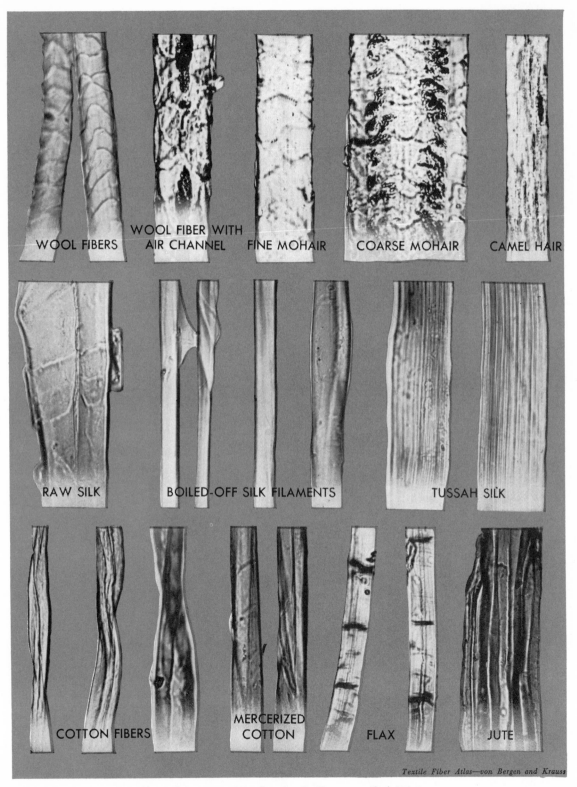

WOOL FIBERS

WOOL FIBER WITH
AIR CHANNEL

FINE MOHAIR

COARSE MOHAIR

CAMEL HAIR

RAW SILK

BOILED-OFF SILK FILAMENTS

TUSSAH SILK

COTTON FIBERS

MERCERIZED
COTTON

FLAX

JUTE

Textile Fiber Atlas—von Bergen and Krauss

These photomicrographs show textile fibers magnified 500 times.

or cotton, these fibers are known as cellulosic fibers. (See SYNTHETIC or MAN-MADE FIBER.)

In March 1960 an act of Congress went into effect, requiring that all textile materials, with a very few exceptions, be labeled to identify the fibers contained in them. Under noncellulosic man-made fibers were 14 generic names. A generic, or general, name is one that describes a class of materials. Trade names belong to a certain company and can be used by that company only. The rules for labeling state that when a trade name is used, it must also be followed by the generic name. For example, the group of fibers called acrylics have the trade names of Acrilan, Creslan, Orlon, and Zefran. Since there are about 75 to 100 trade names for rayon and acetate alone, and other names are added whenever a new fiber or modification of a fiber is developed, it would be almost impossible for the buyer to know what he is getting if the generic name were not given.

Rayon is an inexpensive fiber. It is versatile in that it can be made into fabrics similar to those of any of the other fibers. It may be shiny, or it can be dulled; and it is easy to dye in fast colors. However, it is much weaker when wet than when dry; it lacks elasticity and resilience; and it may shrink or stretch. By special processes of stretch-spinning or cross-linking, it can be made stronger, more crease resistant, and less apt to shrink or stretch.

Acetate is similar to rayon in price, and can be made into as wide a range of materials. It melts if pressed with too hot an iron and is destroyed by acetone, which is found in most nail-polish removers. It requires a different set of dyes from those used on rayon but is generally colorfast.

Nylon, the acrylic fibers, the modacrylics (Dynel, Verel), and the polyesters (Dacron, Kodel, and others) are strong, keep their original shape even when wet, are elastic and resilient, and are not attacked by molds or mildew. They can be set into permanent pleats or creases by heating to a certain temperature. They take up little moisture. They are apt to develop static electricity, so that they cling to the body or other surfaces. They usually can be washed and worn with little or no ironing. Filament yarns may be textured by crimping, twisting, or heat-setting to make a bulkier, softer fabric or one that will stretch.

Man-made fibers may be used alone or may be blended with other fibers. A blend of polyester and cotton fibers, for example, may produce a fabric that needs little ironing, and has a soft and comfortable feel because of the cotton content. A blend of acrylic fiber with wool may make the wool washable and capable of being permanently pleated.

Fabric Finishing

Fibers and yarns may be dyed before a fabric is woven, but most fabrics are "piece dyed" after weaving. As the material comes from the loom, it is called "gray goods" or "greige goods." Unbleached muslin is cotton "in the gray." In addition to bleaching and dyeing, many other finishes have been developed to increase the beauty or the usefulness of a fabric. These finishes may be mechanical, as in calendering (pressing), preshrinking, or embossing; or they may be chemical, as when the nature of the fiber is changed (as in washable wools), or when synthetic resins, which are heat-cured in the fabric and give a permanent finish, are used. Some of the finishes that are used are antiseptic (self-sterilizing), crease or wrinkle resistant, glazed, permanently starched or stiffened, softened, mildew-proofed, moth-proofed, shrink resistant, waterproofed, water repellent, or stain resistant.

Other developments include nonwoven fabrics, in which fibers are bonded or fused by a resin without spinning or weaving; foams are bonded to the backs of fabrics for increased warmth, softness, or stability; wools are made machine-washable; and garments are seamed together by ultrasonic methods instead of by stitching.

The force behind the development of new fibers has not been a shortage of natural fibers but a desire to produce fibers with different properties. The possibilities for further developments in the future seem almost unlimited.

THACKERAY (*thăk'ẽr ē*), **WILLIAM MAKE-PEACE** (*māk'pēs'*) (1811–1863), was one of the great English novelists of the mid-19th century, and was also a talented artist and illustrator. He was born in Calcutta, India, where his father worked for the East India Company. In 1817, the year after his father died, he was sent to England to live with relatives. From 1822 to 1828 he

Culver Service

William Makepeace Thackeray.

attended Charterhouse School. In 1830, after a year at Trinity College, Cambridge, Thackeray traveled in France and Germany. When he returned to England, he studied law.

He then worked for a year as editor of a London magazine, and in 1834 settled in Paris to study art. When Thackeray returned to England, he began writing satires of the popular fiction writers of his day. He also drew illustrations for magazines.

For the next several years he contributed humorous stories and sketches to such important periodicals as *Fraser's Magazine* and *Punch.* Among his books that appeared serially in these magazines during the 1840's were *The Luck of Barry Lyndon* and *The Book of Snobs.*

With the publication of *The Book of Snobs,* Thackeray achieved a great deal of popularity. This popularity was increased with the publication of *Vanity Fair* in 1848, his best—and best-known—novel. It was this novel that placed him among the greatest of English novelists. His portrayal and evaluation of early 19th-century English society, with its follies and vices, was an accurate one. The novel tells the story of two women and the men they associate with. The sweet and virtuous Amelia Sedley provides marked contrast to the ruthless and scheming adventuress Becky Sharp.

In 1850 Thackeray published his partly autobiographical novel *Pendennis.* He followed this in 1852 with a historical novel, *Henry Esmond,* dealing with life in 18th-century England. *The Newcomes,* containing some of the characters Thackeray had written about in *Pendennis,* ap-

peared in 1854. *The Virginians,* a sequel to the Henry Esmond story, appeared between 1857 and 1859, and contains material that Thackeray gathered on lecture tours in the United States in 1852–1853 and 1854–1855.

Thackeray accepted the post as editor of the newly founded *Cornhill Magazine* in 1860, and resigned this position in 1862. He continued to write for the magazine until his death.

THAILAND (*tī'lănd*), **ASIA,** a country in the southeastern part of the continent, is about four-fifths the size of the state of Texas. It is shaped something like a frying pan, with its handle extending southward down the Malay (or Kra) Peninsula to the border of Malaya. Thailand's neighbors are Burma on the west and northwest, Laos on the northeast and east, Cambodia on the southeast, and Malaya on the south. It has a short coastline on the Andaman Sea (a part of the Indian Ocean) and a longer coastline on the Gulf of Siam (the westernmost gulf in the Pacific Ocean). Long known as Siam, the country officially changed its name to Thailand in 1949. Thailand means "Land of the Free People."

Landscape and Climate

The country has three general land regions: the Highland, the Central Lowland, and the Plateau. The Highland includes many short mountain ranges in northern Thailand and a belt of forest-covered mountains that extends along the country's border with Burma and into the peninsula. Elevations in the Highland region seldom exceed 5,000 feet above sea level. Inthanon Peak (8,468 feet) is Thailand's highest point.

The Central Lowland region lies in the heart of Thailand along the Chao Phraya (or Menam), a river that begins in the northern mountains. About 120 miles north of its mouth, the Chao Phraya divides into many smaller streams. These flow southward across an area of flatland, or delta, and empty into the Gulf of Siam. The delta is the most heavily settled part of Thailand.

In eastern Thailand is the low, hilly Korat (or Khorat) Plateau. It is separated from the

Chao Phraya lowlands by a north-south ridge that rises sharply to an elevation of about 1,500 feet. The plateau surface slopes downward to the Mekong River valley in the east. The Mekong forms much of the Thailand-Laos border.

Land regions of Thailand.

Thailand has a tropical climate. Temperatures seldom drop below 64 degrees. Rainfall is heaviest from June to October when the moist monsoon wind blows in from the sea. Most places receive 40 to 60 inches of rainfall a year. The western mountains, however, block the path of the southwest monsoon winds, causing the air to rise and drop its moisture. Much of this region receives more than 80 inches annually.

The vegetation of the western part of the Highland region, of the western edge of the Plateau, and of the Malay Peninsula is dense tropical rain forest. Teak, Thailand's most valuable tree, is found in the forests of the northern mountains. The rest of Thailand has vegetation that is a mixture of trees and tall grass.

The People

The Thai are a Mongoloid people who came originally from the hill country of southwestern China. They are generally slender of build, medium in height, and have straight black hair and light brown skin. More than 80 per cent of the population is Thai.

The Thai culture has been influenced by Indian and Chinese ways of life. Their language, for example, uses mostly words of one syllable, as does the Chinese language. And like the Chinese spoken language, spoken Thai depends greatly on pitch or voice tone. The written language of the Thai people is more like Indian than Chinese script. Many Indian words are used in the Thai language.

From their ancient past in China the Thai brought with them the techniques of growing rice in paddies. From the Indians the Thai gained their religion, Buddhism. Buddhism plays an important part in the life of the Thai people. Thousands of golden-domed pagodas, or temples, have been built throughout the country. Most boys enter a monastery for a short period in their lives to receive religious instruction from the highly respected Buddhist monks. Thai painting and sculpture is largely concerned with showing events in the life of Buddha. The king must be Buddhist, and only Buddhists can hold government jobs.

Several other large ethnic groups live in Thailand. The Chinese, who make up about 14 per cent of the population, began moving to Thailand in the 17th century. The country now has the largest Chinese community in the world outside of China. The Chinese control most of the country's banks, stores, and factories. Many have become citizens of Thailand and consider themselves as Thai. Many others, however, have remained loyal to China.

A much smaller ethnic group is Malayan in the southern part of the country. Unlike the Thai and the Chinese, most of whom are Buddhists, the Malayans follow the Islamic religion.

Smaller minority groups, of unknown numbers, are the various primitive tribal peoples

Locator map of Thailand.

who live in the northern and western mountains.

Bangkok (known officially as Krung Thep), Thailand's capital and largest city, has a population of more than 1,290,000. Although it is 15 miles upstream on the Chao Phraya, the city is the country's leading seaport. Small ocean vessels can travel up to the city. (See BANGKOK.)

Among the other important cities are Thonburi, across the Chao Phraya from Bangkok; Chiangmai, the chief market of the northwest, on the Ping River; Nakhon Ratchasima, Khon Kaen, and Ubon, all of which are trading centers on the Plateau; and Songkhla, a rubber-exporting center of the peninsula.

How the People Make a Living

More than 80 per cent of the working people are farmers. Most own their own farms, which average about four acres in size. Rice is planted on about 85 per cent of the land used for crops. Of the 8,000,000 tons of rice grown annually in Thailand, about 1,200,000 tons are exported. Almost all the rice is grown in small paddies. Dikes are built to hold in the water that must cover the rice to a depth of four inches during the growing season. In the Malay Peninsula, water for the paddies comes almost entirely from rainfall. The delta region gets its water supply both from rain and from the annual flooding of the Chao Phraya River. Elsewhere rice growing depends heavily on irrigation.

Aside from rice, the chief crops are cotton, sugar cane, tobacco, coconuts, corn, and rubber. Corn and rubber are among Thailand's leading exports. Corn is grown largely on the Korat Plateau, and crude rubber comes from the Malay Peninsula.

Irrigation projects are opening up new areas of land for agriculture. In 1957 the Chao Phraya Dam (near Chaimat) was completed. It greatly extends the usable farm land of the Central Lowland. The dam helps control flooding of the Chao Phraya and makes double cropping possible. With water available the year around, two crops can be grown each year.

Wood and charcoal are the chief fuels used in Thailand. Coal and petroleum, needed for industrial use, must be imported. Tin is the only mineral mined in large quantities. Most of the tin mines are on the Malay Peninsula. The country is among the world's chief tin producers. Tungsten, lead, salt, and cement are produced in smaller amounts.

Until recently Thailand had little modern industry. The lack of mineral resources, especially fuels, has held back industrial development. Most of the country's factories process farm or forest products. There are many sawmills, rubber factories, tobacco-processing plants, and textile, rice, and sugar mills. Thailand is known for the quality of its silks.

About three-fourths of the country's freight is transported by water, chiefly over the Chao Phraya and its tributaries. A network of canals connects the many streams in the delta. Thailand also has a good network of railways. Bangkok is the center of rail, water, and air routes.

Education and Government

Thailand places great importance on education. Schooling is required for children between the ages of 7 and 14. The country's five universities are all in Bangkok. The oldest and largest is Chulalongkorn University, named after a famous 19th-century Thai monarch. It was founded in 1917. The others are Thammasart University, the University of Medical Sciences, the University of Fine Arts, and the University of Agriculture. Thailand also has a number of teachers', technical, and commercial schools.

Thailand's government is a constitutional monarchy. Its king has little power but is respected by the people as a symbol of Thai nationalism. The real power rests in the hands of the prime minister, who in theory is the head of the leading political party. Actually, the prime minister is more often an army general who has seized power. Thailand has a one-house legislature called the National Assembly. Half of its members are elected. The other half are appointed by the king on advice of the prime minister and other advisers.

History

About 2,000 years ago the Thai people lived in the southern part of China. By the 7th century A.D. they had formed a powerful kingdom called Nan Chao. It was broken up in the 13th century by the Mongol Emperor Kublai Khan, whose forces swept into southern China. The Thai then fled southward across the mountains to reach the plain of the Chao Phraya. There, in 1257, they formed a new kingdom known as Sukhothai. King Rama Kamheng, who reigned from A.D. 1275–1314, is one of Thailand's national heroes. He established an alphabet for the Thai language, and he was known as a wise and just ruler. During his reign the Thai kingdom expanded southward into what is now Malaya. During the next 400 years the Thai kingdom often fought with the Burmese on the west and the Cambodians on the east. From the Cambodians the Thai eventually won control over the Korat Plateau. Bangkok, the capital, was founded in 1782, after a Burmese attack had destroyed the old capital of Ayutthaya.

Trade with European nations began in the 16th century. The Thai, however, were highly suspicious of Europeans and the Western world, and for 300 years there were few contacts. In the 19th century three wise Thai rulers, King Rama III (1824–1851); King Mongkut (1851–1868); and his son King Chulalongkorn (1868–1910), developed contacts with the West. They made trade treaties with the United States, England, and France. They invited foreign teachers and engineers to live in Thailand and to advise the Thai government. Chulalongkorn established educational and public health programs, built railroads and highways, and started a telephone system.

In the middle of the 19th century Thailand (then called Siam) included what is now Laos and Cambodia, plus a large part of the Malay Peninsula. In 1893 France forced Thailand to give up all of its territory east of the Mekong River. England, which at that time controlled Burma, feared a French movement westward toward their possession. The French likewise feared that the British would move eastward from Burma. As a result, France and England in 1896 agreed to recognize Thailand as an independent nation. Events in the 20th century resulted in the loss of all of Cambodia to France and of a large part of the Malay Peninsula to England. The heart of Thailand, however, was never under European control.

In 1932 a revolution reduced the power of the king and marked the beginning of representative government in Thailand. The Japanese invaded Thailand on December 8, 1941. A government under Japanese supervision ruled Thailand during most of World War II (1939–1945).

After World War II, several important events occurred in Thailand. In 1946 the Thai ruler, King Ananda, was assassinated. He was succeeded by King Bhumibol Adulyadej. In 1947, and again in 1957, revolutions overthrew the leading government advisers without, however, involving the country in civil war.

Thailand is a member of the Southeast Asia Treaty Organization and has given active support to the United Nations. Bangkok is the center for many UN activities in the Far East.

The population in 1960 was 26,257,916.

THAMES (*tĕmz*) **RIVER, ENGLAND,** is the largest and most famous river in England. It rises from several small streams that flow down the grassy eastern slopes of the Cotswold Hills in southwestern England and unite near Oxford.

Below Oxford the river flows in a winding course, or meanders, over a broad, flat valley, then breaks through the Chiltern and Whitehorse Hills in the Goring Gap to reach the manufacturing town of Reading. From there the Thames flows eastward to London and the North Sea. Below London the river is really an estuary, or a long, narrow bay, of the North Sea. The tide reaches nearly 50 miles up this bay, to a few miles above London Bridge.

Above London the river is a slow and placid stream, noted for scenic beauty, fishing, and boating. The tidal estuary below London is a busy harbor filled with tugs, barges, and ships.

Along its total length of 210 miles numerous small tributaries reach the Thames. Many join from the Cotswold Hills or from the Chilterns. Others, like the Medway, flow northward from the Forest Ridge of the Weald. Two small rivers, the Lea and the Roding, join it from the north. The Thames and its tributaries drain 6,000 square miles, about one-eighth of England.

Many reminders in stone and brick along the river recall the events of history. At Oxford rise the gray spires of its famous colleges. Farther downstream is Henley. Still farther down is Eton, and across from it on the right bank is Windsor Castle, which has been a royal residence since the Norman kings. A little way downstream from there is Runnymede, where in 1215 Magna Carta was signed, and the former royal residence of Hampton Court.

The Thames flows through the great city of London itself, past the Tower, Westminster Abbey, and St. Paul's. Within the city the river flows under 15 bridges. Finally the Thames reaches Gravesend and the famous Tilbury Docks where pirates once were hanged in chains as grim warning to the crews of passing foreign ships of England's power.

THANKSGIVING (*thăngks gĭv'ĭng*) **DAY** is a day set aside for people to give thanks for their blessings.

Thanksgiving is an old custom. European and Asiatic nations often set aside special days to give thanks for a military victory or some other blessing. When the Spanish Armada was defeated in 1588, thanksgiving services were held in English churches.

The English often held thanksgiving services when a member of the king's family recovered from an illness.

The best-known Thanksgiving in the United States was held by the Pilgrims in the autumn of 1621 in Plymouth, Massachusetts. Their first winter in the new country had been difficult. Half of the Pilgrims had died. In the spring they cleared the land and planted the fields. They worked hard all summer and in the fall there was an abundant harvest. Governor William Bradford proclaimed a day of thanksgiving.

Great preparations were made for the feast. Indian friends were invited as guests. The Indians had taught the colonists to hunt and fish and plant their crops. They brought wild turkeys and venison from the forests as their share of the feast. There were church services. Then for three days the Pilgrims and Indians feasted together around outdoor tables piled high with food. There were prayers of thanks, sermons, and songs of praise.

Other New England colonies soon adopted the custom of public thanksgiving. It became an annual event after 1680 in Massachusetts Bay Colony. Connecticut held an annual Thanksgiving Day after 1647, except in 1675. In New Netherlands the Dutch had some days of thanksgiving, beginning in 1644.

During the Revolutionary War, several days for prayer and thanksgiving were announced by the Continental Congress. President George

In her painting "Thanksgiving," artist Doris Lee imaginatively captured the spirit of the traditional Thanksgiving Day observations in the United States.

Washington proclaimed a day of thanksgiving for the adoption of the Constitution in 1789. President James Madison proclaimed a day of thanksgiving for peace at the end of the War of 1812.

Many of the states had annual Thanksgiving Days. Many people wanted a national holiday on the same day every year. In 1863 Abraham Lincoln named the last Thursday in November as the first national Thanksgiving Day. Each president followed this custom until 1939 when President Franklin Delano Roosevelt named the next to the last Thursday in November as Thanksgiving Day. This provided more shopping time between the Thanksgiving and Christmas holidays. Some states opposed the idea.

In December 1941 an act of Congress declared the fourth Thursday in November as a national holiday. Some states still observe the last Thursday. In Canada, Thanksgiving is usually the second Monday in October.

THEATER (*thē'ä tēr*). When the beginnings of the drama first developed in Greece, the stage was simply a circle of turf on which the worshipers danced around the altar of Dionysus. The spot chosen was usually at the foot of a hill so that spectators on the slopes could watch the dancing. Following this tradition, the Greek theaters from first to last were semicircles of seats, built into a hillside. The word *theater* is of Greek origin and means *a place for seeing*.

At the theater of Dionysus in Athens, built about 500 B.C., the performance was given in a circular place called the orchestra. This space was about 75 feet in diameter. Rising on the side of the hill, tier above tier, were the seats for the spectators, arranged in the shape of a horseshoe. The theater held 27,500 persons, for the performance was a national festival which the whole free population attended. Erected behind the circle of the orchestra was a rather dignified-looking stage building. It was used as a dressing place for the performers. This *skene* (from which comes the word *scene*) served as a background for the action of the play. It might represent a temple, a palace, or whatever building was called for in the drama. In front of the *skene*, supporting a platform, was a

row of columns, called the *proscenium*. Besides this formal background, very little scenery was used by the Greeks. No artificial lighting was needed, for the plays were presented in the daytime.

It was not until 52 B.C. that the first permanent stone theater was completed at Rome. On the opening night 500 lions and 20 elephants were killed by gladiators. The theaters of the Romans followed a plan similar in outline to that of the Greeks, but were built, almost without exception, on level ground. This necessitated enormous amounts of concrete and masonry for their construction. The Romans were the first to fill the orchestra with seats and present the play on a raised stage behind which was the *skene*.

When the Roman world turned Christian, public opinion condemned theatrical performances. No theaters were built for about 1,000 years. The miracle and morality plays of the Middle Ages were performed in churches or in wooden booths set up in public squares and in yards. The settings were simple, usually consisting of a three-story platform representing heaven, earth, and hell in proper order. The first modern theater was the Teatro Farnese at Parma, Italy, built in 1618 or 1619. Its stage, instead of projecting far out into the orchestra, was built into one of the walls. A curtain was used to separate the stage from the auditorium, thus permitting changes of scenery to be made out of sight of the audience. The proscenium arch, forming a frame in front of the stage, gave a picturelike effect to the action.

English Theaters

Meanwhile English theaters had been developing on different lines. The first permanent English playhouse was built in 1576 at Shoreditch, near London, by James Burbage. It was known simply as The Theater. The famous Globe Theater, in which many of the plays of William Shakespeare were presented, went up in 1599. The Elizabethan theaters were modeled on the inn courtyards where the traveling players had presented the miracle plays. They were either eight-sided or round in plan and completely surrounded by tiers of galleries. There

Scene from *Alice in Wonderland.*

was a central platform for the stage, and grouped around it in the "pit" stood or sat the poorer spectators. They surrounded the stage on all sides but one, which led to the "green-room," or retiring place for the actors. There was no scenery such as is used today. A placard bearing an inscription, such as "This is a street in Venice," served to announce the setting. These native English theaters disappeared in the middle of the 17th century, their place being taken by the newer Italian type.

During the 19th century many elaborate theaters were built in both Europe and the Americas. The ideals of those days may be seen in the opera at Paris, the Metropolitan Opera House in New York City, Covent Garden in London, and La Scala in Milan, Italy.

The modern tendency in the theater is toward making it simpler and tends to increase the feeling of closeness between the audience and the stage. Instead of being built on a horseshoe plan, with a flat or nearly flat floor, several galleries, and boxes, the modern theater ap-

proaches the shape of a fan. Boxes are done away with. The floor of the theater is tilted so that every member of the audience gets a clear view of the stage, and there is only one deep gallery. The ideal of the modern theatrical architect is to get rid of the proscenium arch which frames the action on the stage. The arch gives it an air of unreality. The arch was necessary to hide the top of the drop scenes and back drop, and the pulleys by which they were raised and lowered, but it is no longer wanted.

Revolving, Ready-Set Stages

With the silent power of electricity at its disposal, the modern theater no longer needs an army of scene shifters and complicated machinery. The stage may be lowered into the floor for scene changing or it may be constructed to revolve so that three or more scenes can be prepared before the play starts. These are simply swung into position when wanted. A still better system is to mount the stages on a track which forms the arc of a circle. By moving a lever a

Scene from *Abe Lincoln: New Salem Days.*

In ancient Greece, theaters were built on natural slopes. The stone seats formed part of a circle on the side of a hill, with the orchestra, or stage, forming a smaller circle at the foot. The theater at Epidaurus, one of the most beautiful of Greek theaters, was so constructed that an actor's voice carried the entire distance to the outer rim of seats.

In a modern playhouse, the lighting, the arrangement of the seats, and the tilted floor make it possible for everyone in the audience to get a good view. This picture shows the Goodman Memorial Theatre of Chicago with the stage set for a performance. Occasionally very elaborate scenery is used, but the tendency is to simplify the actual setting and obtain most effects by means of lighting.

Above and right: Courtesy Goodman Memorial Theatre of the Art Institute of Chicago

Courtesy Radio City Music Hall

Radio City Music Hall in New York City is the world's largest theater, seating 6,200 people. The stage is a full city block wide, and the arch over it is 70 feet high. When the stage show is over, a screen will be let down for the showing of a motion picture.

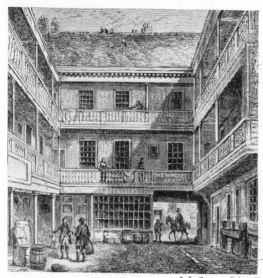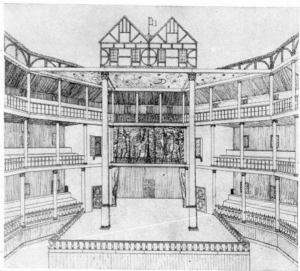

Left: Courtesy Folger Shakespeare Library; right: Joseph Quincy Adams, "A Life of William Shakespeare," 1923

During the Middle Ages there were no theaters, and plays, based on the Bible, were given in churches. In England the earliest nonreligious plays were performed on rolling platforms in yards of inns, like the one at the left. The audience stood around the yard or on the balconies above to watch the play. It is easy to see how the theaters of Shakespeare's time, as shown in the Globe Theater on the right, developed from the arrangement of these inn yards. In these theaters the poorer members of the audience stood below, as in the inn yards, but seats were provided on the balconies for the better class. Usually there were even seats on the stage for some of the audience. Like the Greek theaters and the inn yards, these playhouses were open to the weather. It was not until some time later that they were roofed.

whole set is wheeled into position under the proscenium arch at a moment's notice. Theaters have been designed where the tracks form a complete circle around the auditorium and hold any number of stages, ready set. These are used especially for small spectacular shows such as are given in amusement parks.

Such remarkable effects can now be obtained by skillful lighting that plays are often staged on a single set. This was done with great success in the revival of Aristophanes *Lysistrata* in New York City in 1930. For a time the footlights in front and spotlights in the wings and the gallery were the whole battery of the theater. Lighting today uses all the inventions in the field of optics. The colors are chosen for their effect on emotions and harmonized with the mood of the music and the action. The lights are operated by a keyboard of switches, which resembles the keyboard of an organ except that there are levers instead of keys. This is in charge of an expert electrician who must know the producer's business as well as his own. The backdrop can be done away with, its place being taken by patterns of light thrown on a plaster screen.

Behind the scenes the modern theater has changed but little. The ground occupied by a theater in a large city is usually very valuable. This means that the greatest possible space must be given to the auditorium and the least possible to the actors. The result is that their quarters are cramped. There is a common room for the players, known as the greenroom, a chorus room, a music room, and separate dressing rooms for the principals. The shops of the electrician and the carpenter are large and well equipped. A theater, like a ship, must be prepared to do all its internal repairs and alterations.

THEBES (*thēbz*), **BOEOTIA** (*bē ō'shĭ ä*). In Greek legend Thebes was one of the most famous cities. There are many myths concerning Thebes. They tell of the founding of the city by Cadmus; the building of the seven-gated wall by Amphion; the curse that rested on its royal house and ended in the disasters of Oedipus; and the war of the Seven against Thebes. The city stood on hilly ground to the north of Mount Cithaeron, and was believed among the ancients to be the birthplace of Dionysus and Hercules. Athens was 44 miles away across the mountains. The rivers Ismenus on the east, and Dirce on the west, flow past the site, and between them are many springs.

In historic times Thebes was governed by a group of a few powerful people who were always trying to establish their rule over the other towns of Boeotia. They hated Athens because it helped Plataea to keep its independence. When the Persians invaded Greece, the Thebans' hatred of Athens made them join the Persian side. They fought against their fellow Greeks at Plataea in 479 B.C.

After the war Sparta wished to turn the Thebans out of the Amphictyonic League, but later on took them back as the chief power in Boeotia. Thebes was at one time head of the Boeotian League. The city held out while Athens overran Boeotia between 457 and 447 B.C. The Thebans were allied with the Spartans in the Peloponnesian War, and in 427 B.C. destroyed Plataea. Sparta turned on them after the war, but the Theban military power was rapidly increasing. They withstood the Spartans at Haliartus and Coronea. In 371 B.C., under Epaminondas, the Thebans invaded the Peloponnese and broke the Spartans at the Battle of Leuctra. From that time until the Battle of Mantinea in 362 B.C., Thebes was supreme over all Greece. In 338 B.C. it allied itself with Athens to resist Philip of Macedon, and was defeated at Chaeronea. Two years later the Thebans revolted. The whole city, except for the house where the poet Pindar had lived, was destroyed by Alexander the Great.

The Cadmea, the ancient citadel, was inhabited throughout Roman times and the Middle Ages. It was fought for by Normans, Franks, and Catalans. There is still a village of some 5,000 inhabitants there.

THEMISTOCLES (*thē mĭs'tō klēz*) (514?–449 B.C.). It was Themistocles who made Athens into a sea power and saved Greece from the Persians. He was born of poor parents, and little is known of his early life. Following the Battle of Marathon, he foresaw that another Persian invasion would come. He persuaded the Athenian Assembly to turn the profits of their silver mines at Laurium into building a fleet, instead of distributing it to the people.

When his political rival, Aristides, lost popularity in 482 B.C., Themistocles was left as the acknowledged leader of Athens. He prepared to resist the attack of the Persian King Xerxes with a fleet. He interpreted the prophecy of the Oracle of Delphi, that Athens must put its trust in "wooden walls," to mean that ships must be constructed. He commanded the Athenian fleet, but agreed to fight under Eurybiades, the Spartan admiral commanding the entire allied fleet. Themistocles' aggressive leadership and bribery of the Greeks kept them fighting until finally they forced the Persians to retreat from Greece.

The Greeks at the battle of Salamis broke the naval supremacy of Xerxes. Themistocles became the hero of Greece. The Spartans did not want the Athenians to rebuild their fortifying walls. Themistocles led them to believe that this would not be done but meanwhile the Athenians did reconstruct the wall. Themistocles was thought to be too crafty for even the Athenians to trust. Therefore, he was banished in 471 B.C. by popular vote, and he retired to Argos. He was involved in the treasonable correspondence of Pausanias with the Persians. In 465 B.C. he escaped to the court of Artaxerxes. He spent a year mastering the language and customs of Persia before he would see the king. Artaxerxes gave him a pension and an estate at Magnesia, where he lived the rest of his days.

THEODORIC (*thē ŏd'ō rĭk*) (454?–526). The first great European king to rise after the fall of the Roman Empire was Theodoric. He was the son of one of three brothers who ruled the Ostrogoths living in Pannonia.

When Theodoric was seven years of age he was sent to Constantinople, Turkey, as a hostage. He spent ten years there. In 474 he succeeded his father and for 14 years conducted far-reaching raids into the lands of rival chieftains. With the approval of the Byzantine emperor at Constantinople he set out for Italy in 488. Italy was then ruled by Odoacer. Theodoric won two decisive battles, but Odoacer received aid from the Burgundians and did not surrender until 493. Theodoric, although he had promised Odoacer safety, killed him.

Theodoric reigned for 33 years. It was a period of unbroken prosperity for Italy. He lowered taxes, built harbors, and drained marshes. Instead of importing corn as it had always done, Italy began to raise enough corn to export it. Theodoric belonged to the Arian sect of Christians but he showed complete religious tolerance. He got on well with the Catholics until Justin, the Byzantine emperor, began to persecute the Arians. Theodoric sent Pope John to beg the emperor to stop the persecution. John failed in his mission and Theodoric imprisoned him. The Catholics continued to plot with Justin. Theodoric executed Anicius Boethius, the Christian philosopher, and his son Symmachus. Both of these people later became known as martyrs in the struggle between Catholics and Arians.

Theodoric was buried in his great mausoleum at Ravenna. His tomb is still one of the sights of this town.

THEODOSIUS *(thē ō dō'shĭ ŭs)* (346?–395).
The last man to rule with forceful leadership the whole Roman Empire was Theodosius I, called The Great. He was born in Spain. His father was Theodosius, the famous Roman general who drove the Picts and Scots out of Britain.

In 378 after the Battle of Adrianople, the Emperor Gratian called Theodosius to aid in ruling the Roman Empire. He was assigned the eastern provinces, together with a section of Illyria. The barbarians were pouring over the frontiers, and in 381 Theodosius had to meet two invasions at the same time. He himself fought the Visigoths in Macedonia and Phirus. Promotus, one of his generals, defended the Danube against the Ostrogoths. Both were successful. Theodosius diplomatically influenced Athanaric, king of the Visogoths, to enter his service with 40,000 men.

In 383 Maximus rebelled in Britain, and Gratian was murdered. Theodosius accepted Maximus as his colleague. Yet when Maximus tried to invade Italy in 388, Theodosius attacked and defeated him at Aquileia. Maximus and his son were put to death. The emperor then chose Valentinian II to rule the western empire. Valentinian was murdered and Eugenius ruled in his place. Theodosius defeated the latter in 394, and peace was brought to the Empire. Theodosius died at Milan, leaving the Empire to be shared by his two sons, Honorius and Arcadius.

THERESA *(tŭ rē'sŭ)* or TERESA *(tā rä'sŭ)* OF AVILA, SAINT, (1515–1582), a patron
saint of Spain, won canonization not by martyrdom, but by a long life of faith and religious zeal. She was born at Avila in Old Castile. In about 1535 she entered a local Carmelite convent. She was nearly 40, however, when she began her life work. Deeply moved by the death of her father, and under the influence of her reading of St. Augustine's *Confessions*, she suddenly came upon an image of the wounded Christ. She was so overcome with emotion that she became unconscious. Thereafter she frequently had religious trances and visions.

St. Theresa was greatly distressed by what she regarded as the catastrophe of the Reformation. Carelessness in the convents, she felt, was partly responsible, and she tried to restore the ancient discipline among the nuns of the Carmelite order. With the approval of the pope, she gathered a few followers and started a new convent. There the nuns wore rope sandals, slept on straw, ate no meat, never went out, and lived on alms alone. She habitually scourged herself and wore a painful haircloth garment. Her best known written works are her autobiography, called *The Way of Perfection*, considered a notable work on asceticism, and her collected letters. She spent the last 15 years of her life traveling from place to place, founding new convents of "Barefoot Carmelites."

THERESA or THERESE *(tā rĕz')* OF LISIEUX, SAINT (1873–1897), was a French nun of the
Carmelite order. Her real name was Marie Francoise Therese Martin. She was officially declared a saint in 1925, the first woman to be canonized so soon after her death.

The youngest of four sisters, Therese was

born to devout parents at Alencon, France. When she was a little more than four, her mother died, and the family moved to Lisieux. There, when she was only 15, she entered the brown-habited Carmelite Order.

Her life was one of faith, mortification, and charity. She died at the age of 24. She was made a saint 28 years later, after her autobiography, *The Story of a Soul*, had been published and translated. After her death many healings were credited to her.

She was canonized as St. Teresa-of-the-Child-Jesus, and is called "The Little Flower."

THERMOMETER (*thẽr mŏm'ĕ tẽr*). The thermometer is a very common instrument in use all over the world. The word itself tells what the thermometer does since "thermo" means "heat," and "meter" means "measure"; so you see, a thermometer measures heat.

Heat and cold cause many materials to change. Most are changed in the same way whenever the same temperature is applied. For example, mercury always expands at the same rate according to the temperature around it. When placed in a glass tube and warmed, the mercury always rises to the same point on the tube whenever the same amount of heat is applied. Adding a scale makes a simple thermometer which gives accurate temperature readings in degrees.

A glass thermometer is usually made of four parts: a glass tube, a glass bulb (at the bottom of the tube), a scale, and a liquid. This is called a liquid-in-glass thermometer.

Some time around 1592 (100 years after Christopher Columbus discovered America) Galileo, an Italian scientist, began to experiment with the effect of heat and cold on liquid in a glass tube. In general, his experimental thermometer consisted of a glass tube having a hollow bulb at one end. The tube and bulb were heated to expand the air inside, and then the open end was placed in a fluid, such as water. As the air in the tube cooled, its volume contracted or shrank, and the liquid rose in the tube to take its place. Changes in temperature could then be noted by the rising or falling level of the liquid in the tube.

Liquid Thermometers

It was found that mercury and alcohol provide the best liquids for thermometer use. Mercury reacts quickly to a rise in temperature, expands evenly, and is easily seen. It can stand low temperatures (−38 degrees Fahrenheit) without freezing and high temperatures (+675 degrees) without turning to vapor. Alcohol is excellent for extremely low temperatures (as low as −180 degrees) but poor for high temperatures since it boils easily. Alcohol, however, is colorless; so a dye must be added to make it readable.

In the modern mercury-in-glass thermometer the hole in the tube, or bore, as it is called, is often finer than a human hair and in most cases no larger than the shank of a common pin. The bulb and tube are filled with just the right amount of mercury for the temperature range desired, then sealed in such a way that the upper end of the tube is either left as an almost perfect vacuum or filled with an inert gas such as nitrogen. Since mercury expands more for a given rise in temperature than does the glass, it rises in the tube. When heat is withdrawn, the mercury contracts or recedes.

In order to read a thermometer a scale must be provided. The two scales in most common use (although there are others) are the Fahrenheit scale and the Centigrade scale. These scales are sometimes marked directly on the glass tube itself or on a background of wood, metal, or plastic against which the tube is fitted.

A recording thermometer, or thermograph.

Courtesy Taylor Instrument Companies

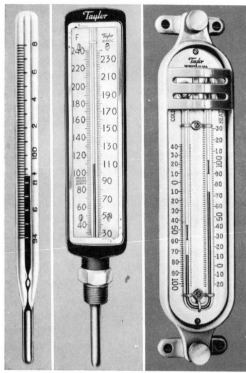
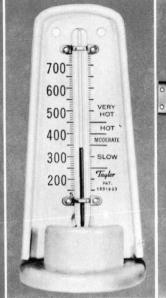
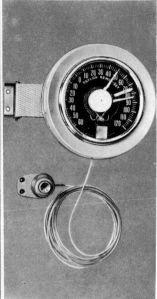

Courtesy Taylor Instrument Companies

(1) A household fever thermometer. (2) An industrial thermometer. (3) A thermometer which records maximum and minimum temperatures. (4) An oven thermometer. (5) A bimetal maximum-minimum thermometer.

On the Centigrade scale the zero point is at the freezing point of water. The boiling point of water is placed at 100 degrees and the space between graduated into 100 equal parts. On the Fahrenheit scale the freezing point of water is at 32 degrees above zero. The freezing point is not at zero because Gabriel Fahrenheit, inventor of this thermometer, fixed zero at the freezing point of a mixture of ordinary salt and water which freezes at a lower temperature than pure water. The space in between the freezing point (32 degrees) and the boiling point (212 degrees) was graduated into 180 degrees. From habit, the Fahrenheit scale is in common use throughout English-speaking countries; however, the Centigrade scale easily fits into the world-wide system of mathematics and therefore is convenient for most scientific purposes.

Good thermometers are calibrated at two or more known temperatures or points, the most common being the freezing point and boiling point of pure water. The freezing point is found by putting the thermometer into a mixture of ice and pure water. This point, indicated by the thermometer liquid, is marked on the tube. The boiling point is found and marked by placing the thermometer in steam from water boiling at normal atmospheric pressure (15 pounds per square inch).

Of great medical importance is the clinical, or fever, thermometer used to determine body temperature. This is a mercury-in-glass thermometer which has a small constriction or bubble just above the bulb which permits the mercury column to remain at its highest reading until shaken down with a quick snap of the wrist. This thermometer is often called a self-registering thermometer.

Bimetallic Thermometer

There is another type of thermometer which has come into widespread use. This is the bimetallic thermometer which operates without the use of liquid-in-glass. A strip of iron and a strip of brass are fastened together in the form of a coil, one end of which is fastened while the other end, connected to a pointer, is free to move. The metals expand and contract at different rates. When heated, the free end of the

Courtesy Taylor Instrument Companies

An outside window thermometer.

coil winds or unwinds as the case may be, and the movement positions a pointer on a dial graduated into degrees to correspond to the Fahrenheit or Centigrade scale. By placing a pen on the pointer and by providing a rotating chart, we have a recording thermometer. The chart is usually divided into hours and days of the week and is rotated by means of a clock.

It would take a great deal of space to list all the many uses of thermometers. Besides the generally known household, cooking, and fever thermometers there is a wide variety of thermometers made especially for industrial and laboratory use. They are generally of the liquid-in-glass type, often protected against breakage by a metal case and stem. (See PYROMETER.)

THERMOSTAT (*thĕr′mō stăt*). A thermostat is a device that regulates temperature automatically.

Like a thermometer, a thermostat also "feels" temperature changes. Instead of merely showing change on a scale, however, a thermostat operates some type of equipment, such as a heating furnace, to maintain temperature at a previously selected point.

For example, if the furnace is to keep your house at a certain temperature, the thermostat dial is set at that point. If the air becomes colder in the house, the thermostat senses, or feels, this and sends an electrical signal to the furnace. This signal causes the furnace to start. When the room warms to the desired temperature, the thermostat automatically sends another signal that stops the furnace. When the room gets cold again, the furnace starts once more.

Instead of using mercury to feel temperature changes, thermostats commonly use a strip of specially built metals. These metals always bend at the same rate according to temperature.

The idea that bending metal could be used to control heating equipment was first described by Andrew Ure, a Scottish chemist, in 1831. A practical system for homes was developed by Andrew Butz, a young Minneapolis (Minnesota) inventor, about 1883. In his automatic system the bending metal contacted a switch to operate an electric motor. The motor opened a door on the furnace. This permitted more air to flow over the fire causing it to burn faster. As the house became warmer, the metal strip bent back until another switch caused the door to close.

While bending metal is most commonly used in controlling heating equipment, changes in air pres-

A diagram of a thermostat. The bimetal (two different metals) strip bends with changes in temperature. By setting it in a certain position it will keep room temperature steady by turning the furnace on or off.

Adapted by courtesy of Minneapolis-Honeywell Regulator Company

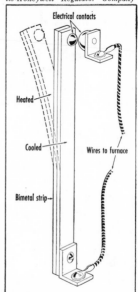

sure or changes in the flow of electricity through a coil of fine wire may also be used to detect temperature changes.

In addition to controlling home heating equipment and heating devices used in industry, thermostats also regulate the temperature of such appliances as electric blankets, irons, toasters, clothes dryers, waffle irons, ovens, and water heaters. In an air-conditioning system, thermostats feel warmth and signal for more cold air from the cooling equipment.

THESEUS (*thē'sūs*). In Athenian legend Theseus is the son of Aegeus, king of Athens. His mother was Aethra, daughter of the king of Troezen. Before he was born, his father hid a sword and sandals under a great stone. He told Aethra that if she had a son who could lift the stone and take the gifts, she was to send the boy secretly to Athens.

When Theseus grew up he easily raised the stone. With the sword and sandals, he set out for Athens. After his arrival in Athens, Medea, who had become the wife of Aegeus, found out who Theseus was and tried to poison him. Theseus drew his sword, and Aegeus, recognizing it, hailed him as his son and successor.

Every year Athens had to send a tribute of seven young men and seven girls to King Minos of Crete. They were delivered to the Minotaur, a monster half bull and half man, that dwelt in a labyrinth—a structure with winding and confusing passageways. Theseus offered to go with the victims and to slay the Minotaur. As usual, the ship departed under black sails, which Theseus promised to change to white if he were victorious.

When Ariadne, the daughter of Minos, saw Theseus, she fell in love with him. She gave him a long thread which he was to use in escaping from the labyrinth. Theseus slew the Minotaur and followed the thread out of the winding passages. Then he set sail for Athens. He forgot to change the black sails to white, and Aegeus, thinking his son dead, threw himself into the sea. This sea was thereafter called the Aegean.

Theseus thus became king of Athens. Later he united various Attic communities into a single state of Attica. He married Antiope, sister of the queen of the Amazons. Later he kidnapped the young Helen of Troy, and even tried to capture the wife of Pluto. But Pluto caught him and imprisoned him in Hades, until Hercules came to his rescue. The Athenians refused to receive their king again. Theseus went to Scyros, where he died.

THIRTY (*thēr'tē*) **YEARS'** (*yērz*) **WAR.** From 1618 to 1648 a war was fought in Europe which caused untold misery and loss of life. During this Thirty Years' War Germany lost half its population and Bohemia lost two-thirds of its population. It was said that 15,000 towns and villages were utterly destroyed.

In this century war had become a business for professional soldiers who were paid and fed by a leader. Supplies for these soldiers were obtained from the countryside by bribery or by the looting of towns. People living in areas where wars occurred often lost everything to these armies of looting soldiers. This was true during the Thirty Years' War.

Germany in those days was a patchwork of little principalities and dukedoms, each under its own ruler. They were independent but owed allegiance to the Holy Roman Emperor, who was the Hapsburg ruler of Austria. The territory ruled by this emperor was divided by religious differences. There was a Union of Protestant Princes and a Catholic League. The Catholic League was supported by the emperor and was the strongest. Many of the German princes had been Protestants for nearly 100 years. They were permitted to rule because the emperor lacked the military power to crush them. But they were outvoted in the imperial councils. The Protestant princes felt that it was only a matter of time before religious persecution would begin against them.

The Fighting Begins

The situation reached a critical point in 1618. Protestants of Bohemia refused to elect the Catholic Ferdinand of Austria to the vacant throne of their country. Instead they offered it to Frederick, the Protestant prince who was the elector of the Palatinate. Frederick accepted and Emperor Ferdinand II of Austria declared war on him. The emperor had a powerful ally in Maximilian of Bavaria. Frederick fought alone at first because the other Protestant princes were jealous of his increased power and refused to help.

The army of the Catholic League, led by Count Johann von Tilly, defeated the Bohemian nobles and executed many of them. The Protestant princes were alarmed by this and Frederick received some support from the princes of Brunswick and Baden-Durlach. Later other princes joined him. They held off Tilly's army for a while but in 1623 suffered another defeat.

Coming to the aid of the Protestant cause, Christian IV of Denmark helped strengthen Frederick's position. But the powerful Duke Albrecht von Wallenstein joined the Catholic cause. He defeated the Protestant forces and marched to invade Denmark. The Protestants were defeated and only the town of Magdeburg remained in arms. The Peace of Luebeck was signed in 1629.

Richelieu Enters the War

Now help came to the Protestants from another source. Cardinal Richelieu, the French minister, was interested in the outcome of the conflict. He did not wish Austria and Spain, the two chief members of the Holy Roman Empire, to become powerful. Although France was a Catholic nation, Richelieu gave money to Gustavus Adolphus, the Protestant king of Sweden. The money was to be used to renew the war.

Tilly's army defeated, burned, and looted the Protestant town of Magdeburg in 1631. Later in that year Gustavus Adolphus led his army into the field against Tilly. The Catholic League Army was defeated and Tilly was fatally wounded. Wallenstein now became the leader of the Catholic forces. After he had forced Saxony into peace, his army met that of Gustavus Adolphus at Luetzen. Wallenstein's army was defeated, but Gustavus Adolphus was killed.

With Gustavus Adolphus dead, the Catholic League met with success. Then Wallenstein

was removed from his position and assassinated. The Holy Roman Emperor had this done because he feared Wallenstein's increasing power. The Catholic League Army was able to defeat the Swedes and the Peace of Prague was signed in 1635.

Again Richelieu came to the aid of the Protestants. France began fighting on all its frontiers. Its armies at first were scattered and it was invaded by the emperor's army. The Swedes met with success, however. They fought their way southward and for the rest of the war the Austrian armies seldom dared go north of the Danube River.

Then France found two outstanding generals in Duke Louis d'Enghien and Viscount Henri de Turenne. French efforts began to meet with success and in 1645 France won the Battle of Allersheim. The emperor was deserted by all his allies except Bavaria, which could not offer much help because it was being reduced to a desert by the enemy.

With French and Swedish armies united in Germany, peace finally came. A committee of diplomats had been arguing over terms of peace for seven years. The Treaty of Westphalia was signed in 1648. Under this treaty the German states won their religious freedom. They were in terrible condition after the 30 years of war, but the power of the Holy Roman Emperor was reduced to a shadow. France received the territory of Alsace. The elector of Brandenburg was given a great deal of territory which, in 1701, became the powerful kingdom of Prussia.

THISTLE (*this″l*). The term thistle is broadly applied to many kinds of plants which have noticeably prickly or spiny leaves or stems. Many of them are troublesome weeds. Others such as the globe thistle and star thistle are grown as ornamentals. The star thistles are close relatives of the cornflowers, or bachelor's-buttons. The Russian thistle, or tumbleweed, is a much-branched spiny plant. It belongs to the same family as the beet. It was introduced into the United States from Russia in flaxseed. When mature, entire plants break off at the surface of the soil. They may be blown long

J. Horace McFarland Company

The common field thistle. Its hairy cup-shaped bracts enclose satiny flower heads. The thistle spreads by means of seeds and long rootstocks.

distances by the wind, thus scattering their seeds. The weed is especially troublesome in the western states.

The more commonly recognized thistles, as well as the globe and star thistles, belong to a special group of the very large family Compositae. The plants are coarsely spiny. Their small tubular flowers are borne in prickly heads. The flowers range in color from purple to white or yellow. Many of them are very attractive. When all the flowers in a head have finished blooming they wither and ripen their small, dry, seedlike fruits. Each fruit develops long silky hairs. The fruit is then easily broken from the head and may be borne away by the wind. Thistles may be spread long distances in this manner.

There are several very troublesome thistles in the United States. One of these is the large bull thistle common in pasture lands and fields in the eastern states. During its first year of growth it develops a large coarse rosette close to the ground. The second year the stem elongates, bears flowers, and matures seed. The whole plant then dies. Probably the most troublesome of all thistles is the lavender-flowered Canada thistle. It is smaller than the bull thistle but is more persistent as a weed. This is because it lives many years instead of only two. The plants spread by means of seeds and also by long underground stems or rootstocks. These stems are not reached nor dug out readily by cultivation tools. They are easily broken, however, and each broken part left in the soil will form a complete new plant. The best way to destroy Canada thistle is to spray it with chemicals such as 2,4-D.

Another effective method is to keep the tops above ground cut down as closely as possible. Eventually the underground stems will be starved for lack of food and will die. In many states there are laws which make it an offense for anyone to allow Canada thistles to come to seed on his land.

THOMAS (tŏm'äs), **THEODORE** (thē'ō dōr) (1835–1905). Had it not been for Theodore Thomas, music might have disappeared from the United States completely during the busy reconstruction days following the War Between the States. He organized symphony orchestras in various large cities. Many of the great symphonic works of European masters were introduced by him to audiences in the United States. His efforts laid most of the foundation for the present nation-wide interest in music in that country.

Theodore Thomas was born at Esens, Germany. An infant wonder as a violinist, he made his first public appearance when he was only five. His family went to New York City when he was ten. In 1851 he toured the country with the orchestra that accompanied Jenny Lind. His true fame rests, not upon his ability as a violinist, but on his work as conductor and organizer of orchestras in New York City; Cincinnati, Ohio; Brooklyn, New York; and Chicago, Illinois. Citizens of Chicago built him the magnificent Orchestra Hall in 1904. He was the first director of the Cincinnati College of

Music, and the first president of the Wagner Union.

THOMAS A KEMPIS (*ŭ kĕm′ pŭs*) (1380?– 1471) was a monk who is famous as the author of influential Christian literature. He was a member of the Augustinian Canons of the Windesheim Congregation at Mount St. Agnes, near the Netherlands city of Zwolle. It was his duty to make copies of the Scriptures.

He was born at Kempen, Germany, from which he took his name. He took vows as a monk at Mount St. Agnes Monastery in 1408 and entered the Brotherhood of the Common Life. His work as a copyist of the Scriptures turned his interest to literature. He began to write works on goodness, self-denial, and the religious life. The most famous work credited to him is *The Imitation of Christ*. It has been translated into every language of the Christian world. Of this work on Christian conduct it was said, "Its author is the Holy Spirit."

THOR (*thôr*), for whom Thursday is named, was the Norse god of war, physical strength, and thunder, and the eldest son of Odin. Thor had three precious possessions. One was the red-hot hammer which he used against the giants and which returned to his hand of its own accord. Another was a pair of iron gloves which he put on when he wished to throw his hammer. His third precious possession was the belt of strength which doubled his might.

In his wonderful palace called *Bilskirnir* (Lightning) Thor lived with his golden-haired wife Sif. When he traveled across the sky in his goat-drawn chariot, lightning flashed from his hammer. Thunder roared whenever he threw the hammer. Thor was the friend of man, particularly of the peasants and laboring classes because he kept the giants from destroying the earth.

Thor had many remarkable adventures. Once he impersonated the goddess Freya and slew the giant who had stolen his hammer. His strangest undertaking was a visit to Jotunheim, land of the giants. On the way Thor and his companions came to a large hall where they spent the night. The hall turned out to be only the glove of the giant Skrymir. Skrymir proposed that they travel together, and they passed the next night under an oak tree. When Skrymir was asleep, Thor hit him on the head with his hammer. The giant woke up and asked if a leaf had struck him. Twice again Thor hit him, but Skrymir only stroked his head and said that twigs or acorns must be falling. The next morning Thor took leave of him.

When Thor and his companions came to Jotunheim, the king of the giants was surprised to see that they were so small. The king made them compete with the giants in various contests. To Thor he gave a large drinking horn, telling him to drain it in three draughts. Thor tried, but the level of the liquor was only a little lower when he had finished. Then the king challenged him to lift a gray cat from the ground. Thor could raise only one of its feet. The third test was to wrestle with a toothless old woman. Thor struggled valiantly, but at last was forced down on one knee.

The visitors were about to depart, feeling very much ashamed of themselves, when the king admitted that he had bewitched them. He himself, he said, was the giant Skrymir. Thor's three blows had not fallen on him, but had driven three great valleys in a mountain. The horn from which Thor had drunk had one end in the ocean. The level of the sea had actually been lowered by Thor's drinking. As for the cat, it was really the Midgard serpent that surrounds the earth. When Thor lifted one of its feet, all the giants had been terrified. The old woman who could get Thor down only on one knee was Old Age herself.

THOREAU (*thôr′ ō* or *thŭ rō′*), **HENRY DAVID** (1817–1862), was a U.S. author, poet, and philosopher who upheld man's right to be an individual. He believed that man could benefit spiritually and culturally from contact with nature. Thoreau stands forth in his writings as a unique and fascinating figure. "A man is rich," he said, "in proportion to the number of things which he can afford to let alone." On that axiom he patterned his life.

He was born in Concord, Massachusetts. As a boy he collected specimens for L. J. R. Agassiz, the naturalist. He entered Harvard College and was graduated without having distinguished himself. He taught school for a while, but abandoned teaching to earn a scanty living by making pencils. He never married.

At the age of 28 Thoreau went to the shores of Walden Pond, near Concord, and built himself a hut. There he lived alone for two years, reading, writing, thinking, and learning the secrets of the wild country in the vicinity. His own affairs

Brown Brothers
Henry David Thoreau.

were simple; he worked only at odd jobs to supply his barest needs. In his most popular book, *Walden, or Life in the Woods*, he describes his experience during this period.

Thoreau knew intimately the philosopher, Ralph Waldo Emerson, the novelist, Nathaniel Hawthorne, and others. However, living in a conservative community, he was bound to get into trouble. He refused to vote or to pay his poll tax, and once spent a night in jail on this account. Almost all his writings are autobiographical and are taken from his journal, in which he kept a record of his thoughts and observations of nature. In addition to *Walden*, other notable volumes are *Early Spring in Massachusetts, Summer, Winter, Autumn*, and *Notes on New England Birds*.

THORNTON (*thōrn'tŏn*), **SIR HENRY** (1871–1933). The life of Sir Henry Thornton reads like a chapter out of a story book. Before his death, he became president of the Canadian National Railways, the largest commercial organization in the British Empire. He was born in Logansport, Indiana, and studied at the University of Pennsylvania. He began his railroad career as a draftsman and rose to become general superintendent of the Long Island Railroad in 1911. In 1914, shortly before World War I broke out, this young U.S. citizen was sent for by the Great Eastern Railway, in England,

which was losing money. He became its general manager and put it on a profit-making basis. During World War I he was made a major general in the British Army. He was placed in charge of all railway transportation for the allied forces in Europe. Thornton was knighted for his services by King George V. He also received the medal of the French Legion of Honor and the Distinguished Service Medal of the United States. In 1919 he became a naturalized British subject.

In 1922 Canada was having trouble with its nationally owned railways, which were losing more than $50,000,000 a year. Sir Henry was put in charge at a salary of $50,000 a year. He performed his task so satisfactorily that in seven years he had changed the huge losses of the Canadian National Railways into a large annual profit.

THORWALDSEN (*tôr'wôld sĕn*), **BERTEL** (*bär'tĕl*) (1770–1844). Denmark's great sculptor, Bertel Thorwaldsen, lived at a time when people thought the greatest sculpture was that of the ancient Greeks. Thorwaldsen did not develop a style of his own but imitated the classic sculptors.

He was born near Copenhagen, Denmark. He went to art school and won many prizes. One of these was a scholarship which entitled him to

The "Lion of Lucerne," by Bertel Thorwaldsen, symbolizes the Swiss guards who defended the royal family in the French Revolution. The lion is wounded, his paw still guarding the fleur-de-lis emblem of the Bourbons.

Ewing Galloway

study in Italy, where he did most of his work. The classic marbles which he studied in Rome had great influence on his early work. As a sculptor of bas-relief, Thorwaldsen was the finest of his day.

His "Lion of Lucerne," cut in natural rock, is a memorial to the Swiss Guards who lost their lives defending the Tuileries against the attack of the mob during the French Revolution. Some of his other works are "Jason and the Golden Fleece," "Christ and the Twelve Apostles," "Cupid and Psyche," and the bas-reliefs, "Night" and "Day."

THRASHER (*thrăsh'ẽr*). A distinctively American bird is the thrasher, closely related to the mockingbird and the catbird. Thrashers belong to the order of perchers, and to the family of mimic thrushes, or Mimidae. The name *thrasher* may have been given to them because of their curious habit of switching their tails about when excited or when imitating other birds. The song is delightful.

The brown thrasher (11 inches long) is a bold and powerful bird. He is known for his pleasing song, which is loud and musical.

The brown thrasher, the best-known member of the group, is about 11 inches long. Nearly half of this length consists of the tail, which is rounded at the tip. The wings are short and also rounded. As its name indicates, the bird is brown, with underparts darkly streaked. It is found all over the eastern part of the United States and occasionally as far west as Colorado. It winters in the southern United States. The thrasher likes to build its nest in clumps of vines or thorny hedges. The nest is loosely and carelessly constructed and contains from three to five eggs, varying from pale green to buff and dull white, with minute brownish specks. When the young are hatched the parents carefully guard them. They will not hesitate to attack any intruder, even man, with their strong beaks. It is well for trespassers to be careful.

A distinctively Western species is the sage thrasher, a smaller bird of a grayish brown color which matches the tints of the sand and sage. Its breast is also darkly streaked. It runs rapidly along the ground in search of insects. Its song rings out clear and sweet across the sandy wastes. Other Western species are the California thrasher, LeConte's thrasher, curve-billed thrasher, San Lucas thrasher, Sennett's thrasher, crissal thrasher, and Bendire's thrasher. The California species has a long sickle-shaped beak. It is grayish brown above and below, and does not have the spotted breast. It is about 12 inches long and is bold and independent, like its Eastern cousin. It is also said to be quite as good a mimic as the catbird and the mockingbird.

THREAD (*thrĕd*) **AND THREADMAKING** (*thrĕd'māk'ing*). Until the end of the 18th century, housewives and dressmakers had no spools of thread in their sewing baskets, for ordinary cotton thread was unknown. Each housewife made her thread of linen fibers spun on her own spinning wheel. The improvements in cotton spinning during the 18th century made it possible to spin cotton yarns strong enough for warps. (See SPINNING AND WEAVING.) About 1790 Samuel Slater, an English cotton mill worker who had gone to the United States, built the first cotton mill in North America. His wife

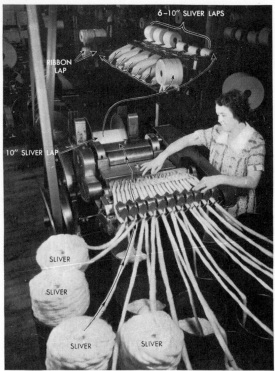

6-10" SLIVER LAPS

RIBBON LAP

10" SLIVER LAP

SLIVER

SLIVER

SLIVER

SLIVER

Courtesy J. & P. Coats Thread Company

Coming from a carding machine, 18 to 22 slivers are combined then drawn out to form a sliver lap about 10 inches wide. Six of these ten-inch sliver laps are shown above being combined and again drawn out into one ribbon lap that is lighter in weight than any one of the original six. This doubling together and drawing out of cotton fibers gives evenness to the finished thread.

is said to have suggested that the new fine cotton yarns be used for sewing thread.

Although thread may also be made of wool, flax, silk, or nylon, by far the most of it is made of cotton. The process of spinning cotton thread is very like the making of cotton yarns for weaving. The best quality of cotton thread is made from long-fibered Sea Island or Egyptian cotton. The matted, closely packed cotton from the bales of cotton is opened, fluffed, and cleaned. It goes into the carding machines, where small wires clean and straighten the fibers. It comes out in the form of soft, flattened ropes of fiber called slivers. These are further straightened and laid parallel by combing. Next a series of drawing frames draws out, doubles, and twists the fibers again and again. Finally, the fine, soft yarn which has been formed, called a roving, is spun into a firm, tightly twisted

strand. Three to six of these strands are twisted together to form a strong, compact thread, which may then be mercerized, bleached, or dyed.

Sometime early in the 19th century it occurred to a thread manufacturer in Scotland to wind the yarn on spools instead of selling it in skeins. The invention of the sewing machine about the middle of the century brought about a great demand for the convenient, smoothly wound spools. In the thread mill the skeins from the dyeing or bleaching vats are wound first on huge bobbins. The spooling machine winds the thread from the bobbins to the spools, automatically cuts the thread when the desired number of yards has been wound, and tucks the end of the thread into a little nick in the rim of the spool.

Threads vary in size from a heavy cord suitable for sewing on the coarsest canvas, to a gossamer-fine strand for dainty hand sewing. The size of the spool generally varies with the size of the thread, from a great spool of heavy cord for a power sewing machine, to a tiny spool of Number 150 cotton, less than an inch in height.

THRUSH (*thrŭsh*). Some of the most famous songbirds belong to the thrush family, or Turdidae. There are about 300 species of this family in the world. Only 14 of the species occur regularly in North America. The young birds of this family, while in the juvenile plumage, have the underparts spotted. Some adults, such as the wood thrush and others, have spotted underparts. Others, such as the robin and bluebird, lose these spots when they molt and have adult plumage. The thrushes are beneficial birds because they eat so many insect pests which they find on the ground or on trees. They feed, too, on spiders and worms. Some are fond of wild berries and other small wild fruits. (See the articles on BLUEBIRD; NIGHTINGALE; ROBIN (AMERICAN) for accounts of three members of the thrush family.)

The wood thrush, also called wood robin, has a clear sweet song, sometimes ending with bell-like notes. Its back is bright cinnamon brown. Its underparts are white, spotted with brownish black. Thickets and woods near water

Sometimes called the "wood robin," the wood thrush is about six inches long. No other American bird has a sweeter song—clear and mellow.

are favorite places. There it builds a mud-walled nest of twigs, moss, or other materials. The eggs are plain greenish blue. The general summer range of the wood thrush is eastern North America. It winters chiefly in Mexico and Central America.

The hermit thrush has been called the American nightingale. But its melody has tones different from the European nightingale's. A name that has been given to the hermit thrush as well as to the wood thrush is swamp angel. Both live in woody swamps. The songs they sing are somewhat similar—enough so that some people find it hard to tell one from the other. Those who recognize both songs are not always agreed as to which is the more beautiful. The hermit thrush, about seven inches long, has a coat that is russet brown above, the underparts being white with dark spots. The nest is usually built in a hummock shaded by ferns, bushes, or an evergreen tree. The three or four eggs are plain greenish blue. During its early spring migration this bird is not too shy to stop to seek food even in city parks. It saves its full glad song for its forest home. It breeds from mountains in Virginia, New Mexico, and California northward over Canada. It winters in

southern United States west to Texas, the southwest, and Mexico.

A bird in the far west has been called "a robin in a different dress," by Edward Howe Forbush, because of its shape and actions. Instead of red, its breast is orange brown, with a broad curved blackish band across its chest. This is the varied thrush, Oregon robin, or Alaska robin. It breeds in spruce forests from Alaska and the MacKenzie Delta in the Arctic Circle to mountains in California. It seeks food in winter in valleys from southern Alaska south to southern California. Its nest is much like that of the eastern robin, but its bluish green eggs are speckled.

Another bird of the deep woods and silent places is the veery, also called the tawny thrush because of its upper coat of tawny brown. It is as timid as the hermit. Although not so well known as a singer, it has a lovely note of its own. Its name *veery* was bestowed in imitation of its oft-repeated call. This is an eastern bird of about the shape and habits of the robin. Its range is from southern Canada to northern Indiana and New Jersey, south in the Alleghenies to northern Georgia. It winters in northern South America. The veery is a little longer than the bluebird and about the same length as the hermit thrush. A western race, the willow-thrush, occurs from southern Canada to Oregon and Iowa, south in mountains to New Mexico. Once found, the nest will have from three to five eggs of a plain greenish blue.

Other American thrushes include Townsend's solitaire, the gray-cheeked thrush, and the olive-backed thrush.

THUCYDIDES (*thū sĭd′ĭ dēz*) (471?–?400 B.C.). The great historian of the Peloponnesian War, Thucydides, actually took part in the war. He was an Athenian of good family. He was said to be descended from a king of Thrace on his mother's side, and also to have owned gold mines and to have had great influence in Thrace. He was stricken with the plague in the second year of the Peloponnesian War and was thus able to give in his history a first-hand account of the great catastrophe.

In 424 B.C. he was commanding a force of

seven ships at Thasos when Brasidas, the Spartan general, took Amphipolis. Because he arrived there too late to save the town, he was banished from Athens. He lived 20 years in exile, writing his history of the Peloponnesian War, and visiting the countries of his former enemies, so that he was able to present all sides of the conflict. The eight books of the history cover the war down to 411 B.C. Thucydides returned to Athens in 404 B.C. and died soon afterward, either there or in Thrace. His work is of great value, both for its impartiality—for which his years of exile were probably responsible—and for its style.

TIBET (*tǐ bět'*), **CHINA,** is a vast region in Central Asia, north of the Himalaya Mountains. Since 1951 it has been part of the People's Republic of China. Because of its high elevation Tibet is often known as "the roof of the world." It is also known as "the Forbidden Land," for its rulers have always tried to keep foreigners out of their country. The area of Tibet is 469,413 square miles, larger than the states of California and Texas put together.

Most of Tibet is a high, cold, windswept plateau, averaging about 16,000 feet above sea level. Along the borders of Tibet are the highest mountains in the world. To the south are the Himalayas, with 29,028 foot Mount Everest on Tibet's border with Nepal. To the west are the Karakorum Mountains, with 28,250 foot Mount Godwin Austen (K-2) just beyond Tibet's border with Kashmir. To the north the high Kun Lun mountains separate the Tibetan plateau from the desert of China's Sinkiang province. To the east, along the border with China, the mountains are cut into narrow ridges and steep-sided valleys. Through these valleys flow some of the largest rivers in Asia: the Brahmaputra, the Salween, the Mekong, the Yangtze, and the Hwang Ho.

The upper Brahmaputra, in southern Tibet, is the most important river. The river valleys form the main farming areas in Tibet. These valleys lie at an elevation of 12,000 feet, much lower than most of the country. Within these southern valleys are three of Tibet's largest cities: Lhasa, the capital (50,000), Shigatse

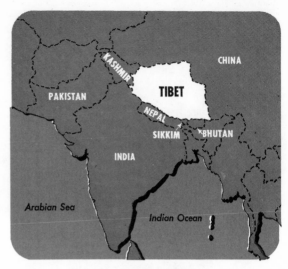

Locator map of Tibet.

(20,000), and Gyangtse (10,000).

Most of Tibet's people live in the Brahmaputra Valley. The vast northern part of the country is a cold, stony desert region known as Chang Tang or Chang Thang. This region is separated from the Brahmaputra Valley by a range of high mountains. Rivers flowing north out of these mountains have no outlet to the sea, but empty into salty lakes.

Because of its high elevation Tibet has a very cold climate. The Himalayas cut off most of the rainfall, leaving the country with little moisture. The Brahmaputra Valley receives about 12 inches of rainfall a year, which is enough for farming. Tibet has two seasons—a slightly moist cool summer and a dry cold winter.

People and Culture

The Tibetan people belong to the Mongolian race. They are short and stocky, with straight black hair, high cheekbones, and narrow eye openings. In their culture the Tibetan people are somewhat like the people of both China and India. The Tibetan language, like the Chinese language, uses single-syllable words. However, the language is written in an Indian script that comes from Sanskrit.

Tibet has a feudal society. Most of the people are peasants who work the land and pay taxes to the nobles. The peasants and nobles live different lives. The peasants wear clothing

Photos by Harrison Forman

(1) Young warriors carrying their rifles. The rifles have two prongs attached which swivel down to form a rifle rest. (2) This six-foot god is carved entirely from colored butter. It is brought out for exhibition on the last day of the "Devil Dance" performance and is illuminated with rows of tiny butter lamps. By dawn the statue melts from the heat of the lamps and the crowds of spectators. (3) These women dress their hair in 108 braids, suggested by the sacred 108 volumes of the "Kanjur." Attached to the ends of the braids is a rectangle of heavy cloth studded with ornaments of silver, gold, coral, turquoise, and other gems.

made of sheepskin. Their food, eaten with the fingers, is barley, meat (mutton or yak), butter, and tea. Their homes are usually small, one-story stone huts, or tents of woven yak hair.

When compared with the peasants, the nobles or landowners live lives of luxury. In dress and manners they imitate the Chinese. They eat Chinese-style food with chopsticks, and wear fancy silk clothing. The houses of the nobles are often several stories high. Even these houses, however, do not have conveniences such as heating or plumbing.

Most of the people of Tibet are either farmers, herders, or traders. Barley is the chief crop, but corn, wheat, peas, beans, and a variety of vegetables are also grown. Methods of cultivating the land are very primitive.

Nomad herders wander from place to place tending flocks of sheep, goats, and yaks. They graze their animals on the plateau for most of the year. In the summer they take their flocks to the colorful fairs in the towns, where the animals are offered for sale. The yak, a shaggy-haired animal like a buffalo, is well-suited to the cold Tibetan plateau. It is used as a beast of burden, and is also useful for its milk, hair, and hide.

Although travel is difficult in mountainous Tibet, a large amount of trading is done. Caravan routes south into India are often used. Hides and gold are traded for Indian cotton, sugar, and metalware. Routes eastward and northward into China are used to carry wool and hides to trade for Chinese silk, tea, and other products. Motor roads built by the Chinese have made travel between Tibet and China easier. India, however, is still connected with Tibet only by steep mountain trails.

Lamaism and Government

Religion is very important in the life of the Tibetan people. The Tibetan religion, a form of Buddhism, is known as Lamaism. Buddhism was brought to Tibet from India in the 7th century A.D. In Tibet Buddhism became mixed with a spirit-worshipping cult known as Bon. Bon includes devil worship, magic, and sacrifice. This addition of spirit-worship gives Tibetan

Buddhism a form unknown elsewhere. However, like other Buddhists, the Tibetans feel that time spent alone in quiet thought is important. Images of Buddha are everywhere.

Monks are the most honored people in Tibet. Usually one boy from every family becomes a monk. The monks live together in monasteries, where they study the Buddhist scriptures. Almost all artistic work in Tibet is done in the monasteries. As a result, most art and literature is of religious subjects.

There are over 3,000 monasteries in Tibet. Each receives contributions from the villagers or herdsmen living nearby. As a result the monasteries are very wealthy. The holiest and most honored of monks are known as lamas.

Tibet has two rulers, both of them religious leaders. One is known as the Dalai (or Chief) Lama, who is regarded by the people as a living god. Tibetans believe that when the old Dalai Lama dies, his soul passes into the body of a newborn baby. The child must be found and identified by a series of signs and religious tests. A peasant boy was selected as the present Dalai Lama in 1940.

The other ruler is known as the Panchen Lama. He is the chief monk in the most important monastery, the Tashilumpo, at Shigatse.

The headquarters of the Dalai Lama is at Lhasa, where the magnificent Potala or palace rises above the city. From all over Tibet pilgrims come to walk around the Potala, the home of the "living god."

History

Tibet was an independent kingdom by the 7th century A.D. The Lamaist form of Buddhism was in practice by the 8th century, and the power of the king passed to the priests. Tibet came under Mongol control in the 13th century. In the 17th century the Grand Lama of Lhasa (the Dalai Lama) became the supreme ruler.

In the 18th and 19th centuries China loosely controlled Tibet through two ambassadors sent to the court of the Dalai Lama. Other foreigners were forbidden to enter the country. In 1904 an armed British expedition gained trading rights with Tibet. In turn Britain officially recognized Chinese control over Tibet.

Keystone View Company

At an elevation of 14,000 feet rises the "Shining Crystal Temple."

The Tibetans declared themselves independent of China in 1912. China did not agree to this but could do little about it. In 1950 the Chinese Communist government sent a military expedition to Tibet, and Tibet became a "national autonomous province." Chinese-built transportation and communication lines connect Lhasa with the Chinese capital at Peiping.

The Chinese were to help out only with Tibet's trade and foreign affairs. Affairs within the country were to be in charge of the Dalai Lama. But the Chinese sent troops and administrators and tried to change the Tibetans to Communists. With their strong traditions of Buddhism, the Tibetans do not want to be changed.

In 1959 Tibetan tribesmen tried to overthrow the Chinese Communists. The attempt was unsuccessful and the Dalai Lama was forced to flee to India. The Panchen Lama, who shared the ideas of the Communists, became Tibet's ruler.

The mountain area along the border of Tibet and India had long been unoccupied territory. In recent years China and India have clashed over lands in the border area.

A Chinese census in 1953 gave the population of Tibet as 1,273,969. Since that time many Chinese settlers have increased the population.

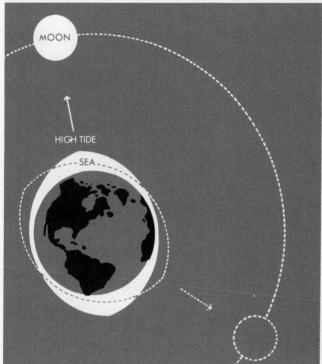

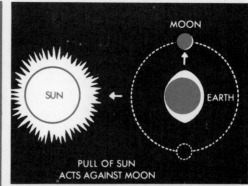

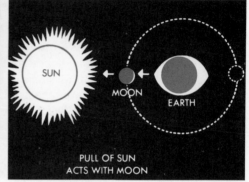

When the moon pulls at the waters of the earth, they pile up on the side toward the moon and on the side away from the moon—where the pull is greatest, and where the pull is least—as in the large drawing. The upper right-hand drawing shows the sun, earth, and moon at neap tide. The lower right-hand drawing shows positions at spring tide.

TIDE (*tīd*) is the regular rise and fall of the level of the seas that takes place twice a day. Tides on earth are caused by the gravitational pull of the moon. This pull of the moon draws the nearest bodies of water toward the moon as a broad swell, or wave. The moon also pulls upon the earth itself, but because the center of the earth is farther away than the forward waters, the pull upon the earth is less than upon the forward waters. Finally, the moon's pull upon the most distant waters is weaker still. The forward waters are pulled away from the earth, and the earth is pulled away from the back waters. The water level, therefore, is high on the side toward the moon, and also on the side opposite. These two heaps, or bulges, of water and the lower level of water between the two heaps remain in about the same position on the earth's surface in relation to the moon.

On an island far from a continent, the water level rises and falls twice daily as the earth turns on its axis. Because of the friction of the water on the ocean bed and because conti-

nents are in the way, the two heaps of water do not quite keep up with the moon as it circles the earth, and, therefore, they are not actually in a direct line from the moon through the earth's center.

If the earth's surface were entirely covered with water, its rotation would cause the two heaps of water, or high tides, to follow each other at regular intervals around the globe. Because the moon also is moving around the earth while the earth rotates, each high tide would come about 12 hours and 26 minutes after the one before it. At a given place, for example, high tide might fall at 1 P.M. and at 1:26 A.M. and 1:52 P.M. of the following day.

The great bulk of the continents, however, interferes with this regular pattern. High tide at a given point, therefore, may come far later than the actual moment when the moon's gravitational attraction is the greatest. Tides occur on lakes, but tidal rise and fall of their waters is small—less than two inches on Lake Michigan, for example.

The sun's gravitational force also affects the

The coastal freighter *Lionel,* beached at low tide (left), is afloat and ready to sail five hours later at high tide (right) in the Bay of Fundy, Nova Scotia.

tides on earth, as is shown in the diagram, but the moon, because it is much closer, has a greater effect. The difference in the power of the moon and that of the sun to form tide is said to be the same as the difference between the numbers 11 and 5. When the sun, moon, and earth are in line, the force of the sun and moon are added $(11 + 5 = 16)$. This makes a very high tide, called spring tide. When the moon is at right angles to the sun, the moon's force pulls against the sun's. The sun's pull then is subtracted from the moon's $(11 - 5 = 6)$. This gives an unusually low tide, called neap tide. Spring tides occur at full and new moon, and neap tides occur when the moon is at its first and third quarters. The moon's pull is greatest when it is nearest the earth.

The difference between high tide and low tide varies greatly. In most of the Mediterranean Sea and in the central Pacific Ocean, the water rises only one or two feet. On coasts that are gently sloping and straight, the incoming tide has room to spread and may not rise very high. Where the incoming tide enters a narrow bay or channel, it cannot spread, and the water may pile up to greater heights. The highest known tides occur in the Bay of Fundy, on the Atlantic coast of Canada. At the narrow head of the bay, the average height of high tide above low tide is more than 40 feet, and at extreme spring tide, the difference may even exceed 70 feet.

Where a river empties into a funnel-shaped bay, the high tide may sweep up the river as a wall of water several feet high, called a bore. Such bores occur on the Severn and Trent rivers in England and the Seine River in France. In a small river near Shanghai, China, the bore is normally 12 feet high. At spring tide it may be as much as 25 feet high.

Ocean tides offer a great source of unused energy. This energy possibly could be put to work as the energy from many waterfalls and rivers is. If a large bay could be dammed so that it did not empty at low tide, the water then could be turned into electric power by directing it through power plants. So far, this has been done only on a small scale. A project of this type was begun at Passamaquoddy, Maine, in 1935, but the necessary dams never were completed.

TIENTSIN (*tĭn'tsĭn'*), **CHINA,** a leading port and industrial center, is the capital of Hopeh Province. The city is located in northeastern China at the point where the Grand Canal and several rivers come together to form the Hai River. Tientsin is about 30 miles inland from the Gulf of Chihli (Po Hai) and about 70 miles southeast of Peiping (Peking). The average annual temperature of the Tientsin area is 52 degrees Fahrenheit. The annual rainfall averages about 20 inches.

Tientsin is in China's third largest industrial

region. A number of heavy industries are located within the city. Iron and steel are leading products. Chemicals, cement, electrical supplies, textiles, and food products also are important. The Grand Canal links the city with the Hwang and the Yangtze rivers, providing excellent water connections for trade and commerce. The rivers that meet in the area, however, present a problem to Tientsin because of frequent flooding. The waterways continually are dredged of silt that is brought down by the rivers, and icebreakers are used to free the port of ice during the cold months. Tientsin is connected with other cities of northern China's industrial areas by railway.

For centuries Tientsin was a military and commercial town. It was opened to foreign trade in 1860, after the second Opium War between China and Great Britain and France. Much of the city was severely damaged twice by war, once during the Boxer Uprising in 1900 and again during a war between Japan and China in 1937. The city has since been rebuilt.

In 1949, during the civil war in China, the Communists captured the city from the Nationalist Chinese forces. Tientsin was an independent municipality governed directly from Peiping, the national capital, until 1958. In that year it was included in Hopeh Province.

The city is the site of Nankai University, Hopeh University, and Tientsin University.

The population of Tientsin is 3,220,000 (1957).

TIGER (tī′gĕr) (*Panthera tigris*) is the largest and most powerful member of the cat family. Adult male tigers have been known to reach a length of more than 10 feet and a weight of 500 pounds. Females usually are smaller, averaging about 8½ feet long and 300 pounds in weight. The only other great cat that approaches this size is the lion. In fact, lions and tigers are similar in structure. The main differences are in their skulls and markings. Tigers do not have true manes, although the fur around their faces often grows quite long.

Tigers vary in size and coloring according to the region in which they live. The Siberian tiger is the largest. Its fur is thick and long, its stripes are pale, and its background color is light yellowish-brown. Tigers of warmer areas have shorter fur. They are more richly colored and are somewhat smaller. The background color of the Indian tiger is reddish-brown and its stripes are dark and distinct. The fur in the ears and around the face is nearly white in color. The underparts are light-colored. The coloring and markings of the Indian tiger blend well with its surroundings of tall grass or shadowy forest. The lighter coloring of the northern tiger is more suitable for concealment in dry, treeless, and snowy areas. Some all-white, or albino, tigers have been found, as well as white ones with black stripes. These are not common, however.

Tigers are found only in Asia. They range from the islands of Java, Bali, and Sumatra through India, Malaya, and China, and as far north as southeastern Siberia. They are not found in Ceylon, Borneo, or the plateau of central Asia. It is believed that they were originally animals of the far north or Arctic regions.

Tigers are strictly meat eaters. Their diets vary according to their surroundings. The tigers of the southern jungles feed on small elephants, crocodiles, and wild pigs, among other things. The cats living in regions of tall grass eat buffaloes, antelopes, and the rodents that live there. Tigers of the north prey on caribou, rabbits, and other available mammals, birds, or fish. Sometimes, when a tiger becomes crippled or too old to hunt wild animals, it will raid herds of domestic cattle. At other times, man himself becomes the victim. Usually, however, tigers are timid and avoid man as much as possible. The big cats often hunt in pairs. One will drive the game toward the other, which then kills it. They kill their prey by leaping on it and sinking their teeth into its throat or breaking its neck or back with a wrench of powerful forelegs.

Tigers have been known to jump long distances but are poor climbers. In an emergency they usually can manage to climb a tree, however. Man has learned that, when hunting a tiger, the safest place to be is high in a tree or on the back of a tall elephant. Man is the tiger's worst enemy, although packs of wild, doglike animals called dholes have been known to worry or starve the big cats to death.

Tigers are among the few cats that truly can roar. This ability is due to the presence of certain small bones embedded in the base of the tongue. Lions and leopards also have this characteristic. Tigers, unlike many cats, are excellent swimmers.

The average number of cubs born to a female tiger is three. They stay with the mother for more than a year, until they are nearly full-grown. Lions and tigers have been known to crossbreed in zoos, producing young that are known as "ligers" or "tigons." (For illustration see CAT, Plate 2.)

TIME (*tīm*), according to Sir Isaac Newton, is that which flows uniformly onward. It is hard to define it in simpler terms. Each of us has a feeling for duration, for a succession of happenings that take place in time and space. With practice we can judge time intervals. Our estimate of time, however, is not reliable. Great events often happen quickly, but in memory they seem to be stretched out. On the other hand, a summer may seem to last forever. Later, when we think back on it, the entire summer seems to have covered a very short time.

We often divide time into past, present, and future. Astronomy and geology examine the distant past of the universe and of the earth. History and archaeology deal with the past of the human race. The exact placement of events in the calendar of the past is called chronology, after the Greek god of time, Chronos.

Throughout history, man has used many periodic events to measure time. These things include the daily passage of the sun or the stars across the sky, the return of the full moon every 29.5 days, and the repeating of the seasons year after year. North American Indians measured time by "moons" and "snows." Many ancient people devised calendars based on the passage of days and of the seasons. Man now measures time by many units. He uses years, months, weeks, days, hours, minutes, and seconds.

To arrive at more exact measurements than ancient man used, the astronomer observes the passage of the sun or stars across a meridian

plane. The meridian plane is an imaginary plane running north and south and extending into the sky directly over the observer. The astronomer measures the time from one passage of the sun or the stars over a selected meridian plane to the next passage. The sun appears over the meridian at the time called noon. The observer's shadow is shorter at this moment than at any other time of day.

Sun and Star Days

Sun days, from noon to noon, vary in length by as much as 51 seconds. The average sun day is called the mean solar day. (See DAY.) Clocks are adjusted to the mean solar day, which is divided into 24 equal hours of 60 minutes each. Each minute is further divided into 60 seconds. This makes 1,440 minutes or 86,400 seconds in a 24-hour day. The time from one passage of a star over the meridian to its next passage is called the sidereal (or star) day. Star days are all almost exactly of the same length. They depend only upon the steady turning of the earth. Each day any one star returns to the meridian nearly four minutes earlier than the day before, as shown by our clocks. Thus, star days are 3 minutes 56 seconds shorter than the mean solar day.

Astronomers wondered whether the turning of the earth was truly steady through the centuries. A system to detect any changes was worked out. By studying eclipses of the sun reported in early times and by computing them, scientists have discovered a very slow retardation of the earth's motion. This is measured as an increase in the length of the day by perhaps one-hundredth of a second in a century. Minor changes in the earth's rotation are observed by checking the rotation with atomic clocks, which have remarkable regularity. Rotating molecules, instead of the rotating earth, are used to pace the atomic clocks.

The measurement of distances and speeds by modern methods has shown the second of time to be extremely long. In radar and other uses of electronics, even a millionth of a second, called a microsecond, is a long interval. It is presently common to measure time down to fractions of a *nanosecond*, or one-billionth of a second. In one nanosecond, light travels only one foot. Radio oscillators can be built to make electric currents vibrate as many as one million-million times per second. Atoms emit light that vibrates at rates in the range of one thousand-million-millions per second.

Standard Time

A man living by himself might forget clocks and regulate his activities by sunlight. Rural people, for example, often work from sunup to sundown. The development of civilization, however, has required accurate timekeeping around the world. Trains, airplanes, and radio and television programs are scheduled by clocks that now have an agreement scarcely dreamed of 50 years ago. Electric clocks, driven by distant generators, keep millions of homes and offices in agreement. Their clock motors keep pace with the massive generators that rotate at steady speed to supply electrical systems. The turning of the generators is checked frequently against the turning of the earth. The earth's rotation is watched by the United States Naval Observatory and by the national observatories of other countries. Radio time signals are sent out to help people in all parts of the world and on ships at sea check their clocks. Yet, clocks are comparatively recent in our history. Three or four hundred years ago only noblemen could afford pocket watches, and the steeple clock

was the community timepiece. (See Clock and Watch.)

Because of the rotation of the earth toward the east, the place where the sun is directly on the meridian (local noon) advances westward at the rate of 15 degrees per hour. Every town has its own local noon. To assure agreement over wide areas, the world has been divided arbitrarily into 24 standard time zones. They often are marked on maps.

Less than a century ago, no agreement on timekeeping existed among the countries of the world. Many kinds of local time were kept. An international conference in 1884 in Washington, D.C., set the present standard time zones. These zones on the earth's surface are about 15 degrees wide and usually differ from the next zone by one hour of time. The zero-degree meridian of longitude passes through Greenwich, England. Thus, Philadelphia near 75 degrees west longitude is five clock hours earlier than Greenwich. St. Louis at 90 degrees west is six clock hours earlier; Denver at 105 degrees west is seven hours earlier; and Los Angeles near 120 degrees west is eight hours earlier.

To say it another way, the sun appears to cross the Denver meridian just seven hours after it crosses the Greenwich meridian. The selection of the zero-degree meridian places the 180-degree meridian, or International Date Line, in the middle of the Pacific Ocean where few persons are affected.

The International Date Line

With the world divided into zones of 15 degrees each, there are 24 zones of one hour each, as we have seen. This also means that only at one instant each day does the whole world have the same day. This is the moment when it is noon in London and midnight at the Date Line. At all other times, it is necessary to consider a change of one day on the two sides of the Date Line.

Suppose an astronaut is launched eastward from Cape Kennedy, Florida, just before sunrise at 5 o'clock on Monday morning, to orbit the earth once every two hours. In only a little more than half an hour, he will see the sun on his meridian and call it noon. About an hour

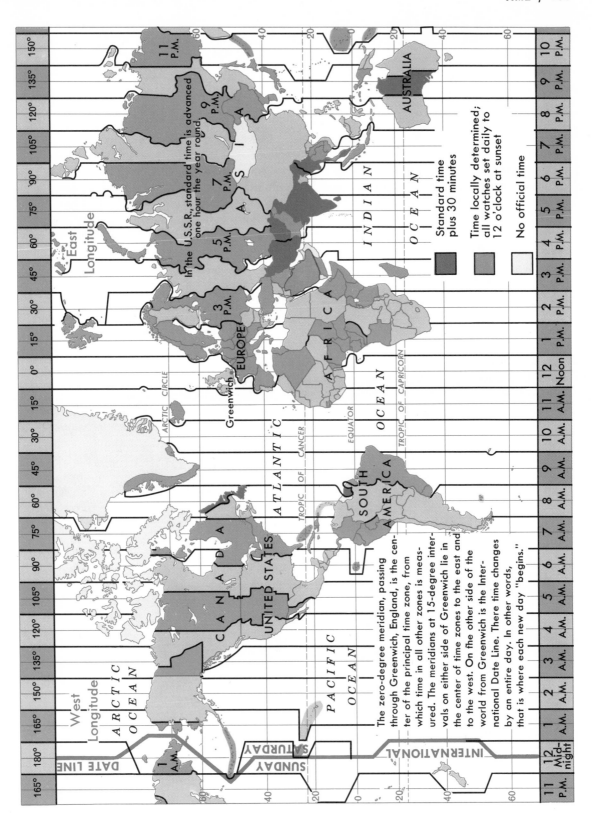

The zero-degree meridian, passing through Greenwich, England, is the center of the principal time zone, from which time in all other zones is measured. The meridians at 15-degree intervals on either side of Greenwich lie in the center of time zones to the east and to the west. On the other side of the world from Greenwich is the International Date Line. There time changes by an entire day. In other words, that is where each new day "begins."

In the U.S.S.R., standard time is advanced one hour the year round.

Standard time plus 30 minutes

Time locally determined; all watches set daily to 12 o'clock at sunset

No official time

after he is launched, he will see the sun set rapidly in the Indian Ocean behind him. Before an hour and a half has elapsed he will reach the Date Line. He is now in Sunday. Soon he will reach the point over the Pacific Ocean where it is midnight, and he will pass back into Monday. As he flies over western United States near the end of his first orbit, he sees the sun rise to the east of him.

On his second orbit the midnight line will have passed the Date Line. Sunday will have gone off the earth. Tuesday will have begun west of the Date Line. The astronaut will then be flying from Monday into Tuesday over the Pacific Ocean and back into Monday at the Date Line. An airplane flying westward from Honolulu to Japan in broad daylight would fly from today into tomorrow at the Date Line.

As we have seen, the world has the same day only when it is noon in London and midnight at the Date Line. Suppose that day is Monday. The midnight line advances westward 15 degrees every hour. As it sweeps Monday ahead of it, Tuesday advances behind it. Twelve hours from the time it leaves the Date Line, it will be midnight in London. Now, the world has half-Monday and half-Tuesday: Monday still lies westward from London across America to mid-Pacific, and Tuesday lies eastward across Asia. In another 12 hours, Monday

will be "swept off the earth" against the east side of the Date Line, and the day immediately following it on the west side of the line will be Wednesday, not Tuesday. Tuesday is already there, wrapped completely around the earth.

Equation of Time

The apparent daily motion of the sun around the earth is caused by the rotation of the earth on its axis. It also is affected by its revolution around the sun. This motion is somewhat irregular. There are two chief reasons for the difference between a steadily running clock and the sun. First, the earth does not move at steady speed in its orbit around the sun; it moves fastest when it is nearest to the sun, in January, and slowest when it is farthest from the sun, in July. Second, the axis of the earth is tilted $23\frac{1}{2}$ degrees from an upright drawn at right angles to its orbit. This tilt is what causes our seasons, as the global dial shows. The sun appears to go $23\frac{1}{2}$ degrees south of the Equator in December, and $23\frac{1}{2}$ degrees north of the Equator in June. (See ROTATION AND REVOLUTION.)

Because of the variations in sun time, a well-regulated clock in a town at the center of a zone may run as much as 16 minutes early, or "ahead of the sun," in early November. It may be as much as 14 minutes late, or "behind the sun," in mid-February. For this reason, the reading of a sundial that is not corrected for the equation of time may be as much as 16 minutes off, even at the center of a time zone. It is possible, however, by making adjustments for these variations, to make a sundial correct to within a few seconds at any time of the year.

Daylight-Saving Time

It becomes clear from watching a globe sundial that, wherever it is summer, every day has more than 12 hours of sunlight. As spring advances, the sun rises earlier and sets later. Many city dwellers like to start the workday earlier and enjoy a longer evening before dark. Daylight-saving time has been established by law in many areas. (See DAYLIGHT-SAVING TIME.) In these places, clocks are set forward one hour in the spring and back again in the fall of the year. The dates for these changes also

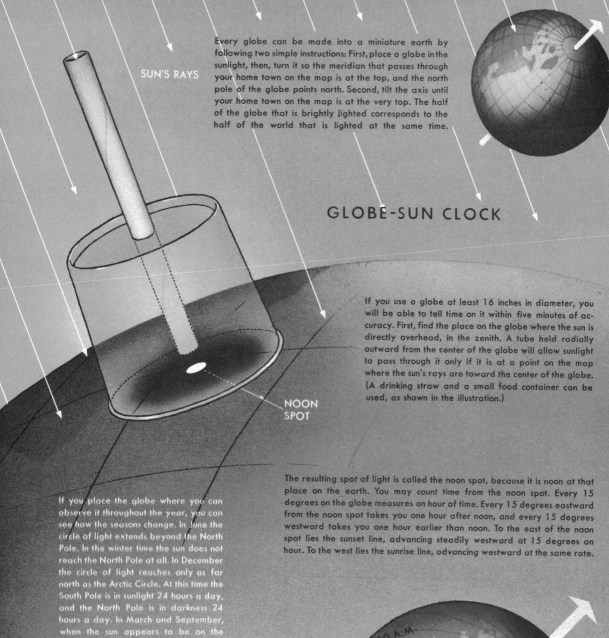

SUN'S RAYS

Every globe can be made into a miniature earth by following two simple instructions: First, place a globe in the sunlight, then, turn it so the meridian that passes through your home town on the map is at the top, and the north pole of the globe points north. Second, tilt the axis until your home town on the map is at the very top. The half of the globe that is brightly lighted corresponds to the half of the world that is lighted at the same time.

GLOBE-SUN CLOCK

If you use a globe at least 16 inches in diameter, you will be able to tell time on it within five minutes of accuracy. First, find the place on the globe where the sun is directly overhead, in the zenith. A tube held radially outward from the center of the globe will allow sunlight to pass through it only if it is at a point on the map where the sun's rays are toward the center of the globe. (A drinking straw and a small food container can be used, as shown in the illustration.)

NOON
SPOT

The resulting spot of light is called the noon spot, because it is noon at that place on the earth. You may count time from the noon spot. Every 15 degrees on the globe measures an hour of time. Every 15 degrees eastward from the noon spot takes you one hour after noon, and every 15 degrees westward takes you one hour earlier than noon. To the east of the noon spot lies the sunset line, advancing steadily westward at 15 degrees an hour. To the west lies the sunrise line, advancing westward at the same rate.

If you place the globe where you can observe it throughout the year, you can see how the seasons change. In June the circle of light extends beyond the North Pole. In the winter time the sun does not reach the North Pole at all. In December the circle of light reaches only as far north as the Arctic Circle. At this time the South Pole is in sunlight 24 hours a day, and the North Pole is in darkness 24 hours a day. In March and September, when the sun appears to be on the celestial equator, there are equinoxes, or equal days and nights, everywhere on earth. You can see why this is: the circle of light and dark runs directly over the two poles of the earth, and every place on the earth has 12 hours of daylight and 12 hours of darkness. Two things make this simple dial work. First, the sun is so far away that its light falls on earth (and on the globe) in very close to parallel rays. Thus, the globe is lighted exactly as the earth is lighted. Second, as the earth turns, the globe turns with it, on an axis parallel to the earth's axis.

NOON
SPOT

10 A.M.

11 A.M.

12 NOON

1 P.M.

2 P.M.

3 P.M.

4 P.M.

5 P.M.

CHICAGO

NEW YORK

LONDON

are set locally, by law. Thus, if you lived where the sun is on the meridian at 12 o'clock civil time during the winter, you would find, under daylight-saving time, that the sun does not reach the meridian until the clock reads 1 o'clock. Nature provides sunlight; man sets the clock to suit his needs and desires. Standard time is one such arbitrary regulation. Daylight saving is another.

(See EQUINOX AND SOLSTICE.)

TIMOR (tē'môr or tē môr'), **EAST INDIES,** is the easternmost of the Sunda Islands. Australia lies to the southeast, New Guinea to the northeast, and Java to the west of it. Western Timor belongs to Indonesia. (See INDONESIA.) The eastern part and the small territory of Oe-Cusse in western Timor and several nearby islands are under Portuguese rule. (See PORTUGUESE OVERSEAS PROVINCES.) The area of Indonesian Timor is 6,120 square miles. The area of Portuguese Timor is 5,763 square miles.

Locator map of Timor.

The island is 294 miles long and is 66 miles across at its widest point. Much of it is hilly or mountainous, and it is cut by deep valleys. The climate is always warm. There is a short rainy season, from January to March, when rainfall ranges from 30 inches on the northern coast to 100 inches in the southwest. During the remainder of the year, it usually is dry. Sandalwood, coconut, and eucalyptus trees grow throughout the island. Animal life includes monkeys, deer, wild pigs, civets, bats and a particular species of wildcat.

The people of Timor are of mixed origin. The main stock is Papuan, mixed with Indonesian and Malayan. Most of the natives have brown skin, black hair, and dark eyes. They speak many languages and dialects and lead primitive lives. Their houses are round in shape, are built of wood, and have roofs thatched with grass or palm leaves.

Most of these people live in villages along the coastal lowlands. They fish, hunt, gather coconuts, and grow rice and corn. Coconut products, sandalwood, hides, cotton, coffee, wool, and pearls are the chief exports.

The main cities of Timor are Kupang and Dili. Kupang, the capital of Indonesian Timor, is the chief port of the island. It is near the southwestern tip of the island. Dili, the capital of Portuguese Timor, is on the northern coast.

In about 1520 the Portuguese came to Timor to trade for sandalwood. The Dutch arrived at the beginning of the 17th century. The border between Dutch and Portuguese territory was disputed for many years. The present boundary finally was set in 1914. During World War II, the island was held by the Japanese. Shortly after the war, western Timor became a part of Indonesia, but eastern Timor remains an overseas province of Portugal.

The population of Indonesian Timor is 822,-915 (1956 est.). The population of Portuguese Timor is 517,079 (1960).

TIN (tĭn) is a soft, silvery-white metal, and one of the earliest elements known to man. Its chemical symbol, Sn, comes from *stannum*, the Latin name for tin. The atomic number of tin is 50, and its atomic weight is 118.69. Tin does not readily corrode or tarnish in air and is resistant to the weak acids of foods. It forms alloys with most of the other metals. Its properties make it an extremely useful metal, especially in the packaging of foods. Small amounts of tin occur naturally, but the bulk of the world's supply comes from the extraction of tin from its principal ore, cassiterite, composed of tin dioxide.

Tin was used as early as 1000 B.C. by the Phoenicians. These people sailed through the Strait of Gibraltar to islands, probably the southern part of England, that they called the Cassiterides, or Tin Islands. It was their word that furnished the name for the important tin ore, cassiterite. Devon and Cornwall, in the southern part of England, continued, for many centuries, to be the best-known source of tin. These deposits are now nearly exhausted, and other regions are the major suppliers. More

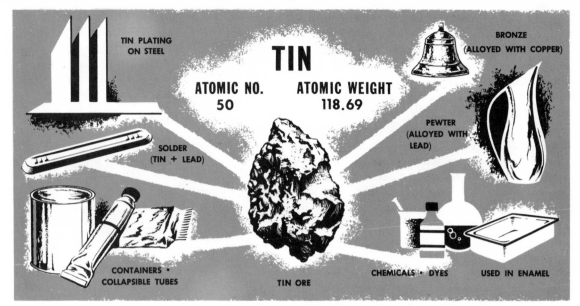

TIN PLATING ON STEEL

TIN

ATOMIC NO. 50

ATOMIC WEIGHT 118.69

BRONZE (ALLOYED WITH COPPER)

SOLDER (TIN + LEAD)

PEWTER (ALLOYED WITH LEAD)

CONTAINERS · COLLAPSIBLE TUBES

TIN ORE

CHEMICALS · DYES

USED IN ENAMEL

than 30 percent of the world production of tin comes from the Federation of Malaysia. Other major producers are China, Bolivia, the U.S.S.R., Thailand, Indonesia, and Democratic Republic of Congo. The amount of tin produced in the world is regulated by international agreement. Tin is not found in valuable quantities in the United States, which imports and uses more tin than any other country in the world.

How Tin Is Processed

Cassiterite occurs and is mined in two forms: primary deposits, which occur as veins, or lodes; and secondary, alluvial, or placer deposits, which are left by water.

After the ore is mined it is crushed, and the lighter particles of sand and clay are washed away, leaving behind the heavier particles of cassiterite. This is necessary as the methods of purification are not very efficient, and the purer the ore delivered to the smelter, the purer the final product will be. The cleaned ore is mixed with coke and limestone or sand and heated in a blast furnace. From the bottom of the blast furnace a crude metallic tin is separated. This crude tin is then refined by either of two processes. In the fire-refining process, the tin is melted in large kettles, into which poles of green wood are thrust. The green wood produces gases that cause a violent boiling, bring-

ing the metal to the surface, where the oxygen in the air can act on the impurities. The film of oxides that forms is removed by skimming, and relatively pure tin remains. In the electrical refining process the metal is dissolved and deposited as pure tin by an electric current. Some tin is recovered through the processing of old tin cans and other tin scrap.

How Tin Is Used

Tin, because it resists corrosion, is used to protect other metals from the action of air. The familiar tin can consists of a sheet of iron with a thin coating of tin on each side. The tin prevents rusting of the iron. Tin also resists weak acids, which makes the cans ideal containers for food. Nearly 90 percent of the tinplate produced in the United States is used in the manufacture of tin cans.

A large proportion of the tin produced is mixed with copper to form bronze, an important alloy. Mixed with lead, tin forms solder, which is used in joining other metals. The lead-tin alloy is rolled out to form tin foil, a thin metal sheet used for wrapping food products and for making collapsible containers for such materials as toothpaste. The compound of tin and chlorine, tin chloride, is used in the textile industry for printing calico and for weighting silk. (See ALLOY.)

TINTORETTO (*tĭn'tō rĕt'ō* or *tēn'tō rāt'tō*) (JACOPO [*yä'kō pō*] ROBUSTI [*rō bŏŏs'tĕ*]) (1518–1594), the last great artist of the Renaissance, was born in Venice, Italy. He was nicknamed Tintoretto, which means little dyer, because his father was a dyer or *tintore*. He is known for his great energy, and original and daring composition. As a boy he drew charcoal figures on the wall and colored them with his father's dyes. He practically taught himself how to paint by studying anatomy and copying masterpieces. On the wall of his studio was his motto and aim: "The drawing of Michelangelo and the coloring of Titian."

Tintoretto did many paintings for small churches and convents in Venice. He refused no request, however small, as long as he was allowed to paint. Soon people recognized his ability, particularly in the painting of light and shadows. He was so anxious to paint that he did two huge canvases without any charge; "The Last Judgment," which is one of the largest oil paintings in the world, and "The Worship of the Golden Calf."

The last important picture by Tintoretto was the huge "Paradise," 75 x 30 feet, one of the finest things ever done. It is so highly imaginative and so rich in color that it is unique among paintings. His masterpiece "The Miracle of St. Mark" is 20 feet square, containing 25 large figures. It is known for its brilliant light and color, dash, and sense of motion. Others are "The Martyrdom of St. Agnes," the "Annunciation," "Marriage at Cana," and the "Crucifixion."

(See Plate 5 with the article PAINTING for an illustration of his work.)

TIROL (*tĭ rōl'* or *tĭr'ōl*), **AUSTRIA,** is one of the Austrian federal states. To the west of it are Switzerland and the Austrian state of Vorarlberg, to the north is Germany, to the south Italy, and to the east two other Austrian states, Salzburg and Carinthia. Most of Tirol is in the great mountain system of the Alps. The highest peaks, in the south along the Swiss and Italian borders, rise to nearly 13,000 feet.

The tourist trade is one of the most important sources of income in Tirol. The beautiful scenery of the Alps attracts many tourists. Also

Locator map of the Tirol region of Austria.

outdoor sports such as skiing, tobogganing, ice skating, swimming and fishing are popular. Other sources of income are milk, cheese, timber, salt, and silver.

Because Tirol is mostly mountain country, there is very little level land for farming. However, there are good pastures on the mountainsides where large herds of cattle graze. Besides lumbering, dairying, and industry, woodworking, spinning, and weaving are very popular in Tirolean villages.

The folk dress of Tirol is well known. In summer men and boys wear shorts made of deerskin; the women dress in embroidered shirtwaists and dirndl skirts. On holidays the men wear dark suits with silver buttons, white handmade socks, and broad-brimmed velvet hats; the women wear velvet skirts, white bodices, embroidered aprons, and gold pins and lockets.

The rivers of Tirol are used to drive great electric turbines and provide electric power. All of the railroads are run by electricity, and some electric power is sent to the rest of Austria, to Germany, and to Italy.

The main river is the Inn. It crosses the state from Switzerland in the southwest to Germany in the northeast. The valley of the Inn is an excellent route across Tirol. The capital city of the state is Innsbruck. It has grown where the Inn River valley meets the route leading to the Brenner Pass. The Brenner Pass is one of the easiest ways across the Alps from Italy to Germany.

During its history Tirol has had many rulers. Nearly the entire period from the 14th century until after World War I (except for a short period when it was under Bavarian rule, 1805–1814) Tirol was a part of the Hapsburg Empire.

In 1919 the part of Tirol south of the Brenner Pass became Italian territory.

The population is 427,000 and the area is 4,883 square miles.

James Sawders

The little valley town is Landeck on the Inn River in the Austrian province of Tirol.

TITANS (*tī'tănz*), **THE.** To Uranus (Heaven) and Ge (or Terra) (Earth) were born 12 giant children, 6 sons and 6 daughters. They were called the Titans. The six sons were Oceanus, Cocus, Crius, Hyperion, Iapetus, and Cronus. The six daughters were Thea, Rhea, Themis, Mnemosyne, Phoebe, and Tethys. Their father, Uranus, fearing their great strength, chained them in the dark Gulf of Tartarus, below the underworld. Their mother, however, released Cronus (Saturn), the youngest, who killed his father and freed his brothers and sisters.

The children then intermarried, and under the rule of Cronus and his wife, Rhea, lived for a long golden age. But Cronus in turn was deposed by his son Zeus (Jupiter). All the Titans joined the father in giving battle to Zeus and the gods of Olympus. Zeus took as his allies his brothers and sisters, the one-eyed Cyclopes, forgers of lightning, and the Hecatoncheires, hundred-handed monsters of the earthquake. Prometheus, one of the sons of Iapetus, also joined with Zeus in the great battle.

The Titans were beaten and again thrown into Tartarus. Atlas, son of the Titan Iapetus, was condemned to bear the heavens on his shoulders. Thousands of years later the Titans were released and dwelt under Cronus in the Islands of the Blest.

TITIAN (*tĭsh'ăn*) (1477?–1576). The greatest colorist of the Venetian school of painting and consequently of the world was Titian. His real name was Tiziano Vecellio. He was born of a noble family at Pieve di Cadore, Friuli, in the Venetian Alps. At the age of ten he made a picture of the Madonna and colored it with natural dyes extracted from flowers. His father was greatly impressed. He sent him off at once to study in Venice with Giovanni Bellini and Sebastiano Zuccati, leading painters of the day. Titian's first work was to decorate the exteriors of buildings with frescoes. He soon established himself as an artist of the first rank.

Not only did Titian work on the Ducal Palace in Venice, but he also painted in Ferrara, Mantua, Augsburg, Milan, Rome, and Bologna. Dukes, kings, emperors, and popes were his friends and employers, and noted artists were his companions.

Titian had a splendid constitution and remarkable energy. Not even in the last years of

"Man with a Glove," by Titian.

Gramstorff Bros.

his long life did his work show any sign of feebleness. He lived in luxury, entertaining and being entertained, loving music, food, all pleasures, and surrounded by beauty, taste, and culture. He died of a plague which swept Venice. All the churches were closed against victims of the plague, yet Titian was given a gorgeous public funeral. By a special ruling he was buried in the Church of Santa Maria de Frari, which he had adorned with his marvelous art.

Titian was sure of his talents. He did nothing in a hurry and would work patiently on each picture until it was perfect. Often he would put in the finishing touches with his fingers instead of with a brush. He used whatever added to his art. He believed that art should not be extreme in composition or thought. Though his work shows deep feeling, it never disturbs nor is violent. He was a healthy man, and his art was healthy. There are many who excelled him in one particular quality, but on the whole he combined more fine qualities than any painter who has ever lived. He was the complete artist, uniting grace and elegance with force, and delicacy with strength. His color was rich but never glaring. His faces are so alive that they look out from their frames. They seem to be those of pleasant people, whom one would choose as friends.

The "Assumption of the Madonna" is one of the greatest pictures ever painted. The "Man with a Glove" is one of the best portraits. The "Entombment," with its rich color and strength of feeling, is perhaps the world's most masterly picture. Others of his masterpieces are "Madonna with the Cherries," "Madonna of the Pesaro Family," and "Madonna with Four Saints," "Christ Crowned with Thorns," "Jupiter and Antiope," "Sacred and Profane Love," "Bacchus and Ariadne," "Perseus and Andromeda," and portraits of his daughter and of Francis I. The Metropolitan Museum of Art in New York City has his "Portrait of a Gentleman."

TITMOUSE (*tit′mous*). Among the smallest and daintiest of North American birds are the titmice, little fellows ranging from four to six inches. Every one of those inches is full of energy and usefulness.

What the bird lacks in size it makes up in appetite. Its keen little eyes find the tiny insects and their eggs which larger birds would pass by.

The titmouse belongs to the great order of perching birds.

The titmouse family includes such common North American birds as the titmouse, the bush tit, the verdin, and the chickadee. There are

The tufted titmouse (about six inches) has a great deal of curiosity and little fear of man.

about 65 species in the family. They are found in various parts of Europe, Asia, Africa, and North America. (See CHICKADEE.)

The tufted titmouse is one of the best-known species of its tribe. It is also called the crested tomtit, from its crest, which rises to a sharp point. Its beak is short and stout. Its color is a slaty gray above. The underparts are paler with a patch of dull red below. Its tail is fairly long and narrow. This bird is widely distributed over the eastern part of the United States and has little fear of man. One observer says that a female titmouse flew in the window and all over the room as if to see everything that was in it. A hanging basket near the window caught its fancy. Deciding that this was a good place to stay, it moved in and built its nest. Ordinarily this bird builds in the hole of a tree or stump. The eggs vary from four to eight and are white, marked with brown.

Others bearing the same family name are the black-crested titmouse and the bridled titmouse. The former is a bird of Texas and Mexico, of the same size and shape as the tufted titmouse, but with a sharply defined black topknot. The crest of the bridled species is black with a large patch of gray. The curious markings around its throat have given rise to its name. It is found chiefly in Arizona and New Mexico. The bush tit, only a trifle over four inches long, has no crest. It builds a remarkable home out of moss, lichens, and fibers—a long, gourd-shaped structure with a hole at the top which leads down into cleverly constructed rooms. In one of these is the nest with from four to seven tiny, pure-white eggs. This species is found from British Columbia to California, western Texas, and Central America.

The verdin, a near relative with a yellow head and often called the yellow-headed bush tit, is not much larger. It is found in southwestern thorny deserts from southern California, southwestern Utah, and central Texas south into northern Mexico. Its nest, similar to that of the bush tit, is a round structure with a hole on one side. The eggs are bluish- or greenish-white. Verdins do not abandon the nest after the young are hatched. The home is kept clean and the birds often live in it the year round.

TOBACCO (*tō băk'ō*). It was a strange story the monk told when he returned to Spain. He had been with an exploring party that went ashore in the new world Christopher Columbus had discovered. The party had met, he said, some natives who held long wooden tubes. These tubes branched at one end to fit into the nostrils. The other end was held in the smoke of smouldering leaves. Thus the smoke was inhaled through the nose.

The natives called the tube a *tobacco*. From this came the name which is applied to the plant. Natives also rolled the dried leaves of the tobacco in corn husks and inhaled the smoke through their mouths. These were the first cigars and cigarettes of which there is any record.

Within about 100 years people in western Europe were smoking tobacco. The habit spread to Turkey, Arabia, and finally to China, Japan, and India. Now tobacco is used in almost every nation or large community.

Where and How Tobacco Is Grown

With use of the plant the growing of tobacco spread until it is now grown in almost all countries. The United States leads the world in production. Practically all of that raised in the United States is grown in the eastern half of the country.

According to type, main areas of tobacco production in the United States are: (1) flue-cured, in southern Virginia, North and South Carolina, Georgia, and Florida; (2) fire-cured, in Virginia and in part of Kentucky; (3) air-cured, including the Burley, in western North Carolina, Tennessee, and Kentucky, the Virginia sun-cured, and the Maryland broadleaf; (4) cigar-filler types in Pennsylvania and parts of Georgia and Florida; (5) cigar-binder types in the Connecticut Valley, Pennsylvania, and Wisconsin; and (6) cigar-wrapper types in the Connecticut Valley and in parts of Georgia and Florida. These type names refer to the method of curing or to the purpose for which it is used.

The size of the tobacco plant varies. Some of the foreign varieties, especially those of Turkey, Arabia, Greece, and India, do not grow so large as those grown in the United States. To-

(1) Gathering leaf tobacco in Connecticut. (2) Planting tobacco plants in rows under muslin. (3) A field of healthy tobacco plants. (4) Tobacco leaves hung in sheds (over charcoal fires) for curing.

Courtesy (1) Connecticut Development Commission; Photos (2, 4) Russell S. Anderson, (3) Caufield & Shook

bacco plants in the United States are usually about as high as the average man. Likewise, the Turkish and related types have small leaves, about three to four inches wide and six to ten inches long. The United States types have much larger leaves—8 to 12 or 14 inches wide and 12 to 20 inches long. The flowers are long and tubelike and are pinkish or yellowish, depending upon the variety.

Tobacco growing is a year-round job. The seeds are sowed in plant beds in the winter or early spring, depending on the climate of the area. About six weeks or two months later the young plants are set in the field. It takes about two months for the first leaves to mature. The last ones are usually ripe four or five weeks later. In some cases, especially with the flue-cured types of Virginia and the Carolinas, the leaves are pulled as they ripen. With most other types the entire stalk is cut when most of the leaves are about mature.

Tobacco is cured by drying in the sun or in barns without heat being applied (sun-cured or air-cured). Another method is curing in barns with open fires (fire-cured). The curing may also be done in barns with a series of flues for circulating the heat (flue-cured). The curing process requires from three to four days for flue-cured to several weeks or even a month or two for the air-cured.

After curing it is packed in piles in a "pack-house." It is allowed to stay there several weeks to develop a good physical condition and a better color. The fire-cured and air-cured develop a rich mahogany color, while the flue-cured becomes a lemon-yellow.

The tobacco leaves are then graded, tied into "hands," and marketed. Nearly all the tobacco in the United States is sold on auction markets. Auctioneer and buyers walk along the rows of tobacco piled on the warehouse floors. Buyers thus can see the quality of the tobacco on sale and can bid competitively for it.

Before tobacco is used to make cigarettes, cigars, or chewing or pipe tobacco, it is packed in "hogsheads" and allowed to age for several years. During this period chemical changes take place which give it a better flavor.

Cigarettes are made mostly from the lemon-yellow, flue-cured tobacco from Virginia and the Carolinas. It is blended with others, especially the Turkish types which have a desirable flavor and odor. The Burley tobacco, common in Kentucky and Tennessee, is used for chewing tobacco and for pipe mixtures. Cigars are made from the cigar-wrapper and cigar-filler types. That from the Connecticut Valley area is especially desirable. Cuba produces a famous cigar tobacco known as Vuelta Abajo from which very expensive cigars are made. Snuff is made by grinding the leaves and sometimes the stems.

TOCQUEVILLE (*tŏk vēl'*), **COUNT ALEXIS** (*ȧ'lĕk'sē'*) **CHARLES HENRI MAURICE** (*mô-rēs'*) **CLEREL DE** (1805–1859), who wrote the first study of the institutions governing the United States, was of the French aristocracy and was born at the family estate in Verneuil,

France. When he was 26, the French government sent him to the United States to write a report about its prisons. On his return to France he published this report, but more important was his next work, *Democracy in America*, which appeared in 1835.

His book made the principles of United States government so clear to the liberty-loving French that the author was elected in 1838 to the French Academy. In a few years 13 editions of the work had been read by French book buyers. It also gained great popularity among lovers of liberal action in England. Tocqueville was a member of the Chamber of Deputies for several years and was its vice-president in 1849. His fame grew in Europe, where he was recognized as a leading authority on democratic forms of government.

TOGO (*tō'gō*), **AFRICA,** is one of the smallest independent countries of the African continent. It has an area of 21,853 square miles, which is about the size of the state of West Virginia. Bordering Togo to the west is Ghana, to the north is Upper Volta, to the east is Dahomey, and to the south the Atlantic Ocean. Togo is a long, narrow country measuring about 350 miles from north to south, and about 85 miles at its widest east-west point.

Togo's 32 miles of coastline are sandy and swampy. Many lagoons and mangrove forests border the coast. The climate of the coastal area is very unhealthful, with high temperatures and high humidity throughout the year. The rainfall is fairly light for this part of Africa, however, averaging only about 20 inches a year. Winds blowing over the cold coastal waters hold little moisture and bring little rain. Also winds blowing from southwest to northeast parallel to the coast do not carry moisture far inland.

Inland the land rises to a low plateau between 300 and 800 feet above sea level. In a mountainous area in the central part of the plateau, elevations are almost 3,000 feet above sea level. Rainfall is heavier in the uplands than on the coast. There are hardwood and oil palm forests inland from the coast. Farther north, grass is the chief vegetation.

Togo is mainly an agricultural country. The chief exports are agricultural and forest products. They include cocoa, palm kernels and palm oil, coffee, copra (dried coconut), peanuts, and cotton.

Most of Togo's exports pass through Lome, the country's chief seaport and capital city. Two short railroad lines extend inland and along the coast from Lome. Lome, with a population of 90,600 (1968 estimate) is the largest city of Togo.

History

In 1884 Germany made Togoland a protectorate. During World War I Germany lost all its African territories. Togoland was divided into two parts by the League of Nations and mandated, or given over for governing, to Great Britain and to France. After World War II, Togoland became a trust territory under the United Nations. It remained divided into British Togoland and French Togoland.

British Togoland

In March 1957 British Togoland became part of the independent state of Ghana. (See GHANA.) British Togoland was the smaller part of the former German protectorate, with an area of 13,041 square miles. It was a long strip of territory along the western boundary of French Togoland. No part of former British Togoland reaches the coast. Before March 6, 1957, British Togoland was administered with the Gold Coast from Accra, the capital of the Gold Coast (now called Ghana). The total population of British Togoland was 383,000.

French Togoland

At the end of World War I, about two-thirds of the area of the former German Togoland was mandated to France by the League of Nations. The mandate gave France the responsibility of setting up a government in the territory. In 1956, French Togoland became a republic within the French Union and asked the United Nations to end its trusteeship. In November 1958 the UN approved of French Togoland's independence and on April 27, 1960, the trust territory became the Republic of Togo.

The Togolese government has a president, a prime minister, and a legislative assembly. The prime minister is head of the government. Togo's first prime minister was Sylvanus Olympio. Togo's population is estimated at 1,746,400 (1968).

TOKYO (*tō′ kē ō*), **JAPAN,** the capital and chief city of the country, is on the Pacific coast of central Honshu, the largest of Japan's four main islands. Tokyo is the largest city in the world. Its metropolitan area, however, ranks second to that of New York City.

Three factors have helped to make Tokyo an important city: its land position, its location on the sea, and its role as an imperial capital. There is little level land in mountainous Japan, and every lowland area is important as a center of population. The Kwanto plain around Tokyo is the largest lowland area in Japan. All the rich agricultural production of the Kwanto plain is funneled through Tokyo to other parts of Japan.

The rail network of Japan centers on Tokyo, and the city is in direct contact by rail with all parts of the country. About one-fifth of the population of Japan lives on the Kwanto plain. This vast labor supply makes Tokyo a good location for industry.

Located at the head of Tokyo Bay, Tokyo is a port for coastal and overseas shipping. The bay is too shallow for large oceangoing vessels to dock at Tokyo. These stop at the port city of Yokohama, 20 miles closer to the mouth of the bay. Dredging operations deepened a channel and created a harbor at Tokyo capable of handling ships up to 10,000 tons. Cargo from larger ships is unloaded at Yokohama and transferred to barges for the trip up the bay to Tokyo. By means of this seaway, Tokyo can receive the raw materials, such as coal and raw cotton, needed in the city's industries.

The ports of Tokyo and Yokohama are combined under the same administrative authority. Tokyo handles the coastal shipping, and Yokohama handles the foreign trade.

The advantages of Tokyo's site were early noted by the rulers of Japan. Although the emperors had their court at the inland city of

Kyoto, the Tokugawa shoguns (military dictators), who ruled Japan from 1603 to 1867, preferred to rule from Tokyo. At that time Tokyo was called Edo. Before the 17th century, Edo was only a small fishing village. The first Tokugawa shogun, Ieyasu, reclaimed the swamplands, built a system of canals, compelled the feudal lords to establish their castles there, and encouraged traders from other parts

When the emperor Meiji was restored officially to power in 1868 he moved his capital from Kyoto to Edo, which he renamed Tokyo, or "eastern capital." Meiji decided to modernize his country and to learn Western methods of education, industry, transportation, and construction. Tokyo became the most modern city in all Asia. As the demand for its products increased, through foreign trade, an increasing

Courtesy (above left, below left, right) Consulate General of Japan, New York, (center left) Japan, Ministry of Foreign Affairs

The soaring 1,092-foot-high Tokyo Tower (right), a central television transmission point, overlooks the city's busy central business district (above left) and its vast industry-lined waterfront (below left). Each working day, millions of commuters crowd fast electric trains (center left) to go to and from their jobs in Tokyo.

of Japan to do business in the new capital. Before long, Edo became a center of learning and culture, and by the time the period of shogun rule came to an end the city already boasted a population of more than 1,000,000. Commodore Matthew C. Perry of the U.S. Navy sailed into Edo Bay in 1853 and again in 1854, demanding from the shoguns the right of the United States to trade with Japan.

number of industries were established in Tokyo. The city grew rapidly in population. As the center of the national government, Tokyo became also the center of banking, commerce, and education.

Modern Tokyo

A great earthquake and fire in 1923 destroyed more than half of Tokyo. The earth-

Tokyo's National Diet Library (above left) is one of the world's largest. Skiers practice at the man-made Sayama Skiing Slope (above right) in suburban Tokyo. The city's Metropolitan Festival Hall (above) has played host to some of the world's great orchestras.

cial and industrial districts. These later were rebuilt. After Japan's defeat by the Allies in 1945, Tokyo was made the headquarters of the Allied military occupation forces under General Douglas MacArthur. Much of the city again had to be rebuilt, and an even more modern Tokyo emerged from the ruins of the war.

The Sumida River, which flows through the Kwanto plain and empties into Tokyo Bay, divides Tokyo into two parts. To the east on the low flood plain is the commercial and industrial area, cut through by a web of canals. The western section, built on an upland, is the residential district. On an upland spur just

quake also had a good effect, however, because it forced the rebuilding of the city. Before the earthquake, attempts at modernization had been only partly successful because of the winding, narrow streets. Following the earthquake, wide, well-paved streets were built to crisscross the city. Bridges were also built, and space was set aside for parks. Water and sewage systems were improved. Modern commercial and apartment buildings were erected. To limit the effects of future earthquakes, no building was built more than eight stories high, and the concrete building material was reinforced with steel.

World War II bombing brought more destruction to Tokyo. This time the heart of the city, where most of the large modern office buildings are located, was spared. Bombs nearly wiped out large portions of the commer-

west of the river is the old shogun castle, which is now the palace of the emperor. A series of moats encircle the palace.

Streets lead out in all directions from the castle, giving a kind of cobweb street pattern to the nearby area. Smaller castles of various feudal lords also have streets leading out from them, with the result that the street pattern of Tokyo is quite complicated.

Tokyo has many points of interest that attract residents and visitors alike. These include, in addition to the Imperial Palace, the parks of Hibiya, Shiba, Ueno, Asakusa, and Sumida Riverside; Tokyo Tower (1,092 feet high); many beautiful Buddhist temples and Shinto shrines; the Meiji Shrine; the Tokyo Art Gallery; Tokyo University and Museum; the *Kabuki* and *No* theaters; and Tokyo's most famous shopping and entertainment district, the Ginza.

The main street of the Ginza has been called the "Broadway of Tokyo." The district includes department stores, banks, and theaters. The Ginza bustles with traffic and crowds of people, including many tourists. At night it is brilliantly lighted by neon and electric signs.

A complete system of bus, streetcar, and subway lines links all parts of the city. Automobiles crowd the main streets in much the same manner as in large U.S. cities. Expressways have been built to accommodate the increasing flow of traffic. Bicycles and motorcycles are common means of transportation. Fast interurban electric trains connect Tokyo with Yokohama. The area between the two cities is almost entirely filled with residential and industrial suburbs, so that it is difficult to tell where one city ends and the other begins. Tokyo International Airport at Haneda serves the city.

Industries in Tokyo are of many different kinds, producing a wide variety of products ranging from textiles to paper, from machinery and tools to toys, and from chemicals to furniture. Electricity is widely used as a source of power since streams in the nearby mountains have been harnessed for hydroelectricity. Coal is also an important fuel. Tokyo imports all its industrial raw materials. There are many large factories in Tokyo as well as small workshops employing 10 to 30 persons.

A cultural center for all of Japan, Tokyo has several large universities, medical schools, technical schools, and other schools of higher learning. Tokyo University, founded in 1869, is one of the leading universities of the world. All forms of sports have been encouraged in Tokyo and recreational facilities—such as baseball diamonds, tennis courts, and swimming pools—are found throughout the city. Sports facilities were expanded to accommodate the 1964 Olympic Games.

Until 1932 Tokyo covered an area of only 32 square miles and had a population of slightly more than 2,000,000. The inclusion of outlying areas within the city limits in 1932, and again in 1936, brought the area to 222 square miles and the population, by 1940, to 6,778,804. In 1943 Tokyo Metropolis was created—including the city area and the area of Tokyo Prefecture. The city lost population during World War II, but since then has experienced steady population growth. The population of Tokyo proper is 8,901,341 (1965).

TOLSTOY (*tŏl stoi′*), **COUNT LYEV (LEO) NIKOLAEVICH** (1828–1910), a Russian novelist, was one of the world's greatest writers. By dignifying labor and showing the corruption of the aristocracy, he helped prepare the way for the Russian Revolution.

Tolstoy was born on his father's estate at Yasnaya Polyana. He went to the University of Kazan and afterward joined an artillery regiment. In 1854 he took part in the Crimean War and was present at the defense of Sevastopol against the English and French. Before this he had written some stories dealing with his boyhood; now he wrote several sketches about military life in Sevastopol. They were strikingly new. No Russian writer before had written with such complete lifelikeness. No writer had ever before exposed to such an extent the cruelty and empty pride of war.

When the Crimean War was over Tolstoy resigned his commission and went abroad. He hoped to find something very different from Russia, but everywhere among working people he found poverty and ignorance. When he came back to Russia he wrote a book called *From the Memoirs of Prince Nekhlyudov* in which he attacked the society of his day. He retired to his estate to live a peasant's life and to spend his time teaching peasant children. In 1866 he completed *War and Peace*, a long novel which depicts the whole range of Russian life during the period of the Napoleonic Wars. *Anna Karenina*, another study of Russian life, appeared in 1875. In 1884 appeared his famous autobiographical work, *A Confession*. In it he proclaimed his disgust

Count Lyev Tolstoy.

with the artificial life he had been leading, and his desire for a life of poverty and humility, as lived by Jesus Christ.

Tolstoy, indeed, wore a peasant's blouse, plowed his land himself, cobbled his own shoes, and disapproved of the ownership of property. Yet he would hardly have satisfied a modern Communist, for he was opposed both to serving the state and to resisting it, and preached that society would never improve until individuals became better. During the latter part of his life, he devoted himself to writing treatises on religion, philosophy, and social questions. In religion he would accept nothing that was not the direct teaching of Christ. He refused to accept the authority of the church or of any interpretations of the Bible. In philosophy he criticized all laws and institutions that stood in the way of the individual. His last novel was *Resurrection* (1899), describing how a worthless aristocrat became an honorable man. The final years of his life were spent in a vain effort to reconcile his hatred of the ownership of property with his continually increasing wealth, which his wife and children insisted that he keep. He is universally recognized as one of the world's greatest novelists and is unsurpassed both in his ability to portray people and to create scenes of life, rich in details.

Courtesy Libby, McNeill & Libby

Tomatoes are grown successfully in light, rich, well-drained soil.

TOMATO (*tō mā'tō* or *tō mä'tō*). The tomato is properly classed as a fruit. It is usually spoken of as a vegetable. In fact, it is the most widely grown vegetable in the United States. It was once considered poisonous. Today it is eaten in many forms.

The tomato is rich in vitamins, especially vitamins A and C. It also contains substances that prevent scurvy, beriberi, and rickets.

The tomato is a relative of the potato and tobacco plants. Like those plants, it was first grown in the Americas. It was introduced into Europe in the century after Columbus discovered America. For a long time, it was called the "love apple."

The tomato plant needs a long growing season and light, rich, well-drained soil. In northern Europe and the northern United States it is often grown in hothouses during the winter. It is also grown in Florida, Texas, Mexico, and Cuba during the winter. Winter tomatoes are picked while green and shipped to northern markets. They ripen on the way to market.

Tomatoes are first planted from February to April in hothouses and on large plots on land in the southern part of the United States. As it gets warmer, six-week-old seedlings are taken to the tomato-growing areas. They must not be planted until after the last frost. Late spring frosts will kill young tomato plants.

The plants are almost a foot high when they are placed in the open field. They are tied to stakes and pruned frequently. Pruning is done by cutting off little branches that form at the base of the leaves. After four or five fruit clusters have formed, the top growing part of the plant is removed. Thus, all the strength of the plant goes into the ripening of the fruit.

The plant has a number of natural enemies. The worst is frost. There are also a number of insects and fungus infections that feed on it. The cutworm cuts off the stem close to the surface of the ground. The grub of the June beetle damages the roots. Other insects and fungus diseases feed on the leaves.

Most of these pests can be controlled. Plants can be sprayed with insecticide poisons that kill many of their enemies. Crop rotation and proper soil and seed treatment also help protect the plants from fungus diseases. (See PLANT DISEASE.)

At the height of the tomato season, most of the crop is canned. Large amounts are canned whole or made into tomato juice, tomato paste, or different kinds of tomato sauces. Tomatoes are also pickled.

TONSILS (tŏn′sĭlz) **AND TONSILLITIS** (tŏn′-sĭ lī′tĭs). When we speak of the tonsils we usually mean the largest pair on either side of the throat just behind the tongue. But there are several pairs of tonsils of different sizes. They are small bundles of lymphoid tissue. They are like the lymph nodes in the way their parts are put together. (See LYMPHATIC SYSTEM.) Because of their location in the throat they have a special job. They are the first line of defense against infections entering through the nose and mouth.

The largest pair near the palate are the *palatine* tonsils. High in the back of the throat are some smaller ones. These are called the *adenoids*. Other small tonsils are found just below the surface in the back of the tongue; still others are in the back of the pharynx.

The tonsils are covered by the same smooth membrane that lines the mouth. In the tonsils this membrane dips down to form deep thin pockets called *crypts*. The crypts trap germs and other harmful material from the mouth. The white blood cells, leucocytes, surround the germs and help to destroy them. (See BLOOD.) Fighting infection is the normal work of the tonsils.

When germs become active within the lymphoid tissue of the tonsils, they may cause inflammation of the whole tonsil. This inflammation is called *tonsillitis*. One, or usually both, palatine tonsils become enlarged, red, and sore. The crypts are swollen and sometimes discharge thick pus. This is acute tonsillitis. It is an infection that happens suddenly and usually goes away in four or five days.

Acute tonsillitis may be caused by different bacteria. A common type is the streptococcus. Such an infection is often called a "strep" sore throat. Drugs may stop this infection, but they do not clear the throat of the bacteria.

Acute tonsillitis develops more often in childhood than in infancy or adulthood. It also happens more often during the winter months, when colds are common.

Infection may not be limited to the tonsils. Lymph nodes high in the neck often become swollen since they drain the region of the tonsils. This can be expected to happen during infections. It becomes serious if the infection spreads into the soft tissues about the tonsils and forms an abscess. (See ABSCESS.) The throat becomes greatly swollen and sore; the patient generally has a fever and appears to be very ill. The abscess may break of itself or it may need to be opened.

After recovery from acute tonsillitis, the patient may develop conditions like those that result from a streptococcus infection.

When a person has many attacks of tonsillitis, it is called chronic tonsillitis. This condition is a drain on his health. It may also be responsible for other inflammations, as in the joints or the kidneys. To prevent such developments, the tonsils are taken out.

TOP (tŏp). The top is a toy shaped like a small fat wheel on an axle. It will spin on the pointed end of the axle. It is one of man's oldest and most popular toys. Eskimos make them from ice, Indians from bone, South Sea islanders from palm wood and volcanic ash.

Pictures from ancient Greece show men playing with tops. One of the most popular was the whipping top. It was kept moving by a whip wound around the upper part of the

Courtesy (left) Gibbs Manufacturing Company, (center) Toy Information Bureau, (right) Sperry Gyroscope Company

Left: This mechanical top balances on a spring which makes it bounce as it spins. **Center:** Skilled top spinners can do tricks with peg tops and string. **Right:** Gyroscope tops can be toys but more often they are used as scientific instruments.

top. The lashing of the whip kept the top going around. Often a slit in the top made a humming noise as it spun.

One of the simplest tops is the whirligig or teetotum. These are spun with a twist of the fingers. The teetotum often has a different letter on each of the four sides.

The most popular top in the United States is probably the peg top. A string, wound around the bottom part, is pulled to make it spin. It is often called a whistling top because of the sharp noise it makes as it moves through the air. There are many games played with the peg top. In one, a player starts his top spinning in a circle. Another player tries to knock the first top out of the circle with a second spinning top.

Top spinning is very popular in Japan and China. In Japan there are tops that play music and tops that spin inside other tops. An African tribe has a top that it can spin in the air with a whip. South Sea islanders often lie on their backs and spin tops on their big toes.

Modern science makes instruments that use the principle of the spinning top. They are called gyroscopes. (See GYROSCOPE.)

TOPEKA (tō pē′kä), **KANSAS,** the capital, is in the northeastern part of the state, on the Kansas (Kaw) River, about 50 miles west of Kansas City. More than a capital, Topeka is a business center for a rich farming area, and a railroad and industrial center. The city has railroad shops, food processing plants, metal, rubber and plaster industries, and a United States air force base.

The first settlers found at Topeka a good crossing for a railroad. A ferry already had been started, and one branch of the Oregon Trail crossed there. As slavery and antislavery people fought for control of the Kansas Territory, there was some question as to the location of the new capital. However, Kansas was admitted as a free state on January 29, 1861, and Topeka became the capital.

In 1869 the first transcontinental railroad was finished. The part known as the Kansas Pacific passed through Topeka. A second railroad, the Santa Fe, crossed the Kansas River at Topeka and continued on to the southwest. With these, Topeka became a railroad center. The city has a commission form of government.

Topeka's population is 125,011 (1970).

TORONTO (tŭ rŏn′tō), **ONTARIO.** Toronto is on the northwestern edge of Lake Ontario, 100 miles north of Buffalo, New York. It stands on land that rises gradually from Lake Ontario and then forms a level plateau. Its island-sheltered harbor has made it a fine Great Lakes port. It is well prepared to handle the ocean shipping coming through the St. Lawrence

Seaway. (See St. Lawrence River.) It is the capital of the province of Ontario and the second largest city in Canada.

The citizens of Toronto were once almost all of British origin. Since World War II thousands of immigrants have made it a city of many races and languages.

Because of its location on the seaway, its nearness to raw materials, and its nearness to hydroelectric and steam generating power plants, it is an important industrial and commercial city. Its factories make agricultural machinery, metal goods, leather, clothing and furs, electrical appliances, aircraft, paper products, furniture and lumber. Its stockyards, slaughterhouses, and meat-packing plants are similar to those of Chicago, Illinois. It is the book publishing center of Canada and the financial center for the mines of northern Canada.

Toronto's new City Hall was officially opened in 1965. The buildings, designed by the Finnish architect Viljo Revell, include two curved office towers that flank a domed council chamber. The three-story base houses offices and a public library.

Toronto is well served by railway lines. Its airport at Malton, on the outskirts of the city, is one of the busiest in Canada. The city owns its transportation system of electric railways, and electric and motor busses. In 1954 it put into use the first subway in Canada.

Among Toronto's notable buildings are the red sandstone Parliament buildings in Queen's Park south of the city's center. The Royal Ontario Museum is also in Queen's Park. Nearby is the old City Hall with its tall clock tower. Nearby too is the University of Toronto, one of the largest educational institutions in Canada. A great public library system, the Royal Conservatory of Music, an art gallery, and a famous symphony orchestra help to make Toronto a center for education and culture.

In 1953 Toronto began a new form of city government. It is a federal system. Twelve towns and villages surrounding Toronto joined it in forming Metropolitan Toronto. Each town or village keeps its own elected council but sends delegates to a metropolitan council of 25 persons. This council controls important matters of common interest, such as finance, water supply, and transportation.

No city organization like this had been tried before in North America.

In 1794 John Graves Simcoe, British governor of the new province of Upper Canada (now Ontario), chose this site for its capital. There had been an Indian village there called Toronto, "the place of meeting." He called the new capital York, in honor of King George III's second son. In 1834 York was incorporated as a city and given its old Indian name of Toronto.

The population of the city proper is 664,584; Metropolitan Toronto has 1,881,691 (1966).

TORPEDO (*tôr pēd'ō*) is a self-propelled guided missile that travels underwater. It carries an explosive warhead and is designed to attack all kinds of ships. Torpedoes can be fired by surface ships or by submarines, or they can be dropped from aircraft. Modern torpedoes may carry atomic warheads that can sink or damage a target without making a direct hit.

Naval mines and some other naval weapons were once known as torpedoes. When the self-propelled torpedo was invented, it was called "automobile torpedo" or "fish torpedo" because it moved under its own power. The self-propelled torpedo was invented by Robert Whitehead, a British-born engineer. His first idea for a torpedo came from an Austrian naval officer, Giovanni Luppis, in 1864. Luppis suggested a self-propelled, explosive-carrying boat that could be steered from a distance by long lines.

Whitehead built a model but decided that it was not practical. He then began work on an idea of his own and, after two years, developed a workable torpedo.

An early Whitehead torpedo was about 14 feet long, 14 inches in diameter, and weighed about 300 pounds, including 18 pounds of dynamite in its nose. It was powered by a compressed-air engine driving a single propeller at the tail. It traveled underwater, and its depth was controlled by rudders driven by a valve that worked by water pressure. According to reports, this torpedo had a speed of 6 knots and a range between 200 and 700 yards. By contrast, the Japanese Navy, during World War II, used a torpedo called the "Long Lance," which was powered by a steam engine and carried more than 1,000 pounds of explosive. It had a range of 22,000 yards and attained a speed of 49 knots.

In 1895 Ludwig Obry, an Austrian, adapted the gyroscope to steer the torpedo. This greatly improved the weapon's accuracy. Soon steam engines were designed to power torpedoes. British manufacturers—especially Armstrong, Whitworth and Company—were most successful in developing steam-powered torpedoes. The E. W. Bliss Company of Brooklyn, New York, introduced a turbine-driven torpedo in the early 1900's. These developments increased the range and speed of torpedoes. Torpedoes powered by electric batteries were perfected

MAJOR PARTS OF A STEAM-DRIVEN TORPEDO

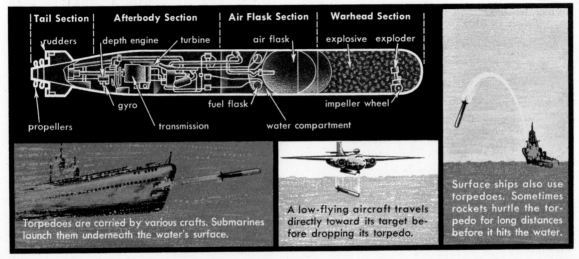

| Tail Section | Afterbody Section | Air Flask Section | Warhead Section |

rudders — depth engine — turbine — air flask — explosive — exploder

gyro — fuel flask — impeller wheel

propellers — transmission — water compartment

Torpedoes are carried by various crafts. Submarines launch them underneath the water's surface.

A low-flying aircraft travels directly toward its target before dropping its torpedo.

Surface ships also use torpedoes. Sometimes rockets hurtle the torpedo for long distances before it hits the water.

between World War I and World War II. Both steam and electric power are used to propel modern torpedoes.

During World War II, Germany introduced homing torpedoes. A homing torpedo carries special devices that detect the presence of a target. The torpedo then steers itself toward the target. Modern torpedoes can be set to search for a target and "home on it" when it is found. Some modern submarine torpedoes are guided by means of signals sent through wires attached to the torpedo.

A torpedo consists of four major sections. In the front is the warhead, which carries the explosive and an exploder mechanism to set it off. Any homing device is attached to the front of the warhead. Next to the warhead is the air flask (in a steam torpedo) or the battery compartment (in an electric torpedo). The air flask contains fuel, compressed air, and water for making steam. The next section is the afterbody, where the engine, the gyroscopes, and the depth-controlling device are installed. The afterbody of the steam torpedo contains the combustion flasks, which convert water into steam. Last is the tail section, which carries the tail fins, the rudders, and the propellers.

Torpedoes are effective because they strike their targets underwater, where ships usually have little or no armor. More shipping has been sunk by torpedoes than by all other naval weapons combined. (See SUBMARINE.)

TOSCANINI (*täs′ kŭ nē′ nē*), **ARTURO** (*är tur′ ō*) (1867-1957), was an Italian musician. He perhaps can be called the greatest conductor of the 20th century. He was born in Parma, Italy, and studied music at the conservatory there and later in Milan.

At the age of 19, Toscanini was engaged as first cellist in the orchestra of an Italian opera company touring in Brazil. There his fantastic memory, which later made him a musical legend even during his lifetime, was first displayed. When a series of events prevented the regular conductor from proceeding with a performance of *Aida*, the young cellist, without previous experience or rehearsals, conducted the entire performance from memory. In 1886 he returned

to Italy to conduct. Though at that time an unknown, Toscanini built his reputation and gradually was invited to conduct all over Italy. In 1898 he was engaged as the chief conductor at Milan's La Scala, Italy's most famous opera house. In 1907 he went to the Metropolitan Opera in New York City, New

Arturo Toscanini.

York. Throughout his life his two centers of greatest musical activity were to be Milan and New York City.

In 1915 Toscanini resigned from the Metropolitan Opera and returned to Italy. He conducted again at La Scala and became its director in 1922. Four years later, however, he returned to New York City to become conductor of the New York Philharmonic Orchestra. He held the position for the next ten years. In 1936 he resigned to conduct the new NBC Symphony, an orchestra organized for him by the National Broadcasting Company. He conducted it until a few years before his death.

Toscanini's outstanding qualities were many. Among them was his versatility. That is, he could conduct the music of many different composers, lands, and periods—all with equal brilliance. Toscanini was an ideal interpreter of the music of Verdi, Beethoven, Brahms, and Wagner. His excellent memory enabled him to remember many works, and so he could conduct without printed music in front of him. His commanding personality gave him a high degree of control over his musicians.

TOTEMISM (*tōt′ ŭ mĭz′ ŭm*) is the belief of many primitive societies in a mystic relationship between individuals or groups of individuals and certain animals, plants, or, at times, natural phenomena, such as the sun or rainbows.

Totemism is most often associated with subdivisions of primitive societies called clans or sibs. The members of such a group believe that they can trace their ancestry to a single source.

This source is the totem. It may be an animal, a plant, or a phenomenon. Whatever it is, the clan members believe the totem to be their oldest ancestor and the founder of their clan. They therefore refer to themselves as "children of" their totem—for example, "children of the bear," or "children of the kangaroo." How the totem ancestor came to found the clan is told in myth.

The members of a totemic clan believe the welfare and survival of the group depend on a close relationship with the totem. The totem is therefore worshiped as a supernatural being. Devotional rites are held by the clan at certain times. These rites —dancing, singing, and pageantry—remind the clan members of their common ties and strengthen the bonds that unite them. The totem is the symbol or badge of this unity.

Members of totemic clans, or similar subdivisions of primitive societies, often depict their totems in statues, paintings, or in symbols painted on their own bodies and in many

Totem poles, such as this one in Alaska, do not represent actual totems. Instead, they are grave markers or emblems.

The Smithsonian Institution

other ways. From the viewpoint of anthropology, various forms of art of primitive peoples have been incorrectly called totemic. The totem poles of the North American Indians of the Pacific coast are an example. These impressive carvings do not represent totems of clans or other such groups, and they are not used in totemic rites of worship. Some are grave markers and are scattered through the native villages. Others are attached to houses and illustrate legendary or real events in the lives of the owners of the houses. Some are the equivalents of coats of arms. (See HERALDRY.)

TOUCAN (*tōō'kăn* or *tōō'kän*) is any of several birds of the family Ramphastidae, which belongs to the order Piciformes. The order also includes jacamars, puffbirds, barbets, honey guides, and woodpeckers. Toucans are divided into 37 species, all of which are native to Central or South America. Many are found in the tropical rain forests of South America's Amazon River Basin.

Toucans are noted for their enormous bills, which are toothed along the margin. In some cases the bill makes up one-third of the entire length of the bird. For its size, the bill is comparatively light in weight, but it gives the bird a grotesque, overbalanced appearance.

Although fruit is the main part of their diet,

Richard Keane

The enormous bill of the toucan makes up one-third of the bird's entire length.

toucans are known to eat a number of different foods. Captive toucans have been trained to exist on a widely varied diet. They are often seen in zoos because they are easily tamed and thrive in captivity.

Toucans have gaily colored plumage and multicolored bills. Feathers may be red, green, orange, blue, yellow, black, and white. Toucans are weak fliers. They are, therefore, rather sedentary and usually move about by climbing or hopping from branch to branch.

TOULOUSE-LAUTREC (*tụ lōōz′ lō trĕk′*), **HENRI DE** (*än rē′ dē*) (1864-1901), was a French artist noted for his vivid paintings of Paris dance halls, cafes, and theaters.

He was born of a noble family at Albi, in southern France. As a child, he was injured and grew up with feeble, shrunken legs. At 18 he moved to Paris to study painting. He lived and worked among the nightclubs of Montmartre, wearing away his health with late hours and overindulgence. He died at the early age of 36 of a stroke brought about by alcoholism.

Lautrec saw and recorded the people of his world with the keen eye and the swift brush of a cartoonist. In his works, which were inspired by Japanese wood-block prints and the paintings of Edgar Degas, expressive lines surround flat areas of color. A face cut by the edge of the canvas, an intruding shoulder, or a chair back often give the effect of a momentary glimpse. Yet Lautrec's compositions are thought out with great care. His draftsmanship shows a great ability to portray the psychology of his subjects. The color patterns in his work often suggest the artificial intenseness of theatrical lighting.

Lautrec worked on canvas, cardboard, or paper, using oil paints, watercolors, and pastels with equal skill. He is among the early creators of the poster as a work of art. During the last ten years of his life he produced more than 300 lithographs and contributed much to the development of color lithography. His finished oil paintings are few. Among them, "At the Moulin Rouge," in The Art Institute of Chicago, is a masterpiece.

TOUSSAINT (*tōō′ săn*) **L'OUVERTURE** (*lōō′- vĕr tụr′*) (1743-1803) was one of the liberators of Haiti. He was born a Negro slave near what is now Cap Haitien in the French colony of S. Domingue on the island of Hispaniola (now Haiti and the Dominican Republic). Toussaint's real name was Francois Dominique Toussaint, but he was called L'Ouverture (the opener) because of his valor in opening the enemy's ranks.

Toussaint's fight for liberation began in 1791 when he joined the slaves of the northern part of S. Domingue in a rebellion against their French masters. He became one of the slaves' leaders and soon commanded a large Negro force. The Spanish invaded Hispaniola in 1793, and with their ally, the British, they tried to take over the entire island. (They already had possession of the eastern part of it.) At first Toussaint, like most of the other Negro leaders, joined the Spanish forces. Soon, however, he switched his allegiance to the French in an attempt to drive the British from the island. In 1798 he succeeded, and the British withdrew.

By 1801 Toussaint had become master of all of Hispaniola and proclaimed himself governor general for life. The power he wielded over his people was astonishing. He was an able administrator, and the country prospered under his rule. In 1801, however, Napoleon Bonaparte sent troops to reconquer the island. After a gallant battle Toussaint yielded. He was treacherously seized and sent to France, where he died in prison. (See HAITI.)

"In the Circus Fernando: The Ringmaster" is one of Toulouse-Lautrec's few oil paintings.

Courtesy The Art Institute of Chicago, The Joseph Winterbotham Collection

TOY (*toi*) is an object used as a plaything, usually by children. The object may be a manufactured toy or it may be any other kind of object that the child uses as a toy, such as a stick or a box. A child's imagination creates toys. A stick found in the street can easily become a hobbyhorse or a spear; an orange crate can be imagined as an automobile or a boat.

Toys are valuable for the role they play in helping children grow up into the adult world. Toys have always been made to imitate objects used by adults. Children themselves imitate adults. Eventually, they may do things in the world as adults that they once did for play.

Similar kinds of toys often develop among peoples who live far apart and have had little contact with one another. Such playthings as dolls, tops, toy weapons, balls, and Yo-Yos all are noted for their universal appeal. The toys of younger children are most notably alike among various cultures.

The history of toys goes back as far as the history of man. In early cultures boys played with toy weapons, imitating the hunting and battle techniques they would need for survival as adults. Girls played with toys related to the domestic activities of the family. Dolls and toy weapons were among the earliest toys. (See DOLL.) Archaeologists have found clappers, rattles, tiny pots, and miniature animals among ancient ruins. The figure of a lion on a wheeled stand, discovered in Iran, is said to date from about 1100 B.C. In Egyptian ruins, tops, balls, and dolls have been found.

Before the era of mass production, toy makers

An intricately designed gondola (right) dating from the 16th century is among the earliest automatic toys existing. It was probably made in Augsburg, Germany.
Courtesy Kunsthistorisches Museum, Vienna

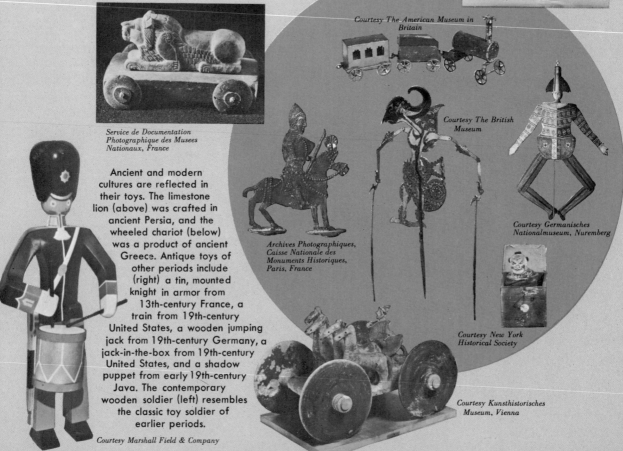

Service de Documentation Photographique des Musees Nationaux, France

Courtesy The American Museum in Britain

Courtesy The British Museum

Courtesy Germanisches Nationalmuseum, Nuremberg

Ancient and modern cultures are reflected in their toys. The limestone lion (above) was crafted in ancient Persia, and the wheeled chariot (below) was a product of ancient Greece. Antique toys of other periods include (right) a tin, mounted knight in armor from 13th-century France, a train from 19th-century United States, a wooden jumping jack from 19th-century Germany, a jack-in-the-box from 19th-century United States, and a shadow puppet from early 19th-century Java. The contemporary wooden soldier (left) resembles the classic toy soldier of earlier periods.

Courtesy Marshall Field & Company

Archives Photographiques, Caisse Nationale des Monuments Historiques, Paris, France

Courtesy New York Historical Society

Courtesy Kunsthistorisches Museum, Vienna

were often craftsmen whose products reflected great skill. Mechanical toys often contained intricate clockworks that made them move realistically. Dolls, toy soldiers, and miniature furniture were often masterfully carved. Many museums have preserved toys of magnificent workmanship.

During the Middle Ages, Nuremberg, Germany, began to develop into a great center of toy making. Skilled workers used such materials as gold, silver, iron, brass, tin, wood, silk, and kid in making toys. A worldwide demand grew for Nuremberg toys. From the 16th to the 18th century, toy makers' guilds in Germany produced beautiful dollhouses, which were the exact copies of the homes of kings and nobles. Germany became the world's leading toy-making and toy-exporting country. Other European countries soon competed with Germany in toy production. Asian countries also developed toy-making craftsmen. In the Far East the making of kites, tops, dolls, and toy furniture has long been highly developed. (See KITE; TOP).

The first settlers in the New World found that Indian children had toys, including hoops, balls, and small bows and arrows for the boys, and dishes and dolls of carved wood or clay for the girls. The children of the settlers also had to be content with toys made in their own homes. Toy making during the early days of the United States was centered in Europe, and imports were costly.

By the mid-18th century a few toys were being made in New England. They were produced chiefly by woodworkers and clockmakers, who were among the first to build workshops in the new country. Dolls, whistles, and other simple toys from American sources began to appear.

Toys largely reflect the culture that produces

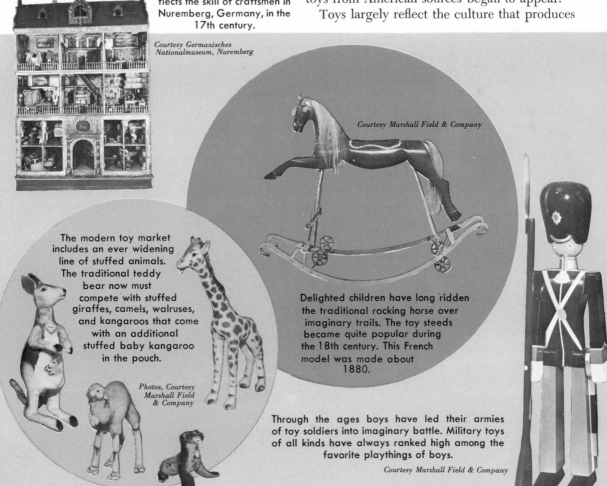

This elaborate doll house reflects the skill of craftsmen in Nuremberg, Germany, in the 17th century.

Courtesy Germanisches Nationalmuseum, Nuremberg

Courtesy Marshall Field & Company

The modern toy market includes an ever widening line of stuffed animals. The traditional teddy bear now must compete with stuffed giraffes, camels, walruses, and kangaroos that come with an additional stuffed baby kangaroo in the pouch.

Photos, Courtesy Marshall Field & Company

Delighted children have long ridden the traditional rocking horse over imaginary trails. The toy steeds became quite popular during the 18th century. This French model was made about 1880.

Through the ages boys have led their armies of toy soldiers into imaginary battle. Military toys of all kinds have always ranked high among the favorite playthings of boys.

Courtesy Marshall Field & Company

Photos, Courtesy
Marshall Field & Company

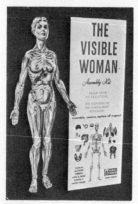

Grotesque robots (above left) fascinate children with battery-operated movements, noises, and flashing lights. Among the popular educational toys of the mid-1960's was Lego (above right), a building set. The Visible Woman (left), a scientific toy, teaches human anatomy to children by letting them put movable body parts into place on a skeleton.

Courtesy Marshall Field & Company

them. During the French Revolution, for example, children played with toy guillotines that beheaded doll aristocrats. Industrial progress and scientific achievement are also represented by toys. Toy weapons often are replicas of the latest in weaponry. Trains became popular in toy form as soon as they became a significant mode of transportation. The invention of electricity added to the mechanization of toys. In the 20th century, model airplanes, replicas of equipment used in space flight, and toy robots became popular. (See MODEL BUILDING and Frontispiece of this volume.)

World Wars I and II had their effect on toy manufacturing, as they did on other industries. Not only did they stop the import of toys from Europe but they also forced U.S. toy makers to turn to nonstrategic materials. Until World War II most toys were made of metal or wood. Manufacturers soon found plastic materials suitable for making toys. In the mid-1960's more than $90,000,000 worth of plastic materials were being used yearly in toy making.

More dolls are sold in the United States than any other type of plaything. Also popular in the United States are nonriding transportation toys (such as small cars and trucks), sporting goods, educational and scientific toys, riding toys, activity toys, musical toys, and stuffed toys (other than dolls). (See RECREATION AND PLAY.)

TOYNBEE (toin'bē), **ARNOLD JOSEPH** (1889-), is an English historian. He was born in London and educated at Oxford. As a young man he embarked on a career in international relations. During World War I and again during World War II, he served in the intelligence division of the British Foreign Office. He also served as a British delegate to the peace conferences at Paris in 1919 and 1946.

In 1915 Toynbee's first book, *Nationality and the War,* was published. *Survey of International Affairs* was published while he was professor of Byzantine and modern Greek language, literature, and history at the University of London. From 1925 until his retirement 30 years later, Toynbee was research professor of international history at the University of London and director of studies at the Royal Institute of International Affairs.

Toynbee's masterpiece, A *Study of History* (1934-1954), was published in ten volumes. In it he compares more than 20 civilizations and in so doing theorizes that civilizations or societies and not nations or periods are the important units of history. These societies develop, says Toynbee, under the guidance of a small group of creative leaders. When the leadership fails, the civilizations decline.

Arnold Toynbee.

Among Toynbee's other books are *The World and the West* (1953), *An Historian's Approach to Religion* (1956), and *Hellenism: the History of a Civilization* (1959).

TRACK & FIELD SPORTS

Photo,
Track and Field News Inc.
Glenn Davis, United States

TRACK (*trăk*) **AND FIELD** (*fēld*) **SPORTS** (*spōrts*) are competitive athletics based upon the most natural and widespread of all play activities: running, jumping, and throwing. Their development grew out of the long human history of catching food, fighting or escaping one's enemies, enjoying friendly competition.

In France and the Commonwealth of Nations, track and field is called simply athletics; the term sports covers all other competitive games. In the U.S.S.R. and Germany, it is called light athletics. In Norway and Sweden, it is called free athletics.

Worldwide Participation

At each Olympic Games, track and field sports make up the largest part of the program; more nations and individuals compete in them, and they are watched by more spectators. Of the 94 countries represented in 1964 at Tokyo, 84 competed in track and field sports.

There are sound reasons for such widespread participation. First, the wide variety of track and field events allows both male and female athletes of various sizes and abilities to compete on a fair basis. Implements can be adjusted in size and weight; distances can be altered.

Second, track and field is an individual sport. A boy or girl can run, jump, or throw in practice whenever it is convenient, with or without a companion or coach. Development can be based on individual interests and capacities, with only a lesser concern for team needs. Track and field teams can vary in size from 1 to as many as 40.

Third, track and field permits a great number of athletes to compete at one time and place. At the Pennsylvania Relay Carnival, for example, more than 5,000 athletes, representing more than 500 institutions, compete on a single track and field for 14 hours over a two-day period.

Organization and Regulations

Associations. The events, rules, competitors, techniques, and officiating of track and field sports vary greatly according to location and level of competition. There is a growing trend, however, toward consistency with the rules of the International Amateur Athletic Federation (I.A.A.F.). In the United States, national associations serve as the regulating bodies for many track and field activities. The Amateur Athletic Union (A.A.U.) of the United States sends representatives to the I.A.A.F. The A.A.U. and the National Collegiate Athletic Association (N.C.A.A.) are both represented on the track and field committee of the U.S. Olympic Association. High-school track and field is largely under the administration of the National Federation of State High School Athletic Associations.

Track and Field Teams. A team in track and field has no fixed number of members. Competing teams may make their own agreements. Usually in meets between two teams as many as three contestants may be started in each event. The number of events in such dual meets also varies, from 9 to as many as 18. Since individual members often compete in more than one event, total team membership is usually less than 25.

Scoring. In dual meets scoring usually counts five points for first place, three for second, and one for third. In three-team meets scoring tends to be similar, but with two points for third, and one for fourth. For the Olympic

SPRINT START A fast start is vital in sprinting. Sprinters begin from a crouch, usually using starting blocks from which to spring. Until the late 1800's, sprinters started from a standing position.

Jesse Owens, United States

Photo, Courtesy Department of Photography, Ohio State University

Games there is no official scoring system, since the International Olympic Committee (I.O.C.) wishes to emphasize individual excellence and de-emphasize national team rivalries. Each country tends to score in accordance with its own traditions and national interests. Medals, however, are awarded to first-, second-, and third-place winners in the various events. Gold is for first, silver for second, and bronze for third.

Measurement Systems. Track and field events may also vary according to the system of measurement used. The United States and the United Kingdom generally use the British system of measurement. That is, events usually are measured off in yards or miles. Most of the rest of the world's countries use the metric system of measurement, which measures off most events in meters and kilometers. Most Olympic Games events are measured off according to the metric system. The United Kingdom has announced plans to switch to the metric system as soon as it is practical to do so. A similar plan is being considered in the United States.

Track and Field Dimensions. Outdoor track events are held officially on 440-yard (400-meter) oval-shaped tracks. This is equivalent to one-fourth of a mile, or four laps to the mile. The track surface is made to provide good footing under all weather conditions. Fine cinders mixed with loam have been most commonly used where rain is a problem; a clay-loam mixture, when it is not. Recently there has been a rapid increase in the use of all-weather synthetic materials. Track events may also be run on dirt or grass. Field events may be held on the area within the oval-shaped track or on an adjacent field. Firm runways, soft landing pits, and measured circles are needed for field events.

Indoor tracks may be made of the same material as outdoor tracks, or they may be made of wood. Special wooden tracks are often banked at the curves. Indoor tracks usually run 8 to 12 laps to the mile. Records for indoor and outdoor track are kept separately.

Track and Field Events

Track Events involve some form of running or, sometimes, walking over a measured distance. Races fall into four categories: sprints, endurance runs, hurdles, and relays.

The sprints (50 to 220 yards) call for a maximum speed throughout. Sprint training, there-

Photo, Track and Field News Inc.

Harrison Dillard, United States

HURDLES Speed, form, and timing are required for hurdling. The hurdler takes an exact number of steps between each hurdle and must clear the hurdle without breaking form. Hurdling form is designed to put the hurdler in the best position to continue sprinting after the jump.

ENDURANCE RUNS The athlete who runs distances must develop a steady, driving form. In the mile, some runners, called pacesetters, take an early lead and try to hold it. Others, called kick runners, save their strength for a driving finish.

Michel Jazy, France

Photo, A.G.I.P.

fore, emphasizes the skills of starting, running, and accelerating.

The endurance runs (440 yards to the marathon, 26 miles 385 yards) require great physical and mental stamina. The athlete must cope with the hardships of running long distances in the shortest possible time. Endurance training mixes steady long running with fast, short runs, gradually increasing pace as condition improves.

The hurdles require the athlete to run certain distances while striding over obstacles 30, 36, or 42 inches in height. The outdoor 120-yard high hurdles and 220-yard low hurdles demand great speed and skill; the outdoor 440-yard hurdles add to these the factor of great endurance. In outdoor events ten hurdles are used; indoor races may include four hurdles at 50 yards, five hurdles at 60 yards, and six hurdles at 70 yards.

The relays, except for the hurdles, require that a baton be passed from one of four team members to another after each completes his leg of the race. Popular relay races include two sprint relays (four legs at 110 yards and four at 220 yards), the mile relay (four at 440 yards), the two-mile relay (four at 880 yards), the four-mile relay (four at one mile), the sprint medley relay (440, 220, 220, 880 yards), and the distance medley relay (880 yards, 440 yards, $\frac{3}{4}$ mile, mile).

Field Events can be classified into jumping events and throwing events. There are four jumping events: the running high jump; the pole vault; the long (broad) jump; and the triple jump (hop, step, and jump).

In the running high jump the athlete may run any distance from any angle in approaching the crossbar but must take off from only one foot. The jumper may use any style and position while trying to clear the crossbar. Almost all jumpers today use a straddle style.

In the pole vault the athlete uses a vaulting

SHOT PUT Great strength, concentration, and development of technique are necessary to successful shot-putting. Improvements in technique have doubled record put distances since the 1890's.

Randy Matson, United States

Photo, Courtesy Texas A. & M. University

HIGH JUMP Athletes use a variety of styles for the high jump, but the greatest heights have been reached by straddle-type jumpers.

John Thomas, United States

Photo, Wide World

pole from 12 to 16 feet in length as an aid in clearing a crossbar. The vaulter develops good momentum during a run of about 100 to 150 feet, places the front end of his pole in a fixed box, then uses it like a pendulum to clear the bar. The vaulter lands on heaped-up soft material, such as foam rubber or fine shavings. Poles may be made of wood, metal, or fiber glass. In the early 1960's fiber glass poles became the most efficient for vaulting. The extra flexibility of fiber glass has enabled athletes to make vaults of more than 17 feet. The best efforts with bamboo and aluminum poles are usually within the 15 to 16 foot range.

In the long jump, distance is measured from a fixed takeoff point to the part of the athlete that lands nearest the takeoff point. Jumpers sprint at top speed for about 100 to 130 feet, leaping as high as possible from the takeoff point to attain the longest jump.

In the triple jump, a hop on the first foot, a step to the second foot, and a final long jump are combined.

There are also four throwing events: the shot put and the discus, javelin, and hammer throws. Throwing events are judged solely on the basis of distance thrown. Accuracy is not considered. The fundamental technique used in throwing each of the implements is similar. The thrower combines body momentum with power from the muscles of the legs, torso, and arms to attain maximum distance.

In the shot put a heavy ball (the shot), usually made of iron or brass, is put (by an over-

hand push) as far as possible, from within a seven-foot circle. The ball must be put from the shoulder with one hand only; actual throwing is illegal. The putter concentrates power behind the shot by combining a quick glide across the circle with an upward drive and follow-through at the toeboard. The shot used by men in the Olympic Games weighs 16 pounds; by women, 8 pounds 13 ounces. High-school boys use a 12-pound shot.

In the discus throw the performer projects a heavy, round, platelike object into the air after whirling about $1\frac{3}{4}$ turns within an 8 foot $2\frac{1}{2}$ inch circle. During the whirl the discus is held against the palm of the hand and behind the body. The men's discus, made of wood and metal, weighs 4 pounds $6\frac{2}{5}$ ounces. (See DISCUS.)

In the javelin throw the action is similar to casting a spear. A good throw requires high body momentum from a rather fast run of about 120 feet. The javelin used in Olympic Games must be at least 8 feet $6\frac{3}{8}$ inches long and weigh no less than 1.76 pounds.

In the hammer throw the implement used

LONG JUMP A successful long, or broad, jump requires speed and form, as well as jumping ability. The jumper must leap as high as he can at the end of his sprint, kicking his legs to gain greater height and distance.

Igor Ter-Ovanesyan, U.S.S.R.

Photo, Wide World

does not resemble a hammer. It consists of a rigid metal loop (the grip) connected to a heavy metal ball by a flexible wire. The overall length of the implement must be between 46.4 and 48 inches, and it must weigh at least 16 pounds. The sport got its name during its early days when a blacksmith's hammer was the throwing implement. For an effective throw, momentum must be built up through two, three, or even four turns of the body and hammer within a seven-foot circle. The grip is with two hands, and the hammer is held in front of the body.

The Decathlon and Pentathlon. Two other major track and field events, the decathlon and pentathlon, require great ability and stamina. The decathlon requires participation in ten events: four track events (100-meter dash, 400-meter run, 1,500-meter run, 110-meter hurdles); three jumping events (high jump, pole vault, long jump); and three throwing events (shot, discus, javelin). Competition takes place over a two-day period. Competitors are scored in each event according to a scoring table. The decathlon is for men's participation only.

The pentathlon requires participation in five events. In men's competition these include the 200-, and 1,500-meter runs, the long jump, and the javelin and discus throws. In women's competition these include the shot put, high jump, long jump, 200-meter dash, and 80-meter hurdles.

History

Track and field has a long history as an organized sport. Homer, in the *Iliad*, describes the running, jumping, and throwing events at the funeral games held after the death of Achilles' friend Patroclus. According to Irish legend, Luguid the Strong founded the Tailtean Games about 4,000 years ago in honor of his beautiful foster mother, Queen Tailte.

The Ancient Games. The main impetus for modern track and field came from the ancient Greek Olympic Games. From the Greeks comes the word athlete. Actually, athletic games were held in many cities of Greece during more than a thousand-year history. The most outstanding of these were at Olympia and at Delphi. The games at Olympia were celebrated every four years. (See OLYMPIC GAMES.)

Events tended to follow the same program in all the various city games. They began as a single footrace. The first recorded victor was Coroebus of Elia in 776 B.C. Later, there were five track and field events: four runs and a pentathlon. The runs included the stade (one length of the stadium, about 200 yards), the diaulos (two lengths), a race in armor (two lengths), and a long-distance race of varying length, but usually of about two miles.

The Modern Games. Today's Olympic Games had many sources. The British had competed in various track and field events since early medieval times. Thomas Hughes' *Tom Brown's School Days* tells of a well-developed organization of school sports before 1850. The Frenchman Baron Pierre de Coubertin tried unsuccessfully to introduce such sports into France in the hope of raising the morale and restoring the fitness of youth. Finally he realized that by recreating the ancient Olympic Games on an international basis, he could accomplish his purpose. The first modern Olympic Games were held at Athens, Greece, in 1896.

Today, the Olympic Games help promote international agreement and goodwill. In the 1964 games at Tokyo more than 5,000 athletes from 94 countries competed.

Track and Field in the United States began mostly as a club sport. The New York Athletic Club was formed in 1868. In that year it held the first U.S. track and field meet. The Olympic Club of San Francisco held meets in 1877 and by 1900 many clubs were operating.

College track and field began in the eastern states. The Intercollegiate Association of Amateur Athletics of America (I.C.4-A.) held its first championships in 1876 with 15 colleges competing. The first national championships conducted by the N.C.A.A. were held in 1921. High school track and field, as in the colleges, began under local, state, and sectional organizations. After the National Federation of State High School Athletic Associations was formed in 1922, national agreement on uniform rules developed.

Women's Track and Field gained considerable importance after the foundation of the Federation Sportive Feminine Internationale in Paris in 1921. The organization held world track and field championships for women in 1922, 1926, 1930, and 1934. Beginning in 1928, women's track and field competition was included in the Olympic Games. By 1952, in the Olympic Games at Helsinki, Finland, 41 countries entered women's track and field teams. After the women's federation dissolved in 1936, the I.A.A.F. became the chief organizer for men's and women's international amateur competition.

Famous Track and Field Athletes

In the history of track and field there have been many truly great performers. Among those who deserve special mention in a list of the all-time greats are the following:

Alvin Kraenzlein, a University of Pennsylvania athlete of the late 1800's, is generally credited with inventing the modern hurdling style. In brief, he ran over the hurdle rather than jump over it. At the 1900 Olympic Games he set world records for the high and low hurdles and the running broad jump. He was also 60-meter-dash champion that year.

Jesse Owens, who attended Ohio State University, has held several world records. In 1935 he broke three world records (broad jump, 220-yard dash, 220-yard hurdles) and tied a fourth

MEN'S OUTDOOR TRACK AND FIELD WORLD RECORDS				
EVENT	**RECORD**	**YEAR**	**NAME**	**COUNTRY**
100-YARD DASH	9.1 sec.	1963	Robert Hayes	U.S.
		1966	Harry Jerome	Canada
		1967	James Hines	U.S.
		1967	Charles Greene	U.S.
		1970	Willie McGee	U.S.
220-YARD STRAIGHT DASH	19.5 sec.	1966	Thomas Smith	U.S.
440-YARD RUN	44.7 sec.	1969	Curtis Mills	U.S.
880-YARD RUN	1 min. 45.1 sec.	1962	Peter Snell	New Zealand
ONE-MILE RUN	3 min. 51.1 sec.	1967	James Ryun	U.S.
TWO-MILE RUN	8 min. 19.8 sec.	1967	Ron Clarke	Australia
120-YARD HIGH HURDLES	13.2 sec.	1959	Karl Lauer	West Germany
		1960	Lee Calhoun	U.S.
		1967	Earl McCullouch	U.S.
		1970	Thomas Hill	U.S.
440-YARD HURDLES	48.8 sec.	1970	Ralph Mann	U.S.
HIGH JUMP	7' 6¼"	1971	Pat Matzdorf	U.S.
POLE VAULT	18' ¼"	1970	Christos Papanicolaou	Greece
LONG (BROAD) JUMP	29' 2⅜"	1968	Bob Beamon	U.S.
TRIPLE JUMP (HOP, STEP, AND JUMP)	57' ¾"	1968	Viktor Saneyev	U.S.S.R.
SHOT PUT	71' 5½"	1965	Randy Matson	U.S.
DISCUS THROW	218' 4"	1968	Jay Silvester	U.S.
JAVELIN THROW	301' 9¼"	1968	Yanis Lusis	U.S.S.R.
HAMMER THROW	242'	1968	Gyula Zsivotzky	Hungary

(100-yard dash). At the 1936 Olympic Games, Owens won three gold medals for taking first place in the 100- and 200-meter dashes and the long jump. He won a fourth gold medal as part of a U.S. relay team.

Emil Zatopek of Czechoslovakia dominated world distance running just after World War II. He held many world records, and at the 1952 Olympic Games at Helsinki he won the 5,000-meter run, the 10,000-meter run, and the marathon—the first athlete ever to win this triple crown.

Parry O'Brien, who attended the University of Southern California, is noted for his great accomplishments in throwing events. During five years of world dominance in the shot put, he moved the world record upward by more than 4 feet, from 58 feet $10\frac{3}{4}$ inches to 63 feet 2 inches. His record put of 60 feet $5\frac{1}{4}$ inches in 1954 was the first to break the 60-foot barrier.

He invented a new and better style of putting, now called the O'Brien style. He took part in the four Olympic Games between 1952 and 1964. In the first two, O'Brien won the gold medal with new Olympic records.

Valery Brumel of the U.S.S.R., during the years 1960 and 1964, advanced the world record in the high jump from the 7-foot $\frac{3}{4}$-inch mark to 7 feet $5\frac{3}{4}$ inches. He was the Olympic Games champion in 1964.

Cornelius Warmerdam of the United States became the first man to pole vault over 15 feet. His record vault, in 1940, was 15 feet $1\frac{1}{8}$ inches. In 1942 Warmerdam set a new record of 15 feet $7\frac{3}{4}$ inches, which lasted for 15 years.

Other athletes who made noteworthy contributions to track and field include Roger Bannister of England, the first man to run the mile in under 4 minutes (3 minutes and 59.4 seconds in 1954); Charles Dumas of the United States, the first man to high jump over 7 feet (7 feet $\frac{1}{2}$ inch in 1956); Ralph Boston of the United States, the first man to attain a long jump of more than 27 feet (27 feet $\frac{1}{2}$ inch in 1961); John Pennel of the United States, the first man to pole vault more than 17 feet (17 feet $\frac{3}{4}$ inches in 1963); and Randy Matson of the United States, the first to put the 16-pound shot over 71 feet.

TRADE (*trād*) is the exchange of goods and services between persons for other goods and services or for money. If goods are exchanged between persons who live in different countries, it is called foreign or international trade. Goods going out of a country are exports; those coming into a country are imports.

How Trade Developed

Trade probably first began among wandering peoples. They exchanged gifts as a way of showing friendship, of making peace, or celebrating religious festivals. They also traded for an economic advantage, to get items, such as food or metals, that they did not have in their own community. The simplest kind of trade that developed was the barter system. Under this system a person gave something that he had to someone else for another item of the same value. A basket maker, for example, might exchange a basket for some fish from a fisherman. The barter system is still used today.

In the early beginnings of Western civilization, trade was still limited to the exchange of a small number of goods. People's wants were few, and most that was needed was nearby. Trade was then an adventure across unknown seas and lands, with pirates and robbers as a danger. Mostly luxury goods were exchanged because they sold for a great deal of money compared with their size and weight. Some goods imported into Egypt 4,000 years ago included silver from Asia Minor, sword blades from Greece, and tapestries from Syria.

Trade was carried on largely by river or by sea. There were few major roads, and these were always in bad repair. Some goods came across the land from China to Europe. Some arrived by boats, which hugged the coast of Asia and after many months arrived at the north end of the Red Sea. Transportation by water was cheaper, safer, and faster than by land. Only after the compass, an instrument for finding direction, was perfected did sailors dare to cross the open seas regularly. Oceans then changed from barriers to highways for trade.

At about that same time, methods of producing goods changed. There were a great many more products for sale. New discoveries and

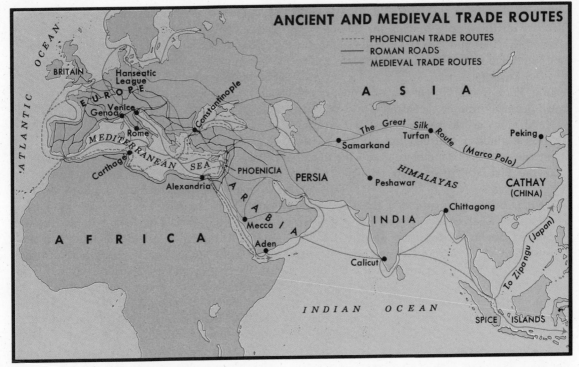

ANCIENT AND MEDIEVAL TRADE ROUTES

- - - - - - PHOENICIAN TRADE ROUTES
————— ROMAN ROADS
————— MEDIEVAL TRADE ROUTES

new inventions made people want more things. In the 20th century few countries have everything they need. Goods of every kind are exchanged. They are moved all over the world by boat, airplane, railroad, and truck.

Why Goods Are Exchanged

There are many reasons why goods are exchanged. In general, people trade because of the specialization of labor. That is, different workers perform jobs in accordance with their skills, interests, and resources. In order to get what other workers make, people trade. People also trade to get goods that are produced only in some areas, like coffee, or found only in a few places, like petroleum. Certain labor skills and raw materials also allow people in some areas to manufacture goods not made elsewhere, such as steel in Pittsburgh, Pennsylvania, or cuckoo clocks in Germany. Everyone who wants these items must get them from the areas where they are produced.

In some places certain goods are produced in greater quantities than needed. The extra amounts are sold to people who do not make enough of the item for themselves. A country

may find it cheaper to buy goods that are expensive for it to make and in exchange to sell other goods that it can produce easily.

People need to buy as well as sell. The person who sells to someone in a foreign country, however, may not want to buy other goods or services himself. Someone must use the money he received to import goods or services, however, or there is nothing gained by exporting.

Trade of Early Times

Thousands of years ago trade was carried along desert routes in camel caravans. The products of Africa and Arabia were brought to fairs in the valley of the Tigris and Euphrates rivers. Olive oil and dyes were exchanged for textiles and metals. Buyers also carried silks and jewels from China to Europe.

The first important seagoing people were the Minoans on the little island of Crete. Between 2500 and 1500 B.C. they ruled the Mediterranean Sea and traded with Egypt and Greece. After the Minoans disappeared, the Phoenicians ruled the sea. They had little agricultural land from which to earn a living. Because their land bordered the eastern Mediterranean, these adventurous people turned to the sea for a living. For more than 500 years they were the principal traders on the Mediterranean Sea. In addition to their large water trade, the Phoenicians carried on land trade from their great cities of Tyre and Sidon. Every corner of the known world was reached by them. (See PHOENICIA.)

After about the 6th century B.C. the Greeks took the place of the Phoenicians as the leading trading nation in the Mediterranean area. The Greeks needed many kinds of food and raw materials. To get these things they traded the goods of gold, ivory, stone, and clay that they were able to make. These were eagerly bought by other countries. Ancient Greek pottery vases, bronze statues, and other goods are still being found in the ruins of cities of North Africa, Spain, Italy, and Egypt, where traders had carried them in the time of Alexander the Great (356–323 B.C.).

The wars of Alexander brought the Western world into more direct contact with the East. After his conquests trade developed with Central Asia and India.

The Greeks expanded trade by spreading the use of coined money. As long as only barter existed, trade was limited. Two persons had to meet, each of whom wanted to sell what the other wanted to buy. With a system of coinage, a trader could sell his wares and accept money in payment instead of goods. This money he later used to buy the goods he wanted. (See MONEY.)

After the Greeks, Rome became the leader in trade. By the 1st century A.D. the Romans had built an empire extending from England across modern Europe to the Persian Gulf and from the Black Sea south to Africa. Rome became a powerful trade center where goods from all over the world were brought. Trade within the Roman Empire was aided by excellent roads, built from the capital city to every part of western Europe. For the first time, paved roads were used along with natural waterways for commerce.

The Middle Ages

During the 5th century, trade continued to grow in the East. The great city of Constanti-

nople (now Istanbul, Turkey) became the commercial center of the world because it linked the East with the West. Beautiful porcelains, mosaics, and engraved metal articles were manufactured there and sold at great trade fairs. Banking and insurance had their beginnings at this time in Constantinople. One of the great eastern trade routes of the Middle Ages passed through the city.

In the West, however, after Rome was overthrown in the 5th century, trade between the parts of Europe gradually died out. As feudalism developed, each small area produced most of what it needed for itself. (See FEUDAL SYSTEM.) Tolls were collected on roads and rivers from the few merchants who remained. By the 9th century the wandering peddler with a few wares on his back was more common than the professional merchant. Salt and spices were almost the only items from outside Europe that were traded.

In Europe the most powerful city of the Middle Ages was Venice. Most trade that continued during the period was controlled by Venetian merchants. Compared with the earlier Roman period or later centuries, however, trade was small indeed. It was largely in luxury goods for the wealthy or for the church.

Revival of Trade

From the 11th to the 13th century, many changes took place in Europe. Feudalism became less common, and manufacturing developed in the growing towns. Many men went from Europe in the fight, or Crusades, to recover the Holy Land. When these men returned, they brought stories of the many comforts of living that they had seen in the Middle East. Marco Polo traveled to the Far East and amazed Venice on his return in 1295 when he told of the wealth to be found there. (See POLO, MARCO.) A new interest in commerce with the East began to develop, which led to a great increase in trade.

When Constantinople was captured by the Turks in 1453, a main route to the East was cut. Explorers began to search for new routes to India and also for new sources of gold. This metal had become scarce in Europe because it

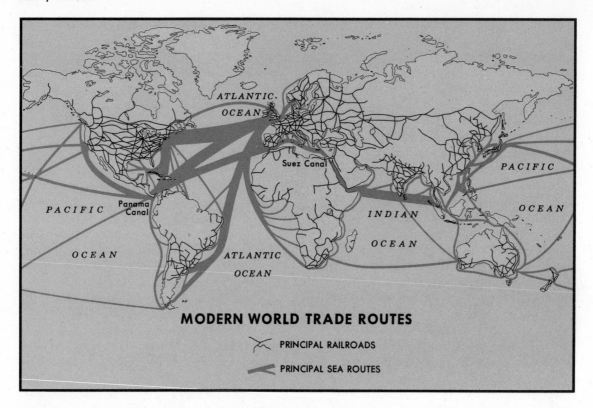

MODERN WORLD TRADE ROUTES

⤬ PRINCIPAL RAILROADS

◄ PRINCIPAL SEA ROUTES

was used to make payments for the growing supplies of goods from the East.

Portugal and Spain were the most powerful countries in the world of commerce in the 15th century. Their explorers reached the New World and around Africa to India. In their wake came traders who established trading stations and colonies.

In the 17th century the Netherlands became the leading commercial nation; France and England, however, fought to gain this leadership. By 1763, as the Industrial Revolution was beginning, England had become the commercial leader of the world.

The 19th Century

Foreign trade changed greatly in the 19th century. Between 1800 and 1850, more new ways of producing goods and new means of transportation were developed. Power machinery and factory production made more goods available than ever before. (See INDUSTRIAL REVOLUTION, THE.) The first telegraph line was opened in 1844; news could then travel faster than men or goods. A worldwide postal service was begun in 1874. Railroads were built, and steamships replaced the old sailing vessels. These changes in communication made it easier for buyers and sellers to do business.

England, with a great colonial empire, carried on the largest world trade in the early part of the century. Although England produced many manufactured items for export, the country needed to import food and raw materials. English leadership in world trade continued until the 1920's. By this time other countries, such as France, Germany, and the United States, were developing as important trading countries.

The 20th Century

In the 20th century the exchange of goods is greater than ever before in the history of the world. Every country has some foreign trade. Certain countries, such as the United States, have many resources and, therefore, are able to produce most but not all of what they need. Others, such as Japan, have to depend on imports for their daily needs.

About 100 million persons are employed today in foreign and domestic commerce. This is about 10 percent of all the world's workers. The importance of trade today is also shown by the fact that world exports in any one year are valued at more than $170 billion. Of this, almost two-thirds is exported from ten industrialized countries; that is, countries that have large industries where such products as steel, chemicals, and machinery are made. These countries include, in order of volume, the United States, West Germany, the United Kingdom, France, the U.S.S.R., Canada, Japan, Italy, the Netherlands, and Belgium-Luxembourg.

The principal commodities now traded in the world are of several types. Wheat, fruits and vegetables, rubber, meat, cotton, and wool are among the major agricultural products. About one-quarter of all exports are the products of agriculture. Coal, crude petroleum, and petroleum products are the major fuel exports. Trade in manufactured goods is made up of many thousands of items. The largest in value are machinery, iron- and steel-mill products, cotton fabrics, and motor vehicles.

The exports of the countries in Asia, Africa, and Latin America are largely food and raw materials. Many of them depend almost completely on one or two export products to earn foreign money. If the world buys less of that product or if the price for that product falls, then the country has to cut its imports, unless aid or investment is provided by another country. These countries import mostly manufactured goods from Europe, North America, and Japan.

Importance of Trade to the United States

Foreign trade helped the United States change from an agricultural country in the 19th century to the leading industrial country in the 20th century. In 1850 the United States exported little of importance except food and raw materials. Now foreign trade is one of the most important business activities in the United States. About 4,500,000 workers are employed in producing or selling goods for export and handling or distributing imports.

To some industries in the United States, it is important to sell to other countries. Many producers export between one-fourth to one-half of all their products. The most important exports are machinery, chemicals, automobiles, electrical equipment, aircraft, munitions, iron- and steel-mill products, other metals, textiles, and coal.

Many other U.S. manufacturers import large amounts of raw materials. All natural rubber, diamonds, tin, and most of the newsprint come from other countries. More than one-half of the

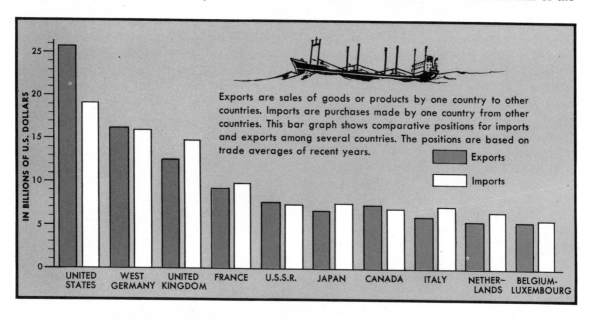

Exports are sales of goods or products by one country to other countries. Imports are purchases made by one country from other countries. This bar graph shows comparative positions for imports and exports among several countries. The positions are based on trade averages of recent years.

Exports
Imports

IN BILLIONS OF U.S. DOLLARS

UNITED STATES · WEST GERMANY · UNITED KINGDOM · FRANCE · U.S.S.R. · JAPAN · CANADA · ITALY · NETHER-LANDS · BELGIUM-LUXEMBOURG

wool and one-fifth of the crude petroleum are also purchased overseas. Many foods are imported, such as tropical products not grown widely in the United States—cocoa, coffee, spices, and bananas. Goods, such as toys, china, and automobiles, that are produced in the United States are also imported. Because of these imports, people in the United States have a greater choice of things to buy. Sometimes imports help reduce prices of products made in the United States.

Barriers to Trade

Almost as long as there has been trade in the world, attempts have been made to limit it. From Greek and Roman times to the 19th century, exports were often taxed as a means of raising money to pay the expenses of government. In some developing countries, export taxes are still commonly used.

There was, however, free trade, or trade without taxation, in the 19th century. It then became usual for most countries to collect duties on their imports. Duties or tariffs are a kind of tax on the value of goods traded. (See TARIFF.)

Many countries allow only certain amounts of some products to enter their country. Sometimes these controls are put into effect to help a country save the money it has for the most needed imports. Almost every country has a list of commodities that are not allowed to enter the country at all. These commodities include goods that might hurt public health or safety.

The greatest barriers to trade in modern times were set up in the 1930's and 1940's during the great depression and after World War II. A new international organization called the G.A.T.T. (General Agreement on Tariffs and Trade) came into being in 1947 to help reduce trade barriers. By 1967 it had been successful in causing reductions in the tariffs of nearly every country in the world and causing many other trade barriers to disappear. (See COMMERCE; INTERNATIONAL RELATIONS, *Trade and Trade Agreements;* TARIFF.)

TRADEMARK (*trād' märk*) is a mark or symbol used by manufacturers or merchants to identify and distinguish goods and services. It may be a word, a picture, a letter, a number, or a combination of these.

A trademark indicates the origin of an item. That is, it tells what manufacturer or merchant is responsible for the product. It also identifies the product so that a buyer can purchase duplicates over and over again and be certain he is receiving the same type of item each time. A trademark also has an important advertising function. Manufacturers spend large sums of money to advertise their products under certain trademarks so that the products will be easily recognized. When a manufacturer puts his trademark on several items, he classes them together as a brand. Usually the brand name is the same as the trademark. A trademark can also identify a service, in which case it is referred to as a service name.

Trademarks are protected by laws throughout the world. The laws provide for registration of trademarks and for penalties against those who use them unlawfully. In 1881 the first effective federal trademark law in the United States was passed. The present trademark act, the Lanham Act, was passed in 1946.

A person who wants to register a trademark must apply at the U.S. Patent Office. The application is granted if the trademark will not confuse the identity of trademarks already registered. Protection is granted for 20 years. It may be renewed, for a small fee, for successive terms of 20 years.

The custom of using trademarks is very old. Among the ruins of ancient Egypt, bricks bearing the manufacturer's name have been found. The name of the maker usually appeared on ancient Greek pottery. Sometimes it had with it a picture, such as a bee, lion's head, or oil jug. Trademarks were used in ancient Roman commercial life in almost the same way as they are in modern business. Roman lamps, tiles, and cheeses all carried them.

The thistle is the trademark of the *Encyclopaedia Britannica.*

17·68

In the 15th and 16th centuries, metalworkers, tapestry weavers, papermakers, printers, smiths, tanners, and armorers used trademarks. At that time strict laws punished those who copied trademarks of others. Nevertheless only a few products bore such marks. Most buyers knew the worker from whom they bought. Today, shoes, flour, clothes, and in fact almost everything people use come from enormous factories whose owners are unknown to buyers. For that reason, trademarks are necessary.

TRAILS (*trālz*), **U.S. HISTORIC** (*his tôr' ik*). Modern highways and railroads all over the world often follow old trails first made by animals and early man. In the United States, early trappers and traders wended their way along Indian footpaths. When the settlers began their trek across the continent, they usually followed these trails, clearing them for their wagons as they went. Emigrants poured through the Appalachian Mountains on the Great Genesee Road into western New York; over Braddock's Road and Forbes Road into the Ohio Valley at Pittsburgh, Pennsylvania; and into Kentucky over the Wilderness Road. Farther west was the Natchez Trace, which followed an old Indian trail from Nashville, Tennessee, to Natchez, a Mississippi River town. The Butterfield Overland Mail had a route from St. Louis, Missouri, through El Paso, Texas, to northern California, and the Old Spanish Trail went from Santa Fe to California. (See WESTWARD MOVEMENT).

The great trail of early America was the Cumberland, or National, Road. The road, built between 1811 and 1852 by the national government, ran from Cumberland, Maryland, to Vandalia, Illinois. It was an important road because it opened the area it reached to waves of settlement. Conestoga wagons carried tons of goods and settlers west along the road, and stagecoaches carried passengers and mail. Farmers hauled their harvest and drove their cattle and hogs along the trail to eastern markets.

Central Overland Trail

The great emigrant trails of the Far West made up the network of central overland trails.

Usually they were nothing but several sets of ruts leading in the same direction. Included among them were the Oregon Trail, the Mormon Trail, and the California Trail. The Union Pacific and Central Pacific railroads and the pony express later followed much of the central route.

Culver Pictures
The first wagon train over the Oregon Trail was taken by fur traders in 1830.

Oregon Trail led from Independence, Missouri, northwest to the Platte River, up the Platte to South Pass of the Rocky Mountains, on to the Snake River, and down it to Fort Vancouver on the Columbia River. It was more than 2,000 miles long and was first used by fur traders. (See FUR AND FUR TRADE.) Missionaries and fur traders took the first wagon over the trail in the 1830's. The migration of settlers to Oregon began in 1841. Each year the number increased, until 3,000 went overland in 1845. Overland pioneers could get some supplies at several trading posts—Fort Laramie and Fort Bridger in Wyoming and Fort Hall and Fort Boise in Idaho—but food was scarce, and prices were high. The hardships of disease and fear of Indian attack further tested the settlers' strength. Nevertheless, thousands survived the grueling trip to settle the land and bring about the organization of the Territory of Oregon. (See OREGON.)

California Trail followed the Oregon Trail beyond Fort Hall and then branched off southward through Utah and Nevada by several routes toward California. Following the gold discovery in California in 1848, thousands of gold seekers pushed their way along the trail.

HISTORIC TRAILS OF THE UNITED STATES

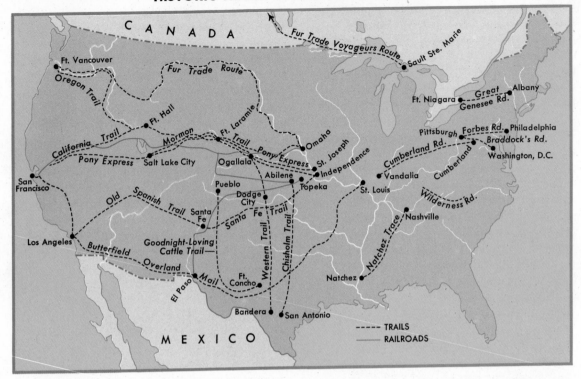

Mormon Trail. The Mormons moved from Illinois to western Iowa in 1846, hoping to find religious freedom farther west. The next year a pioneering band of 143 men, 3 women, and 2 children in 73 wagons started west to find a new home. They drove out the north side of the Platte River, through South Pass, and to the Great Salt Lake Valley. There, under the leadership of Brigham Young, they started a settlement. (See YOUNG, BRIGHAM.) About 80,000 people moved along the 1,100-mile trail before the completion of the Union Pacific Railroad in 1869.

Santa Fe Trail

The people living on the Mexican or Spanish frontier in New Mexico during the early 1800's were about 1,000 miles from the Missouri settlements. They needed clothing, tools, and iron, and markets for their gold, silver, mules, and wool. Three wagons loaded with goods were the first to successfully travel to Santa Fe in 1822. After that, wagon trains wore the ruts in the almost 800 miles that became the Santa Fe Trail. By 1850 more than 3,000 wagons had

traveled the trail. Most of them carried traders and their goods. The Santa Fe Trail was far more important as a trade route than as a settlers' route. After the Atchison, Topeka and Santa Fe Railroad was completed to New Mexico in 1880, the Santa Fe Trail was little used.

Chisholm Trail

The Spanish brought the first cows, horses, and sheep into the Southwest. Texas became a great cattle-ranching country, but the ranchers had the problem of finding markets for their cattle. Some drove herds to California to sell to the miners. Others drove their longhorned cattle to Iowa and Illinois to sell to farmers. Then in 1867 Joseph McCoy built pens at the end of the Kansas-Pacific Railroad in Abilene, Kansas. Texans drove their herds there and shipped them east on the railroad. This trail from Texas to Abilene was the Chisholm Trail.

As the railroads and settlers pushed westward across the plains, the Chisholm Trail lost much of its importance. Among the other cattle trails were the Western Trail, from Texas to

Dodge City, Kansas, and Ogallala, Nebraska; and the Goodnight-Loving Cattle Trail up to Pueblo, Colorado. Over these dusty trails five million cattle moved northward to the cow towns or to stock the ranches of the plains. After the railroad came, the cattle rode to market. (See CATTLE; COWBOY.)

TRANSFORMER (*trăns fôr′ mēr*) is an electrical device that is used primarily to increase or decrease the amount of voltage between two circuits. (See ELECTRICITY.)

A transformer is made of two separate coils of wire positioned near each other. The coils are placed on rods or other shapes of iron or other magnetic materials. A changing, or alternating, voltage applied to one coil causes another alternating voltage to appear in the circuit containing the other coil. This effect, electromagnetic induction, was discovered by Michael Faraday in 1831. (See FARADAY, MICHAEL; MAGNET AND ELECTROMAGNET.)

Faraday wound two coils of wire on an iron ring. When he connected one coil to a battery and the second coil to a current-measuring instrument, he expected to find a current flowing in the second coil. He found, however, that no current flowed in the second coil until he disconnected the battery from the first. At that instant a brief surge of current flowed through the second coil. When he reconnected the battery to the first coil, another short surge of current was produced in the second coil.

Faraday found that whenever the current in the first coil was changed in any way—by starting, stopping, increasing, or decreasing—there was a surge of current in the second coil. He explained this "link" between the two coils by the presence of a magnetic field that was produced by the current in the first coil. He explained that the field surrounded both coils. When the current in the first coil changed, the field that surrounded the coils changed. This caused the magnetic field to move through the second coil. The motion of the field caused an induced current to flow in the second coil.

Faraday's iron ring wound with two coils of wire was the first transformer. He recognized that electromagnetic induction could be used for converting mechanical energy into electrical energy. With this in mind, he made the first electric generator, which converts the energy of a rotating shaft to electrical energy. (See GENERATOR, ELECTRIC.)

The voltage in each coil, or winding, is proportional to the number of turns of wire. If the

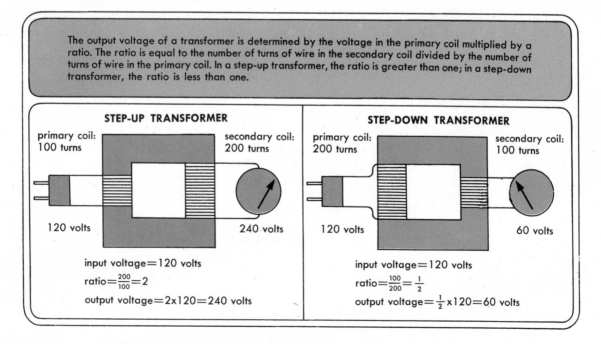

The output voltage of a transformer is determined by the voltage in the primary coil multiplied by a ratio. The ratio is equal to the number of turns of wire in the secondary coil divided by the number of turns of wire in the primary coil. In a step-up transformer, the ratio is greater than one; in a step-down transformer, the ratio is less than one.

STEP-UP TRANSFORMER

primary coil: 100 turns

secondary coil: 200 turns

120 volts

240 volts

input voltage = 120 volts

ratio = $\frac{200}{100}$ = 2

output voltage = 2 x 120 = 240 volts

STEP-DOWN TRANSFORMER

primary coil: 200 turns

secondary coil: 100 turns

120 volts

60 volts

input voltage = 120 volts

ratio = $\frac{100}{200}$ = $\frac{1}{2}$

output voltage = $\frac{1}{2}$ x 120 = 60 volts

primary has 100 turns, for example, and the secondary has 200 turns, and the primary is connected to a 120-volt wall outlet, the secondary voltage will be 2 × 120 volts, or 240 volts. The same voltage would result if the primary has 200 turns and the secondary has 400 turns. In each case, the secondary has two times the number of turns of the primary. A transformer that increases voltage is a step-up transformer.

If the primary has 200 turns and the secondary has 100, and the primary is connected to a 120-volt wall outlet, the secondary voltage will be $\frac{1}{2}$ × 120 volts, or 60 volts. In this case the secondary has one-half the number of turns of the primary. A transformer that decreases voltage is a step-down transformer.

The amount of current in each winding is calculated in the reverse way. The coil that has the greater number of turns has the lesser amount of current. If a current of one ampere, for example, passes through a primary of 100 turns, the current in a secondary of 200 turns will be $\frac{1}{2}$ ampere.

Power transformers are used to distribute power from generating stations to homes and factories. Without transformers it would be im-practical or impossible to transmit power over long distances. The distance that electric power can be economically transmitted depends on the amount of current used. The power-station generators produce power at high current and somewhat low voltage. If such power were to be transmitted directly to homes, the wires necessary to carry it might be as big around as a telephone pole and enormously expensive. Generating stations, therefore, first pass the power through step-up transformers, which raise the voltage to hundreds of thousands of volts at a much reduced current. Along the power-line routes step-down transformers reduce the voltage several times. The wiring in homes and factories is connected to transformers that produce 120 and 240 volts.

In many applications where transformers are used, the power in watts is almost equal to voltage multiplied by current, or the number of volt-amperes. In theory, the volt-amperes in the primary are equal to the volt-amperes in the secondary. In real transformers there are losses of energy in the form of heat, and the number of volt-amperes is always slightly less than the primary—usually a few percent.

Transformers have other uses. Television sets, radios, phonographs, and other household appliances contain small transformers for converting the wall-outlet power to that required by the appliance. These transformers have windings on a core of magnetic material. The core is often of thin steel strips, or laminations. Laminated cores are used because they produce less heat than a solid, one-piece core.

Transformers used in radio circuits may have iron-oxide cores or no cores at all other than air. Air-core and iron-oxide types must be used where the frequency, or the number of times the current changes direction, is hundreds of thousands to millions of times per second.

TRANSISTOR (*trănz ĭs′tēr*) is an electronic device used for amplification, rectification, and other purposes in an electronic circuit. It is usually made of a tiny amount of solid material. Since its invention in 1947, the transistor has almost replaced the vacuum tube. (See INVENTION; RADIO.)

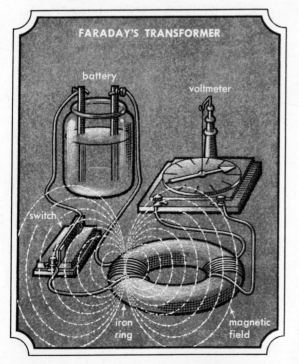

FARADAY'S TRANSFORMER

battery
voltmeter
switch
iron ring
magnetic field

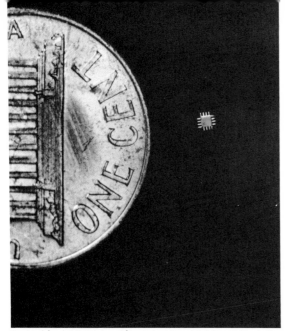

enlarged inside view
of the metal enclosure

actual size (¼ x
⅜ x 1/16 inches)

Courtesy (above) Bell Telephone Laboratories, (above right) General Electric Co.

Many transistor circuits can be sealed in one small metal enclosure, above. Other circuits can be sealed directly onto the transistor material, left, without an extra enclosure.

A transistor is a kind of control valve. A small amount of force on a mechanical valve, below left, allows a big "whoosh" of high-pressure spray. A small amount of electrical force from the microphone, below right, that reaches the transistor allows a large push of electrical force from the power supply to pass through. A whisper into the microphone can become a booming voice from the loud-speaker.

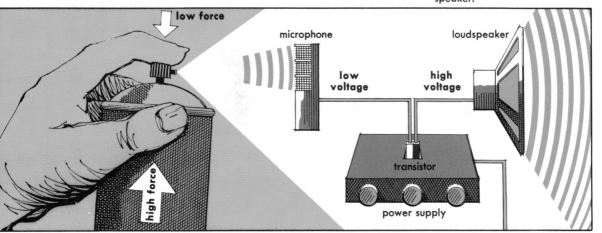

The main purpose of the vacuum tube is to amplify, or strengthen, weak electric signals. The transistor can also amplify, but it does so with much less power and more reliability, and it is much smaller than the vacuum tube. A transistor is a current amplifier, and a vacuum tube is a voltage amplifier.

Most vacuum tubes control current flowing through a vacuum within a glass tube. Such currents flow by the motion of negatively charged electrons that come from certain heated materials. In a vacuum tube, this material is the cathode. A hot cathode, however, uses a great amount of power to reach its operating temperature. (See ELECTRON; ELECTRICITY.)

The transistor, on the other hand, controls electric currents flowing through a solid material. The electric current may be caused by either negatively charged electrons or positively charged holes. The passage of these currents takes place inside the solid material. The charged particles need not be forced outside the material, as are the electrons in a vacuum tube. This is the reason why large amounts of power are not needed for a transistor.

All matter may be classified as conductors, semiconductors, or insulators. In conductors—such as copper, aluminum, and steel—the electric current is always carried by negatively charged electrons. In insulators—such as glass, mica, and ceramics—no electric current at all can be carried. Semiconductors—such as silicon, germanium, and carbon—will carry current but not so efficiently as the conductors. Semiconductors, however, will conduct current either by electrons (negative charges) or holes (positive charges). Transistors are made of semiconductors. (See MATTER; SOLID.)

Current conduction by holes may be compared to the movement of cars in a parking lot.

The figure below shows a car trying to park in a lot. The only remaining space, however, is at the rear of the lot. The parking attendant, by repositioning the rest of the cars

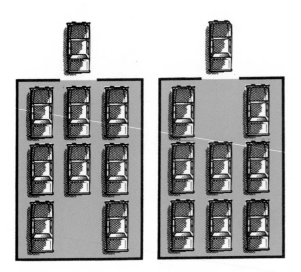

in the lot, finally makes an empty space at the entrance to the lot. The waiting car can then enter. The parking space, or hole, has "moved" from the rear of the lot to the front.

A current applied to a semiconductor produces a random but directed pattern of holes and moving electrons. An electron, with a negative charge, skips off one atom only to settle on another atom. A hole, or positive charge, is produced in the first atom. Another electron settles on the first atom, leaving behind another hole. The holes move through the solid much as bubbles through a liquid. The cars in the example may be thought of as electrons.

A semiconductor having more electrons than holes is an N-type, or negative, material. Similarly, a semiconductor with more holes than electrons is a P-type, or positive, material. A semiconductor material is made N- or P-type by a kind of alloying. (See ALLOY.)

Transistors are made by joining together layers of P- and N-types of semiconducting material. Batteries are connected between these layers to control the direction and amount of current flow. The most common kinds of transistors are the PNP and NPN transistors. The first is a sandwich of N-type between two layers of P-type material. The NPN is a sandwich of P-type between two layers of N-type material. The electric leads connected to the outer layers are the emitter and collector of the transistor. The lead connected to the middle layer is the base. The grid of a vacuum tube is similar to the base of a transistor. The cathode corresponds to the emitter, and the plate corresponds to the collector.

The extremely small size of the transistor makes many things possible. Because it is so small and dependable, and because it requires so little power to operate, the transistor reduces the size of the electronic equipment mounted in a space capsule. For the same reason, computers are built with transistors. Hearing aids, using transistors, are almost invisible. (See COMPUTER.)

Transistors today do more than merely replace some vacuum tubes. The light-activated transistor, or photo transistor, operates on light that strikes its surface. The unijunction transistor makes possible extremely accurate timing circuits. The gate-controlled switch can replace certain mechanically operated switches.

The search to make the transistor as small as possible forms a new branch of electronics. It is microelectronics. Scientists and engineers in this field have produced one device so small that 50,000 of them will fit in a thimble. This transistor is a square, $\frac{1}{32}$ inch by $\frac{1}{32}$ inch. It is so thin, about 60 millionths of an inch, that about 50 of them stacked up one on top of another would be as thick as a sheet of newspaper.

TRANSPORTATION

(*trăns′ pŭr tā′ shŭn*) is the means by which goods and passengers are moved from one place to another. Modern transportation has speeded up people's lives, broadened their activities, and affected them in many other ways. The United States, for example, has a vast network of railroads, highways, waterways, and airways.

In many parts of the world the rivers, lakes, and oceans are busy water routes and channels. Trains carry passengers and freight, and so do great ships that cross the oceans. Airplanes, carrying mail and passengers, fly overhead at supersonic speeds, and everywhere people dash about in automobiles. The world is made smaller in terms of the time it takes to get from one place to another.

Most of the great inventions that make possible today's transportation system have taken place since the latter part of the 18th century. Before then, travel and transportation were slow, difficult, and costly.

In primitive times human muscles were the only means of moving things from one place to another. Man was his own beast of burden. He carried wood for his campfire. He carried water from the spring. He carried home animals that he had killed for food. When a tribe moved, the women and children carried their belongings on their backs. The men carried their weapons ready for use. They traveled on foot at only a few miles an hour.

A native of Bombay, India, carries a huge load of basket-like goods on his shoulders.

H. Armstrong Roberts

Movement from one place to another became easier when man tamed certain animals and taught them to carry riders or other loads. In Egypt and other countries around the Mediterranean Sea, people trained the ox and the donkey. In India and China people trained the water buffalo and the bullock. Wandering tribes in Central Asia trained horses to wear bridles and saddles and to carry goods and people.

People tamed and trained those animals that lived in their region that were best adapted to

(Left) Arizona Photographic Associates, Inc., (right) Sergio Larrain—Magnum

Camels still are used for transportation by the Bedouins of Saudi Arabia, left. Only llamas, right, and donkeys can travel safely the steep, narrow mountain paths of Peru. The llama is an animal that is related to the camel but does not have a hump.

The first kind of sledge was probably used in the northern countries to travel over ice and snow.

Courtesy Chicago Museum of Science and Industry from The Dunbar Collection

the region. In Tibet, for example, the yak was used because its heavy coat protected the animal during the cold winters. The desert people trained the camel because it can endure extreme heat and can travel for days without water or food. In addition, the camel has broad padded feet that keep it from sinking into the sand. The Indians of South America trained the llama to carry burdens in the Andes Mountains. The llama is a surefooted animal that can travel steep trails without slipping.

After man found animals to carry him and his belongings he was satisfied—for a while. The load had been taken off his back and placed on a beast of burden. So long as animals were used only to carry burdens, however, there could be no great increase in the amount of goods carried.

The next improvement in transportation was the means by which animals could transport more goods. Animals can transport more goods by pulling things behind them than they can by carrying things on their backs. At first man had only the crudest sorts of drags and sledges to hitch to his animals. Flat-bottomed sledges and sleds with runners move smoothly in snowy regions. Such vehicles are pulled by reindeer or by dogs. Without snow, sleds and sledges are almost useless, although sleds can ·be dragged over fairly smooth ground.

The Indians of North America used poles instead of flat drags. Two long poles were tied to the back of a horse or a dog, so that the ends trailed on the ground. On this device, a travois, goods could be dragged along. (For illustration, see INDIANS, NORTH AMERICAN.)

Man Invents the Wheel

One of the greatest events in the history of transportation was the invention of the wheel. The first wheels were probably small sections of logs that were used as rollers under a drag or a platform. When the platform was pulled, the logs under it rolled. This made the work easier than pulling the platform along bare ground. As the platform moved along, it passed completely over the logs. Then the logs were picked up and again put under the front end of the platform, and the process was repeated.

After a long time, someone thought of cutting a slice from the end of a log and making a hole in its center. When two such wheels were

An all-wood wheel used by the Romans was found near Newst End, Scotland.

Courtesy National Museum of Antiquities, Edinburgh, Scotland

joined by a shaft, or axle, and the axle fastened to a platform, man had made a crude cart. Solid wooden wheels were heavy and clumsy; they wore down quickly when used on rough ground. Solid wheels made it possible, nevertheless, to move heavier loads with less effort.

In the course of thousands of years, man improved the wheel. He built wheels with separate hubs, spokes, and rims, which made the wheels lighter and more efficient. He made rims and tires of copper or iron so that the wheels would last longer. Eventually he learned to use rubber tires for easier riding.

The invention of the wheel alone did not solve immediately all of the problems of transporting people and goods. Early people had poor roads. They traveled on paths that were wide enough for pack animals but not for carts or wagons. There were swamps, deserts, mountains, rivers, and plains to be crossed. A man with an oxcart might have to travel far along a river before he came to a shallow place where he could cross, or ford, the stream. He had to find passes to get through mountains. In addition, travel was dependent on good weather. He was always fearful of floods, snow, or impassable mud.

Because of all the problems, early traders traveled in caravans or groups. Then they could help each other across swamps, mountains, and rivers. They gathered at a meeting place, usually once a year, and started out together. This was safer than traveling alone, but it was very slow. The caravans that brought tea from western China to the Russian city of Gorki, for example, were supposed to make that trip in a year. Often it took two years, and sometimes three, before a caravan arrived at its destination.

There are millions of people today who still depend on pack animals and crude-wheeled vehicles for transportation. In certain parts of Africa, Australia, Asia, South America, eastern Europe, and even in some parts of North America, this primitive transportation is the only kind available.

Good Roads Increased Trade

The Romans were the first people in Europe to build good roads. They wanted to send soldiers and messengers swiftly to all parts of their vast empire. They wanted to bring in goods from their faraway provinces. In order to do this, they needed good roads as well as ships. They built thousands of miles of roads, all leading to Rome. Roman roads were wide and straight, and sometimes paved with slabs of rock. There were milestones, signposts, and resting-places for travelers, with stables for their oxen and horses. Bridges of wood or stone made it easy to cross rivers. Soldiers were stationed along the routes to protect travelers and their goods from robbers. (See ROME, ANCIENT.)

For the first time, wagons were really useful for transporting goods, because smooth roads were available. Goods were not so likely to be damaged when carried on smooth roads. The wagons, however, were not very comfortable for passengers. Important people rode in light, two-wheeled carriages or in chariots, but most travelers went on horseback or on foot. Bad weather no longer made travel impossible. The Roman roads, with their solid foundations and hard surfaces, could be used in any weather.

In the early 1800's the horse-drawn English carriage provided a bouncy ride.

Courtesy Chicago Museum of Science and Industry from The Dunbar Collection

For about 200 years after the birth of Christ, the strong Roman government enforced law and order. The ancient world had never known such a time of peace and prosperity, and trade flourished. Later, however, the barbarians crowded into the Roman Empire and destroyed Roman power. A period of disorder and strife began that lasted for several centuries. Once again travel became difficult and dangerous. Because there was no strong central government, local rulers began to collect tolls, or taxes, on goods that crossed through their lands. A trader transporting goods sometimes had to pay a toll every few miles along the way. In addition, bands of outlaws attacked travelers and robbed them. The fine Roman roads, no longer kept in repair, became muddy or dusty or full of frozen ruts, depending on the weather. Most of the time roads were impassable for wheeled vehicles, but pack animals and riders on horseback could still make their way. (See TRADE.)

When strong central governments again developed in western Europe, commerce and travel started up again, chiefly by private carriage. Finally public stagecoaches made trips on regular schedules in spite of mud and bumps. Better roads, however, were badly needed.

Courtesy The National
Museum of Wales

In about the 1st century B.C., Celts traveled in this horse-drawn chariot.

The queen of ancient Persia is said to have traveled in a richly trimmed "car" carried by two camels.

In about 1800 a Scotsman, John McAdam, began to experiment with a new kind of road. On a base of stones he laid a layer of crushed rock. The rock was bound together with mud or tar. This kind of road was usable even in wet weather. It had the best foundation and surface of any road built since the time of the Romans, about 1,500 years before. McAdam's name is still recognized today because some present-day highways are macadamized, that is, made of crushed rock bound together by a tarlike substance.

To pay the cost of construction and to make a profit for the builder, many of the early improved roads were toll roads. They could be used only by travelers who were willing to pay a toll, or fee. This practice slowed traffic because of frequent stops at tollgates. The expensive tolls also discouraged many travelers. The time saved in travel over the improved roads, however, was often worth the added cost.

Some early roads were built with rails, or tracks, on which wagons moved. Rails were first used in coal mines, where horses or windlasses were used to haul heavily loaded wagons from the mine. When a horse pulled a wagon running smoothly on rails, it could draw a heavier load. Later, tracks were laid for greater distances, and horsecars for passengers traveled along them.

That was the state of things in about 1800. The people of Europe still depended on animal power to transport them from place to place. Their rate of travel was held down to the speed of a horse.

Transportation on Water

For many thousands of years, people have traveled on the water. During the Stone Age man learned to build rafts. He tied together logs or bundles of reeds to form rafts. The rafts could either drift with the current or be propelled by poles. Finally he learned to make canoes. The first canoes were made from logs that were hollowed out by burning and scraping. Sometimes called a dugout, this canoe is still used by some peoples today. Canoe making became easier when frames of wood

Courtesy Chicago Museum of Science and Industry
from The Dunbar Collection

A native of Porto-Novo in Dahomey, Africa, uses a canoe, called a pirogue, that has been hollowed out of wood.

were covered with bark or with the skins of animals. Canoes were better than rafts because with paddles canoes can travel upstream as well as downstream.

On water, as well as on land, human muscles supplied the power needed for transportation. After thousands of years of paddling canoes, man invented oars for rowing larger boats. Paddles are good enough for making light boats and canoes move, but they are not efficient for moving large boats.

In time the peoples of Phoenicia and Venice developed ships, called galleys, that used as many as 200 or 300 rowers, or oarsmen. The rowers sat, one behind the other, along the sides of the ship. Seats were arranged so that there were two, and sometimes three, rows, one above the other. Working together, and directed by drivers, the rowers pulled on the oars. The ship moved swiftly through the water by the power of human muscles. This backbreaking work was performed by galley slaves, who were the "machines" in those days.

Sails Introduce a New Form of Power

Another important discovery in water transportation came when man learned to catch the wind in sails. He made the power of the wind move his ships. With sails, man could travel farther than in ships that depended entirely on man power. Sails alone, however, were not enough. If the wind died down, a ship might not move for days. For many hundreds of years, therefore, most ships made use of both sails and oars. In such ships the Egyptians traveled up and down the Nile River and even ventured out into the Mediterranean Sea. (See EGYPT, HISTORY OF.)

The Egyptians and their neighbors, the Phoenicians, became the first great travelers, traders, and explorers of the sea. The Phoenicians were especially daring. They sailed from one end of the Mediterranean to the other. They also made their way through the Strait of Gibraltar into the Atlantic Ocean. They traveled as far as Great Britain in their search for tin. (See PHOENICIA.)

At a later time, the Vikings, or Northmen, were daring seafarers in small oar-and-sail ships. They went farther and farther across the Atlantic. They traveled to Iceland, to Greenland, and, it is believed, even to North America, almost 500 years before Christopher Columbus. These were truly great accomplishments for early peoples. (See NORTHMEN.)

There were many difficulties that early sailors had to overcome, even in inland waterways. Because the water level in rivers changes from season to season, their boats were in danger of being stranded. In some streams, the level of the bottom of the river changes rapidly, and only the most skillful sailor can steer a boat safely. Going against the current was always a serious problem. Often men or draft animals were used to tow boats upstream. If the current was strong, even towing was almost impossible. Whirlpools and reefs were other dangers that made early transportation by water difficult. (See BOAT.)

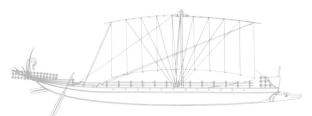

From "The Ship" by Bjorn Landstrom. Copyright © 1961 by Bjorn Landstrom. Reprinted by permission of Doubleday & Company, Inc.

A bireme, above, was an ancient Greek ship sometimes used in battle. It was manned by many oarsmen who were seated at two levels along each side of the ship and was used in about 300 B.C. The Nina, right, was one of the three ships used by Columbus on his trip to America in 1492.

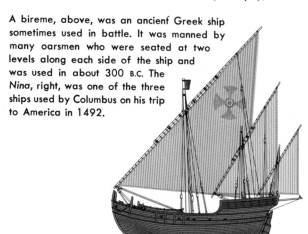

Travel on the sea seemed especially dangerous, full of all the terrors of the unknown. Until the use of the modern compass in the 12th century, ships usually sailed in sight of the coast. (See COMPASS.) At night, travel was halted as ships spent the night at shore. The crews slept on shore; therefore there was no need for sleeping quarters on the ships. Because ships seldom sailed far from land, where food was available, few provisions or supplies were carried. The ships of ancient days, therefore, did not need to be large. For long voyages, however, larger ships were needed. Room was required for a many-months' supply of food and water, as well as for sleeping quarters for the crew. Storage space for a good-sized cargo was needed to make the voyage pay.

The ships of Columbus and other explorers seem small by modern standards, but they were large and seaworthy for those days.

Seamen began to depend on sails alone. They used more and taller masts and larger sails. They learned more about navigation and the art of sailing. They even learned how to tack, or sail at an angle into the wind. Even with all their skill, however, travel by water was still slow, for when there was no wind the ships had to stand still. (See SAILBOAT AND SAILING.)

Some of the finest and fastest sailing ships of all times were built in the United States early in the 19th century. They were the clipper ships—long, slender, and graceful, with towering masts and many sails. They could go as fast as 15 miles an hour in a good wind. Before the clippers came into use, sailing ships took five or six months to go from New England to China. The new ships made the voyage in about three months. The *Dreadnought*, a famous clipper, crossed the Atlantic in ten days, a record no other sailing ship has equaled. The clipper ships were often faster than early steamboats. (See SHIP.)

The Steam Engine Replaces Sails

The clippers were so swift that for a time they were able to compete successfully with the new steamboats. In the end, however, it was a losing race because the clippers had to depend on nature's power—the wind. As more

Culver Pictures

The *Great Eastern*, launched in 1858, was a steamer operated both by paddle wheel and screw (propeller).

powerful steam engines were developed, steamships became the masters of the sea. Although the first steamboats had been considered impracticable, eventually they completely changed transportation on water.

Toward the end of the 18th century, many European, British, and U.S. inventors had experimented with steamboats. One U.S. inventor, John Fitch, experimented with different kinds of paddles and even with the screw propeller. In the 1780's he built a steamboat that traveled up and down the Delaware River at speeds of several miles an hour. No one, however, was sufficiently interested in the new boats to invest money in them.

Robert Fulton was the first man to run a steamboat at a profit. His *Clermont*, a vessel 135 feet long, in 1807 made the trip upstream from New York City to Albany, New York, a distance of 150 miles, in 32 hours. (See FULTON, ROBERT.) After the success of the *Clermont*, many other steamships set new records. In 1819, for example, the *Savannah*, using steam and sails, crossed the Atlantic Ocean in less than 30 days.

In the early 1800's the people of the United States had great need for good transportation. Settlers had moved westward across the Appalachian Mountains bound for the Ohio and Mississippi valleys. These settlers depended on the East for tools, farming implements, cloth, needles, thread, salt, nails, and other necessities that they could not make or produce. In return, they wanted to sell their furs and farm produce on the eastern markets.

Wagons were used to some extent, but water transportation was also necessary. Goods were loaded on flatboats that floated down tributaries to the Mississippi River to New Orleans, Louisiana. There the goods might be transferred to sailing ships, which would carry them to ports on the Atlantic coast. This route was slow and indirect, but the settlers had no better way to send their goods to eastern markets.

Another water link connecting the Middle West with the East was the Erie Canal. This canal, completed in 1825, led from Buffalo, New York, at the eastern end of Lake Erie, eastward along the Mohawk Valley to Albany, New York. Albany was connected with New York City on the south by the Hudson River. The increase in commerce caused by the use of the Erie Canal was tremendous. Farm products from the Great Lakes states were readily exchanged for eastern products as the horse-drawn or mule-drawn canalboats traveled back and forth. Freight rates between Buffalo, New York, and New York City dropped from $100 per ton by wagon to about one-tenth that amount by canal barge. New York City soon became the most important Atlantic port. (See ERIE CANAL.)

After the success of the Erie Canal, an era of canal building began. Other cities wanted to become rich trading centers in the

Courtesy Chicago Museum of Science and Industry from The Dunbar Collection

Some people thought that sails could efficiently drive a railroad car.

manner of Buffalo and New York. Some, however, were situated where natural barriers prevented the building of canals. Between Baltimore, Maryland, and the Ohio River, for example, there was no water-level route. No other canal in the United States ever attained the success of the Erie Canal.

The screw propeller was invented in 1836, and iron hulls were introduced in about 1820. Most oceangoing ships made use of these improvements. Wooden steamboats, nevertheless, with paddle wheels on the sides or at the stern, remained popular on inland waterways. The number of steamboats on the Ohio and Mississippi rivers increased from 21 in 1813 to 3,566 in 1860. After the U.S. Civil War, river steamboats lost much of their business to the railroads. Today, however, on rivers and canals, barges carry much of the heavy freight that does not need to be moved rapidly.

After 1919, oceangoing steamships competed with motor-driven ships. The motor ship, like the automobile, develops its driving power directly from the expansion of burning fuel in the cylinders. The steamship, on the other hand, must get its driving energy by the roundabout method of burning fuel to turn water into steam. Steam, at high pressure, is then fed into an engine, or a turbine, which propels the ship. (See INTERNAL-COMBUSTION ENGINE; STEAM ENGINE; TURBINE.)

Many of the dangers and difficulties that limited early water transportation have been removed. Channels in rivers and harbors have been deepened and straightened. Canals, such as those at Panama and Suez, have greatly

At one time horses and mules towed barges through the Erie Canal. Today modern barges that use the canal are diesel powered.

Culver Pictures

Courtesy Chicago Museum of Science and Industry
from The Dunbar Collection

The general shape of coal-fired locomotives remained the same for many years.

shortened distances. Scientists better understand water and wind currents and have compiled information for ship captains to use. Lanes of travel on the ocean have been mapped and charted much as highways are on land. Dangerous stretches of coastline are marked with buoys and lighthouses. Best of all, vessels are equipped with new inventions, such as radar, which allow ship captains to receive warnings of storms and other dangers. Other instruments help the captains find their way across thousands of miles of water. (See NAVIGATION; PANAMA CANAL; SUEZ CANAL.)

In the last hundred years, there has been a complete change in ways of carrying passengers and freight over the waterways of the world. Ships now run on regular schedules and are specialized, just as railroad cars are. The express liners carry passengers and expensive freight. They represent luxury in travel. The largest liner today is more than 2,000 feet long and carries 1,000 or more passengers. The liners average more than 30 miles an hour and cross the Atlantic, from New York City to England, in about four days. Smaller liners, which are not so fast, carry passengers and freight at cheaper rates. Among the freighters, some are especially constructed to carry certain products. There are oil tankers, ore boats, fruit ships, refrigerator ships, and other specialized vessels. Some freighters also carry a few passengers. There are tramp freighters, which are usually smaller ships, that go from port to port without regular schedules, picking up cargo wherever it is available.

As ships have been made larger, they have been able to carry more passengers and more freight. This has often meant a reduction in passenger and freight rates. Lower rates are an advantage to everyone. Even though one may never take an ocean trip, he almost certainly uses products, such as coffee, bananas, rope, rubber, and drugs, that are carried by ship.

The Development of Railroads

The invention of the steam engine introduced a new source of power. At first, steam engines were used to pump water and to run spinning and weaving machines. Some men began to wonder whether steam engines might also be used to move things. Richard Trevithick, a British engineer, in 1801 was one of the first men to use a steam engine to drive a wagon. Eventually, his steam wagon was put on rails and used to haul coal out of the mines. In 1812 William Hedley, another British engineer, built a steam wagon, "Puffing Billy," to be used in hauling coal. Hedley's was the first steam wagon that looked like a locomotive. (See RAILROAD.)

In 1825 British engineer George Stephenson built a locomotive that hauled a train of 34 cars at an average speed of about 15 miles an hour. Stephenson was a practical engineer who made improvements in the early steam wagon. Four years later he built another locomotive, the "Rocket," which traveled at a speed of 30 miles

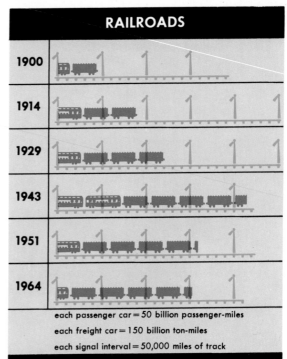

RAILROADS

1900	
1914	
1929	
1943	
1951	
1964	

each passenger car = 50 billion passenger-miles
each freight car = 150 billion ton-miles
each signal interval = 50,000 miles of track

an hour. English businessmen were convinced that the railroad was a success. Tracks were built connecting the larger cities, and branch lines were extended to the smaller ones. The iron horse had triumphed in England, and a little later it was accepted in the United States.

In the 1830's and 1840's railroads were being built in the eastern and the middle western sections of the United States. At the same time, settlers had pushed on to the land west of the Mississippi River. There the roads were poor, and transportation by covered wagon and stagecoach was slow and difficult. The settlers needed good roads and railroad service. After 1849 the California gold rush increased the demand for a railroad across the continent. During the U.S. Civil War, rapid transportation of soldiers and supplies was necessary. Congress passed bills giving grants of land and loans of money to two private companies interested in a transcontinental railway. The work was rushed to completion.

In 1869 the Union Pacific Railroad tracks, from the east, and the Central Pacific Railroad tracks, from the west, met in Utah. At last the East and the West were linked by rail. During the next few years other lines were extended to the Pacific Coast. Hundreds of thousands of people moved west. They settled on farms and ranches along the railroads. They knew that now they could easily send their grain and cattle to markets in the East.

Inventions Improve Railroad Transportation

In 1830 there were fewer than 50 miles of railroad track in the United States. In 1963 there were about 200,670 miles of track. The first trains traveled at about 15 miles an hour. Some of the streamlined trains of today can travel at more than 100 miles an hour. They average more than 60 miles an hour on a long trip. The first engines burned wood, instead of coal, to produce steam. Modern trains no longer depend on steam for power. They use diesel engines or electricity from overhead wires or third rails. (See DIESEL ENGINE.)

Many inventions and improvements have made railroad transportation different from anything imagined a century ago. In about 1835, rails were first rolled into the T-shape familiar today. Later, steel replaced iron in rails. Sleeping cars were built by U.S. inventor George Pullman in about 1860. The block-signal system, which does so much to insure safety, was first used in the United States in 1863. The air brake was invented by U.S. inventor George Westinghouse in 1869. In 1877 U.S. meat-packer Gustavus Swift successfully used the first refrigerator car. Hundreds of other improvements, such as automatic train control and interlocking signal systems, helped make railroads a swifter, safer, and more adequate means of transportation.

The railroads today are important, but they do not carry so large a portion of the total passenger and freight traffic as they did at one time. The rise of motor and air transportation has decreased the use of the rails.

In 1940 the railroads of the United States carried about 62 percent of the total freight moving between cities and about 61 percent of the passengers. In 1967 they carried only 42 percent of the freight and 12 percent of the passengers. In 1940, motortrucks carried about 8 percent of the intercity freight, but by 1967 their share of this business had increased to more than 22 percent of the total. In 1940 the airlines carried only about 2 percent of the passengers. In 1950 their share had grown to about 13 percent of the total intercity passenger business. In 1957, airplanes were carrying more passengers than railroads in the United States, and by 1967 the airlines were carrying about 60 percent of the passengers.

The chief decline in railroad passenger use

The hustle-bustle in a railroad station is much the same today as it was in years past.

has been caused by the greater use of the private automobile for long trips. Today 93 percent of all railroad income is from freight. Only 7 percent of railroad income is from passenger service, which usually results in a non-profitable financial operation.

Automobile Transportation

Except for the railroad, methods of land transportation changed little during the 19th century. The farmer in 1890, as did the farmer in 1790, hitched his horse to a wagon. He hauled his produce along a dirt road to the nearest village. Merchants in the cities used horses to deliver their goods. Travel was still slow, but people had discovered that it could be fun, too. They took pleasure trips in their carriages, rolling along in comfort on solid rubber tires. A craze for bicycling gave men, women, and children a new sense of freedom and speed. (See BICYCLE.) The bicycle, of course, was not fast enough. Eventually, the automobile gave them what they wanted. (See AUTOMOBILE.)

During the period of railroad expansion, some inventors kept working on the problem of making smaller engines that would give more power. They tried many kinds of fuel: illuminating gas, kerosene, benzene, gasoline, and so on. In 1883 Gottlieb Daimler, a German engineer, built an engine that had more power and

A Benz motorcar patented in 1886 was considered the height of elegance in its day.

Courtesy Mercedes-Benz of North America Inc.

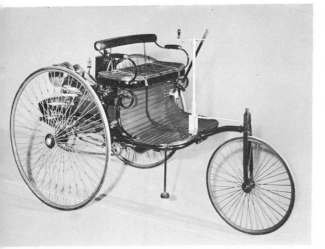

was much lighter than any built previously. In 1885 Carl Benz, another German engineer, installed a gasoline-burning internal-combustion engine on a tricycle, a three-wheeled vehicle, and the automobile became a reality. Many U.S. inventors experimented along the same lines. Charles E. and Frank Duryea in 1892 built a self-moving "buggy" that used a similar gasoline engine. In the next few years Henry Ford, Elwood Haynes, and Ransom E. Olds built their first experimental automobiles. Many early manufacturers of automobiles had been makers of bicycles or carriages.

Inventors and builders continued to make improvements of all kinds. They built stronger frames, closed bodies, and self-starters. They improved tires and springs and introduced shock absorbers. Through the efforts of many men, the automobile became the swift, reliable, and comfortable means of transportation that it is today.

Henry Ford introduced mass-production methods and built thousands of automobiles in a single year. Eventually he built hundreds of

AUTOMOBILES AND HIGHWAYS	
1925	
1935	
1945	
1955	
1964	

each automobile = 10 million automobiles
each milestone interval = 500,000 miles of road
each milestone interval = 500,000 miles of surfaced road

thousands a year. Other automobile manufacturers also used his method of construction. Each leading automobile manufacturer makes its cars with standardized parts. Travelers, therefore, can have their automobiles repaired easily wherever they travel.

Automobile transportation requires good roads. Before automobiles could be widely used, roads had to be improved to be usable in any weather. As better roads were made, more automobiles appeared, creating a demand for more good roads. Today every large city has paved streets. A network of first-class highways and graded dirt or graveled roads covers many countries. More than three million miles of roads in the United States contribute to the comfort of travel. (See ROAD, HIGHWAY, AND STREET.)

In 1967 there were 7,412,659 passenger cars made in the United States. A total of 8,976,000 of all kinds of motor vehicles were made in that same year. With so many passenger automobiles and other swift-moving vehicles on the streets and highways, accidents are frequent and serious. Highway accidents in the United States killed 55,000 people in 1968 and injured 2,000,000 others. This high accident rate is an undesirable result of the use of motor vehicles.

Air pollution, partially caused by gasoline-engine exhaust, is a serious problem. In the mid-1960's several manufacturers started developing electric-motor-powered automobiles.

Air Transportation

The first persons who experimented with airplanes built gliders. They launched them from the tops of hills and flew them as far as they could on air currents. Gliders have no engines, but by working with them man learned a great deal about air currents and how to control planes in the wind. (See AIRPLANE; AVIATION; GLIDER AND SAILPLANE.)

Many inventors in Europe and the United States tried to put engines on gliders before someone finally was successful. Samuel P. Langley, a U.S. physicist, put a gasoline engine in his plane and tried to make several flights. Although his model-sized aerodromes, as they were called, were successfully flown, a full-sized aerodrome was damaged in attempting to take off. Later, however, it was flown successfully. Langley's efforts encouraged others to carry on experiments with smaller and lighter gasoline engines.

Two brothers, U.S. inventors Orville and Wilbur Wright, made the first successful man-carrying flights in an airplane in December 1903. They continued to improve the engine and other parts of the machine. By 1908 they had built a plane that could stay aloft for more than an hour. They traveled through Europe, exhibiting and demonstrating their plane. They aroused great interest in this new form of transportation. (See WRIGHT, ORVILLE AND WILB[...])

Strangely enough, the United States [...] slower to accept the idea of aviation than we[...] European countri[...] [du]ring World War[...]

Courtesy (top) Lockheed-California Compa[...] [Ph]oto, (below) So[vf]oto

Growth in airplane capacity has been rapid. The Vega, above, which carried five passengers, was built in the United States in 1927. The huge U.S.S.R. airplane, below, which can carry 80 tons of cargo or 720 passengers, was built in 1965.

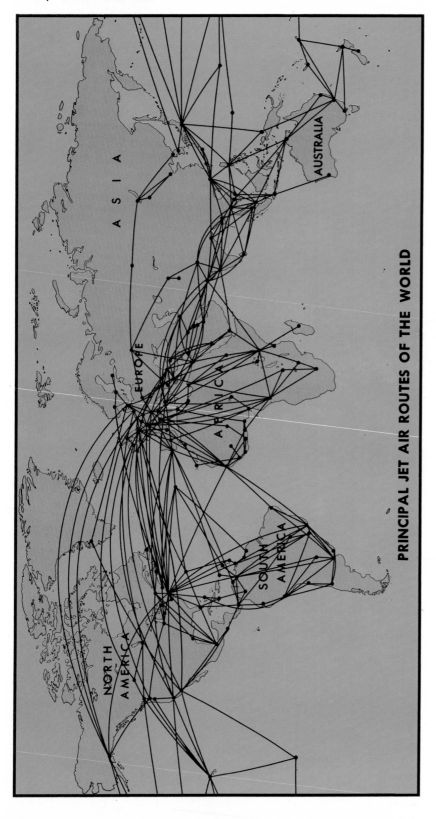

PRINCIPAL JET AIR ROUTES OF THE WORLD

(1914–1918) flying and airplane building developed rapidly. At the beginning of the war, there were few planes in service. At its close, there were tens of thousands of planes and thousands of young men trained as flyers. These trained men and other aviators were eager to fly commercial planes after the war. They carried mail and passengers on the developing airlines.

Airplanes have been vastly improved since commercial aviation's pioneer days in the 1920's. Traveling by air is a pleasant experience today. Passengers ride in comfortable surroundings. Jet-propelled planes often carry their passengers at a speed of more than 600 miles an hour.

The comforts and the time saved by air travel have greatly increased the airlines' passenger business. In 1967, air passengers traveled 87,241,000,000 revenue passenger-miles over the 271,959 miles of certified airway routes in the United States. In addition to this, many passengers were carried on other national and international airlines. An added reason for the public's willingness to travel by air is the safety record made by the airlines.

In the United States, the Civil Aeronautics Board provides a variety of services to promote safe air transportation. Among them are beacon lights and radio information on weather conditions. Radio beams make it possible to fly "blind." Intermediate landing fields are available for use in emergencies. Instrument landing systems and other safety facilities are provided and controlled by regulations. (See Airports and Air Routes.)

Transportation in Urban Areas

The 1960 census revealed that 70 percent of the people in the United States live in cities, or urban areas. This is an increase of 6 percent over the 1950 census figures. With more and more people living in cities, a greater number of transportation problems are present. The downtown business areas are becoming more congested with automobiles.

Middle- and higher-income families are moving out to the suburbs, and lower-income families are moving into the cities. The upper-income families continue to work in the city. They use the city's cultural and recreational facilities and usually do not support the city facilities by paying taxes. The same suburban residents make up a large percentage of those who create urban transportation problems by driving their automobiles into the central city to work. An engineering survey has shown that it costs a city such as Washington, D.C., 50 cents per day for every car that comes in from the suburbs. This includes the cost of traffic controls, parking facilities, and the like.

The crisis of city transportation is not only the congestion caused by automobiles and the resulting air pollution. Urban transit facilities—which include subways, elevated transit service, commuter railroads, streetcars, and buses—have also decayed. Between 1950 and 1960, the mass-transit industry owned 24 percent fewer vehicles, drove 25 percent fewer vehicle miles, lost 45 percent of its passengers, and suffered a 25 percent decline in net revenue. (See City, *Transportation in Cities*.)

Mass transit primarily serves central business-district trips, especially those of city workers,

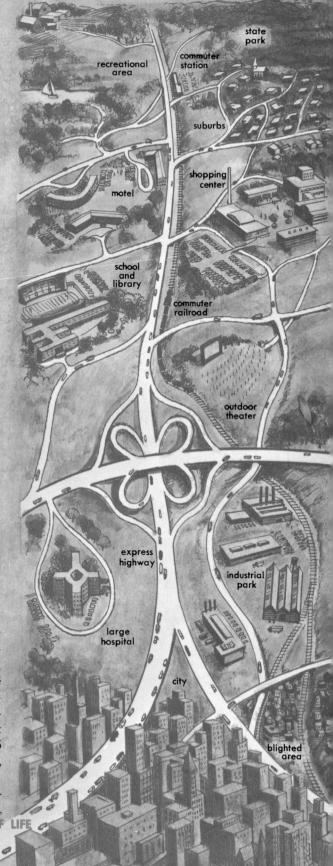

although many outlying areas are also served. In general, mass transit continues to be used heavily during weekday rush hours while people are getting to and from work. It is used little at other times. Mass transit remains profitable during the rush hours but not profitable enough to make up the losses of all the other hours.

When the city of Chicago, Illinois, constructed

Courtesy Chicago Transit Authority

Laurence Lowry from Rapho—Guillumette

A train of the city transport system runs in the middle of the Eisenhower Expressway, above, in Chicago. The interchange on Route 128 at the Massachusetts Turnpike, below, has many twists and turns.

its huge east-west Congress Street Expressway, since renamed the Eisenhower Expressway, it included rapid-transit tracks in the center of the right-of-way. On this expressway the two lines of the rapid transit can serve approximately 50 percent more people than the eight lanes open to automobiles.

It is estimated that it would cost 31 billion dollars to handle the automobile traffic that would be needed to replace the commuter railroad service now operating in the cities of New York, New York; Chicago; Boston, Massachu-

setts; Philadelphia, Pennsylvania; and Cleveland, Ohio. In San Francisco, California, it would take five times as much money and four times as much land for automobile roads to carry as many people as that city's 75-mile rapid-transit network now under construction.

Cities badly need bypass express routes to permit vehicular traffic to go around them, if possible. The Bay Tunnel bypass of Baltimore, Maryland, cuts that city's downtown traffic by 30 percent, greatly relieving traffic congestion.

Some cities are spread out too much for an efficient and self-supporting public transit service. Los Angeles, California, covers an area 25 percent larger than New York City but has less than one-third as many people. Because of this, four-fifths of the people in Los Angeles drive their own cars instead of using the city's 1,700 buses and trolleys. Metropolitan areas of the future with less than 10,000 people per square mile, such as Los Angeles, will probably emphasize the further development of freeways for automobile transportation.

Chicago, which has about 16,000 people per square mile, directs most of its rapid transit and commuter railroad lines to the central business district. Approximately two-thirds of all passengers entering Chicago's downtown area arrive on some type of public transit. In 1947 the Chicago Transit Authority (CTA), a municipal corporation, took over control of the city's transit lines and has since made sweeping changes in operating procedures. The surface lines (buses and trolleys) and the elevated and subway lines have uniform fare and transfer privileges. In attempts to provide better and faster service, the CTA has installed much new equipment and established the "A and B stop" service. The elevated transit stations that do not handle a great deal of passenger traffic are now designated either A or B stations, and only A or B trains stop at their respective stations. More important stations are designated "all-stop" stations, where both A and B trains stop.

One answer to the problem of urban transportation is to make public transportation efficient, convenient, and attractive enough so that people will not drive their automobiles into the core of the city. In 1964 the United States set aside $375 million to aid urban mass transit. This was a strong first step in trying to unchoke cities' streets and highways.

Competition Improves Transportation

There has always been competition between the several kinds of intercity transportation. When railroads began, owners of stagecoach and wagon freight lines fought them vigorously but unsuccessfully. Sailing ships did their best to compete with steamships and for a time were successful. Canalboat owners and steamship companies fought the railroads. Railroads even fought each other, trying to get business in the same territory or attempting to gain control over connecting railways. After the railroads became established, they, in turn, had to face competition from private automobiles, buses, trucks, and airplanes.

Many people prefer to travel in their own cars, free to go where and when they please. Cross-country buses, too, offer a wider choice of routes than do railroads. In many cities buses have replaced the old street railways because buses can be better adapted to new routes. Railroads do not reach every small community and cannot always give frequent service to the towns through which they pass. Buses are necessary, therefore, to provide transportation for people who might otherwise be neglected. (See Bus.)

There has always been competition in freight transportation. Formerly, farmers and city people had to have their goods hauled to the nearest railway station before the goods could be started on their way. When the goods arrived at the end of the railroad trip, another means of transportation was needed to reach the final destination. Sometimes trucks were used to go to and from the railroad. Motor-trucks can give door-to-door pickup and quick delivery service. This saves charges for extra handling at each end of the trip. (See TRUCK AND TRUCKING.)

The railroads and steamship lines now use motortrucks for pickup and delivery services at their terminals between their stations. Trucks benefit because they are willing to haul small loads that the railroads do not find profitable.

Faced with a serious loss of business, the railroads began to improve their service. They now offer faster freight service. They also handle shipments of less-than-carload size, and they provide to-the-door pickup and delivery of the goods transported.

All the forms of transportation that have developed since 1800—on land, on water, and in

Courtesy Aero Spacelines, Inc.

Courtesy Consulate General of Japan, N.Y.

The Super Guppy (above) is an air cargo plane that has transported Gemini capsules; its tail is about as high as a five-story building. The world's largest oil tanker is the Japanese *Idemitsu Maru*, which displaces more than 200,000 tons.

the air—have a place in the modern transportation system. Each has certain advantages and disadvantages. Together they offer a wide choice of services in transporting goods and people. There is a service to suit any customer's time, money, and convenience.

For short trips, passenger trains and buses offer just about the same service in terms of time and cost. For long trips, trains save time, but their fares are higher than bus fares.

Railroads are generally more economical than

A man can travel 60 miles per hour and reach 85 feet with the personal rocket lift-device.

A "skybus" runs on an elevated, automated transit system. The bus is powered by electricity and rides on rubber tires.

The highway truck Turbo Titan III, above, is powered by a gas turbine that is smaller and lighter than a diesel engine.

motor vehicles for large shipments of freight over great distances. One freight train, run by a crew of a few men, can carry goods that would require a large fleet of motortrucks. For transporting smaller loads, motortrucks are fast, efficient, and economical.

Ships on inland waterways and along the coast compete with the railroads. Wherever they serve the same territory, railroads have the advantage of saving time, but they usually charge higher rates than the ships. When time is not important, transportation by water is efficient and economical, particularly for shipment of heavy, bulky goods, such as iron ore and grains.

Steamships and motor ships still carry the bulk of the world's trade across oceans. The luxury passenger liners compete for passengers with the giant airplanes that have cut days of travel time from overseas trips. Ships, however, are still masters of the sea for carrying intercontinental cargoes. No matter how large airplanes become, it would take vast numbers of them to replace the thousands of roomy cargo ships that deliver most of the goods on which the world's commerce is based. The cost of moving heavy cargo by air is much higher than by steamship. (See COMMERCE.)

The transportation system serves the public, and it is important to the welfare of the public. To protect the public interest, therefore, some governments keep a control on transportation and make regulations for the good of the public. In general, these regulations are made to insure a safe, efficient, and economical service that is sufficient to the public needs. The regulations provide fair rates for all—shippers, travelers, and carriers. In many countries, government protects the interests of the transportation companies, too, because they also are part of the public. Certain regulations provide that the

Air-cushion vehicles, above, skim the surface of land or water on a cushion of air.

The French Aerotrain, left, an air-cushion vehicle, is guided by a concrete rail and is driven by a turboprop engine mounted at the rear.

FAMOUS TRIPS AROUND THE WORLD

Traveler	Time	Terminal	Date(s)
Ferdinand Magellan, by boat	1,083 days	Seville, Spain	1519-1522
Sir Francis Drake, by boat	1,052 days	Plymouth, England	1577-1580
Thomas Cavendish, by boat	781 days	England	1586-1588
"Phileas Fogg," Jules Verne's fictitious character, by boat and train	80 days	London, England	1872
Nellie Bly, by boat and train	72 days 6 hours 11 minutes	New York, N.Y.	1889
George Francis Train, by boat	67 days 12 hours 3 minutes	New York, N.Y.	1890
Charles Fitzmorris	60 days 13 hours 29 minutes	Chicago, Illinois	1901
J. Willis Sayre	54 days 9 hours 42 minutes	Seattle, Washington	1903
Henry Frederick	54 days 7 hours 2 minutes	Seattle, Washington	1903
Col. Burnlay-Campbell, first use of Trans-Siberian Railway	40 days 19 hours 30 minutes		1907
Andre Jaeger-Schmidt, by boat and train	39 days 19 hours 43 minutes	Paris, France	1911
John Henry Mears, by boat and train	35 days 21 hours 36 minutes		1913
U.S. Army planes, first circumnavigation by air; flying time 14 days 15 hours	175 days	Seattle, Washington	1924
Edward Evans and Linton Wells, by boat, automobile, and plane	28 days 14 hours 36 minutes		1925
John Henry Mears and C. B. Collyer, by plane and boat	24 days 15 hours 21 minutes	New York, N.Y.	1928
Graf Zeppelin	21 days 7 hours 26 minutes	Friedrichshafen, Germany	1929
Wiley Post and Harold Gatty, by plane	8 days 15 hours 51 minutes	New York, N.Y.	1931
Wiley Post, by plane	7 days 18 hours 49½ minutes	New York, N.Y.	1933
U.S. Air Force plane, first nonstop flight around the world	3 days 22 hours 1 minute	Fort Worth, Texas	1949
Howard Hughes, by plane	3 days 19 hours 8⅙ minutes	New York, N.Y.	1938
Milton Reynolds, by plane	3 days 6 hours 55½ minutes	New York, N.Y.	1947
William Odom, by plane	3 days 1 hour 5 minutes 11 seconds	Chicago, Illinois	1947
U.S. Air Force planes	1 day 21 hours 19 minutes	Merced, California	1957

transportation companies and their investors may receive a reasonable return on the money they have invested. Other regulations seek to prevent harmful competition between the same and different types of transportation companies.

Today people are more dependent on one another than ever before. In earlier times, each family had to be self-sufficient. Pioneers living on the frontier of the United States, for example, had to raise their own food, make their own clothing, and provide their own shelter. Because there was no efficient way of transporting goods from one place to another, they had to do everything for themselves. They could not have all the comforts and conveniences that are taken for granted today.

With improvements in transportation, men and regions were able to specialize. Men can spend their working hours doing the work for which they are best fitted and still have time left for leisure. Regions are able to specialize in goods that they can produce best or manufacture most cheaply. Trains, trucks, ships, and airplanes carry their goods to other localities and bring back whatever is needed. Factory workers in the city depend on the farmers for food and raw materials. Farmers depend on the factory workers for clothing, machinery, and other manufactured products, and even for prepared food products. They—and everyone else—in turn, depend upon the transportation facilities and the army of transportation workers who move goods and raw materials from one part of the world to another.

Transportation in the Future

A number of recent transportation improvements are either already in operation or in the development stage. Several or all of these could prove to be of great importance either as individual or mass transportation methods in the future.

The monorail railroad runs along a single rail positioned above or below the railroad car. Monorails cost less to build and operate than subway systems or two-rail elevated railroads. They can operate above a heavily traveled street. Detroit, Michigan, has considered building subways that may cost up to $15 million a mile. A monorail, including the price of separate rights-of-way, would cost between $2 million and $5 million per mile. The monorail is being considered for use in many major U.S. cities. It has been in operation on a limited basis in Houston, Texas, since 1956. Both Seattle, Washington, and New York City built monorails for their world's fairs, held in 1962 and 1964–1965, respectively.

High-speed trains with pressurized cabins, similar to those on airplanes, are now being proposed for operation between Washington, D.C., and New York City. Similar trains are already in operation between major Japanese cities. (For illustrations, see JAPAN.)

Another new idea in transportation has already been tested to a limited extent in Japan. An excellent highway route through one of Tokyo's most congested sections is the roof of a mile-long building. The two-story building beneath the highway contains shops and offices. A five-road network of the same type of construction is planned for Tokyo at a cost of approximately $200 million. The joining of these arteries will make up the core of Tokyo's highway transportation system.

Conveyor belts, once used only for moving goods, are becoming more important as a means of moving people from one place to another. Today many buildings use moving sidewalks, which are flat conveyor belts with handrails. Some of them can accommodate as many as 15,000 people per hour. Escalators are conveyor belts that form stairs as they move. (See ESCALATOR.)

The air-cushion vehicle is a new concept in transportation now under study. This vehicle moves over land and water on a cushion of air and can move in any direction. In France, a monorail train moving on $\frac{1}{10}$ inch of air has traveled faster than 200 miles per hour.

At one time, pipelines were used only to carry water, gas, and oil. Today, however, coal in small lumps, mixed with water, is being pumped through pipelines. There is, for example, a 108-mile line from Cadiz, Ohio, to Cleveland, Ohio, that can transport 1,200,000 tons of coal per year. Soil for fill, mixed with water, has also been carried by pipeline.

Special containers of standard sizes have been developed for use on trucks, railroad cars, and ships. They can be loaded and unloaded with greater ease and speed than ordinary containers that differ in size. Extensive use of "containerization" is expected in the future.

One other new type of transportation is the rocket belt, which enables man to fly. In 1961 the U.S. Army first demonstrated this self-propulsion device. The rocket belt is strapped onto an individual and permits him to fly as high as tall buildings.

Amazing transportation advances have occurred in the past years, but even these may be overshadowed in a few years by interplanetary space flights. (See SPACE EXPLORATION.)

TRAP (*trăp*) **AND TRAPPING** (*trăp′ing*). A trap is a device used to catch an animal and hold it so that it cannot escape. Some traps injure or kill animals; others capture them alive and unharmed. The way traps are made depends on the kind of animal to be caught, how the trapper wants to catch it, and the materials used.

In early times trapping was an important way of getting food, clothing, and shelter. Trapping is carried on today to provide not only these necessities of life for primitive people but also such luxuries as furs and feathers. The trapping of fur-bearing animals became such an important business in early America that special fur-trapping and trading organizations were formed. One of the most famous of these is the Hudson's Bay Company, begun in 1670. The trappers of this and other companies covered most of North

America during the 17th and 18th centuries. They were among the first explorers of the new continent. (See FUR AND FUR TRADE.)

Kinds of Traps

A net is one of the oldest kinds of traps. Nets have been used to capture animals as small as insects and as large as sea turtles. Before string and wire were available, they were made of sticks and vines. Nets are often used in fishing. Sometimes a fence made of stakes, called a weir, is placed in the water to steer fish into the net. Fences can also be used on land to capture wild animals.

Animals also can be caught in pitfalls. A pitfall is simply a deep hole, or pit, in the ground. The pit may be dug in the middle of an animal trail and covered with sticks and leaves to make it look like the ground. Bait may be placed on the sticks and leaves. When the animal steps on the covering, it breaks and the animal falls into the pit. The pit is too deep for the animal to jump out, and the sides are too steep to climb. If the trapper wishes to kill the animal, he may stick spears into the ground, points up, at the bottom of the pit, so that the animal falls on them and is killed.

Small pitfalls, often called molasses traps, are used in capturing certain kinds of insects. A molasses trap may be a glass fruit jar buried so that its opening is level with the ground. A little molasses, mixed with an equal part of water, serves as bait. After an insect falls in, it cannot crawl out because of the smooth walls of the jar and the sticky bait.

In the past the deadfall was usually made of two logs, one above the other. The bait was placed in such a way that when it was moved

KINDS OF TRAPS

Simple Snare

Bent-Branch Snare

Steel Trap

Deadfall with Figure 4 Trigger

The deadfall, a primitive trap once used widely by trappers, may be fashioned from one or two logs. When two are used, the top one is propped up with a trigger containing bait. When the bait is removed, the upper log is jarred loose and sent crashing onto the lower log.

Deadfall

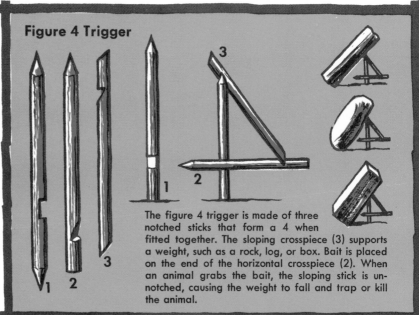

Figure 4 Trigger

The figure 4 trigger is made of three notched sticks that form a 4 when fitted together. The sloping crosspiece (3) supports a weight, such as a rock, log, or box. Bait is placed on the end of the horizontal crosspiece (2). When an animal grabs the bait, the sloping stick is unnotched, causing the weight to fall and trap or kill the animal.

it pulled a trigger, which released the upper log to fall against the bottom log. The animal was caught and crushed between the two. If necessary, the fall log was weighted with stones. Instead of a heavy weight, the falling piece might be a box, which traps the animal alive. The common mousetrap is a type of deadfall. In this case a spring gives great force to the falling part of the trap.

One type of trigger is called a figure 4 because of its shape. It is made of three sticks. One is usually driven into the ground to form a strong support. Another, which has a notch on the underside near its upper end, hooks over the top of the stick in the ground and hangs down as the sloping side of the figure 4. The upper end of this sloping stick supports a weight (usually a box or cage), while the lower end is held in place by a notch in the third stick, which forms the crosspiece of the figure 4. The bait is placed at the other end of the crosspiece. When an animal bites the bait, the sloping stick is unhooked from the notch, which lets the weight fall.

The noose, with or without a trigger, is widely used in trapping animals. The cowboy's lariat, or lasso, is one type. Another type is the snare, which is usually supported by a spring. A spring can be made by bending a flexible sapling. The noose may be made of a wire loop, with a string holding the sapling down and acting as the trigger. The string is covered with salt and breaks when the animal gnaws at the salt. The sapling then springs upward, drawing the noose tight around the animal and lifting it off the ground. The snare is an unlawful device in some states.

The steel trap has long been the one most often used for capturing fur-bearing animals. A steel trap was made in New York State as early as 1823. Twenty years later such traps were being produced in large numbers.

The steel trap is made of two metal jaws that are hinged to spread apart when the trap is set. They are held apart by a trigger attached to a pan set between the jaws. When an animal steps on the pan, it sets off the trigger. The jaws then snap together by means of a spring, catching the animal's leg. Once closed, the jaws

lock. Traps for large animals have a spring at each end of the jaws.

All steel traps are equipped with a chain. Often they are anchored to the ground with a stake or chained to an anchor, such as a log. Two or three pointed metal drags are sometimes used instead of stakes. These drag hooks entangle the trapped animal as it attempts to escape. Traps for beaver and muskrat are set in water so that the animal drowns soon after capture.

Live traps catch animals alive and unharmed. The box type of deadfall is an example of a live trap. Most modern live traps, however, are made of a box with a trapdoor. Trapdoors usually are released by some kind of trigger. The trigger may be part of the floor, so that as soon as the animal steps on it the door closes. Some live traps are large and strong enough to catch bears, lions, and tigers. Others are small enough to catch mice. Traps like these are used to capture animals for circuses and zoos.

Live trapping and tagging provide valuable information about animals. Birds, for example, have been marked by numbered bands on their legs. They are then set free, and, when they are later recaptured, it is possible to learn the routes they travel between their northern nesting places and their southern winter quarters. In the same way, tags have been placed on the fins or backs of young salmon. The distant places where these fish have been recaptured show how far and how fast they travel in making their long journeys to the sea.

TREATY (*trēt′ē*) is a formal, binding agreement between two or more states. It pledges the states to undertake certain responsibilities in their relations with each other. Treaties are usually in written form and are negotiated, or worked out, by official representatives of governments. The laws and rules that countries follow in their dealings with one another are set down in treaties. These agreements are therefore necessary for cooperation and harmony between modern nations.

General Nature of Treaties

The history of treaties goes back almost 5,000

years to ancient Mesopotamia. Today, well over 15,000 treaties on record show the many and varied relations states have with one another.

A bilateral treaty is a formal, written agreement between only two states, while a multilateral treaty is an agreement between three or more states. Other names for treaties include convention, covenant, and charter. Usually a convention is a treaty that deals with some specific subject. Such an agreement is the Convention on the High Seas of 1958, in which many states accepted obligations concerning their ships and planes. The League of Nations Covenant and the United Nations Charter both are multilateral treaties establishing world peace and security organizations. Treaties may also go under the names of declarations, pacts, and protocols.

During the course of history, many treaties among states have been secret, especially when states have promised to support each other in case of war. In 1918 U.S. President Woodrow Wilson called for all treaties to be negotiated publicly and then published for all the world to see. Although some agreements among states are still made secretly, most treaties are now matters of public record. Practically all agreements among states since 1920 may be found in the League of Nations' *Treaty Series* (1920 to 1946) and the United Nations' *Treaty Series* (1946 to the present).

Kinds of Treaties

Although there is no formal classification of treaties in international law, they may be grouped according to the functions they perform. A treaty of friendship and commerce is a basic treaty between two states. It sets forth promises of goodwill and friendly relations in world affairs. It also contains provisions for the conduct of business by citizens and corporations of each state within the other. More than 10,000 bilateral treaties of friendship and commerce have been negotiated among the more than 130 sovereign states of the world. These agreements indicate the vastness of the network of treaty obligations and the importance that nations place upon them.

Treaties in the area of war and peace play a prominent part in the search for security by states. Many states are bound by treaties with other states in which they promise to aid one another if attacked by a hostile country. The North Atlantic Treaty of 1949, which established the North Atlantic Treaty Organization (NATO), is one example of a collective defense treaty. There are many treaties dealing with rules of warfare. They include such matters as blockades, preventing attacks on civilian populations, and humane treatment of prisoners of war. The Hague Conventions of 1899 and 1907, as well as a number of agreements under the League of Nations and the United Nations, contain many provisions on laws of war. (See LEAGUE OF NATIONS; NORTH ATLANTIC TREATY ORGANIZATION (NATO); UNITED NATIONS.)

After most wars, peace treaties have been negotiated and signed. They deal with obligations of the defeated states toward the victors, changes of territory, and exchanges of people. The Treaty of Versailles of 1919, at the end of World War I, and the many peace treaties following World War II put penalties on the defeated states. They also provided for new arrangements in the relationships among the states fighting in these wars. In any war, victors force the peace treaty upon the losing states, and thus all treaties are not entered into freely by states.

Many treaties establish international organizations and other agencies concerned with orderly relations among states. The United Nations and its many specialized agencies are all based on treaties. These treaties not only created the agencies but also define their powers and responsibilities.

There are many other kinds of treaties as well. Some define borders among states. Others are concerned with the authority states have over citizens of other states. Guarantees of human rights and the jurisdiction of states over territories and seas are also matters that are defined in detail in treaties.

Treaty Making

Official representatives of governments of states (or, in rare instances, heads of governments or states) are the negotiators of treaties.

An official acting for a head of government or state is a plenipotentiary. He must be fully authorized by his government to take part in the making of a treaty. Treaties may be negotiated in small groups of two or more officials, or they may be developed at large conferences, such as the United Nations Charter conference at San Francisco in 1945. Treaties may also develop within the United Nations General Assembly.

Much bargaining and research go into the writing of a treaty. Once agreement is reached and the treaty has been signed, it is taken back to the government of each state for ratification. The U.S. Constitution requires that the Senate, by a two-thirds vote, give its "advice and consent" to the president before he can ratify a treaty. Occasionally, governing bodies, such as the Senate, call for changes in a treaty. When this is the case, the other parties to the treaty must agree to any changes before the treaty goes into effect. The U.S. Senate in 1920 wanted to make many changes in the Treaty of Versailles, which ended World War I and established the League of Nations. President Woodrow Wilson did not agree with the proposed changes. Two-thirds of the Senate, therefore, refused to approve this important treaty. (See WILSON, THOMAS WOODROW.)

Effect, Enforcement, and Interpretation of Treaties

Once a treaty has been negotiated, signed, and ratified, the parties to the agreement must be faithful to its terms. The constitutions of most nations make this point quite clear. Article VI of the U.S. Constitution declares that "all Treaties made, or which shall be made, under the Authority of the United States, shall be the supreme Law of the Land; . . ." Article 98 of the Constitution of Japan of 1946 states that "treaties concluded by Japan and established laws of nations shall be faithfully observed." Occasionally, however, legislation in the United States and in other nations is necessary to make clear how much the provisions of a treaty actually are the law of the land.

There is no international government or police force that enforces treaties. The power of public opinion and the need to have good relations between states, however, persuade states to abide by their treaties.

The contents of treaties are sometimes unclear and can be interpreted in many ways. Article 51 of the United Nations Charter, for instance, states that nations may take measures in "individual or collective self-defense" in case of an "armed attack." It is unclear, however, whether a nation must wait until the attack has actually taken place before defending itself. This is particularly important today, in view of how quickly a nuclear attack can destroy any country. Furthermore, many countries have organized for "collective self-defense" (such as the NATO members) in case an armed attack takes place.

Language differences among parties to a treaty often lead to confused interpretation. The International Court of Justice and the courts of many nations, such as the U.S. Supreme Court, have tried to interpret provisions of treaties. Deciding exactly what treaties mean, however, really rests on whether the parties to the treaty are willing to abide by its provisions in good faith.

Termination and Change of Treaties

Many treaties provide for the period of time they are to be in effect. At the end of that period, parties to the treaty may continue the agreement, amend it, or terminate it. If a country feels that after a period of years conditions have changed and the treaty is out of date, it may declare that it is going to ignore the agreement. Adolf Hitler in the 1930's often stated that the provisions of the Treaty of Versailles were outdated and that Nazi Germany had a right to act contrary to the treaty's provisions. Such action is breaking the contract, and most countries do not want to be accused of acting in bad faith. Instead, they often ask to renegotiate the treaty and bring it up to date. All the parties to the treaty must then be willing to accept change. Each country tends to view change or termination of a treaty in the light of its own national interests. Each country, however, also must be flexible so that treaties can be adjusted to the rapidly changing world.

PLATE 1 TREE Common trees. Above left: Aspens in fall color line a roadway in Arizona. Above right: A majestic American elm. Below left: A white ash in the Massachusetts countryside. Below right: A white oak in the fall.

PLATE 2 TREE Common trees. Above left: The Joshua tree is a familiar part of the Mohave Desert landscape. Above right: Tall black locusts at a pond's edge. Left: Sugar maple in brilliant red fall color. Below: The weeping willow's name comes from its rather drooping appearance.

(*Above left, above right*) *Rutherford Platt*, (*left*) *W. H. Hodge*, (*below*) *J. Horace McFarland Company*

PLATE 3 TREE Flowering trees. Above left: Red flowering dogwood in full bloom. Above right: The magnolia, grown in southern United States, is famous for the fragrance of its flowers. Right: Colorful blossoms of the quince. Below: An apple orchard in bloom.

PLATE 4 TREE Conifers. Above left: Mountain hemlocks on the shores of Crater Lake, Oregon. Above right: White spruce. Small spruces, firs, and balsams are commonly used as Christmas trees. Left: Unlike most conifers, bald cypresses grow in swamps and lose their foliage in winter. Below: White pines are commonest in northeastern United States and Canada, and are valuable for their timber.

(Above left, above right, and below) Rutherford Platt, (left) W. H. Hodge

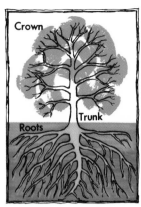

The main parts of a tree are its roots, crown, trunk and flowers or cones.

TREE (*trē*) is a woody plant usually with a single stem. A large elm or oak is easily recognized as being a tree. It has one main stem, or trunk, and a crown of branches. The woody plants called shrubs are usually smaller than trees and have usually more than one main stem. The difference between trees and shrubs, however, is not always clear. Some plants that normally are considered to be trees may, under certain conditions, be shrublike. Others, normally shrubs, may at times be tree-like.

Foresters are not in agreement as to a definition of a tree, but they commonly say that a tree is a woody plant having one erect stem at least 3 inches in diameter, a crown of branches, and a height of at least 12 feet. There are, however, plants that do not come under this definition but nevertheless are considered trees. They include bonsai and dwarf trees.

Parts of a Tree

The main parts of a tree are the roots; the crown, which is composed of branches and leaves; the trunk; and the reproductive parts (flowers, fruits, or cones).

Roots anchor a tree and absorb water and minerals from the soil. Only the tiniest roots take part in absorption. The root system of a tree generally takes up more room underground than the crown and trunk do above the ground. The roots, like the branches, are covered with bark and consist mostly of wood.

Leaves are the food-manufacturing centers of plants. From the sunlight, air, and water, they make the food that trees need to grow and to form flowers or fruits and seeds. In this process, called photosynthesis, leaves manufacture sugar from water that they get from the soil, and from carbon dioxide that they absorb from the air. Sunshine furnishes the energy needed for the manufacturing process. Green plants, unlike animals, are able to make their own food; animals must get theirs ready-made, either directly or indirectly from plants. (See Botany; Leaf.)

The trunk supports the crown. The branches, the trunk, and the roots contain many tiny tubes through which liquids are carried. Food materials made in the leaves move to the roots through the phloem tissue, which is the inner lining bark tissue. Stopping the flow of food to the roots by removing a ring of bark from around the trunk will eventually kill a tree. This removal of bark is called girdling. Water, with dissolved minerals from the soil, moves to the leaves through the xylem tissue, which is the wood of the tree; however, only the outer layers of the wood, called sapwood, carry water and minerals. The main part of the tree, called heartwood, serves only to give strength to the tree. Removal of the heartwood from a tree trunk weakens the tree but does not interfere with the supply of water going to the leaves.

Flowers and fruits, which include cones, are reproductive structures. Without them, trees cannot make seeds. Tree flowers may be small

REPRESENTATIVE TREES

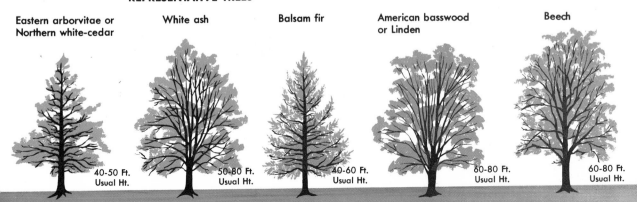

Eastern arborvitae or Northern white-cedar
40-50 Ft. Usual Ht.

White ash
50-80 Ft. Usual Ht.

Balsam fir
40-60 Ft. Usual Ht.

American basswood or Linden
60-80 Ft. Usual Ht.

Beech
60-80 Ft. Usual Ht.

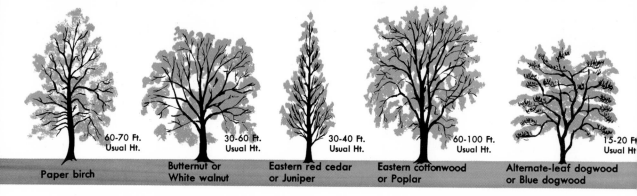

Paper birch	Butternut or White walnut	Eastern red cedar or Juniper	Eastern cottonwood or Poplar	Alternate-leaf dogwood or Blue dogwood
60-70 Ft. Usual Ht.	30-60 Ft. Usual Ht.	30-40 Ft. Usual Ht.	60-100 Ft. Usual Ht.	15-20 Ft. Usual Ht

and inconspicuous, like those of elms and oaks, or large and showy, like those of magnolia and flowering crabapple. (See FLOWER.) Tree cones range in size from the small ones of the eastern hemlock to the large ones of the sugar pine. The latter may be as long as 18 inches.

With the exception of the tree ferns of the tropics, which reproduce by means of spores, all trees reproduce by means of seeds. All trees and other plants that bear seeds are either gymnosperms or angiosperms. The seeds of gymnosperms are usually borne in cones. Trees that are gymnosperms are commonly known as conifers. Familiar conifers are pines, spruces, bald cypresses, redwoods, and sequoias. They are called softwoods. Angiosperms produce flowers; their seeds are enclosed in fruits, such as apples and walnuts. Most trees that are angiosperms are commonly called hardwoods. Familiar hardwood trees are elms, ashes, poplars, willows, oaks, maples, and birches. The wood of most hardwood trees is harder and heavier than that of most softwood trees. (See WOOD.) Hardwood trees are usually broad-leaved trees; that is, their leaves are broad and flat. Most softwood trees are narrow-leaved trees. Their leaves are long and narrow (for example, the needles of pines), although some may be scale-like and small (like those of junipers).

Some trees lose all their leaves at the start of the cold or dry season; they are deciduous trees. Other trees keep their leaves all year around; they are evergreens. (See DECIDUOUS; EVERGREEN.)

Geographical Distribution

In some regions, trees are scarce or missing from the landscape. The regions may be grasslands, such as the prairies of central North America; deserts, such as the Sahara; or areas that are too high or too far north or south for trees to grow. (See LAND TYPES.) The timberline on high mountains is the line above which trees cannot survive. Treeless areas in the far north are called the Arctic; they are beyond the continental tree line, which marks the northern limit of tree growth. Similar treeless areas occur in the far southern parts of the southern hemisphere. No trees at all grow on Antarctica, the only treeless continent.

The greatest number of kinds of trees is found in the tropical regions of the world, especially in rain forests. Such forests, even those of relatively small size, may contain as many as 500 species of trees. As distance north or south of the tropics increases, the number of tree species

Honey locust   **Sugar maple**   **White oak**   **White pine**   **Sassafras**

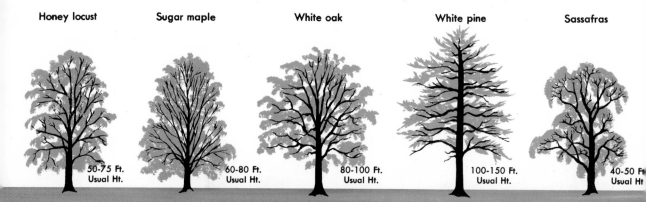

Honey locust	Sugar maple	White oak	White pine	Sassafras
50-75 Ft. Usual Ht.	60-80 Ft. Usual Ht.	80-100 Ft. Usual Ht.	100-150 Ft. Usual Ht.	40-50 Ft. Usual Ht

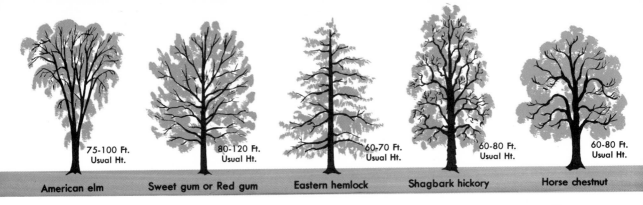

American elm 75-100 Ft. Usual Ht.

Sweet gum or Red gum 80-120 Ft. Usual Ht.

Eastern hemlock 60-70 Ft. Usual Ht.

Shagbark hickory 60-80 Ft. Usual Ht.

Horse chestnut 60-80 Ft. Usual Ht.

decreases until, in the polar regions, it reaches zero. Only five species of trees, for example, make up the vast forests of far northern Canada.

Continental United States (including Alaska) has about 840 species of native trees. Canada has about 150 species of native trees, and the British Isles have about 55.

Size and Age

The world's tallest, largest, and oldest living things are trees. The tallest living thing is a redwood growing in California. In 1964 it measured 367.8 feet in height. Placed bumper to bumper, 21 average-size automobiles would reach almost as far as this tree is high. The largest living thing, that is, the living thing with the greatest volume, is the General Sherman Sequoia in California's Sequoia National Park. It is about 272 feet tall and has a trunk diameter of 37 feet at the base. Two average-size automobiles, bumper to bumper, could fit inside the trunk with room to spare. Until recently, the sequoias were considered the oldest living things. The oldest precisely dated sequoia, cut down in 1892, was 3,212 years old. (See SEQUOIA.) Certain bristlecone pines, also in California, however, have beaten this record: one

of them is reported to be 4,600 years old.

Fossils reveal that trees were growing on the Earth many millions of years ago. Most of the ancient trees were much different from trees of today, although some of them, such as the ginkgo, have changed little over the ages. (See GINKGO TREE.) In swampy forests of the Carboniferous period (about 300 million years ago) there grew giant seed fern, club moss, horsetail, and cordaitalean trees. These trees, now all extinct, are of importance because they contributed to the formation of coal. At one time there were trees in the now treeless Arctic and Antarctic. Beech, maple, oak, and sycamore, for example, grew in Greenland 40 million years ago. (See FOSSIL.)

The age of a tree can be told by counting the rings in the trunk. In most kinds of temperate trees, new wood is formed each year in a layer outside the wood of the previous year. The layers of wood, as seen on the cut end of a felled tree, are circular and are called annual rings. Each ring in the wood of the trunk represents one year of the tree's life. In a year of good rainfall, the ring formed is wider than one formed in a drier year. A record of rainfall can thus be read in tree rings.

It is not necessary to cut down a tree to

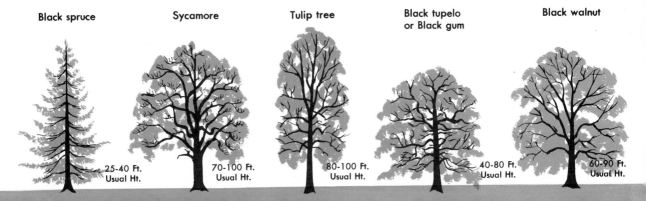

Black spruce 25-40 Ft. Usual Ht.

Sycamore 70-100 Ft. Usual Ht.

Tulip tree 80-100 Ft. Usual Ht.

Black tupelo or Black gum 40-80 Ft. Usual Ht.

Black walnut 60-90 Ft. Usual Ht.

discover its age. Using an instrument called an increment borer, it is possible to remove a narrow piece of wood extending from the bark to the tree's center. From this piece, called a core, the number of rings in the tree's trunk can be counted.

Trees not only increase the diameter of their trunks and branches each year but also grow in height. This growth in height comes about by the annual addition of many new cells to the tips of the twigs. The new cells make the

Courtesy U.S. Forest Service

The gnarled bristlecone pines of California are the oldest known living things—4,600 years old.

twigs longer and the tree taller. Because growth in height takes place only at the tips of the twigs, it is easy to understand why a nail driven into a trunk never moves further from the ground than it was at first. Trees continue to grow larger every year; they are not of limited size as are animals.

Value of Trees

Trees are of great importance to man. They supply wood, which is used for fuel and is made into lumber, paper, plywood, plastics, fence posts, railroad ties, and countless other products. Certain trees are of value as sources of foods, including fruits—such as apples, oranges, peaches, and dates—and nuts—such as pecans, walnuts, almonds, and cashews. Well-known spices that come from trees are cinnamon, cloves, and nutmeg.

Coffee and cocoa are beverages made from tree seeds. Among other tree products are cork; tannins (from wattle bark and quebracho wood), used to make leather; rubber; turpentine; useful gums and resins (gum Arabic, amber, and myrrh); essential oils (camphor and eucalyptus); fatty oils (olive and tung); waxes (carnauba); sugars (maple and palm); medicines (quinine and cascara); and fibers (kapok). In addition, man plants trees for ornament, shade, and soil erosion control, and as windbreaks. Millions of trees are cut annually for use as decorations at Christmas. Trees, providing shelter and food, are necessary for wildlife. Certain trees are poisonous, causing skin irritation when they are touched or injury to health when their foliage or fruits are eaten. (See articles on individual trees.)

TREE CREEPER (*krē′ pēr*) is any bird of the family Certhiidae. It is found throughout the northern hemisphere. The Australian tree creepers are usually classed in the family Climacteridae, although some experts class them in Certhiidae.

Certhia familiaris is the principal species of the Certhiidae family. It is called the tree creeper in Europe and the brown creeper in North America.

The plumage of creepers is brown to chestnut above, streaked with buff, and gray to white below. The bill is slender, long, and curved downward to the tip, and each feather on the long tail is stiff and pointed. The claws are curved and sharp.

Creepers, as the name suggests, creep about tree trunks and branches, cliffs, and walls, hunting for insects and spiders in the crevices. The brown creeper usually flies to the bottom of a tree trunk and works its way upward in a spiral

The brown creeper (*Certhia familiaris*) follows a spiral course up the trunks of trees in search of insects.

course. Its sharp claws, supporting tail feathers, and curved bill make the creeper admirably suited for this type of food hunting. When it has gone up the trunk, it flies to the next tree and repeats the performance. Its hunting method is nearly the reverse of the nuthatch, which usually starts at the top and works downward, head first. (See NUTHATCH.)

The nests of creepers are placed in trees behind loose bark. They are made of moss, grass, and bark and are lined with hair and feathers. The female lays five to seven white or flesh-colored eggs spotted with brown.

TRENT (*trĕnt*), **COUNCIL** (*kaun'sŭl*) **OF,** was a meeting of the leaders of the Roman Catholic church. The council took place between the years 1545 and 1563, but there were two long interruptions of its work: between 1547 and 1551; and between 1552 and 1562.

This council, considered the 19th ecumenical or general council, was probably the most important of all (at least up to the Second Vatican Council) for two reasons: Trent issued more decrees and on a much wider variety of topics than any previous church council; and the beliefs, practices, and lives of all Roman Catholics have been deeply influenced by what was done at Trent.

The century of the Council of Trent was the time when Catholic unity was destroyed in Europe as a result of the work of the Protestant reformers. These men, such as Martin Luther and John Calvin, insisted that they had no wish to destroy the Christian church. But they were concerned that the corruption of the church, especially in Rome, was so deep seated and widespread that it threatened to destroy the very idea of the Christian religion. At length they withdrew from the church of Rome in order to work to rebuild the Christian church on the firm foundation of the gospel. As time went on the reformers came to deny the truth of certain teachings of the Roman church. These teachings were believed by Catholics to be basic to the Christian religion as presented in the New Testament.

Meanwhile, many Catholics generally agreed with the reformers that there were numerous church practices that called for drastic reform. They did not believe, however, that it was necessary to leave the church in order to bring about the reforms. Both sides agreed that a general council should be called. At such a meeting all the disputed matters could be dealt with, and reform measures could be enacted.

Complications, however, arose because of the political situation in Europe. The Holy Roman emperor, Charles V, was in favor of a council. Francis I, king of France, and the pope, Clement VII, were against the idea. Clement died in 1534, and his successor, Paul III, almost immediately set about preparing for a council. When Pope Paul first presented the plan to the cardinals, nearly all were opposed. Nevertheless, he summoned the council, and in 1545 work finally began.

In its 25 sessions the Council of Trent practically restated the whole of Roman Catholic teaching in clear and unmistakable terms. It issued a great number of regulations concerning all phases of the church's life and organization. Even though it failed to satisfy the Protestants, the council established the solid base that is the teaching of the Roman Catholic church of today.

TRENT AFFAIR was an incident that occurred during the U. S. Civil War and nearly caused England to declare war on the Union.

The Confederate States had chosen two men

to represent them in England and France. The commissioners, James Murray Mason and John Slidell, were sailing to Europe on the *Trent,* a British ship. A Union ship, the *San Jacinto,* commanded by Captain Charles Wilkes, stopped the *Trent* on November 8, 1861. Acting without authority, Wilkes searched the ship, arrested the commissioners and their secretaries, and took them as prisoners to Boston, Massachusetts.

The people of the North were pleased, and Wilkes became a hero. The British, however, were angry, claiming that the United States had violated freedom of the seas. The British demanded an apology and the release of Mason and Slidell. They claimed that the United States had no right to take men off the ship of a neutral nation. In the War of 1812 the United States had fought England to defend the same principle. A new war was now threatening.

Most people in the North did not want to free Mason and Slidell. There were lengthy discussions in the cabinet, and President Abraham Lincoln, backed by Secretary of State William Seward, decided to free the commissioners. Meanwhile, in England, Prince Albert, Queen Victoria's husband, persuaded British leaders to take a more peaceful attitude. Soon after, the two were freed, and relations between the two countries again became friendly.

TRENTON (*trĕnt' 'n*), **NEW JERSEY,** is the state capital and an industrial city on the Delaware River, about 30 miles northeast of Philadelphia, Pennsylvania. Early Indian trails, post roads, and railroads came through the city. Nearby waterpower and coal helped its early industrial growth.

The city is one of the world's largest makers of wire ropes and cables. Steel cable from Trenton has been used in many famous suspension bridges of the world. The city is renowned for pottery making, which it began in colonial times. The potteries of Lenox, Inc., make one of the finest porcelains in the world. Among the many other industrial works in the area are iron and steel plants and rubber, linoleum, electrical products, machine, and wool factories.

Trenton is served by two major railroad lines. Airlines use Mercer County Airport west of Trenton, and there are shipping facilities on the Delaware River.

There are many buildings, parks, and monuments that reflect Trenton's rich colonial history. These include the Old Barracks, originally built to house British troops during the French and Indian War; the Battle Monument, marking the place where George Washington opened fire on the British in 1776; and Washington Crossing Park, site of George Washington's Delaware River crossing. The gold-domed State Capitol and other state buildings are located along the riverfront.

In 1679 Mahlon Stacy, a Quaker, built a grain mill and a log house on the site of Trenton. Stacy's son later sold the mill and land to William Trent of Philadelphia, and the village was named in his honor. Trenton served as the temporary national capital in 1784 and 1799. It became the state capital in 1790. By the mid-19th century the city was well known for steel products and pottery. Trenton's economy was aided in the early 1950's when one of the country's largest steel plants was established across the river, at Morrisville, Pennsylvania. Trenton has a mayor-council form of government. The population is 104,638 (1970).

TRIESTE (*trē ĕst'* or *trē ĕs'tē*), **ITALY,** is an important seaport and commercial city on the Adriatic Sea. It lies along Italy's border with Yugoslavia, south of Austria. During its history, Trieste has been held by each of these countries.

Trieste is built on a series of terraces that rise from the sea. The old part of town is on and around the Hill of San Giusto. At the top of the hill is a castle, dating from medieval times, and the cathedral of San Giusto. Much of the newer part of Trieste is built on level ground adjoining the bay. Two important centers of commercial activities in the newer section are the Piazza Oberdan and the Piazza dell' Unita. Among the important buildings are a museum of Roman remains and the municipal buildings.

Trieste has important shipbuilding yards, petroleum refineries, steel mills, ironworks, cement factories, and stone quarries. It is also noted as a center for insurance companies.

The Castle of Miramare is located on the Adriatic coast just north of Trieste. A Viennese architect designed the building for Archduke Maximilian of Austria.

Authenticated News

History

The history of Trieste is long and filled with many conflicts. Trieste grew rapidly when the Roman Empire was at the height of its power. After the downfall of the Roman Empire, Trieste declined. The city acquired some independence in the 10th century, but in 1202 it was captured by Venice. The Venetians ruled Trieste until 1382, when the city accepted the protection of Austria. But Austria did not give much attention to Trieste until 1719, when it made the city a free port.

The city grew rapidly during the 19th century as a center of trade and commerce. The Austro-Hungarian Empire began to use Trieste as its main port leading to the Mediterranean, and it became the chief port for much of southeast and central Europe. Trieste's population had become largely Italian, and many Italians of the period believed that Trieste should become a part of Italy. When Italy entered World War I, one of its objects was to gain control of Trieste. This finally happened through the Treaty of St. Germain, signed in 1919.

Toward the end of World War II, Trieste was occupied by Yugoslavia, which was determined to hold it. Italy was equally determined to regain control. The Allied forces, wishing to settle the matter peacefully, divided the territory into two zones: zone A, including the city of Trieste, under U.S.-British administration, and zone B, under Yugoslav administration. In 1947 the Allies established the Free Territory of Trieste, which was to be an independent state. A free state of Trieste, however, did not develop.

In 1954, Trieste territory was divided between Italy and Yugoslavia. The city, as a free port, and a narrow strip of coastal land became a part of Italy, while a larger area of land south of the city went to Yugoslavia. Trieste has a population of 272,900 (1961).

TRILLIUM (*trĭl'ē ŭm*) is any of several species of flowering plants of the lily family, Liliaceae. The plant's name comes from the Latin word for three. The blossoms of trilliums have three petals, three sepals, six stamens, a three-celled ovary, and a cluster of three leaves. A solitary flower blooms above the cluster of leaves.

The great white trillium has three broad, white petals.

Roche

Trilliums are woodland plants native to North America and Asia. They grow in damp, shaded areas. About 30 different species are known. Some bloom in early spring before the robins come. Thus the name wake-robin is given to them.

One of the species of trillium with large flowers is the great white trillium, or trinity lily (*Trillium gran-*

diflorum). Its blossoms have broad petals, each two or three inches long, and a pleasant scent. Days after blooming, the flowers change from white to pink. The so-called purple trillium (*T. erectum*) really has dark-red petals. The blossom is beautiful but has a most unpleasant odor.

Perhaps the prettiest of the trilliums is the painted trillium (*T. undulatum*), also called painted wake-robin or smiling wake-robin. Its narrow, pointed petals are white marked with deep pink or maroon. The nodding trillium's (*T. cernuum*) white flowers droop and are almost hidden by the leaves.

When trilliums are picked, they wilt quickly, and the plant forms no seed for the next year. It is best, therefore, to let the flowers stay in their natural woodland home.

In 1927 the trillium was made the official flower of Ontario, Canada.

TRINIDAD AND TOBAGO (*trĭn′ ŭ dăd′* and *tŭbā′ gō*), **WEST INDIES,** are two islands off the coast of Venezuela that together form a single independent country. They are part of a sunken segment of the Andes Mountains that at one time was part of the South American mainland. Trinidad is by far the largest and most populous of the two islands.

Mountain ranges cross Trinidad in the north and south, and the Central Range crosses it diagonally. The highest elevation is El Cerro del Aripo (3,085 feet) in the Northern Range. In the south the ranges are less than 1,000 feet high. Trinidad takes its name from the Trinity Hills in the Southern Range.

Vegetation on Trinidad has some characteristics of the nearby mainland. It includes tropical rain forest, tropical deciduous forest, and some savanna. Much of the original vegetation, however, has been cleared for agricultural purposes. All of the island has constantly warm temperatures and considerable rainfall. Average monthly temperatures range between 75 and 80 degrees Fahrenheit. Most of the island has a wet season, from June to December, and a dry season, from January to May.

Tobago's climate and vegetation are typical of a Caribbean tropical island. It has received serious damage from Caribbean hurricanes, though these usually strike farther north. Trinidad, farther south, is seldom affected by hurricanes.

The population of Trinidad and Tobago is quite mixed. More than 40 percent of the people are of African descent. Asian Indians make up the next largest group, and most of the remainder are Chinese, Syrian, Portuguese, Spanish, French, and British. Roman Catholics form the largest religious group, followed by Hindus and Anglicans. The most populous city is Port of Spain, the country's capital and chief port. (See PORT OF SPAIN.)

Trinidad first became important for its cacao and coconuts, which grew wild and were easily harvested. After the British seized the island in 1797, sugar-

Locator map of Trinidad and Tobago.

FACTS ABOUT TRINIDAD AND TOBAGO

CAPITAL: Port of Spain.
AREA: 1,980 square miles (Tobago 116 square miles).
POPULATION: 827,957 (33,333 on Tobago) (1960); 974,700 (1965 estimate).
HIGHEST POINT: El Cerro del Aripo (3,085 feet).
FORM OF GOVERNMENT: Parliamentary State.
CHIEF OF STATE: Queen.
HEAD OF GOVERNMENT: Prime Minister.
POLITICAL DIVISIONS: Three municipalities and seven counties.
CHIEF PRODUCTS: *Manufactured,* petroleum and petroleum products, sugar; *Agricultural,* cacao, citrus fruits, coconuts, coffee, sugarcane; *Mined,* asphalt, natural gas, petroleum.
CURRENCY: Dollar; two dollars equal one U.S. dollar.

cane was introduced and is today the leading agricultural export. Other crops include citrus and other fruits, coffee, and vegetables.

Petroleum is the country's most important product. About three-fourths of the total value of exports is made up of petroleum and petroleum products. Pitch Lake, near the southern shore of the Gulf of Paria, long has furnished asphalt to the world. There are also considerable reserves of natural gas.

Petroleum refining and chemical fertilizers are important industries. Traditional manufactured products of the country include sugar, rum, beer, angostura bitters, and processed citrus fruits. Textiles and lumber add to the economy.

Primary education is free in Trinidad and Tobago, and secondary education is free to those who qualify. Higher education is offered at the Trinidad branch of the University of the West Indies.

Trinidad was discovered and claimed for Spain by Columbus on his voyage of 1498. The island was inhabited by Indians whose numbers were greatly reduced when Spanish colonists forced them to labor in mines. No precious metals were found, however, and the island received little attention from Spain.

In the 18th century, Spain agreed to let French planters settle in Trinidad to cultivate the virgin soil. From that time the colony grew rapidly. In 1802 Spain ceded Trinidad to Great Britain and Tobago to France. Tobago went to the British in 1814.

The two islands were politically united in 1889. The British granted independence to Trinidad and Tobago on August 31, 1962. Eric Williams became the first prime minister. The new country joined the Commonwealth of Nations, the Organization of American States, and the United Nations.

TRINITY (*trĭn′ŭt ē*) is the Christian belief in God as a threefold being. According to this doctrine God is really one, but He has three distinctive ways of acting and of showing Himself. The one God is Father, Son, and Holy Spirit.

The word *Trinity* is not present in the Bible, but the doctrine does seem to have its roots there. The name given to God by the early Christians was Father. The Father, however, was known through his Son, Jesus Christ, who was also called the Lord. It was thought that man is moved to believe in the Father through the Son by the Holy Spirit, and that this is the way the one God shows Himself to man.

In the Bible, however, Yahweh (the Old Testament term for God) was also called Lord. Occasionally in the New Testament, Lord was applied to the Spirit also; and sometimes the Spirit was referred to as the Spirit of Jesus Christ. This presented a problem to the early Christians: if God is really one, what is the relationship between the Father, the Son, and the Holy Spirit? Some answered that the world was created by an imperfect god and saved by a perfect god. In other words, there are two gods. Others held that although there is only one God, there is a being who is neither God nor man but rather a being in between—the Son.

In the 3rd and 4th centuries the Christian church tried to find a way to state its belief that God is both one and threefold. The formula that came to be accepted in the Western church was "three persons in one substance." This formula can be taken to mean that God is like an actor who plays three roles while remaining one individual. (See CHRISTIANITY.)

TRIPOLI (*trĭp′ō lē*), **LIBYA,** is the largest city and principal commercial center of the country. It is a Mediterranean seaport in the sub-province of Tripoli. Tripoli is one of the two capitals of Libya. The second capital city is Bengasi on the Gulf of Sidra. The government moves from one capital to the other every two years. (See LIBYA.)

Tripoli is a beautiful city built on low terraces which rise from the shores of the harbor. Summers are very hot and humid; winters are generally short and rainy. There are many mosques, which have tall, slim towers called minarets. The old part of the city has narrow, twisting streets which are roofed over by buildings and arches. Many buildings in the business section are very modern.

Promising oil wells have been drilled in Libya, and oil exploration teams from the United States and Europe have their headquarters in Tripoli. Wheelus Air Force Base, one of the largest United States overseas bases, is seven miles east of Tripoli. New businesses and housing for the oilmen and airmen, and their families, brought new prosperity to the city.

Many nations have been interested in controlling Tripoli because of its important location. It is a trading center, a seaport, a station on the coastal road across North Africa, and the northern end of several caravan routes which cross the Sahara Desert from central Africa.

Farming, fishing, and livestock raising are the chief occupations in the area about Tripoli.

The waterfront fort at Tripoli was attacked by U.S. Marines in the 1805 war against pirates.

Wide World

The city has some small industries, such as the production of salt, cigarettes, cloth, and carpets. An important export is esparto, a grass used in making fine paper. Among the chief imports are foods, automobiles, machinery, and petroleum.

History

Tripoli is a very old city with a colorful history. It was probably founded by the Phoenicians, and later had many different rulers. At times it was ruled by Carthage, Rome, the Vandals, the Ottoman Empire, and Italy. During World War II, Tripoli was held by the British, who governed the northern part of Libya until 1951. Libya became an independent Arab nation and King Mohammed Idris I es-Senussi took the throne in December 1951.

During the period of Turkish control (between the 16th and 19th centuries), many seamen of Tripoli were pirates. Between 1801 and 1805, the United States fought against the notorious pirates of Tripoli. (See PIRATE AND PIRACY.) During this war, Stephen Decatur won fame by destroying the ship *Philadelphia* which the pirates had captured and were using against the United States.

The population of Tripoli is 213,506 (1964).

TROGON (*trō'gŏn*), any bird that belongs to Trogonidae, a family of about 34 species found throughout the tropics. It has a strong, somewhat hooked bill and small weak claws. Trogons have two front and two back toes on each foot. The feathers on the lower parts of the body are generally colored with yellows, reds, and blues while on the upper parts they are metallike greens. Their tails are long.

While the species that live in the New World eat mainly fruit and some insects, those in the Old World eat mostly insects with some fruit. All trogons lay their two to four, white or pale blue eggs on loose wood chips in tree hollows, usually a deserted woodpecker hole.

Trogons are from 10 to 12 inches long except for the quetzal, the national bird of Guatemala. The quetzal has a tail about 30 inches long on a body only 14 inches long. However, his long plumes are not true tail feathers used for flying but grow from just above the tail.

Trogons are about 12 inches long and their plumage is brightly colored.

The coppery-tailed trogon is the only kind in the United States. It is found in the mountains of southeastern Arizona. Like the rest of his family, it is not a song bird, but has a number of calls. About a foot long, it usually has a brownish green back and red breast.

TROTSKY (*trôts'kē* or *trŏt'skē*), **LEON** (*lē'ŏn*) (1879–1940), was one of the top leaders under Nicolai Lenin in the Russian Revolution of November 1917. Born of Jewish parents near Odessa, Russia, Trotsky's real name was Lev Davidovich Bronstein. After he left the University of Odessa, he joined with those planning a revolution in Russia. At this time many Russians were unhappy under the harsh, undemo-

Leon Trotsky.

Brown Brothers

cratic government of the czars, the rulers of Russia. Because of this work, he was arrested in 1898, and exiled to Siberia. In 1902 he escaped by using the name Trotsky on a forged passport. He then took this name as his own.

After escaping from Siberia, Trotsky went to London where he met Lenin. A few years later he returned to Russia to again work for the revolution, but he had to flee in 1910. For a number of years he lived in many European cities where he lectured against the systems of government and World War I. In January 1917 he went to the United States to edit a Russian-language newspaper in New York City. However, when the revolution broke out in Russia in March, he returned to join in the struggle.

Trotsky soon became a Bolshevik, as the Communists were called at that time. He quickly rose to leadership within the party, to a position second only to Lenin. The Bolsheviks overthrew Alexander Kerensky's Provisional government (which was trying to set up a democracy) in November 1917, and set up their own Soviet government. Trotsky became the Bolshevist people's commissioner for foreign affairs. He later took charge of organizing the Communist armies.

After Lenin's death in 1924, Trotsky was opposed by Joseph Stalin in the bitter struggle for power. Trotsky lost and was exiled in 1928. He finally settled in Mexico City. Twelve years later a political enemy murdered him in his home there. Many believed the murderer was acting on orders from Stalin.

Trotsky wrote numerous books; some are in English, including: *Defence of Terrorism* (1920), *Lenin* (1924), *Problems of Life* (1924), and *The Revolution Betrayed* (1937). (See COMMUNISM; LENIN, NICOLAI; STALIN, JOSEPH VISSARIONOVICH.)

TROUT (*trout*) are among the finest of game fish. They belong to the Salmon family and are very good as food. Like salmon they have small, soft, fatty fins on their back just in front of the tail. Their mouths are unusually large, with sharp teeth. They live on insects, shellfish, and smaller fishes. Colored in shades of red, yellow and green, most of them weigh less than 20 pounds.

Trout are divided into three groups or *genera*. The *Salvelinus* group, called chars, include the brook trout, Sunapee trout, Arctic char, Greenland char, and Dolly Varden trout. The best known of the *Salmo* group are the brown trout, rainbow trout, and cutthroat trout. In the *Cristovomer* group is the lake trout.

Females of the *Salmo* and *Salvelinus* group use their tails to dig holes called *redds* in the bottom of a stream just above a pool. Into the redd the female lays her eggs. At the same time a male deposits on the eggs a substance called *milt* which fertilizes them and makes them grow. The female digs many redds, until all of her eggs are laid. Each time she covers the hole with gravel to protect them. Lake trout do not build redds, however, and fish eat the unprotected eggs.

When the young trout hatch and leave the gravel holes they are called *parrs*. Many of these young trout are eaten by other fish. When they start to swim downstream they are called *fry*.

Brook trout are the favorite sport fish of the United States. They are native in eastern streams, but they are now growing in streams of western United States and many other countries. Generally, they are an olive green color above and reddish below. Marked with black, they also have red spots. Their lower fins are red or orange with bands of black and white at the edges. At one time brook trout weighing ten pounds were common. So much fishing has been done, however, that today a one-pound brook trout is considered a good catch. They may be up to 18 inches long, but most are half that length.

Although brook trout live best in cool streams with strong currents, they are also found in cold water lakes. Even when they swim into the ocean, they return to streams to lay their eggs. When they live in lakes they may lay the eggs where spring water enters the lake.

The Dolly Varden trout is found in Montana, Idaho, Washington, Oregon, and California. It is quite like the brook trout, and will also swim to the sea. Larger than the brook trout, however, it averages 5 to 12 pounds, and has

The brook trout (up to 18 inches long) is also known as the "speckled trout." It likes cold water and streams with gravel beds.

orange spots.

The rainbow trout is native to western mountain streams but it has been brought into eastern United States, Canada, Europe, and New Zealand. It can live in warmer water than the brook trout. Fishermen like this fish because it leaps out of the water for an artificial fly and also leaps when hooked. It weighs up to ten pounds and has large scales and black spots on its sides. The name, rainbow, comes from a red streak sometimes found on its side.

Cutthroat trout have two red streaks on their lower jaw. They are found in cold mountain streams from Alaska down to northern California. They may weigh as much as 20 pounds but are usually about 5 pounds. When cutthroats and rainbows run to the ocean, they lose their bright colors. They are then called steelheads. For many years steelheads were believed to be a different species of trout.

Brown trout were brought to the United States from Europe in 1883. They are brown with large, black spots and some light red spots on their sides. They, also, live in water that is too warm for brook trout. Some brown trout have been caught which weigh 40 pounds and it is not uncommon to catch a 10 pound fish.

The lake trout is also called the Mackinaw trout. In Canada it has the Indian name, "Namaycush." Although it may weigh up to 100 pounds, the average size is 10 pounds. In the United States it ranks next to whitefish in commercial importance as a Great Lakes fish. In other large lakes it is considered a sport fish.

It feeds on herring, smelt, whitefish, and other fish. It is a grayish fish marked with white or yellow spots.

TROY (*troi*), **ASIA MINOR,** was an ancient city situated on the northwest coast of what is now Turkey. Troy is of great importance in both literature and archaeology. Where the city once stood is Hissarlik, a mound near the Menderes River. This site is about three miles south of the Dardanelles, gateway to the Black Sea. Troy was an important stop on a trade route to and from the Black Sea. The city was made famous by the stories of the Greek poet Homer. Homer's *Iliad* and *Odyssey* were based on a long war between the Trojans and the Achaean Greeks early in the 12th century B.C.

Archaeological Discovery of Troy

In 1870 Heinrich Schliemann went to Asia Minor to find the city of Troy. He and his assistants began digging at the mound of Hissarlik (meaning "place of fortresses" in Turkish) and during 1872–1874 found many small cities or fortresses built one on top of the other.

At that time very little was known about the early history of the Greeks and their neighbors. The tools, weapons, household goods, and other remains of different periods of man's history in Asia Minor had not been found and arranged in correct historical order by archaeologists. So although Schliemann thought he had found seven cities, he had not correctly identified the Troy of the Trojan War. In digging through the layers of remains of buildings, Schliemann found many treasures of cups, bowls, pitchers, ornaments, weapons, and other objects, most of them made of gold. These helped convince him that the settlement he called Troy II was the Troy of Homer and the Trojan War. In honor of the Trojan ruler Priam in Homer's story he called the discoveries "Priam's treasure."

After Schliemann's death in 1890 his assistant Wilhelm Doerpfeld continued digging at Troy until 1894. Doerpfeld decided that there were nine major levels at Troy and that Troy II existed more than 1,000 years before the Trojan War. Doerpfeld identified Troy VI, a fortress with thick walls and towers, as the Homeric city.

In 1932 Carl W. Blegen of the University of Cincinnati began a series of expeditions to Troy to re-examine the site. He accepted the nine major cities described by Doerpfeld but identified Troy VIIA as the Homeric city.

Archaeological History of Troy

The first city of Troy was a small settlement about 150 feet across, surrounded by a wall eight feet thick. The city's houses had stone foundations. The people used stone implements, a few copper tools, and pottery. This first settlement at Troy was probably built shortly after 3000 B.C.

Around 2600 B.C. Troy II arose. It was a larger fortress, about 300 feet in diameter. Twelve-foot-thick walls and a huge tower gate protected the simple houses of sun-dried brick on stone foundations. In the ruins were many treasures of gold and silver objects. The so-called Priam's treasure should be dated about 2300 to 2200 B.C. when Troy II was destroyed by fire. Troy III, IV, and V seem to have been less important than Troy II. The small objects and the pottery found in the levels of these settlements were somewhat like those of Troy II.

The Troy VI period probably began in the last half of the 18th century B.C. and ended when an earthquake destroyed it about 1275 B.C.

Locator map of Troy.

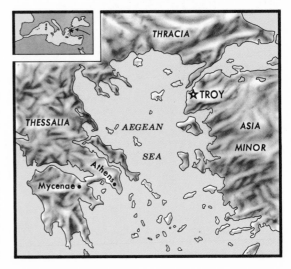

During these centuries a strong fortress-city grew up. The settlement which followed, Troy VIIA (about 1275 to 1185 B.C.), identified by Blegen as the Homeric city, was in part a rebuilding of Troy VI. Fire destroyed Troy VIIA in the early part of the 12th century B.C.

Early History of Troy

Most Homeric scholars believed that Homer lived in the 8th century B.C. He used earlier songs and stories in writing his two great epics, the *Iliad* and *Odyssey*. Evidence suggests that there really was such a war as the Trojan War.

The historical date for the destruction of Troy in the early 12th century B.C. fits the

Unaware that it holds armed Greek warriors, Trojan soldiers push the monumental wooden horse into their city.

archaeological dates for the destruction of Troy VIIA. During this period in the eastern Mediterranean region there were wars and invasions involving Greece, Asia Minor, Phoenicia, Palestine, and Egypt. The Hittite empire in Asia Minor disappeared; Philistines and Hebrews moved into Palestine. Both written material and archaeological remains show that many strange peoples raided widely throughout the eastern Mediterranean area. These peoples included the "Ahhiyawa" and "Danuna," who possibly were linked with the Achaean Greeks.

The Achaeans of Homer's stories had a leader named Agamemnon, king of Mycenae. This city of southern Greece seems to fit into the archaeology and history of the early 12th century B.C. By 1400 B.C. a prosperous people were living in southern Greece around Mycenae, where rich kings lived in large palaces. The Mycenaean culture, as it is called, was partly Cretan in origin. By the 12th century B.C. this culture had spread over much of Greece and to the nearby Aegean Islands. Trade was carried on with Egypt, Palestine, Sicily, Cyprus, and Asia Minor.

Many scholars believe that the Mycenaean culture is the same as that of the Achaean Greeks of the Homeric epics. They date the beginning of the Dorian Greek invasion soon after the fall of Troy. Aside from the romantic tale about the cause of the war and the myths about the gods, the story of the Trojan War grew out of a period of war and invasion. Since Troy had an important location at the entrance to the Black Sea it became involved in war as peoples became interested in trade, colonization, and empire building in that area.

Greek legend, added to by classical and medieval writers, gives a much more colorful story of Troy (Ilium or Ilion) than do archaeology and history. Homer's two long epics tell a large part of the story of Troy. The *Iliad* tells stories about Achaean heroes and leaders who fought a ten-year war against the city of Troy. The other epic, the *Odyssey*, tells of the wanderings and adventures of Odysseus (Ulysses), one of the Greek heroes, on his return home from Troy. (See ILIAD; ODYSSEY.)

The rest of the legendary history of Troy

is largely told in the *Aeneid*, another dramatic epic. The *Aeneid* was written by the Roman poet Virgil in the 1st century B.C., during the reign of Emperor Augustus. (See AENEID; VIRGIL.)

Later History of Troy

In Greek and Roman times Troy (Ilium or Ilion) was often mentioned in written records and was thought to be a city of religious and historical importance. King Xerxes of Persia sacrificed to Athena at Troy in 490 B.C. on the way to his war in Greece. Alexander the Great visited there in 334 B.C. before he set out on his campaign against the Persians. Troy was rebuilt about 300 B.C. but lost its strength again in the following century. Even after it had suffered decline and decay, Greek and Roman leaders continued to visit Troy and often aided in restoring and rebuilding the city. However, with the decline of Rome in the 4th century A.D. Troy also slowly disappeared.

Evidence of Troy's existence after its destruction by the Achaeans in the early 12th century B.C. was found in the levels of Troy VIII and IX. There were fortifications and temple remains of the classical and the Hellenistic and Roman periods. After Roman times there was no important settlement at Hissarlik mound.

TROYON (*trwä yôn'*), **CONSTANT** (*kôns tän'*) (1810–1865). Animal painting was changed completely in the 19th century by the French painter Constant Troyon. He had made a reputation as a landscape painter, and did not begin painting animals until he was 40 years old. However, his real fame came from his simple, real-looking animals, particularly cows.

Troyon was born in Sevres, France. His father worked in the porcelain factory and Constant entered it as a porcelain decorator. When he was 20, he decided to start as a painter.

Troyon worked with the artists who painted around the village of Barbizon. They painted directly from nature. When he went to Paris two years later, his landscapes attracted attention.

In 1847 he traveled in Holland. There, he studied the animal painting of the famous artist

Courtesy, Museum of Fine Arts, Boston

"The Hound Pointing" by Constant Troyon.

Paul Potter. From that time, Troyon's chief interest was in painting animals. He painted them as part of his landscapes.

Among his better-known pictures are "Oxen Going to Their Work," in the Louvre Museum, Paris, France; "Landscape with Cattle," in the Glasgow Corporation Gallery; and "Going to Market," in the Corcoran Gallery of Art, Washington, D.C.

TRUCK (*trŭk*) **AND TRUCKING** (*trŭk'ĭng*). There are four major types of freight transportation, railroad, truck, boat, and airplane. Only the truck, however, can provide the complete service from picking up the articles from the sender to delivering them to their final destination.

Almost all products we eat, wear, or use travel at some time by truck. A chair first is carried on a truck as a newly-cut tree, then on another truck as lumber or plywood, then to a factory, and finally on other trucks to a store and the buyer. A dress is carried in a truck first as cotton, silk or man-made fiber, then as

Courtesy White Motor Company

Early delivery trucks were difficult to handle and often broke down.

a bolt of cloth, then as a finished garment, and finally to a store and home. Most foods, in the same way, are carried by trucks many times before they reach the table. The trucks that perform these services and the thousands of home delivery trucks are all part of the huge trucking industry.

There are many reasons for the rapid growth in trucking. Unlike other kinds of transportation, trucks are able to go any place where there is a road. They can also deliver goods quickly and at low cost. The trucking industry has become so large in the United States that it employs more than 7 million persons, which is second only to agriculture.

The First Trucks

The date of the first truck is not known. Many experiments were made with different kinds of electric, steam and gasoline engines in the early 1890's. Most of the trucks seen at that time were simply automobiles with a box in back instead of the rear seat. By 1898, trucks were being used more and more for local delivery. Owners, however, were still afraid to send their "horseless carriages" too far from home for fear they would break down. When the federal government bought its first three delivery trucks in 1899, they had them built so that a mule could be hitched to them, in case they would not run. At that time, many people thought that a truck was nothing more than a noisy machine that scared the horses. They would

often break down and it was difficult to find someone who knew enough to repair them. Nevertheless, to others, trucks were a valuable replacement for the horse and wagon.

In 1903, the contest committee of the Automobile Club of America held a contest in New York City for business vehicles of all types. This included heavy trucks and delivery wagons, as well as light delivery wagons, run by gasoline, steam and electricity. They hoped to find out by this contest which was better, self-propelled vehicles or horse-drawn vehicles. The results of the contest showed that trucks were better than most people had believed.

Trucking continued to grow and by 1904 there were 700 such vehicles registered in the United States. When the United States entered World War I (1917) this number had grown to about 315,000. By the time the war was over there were more than one million trucks. The truck of that day, however, was still hard to handle compared to the modern vehicles.

People now saw that trucks were a practical and economical means of transportation. They were of less use in transporting freight between distant points for there were few good roads. There were a few paved highways but most routes were winding dirt roads which turned to mudholes in rainy weather.

During the 1920's people became interested in a "Good Roads" movement. Organizations were formed all over the United States to encourage the building of new, hard surfaced roads. This program was the real beginning of the present highway system. It also helped to change trucking from a local service into a national industry.

Kinds of Trucks

The new roads made it possible for trucks to serve new areas. They could carry products that had traveled before only by railroads. To do this, new types of trucks had to be made. Tank trucks were developed to carry kerosene, gasoline, and fuel oil. Special trucks also were built to carry livestock, farm produce, poultry, milk, and meat. Other trucks transported automobiles, huge loads of steel, farm machinery, telephone cable, and thousands of other products.

Courtesy Dealers Transit, Inc.

An automobile carrier transports cars and trucks from a factory or railroad terminal to local dealers. The vehicles are anchored to the truck by chains. At their destination, they are driven off the back of the truck.

Most of the new trucks were *straight* trucks, that is the engine and box or van are part of the same unit. A large number of *tractor-trailer* trucks also were built. In these the engine in the tractor is separated from the load box and this allows a small but powerful tractor to pull many kinds of specialized trailer bodies. Inter-city transportation, with special types of trailers designed to carry almost every type of freight, made trucking important in the growth of large industries in the United States.

Although most trucking companies were still small businesses, the size of the trucking industry was growing rapidly. The federal government then decided that there should be some controls over this new form of transportation. The railroads had long been regulated by the Interstate Commerce Act and, in 1935, Congress formed a new section of the Act to cover trucks. (See INTERSTATE COMMERCE COMMISSION.)

Trucks were then divided into two basic groups, *for-hire* and *private* carriers. The for-hire trucking firms are paid to carry goods which belong to others. Many large companies, however, have their own trucks which carry only their own products. These trucks are private carriers.

Common Carriers

Within the for-hire group, there are common and contract carriers. Each common carrier truck line has a franchise, or government permission, to serve certain places. A person with freight to send would call the common carrier

who has the right to serve the particular place where the shipment is going. These franchises are granted by the Interstate Commerce Commission (ICC) and may cover cities or communities in many states. Some truck lines, especially furniture movers, may cover the entire United States. Most common carriers haul any item that someone wants sent. Certain things, however, need special equipment to transport them so only particular trucks can carry them. These include automobile transporters, tank trucks, household goods movers, and heavy haulers.

Besides granting operating certificates, the ICC closely governs how much trucks may charge. The Commission protects people by requiring the trucking companies to show the ICC their rates. If the rate is too high, the ICC orders the trucking company to lower it. In some cases, a very low rate may be made which

Delivery trucks are used mostly for short distances. They carry nearly all home deliveries, such as milk, laundry, groceries, and department store purchases.

Courtesy Ford Motor Co.

Courtesy (above) Kenworth Motor Truck Company, (right) Consolidated Freightways, Inc.

Above: Semitrailer tanks are used to haul liquids. Right: One tractor can haul more goods when a tandem set-up is used as with these refrigerated trailers.

might cause another trucking firm to go out of business. If the ICC finds that the public would suffer it would not allow the lowered rate to be charged.

Contract and Private Carriers

The second type of for-hire carrier is the contract carrier. These carriers haul goods only for persons with whom they have written contracts or agreements. For instance, a tool manufacturer may make an agreement with a contract carrier to haul his tools to market. The carrier cannot then accept shipments from anyone else who calls him.

The ICC governs only carriers that operate in interstate commerce (those that do business in two or more states). A carrier which operates entirely within one state would be governed by that state's public utilities commission.

Private carriers do not come under the ICC's rate regulations. They must still obey the safety regulations set up by the Commission. Of the 11,000,000 trucks registered in the United States in 1959, about 85 per cent of them were operated by private carriers.

Throughout the 1930's, more and more people and companies used truck transportation because it was fast and not too expensive. New routes were developed and new services were performed. Many smaller communities were reached by trucks. Today there are more than 50,000 communities in rural United States where trucks are the only kind of freight service.

Trucks in World War II

When the United States entered World War II (1941), nearly five million trucks were op-

erating on the nation's highways. Many of these trucks were put to use hauling materials and finished products to and from defense plants. To make a completed gun, tank or airplane, parts were needed from factories hundreds of miles away from the plant where they were finally finished. One large plant put together anti-aircraft guns made of 200 parts. Since they only made 20 of those parts themselves, trucks had to bring the other 180 parts long distances from many plants. These parts had to arrive at a set time or the assembly line would be stopped. Trucks became a part of the assembly line.

Trucks were also used during the war to supply the fighting men at the front with food, clothing and ammunition. When the armies moved, trucks would be driven day and night to keep them supplied. One of the most famous supply lines was the "Red Ball Express" which operated from the beaches of Normandy, France far into Germany until the war was over. Trucks also performed a necessary service on the Pacific islands where they were the only means of delivering supplies. When the war was over and the factories went back to making peacetime products, trucks continued to serve these industries.

Trucks in Rural Communities

Trucks have made possible one of the biggest changes ever to take place in the United States. Before World War II most factories were located within large cities, close to sources of raw materials or water or rail connections. When the war was over, there was a growing demand for all kinds of products that had not been available during the war. Businesses found that they needed larger factories. There was very little room left in cities, however, and the price of property on which to build was very high. Many of these companies then decided to move out of the city limits and a growing highway system opened up whole new areas where these plants might relocate. Plants also wished to be near other plants which supplied parts, and most of all, near to the markets. This new pattern of production and distribution depended heavily on roads and trucks.

People, too, began to leave the cities. Shopping centers were built to supply these people with the things they needed. Almost anything that could be bought in cities was now available to them near their homes. All of these stores had to be supplied by truck as no other means of transportation reached them. Therefore, it can be said that trucks changed where people could live.

The farmer has also received many benefits from truck transportation. At one time, he had to take his fresh fruits and vegetables to markets close to his farm. If he tried to ship them too far, they would either spoil on the way or the high shipping charges would raise their cost

Trailer bodies filled with cargo being loaded on a ship.

Courtesy Consolidated Freightways, Inc.

so much that few people could afford to buy them. When truck service became available, the farmer could send them to distant markets in such a short time that very few spoiled. The cost of shipping them was also low enough to permit a good profit. The freezing of foods and the refrigerated truck allowed the farmer to sell to even more distant markets.

Today, large and small grocery stores all over the country carry fresh fruits and vegetables grown on farms thousands of miles away. A few years ago, certain foods were in stores only "in season" but now they can be purchased fresh, packaged or frozen, at any time of the year. As a growing season ends in one part of the country, the season may be just beginning in another part. Today, a family in Michigan can buy Florida oranges, Maine potatoes, or Georgia peaches—brought to them by truck. Trucks haul 61 per cent of all fresh fruits and vegetables; 100 per cent of the live poultry and fresh eggs; 95 per cent of the dressed poultry; 87 per cent of the livestock to stockyards; and 69 per cent of all butter.

There is no end to the number of jobs the truck performs in our daily life. One can see them at work every day—milk trucks, mail trucks, fire trucks, garbage trucks, telephone trucks, laundry trucks, trucks hauling food, building material, machines, toys, furniture and thousands of other items.

TRUDEAU (*trōō'dō*), EDWARD LIVINGSTON

(1848–1915), was the founder of the first modern tuberculosis sanatorium in the United States. He was one of the first to treat this once hopeless disease by using fresh air and rest.

Born in New York City, Trudeau was educated in Paris, France, until the age of 17 when he returned to New York. He then nursed his older brother during a fatal attack of tuberculosis in the closed, airless room recommended at that time. Trudeau caught the disease himself. He turned to the study of medicine however, and graduated from the College of Physicians and Surgeons in New York in 1871. After practicing and teaching medicine for a short time, he fell sick of tuberculosis, then considered as certain death. To rest, he went to the wild

Adirondack region where he hunted and fished for seven years. Instead of dying, he grew stronger. Thus he learned that rest and fresh air could help a person with tuberculosis.

In 1884 he founded the Adirondack Cottage Sanatorium, later called the Trudeau Sanatorium, at Saranac Lake, New York. At this first hospital of its kind in the United States, Trudeau cared for tuberculosis victims who had little money. His methods of treatment were soon widely followed by others. Shortly after, Trudeau proved, as the German Robert Koch had done, that tuberculosis is caused by a germ, the tubercle bacillus. The little, homemade laboratory in which he worked soon grew into an important center. Studies were made there on immunity, or resistance, in patients who had tuberculosis. In 1915, after an active career in which he was honored with the presidency of several national medical societies, Trudeau died of tuberculosis. His *Autobiography* appeared shortly after his death. (See TUBERCULOSIS.)

TRUMAN (*trōō′măn*), **HARRY S.** (1884–   ), was the 33d president of the United States. He took office on April 12, 1945, a few hours after the sudden death of President Franklin Delano Roosevelt.

Like several other vice-presidents who suddenly became president, Harry S. Truman was almost unknown to most Americans when he took over the highest office in the land. There had been little reason to believe that he would ever become president. It has, in fact, been called an accident of history that he became chief executive when his country was engaged in the most terrible war in its history.

Thus, when Truman was sworn in as president, his tasks were heavy and his problems many. The war that was being fought all over the world had to be won. More important was the need to win the peace after victory.

The war was only part of the burden that fell on President Truman. There was also the problem of following Roosevelt in the presidency. People of the United States and the rest of the world had thought of Roosevelt as a symbol of the hopes of mankind for lasting peace.

Harris and Ewing

Harry S. Truman, U.S. President, 1945–1953.

Whether Roosevelt could have achieved these lofty aims and ideals was not to be known. The people of the United States turned hopefully to his successor. A plain citizen, born of the common people, Truman took up his new responsibilities, determined to do his best.

Roosevelt was known as a fighting liberal, a defender of the rights of man at home and abroad. Truman was a neutral, who believed in "middle-of-the-road" policies, and was hardly known abroad. If Truman did not have the strong personality of Roosevelt, he had other qualities. He was a shrewd politician with a lot of common sense. He was honest and loyal, able and efficient, friendly and likable.

Youth

Harry Truman was born on May 8, 1884, in Lamar, Missouri, the son of Martha Ellen and John Anderson Truman. His father was both a farmer and a horse trader who made a comfortable living for his family. As soon as Harry was old enough, he was taught to help with chores on the farm. While he disliked these tiresome tasks, he did them well.

Harry went to school at Independence, Missouri, and was a good student. His teachers recall that he loved books and learned to play the piano. Harry finished high school at 17. He won an appointment to the United States Military Academy at West Point, New York, but he failed the eye test and could not enter.

Harry wanted to go to college but the family could not pay his tuition. Disappointed, he left the farm and went to work in Kansas City, Missouri. There he did a number of things, such as working in the mail room of a newspaper, clerking in a bank, and acting as timekeeper for a railroad construction crew.

By the time Truman was 22 years old, his earnings were about $100 a month. Unhappy in the "big city," he went back to his father's farm. There he seemed to be happy.

Truman had joined the National Guard while in Kansas City. When the United States entered World War I, he was called up for service and sailed for France as a lieutenant in the artillery. His battery was in the fighting at St. Mihiel, France, and in the Meuse-Argonne, also in France. Toward the end of the war, he was promoted to captain.

On Truman's return to civilian life he married a schoolteacher, Bess Wallace, of Independence, Missouri. He had known her from the time he was six years old. They had one daughter, Mary Margaret. He and a war comrade then invested their savings in a clothing store in Kansas City. In the depression of 1921 the business failed. Instead of declaring himself bankrupt, Truman spent more than ten years repaying his creditors.

Enters Politics

At this unhappy period in Truman's life, another comrade-in-arms introduced him to "Big Tom" Pendergast, the political "boss" of the Missouri Democratic party. With Pendergast's support, Truman was elected, in 1922, a county judge of Jackson County. These judges had few judicial duties. They were really county commissioners who let contracts and supervised the building of highways and other public works.

Under Judge Truman, Jackson County received a good network of roads. He was defeated for a second term in 1924 but was returned to office in 1926 as presiding judge, and was re-elected in 1930.

In 1934 Pendergast urged Truman to run for the United States Senate. With the aid of the powerful Democratic machine in Missouri, Truman was elected. In 1940 he ran for re-election. Although his personal honesty and sincerity had never been questioned, the machine that had backed him in earlier years was by that time broken and disgraced. "Big Tom" Pendergast himself was sentenced to prison.

The majority of Missouri's voters believed that while the Pendergast political gang might have been dishonest, Truman was not. They re-elected him for a second term in the Senate.

When Truman became a national figure, his enemies often used his connection with the Pendergast machine to attack him. To his credit, Truman never tried to hide this association. His views were that in this imperfect world, a practical man needed machine support to get elected.

Truman's career as senator started modestly. He served for a time with the Senate committee investigating railroads. His big opportunity came after his re-election in 1940, when he discovered corruption, waste, and dishonesty in defense construction. He urged the Senate to take some action. The Senate agreed and in February 1941 made him the head of a special Senate

Truman as a captain of artillery in World War I.

United Press International

Harris and Ewing

Bess Truman.

committee to investigate the national defense program.

The Truman committee investigated all parts of the defense program. After taking down millions of words of testimony, they issued 31 reports which attacked those who were guilty of negligence or misconduct in the war effort.

Overnight, Truman became a figure of national importance. His skill in getting the Republicans and Democrats on his committee to work together brought him to President Roosevelt's attention.

Roosevelt had the support of the party in his decision to run for a fourth term. But the Democrats were split over renaming Henry A. Wallace for the vice-presidency. When the Democratic National Convention met in Chicago in July 1944, the president informed the delegates that if Wallace were rejected, Truman would be acceptable to him as a running mate. Truman was nominated on the second ballot and became vice-president when Roosevelt was re-elected.

Becomes President

As vice-president, Truman's life was quiet and uneventful for a few months. All this was changed by Roosevelt's death, April 12, 1945. Four days later (April 16), Truman, in his first speech before Congress, promised to continue the policies of Roosevelt both at home and abroad.

For the new president things went well during his first few months in office. Germany surrendered May 7, 1945. In the summer of 1945, the president went to Potsdam, Germany, for a meeting with British and Soviet leaders. There the Big Three made plans for rebuilding a new Europe out of the ruins of war, for bringing the war with Japan to an end, and for the peace to follow.

Shortly after Potsdam, the first atomic bomb was dropped, August 6, 1945, on Hiroshima, Japan. (See BOMB.) The decision to use this destructive weapon had been a most difficult one for Truman to make. He wanted to shorten the war and save American lives. A second atom bomb, this on Nagasaki, hastened Japan's surrender. On August 14, Japan surrendered and on September 2, the surrender agreement was signed. The war was over. (See WORLD WAR II.)

Meanwhile, Congress co-operated with the president and approved his request to pass the United Nations Charter. The United States was now prepared to work with other nations in preserving world peace. It had refused to support this kind of "collective security" after World War I.

With the end of the war Truman's relations with Congress became more difficult. The people of the United States were glad that the war was over. They wanted to get rid of all controls and "return to normalcy," as they have tried to do after every war. They demanded the quick return home of men in the armed forces and the change-over of industry from defense production to peacetime needs. They wanted an end to rationing and price controls. The armed forces were quickly reduced in size, rationing was ended, and controls were removed. Prices went up and inflation increased.

In 1946 there were troubles between labor and management. During the war labor unions had promised not to strike. With the war over, trouble broke out when union demands were not satisfied. Strikes in the coal mines, steel mills, and on the railroads in some cases brought government control. Under this arrangement the mines, trains, and factories were run temporarily by the government until management and the workers agreed to new contracts. In 1947 Congress passed the Taft-Hartley Act over Truman's veto. This law limited many practices of labor unions and cut down their power. (See LABOR ORGANIZATIONS.) In his handling of the strikes of 1946 and later, Truman was criticized by both friends and enemies of organized labor.

After having first tried to follow the program of Roosevelt, President Truman turned for a short time to more conservative domestic and foreign policies. The result was that he lost the support of many of the New Deal members of his party. In the elections of November 1946 the Republicans won control of both Senate and House of Representatives.

The Fair Deal

Faced by a legislature that opposed him, the president proposed a program that did not fit his conservative policy. When Congress opposed most of his program, he called it a "do-nothing" Congress.

Nevertheless, this program, later called the "Fair Deal," was to have great influence in the years that followed. In his State of the Union message of January 1949, Truman said that "every segment of our population and every individual has a right to expect from his government a fair deal." This idea that the federal government should be concerned with the welfare of all the people was followed in many of his proposals.

Truman asked for laws that would protect civil rights of all citizens; provide good housing; broaden both unemployment insurance and social security benefits; and give health services and medical care to all. He wanted to give control of the atomic energy program to civil-

ians; to enlarge the conservation program by creating projects like the Tennessee Valley Authority; and to provide more aid to farmers.

Even though Congress passed few of these bills, the president made some gains. Government contracts, for instance, were not given in some cases to companies who did not follow the rules on discrimination. (See FAIR EMPLOYMENT PRACTICES COMMISSION.) Also, he kept these issues before the nation.

Truman appointed a commission under former President Herbert Hoover to study the operation of the federal government. Many changes came from the report of the Hoover Commission. Steps were taken to form the Department of Health, Education, and Welfare, and later to complete the St. Lawrence Seaway Project.

In 1948 Truman won renomination by the Democrats only after strong attempts were made to defeat him. Senator Alben Barkley of Kentucky was nominated for vice-president. So great was the anti-Truman feeling in the southern branch of the party that a group called the "Dixiecrats" ran J. Strom Thurmond as a third-party candidate. Another group that did not think Truman liberal enough supported former Vice-President Henry Wallace. Many people were sure that Republican Thomas E. Dewey would be the winner, but Truman was re-elected by a comfortable margin.

As has been the case in most postwar presidencies, charges of corruption were made against members of his administration. Investigations of these charges and those of the Un-American Activities Committee, which was searching for disloyal citizens, gained many headlines.

World Power

The cold war with the U.S.S.R. grew in bitterness. In 1945 President Truman had found out from both the San Francisco and Potsdam conferences that relations with the U.S.S.R would not be peaceful. The Communist governments were set up in many eastern European countries in violation of previous agreements. Then, in 1948, the Communists overthrew the democratic government of

TRUMAN'S LIFETIME

		Truman's Terms of Office (1945–1953)	
1884	Truman born.		
1892	1st auto in U.S.	1945	Atomic bomb dropped.
1898	War with Spain.		End of war.
1903	1st airplane flight.		Nuremberg trials.
1914	Panama Canal opens.		Postwar strikes begin.
1917	U.S. enters war.		United Nations formed.
1919	Prohibition.	1946	Philippine independence.
1920	Woman suffrage.		
1921	Truman store fails.		Seizure of coal mines.
1922	Truman county judge.	1947	Truman Doctrine.
1929	Depression begins.		Hoover Commission.
1933	New Deal begins.		Loyalty investigation.
1934	Truman to Senate.		Taft-Hartley Act.
1939	War begins in Europe.	1948	Berlin airlift.
1941	Pearl Harbor attack.		Marshall Plan.
	Truman committee investigations.	1949	NATO.
			Point Four.
1944	Truman vice-president.		Russians explode atom bomb.
	G.I. Bill of Rights.		
			Trial of Communist leaders.
	PRESIDENT		
1953	Korean War ends.	1950	Internal Security Act.
1954	School segregation ruled illegal.		Korean War.
		1951	22nd Amendment.

United Press International

The "Summer White House" at Independence, Missouri.

Czechoslovakia. At the same time, the iron curtain ended free contact between the U.S.S.R. and the United States. For these reasons the foreign policy of the United States became aimed at keeping communism from spreading throughout the world. This was called the policy of containment.

President Truman backed the United Nations. It was most important in United States foreign policy. Nevertheless, at times he continued in his policy of containment.

The first major step in containment was the so-called Truman Doctrine of 1947. Military and economic aid were promised to Greece and Turkey, who were then afraid of being taken over by the Communists. The European Recovery Program began giving food and dollars in 1948 to help these countries rebuild. It was called the Marshall Plan because it was suggested by Secretary of State George C. Marshall. The dramatic Berlin airlift of food and other supplies was the answer to the U.S.S.R. blockade of routes into West Berlin. The U.S.S.R., occupying East Berlin, tried this threat of freezing and starving West Berlin as a way of getting it to agree to Communist terms. (See BERLIN.)

From President Truman's inaugural address of 1949 came two new important developments. The North Atlantic Treaty Organization (NATO) was a military alliance of North American and West European nations. It bound the western countries together against the Soviet bloc. It was the first peacetime alliance for the United States.

Perhaps more important was the so-called Point Four program. This gave, through the UN, economic aid to underdeveloped regions and countries. It tried to give these underdeveloped countries the knowledge they needed to improve their own standard of living. In both these policies, NATO and Point Four, Truman owed much to Republican Senator Arthur H. Vandenberg of Michigan, who won support from both parties in Congress for these measures.

On June 25, 1950, North Korea invaded South Korea. Backed by the UN, Truman sent United States armed forces to help South Korea. After the Communist North Koreans were turned back by UN forces under General Douglas MacArthur, Communist China began to give open aid to the North Koreans. (See KOREAN WAR.) General MacArthur several times spoke out publicly against Truman's refusal to allow bombing or invasion of Chinese territory. The president did not want the "police action" in Korea to become a general war. He finally removed MacArthur, though this led to protests throughout the country.

The MacArthur incident clearly showed Truman's ideas of the presidency. A president, he felt, should have and should use broad powers. He must be willing to take unpopular actions when they are necessary.

Truman's United States

While Truman was president, the nation quickly changed from wartime to peacetime ways of living. Millions of men were released from the army and navy and returned to civilian life. This was made easier by the GI Bill of Rights, a group of laws passed in 1944 while the war was still on. This bill helped ex-soldiers by providing credit, weekly benefits for the unemployed, and money for job training and education. One result was the largest college enrollment in the nation's history, passing two million in the autumn of 1946.

Industry also shifted to peacetime ways very quickly. For four years people had not been able to buy cars, refrigerators, and other goods they wanted. The demand was so great that factories could not produce enough goods. New factories were built and there were plenty of jobs. One of the nation's newest industries, television, was growing. In 1946 a TV set was a luxury owned by few. By the time Truman retired most families owned a set.

In Europe the people in German concentration camps were freed and many Nazis were brought to trial before the International War Crimes Tribunal at Nuremberg, Germany. In Asia a new nation was formed when the United States gave independence to the Philippine Islands. At the same time, the United States took over the Japanese-held islands in the Pacific and ran them as a UN trust territory.

Progress was made in scientific research. In order to defend the country, scientists developed better methods of defense such as jet planes, missiles, and the hydrogen bomb. At the same time, other scientists were trying to conquer cancer, heart disease, and poliomyelitis, and new drugs such as ACTH, cortisone, Terramycin, and Aureomycin were saving thousands of lives. More people worked for the government than ever before. Taxes were high, but the times were prosperous.

Retirement

In 1951 the 22nd Amendment to the U.S. Constitution was passed, limiting a president to two terms. Although Truman could have run, he was not a candidate for the 1952 election.

As the end of his second term neared, he began to arrange for a smooth changeover to the incoming Eisenhower administration. Truman invited the men chosen for high positions to meet with those still in office.

Truman retired in 1953 to his home in Independence, Missouri, but he continued to speak up on public issues. The Harry S. Truman Library was opened in 1957 to house his presidential papers.

President Truman was a man with the "common touch." Those who heard him in person, or met him, felt his personal appeal, whether they agreed with him or not. As one editorial

writer said, he was "a man of many faults; but he was also a man of good will and a man of courage."

TRUMBULL (trŭm'bŭl), **JOHN** (1756–1843). In the rotunda of the Capitol at Washington, D.C., are four paintings by John Trumbull showing important events in the American Revolution. They are "The Signing of the Declaration of Independence," "The Surrender of Cornwallis," "The Surrender of Burgoyne," and "The Resignation of Washington."

Trumbull was born in Lebanon, Connecticut. He graduated from Harvard College and then studied painting in Boston. When 19, he served as a map maker for George Washington. After he had retired from the army Trumbull went to London to study under Benjamin West.

Among his best portraits are those of Washington, Alexander Hamilton, and Rufus King. Trumbull's paintings are known for their fine coloring and good grouping.

Although Trumbull served his country as a soldier and diplomat, and continued his interests in architecture and map making, he never gave up his painting. Toward the end of his life he sold his remaining work to Yale University, where it became the beginning of the famous Yale Art Gallery.

TRUST (trŭst), in law, is the holding of real or personal property by one person, or trustee, for the use and benefit of another person, or beneficiary. An example of a trust would be one where a man entrusts money or property to a bank to be held and used by the bank for the benefit of his children.

In medieval times in England, land was owned under the feudal system. If a landowner died leaving children to inherit his property, the use of the property went to his overlord until the children became of age. If the land contained coal or forests, the overlord might dig all the coal and use all of the trees before the orphaned children were of age and claimed possession. In addition, the overlord was entitled to certain money payments from the children. If the landowner, however, gave his land to a trustee to hold for the use and benefit of his children, the wasting of the land and the feudal dues were avoided. By use of the trust the orphaned children of a landowner were protected.

In 1279 a law was passed in England called the Statute of Mortmain. Under this law no one could give land to religious corporations, orders, or churches. In order to avoid the Statute of Mortmain, people could give land to a trustee who would hold it for the use and benefit of religious groups. Used in this way the trust was a device to circumvent or cheat the law. Because of this, courts refused to approve of trusts. When land was given to a trustee, he could, therefore, claim it for his own and refuse to give it up to the beneficiaries. The beneficiaries could get no relief in the courts of law. This situation remained for about 300 years. Beneficiaries began to complain directly to the king. Relief was finally given in the name of the king by the lord chancellor, who was the "keeper of the king's conscience." Courts of chancery grew strong, and in such courts, called courts of equity, the trustees were ordered to carry out their trusts. (See LAW.)

Gradually the useful trust idea was expanded. Trusts were made to cover not only land but also money, stocks, bonds, and all other property. Because modern trusts are lawful, they do not circumvent or cheat the law. Nevertheless, in most states they are still enforced in courts of equity and not in courts of law.

Types of Trusts

The modern trust is created by the donor, or giver, of the money or property. He usually writes out a statement of what he wants done with the property on a document called articles of trust. In the paper he names the person, persons, or corporation that he wants to be trustee, and he names those he wishes to be beneficiaries.

The property is then transferred to the trustee, who becomes the legal guardian of it, subject to the duty of carefully conserving it. He must turn over all proceeds, income, or profits to the beneficiaries. He must finally turn over the property, or corpus, itself to the proper beneficiaries under the terms of the trust.

Where the benefits of a trust are to be given to clearly named individuals, it is a private trust. Charities for the benefit of poor and needy people, of orphans, of the sick, and of the aged are the subject of many trusts. Where money or property has been given to a trustee for the benefit of such persons, it is an eleemosynary or charitable trust. Trusts are often provided for hospitals and for institutions that promote medical research.

Money or property given to trustees to found and maintain schools and colleges creates educational trusts. Money or property given to a city or state to be used for the benefit of the people creates public or governmental trusts. Many playgrounds, parks, shelters, museums, and public buildings are the result of trusts established for the benefit of the public.

Many towns, cities, and villages use a form of trust for the benefit of the community. Such trusts are often called Community Chests, Community Funds, or Community Crusades. This form of trust allows a committee to use funds collected from members of the community in many different ways to help other members. Help for the needy and the handicapped usually comes first, but the money may also be used for the aid of hospitals, clinics, and schools, or for such organizations as the Red Cross, Girl Scouts, and Salvation Army.

Private trusts must be ended within a rather short period of time, as specified by law. Public trusts may go on forever.

Trustees and Trust Companies

In early times it was usual for a trust to be established with individuals as trustees. Property was turned over to them because the creator of the trust had confidence in the honesty and wisdom of the trustees. Unfortunately, some trustees were honest but not capable or wise. They sometimes died without having kept a good record of the property entrusted to them.

Because companies, or corporations, do not die, companies were formed to act as trustees. Such companies are generally authorized by state law to assume the duties of a trustee. Before they may administer trusts, they must qualify by showing that they are financially responsible. Because trust companies are able to hire officers and advisers who are competent and experienced, they may be able to offer efficiency and security beyond that of individual trustees. Many state and national banks are also authorized to act as trustees.

Trust Combinations and Monopolies in Business

A second use of the word *trust* arose and is still applied to large corporations or monopolies. It was the result of the transfer of stock of several competing businesses to a single group of trustees. The trustees issue trust certificates to the member firms. The trustees elected from the membership of the trust then control all the member firms.

The trust form was popular during the 1880's, when there were oil trusts (cottonseed, linseed, and petroleum), a salt trust, a sugar trust, a leather trust, and many others.

The holding corporation, or trust, was able to control prices for goods and services among all companies whose stock it held. The result was monopoly and the destruction of competition in trade and transportation.

Public opinion was aroused by the fear that all business would be dominated by a few large holding corporations. The scheme was called "a conspiracy in restraint of trade." In 1890 Congress passed an important law, the Sherman Anti-Trust Act, to restrict the power of trusts.

The first case to come before the Supreme Court under the Sherman Act was *United States v. E. C. Knight Company* in 1895. The case involved a sugar trust that controlled 98 percent of all sugar refined in the country. The court ruled that neither trade nor commerce had been restrained and did not rule the sugar trust in violation of the law.

Additional laws were passed by Congress to counteract evasive practices that had been possible under the Sherman Act. One of these acts created the Federal Trade Commission in 1914. This was a body of experts created to help where the courts were inadequate. The law declared that unfair methods of competition in business are unlawful. Another law of 1914, the Clayton Anti-Trust Act, prohibited price cutting and price fixing. Despite these laws, some large industrial combinations and centrally controlled "big business" still flourish.

TSINGTAO (*chǐng dou*), **CHINA,** is a major seaport on the south coast of Shantung Province. Located at the entrance to Kiaochow Bay, it has an excellent sheltered deepwater harbor equipped with modern facilities. The city is about equidistant between Peiping (Peking) and Shanghai and is connected to the interior by a railroad across Shantung to Tsinan.

Tsingtao was a fishing village until late in the 19th century, when it was leased by treaty to Germany. The Germans built up the city and created a free port in 1899. It was captured by the Japanese in 1914 and held until 1922, when it was returned to the Chinese. The Japanese again controlled Tsingtao from 1938 to 1945. Following World War II, the United States briefly occupied the city. It was the headquarters of U.S. naval forces in the Pacific until the Communists gained control of the Chinese mainland in 1949.

The Communists have emphasized industrial development in Tsingtao. In recent years a major steel plant has been constructed in the suburbs. Other industries produce cotton, silk, paper, leather, flour, oilseed, machinery, cement, locomotives and other rolling stock, and ships. Shantung University is located at Tsingtao, and the city is a resort center with excellent beaches and climate. The population is 1,121,-000 (1957 estimate).

TUBERCULOSIS (*tū bĕr′kū lō′sĭs*) is an infectious disease of man and animals caused by a germ known as the tubercle bacillus. The disease is also called consumption and is common in all parts of the world.

There are three main types of tubercle bacillus—human, bovine (cow), and avian (bird). Man can be infected by all types, but infection by the avian bacillus is extremely rare.

The course of the infection depends on the number and strength of the bacilli, the patient's resistance, and the part of the body infected. The disease most often infects the lungs. This is called pulmonary tuberculosis. When the infection spreads to other parts of the body, it becomes nonpulmonary tuberculosis.

Tuberculosis usually begins by breathing airborne bacilli into the lungs. Less frequently, the bacilli enter the body by swallowing contaminated sputum or food. The first infection, or primary lesion, is an inflammation and breakdown of the tissues. Instead of white blood cells, leucocytes, which ordinarily fight infection, the body sends out another type of white blood cells, plasma cells, to fight the tubercle bacillus. (See BLOOD.) The plasma cells are changed by the bacilli into clusters of long cigar-shaped forms and giant cells. These growths are called tubercles.

In time the body may develop resistance, and the primary lesion heals with thick scar tissue. Or, tubercles may continue to form, and the disease progresses. The bacilli spread through the lungs, causing the tissue to soften and break down into cavities. A cavity may become as large as a fist, and hemorrhaging into the cavities may be very serious. The patient coughs up this infected dead tissue. Germs in the dead tissue easily spread to other people.

A person may be infected by tubercle bacilli, be healed, and never be aware of it. Sometimes bacilli remain in the body in an inactive state, causing no harm. It is also possible to be reinfected. This may be a new infection coming from outside of the body, or it may be an old one becoming active again.

In nonpulmonary tuberculosis the bacilli may enter the bloodstream and be carried to other parts of the body. The organs that are usually infected in this way are the lymph nodes, the kidneys, the bones and joints, the adrenal glands, and the skin.

The symptoms of tuberculosis are coughing, fever, heavy sweats, loss of appetite, loss of weight, and weakness. Treatment consists of drugs, rest, improved nutrition, and sometimes surgery. Surgical treatment involves actual removal of the infected parts of the lungs. The most important drugs used are isoniazid and streptomycin. Treatment with drugs usually continues for many months.

Tuberculosis is most common where people live in crowded, unsanitary conditions and have poor nutrition. Fortunately, man has strong resistance to the infection. Many people are infected, but only a small fraction develop the disease. With improved preventive measures and treatment, the mortality rate throughout the world has been greatly reduced. In the year 1900, about 200 of every 100,000 deaths in the United States were due to tuberculosis. In 65 years this figure dropped to about 6 of every 100,000.

A skin test is commonly used to detect a tuberculous infection. This is called the tuberculin test. A small amount of tuberculin is injected into the skin. If the area becomes swollen and red, the result is said to be positive. It means that the tubercle bacillus is or has been present in the body. Immediate steps can then be taken to arrest the disease or to prevent its occurrence in the future. A tuberculosis infection may also be detected by examination of the sputum.

In the United States most tuberculosis results from infection by the human tubercle bacilli. The bovine-type bacilli cause the infection when the germs enter the stomach and intestines from milk of infected cows. Bovine tuberculosis has been nearly eliminated in the United States and the Scandinavian countries by thoroughly examining the cows and pasteurizing the milk.

Tuberculosis has been known from ancient times. In 1865 a Frenchman, Jean Antoine Villemin, showed that it was contagious. The cause of the disease, however, was not known until 1882, when a German physician, Robert Koch, discovered the tubercle bacillus.

TUBEROSE (*tūb'rōz* or *tū'bĕr ōs*) is a garden plant (*Polianthes tuberosa*) of the Amaryllis family (Amaryllidaceae). It is native to Mexico but has never been found growing wild.

The plant grows to about three feet tall. The blossoms are funnel-shaped and waxy white in color. They are noted for their extremely sweet fragrance. The leaves are long and slender.

The tuberose was so named because it forms a thick, bulb-like underground stem called a tuber. New plants develop from these tubers. They are planted in spring when all danger of

The blossoms of the tuberose (*Polianthes tuberosa*) grow on long, slender stems. They are waxy white and extremely sweet-smelling.

John H. Gerard

frost has passed. The new plants bloom in late summer. In the fall they are dug up and stored in a cool, dry place. The most popular varieties of tuberoses are the Mexican Single, Dwarf, and Pearl Excelsior.

TUCSON (*too'sŏn*), **ARIZONA,** is a city located in the southern part of the state, in the mountain-rimmed valley of the Santa Cruz River. Because of its year-round mild, dry climate and abundant sunshine, Tucson attracts many vacationers. The city is an important railroad center and is surrounded by irrigated farms and cattle ranches. Its factories produce aircraft, electronic equipment, iron products, paint, bricks, and tiles.

The University of Arizona and the Arizona School for the Deaf and Blind are located in Tucson. The mission of San Xavier del Bac dates from 1700. In the city is the Arizona-Sonora Desert Museum. Nearby is the Saguaro National Monument, set aside so that visitors may view the giant cactuses that grow there.

Tucson was originally an Indian village. A fort was established there by the Spaniards in 1776. The United States acquired the settlement as part of the Gadsden Purchase in 1853. It grew into a city after silver and copper were discovered nearby in the 1890's. A large open-pit copper mine is located just outside Tucson.

Tucson has a council-manager form of government. It is Arizona's second largest city, with a population of 262,933 (1970).

TULIP (*tū'lĭp*) is any of the flowering plants that make up the genus *Tulipa*. This genus belongs to the lily family (Liliaceae). There are about 160 species of tulips. They grow wild in the Mediterranean region, eastward across Asia to Japan. Common garden tulips are thought to have developed from only a few of these wild species. Plant breeders have produced thousands of garden varieties in a wide range of colors, sizes, and shapes.

The blossoms are bell shaped. They grow on top of a long stem and point upward. When turned upside down they look something like a turban, and the word "tulip" means turban in Turkish. The plants grow from bulbs. They do not fare well in hot climates. A cool winter period is necessary to mature the bulbs. Most garden soils are suitable for tulips. They should be planted in well-fertilized soil. In Europe, the United States, and Canada the bulbs are planted in the fall. The bulb contains a stem and the beginnings of the next year's

Tucson was an adobe Indian village when the Spanish settled there in 1776. It is now a sprawling city and popular tourist center.

Courtesy Tucson Chamber of Commerce

Diana (foreground) and Rising Sun (rear) are two of the many varieties of tulips that have been developed.

flower and leaves, which were formed while the plant was in bloom. (See Bulb.)

There are two main classes of tulips: the early flowering, which usually has relatively short stems and either single or double blossoms; and the late flowering, which has tall stems. There are many kinds of late tulips, such as Darwin, Cottage, Breeder, Rembrandt, Double (or Peony-flowered), Parrot, and Lily-flowered. These are mainly color classes, although some have different shapes as well.

Tulips came to Europe from Turkey, where they were being grown before the year 1500. The Austrian ambassador to Turkey brought tulips to Europe about 1554. They reached the Netherlands a few years later and became extremely popular there. The Hollanders became so skillful in raising them that they still are the leading growers of tulip bulbs. They ship large quantities to all parts of the world. At one time tulips were so popular in the Netherlands that people paid huge prices for new varieties. During this period, known as the time of the "tulipomania," the plants were the object of much gambling and speculation.

TULIP TREE (*Liriodendron tulipifera*) is a large tree of the magnolia family. Most members of the family have large, showy flowers, but the tulip tree has medium-size flowers that are greenish-yellow and shaped like tulips. The trees grow wild in the central and eastern parts of North America, where they may reach a height of 190 feet, although most of them are not that large. The straight trunks may reach a thickness of 10 feet at the base. The trees grow naturally in woods and reach their greatest size along streams where the soil is deep and moist.

The bark is deeply ridged and gray in color. The wood is fine grained and light yellow. For this reason the wood is called yellow poplar in the lumber trade.

The tulip tree is often grown as an ornamental shade tree. In addition to its lovely flowers, the tree's oddly shaped leaves are quite attractive. Like all members of the magnolia family the tree should be transplanted only in the spring, as the roots are thick and fleshy and easily injured. They do not heal well in the fall.

The tulip tree is a large flowering tree that grows in the eastern half of the United States. Its attractive, greenish-yellow blossoms resemble tulips.

Below, F. E. Westlake; right, U.S. Forest Service

TULSA (*tŭl′sä*), **OKLAHOMA,** is a city in the northeastern part of the state. It is located on the Arkansas River, in the center of rich oil and natural-gas fields. Most of the city's business depends on oil. Refineries and offices connected with the petroleum industry are scattered throughout Tulsa. The city is also in the center of a farming region and near an area rich in minerals. It serves as the financial and marketing center for this region. The aviation industry is second in importance to the petroleum industry. Other manufactured products include oil-well tools and equipment, glass, cotton textiles, chemicals, furniture, automobile bodies, steel, and brick and tile.

Tulsa is a modern city with tall office buildings, which can be seen for miles from the surrounding plains. The University of Tulsa, located there, is famous for petroleum engineering. The city has a symphony orchestra, and its cultural institutions include the Philbrook Art Center, the Thomas Gilcrease Institute of American History and Art, and the Indian Museum.

Creek Indians who were removed from the eastern part of the United States under the Indian Removal Act first came to live in the Tulsa area in 1836. They set up a trading post which came to be known as Tulsy Town. White settlers arrived after a railroad reached the post in 1882. Tulsa was incorporated in 1898, and it grew rapidly after oil was discovered there in 1901. The city became known as the oil capital of the world, and it is the home of the International Petroleum Exposition.

Tulsa is governed by a mayor and a commission. It is Oklahoma's second largest city, with a population of 331,638 (1970).

An aerial view of Tulsa clearly shows how the city has grown up along the banks of the Arkansas River.

Hopkins Photography

TUMOR (*tū'mĕr*) is a mass of abnormal tissue. The word *tumor* in the broad sense means simply a swelling. Modern medical usage, however, has restricted its meaning to refer to enlargements due to new growths or abnormally growing tissue. The simplest swellings, due usually to such inflammations as boils or abscesses, are not true tumors.

The cause of true tumors is not known. Normal growth is controlled by laws. Plants and animals grow to maturity according to these laws and then stop growing. (Sometimes an animal or plant grows to giant size or remains dwarfed, but this occurs only under unusual circumstances.) In the same way, when tissue is injured, it heals according to certain laws. (See GROWTH.) When healing has been completed, the new growth stops. The laws of growth are not fully understood, but enough is known about them to make it clear that tumors develop when these laws are overthrown, and growth goes wild. Then tumors, or new growths (neoplasms), are formed.

Tumors are of two main types—benign and malignant. A benign tumor is one that continues to grow in the place where it starts. It sends out no branches into neighboring tissues, and no wandering cells to become new islands of tumor growth in distant parts of the body. Malignant tumors (called cancers) invade the body and start new islands of growth.

Either benign or malignant tumors may arise from any kind of tissue in the body—skin, mucous membrane, bone, cartilage, muscle, or glands. Malignant tumors of the glands, membrane, or skin are carcinomas. Malignant tumors of muscle, bone, or cartilage are sarcomas. (See CANCER.) The most common benign tumors are fatty tumors under the skin and muscle tumors of the uterus. The fatty tumors cause no trouble. The muscle tumors may be a serious threat to life or health because of bleeding, size, or pressure on nearby structures. Hollow tumors filled with fluid are cysts. They may be benign or malignant.

Tumors may or may not require treatment, depending on their size, location, growth, and malignancy. A small benign tumor in certain locations may be ignored. A malignant tumor, however, must be tended no matter where it is or how small it is. Life depends on removal of the malignant growth before it can spread into neighboring organs. Removal may be by surgery, radium, X-ray, or by a combination of these, again depending on the size, location, and character of the tumor. Chemotherapy (treatment with chemicals) has been successful in treatment of certain kinds of tumors.

TUNA (*tū'nă*) is any of several varieties of fishes belonging to the subfamily Thunninae of the mackerel family. In general, a tuna can be recognized by its cigar-shaped body which tapers sharply toward both ends. At the rear it ends in a narrow "stem" from which flares the wide, crescent-shaped tail fin. The two dorsal (back) fins are extremely close together. This characteristic separates tuna from mackerels and bonitos, which are similar. The dorsal fins of mackerels and bonitos are farther apart than those of tuna.

There are many species of tuna ranging from about 3 to 14 feet in length. Bluefins are the largest. The albacore is a medium-sized bluefin in great demand for its white meat. Skipjack are also economically important tuna. Others are the yellowfin of tropical waters and the spotted tuna.

Tuna are found in nearly all of the oceans of the world. They prefer relatively warm waters of not less than 50 degrees Fahrenheit. They are strong swimmers and migrate with the seasons. Schools of tuna from the Caribbean move northward along the Atlantic coast in the spring and early summer, going as far north as Newfoundland as the waters grow warmer. Studies have shown that Pacific tuna

Joe Pazen from Black Star

Commercially, most tuna are caught today by giant nets, or seines, although spearing, trapping, trolling, and the one-pole, baited-water method of fishing (above) are also used.

from the waters around California have traveled at least as far as Japan in a single year. Studies are being made to gain more information about their breeding habits, spawning grounds, and migrating habits.

Tuna feed on smaller fishes, such as small mackerel and herrings, and on other animals, such as shrimp and squid. Warm water tuna are generally smaller than those of cooler waters because they have a smaller food supply.

Tuna are among the oldest and most valuable food fishes in the world. The Japanese fishing industry alone catches more than 460 million pounds a year. In recent years the United States has far outranked any other country in the canning and consumption of

Skipjack tuna (*Euthynnus pelamis*) swim in schools in all tropical seas. Adults weigh about 50 pounds and are about three feet long. They seldom live more than four years. The skipjack are economically important and supply many fisheries around the world.

Courtesy Bureau of Commercial Fisheries, Honolulu Biological Laboratory, U.S. Fish and Wildlife Service

tuna. Commercially, tuna are caught today by giant nets, or seines. Large traps or baited hooks and lines are still used as well. Tuna are also excellent game fishes.

TUNGSTEN (*tŭng'stĕn*) is a heavy steel-gray to silver-white metal. It does not rust, and it is extremely hard. Its melting point is 3,410 degrees Centigrade (6,170 Fahrenheit), the highest of any metal. *Tungsten*, a Swedish word, means "heavy stone." It was discovered in 1783 by the Spanish mineralogist brothers Juan Jose and Don Fausto d'Elhuyar. Its chemical symbol, W, is from wolfram, the German name for tungsten. Its atomic number is 74, and its atomic weight is 183.85. Tungsten minerals are found mostly in the rocks of mountainous regions. Wolframite, scheelite, ferberite, and hubnerite are the chief tungsten minerals. The primary source areas are located in China, Burma, Korea, Bolivia, Brazil, Portugal, the Soviet Union, and the United States.

In the production of tungsten, the ores are first crushed and washed with water. Heavy tungsten minerals settle, and the lighter rock particles are washed out. The concentrated ore is chemically treated to produce a soluble tungsten compound. This is dissolved and leaves behind insoluble impurities. Chemical refinement continues until WO_3, or tungsten trioxide, is obtained. Heating the tungsten trioxide in hydrogen gas yields a pure tungsten powder at between 800 and 1,000 degrees Centigrade. Its high melting point makes it commercially impractical to melt tungsten. The powdered metal is compressed into bars in great hydraulic presses. The bars are heated in electric furnaces to a temperature of 1,500 degrees Centigrade and placed in swaging, or hammering, machines. These machines pound the bars into rods of smaller diameter. The rods can be rolled or hammered into sheets, or they can be drawn through diamond dies to produce fine tungsten wire.

The most important use of tungsten is in the manufacture of tough steel alloys, which retain their hardness and strength at high temperatures. These alloys are used in jet engines, missiles, and high-speed cutting tools. Tungsten carbide, one of the hardest materials made by man, is used in place of diamonds for cutting and drilling. Pure tungsten is used primarily in the electronic and electric industries. Electrical contact points in the distributor and spark plugs of many engines are made partially of tungsten. In the national interest, the U.S. government maintains a stockpile of this valuable metal.

TUNIS (*tū'nĭs*), **TUNISIA,** is the capital and largest city of the country. It is near the country's northern coast on a shallow inlet (Lake of Tunis) of the Gulf of Tunis. A channel six miles long across this lake connects Tunis with the port of La Goulette. This places the city near the east-west trade routes through the Mediterranean Sea. The ancient Phoenicians saw the strategic advantages of this location and founded the city of Carthage near present-day Tunis. The climate of Tunis is Mediterranean, with cool, wet winters and hot, dry summers.

A pleasant mixture of Muslim and European atmosphere exists in the city. The narrow, winding streets of the Muslim section are an interesting contrast to the wide streets and modern buildings of the European section. A part of the Muslim section is the ancient native area, called the Medina. It has changed little in modern times. One of the entrances to the Medina is through a large structure known as the Bab el Khadra Gate. In the Medina are many individual markets, or *suqs*, where the products of the city's handicraft industries are sold. They include carpets, textiles, pottery, and leather and metal goods. The factories are mainly concerned with processing the products of the rich agricultural area that surrounds Tunis. Beer, soft drinks, chocolate, canned fruit and vegetables, chemicals, and tobacco are the chief products.

Tunis existed during the Carthaginian period. It did not become important, however, until the Arabs took control of the area in the 8th century and later made it their capital. The city was conquered at various times by the Spanish, Algerians, and Turks.

In recent years Tunis has grown rapidly, so

Carl Frank—Photo Researchers

In the European section of Tunis, modern buildings rise along wide avenues.

The majority of Tunisians are Arabs and Berbers. Most of them are Muslims, and Islam is the state religion. Arabic is the official language. The population is unevenly distributed throughout the country. Most of the people live in the north and along the east coast. In the dry areas, where the population is sparse, many of the people are nomads. Only about one-third of the people live in cities. Most of the cities are coastal ports. Tunis is the capital and largest city. Other important port cities are Sfax, Sousse, and Bizerte. Kairouan, in the interior, is one of the holiest Muslim cities, as well as a rug-making center.

Agriculture is the principal economic activity of Tunisia. Crops are cultivated in the north, along the coastal plains, and in the oases of

that now it is by far the largest and most important Tunisian city. It is more than ten times larger than Sfax, the second largest. The population of Tunis, according to the 1966 census, was 462,979. That of the entire metropolitan area was more than 750,000.

TUNISIA (*tū nĭzh'ĭ ä*), AFRICA, is a small country in the northern part of the continent. On the north and east it is bounded by the Mediterranean Sea. On the west it is bordered by Algeria, and on the southeast by Libya.

The northern part of Tunisia is a region of low mountains and valleys. The eastern extension of the Atlas Mountains crosses that part of the country parallel to the northern coast. Only a few peaks reach more than 4,000 feet above sea level. The agricultural valley of the Medjerda River is in this area.

A fairly broad coastal plain extends along eastern Tunisia. Toward the interior from the mountainous north and the eastern coastal plain there is an area of interior drainage basins with many shallow salt lakes, or shotts. The southern part of Tunisia is in the Saharan Plateau, where elevations average between 500 and 1,000 feet.

The northern part of Tunisia has a Mediterranean climate, with hot, dry summers and cool, rainy winters. The climate becomes drier toward the interior. The southern part of the country has a desert climate, with less than four inches of rain a year. There are several oases in the south and interior.

The native markets, or *suqs*, of the Muslim section of Tunis hold many shops that open onto narrow walkways.

Carl Frank—Photo Researchers

Locator map of Tunisia.

FACTS ABOUT TUNISIA

CAPITAL: Tunis.

AREA: 63,378 square miles.

POPULATION: 4,560,000 (1967 estimate).

HIGHEST POINT: Jabal ash Sha'nabi (5,066 feet).

FORM OF GOVERNMENT: Republic.

CHIEF OF STATE AND HEAD OF GOVERNMENT: President.

POLITICAL DIVISIONS: 13 governorates.

CHIEF PRODUCTS: *agricultural*, barley, citrus fruits, dates, grapes, olives, wheat; *manufactured*, olive oil, wine, beer, phosphates.

MONETARY UNIT: Tunisian dinar; one dinar equals 1.92 U.S. dollars.

the interior. The chief crops are wheat, corn, barley, grapes, olives, citrus fruits, and dates. Olive oil, citrus fruits and vegetables are exported.

Mining is an important activity in Tunisia, which is one of the world's leading producers of phosphates; they are the country's major export. Iron, lead, and zinc are also mined and exported. Sponge fishing is important in the Gulf of Gabes, off the southeast coast.

The manufacturing industries of Tunisia are mainly concerned with processing agricultural and mineral products. The factories produce olive oil, wine, flour, spaghetti, and canned fruit, vegetables, and fish. There are also fertilizer factories for processing phosphates, and smelters for reducing lead ores. Most of the factories are in the principal cities. Handicraft industries which produce rugs, cloth, leather, and pottery, are widespread.

Tunisia has been under the domination of many peoples during its history. Phoenician merchants established trading ports there and founded the city of Carthage in 814 B.C. After Carthage was defeated in the Punic Wars, the area became an important part of the Roman Empire. In A.D. 439 the Vandals overran Tunisia. In the next century the Byzantines extended their influence into the area, and later, in the 8th century, Tunisia came under Arab rule. In 1574 Tunisia became a province of the Ottoman Empire, and remained under Turkish rule for more than three centuries. In 1881 it became a protectorate of France, with the bey

of Tunis as titular ruler. In 1956 France recognized Tunisia's independence. One year later the monarchy was abolished, the bey was deposed, and a republic was proclaimed.

Tunisia adopted a new constitution in 1959. The country is governed by members of the national assembly and a president. Tunisia is a member of the Arab League, the Organization of African Unity, and the United Nations.

A portion of Tunisia's fishing fleet docks at Djerba, an island lying close to the mainland. The catch consists of tunny, bonita, sardines, and sponge.

Inge-Morath from Magnum

TUNNEL

The methods of tunnel construction vary according to length, depth, purpose, location, and type of material to be excavated. The most common kinds of tunneling are soft-ground, hard-rock, and trench-type tunneling.

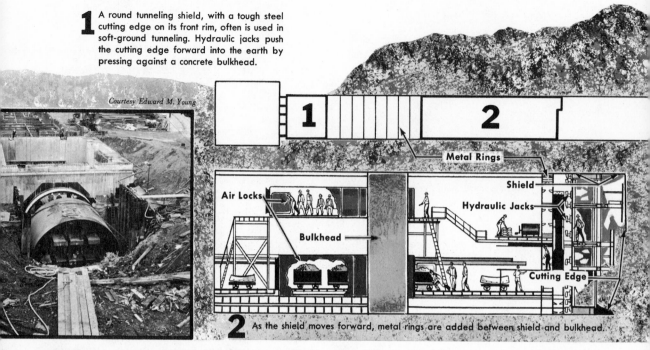

1 A round tunneling shield, with a tough steel cutting edge on its front rim, often is used in soft-ground tunneling. Hydraulic jacks push the cutting edge forward into the earth by pressing against a concrete bulkhead.

Courtesy Edward M. Young

Metal Rings

Air Locks

Bulkhead

Shield

Hydraulic Jacks

Cutting Edge

2 As the shield moves forward, metal rings are added between shield and bulkhead.

TUNNEL (*tŭn'ĕl*) is an underground passageway. Some are the result of natural forces. Probably the first man-made tunnels were dug by cavemen trying to improve their crude dugout homes. Early man tunneled into the earth to find better stone for his tools and weapons. Eventually, he tunneled for the ore to make copper and bronze implements. Later, he dug tunnels for burying the dead, for temples, for military purposes, for sewers and water supply, and for foot and vehicle passageways.

Some of the earliest civilizations built remarkable tunnels. By 2160 B.C. the Assyrians had built a 15-foot-wide tunnel under the Euphrates River. To accomplish this, their engineers changed the course of the river so it no longer flowed where the tunnel was to go. Then they built a brick tunnel in a trench, covered it over, and let the river flow back into its original bed. Although many tunnels were built after that time, centuries passed before another tunnel was built under a river.

The ancient Greeks were said to have built tunnels as early as 1500 B.C. In India, temples were built in solid rock tunnels around 260 B.C.

The Old Testament reports the construction of a water supply tunnel in Jerusalem.

Egyptians and Romans developed methods for digging through even the hardest rock. The Egyptians used drills made of hollow reeds. Very hard rock dust, like emery, was poured around the spinning drill, and the abrasive action wore a hole in the rock. The Romans heated rock with fire and then threw cold water on it, causing it to fracture and break.

Canal and Railroad Tunnels

As transportation methods improved, tunnels became increasingly important. Some of the earliest major tunnels were built for boats and barges. The first large tunnels built in the United States also were for canals. By 1850, however, more than 50 U.S. tunnels had been built for railroads.

The first American tunnel built with power drills and high explosives was the Hoosac Railway Tunnel in Massachusetts. This 4.73-mile bore was begun in 1855 but was not completed until 1876.

The first long railroad tunnel, the Mont Cenis,

3 In trench-type tunneling under shallow bodies of water, prefabricated sections of tubing are capped and floated to position over a dredged trench. They are sunk by filling the hollow walls with concrete and are then attached to the previous section and uncapped.

Courtesy "Engineering News-Record"

3　　　　　　　　　**4**

4 Hard-rock tunnelers drill a required number of holes to specified depths (left), and the holes are then filled with explosives (right). After the blast is set off, machines take out the rock fragments—and the process is repeated.

was started through the Alps between France and Italy in 1857. It took 13 years to finish the 8.5-mile-long tunnel. Another famous Alpine tunnel, the 9.3-mile St. Gotthard Tunnel, was started in 1872 and completed in 10 years despite serious trouble with water.

Some other famous railway tunnels are:

Name	Location	Length in Miles
Simplon	Switzerland-Italy	12.3
Apennine	Italy	11.5
Loetschberg	Switzerland	9.1
Hudson and Manhattan Tube	New York City	8.5

Automobile Tunnels

Tunnels for automobiles are not as long as some other types but they are more complex in design. The exhaust gases developed by cars, trucks, and buses are a major problem. Automobile tunnel lengths always have been limited by the engineers' ability to ventilate them.

Many highway tunnels have more than one tube. New York City's 1.6-mile Lincoln Tunnel has three tubes, each two lanes wide. Exhaust gases are drawn out through grills in the ceiling, while fresh air is pumped in from under

the roadway.

Some other famous automobile tunnels are:

Name	Location	Length in Miles
Mont Blanc	France-Italy	7.25
Mersey	England	2.6
Brooklyn-Battery	New York City	1.7
Holland	New York City	1.6
Hampton Roads	Virginia	1.5
Baltimore Harbor	Baltimore, Maryland	1.4

A recently completed tunnel in Japan, the Kanmon Tunnel, is 2.2 miles long. It has a lower level for automobiles and upper level for pedestrians and cyclists.

Water and Sewer Tunnels

The longest tunnel in the world is a water supply tunnel, the Delaware Aqueduct, in New York state. This 85-mile-long hard rock tunnel delivers fresh stream water to the city. It was completed in 1944. A sister tunnel, the 44-mile-long West Delaware Tunnel, is the second longest ever built. It was scheduled for completion in 1965.

Water tunnels are usually built to avoid pumping water over mountains. The heavily populated regions of southern California are semidesert and long ago outgrew their natural water supplies. As a result water must be brought hundreds of miles from the Colorado River in giant aqueducts. The Colorado River Aqueduct crosses the Sierra Nevada Mountains and includes more than a dozen tunnels.

One of the more recent uses of large tunnels is for sewage disposal. Probably the first sewer tunnels were the Paris Catacombs, carved under the French city by ancient underground streams. The Parisians drained their wastes into the underground streams. Only recently, however, have large cities begun boring large tunnel networks to serve as giant sewer pipes. Such tunnels usually lead to a treatment plant where the waste water is purified.

Tunnel Construction

The methods of building a tunnel differ primarily according to the material the tunnel must go through. To bore through hard rock, tunnelers use large power drills and explosives. Tunneling through rock is difficult and slow, but the rock tunnel usually supports itself and does not cave in. When a tunnel is driven through softer rock or dirt, the digging is easier, but the roof usually needs support. If the tunnel is running through mud or sand, the entire tunnel must be lined with curved metal or concrete plates. As a result, soft-ground tunneling is often slower and more difficult.

Not until 1818 did soft-ground tunneling become relatively safe. That year, Mark I. Brunel, an English engineer, invented the tunneling shield. Basically, the shield looks like a giant tin can with its ends cut out. The front edge of the shield is equipped with a tough steel cutting edge. The back edge of the shield has powerful hydraulic jacks on it. The jacks push against a concrete bulkhead or the metal rings of the completed tunnel behind the shield. As the jacks move the shield ahead, the cutting edge presses forward into the earth like a cookie cutter. Workers inside the shield dig out the "cookie" of earth in the center.

Trench-type tunneling involves digging a trench, building the tunnel tube of brick, metal, or concrete, and then filling in the trench.

Water is one of the tunnelers' biggest prob-lems. Underground water often occurs deep in the ground in rock formations and almost always near the surface in the soil. When tunnelers strike water, it often gushes in, floods the tunnel, and stops work until pumps can remove it. To keep the water out of a soft-ground tunnel, air is pumped into the tunnel. The pressure of the air is kept higher than the pressure of the water trying to enter the tunnel. Because keeping a long tunnel under air pressure is difficult and expensive, usually only the portion near the heading is pressurized. This is done by placing an air lock behind the digging. The air lock is made by building two airtight walls across the tunnel. Both walls have doors in them, but both doors are never opened at the same time. In this way men and machines can pass from the pressurized part of the tunnel to the unpressurized part.

The latest tunneling machines are shieldlike devices with rotating wheels at the front. The wheels have cutting teeth that gnaw away the earth and rock. Another wheel with buckets on it picks up the material and loads it on conveyor belts that carry it out of the tunnel.

Trench-type tunneling is becoming the most common method used to build tunnels under shallow water. A trench is dug in the riverbed by dredging the mud and silt. Next, the tunnel is built on land in sections that look like pipes. The tunnel section is equipped with its roadway, lights, and ventilating ducts and then capped on the ends. These tube sections are then floated out over the trench. The tubes have double walls of steel that help to keep them afloat. When a tube is ready to be sunk, it is spotted directly over the trench, and concrete is poured between its double walls. As it sinks from the weight of the concrete, men in diving suits guide the tube into position and bolt it to the previous tube. Once the outside shells are watertight, the end caps are removed and the sections become a continuous tunnel.

TUPELO ($t\overline{oo}'p\breve{e}\,l\overline{o}$), is any tree of the *Nyssa* genus of the tupelo family (*Nyssaceae*).

Black tupelo, sometimes called black gum, sour gum, or pepperidge, is a small-to-medium-sized tree. It grows in all of the United States east of a line from Chicago, Illinois, to central Texas. It lives on well-drained soil in the southern states but may be found growing along moist roadsides and in woods in the more northern states. The oval leaves are smooth and shiny. They turn a brilliant red in the fall. The small, dark blue fruit is eaten by birds and small mammals. The wood of the black tupelo is used in making barrels, crates, and baskets. A characteristic of this tree is its sharp, horizontal twigs and branches.

Courtesy U.S. Forest Service
The water tupelo (*Nyssa uniflora*) is a tall, thin tree that grows in wet or swampy places.

Water tupelo, also known as tupelo gum or cotton gum, grows in wet or swampy places in the southeastern and southern United States. It may be found as far north as southern Illinois. Water tupelo is usually larger than black tupelo and may grow to a height of more than 70 feet. The wood is used in the manufacture of furniture. The swollen base of the trunk and roots is composed of a soft, light wood used to make floats for fishnets. The blue fruit resembles olives in size and shape.

All kinds of tupelo wood look the same under a microscope. The light-colored sapwood gradually shades into the light brownish-gray heartwood. The growth rings are not clear. The wood fibers are twisted together, and only careful curing prevents warping.

TUPPER (*tŭp'ẽr*), **SIR CHARLES** (1821–1915), was one of the founders of modern Canada. He was born in Amherst, Nova Scotia. He went to Scotland to study medicine at the University of Edinburgh and was graduated in 1843. In 1855 the young doctor was elected to the Nova Scotia Assembly. In 1864 he became prime minister of the province and helped set up a system of free public schools.

At that time Nova Scotia was governed separately from the rest of Canada. Tupper became a leader of the movement to join the Canadian provinces under one government. In 1867 the movement was successful, and the provinces agreed to join together in the Dominion of Canada. (See CANADIAN HISTORY.)

Tupper held a number of high positions in the Conservative government headed by Sir John Macdonald, the first Canadian prime minister. (See MACDONALD, SIR JOHN ALEXANDER.) In 1879 Tupper became Canada's first minister of railways and canals. In this position he worked for the construction of a railroad to connect British Columbia on the Pacific Coast and Canada's eastern provinces on the Atlantic. The result was the Canadian Pacific Railway.

In 1884 Tupper became Canada's high commissioner in Great Britain. He returned to Canada in 1896 and served briefly as prime minister. Later that year the Liberal party won an election, and Tupper became opposition leader. In 1900 he was defeated in a re-election campaign and retired from public life. In 1909 he returned to Great Britain, where he spent his last years.

Sir Charles Tupper.

Tupper was a founder, as well as first president, of the Canadian Medical Association.

TURBINE (*tẽr'bĭn*) is a machine that changes the energy of a fluid into mechanical work. This fluid may be steam, water, or gas.

The turbine is a type of engine. It differs from a reciprocating, or back and forth, engine in that its working motion is entirely rotary, or circular. It differs from a jet or rocket engine in that it produces power from a rotating shaft rather than from thrust. (See ENGINE.)

A turbine has certain advantages over a reciprocating, or piston, engine such as the gasoline or diesel engine. Because the working motion of the turbine is entirely rotary, the power produced is much smoother and more even than that of a piston engine. The turbine also operates with much less vibration and produces greater horsepower in a single unit. Some are capable of as much as 150,000 horsepower, and they are relatively compact considering the output of a single machine.

Steam turbines have come to be used almost exclusively for large ships and large electric power generating stations. The huge horsepowers they produce efficiently and their low vibration make steam turbines especially advantageous for ships.

Turbines are also used to power aircraft. The turbojet engine, though not actually a turbine engine, uses a turbine-driven compressor to compress the incoming air. In the turboprop engine a combustion-gas turbine turns the propeller shaft. (For illustration, see AIRPLANE.) Combustion-gas turbines have been built for railroad locomotives, electric power generation, industry, and experimental automobiles.

Giant hydroelectric power generating stations use hydraulic, or water, turbines to turn the electric generators. Water entering the turbine from a height is the source of energy for the water turbine. A crude form of water turbine is the old waterwheel operating in a stream to power a small sawmill. The water striking the paddles on the wheel rim causes it to turn. For a hydroelectric station, water is trapped behind a dam in order to raise the level of the water above that of the inlets to the turbines located near the bottom of the dam.

An air turbine is another type of turbine. Many factories use compressed air wrenches, drills, and screw and nut drivers. These small tools are powered by air turbines and are light and easy to control. Some

automobile windshield wipers use air turbines.

How Turbines Work

The main part of a turbine is a rotor. It is the moving part of a turbine. It is mounted on bearings and enclosed in a housing that has an inlet and an exhaust for the fluid. At the center of the rotor is a round shaft. Mounted on the shaft is a wheel that is equipped with a row of blades or buckets. A stream of fluid is directed into the buckets through a row of stationary vanes within the housing. These stationary vanes act as nozzles or guides depending on the type of turbine. The action of the fluid stream produces a force on the buckets that causes the shaft to turn and produce mechanical work.

Consider the steam turbine as an example. A turbine is a single-stage machine if it contains only one wheel and one row of buckets. If it has two or more wheels mounted on the same shaft it is a multistage machine. In a multistage turbine partly expanded steam from the preceding stage is redirected by another set of nozzles or stationary blades acting as guides for use by the succeeding row of buckets. A set of nozzles or guides precedes each row of buckets. Because the steam expands every time it passes a stage, the buckets at the exhaust end of the rotor must be larger than those at the inlet end. Therefore, the smallest wheel is the first stage and the largest wheel is the last stage.

In a steam turbine the first-stage buckets may be only a few inches long, while the final-stage buckets may be two or more feet long.

There are two main classes of turbines: the impulse, or velocity, type and the reaction, or pressure, type. In the impulse turbine, the fluid is accelerated in the stationary nozzles to a high velocity and directed at the buckets. The force of the fluid on the buckets causes the rotor to turn. This principle can be illustrated by directing the jet of an air hose or

An early turbine, possibly the world's first, was built by an Italian, Giovanni Branca, in 1629.

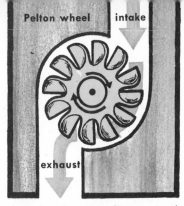

Pelton wheel **intake**

exhaust

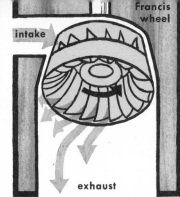

Francis wheel

intake

exhaust

Turbines change the energy of a moving fluid into work. The fluid—gas, steam, or water—is directed against buckets or blades within the turbine. They in turn direct the fluid in such a way as to cause a shaft to turn.

The two types of turbines are impulse and reaction. Examples of these turbines are the Pelton wheel (impulse) and the Francis wheel (reaction). The principles of impulse and reaction can be seen by the effect that moving water would have on a man standing on a wagon.

In the impulse turbine (Pelton wheel), buckets are mounted on the rim of the wheel. Water directed against the buckets creates the force that turns the wheel and shaft. The wheel moves in the same direction as the water.

In the reaction turbine (Francis wheel), water is directed against blades or spokes of the wheel. When the water strikes the blades it changes direction, thus creating the force that turns the wheel and shaft. The wheel moves in a direction different from the water.

IMPULSE

If a stationary hose is turned on the man on the wagon, the force (impulse) will move him in the direction of the flow of the water.

REACTION

If the man holds the hose in his hand, the force (reaction) will move him in the opposite direction.

The steam turbine is more complicated than the hydraulic turbines. It may operate on either the reaction or impulse principle. The main part of the turbine, the rotor, is made up of several rows of stationary blades and moving blades. The moving blades are wheels mounted on a shaft. Steam passing through the rows of blades causes the shaft to rotate.

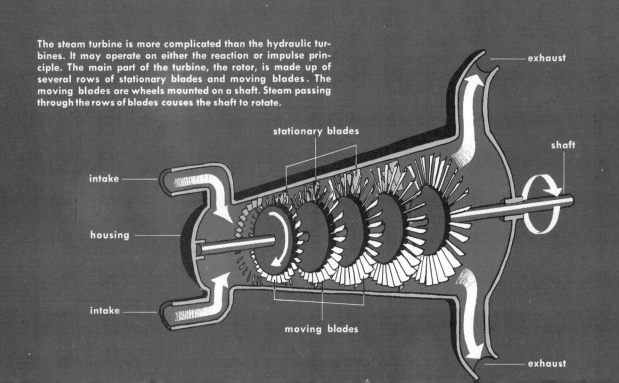

exhaust

stationary blades

shaft

intake

housing

intake

moving blades

exhaust

garden water hose against the cupped hand. A strong force is felt against the hand, and the hand tends to move. The force is increased if the flow of the fluid is increased. It is this force that the buckets of the impulse turbine receive as they are struck by a fluid.

In the reaction turbine, the force against the blades is developed in another way. Using again the steam turbine as an example, the expansion of the steam takes place within the rows of the buckets. Between these moving buckets are stationary blades that expand and guide the steam flow. In passing through the stationary blades, the steam further expands. The energy of the expanding steam is transmitted to the blades that can move. This force causes the rotor to turn. If an air or water hose is held in the hand, a force can be felt pressing against the hand in the direction opposite the direction to the flow of the fluid stream. If the hose is dropped from the hand with the fluid still escaping, the hose thrashes wildly as the reaction force pushes the hose in the direction opposite that of the fluid stream. The spaces between the blades are actually rows of moving nozzles. If an air or water hose could be properly mounted on the rim of a wheel, the wheel would turn as soon as the fluid was allowed to escape.

Steam Turbines

Steam turbines are of both the impulse and reaction types, but the greatest number built today are of the impulse type. The impulse steam turbine is the stronger and least costly to maintain.

Steam turbines are further classified by the way they are used. If the exhaust steam is simply discharged through a smokestack, the turbine is a noncondensing turbine. In most uses, especially if the turbine is large, the exhaust steam is passed into a condenser where it is condensed back to water. The water is then pumped back into a boiler where it is again reheated to steam. Except for necessary additions of new water, the same water is used over and over. A turbine operated in this way is a condensing turbine.

Sometimes the exhaust from a high pressure turbine doing work on one shaft is fed into a low pressure turbine doing work on another shaft. The two turbines together are called a compound turbine.

Sometimes a certain amount of the total steam going through a steam turbine is taken off at some intermediate stage and used for another purpose. If this steam is not used to heat the condensed steam (condensate), then the turbine is called an extraction turbine. The condensate leaving the condenser may be heated by passing it through a heat exchanger before it is pumped back into the boiler. If steam taken off from the turbine is used to supply heat for this heat exchanger, then the turbine is a regenerative one.

In some cases steam, exhausted from a high pressure turbine, is heated again in a heater located in the boiler. The heated steam is then passed into a low pressure turbine before it exhausts into the condenser. This turbine is a reheating one.

In the simplest use the steam entering a turbine is fully expanded and exhausted without any extraction, reheating, or other changes. Such a turbine is called a complete expansion turbine.

The speed of a steam turbine is controlled by a governor that operates the steam inlet valves. As the load demand on the turbine shaft is decreased, the tendency of the turbine to speed up is checked by the automatic closing of the inlet valves. If the load demand on the turbine is increased, the opposite takes place. If the load is suddenly removed, an emergency valve completely shuts off the steam supply as the turbine tries to speed up. This control is an overspeed governor. If it were not used and if the steam could not be shut off quickly, the turbine would continue building speed until it was rotating so fast that its rotor flew apart. The normal operating speeds of many turbines are very high, some exceeding 10,000 revolutions per minute.

Steam is supplied to some of the largest turbines at pressures up to 2,400 pounds per square inch and at temperatures more than 1,000 degrees Fahrenheit. The pipes feeding the steam to the turbine glow dull red with the heat. One large generating station producing at the rate of 200,000 kilowatts uses 89 tons of coal per hour and the station uses more than one million pounds of water per hour to produce the steam. The building housing this station is 17 stories tall. All steam turbines do not run at such high steam pressures and temperatures. However, the higher they are, the higher will be the efficiency of the overall installation. That is to say, the higher will be the mechanical work that can be obtained per unit of fuel used to heat the steam.

Water Turbines

The impulse water turbine uses the Pelton wheel. This wheel has cups, or buckets, bolted to its rim. When a high speed jet of water is directed at these buckets, the force of the impact turns the wheel. A Pelton wheel turbine is a high speed machine and requires a source of water that is far above the inlet to the turbine. The principle is nearly identical to that of directing the jet of a garden hose against the cupped hand.

The reaction water turbine uses the Francis wheel and is also known as a Francis inward-flow turbine. It is a wheel that has a number of curved vanes, or spokes, between its hub and rim. The wheel is housed in a casing shaped like a snail shell. The casing shape causes the water to approach the moving vanes from the proper direction. As the water strikes the vanes, the curve of the vanes forces the water to change direction. This change of direction accelerates the water, which in turn produces the force that turns the wheel. A reaction force due to acceleration of a fluid is created either by increasing the speed of the fluid or by changing its direction. Francis wheel turbines operate at moderate speeds. They are used for hydroelectric generating stations where the level of the water above the turbine, or the head, is not very high but where the quantity of water is great.

The Kaplan wheel turbine has blades like a propeller. It is useful where the quantity and head of the water supply varies from time to time. The angle of the blades can be adjusted to suit the water pressure while the turbine is operating. (See WATER POWER.)

Gas Turbines

A gas turbine may operate with air as its working fluid, or it can use a mixture of air and combustion gases. The gas turbine may be an internal or external combustion engine.

The fluid enters a turbo-compressor and is compressed to several times atmospheric pressure. After compression it is heated, further raising the temperature and pressure. The fluid is then expanded against a set of turbine blades, causing a shaft to rotate and produce mechanical work. The compressor and the turbine are both on the same shaft. Part of the mechanical work produced by the turbine, therefore, is used to operate the associated compressor.

A gas turbine may be considered an internal combustion type if the burning of the fuel takes place in combustion chambers within the engine. Such a machine is said to work on an open system. The fuel is burned with air, and the heated air and combustion products are exhausted into the atmosphere after they have been used by the turbine. (See INTERNAL-COMBUSTION ENGINE.)

A gas turbine may be considered an external combustion type if it works on a closed system, as does a condensing steam turbine. The compressed fluid is led from the compressor through a heat exchanger in the heater. There it receives the heat energy that raises its temperature and pressure. The heated fluid is then admitted to the turbine and expanded to produce work. It is then led through another heat exchanger where it is cooled before it re-enters the compressor. In this system the fluid never contacts combustion products and remains clean, reducing wear and damage to the turbine blades. A low-cost fuel can be used and a fluid other than air is possible.

In gas turbines such as the turbojets and turboprops used on aircraft, the temperature of the combustion gases reaches about 3,500 degrees Fahrenheit. This temperature is far too high for the materials of the turbine blades to withstand. As a result, about two-thirds of the air flowing through the engine is used to cool the other one-third used for combustion. Gas turbine blades are now designed that can withstand temperatures greater than 1,500 degrees Fahrenheit.

Today engineers are searching for better materials for turbine blades so that gas turbines will be able to operate at higher temperatures. These new materials may be ceramics rather than metals. At present the gas turbine finds widest use in aircraft engines and smaller electric power generating stations. Steam turbines and diesels are still preferred for generating electric power (where a hydroelectric station is not possible) and for powering ships, although gas turbines are becoming increasingly popular for these uses. Also the diesel is preferred for railroad locomotives. The gas-turbine automobile is still experimental and available only on a limited basis.

TURGENEV (*tur gĕn'yĕf*), **IVAN SERGEYEVICH** (1818–1883), was a leading Russian novelist, storywriter, and playwright. He was born in Orel of wealthy, landowning parents. He was educated at the universities of Moscow and St. Petersburg, and in 1838 he went to Berlin to study philosophy. There he met educated Russians who were "Westerners," or Russians who admired Western European culture and government. Turgenev joined them and remained a Westerner all his life. After returning to Russia in 1841, he began writing short pieces about country life on Russian estates. These pieces, condemning serfdom, were collected in 1852 under the title *A Sportsman's Sketches*. That same year Turgenev was banished to his estate by czarist authorities for praising the Russian author Nikolai Gogol.

Ivan Turgenev.

He began work on his novels, and *Rudin* was published in 1856; *A Nest of Gentlefolk*, in 1859; *On the Eve*, in 1860; and his masterpiece, *Fathers and Sons*, in 1862. In this great novel he portrayed the new generation of radical Russian youth. The book was unfavorably received in Russia, however, and Turgenev, hurt by its reception, began spending more and more time in France and Germany. His last major novels, *Smoke* (1867) and *Virgin Soil* (1877), did not regain his lost favor in his homeland. Turgenev was worldly, sophisticated, and brilliant; and he was the first Russian novelist whose works were admired throughout Europe. He died in France.

TURIN (*tūr'ĭn*), **ITALY**, is an important industrial and transportation center in the northern part of the country on the banks of the Po River, in a rich agricultural area. The main railroad line leading to France and western Europe from Italy passes through the city.

Swift-flowing streams from the Alps to the north provide hydroelectric power for the city's factories. They turn out textiles, clothing, metal goods, rubber, paper, and glass. Turin is most important, however, as the center of the Italian automobile industry. One of the city's most famous industrial establishments is the Fiat automobile works.

Turin is a city of elegant squares lined with arcades and palaces. Most of these features date from the 17th and 18th centuries, when Turin became an important city. Outstanding buildings include Palazzo Madama; Palazzo Reale (royal palace); the red brick Palazzo Carignano; Academy of Sciences; Chapel of the Holy Shroud in the Cathedral of St. John the Baptist; and several other baroque churches. Among the most imposing squares are Piazza San Carlo and Piazza Castello. A beautiful park, the Parco del Valentino, stretches along the banks of the Po.

The University of Turin, founded in 1405, is famous for its medical and scientific departments. A polytechnic school is housed in the Castello del Valentino. Remarkable museum collections are in the Academy of Sciences Building and in the Palazzo Reale.

Although founded as a Roman town, Turin's growth did not begin until the 13th century, when it was made the capital of the dukedom of Savoy. During the following centuries it became one of the great cities of Europe. In 1720 it was made the capital of the kingdom of Sardinia. In the middle of the 19th century, the kings of the Italian states met in Turin to plan the union of Italy into one kingdom. From 1861 until 1865 Turin was the capital of Italy.

Because of its importance a   al and transportation center, T   get of heavy aerial bombi   ing World War II. The   largely repaired by the 1960   lation is 1,050,910 (1961 censu   ).

TURK (tĕrk), or Turkic, is anyor   longs to any of the groups of people wh   eak a Turkish language. Some of these peop.e live in modern Turkey, but most belong to tribes scattered throughout the mainland of Asia. These peoples differ greatly in customs, religion, and appearance.

Turkish-speaking people may be divided into two main groups—the eastern Turks and the western Turks. Most of the eastern Turks (Tatars, Kazakhs, Uzbeks, and others) live in the southern parts of the Soviet Union and in the great steppes of central Asia. Turkic people are found as far away as eastern Siberia and northern Mongolia. Others live in the Chinese province of Sinkiang. The eastern Turks who are closest to Europe—like the Turkomans near the Caspian Sea—usually live on little farms. The others are nomads who travel on horseback constantly from place to place. In religion most are Muslim, although some are pagan.

The western Turks were the Osmanli, or Ottomans, whose descendants formed the modern country of Turkey. They live also in nearby countries, as in the Macedonian provinces of Yugoslavia and Greece and in the northwestern part of Iran. Most of them are farmers. In religion they are Muslim.

History

A Chinese history, written in the 6th century, is the earliest record of the Turks. At that time the Turks had a huge empire. It stretched from Mongolia and northern China on the east, to the Black Sea on the west. But in the 7th century the Chinese ruled a part of this empire for a short while. This was a section near the Altai Mountains, just west of Mongolia. Some people think the Turks may have taken their name from Turku, a helmet-shaped hill in this area.

In the 7th century a Chinese traveler, Yuan Chwang, wrote about the Turks. Yuan was a Buddhist pilgrim. He traveled through their country, now called Turkistan. He told how he was led before their ruler, or khan, and how warlike the Turks were. They made many successful raids on neighboring countries, although by this time they had given up their nomadic ways and settled in cities. Among them were farmers, traders, and skilled craftsmen.

At the beginning of the 8th century the Arabs conquered Persia (modern Iran). The Arabs brought with them the Muslim religion, Islam. Soon the Turks in nearby Turkistan became converts to it. They were ruled by the Arab conquerors under the caliph of Baghdad (capital of modern Iraq). But gradually different tribes, or branches, of Turks set up strong kingdoms of their own. In about 1000, one of these, the Seljuks, conquered Baghdad. By 1100 they had a large empire in Asia Minor.

The Arabs, when they held Jerusalem, let the Christians visit the city freely. The Turks, however, were cruel to these visitors and even destroyed holy places. Europeans were angry over this behavior of the Turkish infidels. The Christians decided to free the Holy Land, and as a result the Crusades began. (See CRUSADES.)

In these unending wars the Seljuks were victorious. They built a great civilization, with beautiful buildings and great universities. Their empire finally ended in the 13th century when the Mongols defeated them.

The Mongols, under their powerful leader Genghis Khan, conquered almost all the areas of Asia and Asia Minor where Turkic people lived. But as the Mongols lived among the Turks, they became converts to Islam, and the two groups blended.

Another group of Turks, the Ottoman, or Osmanli, became powerful in the 13th century. They had fled westward ahead of the armies of Genghis Khan. They settled on land given them by the Seljuks, in what is now modern Turkey. Their leader was Ertoghrul. After his death in 1288 his son Othman, or Osman, was given still more land by the Seljuk sultan. After the sultan died, Osman became the new sultan. His tribe became independent in about 1299, the beginning of the powerful Ottoman Empire. The Ottoman Turks conquered most of the lands at the eastern end of the Mediterranean. They were the ancestors of the people living in present-day Turkey. (See TURKEY, section on *History*.)

TURKEY (*tĕr'kē*), **EURASIA,** is a country that lies mostly on a peninsula between the Mediterranean and Black seas. It is officially called the Republic of Turkey. The area occupied by the Turkish republic is all that remains of an empire that once stretched from near Vienna, Austria, to Yemen in southwest Arabia. It included much of the coastal zone of North Africa.

The historic waterway formed by the Dardanelles (Hellespont), the Sea of Marmara, and the Bosporous divides Turkey into two parts: Turkey in Europe to the west and Turkey in Asia to the east. European Turkey has

an area about equal to the state of New Hampshire and is bounded by Greece on the west and Bulgaria on the northwest. Asian Turkey, or Anatolia, is about 32 times larger than the European section. It is bounded on the north by the Black Sea, on the west by the Aegean Sea, on the south by the Mediterranean Sea, Syria, and Iraq, on the east by Iran, and on the northeast by the U.S.S.R.

Landscape

European Turkey consists of two ranges of mountains and the valleys of the Maritsa River (Evros) and its tributary the Ergene. Rainfall is moderate, ranging between 20 and 30 inches a year. The winters are fairly cold, and the summers are hot. Much of the land is covered by low-growing scrub or grass, and in the Istranca Mountains there are forests.

Asiatic Turkey consists generally of a central plateau surrounded by mountains. The plateau ranges up to about 6,000 feet above sea level. On the north it is bounded by the Pontic (Pontus) Ranges and on the south by the Taurus Mountains. On the east the plateau merges with a huge mountain group, the Armenian Highland. The highest point in the highland is Mount Ararat (16,945 feet), located near the intersection of the Turkish, Soviet, and Iranian borders. According to ancient stories, Mount Ararat is the place where Noah's ark landed after the flood. Many other peaks in the group reach elevations of more than 10,000 feet. On the west the plateau is cut by the deep valleys of short rivers that flow to the Aegean and Mediterranean seas.

The central plateau is the core of Turkey. It is a high, rolling plateau, and lava flows and volcanic ash cover large areas. The plateau is in part drained to the Black Sea by the Sakarya and Kizil Irmak rivers and to the Aegean and Mediterranean seas by the Menderes, Gediz, and Seyhan rivers. Much of the plateau, however, has no outlet to the sea. Many rivers that carry water only part of the year flow into shallow lakes, or their waters disappear into the sands of the plateau. The Tigris and Euphrates rivers have their headwaters in eastern Turkey. The largest lake is Lake Van. Although Tur-

Locator map of Turkey.

Courtesy Turkish Press Broadcasting & Tourist Department

The beautiful mosque of Sultan Ahmed I, commonly known as the Blue Mosque, is an excellent example of Turkish religious architecture. It was constructed in the early 17th century.

key has more than 3,000 miles of coastline, there are few good natural harbors. Earthquake tremors are common in Turkey.

The climate of Asiatic Turkey is largely controlled by elevation. Turkey's southern and Aegean coasts have a mild Mediterranean climate. Average yearly temperatures in these regions range between 57 and 70 degrees Fahrenheit, and the annual rainfall is moderate. The Black Sea coast also has a mild climate, though it is wetter. The Anatolian plateau is noted for its hot, dry summers and cold winters.

Because of differences in elevation and precipitation, the plateau has a wide variety of plant life. The natural vegetation of the plateau is grassland. On rising ground the grass gives way to scrub plants of stunted trees and bushes, and in the mountains there are stands of various coniferous and some deciduous trees. Valonia oak and olive trees grow in the southwest. Wild animal life in Turkey includes the hare, boar, wildcat, marten, deer, mouflon, bear, fox, wolf, gazelle, and lynx.

The People

The Turks are a mixture of peoples. Before the Turks occupied Anatolia, the area had been influenced by the Macedonian, Roman, and Byzantine empires. Other ancient groups had been there even earlier. Late in the 11th century a Turkish-speaking people from the northeast invaded and conquered Anatolia, ending Byzantine rule there. During the centuries of the Ottoman Empire, conquest and invasion brought the intermingling of many nationalities. By the mid-20th century, however, the people of Turkey had developed into a fairly unified nationality group. Only about 15 percent of the people are classified as racial minorities. Of these, the Kurds, with a population of more than 1,800,000, are the largest minority group. There are small minority groups of Arabs, Greeks, Armenians, and Jews.

Religious freedom is provided by the constitution. Almost 99 percent of the population is Muslim, although there is no official state religion. The state does, however, maintain some mosques and other Muslim religious properties.

PRODUCTS OF TURKEY

LAND USE

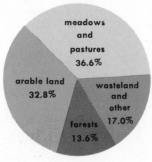

- meadows and pastures 36.6%
- arable land 32.8%
- wasteland and other 17.0%
- forests 13.6%

KEY TO PRODUCTS

- CATTLE
- CHEMICALS
- CHROME ORE
- CITRUS FRUIT
- COAL
- COTTON
- GRAINS
- GRAPES
- IRON AND STEEL
- IRON ORE
- LIGNITE
- PETROLEUM
- SHEEP AND GOATS
- SUGAR BEETS
- TEXTILES
- TOBACCO

VALUE OF PRINCIPAL PRODUCTS

AGRICULTURE	$2,345,500,000
animal products	$619,212,000
grains	$539,465,000
vegetables and fruit	$445,645,000
industrial crops	$272,078,000

MANUFACTURING	$1,773,390,000
food products	$485,500,000
textiles	$381,077,000
tobacco	$178,266,000
chemicals	$146,912,000
metals	$128,469,000

MINING	$82,674,000
coal	$45,057,000
lignite	$20,835,000
chrome ore	$11,326,000
iron ore	$4,712,000

There are also small minority groups of Greek Orthodox, Gregorians, Roman Catholics, Jews, and Protestants in Turkey.

About 68 percent of the population lives in rural areas, and 32 percent lives in cities. The traditional country village usually includes buildings of sun-dried brick or rough stone. Little wood is used because of the scarcity of lumber. The floors of the houses are frequently of earth covered only with straw mats. In the cities the houses vary from primitive to modern. The government is building many homes to improve the poor housing in many sections of the country.

How the People Make a Living

The Turkish economy today, as in past centuries, is based mainly on agriculture. Most farmers can grow only enough food to feed their families. Agriculture for commercial purposes is largely limited to the coastal lowlands. Although agriculture is important, major attempts to modernize it did not occur until after World War II. Farming methods are still primitive in many sections of Turkey. Poor farmers still often cultivate their land and harvest their crops with the ox-drawn wooden plow and the hoe and sickle. Some labor-saving machinery, however, has become available, and modern farming methods have begun to replace traditional methods. Of the land area of Turkey, about 33 percent is cultivated. This includes land in tree crops and vineyards, as well as other crops. About 14 percent of the land is in forests.

Because of the varieties of climates found in Turkey, the number of crops produced is considerable. Grain is the most important crop. It occupies about 75 percent of the arable land, tree crops and vineyards occupy 12 percent; and the remaining 13 percent of the land is in crops for industry, such as cotton and tobacco.

Of the grain crops, wheat is first and barley second in importance. Other grain crops include corn, rye, oats, rice, and millet.

Along the coasts of Turkey the subtropical valleys and lowlands are intensively cultivated. This region supports most of the farmers of the country. In the rainy valleys along the Black Sea, corn, oats, millet, tobacco, peanuts, and tree nuts are produced. Along the drier Aegean and Mediterranean seacoasts the farmer turns to such crops as figs, olives, and grapes. If water is available, he grows citrus fruits, tobacco, and cotton, as well as wheat and barley.

The grass-covered plateaus and mountains of Turkey provide grazing lands for livestock. The most important animals are sheep and goats. During the summer they are grazed in the mountains to take advantage of the fresh, green pastures. In spring and autumn, flocks feed on the fresh grasses of the plateau. Other livestock includes hens, cattle, donkeys, horses, water buffalo, and camels.

After the Turkish republic was established by Mustafa Kemal in 1923, a great effort was made to develop the country's natural resources and industries. In the past, Turkey's industries were almost entirely home industries—the weaving of soft woolens and beautifully decorated carpets and the making of lace. New industries, aided by the government, are now making textiles, iron and steel, cement, paper, and glass, and others are preparing tobacco, refining sugar, and processing other foods. With U.S. aid, Turkey manufactures a large amount of military equipment. Larger towns, such as Ankara and Istanbul, have been transformed into industrial centers.

Turkey possesses a wide variety of minerals. Deposits include coal, lignite, iron ore, chromite, copper, lead, zinc, tungsten, manganese, antimony, petroleum, emery, sulfur, meerschaum, boron, and others. The mines are few in number and support only a few people. Turkey is a world leader in the production of chromite, emery, and meerschaum.

Another resource of Turkey is its fisheries. All along the coastline, and especially at the mouth of the Black Sea, tuna, anchovies, mackerel, and mullet are caught in large quantities. There are also catches of shrimp, lobster, and freshwater fish, such as carp.

Transportation, Communication, and Education

The lack of efficient transportation has been a major handicap to the development of Turkey. Railroads have made considerable progress but are still not adequate. The 5,000 miles of railroads are state owned and operated. In 1951 a road-building program was begun, and the country now has about 39,000 miles of

Trebizond, a historic port on the Black Sea and capital of Trebizond province, is in northeastern Turkey. It is in a market area for vegetables, fruits, nuts, tobacco, and wool.

Marc Riboud-Magnum

The architecture of the Ishak Pasha Palace, near Mount Ararat in eastern Anatolia, reflects many cultures and periods of building. It was most recently restored by an Ottoman nobleman between 1745 and 1775.

State schools are free. Major universities include those located at Istanbul, Ankara, and Izmir.

Government

Turkey is a constitutional republic. Legislative power is held by the Grand National Assembly, which corresponds roughly to the Congress of the United States. Like the Congress, it has two houses: the National Assembly, composed of 450 members elected every four years; and the Senate of 150 members who hold office for six years. An additional 15 members are appointed to the Senate by the president. The whole Assembly elects the president for a term of seven years. Executive power is held by the Council of Ministers, which is led by the prime minister. The president appoints the prime minister.

The whole country is divided into 67 provinces called *ils*. Each *il* is governed by a *vali*,

roads, including about 28,000 miles of all-weather roads. Turkey has a state-owned airline system, which connects the major cities and provides flights to nearby countries. Foreign lines into Istanbul and Ankara link Turkey with many of the world's major cities.

Despite many miles of coastline, Turkey has been of minor importance in the shipping world. Istanbul, Izmir, and Iskenderun have the best harbors. In the 1960's, however, the Turkish government began extensive port improvements.

Postal, telephone, and telegraph services are owned and operated by the government, as are the radiobroadcasting stations. There are more than 2,500,000 radios within the country, although television is still in an early stage of development.

Freedom of speech and the press is guaranteed by the Turkish constitution. The adoption of the Latin alphabet in 1928 was a revolutionary step that has made it easier for the people to learn to read. Literacy in the country has greatly increased since that time.

Education is compulsory by law for all children aged 7 to 12. Because of the lack of teachers and school facilities, however, many children do not have the opportunity to attend school. Only about 40 percent of the population over 6 years of age can read and write.

This modern hotel in Istanbul, the ancient capital of the Byzantine Empire, overlooks the Bosporus.

an officer appointed by the national government. There are provincial assemblies for each *il*. *Ils* are in turn divided into smaller administrative districts called *ilces*.

The government health and welfare programs have been well developed. Turkish citizens who cannot afford to pay may receive free medical care at state hospitals or health centers. Health conditions are still rather poor in many rural areas. A social security system, begun in 1936, provides industrial accident and sickness, old age, and maternity insurance.

History

Turkey has had a long history of great conquests and bitter defeats. The Seljuks were the first Turks to arrive in Anatolia. They overthrew the Byzantine conquerors and established themselves as rulers in the 11th century. The first Ottoman Turks arrived in the 13th century and soon became the ruling group. The first Ottoman sultanate was established by Osman I in about 1281. For more than 200 years the Turks added to their conquests. In 1362 Adrianople was seized by Murad I, who made the city the capital of the Ottoman Empire. In 1389 Murad I defeated the Serbs at the greatest of the battles of Kossovo and extended the Ottoman Empire to the Balkan Peninsula. The Turkish forces were beaten by Tamerlane (Timur) and the Mongol horde in 1402, and their conquests were temporarily halted. Through the reigns of Mohammed I and Murad II, from 1413 to 1451, new conquests were made in Asia Minor and Macedonia, and part of Greece was taken.

Finally, under Mohammed II the Conqueror,

the Turkish forces stormed the walls of Constantinople (Istanbul), the capital of the Byzantine Empire. In 1453 it fell, and the 1,000-year reign of the Byzantine Empire came to an end.

Conquest after conquest was made by the Turks. In 1517 Selim I the Grim conquered Syria and Egypt and became overlord of some of the holy Muslim cities. His successor, Soliman (Suleiman) the Magnificent, took Belgrade (now capital of Yugoslavia) and extended the empire over most of Hungary after capturing Budapest. He laid siege to Vienna in 1529 and

Authenticated News

At Alanya, an ancient port on the Mediterranean Sea in southwestern Turkey, a 700-year-old Seljuk shipyard is still in a fine state of preservation and even today produces ships for the area.

brought the empire to the height of its power.

The Ottoman Empire suffered a serious blow in 1571 when the Turkish Navy was defeated at the Battle of Lepanto, near Greece, by the Holy League of Venice, Spain, and Pope Pius V. In 1683 the Turks again besieged Vienna but were defeated. This defeat clearly marked the beginning of the decline of Ottoman power. The Turks lost much of their Western territory to Christian powers, such as Austria, Venice, Russia, and Poland. In the 18th century, Russia reconquered the northern and eastern shores of the Black Sea and became the official protector of the Orthodox Christians under Turkish rule. In the mid-19th century, Turkey declared war on Russia, and, after Russia defeated a Turkish fleet in the Black Sea, England and France came to Turkey's aid. This conflict was the Crimean War (1854–1856), which was lost by Russia.

In 1877, after a conference failed to settle disputes between Russia and Turkey over several Balkan territories, the Russians declared war on Turkey. Because of its cruel treatment of Bulgarians, the European powers refused to aid Turkey, and Turkey was defeated. Serbia, Rumania, and Montenegro became independent, and a principality of Bulgaria was formed. Turkey gained a constitution in 1876, but it was suspended the following year.

In 1908 the Young Turks, a secret revolutionary group, many of whom had been educated in Europe, demanded that the constitution of 1876 be restored. They gained control of the army and began reorganizing the affairs of the country. The government of the Young Turks was enthusiastic but inexperienced. In a war with Italy (1911–1912) Turkey lost Tripolitania and Cyrenaica in Libya, and most of its islands in the Aegean. Then the Balkan states formed an alliance and defeated Turkey

FACTS ABOUT TURKEY

CAPITAL: Ankara. FORM OF GOVERNMENT: Republic.

NATIONAL ANTHEM: *Istiklal marsi* ("The March of Independence").

AREA: 301,380 square miles (including 3,238 of inland water).

POPULATION (1960 census): 27,754,820; 93 persons per square mile; 32 percent urban, 68 percent rural.

MOUNTAIN RANGES: Pontic Ranges, Taurus Mountains, Armenian Highland.

HIGHEST POINT: Mount Ararat (16,945 feet).

LARGEST LAKE: Lake Van (1,453 square miles).

MOST IMPORTANT RIVERS: Kizil Irmak, Sakarya, Menderes, Seyhan, Tigris, Euphrates, Maritsa.

PLACES OF INTEREST: Istanbul, ancient capital of the Byzantine Empire; Troy, site of the ancient Trojan city.

CHIEF OF STATE: President.

HEAD OF GOVERNMENT: Prime Minister.

LEGISLATURE: Two-house legislature (Grand National Assembly).

VOTING QUALIFICATIONS: Citizens 21 years and older.

POLITICAL DIVISIONS: 67 provinces called *ils*.

CHIEF CITIES: Istanbul (1,466,535), Izmir (296,635), Adana (231,548), Ankara (129,934).

CHIEF MANUFACTURED PRODUCTS: Processed foods, textiles, tobacco, chemicals, metals.

CHIEF AGRICULTURAL PRODUCTS: Livestock, wheat, barley, and other grains, cotton, vegetables, fruits, and nuts.

FLAG: See FLAG, *Plate 12*.

MONETARY UNIT: Lira; about 9 lira equal one U.S. dollar.

in the First Balkan War (1912–1913). After the Second Balkan War, Turkey lost all of its territory west of the Maritsa River. Turkey sided with Germany in World War I and afterward lost all of its outlying territories. This ended the era of the Ottoman Empire.

After World War I the Turkish government was in a disorganized state. However, a government under Mustafa Kemal (later called Mustafa Kemal Ataturk) was organized in 1922. By the following year the Kemal government negotiated the Treaty of Lausanne with the Allies. This restored to Turkey all purely Turkish lands, and the country has had virtually the same boundaries ever since. In 1923 Turkey was declared a republic, and Mustafa Kemal became its first president.

During the next decade a series of social, legal, and political reforms were accomplished, which greatly modernized the country. They included the substitution of civil law for religious law, adoption of a democratic constitution, and introduction of the Roman alphabet. In actuality, Mustafa Kemal maintained dictatorial powers until his death in 1938.

In World War II, Turkey remained neutral until 1945, when it declared war on the Axis. It then became a charter member of the United Nations. In 1947 the Truman Doctrine pledged U.S. support to Turkey because of mounting Soviet pressures. Turkey joined alliances against possible Soviet aggression—including the North Atlantic Treaty Organization (NATO) and the Central Treaty Organization (CENTO).

TURKEY is a large fowl, or bird, belonging to the family Meleagrididae. On the sides of the head and on the upper neck are folds of skin known as wattles. The wattles of the common, or North American, turkey are pink. They fill with blood and turn bright red when the bird is excited. The legs and feet are covered with scales and lack feathers. The males, called toms or gobblers, have a sharp point or spur on the back of each leg. The male common turkey has a beardlike tuft of bristles on his chest.

There are two living species of turkey. Both are native to North and Central America. The common turkey (*Meleagris gallopavo*) is the source of all domesticated turkeys found throughout the world. It is native to the region extending from eastern United States to southern Mexico. It is one of the largest American birds, reaching a length of about 4 feet. The ocellated turkey (*Agriocharis ocellata*) lives in British Honduras, Guatemala, and the Yucatan Peninsula. This bird is smaller than the common turkey, growing to about 3 feet in length. The ocellated turkey gains its name from the eyelike spots on its tail feathers. The head and neck skin are blue rather than pink, and there is no chest tuft.

Wild turkeys live in open forests. They feed on nuts, seeds, and berries, and they roost in trees at night. They are strong fliers for short distances. They live in flocks and do not migrate. The females, called hens, build their nests on the ground, carefully hidden from foxes, skunks, and other turkeys. They lay from 8 to 15 spotted eggs that hatch in about a month. The young are called poults.

When the Spanish conquerors came to America, they found the Aztec Indians of Mexico keeping turkeys for food. The Spaniards sent several of the birds back to Europe. The Pilgrims found the forests of northeastern United

Allan D. Cruickshank from National Audubon Society

The wild common turkey, native to North America, was first domesticated by the Aztecs. In Colonial times the huge flocks were nearly wiped out, but are now increasing.

The domestic common turkey, one of the largest American birds, grows to about four feet long. It has feathers of brown and white that are tinted bronze-green.

Harold M. Lambert

States filled with wild turkeys. Turkey was an important part of the first Thanksgiving feast and has been the traditional holiday bird ever since. It was an extremely plentiful bird until the forests began to be cleared away. The last wild turkeys disappeared from New England more than 100 years ago. They can still be found in some mideastern and southern states, however, and are a favorite among hunters.

The origin of the bird's name is not certain. Some believe it to be from the "turk-turk" sound that the birds make. Another explanation is that the name may have come from the Hebrew word for peacock—*tukki*.

TURKISTAN (*tẽr′kĕ stăn′*), **ASIA,** is the vast region of mountains and desert lowlands of central Asia that stretches between the Caspian Sea on the west to the Gobi Desert on the east. The Tien Shan Mountains separate the region into Western, or Russian, Turkistan and Eastern, or Chinese, Turkistan. Russian Turkistan lies almost entirely within the Soviet Union. It roughly covers the area of Kirghiz, Tadzhik, Turkmen, Uzbek, and Kazakh Soviet Socialist Republics. Chinese Turkistan is the geographic area known as the Tarim Basin, which covers most of the Chinese province of Sinkiang.

Most of Turkistan is a vast steppe and

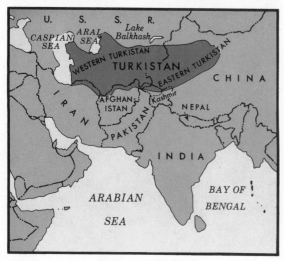

Locator map of Turkistan.

desert, peopled only by nomads who raise sheep, cattle, camels, and horses. At the base of the mountains, where most of the people live, irrigation has made small areas of the desert into fertile basins where melons, citrus fruit, peaches, pears, grapes, cotton, wheat, rice, and barley are grown. Russian Turkistan produces many subtropical agricultural products for the Soviet Union.

Russian Turkistan is mainly an agricultural region, but in recent years an industrial economy has been developing, especially in the cities from Dushanbe, through Tashkent, to Alma-Ata. A cotton textile industry thrives in the region. Other industries based on the agricultural economy include the production of fertilizer and agricultural machinery. The mineral wealth of the region is also providing a basis for manufacturing, including iron, steel, and chemical production, lead smelting and refining, and petroleum refining.

Caravan routes have crossed Turkistan for centuries. Ancient trade centers developed at the oases along these routes. In Russian Turkistan are Bukhara, Samarkand, and Tashkent. In Chinese Turkistan are Khotan, Yarkand, and Kashgar. Some of the cities have been destroyed again and again—by the armies of Alexander the Great, Genghis Khan, Tamerlane, and other desert raiders.

The people of Turkistan are a mixture of the Caucasian and Mongolian races. Most speak a Turkic language. The main groups include Uzbeks, Kazakhs, Kirghiz, Tadzhiks, and Turkmens. In the 20th century many Russians have also settled in this region. Most of the people are followers of Islam. A few are Russian Orthodox Christians.

About 32,000,000 persons live in Turkistan.

TURKMEN (*tẽrk'mĕn*) **SOVIET SOCIALIST REPUBLIC, U.S.S.R.,** is a union republic of the U.S.S.R. located on the eastern shore of the Caspian Sea. The republic is also called Turkmenistan. It is bordered by the Kazakh Soviet Socialist Republic to the north, the Uzbek S.S.R. to the north and east, and Iran and Afghanistan to the south. Turkmen S.S.R. is an extremely dry land with great extremes of temperature. January temperatures in some places average about 25 degrees Fahrenheit, and July temperatures may rise to an average of about 90 degrees Fahrenheit. Most of the republic has only 4 to 8 inches of rainfall yearly.

More than four-fifths of this land is covered by the dry Kara Kum (Black Sand) Desert, a lifeless wasteland with little vegetation or water. The people live mostly on the fringes of the desert, near the Kopet Dagh Range along the southern border, or along the Amu-Darya, Murgab, and Tedzhen rivers.

Most of the people are Turkmen, and they speak a language that resembles the Turkish of Turkey. Before Turkmenistan became a part of the Soviet Union, these people were largely nomads. They raised livestock and moved sea-

Locator map of Turkmen S.S.R.

On small farms, when modern equipment is not readily available, Turkmens use the primitive methods of the region to plant and harvest their crops. In place of a combine or threshing machine, animals tread the wheat to separate the grain.

sonally to favorable pasture lands. After they came under Soviet control, many of the people settled in villages. They began raising crops with the aid of irrigation in addition to livestock. Many Turkmens were also trained to work in manufacturing. Russians now make up about 17 percent of the population, and Uzbeks another 8 percent. The Russians generally hold the positions of leadership, and the Russian language is taught in schools.

In the cities, western dress is common, but the traditional Turkmen costume is still worn in rural areas. It consists of long red gowns and large black fur hats for the men, and red dresses and shawls for the women. Most Turkmens are Sunni Muslims.

The major resource of the republic is petroleum, which is mined in the west. Turkmen S.S.R. is the third largest petroleum producer in the Soviet Union. A pipeline transports petroleum to a refinery on the Caspian Sea. Other important minerals include Glauber's salt from the Kara-Bogaz-Gol area on the Caspian Sea, and sulfur from the Kara Kum. Fisheries are located on the Caspian Sea.

Light manufacturing industries have been developing in the major cities of Turkmen S.S.R. Ashkhabad, the capital, has important cotton and silk textile industries. Other major cities in the republic include Chardzhou, Krasnovodsk, and Mary (Merv). Turkmen industry depends mostly on railroads for transportation. Industry has surpassed agriculture in value, but many Turkmens still farm and raise livestock. Principal crops include cotton, silk, grapes, corn, and wheat. Karakul sheep, horses, and camels are the chief forms of livestock.

The Turkmens occupied the region east of the Caspian Sea in the 11th century. After its defeat by the Russians in 1881, Turkmenistan became a part of the Russian Empire. It became a Soviet Socialist Republic in 1924. The Turkmen S.S.R. has an area of 188,417 square miles. The population is 2,158,000 (1970).

TURNER (tẽr′nẽr), **JOSEPH MALLORD** (măl′ẽrd) **WILLIAM** (1775–1851), was an English artist who gained worldwide fame for his oil paintings and watercolors of sunsets and landscapes. He was born in London, the son of a barber. He used to display his youthful drawings in his father's shop window. At the age of 14 he began studying at the Royal Academy.

Turner traveled in England, Scotland, and Wales, as well as in France, Switzerland, and Italy. He was successful all through his life. When he died he left a large fortune as well as many paintings that he willed to the nation. He had few friends, and as he grew older he withdrew from society and became secretive.

Although he had little formal education, he liked to paint classical and learned subjects. Tu great glori poetic ima his cleve picturing his sen Many of ings have of age beca lack of knowle i mixing oils. His many paintings of Venice,

Joseph Turner.

"The Grand Canal, Venice," by Joseph Mallord William Turner.

Italy, show his active use of imagination, because they were not done with any idea of making faithful representations. Instead, they were idealized and vivid dreams of what Venice meant to him.

As he grew older, he became more and more fascinated with color. Form and subject mattered little if he could use beautiful reds, blues, and oranges. His colors still glow, particularly in his picture "The Fighting Temeraire." Others of Turner's famous pictures are "Crossing the Brook," "Dido Building Carthage," and "Ulysses Deriding Polyphemus." The largest collection of his paintings is in the Tate Gallery, London, England.

TURNIP (tûr′nĭp), or *Brassica rapa*, is a member of the mustard (Cruciferae) family of plants. Brussels sprouts, horseradish, and cauliflower belong to the same family. All of these plants have parts that are good to eat. The root of the turnip is generally eaten, but the tender young leaves are also popular. The large, fleshy roots are usually white, although they are often purplish where they reach aboveground. Turnips are popular in home gardens. They grow well with little attention, store easily, and are high in food value. They may be used as a food for livestock.

Turnips have long, green leaves. They cluster near the roots during the first growing season. In the second year, the leaves grow along the stem, which may reach three feet in height. The small flowers are usually yellow. The fruits are about two inches long and contain round seeds which germinate quickly. Seedlings should be thinned to about six inches. Turnips do not grow well in hot weather. In the United States, they are raised as an early season or summer crop in the north and as a

John H. Gerard

The turnip (*Brassica rapa*) has long, green leaves and a large, fleshy root.

winter crop in the south.

The origin of the turnip is probably eastern Asia, and it grows wild in the U.S.S.R. Under cultivation turnips spread throughout Europe and the Middle East. They were introduced to Mexico by the Spanish during the 16th century, and were first planted in the United States in Virginia in 1609.

TURPENTINE (*tẽr'pĕn tīn*) is a colorless, oily liquid with a strong, pungent odor. Chemically it is a mixture of hydrocarbons. Its prime ingredient, pinene, is a compound of carbon and hydrogen, with a formula of $C_{10}H_{16}$. Oil or spirit of turpentine is obtained from a resinous substance that generally oozes out of pine trees. Its chief use is in making paint, varnish, and paint thinner. It is also an important part of shoe polish, leather dressing, and liniment and other medicines.

Turpentine is made from the resin in the sapwood of pine trees in three ways: (1) by collecting the slow-flowing sap or gum from the living tree and distilling it; (2) by grinding and distilling the stumps of old pine trees after they have been cut for lumber; and (3)

by collecting and condensing turpentine gases formed during cooking of pine chips in the sulfate process of making kraft paper.

Collecting gum from the living tree is the oldest method. V-shaped cuts are made in the tree trunk, and pans are hung under the cuts to catch the gum as it oozes out. Usually only the bark is removed so that little damage is done to the inner wood. This is important when the worked-out tree is later sold for lumber. The gum flows in the warm season, usually from March to November in the pine forests of the South. Fresh cuts are made every week. Sulfuric acid may be sprayed on the cut to increase the flow.

In the distillation plant, the gum is heated until the gases are driven off. When the temperature of the gum is near 212 degrees Fahrenheit, distillation starts. The hot steam and turpentine vapor go through a cooled spiral copper pipe that empties into a separator tank. The condensed water is heavier than condensed turpentine and it goes to the bottom of the tank where it is drawn off. The turpentine on top is put in storage tanks.

The remainder of the distilled gum, a liquid called rosin, is strained and run from the still into barrels to harden as it cools. Rosin has many uses. Baseball pitchers use it on their hands to grip the ball, and boxers use it on their shoes to prevent slipping. It is used to make sealing wax, cement, varnish, soap, and calking for the seams of boats. The greatest demand for rosin is for sizing in papermaking. Size is a coating that gives paper stiffness and

SCRAPING GUM AND CUTTING NEW NOTCHES   EMPTYING GUM BUCKETS   COLLECTING AND EMPTYING GUM INTO BARRELS

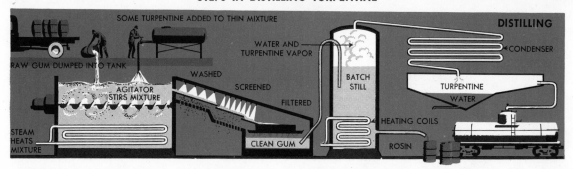

DISTILLING

SOME TURPENTINE ADDED TO THIN MIXTURE

WATER AND TURPENTINE VAPOR

CONDENSER

RAW GUM DUMPED INTO TANK

WASHED

SCREENED

BATCH STILL

TURPENTINE

WATER

AGITATOR STIRS MIXTURE

FILTERED

HEATING COILS

STEAM HEATS MIXTURE

CLEAN GUM

ROSIN

smoothness and prevents the spread of ink.

Only one-fifth of the U.S. turpentine is made from gum. A little less than one-fifth is a by-product of the sulfate process of papermaking. Most turpentine and rosin are made by distilling ground-up pine stumps. Although the supply of pine stumps is being used up, the fast-growing sulfate papermaking industry can make much more turpentine as a by-product. The United States produces more than 500,000 tons of rosin and 650,000 barrels of turpentine a year. This is more than 50 percent of the world's total production. Most of it is produced in southern Georgia and northern Florida, with some from South Carolina, southern Alabama, and Mississippi.

TURTLE (tĕr′t′l) is a four-legged, slow-moving reptile of the order Chelonia. It has a scaly skin and a protective shell enclosing much of its body. It breathes air, using lungs, and it has a sharp, horny beak instead of teeth. The feet usually have five claw-bearing toes. In some cases there are webs between the toes for swimming. Some turtles that live mainly in the water have legs that are modified into flippers for swimming. The shell is usually made of bony plates covered by horny scutes, or scales. The upper portion of the shell is the carapace, and the lower part is the plastron. Many of the vertebrae, or bones of the back, are actually part of the carapace. The bones of the neck have very complicated joints so that the turtle may fold or draw its head and neck into its shell.

The turtle's senses of sight, taste, and touch are well developed. Although there is no visible, outside ear, the turtle can hear relatively well.

Turtles have no vocal cords and no true voice. Most can make hissing or grunting noises by exhaling their breath, and some can make a squeaking sound by rubbing their jaws together.

Although *turtle* has been the most common name for these reptiles in the United States, *tortoise* has been used in the British Isles for all except a few of the water species that have flippers. *Terrapin* refers to some edible species. In trying to standardize the names, most zoologists now use *turtle* for all reptiles with shells and *tortoise* as a secondary name for the slow-moving land turtles. Turtles are of one of the earliest groups of animal life on Earth, and they have changed little in more than 175,000,000 years. There are more than 200 living species. They range in size from the little bog turtle, which reaches a length of only about three inches, to the huge leatherback turtle, which reaches a length of more than eight feet. All lay eggs that are deposited on land, and all are long-lived, some reaching an age of more than 100 years.

During the winter months in temperate climates turtles, like all reptiles, hibernate. Turtles that live in water usually bury themselves in the mud at the bottom, and land turtles bury themselves in the ground to keep from freezing. Many turtles migrate great distances,

The common snapping turtle (*Chelydra serpentina*) has a long tail and very strong jaws.

The shell and body of the painted turtle (*Chrysemys picta*) are beautifully colored.

then apparently return after several years to where they were born to lay their eggs. The green turtle is the most systematic migrant.

Most turtles like a varied diet of worms, insects, and some plant life. They can survive long fasts if need be, living on weekly or even monthly meals. They can store water and survive extended droughts. Pet turtles, however, should be fed chopped raw fish or beef daily, with bone meal and cod-liver oil, until they are several years old. Then feeding twice a week will do. Adult turtles fare well on artificial foods if supplemented with vegetable greens, water plants, worms, and insects.

Sea Turtles

Sea turtles spend nearly their entire lives in the ocean, coming out on to land only long enough to lay their eggs. These turtles are divided into two families, the leatherback turtle and the true sea turtle. The leatherback is the largest of living turtles, sometimes weighing more than 1,500 pounds. The shells of leatherbacks are covered with a thick layer of smooth, leathery skin instead of horny scales. The ribs and backbone are not joined to the shell as they are in other turtles. Leatherbacks are found in most warm seas.

The true sea turtles include the green turtle, the loggerhead, the olive-backed turtle, the hawksbill, and the ridley turtle. The green turtle may weigh up to 500 pounds and reach a length of about four feet. It is important throughout the world as food. Soup is made from its flesh, and the eggs are also eaten. The female green turtle lays up to 200 eggs in a deep hole on the shore. After she covers the hole, she returns to the sea. The heat of the sun usually causes the eggs to hatch within a

Herb and Dorothy McLaughlin

In spite of its menacing appearance, the giant land tortoise is a gentle creature who does not object to riders on its heavy, domed shell.

few weeks, and the young turtles instinctively head for the water. Despite the large numbers of eggs produced, green turtles are growing less common because of man's destruction of them. The loggerhead resembles the green turtle but is not so popular as food because of its strong taste. The hawksbill is another sea turtle that was once threatened with extinction by man. Before the invention of plastics, the yellow-and-brown marbled, horny shell-covering of this turtle was used to make items of "tortoise shell." Hawksbills are the smallest of sea turtles, rarely growing more than three feet long. They are found in warm and temperate seas.

The diamondback terrapin inhabits salt or

The unusual matamata turtle (*Chelys fimbriata*) has a heavy, lumpy shell and a long, thick neck.

The green turtle (*Chelonia mydas*) is a huge marine creature.

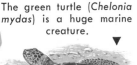

The box turtle (*Terrapene carolina*) has a high rounded shell that is handsomely marked.

◄ The spiny soft-shelled turtle (*Trionyx spinifer*) is a surprisingly swift and active creature.

brackish water but is not a true sea turtle. It has webbed feet with claws. Its gray body is covered with a shell made up of six-sided plates. Females may reach a length of about eight inches; males are smaller.

Fresh-Water Turtles

The largest fresh-water turtles are the snapping turtles. The alligator snapping turtle inhabits the lower Mississippi Valley and the southeastern United States. It is the largest fresh-water turtle in the world, sometimes reaching a length of more than two feet and a weight of more than 200 pounds. Since their shells do not cover them completely, snapping turtles depend upon sharp, strong jaws for protection. The common snapper lives in the mud at the bottom of shallow lakes or rivers. Its mud-colored shell often becomes so covered with moss that it looks like a large stone. Snappers eat almost any available food including fish, frogs, and sometimes young ducklings. Similar to the snapper in coloring are the mud and musk turtles. They are much smaller, however, reaching only about five inches in length. Both of these turtles live in the mud and give off a strong odor when disturbed. The soft-shelled turtle also lives in fresh water. It has a flat, pancake-shaped shell with a leathery covering. It is often used as food. The painted turtle is common in the eastern United States. Its dark, smooth shell averages about six inches long and is edged with lines of yellow. Its head carries yellow and red markings. It lives in ponds and streams but spends much of its time on logs or rocks, basking in the sun. The spotted turtle is similar in size and habits. It has a dark shell marked with yellow spots. Another fresh-water turtle is the red-eared turtle commonly sold in pet shops.

Land Turtles

Land turtles, or tortoises, have heavier, more domelike shells than do water turtles. Their feet are not webbed for swimming but are adapted for walking and digging. The gopher tortoises of the southeastern United States and Texas dig long burrows which they inhabit for many years. The huge tortoises of the Gala-

pagos Islands off the west coast of South America are the largest land turtles in the world. They often reach a length of more than five feet and a weight of more than 500 pounds. These giant tortoises were once common, but sailors and colonists slaughtered them for food. Today, they are almost extinct. The most common North American tortoise is the wood turtle. It has a rough, grayish-brown shell and bright orange-red skin. It eats plants, and meat in the form of insects and worms. It lives in wooded areas near water. The box turtle is another land turtle that lives in moist fields and woodlands. This turtle has a hinged plastron that it can pull up against the carapace at the front and back. This enables it to completely enclose its body in a tight box when frightened. The common species of the eastern United States is usually black with brown or yellow blotches.

TWAIN (*twān*), **MARK** (Samuel Langhorne [*lăng'hôrn*] Clemens [*klĕm'ĕnz*] (1835–1910), created Tom Sawyer and Huckleberry Finn. His real name was Samuel Langhorne Clemens; however, he chose Mark Twain as his pen name. "Mark Twain" was the call used by Mississippi River pilots to tell that the water was "two fathoms deep." He became the United States' best-known humorist and one of its most accomplished writers. (See American Literature.)

Twain was born in 1835 in the village of

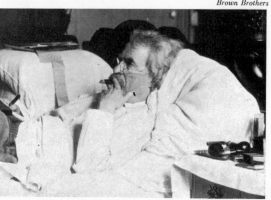

Mark Twain did much of his writing while lying in bed. In his later years he wrote almost constantly in an effort to pay debts incurred when his business failed.

Brown Brothers

Culver Service

Tom Sawyer and Huckleberry Finn are two of Mark Twain's unforgettable characters. Tom whitewashing the fence and Huck curing warts with the carcass of a dead cat are as amusing today as they were a generation ago.

Florida, Missouri. He grew up in the Mississippi River town of Hannibal, Missouri. He described the life of a boy living on the Mississippi in the days of the picturesque river traffic in *The Adventures of Tom Sawyer* and in *The Adventures of Huckleberry Finn*.

In 1848 the young boy was apprenticed to a printer. He became restless and from 1853 to 1856 he traveled, working as a journeyman printer and journalist on newspapers in Missouri, New York, Pennsylvania, and Iowa.

In 1856 he started down the Mississippi on a trip to South America. His boyhood interest in river boats returned, and he became apprenticed to the pilot of the boat he was on. He described his four years as a steamboat pilot in *Life on the Mississippi* (1883). Later he worked in Nevada and California as a miner, a printer, and a reporter. When a magazine published his short story "The Celebrated Jumping Frog of Calaveras County" in 1865, he became known as a humorous writer.

While on a tour of Europe and Palestine in 1867, Twain became attracted to the picture of the sister of a young man he had met. When he returned home, he met her, and in 1870 they were married. He wrote a book about his travels, called *The Innocents Abroad* (1869).

In 1872 he published *Roughing It*, an account of his adventures in the Far West. He then published a number of very popular books, including *The Adventures of Tom Sawyer* (1876), *The Prince and the Pauper* (1880), *The Adventures of Huckleberry Finn* (1884),

and *A Connecticut Yankee in King Arthur's Court* (1889).

In his later years he spent almost all his time writing in order to make enough money to pay off business debts. Before he died in 1910, he had been given honorary degrees by Yale University in the United States and Oxford University in England.

TWEED (*twēd*), **WILLIAM MARCY** (1823–1878), born in New York City, was a political boss who cheated the people of his city out of millions of dollars.

In 1852 Tweed was elected alderman of the New York city council. From 1854 to 1856 he was a member of the United States House of Representatives. But he liked local politics better and became a member of the New York city board of supervisors. At about the same time, he became head of Tammany Hall, the group that ran the Democratic party in New York. (See TAMMANY HALL.)

From 1858 to 1871 Tweed controlled the city government. He put his friends in important jobs. He often bribed people to get what he wanted done, and he took bribes from people who wanted his help. In 1869 Tweed and his friends organized the "Tweed ring" to try to get even more money. The exact amount they took is not known. Estimates run from $45 million to $200 million.

In 1870 Thomas Nast, a cartoonist with *Harper's Weekly*, began using his cartoons to attack Tweed. A reform group led by Samuel

J. Tilden was able to get Tweed arrested and in 1873 he was sentenced to 12 years in prison. He escaped in 1875, but was caught in Spain, brought back and died in prison.

TYLER (*tī′lẽr*), **JOHN** (1790–1862), became the tenth president of the United States upon

Courtesy Smithsonian Institution
John Tyler, U.S. President, 1841–1845.

the death of William Henry Harrison. He was the first vice-president to become chief executive upon the death of a president. All his life John Tyler was a man of strong beliefs. As president he disagreed with the program of his own political party. As a result, for most of his term of office, he was a president without a party.

John Tyler was the second son of John Tyler, a judge and governor of Virginia. His father was a planter and a friend of Thomas Jefferson and Patrick Henry. The future president was born on March 29, 1790, at the plantation of Greenway in Charles City County, Virginia. His early years were spent enjoying the comfortable life of a son of a wealthy Virginia

planter. After attending the College of William and Mary in Williamsburg, Virginia, John read law under his father's direction for two years and then became a lawyer.

In 1813 Tyler married Letitia Christian. There were seven children in the family. Mrs. Tyler died in 1842. Two years later, when he married Julia Gardiner, he became the first president to marry while in office. He and his second wife had seven children.

Political Career

Tyler started his political career in 1811 with his election to the Virginia House of Delegates. After serving for five years, he was elected to the United States House of Representatives. He was a representative from 1816 until 1821, when poor health forced him to resign. During these years he supported states' rights against the federal government. (See STATES' RIGHTS.) He voted against federal help for internal improvements such as roads. He opposed a high tariff, and was against the government stopping slavery in the United States territories. Tyler wanted to see slavery disappear, but he believed that as long as there was slavery it should be protected by law the same as any other property.

When Tyler left Congress he returned to Greenway. However, he could not stay out of politics and within two years was back in the Virginia House of Delegates. Next he served two terms (1825 and 1826) as governor of Virginia, and then was elected to the United States Senate (1827). In 1832 South Carolina declared that a tariff act passed by Congress was unconstitutional and the state would not obey it. Congress then passed the Force Bill to permit the president to use the army and navy to collect the tariff in South Carolina. (See JACKSON, ANDREW.) Tyler thought that this was against the rights of a state and he cast the only vote in the ‘Senate against it.

As senator, Tyler supported President Andrew Jackson on some matters and opposed him on others. Finally he split with Jackson and joined a group of Southerners in a new political party called the Whigs. This party was made up of those who opposed Jackson. (See

Whig Party.) In 1833 Tyler was re-elected to the Senate. In 1836 his opposition to Jackson finally led him to resign his Senate seat. At that time the Senate had passed a resolution criticizing President Jackson. When the Virginia legislature told Tyler to vote to do away with the resolution, he resigned rather than vote against what he believed.

When the Whigs met to nominate candidates for the election of 1840 they had little in common except their opposition to the Democrats. They selected a military hero, William Henry Harrison, to run for president. In order to get southern votes they picked John Tyler as their vice-presidential candidate. In the campaign that followed there was no serious talk on the issues. The Whigs chanted "Tippecanoe and Tyler too" and won a landslide victory in the election.

The Presidency

Within one month of his inauguration Harrison died of pneumonia, and John Tyler became president. At first all seemed peaceful among the Whigs. Tyler kept Harrison's cabinet. He agreed to a new tariff act which helped the manufacturers.

The Bettmann Archive

Letitia Tyler, the first wife of President Tyler.

Tyler's troubles came over the big issue of the day: the bank question. Until the time of Jackson the national government had deposited its money with the Bank of the United States. This was a private corporation, chartered by Congress, with one-fifth of the stock owned by the government. (See BANK AND BANKING, section on *The History of Banking*.) President Jackson thought the bank was a monopoly which helped the rich, but not the poor. He also believed it to be against the Constitution. In 1832, when Congress passed a bill to renew the bank, Jackson vetoed it. Van Buren, who followed Jackson as president, started an Independent Treasury system by which the government kept its money in its own treasuries.

Most of the Whig leaders favored setting up another Bank of the United States. Tyler, however, believed that such a bank would interfere with the rights of the states. He favored a kind of "states' rights national bank," which would operate in the District of Columbia and have branches in the states only with their consent. When the Whigs in Congress under the leadership of Henry Clay passed a bill for a strong Bank of the United States, Tyler

Historical Pictures Service

Julia Tyler, the second wife of President Tyler.

vetoed it. They then passed another bank bill. Again, he vetoed it.

The Whig party was very angry at the president. All of his cabinet except Daniel Webster, the secretary of state, resigned. Webster stayed on to complete his work on a treaty with the British. Tyler was a president without a party for the rest of his term of office.

Tyler's Accomplishments

Despite Tyler's disagreements with his own party a number of worthwhile things were done during his administration. The Navy Department was reorganized. The Seminole Indians of Florida ended their war against the United States and agreed to be moved to lands west of the Mississippi River.

In these years the United States started diplomatic relations with China. Ever since the end of the American Revolution United States ships had taken part in the China trade. By the 1840's this trade was becoming important. In 1842 England forced China to open certain ports to foreign trade. Merchants in the United States wanted the same rights, so Tyler sent a commissioner to China to arrange a treaty. The Chinese granted him just about everything he asked.

The relations between England and the

United States changed in the years Tyler was president. There had been difficulties between the two countries for a number of years. United States support for Canadians who rebelled against England in 1837 was one reason; British demands to search United States merchant ships for slaves was another. Most serious of all was the boundary dispute between Maine and Canada. This boundary had been in question since the signing of the treaty ending the American Revolution. Now England and the United States decided to do something about it.

England sent Lord Ashburton to talk with Secretary of State Webster. Both men were willing to compromise to reach agreement. The result was the Webster-Ashburton Treaty of 1842, which set the present boundary of Maine.

Tyler's United States

John Tyler served as president at a time when the nation was changing rapidly. Florida became the 27th state to enter the Union. People were moving into the western states and territories. Expansion was in the air. Settlement had reached the first row of states beyond the Mississippi River. John C. Fremont was exploring unsettled areas of the West.

The northwest section of the United States and the southwest section of Canada was known as the "Oregon country." It was jointly occupied by the United States and England. In the 1830's some missions were started in this region, and by the 1840's the "Oregon fever" struck the frontier people. Independence, Missouri, was the jumping-off place for wagon trains that crossed the plains and mountains to Oregon. In 1843 more than 1,000 men, women, and children moved over the Oregon Trail to the valley of the Willamette River. United States settlers wanted to take over the whole of Oregon as far north as the latitude of 54° 40'.

People were on the move. Tyler helped settlers who wanted to own their own land. He signed a bill, the Pre-emption Act, by which any person not already the owner of 320 acres or more could stake out 160 acres in the public land and pay for it later at the rate of $1.25 an acre. (See LAND, PUBLIC.)

While many settlers moved to the Oregon country, others headed for the southwest, into territory owned by Mexico. A few under Stephen Austin had made the first American settlement in Texas as early as 1821. Settlement grew and by 1836 Texans under the leadership of Sam Houston were in revolt against the Mexican government. After the victory at the Battle of San Jacinto, Texans declared their independence of Mexico and set up their own government as the Lone Star Republic. A treaty for the annexation of Texas was defeated in the United States Senate. However, at the end of Tyler's term of office, both houses of Congress passed a resolution to admit Texas as a state.

During Tyler's term of office Samuel F. B. Morse proved that his telegraph worked. On May 24, 1844, he sent the first public telegram over a line between Washington, D.C., and Baltimore, Maryland. With the famous words "What hath God wrought!" a new system of communications began.

The Mormons continued to be persecuted for their religious beliefs. In 1844 in Carthage, Illinois, a mob killed their leader, Joseph Smith.

Until the early 1840's only people with property could vote in Rhode Island. To change

TYLER'S LIFETIME

1787	Constitutional Convention.
1790	Tyler born.
1803	Louisiana Purchase.
1807	Graduates college.
1812	War with England.
1813	Tyler marries.
1816	Tyler to Congress.
1825	Erie Canal opened. Tyler Governor of Virginia.
1827	Tyler U.S. senator.
1830	1st passenger railroad.
1832	Nullification issue.
1833	Tyler re-elected senator.
1836	Texas revolt. Tyler resigns.
1837	Revolt in Canada.
1840	Tyler vice-president.
1841	Harrison dies.

Tyler's Term of Office (1841–1845)

1841	Veto of bank bill. Cabinet resigns. Pre-emption Act.
1842	Croton Aqueduct. Webster-Ashburton Treaty. Dorr's Rebellion. Massachusetts Child Labor law. Anesthesia used. End of Seminole War.
1844	1st telegraph message. Treaty with China. Murder of Joseph Smith.
1845	Annexation of Texas. Florida enters the Union.

PRESIDENT

1846	Mexican War.
1849	California Gold Rush.
1861	War Between the States.
1862	Tyler dies.

this, Thomas Dorr led a campaign for several years. Dorr was arrested, but in 1842 the Rhode Island constitution was changed so that people without property could vote.

While people were moving west, others were moving to the cities to take factory jobs. New York City grew so large that the Croton Aqueduct had to be built to carry water 40 miles to the city. In many places children were being hired to do factory work. Massachusetts passed a law that children under 12 could not work more than ten hours a day in a factory. (See CHILD LABOR.)

Later Years

Some Democrats favored nominating Tyler for the presidency in 1844. However, when the regular Democratic convention selected James K. Polk, Tyler withdrew his name. He retired to his country home, called Sherwood Forest. The War Between the States called him back into public life.

At first Tyler was against the idea of the southern states leaving the Union. He believed that a compromise could be worked out between the North and the South. In February 1861 he was chairman of a convention of the states which met in Washington, D.C., to consider compromises. The convention failed, and in the next month Tyler served as a member of the Virginia convention which met to discuss secession. When all compromises failed, he supported secession as the only honorable action possible for the South. He was elected to the Confederate House of Representatives. However, he died before that body met.

TYNDALE (*tin'dăl*), **WILLIAM** (1492?–1536). Translator of the New Testament and part of the Old Testament, William Tyndale was probably born in Gloucester, England. He was at Oxford University in 1510 and had entered the church by 1521.

He was persecuted by the clergy because of his views. He determined to translate the Bible into the vernacular so that the people could read the testaments. In the 16th century Tyndale translated into English the Pentateuch (the first five books of the Old Testament). He was forced to go to Germany to get his work published, and copies were later smuggled into England.

Eventually Tyndale was tried for heresy, convicted, and burned at the stake near Brussels, Belgium.

His translations from the Bible proved popular and went through several editions. His translation from the Greek of part of the Lord's Prayer reads: "O oure father which art in heven, halowed be thy name. . . . Thy wyll be fulfilled, as well in erth, as hit ys in heven, . . . but delyure ys from yvell . . ."

TYNDALL (*tin'd'l*), **JOHN** (1820–1893). Until the appearance of John Tyndall few scientists troubled to make their discoveries understandable to the average man. Tyndall believed it ridiculous for scientists to use long and mysterious words which only they could understand. A part of his fame is the result of his efforts to explain physical science in simple terms.

Tyndall was born in County Carlow, Ireland. He attended secondary school, enlisted in the Ordnance Survey, and later went to England to study technical subjects. In 1844 he became a railway engineer and three years later an instructor in physics at Queenwood College in Hampshire.

His mind was forever reaching for more information and though without funds he determined to study in Europe. While on the Continent he met the great scientists Michael Faraday and Thomas Henry Huxley. He was thereafter constantly associated with them. He accompanied Huxley to Switzerland where they both made detailed studies of glacial movements.

Upon his return he was appointed professor of natural philosophy at the Royal Institution in London. Tyndall succeeded Faraday as superintendent of the institution and as advisor to the Board of Trade.

He made important discoveries in the fields of light and heat, improved methods of sterilization, and explained why the sky is blue. Tyndall lectured in the United States in 1872–73 giving his fees to a trust fund to benefit United States scientists.

TYPE (*tīp*). A piece of type is a small metal block which has a letter carved or molded on one end. These blocks are assembled into words, lines, and paragraphs for printing.

Movable type, that is, type in which each letter is carved on a single block, was first used by Johann Gutenberg, a German printer, about the year 1450. Before that time, it was necessary to carve a whole page upon a single block of wood. When that page had been printed the block was no longer of any use and was thrown away. Gutenberg's method of making each letter or character a separate piece made it possible to use the same letters over and over again. The type was used to print one page and was then taken out of the page printed and reset into different words to form another part of the book. The type used in making a single set of letters could thus be used over and over again.

Following the lead of Gutenberg, other printers soon began to use his method. At first the printers copied the style of letters used in the hand-written books and manuscripts. Presently, the printers began to make distinctive designs of their own. Adolph Rusch was the first to use roman type instead of the black script copied

This picture shows a type used in hand composition, with the technical names used by printers for its parts.

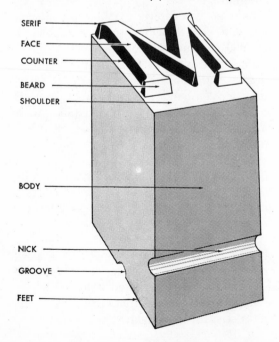

SERIF
FACE
COUNTER
BEARD
SHOULDER
BODY
NICK
GROOVE
FEET

A printer must "learn the case," that is, the arrangement of the characters in the drawer holding a font of type.

from the old manuscripts. Other printers followed, and Nicolas Jenson, a Frenchman, perfected a beautiful style of roman type about 1470. The roman face is now the most widely used style of type. It has become so common that the other types are used only to call attention to a word or sentence. Most commonly used for this purpose of lending emphasis is the type called *italic*. This light slanting face was designed first in 1501 by Aldus Manutius, one of the most famous of the early Italian printers.

From these beginnings thousands of different type faces have been designed by printers of all nations. Among the most famous designers were Ludovico Arrighi in Italy and William Caslon, an 18th-century Englishman who was the outstanding English printer of his day. Among the 20th-century designers, Frederic W. Goudy from the United States is one of the best known.

Today many new type faces are in use in addition to all the older types. A modern print shop has hundreds of these faces, each of which looks different and serves a different purpose. For example, a type such as will make a fine headline would make hard reading for the story beneath, while the type used to tell the story isn't black enough to attract attention as a head. Other types are best suited for use in advertisements where their design gets quick attention from the busy reader. Most printing plants employ expert *typographers*, men who know these many type faces. It is their work to select for each book or piece to be printed, the particular type face which will best serve the purpose. Though there are many faces of type, all English and United States type faces must conform to certain rigid standards. All presses are built to these standards, and a type which did not fit these presses would be useless.

The Parts of a Piece of Type

The important part of a piece of type is the letter which is carved on one end, and which leaves its impression on the paper. This is called the *face*. The larger piece of metal on which the face is carved is called the *body*. In all type faces this body must be exactly .918 of an inch long. This distance is *type-high* according to U.S. and British standards—the distance from the base of the body of the type to the face which touches the paper. The size of a piece of type is determined by the height of the type face, that is, the distance from the top to the bottom of the printed letter, and is measured in *points*. A point is about $\frac{1}{72}$ of an inch, since there are 72.46 points per inch. The amount of room a piece of type will take in a line depends, of course, on which letter it is. The letters "l" and "i" are very narrow and occupy little space, while "m" and "w" are much wider than these, and somewhat wider than other letters such as "c," "h," and "d." Lines of type are measured for width in *picas*. Each pica is about 12 points, or one-sixth of an inch. The printers' measure called an em varies with the size of the type. It is a square of the height of a single piece of type.

So that you may check these measurements, this book is set in 10 point face on a 12 point body. The face is called Caledonia. Each column is 17½ picas wide with one pica between columns, making the type page 36 picas wide. How deep is the type page? That is, how many picas is it from the top of the first line of printed matter at the top of the page to the bottom of the bottom line?

A Font of Type and Matrixes

A complete assortment of any one type face is called a *font*. A font usually has in it the capital letters and the small letters (called by printers, "caps and lower case") numerals, punctuation marks, all proportioned in the assortment according to the number of times each letter is used. The letter "e," for example is by far the most-used letter in the English language, so it has the largest cubbyhole in the case or box

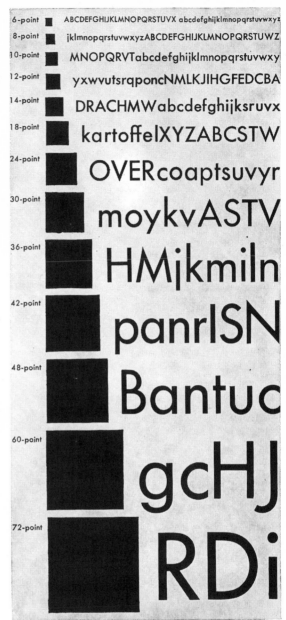

The above squares show one em of the sizes stated. The letters show the size of face made on the body.

containing the pieces of type. Other fonts sometimes contain SMALL CAPITALS, **bold face roman,** *italic,* and ***bold face italic.***

For many hundreds of years type was made by hand. Each letter was cut from a design onto a steel *punch* which was used to punch a mold, or *matrix* of the letter in copper or brass. The matrix was fastened tightly over a body mold and then molten type metal was poured in. When cool, the completed type came from the mold with the raised letter on the face of the body. Type metal is a mixture (alloy) of lead, tin, and antimony, with sometimes a little copper added. Nowadays type is made by machine in type foundries, and sold in font assortments to printers. More commonly, however, for all the ordinary styles and sizes, the larger printing houses make their own type on monotype machines when the latter are not setting "copy."

TYPESETTING (*tīp′sĕt ĭng*) **MACHINE** (*mä-shēn′*). After the invention of movable type shortly before 1450, and until late in the 19th century type was set by hand. For four centuries compositors stood before their composing frames in the print shops of the world and assembled the individual letters into words and sentences. The compositor picked out the letters from the little boxes in the case (see TYPE) with his right hand and put them into the *stick* which he held in his left hand. The stick is a

This man is setting written material in type at the keyboard of a linotype machine.

Chicago Daily News

small metal rack which can hold six or eight lines of type at a time. When it is full, the compositor has to empty it, and transfer the type from the stick to a metal tray called a *galley*. Each page of a book takes many sticks of type, so handsetting a book is a long and expensive process.

By the end of the 19th century the growth of newspapers with many daily readers and magazines with wide circulation brought the need for a faster and more economical way of setting type. The machines which today set nearly all type were invented to fill this need. The two most frequently used are the linotype and the monotype. Both came into wide use about 1900.

The Linotype

As the name indicates, the linotype sets a line of type at a time, casting the whole line on a single piece of metal, called a *slug*. The machine was invented in 1886 by Ottmar Mergenthaler, of Baltimore, Maryland. As you see in the picture, the linotype is a large machine. It is run by an operator who sits at the keyboard. This keyboard operates much like a typewriter except that it has many more keys to control the many characters which the linotype can set.

When the operator touches a letter on the keyboard, a mold, or *matrix*, of that letter falls from the magazine at the top of the machine and is carried to its place beside the other letters in the line. After each word the operator presses a key which inserts a wedge-shaped space bar between the words. When the complete line has been set, these space bars are pushed up so that the line is tight and the space between words is equal. The line of matrices is then pressed against a mold. Molten metal is forced into the mold of the letter which each matrix bears. The letters are all molded on a single slug, which then drops into a tray beside the operator. The matrices are then returned to their correct boxes in the magazine of the linotype machine by a system of notches in the ends of the matrices. These are so arranged that each letter has its own kind of notch, and can drop off the return device only when its own box is reached.

Linotype composition is the fastest kind of machine composition, and for that reason is used almost exclusively for newspaper work. Also, the fact that each line is a single piece of metal makes it easy for the compositors to assemble the galleys full of slugs into columns and pages in the paper.

An interesting development now in use with the linotype is the teletypewriter. Using this device an operator in one place may sit at his keyboard and by electricity operate a linotype machine in another building or city, or in several places at the same time. Such speedy devices as this are needed to give the rapid, up-to-the-minute news the daily papers carry.

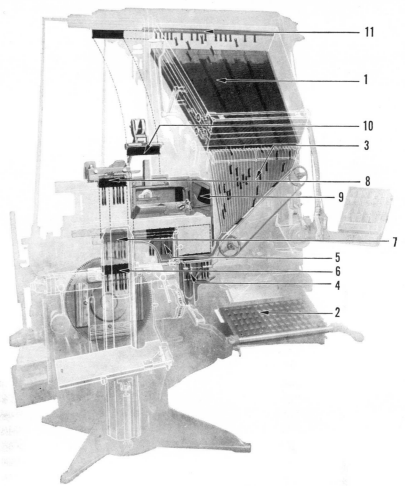

Courtesy Mergenthaler Linotype Company

This is a diagram of a linotype machine. The operator sits at the keyboard. When he touches a letter on the keyboard, a matrix (mold) of the letter falls from the magazine and is carried to its place beside the other letters in the line. (1) is the magazine carrying the type molds or matrices. (2) The keyboard. (3) Matrices dropping to the assembly belt. (4) Assembled matrices. (5) Matrices and spacebands being carried automatically to the casting mechanism. (6) Matrices and spacebands at the casting point. (7) Matrices and spacebands on way to distribution. (8) Point of separation for returning spacebands and matrices. (9) Spacebands returning to storage. (10) Matrices continuing to magazine. (11) Riding distributor bar to channels indicated by variable teeth.

The Monotype

The monotype was invented by Tolbert Lanston of Washington, D.C., in 1887. This machine casts each letter separately, and because it does not cast a slug, but rather individual pieces of type, it also casts spaces to put in the needed space between words.

Setting type by the monotype is a two-part operation. First comes the keyboarding. The operator sits at a keyboard arranged like a typewriter, but with several sets of keys on the same machine. The extra sets of keys are needed because the monotype, like the linotype, sets capitals and small letters, small capitals and numerals and each character has its own key on the keyboard. On top of the machine is a roll of paper like that on an adding machine, except that it is wider. As the operator strikes a key, a small hole is punched in the roll of paper, which moves from one spool to another as the machine is operated. The hole is punched by compressed air. Each letter has a different place on the roll in which its punch always appears. A completed roll looks very much like the rolls used on a player piano.

The roll of paper is then put into the casting machine, the second part of the monotype method. The caster contains a die case, which holds the mold for the letters and figures which the keyboard operator punched when making the roll. As the roll of paper is unrolled and passed through the machine, the holes in it control the movement of the die case, through compressed air. As the air blows through the paper, the letter corresponding to that hole is moved over the mold, and a piece of type with that letter upon it is cast and pushed out of the caster into the galley which holds the type as it is cast. The caster operates very fast, and the little die case moves and sets 140 letters a minute.

The caster can also be adjusted to make type, holding the die case in one position until a sufficient quantity of that letter has been cast. This process is continued until enough pieces of each letter have been made. When the caster is making type this way, it is said to be casting *sorts*. This is the method used by most modern print shops to make type for handset corrections and other hand composition.

Monotype composition is used in cases where a fine flexible sort of composition is wanted, or where a lot of corrections are to be expected. Corrections are made more easily than by linotype, for on the monotype a single word or letter can be inserted without difficulty, while the linotype must reset the entire line. The monotype material is also used where the makeup of a page or a book is complicated and shows very long lines, pictures to run around or unusual composition of any sort. The monotype is better adapted to this sort of makeup than the linotype slug which can not be changed by the compositor, but must be reset if it does not fit.

The Ludlow System

The Ludlow system is used principally for setting display and advertising material. For that reason it is made only in the larger sizes of type. It is only partially a machine-set method, for the compositor has to assemble the molds for the line he wishes to set in a metal rack similar to a compositor's stick. The molds are then inserted in the casting machine, and the line is cast on a single slug.

Machines set virtually all the type in modern print shops. In newspapers they even set the headlines and most of the display work in the advertisements. The hand compositor now sets only an occasional correction or two. His work nowadays is makeup, that is, taking the type from the machines and making it up into pages, putting in page numbers, and locking the pages up either for the making of plates or for the press. Far from putting compositors out of work, the typesetting machines set so much type that more and more compositors are needed to get it ready for the presses.

TYPEWRITER (*tīp′rīt′ēr*). Modern business depends greatly upon a machine that makes it possible to write with much more speed than with a pen. This machine, the typewriter, prints letters of the alphabet as keys are punched by the typist, or operator.

The actual act of typewriting is fairly simple. The main task is to learn by memory the arrangement of letters, numerals, and punctuation marks on the keyboard. This is best done by practice. Letters are arranged on the keyboard in a standard manner.

Paper is inserted in the cylinder, which is located on a carriage riding from right to left as the keyboard is operated. A roll of inked ribbon is constantly fed through a narrow space before this cylinder. Type bars containing raised impressions press against this ribbon to make an impression on the paper.

In addition to the actual printing, typewriters have other arrangements to make typing faster and more accurate. A *line space lever* is usually attached to the carriage. When pushed by the hand, it spaces the paper forward to a new line of writing and returns the carriage to the right. There usually is a *line space adjusting lever* which can be set to control the amount of white space between lines. *Margin stops* may be set so that the lines of print begin at exactly the same position on the left. A margin stop for the right permits fairly even lining-up on the right side of the paper. A *shift key* is used to type capitals. A *shift lock* can be set to hold the carriage to write all capitals.

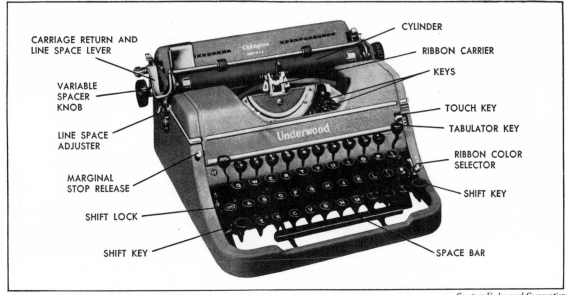

CARRIAGE RETURN AND
LINE SPACE LEVER

VARIABLE
SPACER
KNOB

LINE SPACE
ADJUSTER

MARGINAL
STOP RELEASE

SHIFT LOCK

SHIFT KEY

CYLINDER

RIBBON CARRIER

KEYS

TOUCH KEY

TABULATOR KEY

RIBBON COLOR
SELECTOR

SHIFT KEY

SPACE BAR

Courtesy Underwood Corporation

This portable typewriter has a standard keyboard. The variable spacer knob on the left side, when pulled out, permits the cylinder to be turned smoothly by hand and stopped at any point.

The *space bar* is pressed by the thumb to provide white space between words. A *back spacer* also is provided so that the typist can space back to correct material already printed in a line. Some machines carry a touch-tuning device. This device adjusts the keyboard to suit each typist's individual way of touching the keys.

Development of the Typewriter

Typewriters did not come into general use until the 20th century although a patent for such a machine was issued as long ago as 1714. This typewriter was the invention of an Englishman Henry Mill. It was never manufactured.

At first typewriters were patented as devices to aid the blind. In the United States the first typewriter was patented by William A. Burt in 1829. It was called a typographer but no example of it has survived. In 1833 a Frenchman Xavier Progin invented a machine which used type bars with a key lever for each letter.

In 1843 an American Charles Thurber patented a machine which made use of a set of type bars placed around a brass wheel. The wheel moved on a central pivot. It was brought around by hand to the letter desired, and the inked type struck directly upon the paper be-

low. Naturally, the operation was too slow to make this machine of practical value. In 1856 A. E. Beach, also of the United States, patented a typewriter. His machine made the first use of the principle of a circle of type bars making the impression upon a common center. The following year a typewriter was patented by S. W. Francis. This used a keyboard, somewhat resembling the keyboard on a pianoforte, to operate the type bars.

The first practical typewriter, and one that could be manufactured on a large scale, was the work of three U.S. inventors. They were Christopher Latham Sholes, Samuel W. Soule, and Carlos Glidden of Milwaukee, Wisconsin. Sholes, with the aid of suggestions and financial help from James Densmore, perfected his typewriter in 1873 to the point where it could be sold.

This machine contained most of the principles of the modern machine. It used a set of type bars pivoted on a horizontal ring, which was operated by levers, connected in turn by rods with the levers of the keyboard. The paper was inserted around a rubber cylinder, and the type struck an inked ribbon which registered the letter on the paper. This machine also had reversible spools for the ribbon and a moving

This model of the typewriter made by Christopher L. Sholes, Samuel W. Soule, and Carlos Glidden is in the United States Patent Office.

carriage. The carriage could be shifted back into place when the end of a line was reached.

One defect of this machine was that the cylinder was placed over the key basket. The type struck below the surface of the eyes so that the typist could not see what he was writing. At the time this was not seen as an objection. This machine used only capital letters.

Later inventions added the shift key, by means of which each bar could contain both the capital and the lower-case letter, the cylinder being raised or dropped to receive either the one or the other letter. In 1896 Franz X. Wagner patented the first successful front-stroke, visible-writing machine. It overcame the operating deficiencies of the attempts by other inventors. The introduction of this front-stroke typewriter was destined to revolutionize the entire typewriter industry.

A machine invented by James B. Hammond in 1880, and afterward improved, made it possible to substitute any sort of type desired. Thus, one machine could be used for the writing of many languages. This was made possible by using a revolving type wheel, around which could be set removable plates containing the type. The depression of the key brought the type into position. A hammer struck the paper against the type, making the desired impression.

Modern Improvements

Other improvements upon the typewriter include the portable typewriter, a compact and light machine which can be easily carried around. In the noiseless machine a weight on the back of the type makes the impression on the paper; so the noise of the type's striking the paper is eliminated. Bookkeeping machines exist which can typewrite the entry and add the totals.

Electric power has been harnessed to the typewriter to make the machine more efficient. Power application was perfected in 1920 by a Kansas City inventor James F. Smathers. Every action of the electric machine, including release of the keys, returning the carriage, shifting for capitals, line spacing, and back spacing is done by finger-tip touch. The motor does the work. It can be adjusted to provide a heavy impression, enabling the typist to prepare a large number of legible carbon copies at one typing.

The latest major development in the electric typewriter is the proportional spacing model. In this model carbon paper ribbon provides a continuous supply of fresh carbon deposit. It allows the proper amount of space to each letter according to its width, automatically compensating for small letters such as "i" and large such as "M."

Even young children can learn to use modern typewriters with success, as these second graders are doing.

Courtesy Avery Coonley School

TYPHOID (*ti'foid*) **FEVER** (*fē'vẽr*), also called enteric (or intestinal) fever, is a disease caused by the typhoid bacillus. It is a very serious disease. Death can result even with the most modern treatment. However, because of vaccination and sanitary measures, typhoid fever is now a rare disease.

The typhoid bacilli are bacteria. (See BACTERIA.) They can enter the body with food or water. The germ then settles in the small intestine, where it multiplies. About 10 to 14 days afterward, the illness begins. The patient feels tired. He has no appetite and may have a bad headache. Constipation is usually present. The fever rises by steps, getting a little higher every day until it is about 104 degrees Fahrenheit on the seventh day. At this time, rose-colored spots appear on the skin and the patient's spleen may be enlarged. The patient becomes exhausted. He loses much weight. He may become delirious (out of his senses) and unconscious.

For the next week or two the fever continues. All the symptoms may continue too. The fever gradually disappears during the last week of the illness. Meanwhile, however, serious complications may arise. The wall of the small bowel is invaded by the bacillus. It may bleed, which leads to shock. Sometimes the bowel ruptures, causing the infection to spread with very serious results.

The doctor must discover typhoid fever early in order to treat the patient quickly and to prevent the spread of the disease. At different stages of the disease the bacillus of typhoid fever can be found in the blood, urine, or feces. During the second week of the disease, tests will show antibodies that have formed in the blood to fight the bacillus.

Treatment

Many years ago, typhoid patients were placed on starvation diets. They did badly and many of them died. The modern treatment aims to support the patient's health through proper diet, the prevention and cure of complications, and the use of antibiotics.

One of the greatest advances in the treatment of typhoid fever patients was the discovery that they needed special diet and fluids. During the period of fever, fluids are given in large amounts. Also, a diet of enough calories and vitamins is given. If the patient cannot eat, the food is given either by stomach tube or through a vein. Hospitalization and skilled nursing are needed for proper care of the patient and to prevent the spreading of the disease. Doctors and nurses are necessary in order to follow every little change in the disease. These changes may come before the serious complications and will call for prompt treatment. In recent years, the antibiotic chloramphenicol has brought about swift improvement in patients with typhoid fever as well as in "carriers," persons who carry the germ. (See ANTIBIOTICS.)

Prevention

Modern sanitary science has shown the importance of preventive measures against typhoid fever as well as many other diseases. Early discovery of the disease and immediate isolation of the patient is absolutely necessary. Feces and urine are very infective. Bed clothes, eating utensils, and sometimes contact with the patient may also spread the disease. The sick person who is properly cared for is rarely the cause for large outbreaks. A person who has recovered from typhoid fever may still carry the germ in his small intestine or gall bladder. These people are called "carriers." One famous carrier, "Typhoid Mary," was a cook who, around 1900, unknowingly spread the disease to more than 50 persons.

Some carriers can be discovered by tracing the history of known cases. Many carriers can be cured by medicines or by removal of the gall bladder. Carriers should not be permitted to cook or serve food.

Since it is not always possible to discover carriers, it is important to guard against infection of food and water. Water sources and pipelines must be kept away from sewage, which can carry the germs. To insure pure water, chlorination is now practiced almost everywhere. Milk must not only be pasteurized but shipped in containers cleaned with purified water. Food handlers in stores and restaurants must be free of disease and must wash their hands thoroughly after going to the toilet. Shellfish from infected waters must not be sold. Flies may spread the disease by carrying the germs from the excreta of sick people to food and milk. Insect sprays are now helpful in controlling flies. (See INSECT.)

These methods of protection are public health measures; they protect everyone. In addition, each individual can protect himself by getting a typhoid vaccination. It is recommended for those who are in close touch with patients and those who are traveling to infected areas. This probably was the most important measure in lowering the death rate from typhoid during the World Wars I and II. By vaccination, one injects dead typhoid bacilli into the system. This starts the body's defenses by forming antibodies against typhoid without causing an actual infection. Persons who are vaccinated against typhoid are protected against the disease for two years. (See IMMUNITY AND RESISTANCE TO DISEASE.)

The battle against typhoid fever illustrates the great advances in sanitary and medical sciences. Until the turn of this century, typhoid fever and related intestinal infections were one of the great dangers to human life. During wars, more soldiers were killed by typhoid fever than by enemy troops. More than ten per cent of the United States troops in the Spanish-American War had typhoid fever and many died.

In 1856 the disease was first suspected to be contagious. In 1880 the typhoid bacillus was seen in the tissues of patients. Four years later the bacillus was isolated. During the Russo-Japanese War (1904–1905), the Japanese reduced the cases of typhoid fever by forcing troops to obey strict sanitary measures. Since 1913 the use of vaccination has made typhoid fever a rare disease.

TYPHUS (*tī'fŭs*) **FEVER** is a serious infectious disease. The germ causing the disease is smaller than bacteria and is called a *rickettsia*. It is carried from an infected to a healthy person by body lice. Because it spreads in this way, typhus fever is most common during wars and famines. If people eat poorly and live crowded together without sanitary facilities, the body louse can quickly spread the disease from person to person.

Between one or two weeks after the bite by an infected body louse, there are sudden chills, fever, and severe headache. Nose bleeds, eye soreness, and mild cough may then appear. During the first week a rash develops. Fever continues into the second week when delirium (loss of senses), unconsciousness, and finally heart failure may appear.

A doctor will suspect typhus if a person develops these symptoms and if there is any chance that he might have been bitten by body lice. The disease can be shown to be present by the antibodies that form in the patient's blood to fight the rickettsia. Skillful nursing care is needed to support the patient's health and to prevent complications that might develop. Patients must receive the right amount of fluid and proper diet. More recently the use of antibiotics has greatly improved the chances for cure of typhus.

Typhuslike epidemics have been described since the 16th century. However, typhus fever was not clearly shown to be different from typhoid fever until 1837. Some of the symptoms and even much of the modern treatment are the same for both diseases. (See TYPHOID FEVER.)

Typhus fever and malaria are probably the world's most serious infectious diseases. Malaria is being controlled by draining swamps, by killing mosquitoes with such sprays as DDT, and by the use of various new drugs. (See MALARIA.)

The spread of typhus fever now can be controlled by isolating the sick, by vaccinations, and by delousing. Delousing means cleaning and then spraying exposed people with DDT. (See INSECT.)

During World War II, great numbers of refugees, prisoners of war, and exposed military personnel were deloused. Cases of typhus were probably fewer than in any other war. There is no vaccine as yet that gives complete protection. However, there is much less risk of death for people who have been recently vaccinated. (See IMMUNITY AND RESISTANCE TO DISEASE.)

UGANDA (*ū gǎn'dä* or *ōō gän'dä*), **AFRICA,** is a country in the eastern part of the continent. The total area of Uganda is 91,076 square miles, of which 16,386 are inland water and swamp. It is bordered on the north by Sudan; on the east by Kenya; on the south by Tanzania and Rwanda; and on the west by the Democratic Republic of the Congo. The Equator crosses southern Uganda.

Most of Uganda is a plateau about 4,000 to 5,000 feet above sea level. Rising high above the plateau in the southwest is the beautiful Ruwenzori mountain range (sometimes called the Mountains of the Moon). Several peaks in the Ruwenzori are snow capped. The highest is Margherita Peak with an elevation of 16,763 feet. Another highland area lies along Uganda's eastern border and includes Mount Elgon (14,-178 feet). A branch of the Great Rift Valley crosses western Uganda from north to south. This long and deep valley extends almost continuously from southwestern Asia through eastern Africa to Mozambique.

Although Uganda is a landlocked country, it has many miles of shoreline on three large lakes—Victoria, Albert, and Edward. Lake Victoria, Africa's largest lake, is on the border between Uganda, Kenya, and Tanzania—each of which controls a part of it. Lakes Albert and Edward are in the Great Rift Valley. Another major lake, Kyoga (or Kioga), is in central

Uganda and is surrounded by swampy land. All four lakes are linked together by rivers. The Victoria Nile River flows north and west from Lake Victoria to Lake Albert. The Albert Nile flows north to Sudan. The Semliki River, near the western border, flows from Lake Edward to Lake Albert. This series of connected lakes and rivers is a part of the great Nile River system. Owen Falls Dam, on the Victoria Nile near Jinja, is important as a source of electric power and for controlling the flow of water to Sudan and the U.A.R. (Egypt). (See NILE RIVER, AFRICA.)

Temperatures in most of Uganda are high throughout the year. At the city of Entebbe, on the northern shore of Lake Victoria, the average temperature for January, the hottest month, is 73 degrees Fahrenheit. July, the coolest month, averages 70 degrees. Temperatures are lower in the highland regions. Rainfall is generally heavy in the south, and decreases toward the north. On the average, however, most of Uganda receives from 40 to 60 inches a year. Most of the rain falls during two wet seasons: March to May and September to November. Vegetation ranges from tropical rain forests in the wet areas to grasslands in the dry areas.

There are many wild animals in Uganda. Thousands of elephants and hippopotamuses are found in the area near Lake Albert. Other animals include crocodiles, rhinoceroses, giraffes, chimpanzees, monkeys, lions, leopards, antelopes, and many varieties of birds. The tsetse fly, an insect that carries sleeping sickness, is a problem in the lowlands and swampy areas.

Copper, the chief mineral resource of Uganda, is mined at Kilembe in the foothills of the Ruwenzori. Many other mineral deposits have been discovered, but only phosphate rock, lime, and salt are produced in large amounts. Uganda's forests produce mahogany, teak, and bamboo.

Most of the people of Uganda are Negroid. A number of languages are spoken, but Luganda and Bantu with its related languages are the most widely used. The Ugandans live chiefly in small villages. Kampala, Uganda's capital and chief center of commerce and

Uganda (in black) and neighboring countries.

U

education, has a population of 76,597 (1965 estimate). Jinja, Uganda's second largest town and an industrial center, lies east of Kampala.

Most of the people are farmers. They grow corn, peas, beans, sweet potatoes, bananas, nuts, and cassavas—mainly for their own use. They also raise livestock. Commercial crops include cotton, coffee, tea, sugarcane, and tobacco. Coffee and cotton, along with copper, are the chief exports.

Camera Press—Pix from Publix

The Owen Falls Dam was opened on the Nile River in 1954. It produces electric power for Uganda and Kenya and stores water for Sudan and Egypt.

Manufacturing in Uganda is mainly connected with the processing of farm products. There are a number of cotton ginneries; tea-, tobacco-, and coffee-processing plants; and sugar refineries. Other industries include metalworking, cement manufacturing, furniture and textile making, copper smelting, brewing, and fishing.

Transportation facilities are not well developed in Uganda. The one main railroad extends from Kampala to the eastern border where it links with the Kenya rail system. The bulk of Uganda's exports are sent by rail to the seaport of Mombasa in Kenya. Several spur lines extend northward, and one westward to Kilembe. Except in the area near Lake Victoria, many of the roads are not usable during the rainy seasons. An airport in Entebbe handles international flights. Small steamers maintain transportation service on Lakes Victoria, Albert, and Kyoga.

Arabian traders visited the region in the 1840's, and British explorers reached the area in 1862. Missionaries from England worked in Uganda during the late 1870's but were forced to leave in 1882. In 1888 the British government gave the Imperial British East Africa Company the right to administer and trade in Uganda.

Much of Uganda became a British protectorate in 1894. Until March 1962 Uganda's government was largely controlled by an appointed British governor. After that it was controlled by a prime minister, a cabinet, and an elected National Assembly. In October 1962, Uganda became a fully independent country with membership in the Commonwealth of Nations. The capital was moved from Entebbe to Kampala. The population of Uganda is 7,934,000 (1967 estimate).

UKRAINIAN (*ū krān'ĭ ăn*) **SOVIET SOCIALIST REPUBLIC, U.S.S.R.,** is the third largest republic in the Soviet Union. It has an area of 232,046 square miles. On the southwest it is bordered by the Moldavian S.S.R.; on the west by Rumania, Hungary, Czechoslovakia, and Poland; on the north by the Belorussian (White Russian) S.S.R.; and on the northeast and east by the Russian S.F.S.R. The Ukraine is in the agricultural area of western U.S.S.R. that borders the northern shores of the Black Sea and the Sea of Azov.

Most of the Ukraine is a flat to gentle rolling steppe lowland. A line of low hills crosses the republic from northwest to southeast. Elevations seldom reach more than 1,000 feet above sea level except in the foothills of the Carpathian Mountains in the far western part and the Donets Ridge in the far eastern part. The northwestern corner of the Ukraine is low and swampy. The chief river is the Dnieper, which flows in a general north-south direction across the Ukraine into the Black Sea.

Winters in the Ukraine are cold. Summers are warm and sometimes very hot in the south. Rainfall is generally light. It ranges from 12 inches a year in the south and east to about 24 inches in the northwest. About ten per cent of the Ukraine—chiefly in the northwest and in the hilly areas—is covered with birch, beech, maple, larch, and ash forests. Most of the Republic, however, is grassy, treeless plains.

The Ukraine is a major Soviet agricultural and industrial area. Many of the farms have been collectivized. Farm machinery is widely used, but horse-drawn wagons and hand labor are still common. Ukrainian farmers produce large amounts of bread grains—wheat, rye, oats, and barley. The republic, therefore, sometimes is called the "bread basket of the Soviet Union." The farmers also cultivate sugar beets, corn, fruits, and vineyards. Livestock raising—cattle, pigs, sheep, and goats—is of major importance.

The Ukraine is rich in iron ore, coal, manganese, and oil. Huge dams at Dnepropetrovsk, Zaporozhe, and other sites on the Dnieper River provide hydroelectric power. Because of rich deposits of iron ore at Krivoi Rog and of coal in the Donets Basin, a steel industry has grown up. The republic produces about 40 per cent of the Soviet Union's steel, 33 per cent of its coal, and 57 per cent of its iron ore. Ukrainian factories turn out one-fifth of the Soviet Union's machinery and chemicals. The Ukraine also has an important tourist industry. People from all over the Soviet Union spend their vacations at the many resorts along the Black Sea.

The Ukraine is one of the most densely populated republics of the U.S.S.R. About one-fifth of the Soviet population lives in the republic. The Ukrainians are a Slavic people. About 76 per cent of them are of Ukrainian nationality; 18 per cent Russian; and the remainder, various other national groups, including Belorussians, Poles, and Moldavians. The Ukrainian language

Locator map of the Ukrainian Soviet Socialist Republic.

is similar to the Russian language, but also resembles the Slovak and Bulgarian languages. Many of the people of the Ukraine belong to the Russian Orthodox Church. There are also large groups of Jews and Roman Catholics.

All of the largest cities of the Ukraine are important Soviet industrial centers. The capital of the republic is Kiev. Other major cities are Kharkov, Donetsk, Dnepropetrovsk, Lvov, Zaporozhe, Krivoi Rog, and Odessa. (See KHARKOV; KIEV; ODESSA.)

About 2,000 years ago, Slavic tribal peoples moved eastward from the area north of the Carpathians into the Ukraine. Attacks by Turkic horsemen from central Asia caused the Slavic peoples to move northward into the forest. There, they organized their first state, which was centered at Kiev, and named it Kievan Rus. (See KIEV.) It lasted from the 9th to the 13th century. During this time the Slavic peoples came in contact with the great trading center of Constantinople and adopted Eastern Orthodox Christianity.

In the 13th century the Tatars (a Turkic people of Mongolia) completely overran the Ukraine and destroyed the Kievan Rus. In the 14th and 15th centuries a new Russian state, centered at Moscow, grew up deep in the northern forests. It was not able, however, to extend its authority over the southern grasslands for many centuries. The southernmost part of the

Ukraine remained under Tatar, or Turkic, control until the end of the 18th century. The northern and western parts of the Ukraine were taken over by Lithuania (later the joint kingdom of Poland and Lithuania) from the middle of the 14th century to the end of the 18th century. During this long period a separate Ukrainian nationality developed that was different from that of Russia.

Led by a group of Ukrainian patriots known as the Cossacks, the Ukrainians revolted against Polish rule several times. They asked the Russians for help, and in the 17th century the Cossacks freed much of the Ukraine and set up a Cossack state. Gradually, however, the growing Russian state took control of the Ukraine. In 1654 the Cossack state entered a union with Russia. The area to the west of the Dnieper River was taken over by the Russians in the 1790's, as well as the Turkic area in the southernmost part of the Ukraine.

During the 19th and early 20th centuries a Ukrainian nationalist movement developed, but the Ukrainians never succeeded in breaking with Russia. During the Russian Revolution (1917–1918) a democratic Ukrainian state was declared, but this declaration was not recognized by the Russian Communists. The Ukraine was the scene of fierce struggles in the next few years. Finally, in 1922, the Ukrainian S.S.R. officially joined the Union of Soviet Socialist Republics. Since 1939 the area of the Ukraine has been increased by the addition of parts of Poland and Rumania. In 1954 the Crimean Peninsula was added to the Ukraine. Since 1945 the Ukrainian Soviet Socialist Republic has held a seat in the United Nations, although it is not an independent nation.

The population of the Ukrainian S.S.R. in 1970 was 47,136,000.

ULAN (ōō'län) **BATOR** (bä'tôr), **MONGOLIAN PEOPLE'S REPUBLIC,** is the capital and largest city of the country. It is located on the Tola River, which cuts through a high, windswept plain that is almost enclosed by mountains. The city has grown rapidly since Mongolia's independence, and construction has been unable to keep up with the expanding population. As a result, many residents still live in traditional round, domed, felt tents called *yurts*. In sharp contrast are the city's white or pastel-colored modern apartment buildings. Many of these are supplied with heat and hot water by the city's central power plant. The buildings are seldom built higher than four stories because Ulan Bator is located in an earthquake zone.

The climate of Ulan Bator is quite severe in winter, when temperatures drop as low as 50 degrees Fahrenheit below zero. Summer temperatures, however, may reach 80 degrees above. Ulan Bator lies at an elevation of about 4,300 feet above sea level.

The city is the Mongolian Republic's center of commerce and culture. It dates from the mid-17th century when the Da Khure Monastery was established. A trading center serving Russia and China soon grew up around the monastery. The Russians called the town Urga. In 1911 it became the capital of Outer Mongolia (now the Mongolian People's Republic). In 1924 Urga was renamed Ulan Bator (Red Hero) in honor of Sukhe-Bator, leader of the Mongolian revolution. Sukhe-Bator is further honored by a large statue and by the central city square, which is named for him.

Sukhe-Bator and Choibalsan, the other major builder of Mongolian independence, are buried in a mausoleum fronting on the square. A large government building, the National Theater, and the Hotel Altai are also on the square. Cultural institutions in Ulan Bator include a university, a medical school, the Academy of Sciences, and the Gandan Monastery. A large department store was completed in time for the celebration of Mongolia's 40th independence day in 1961. Industry, located mainly on the outskirts, includes a large flour mill, a tannery, a boot and shoe factory, a large, modern textile mill, a printing plant, a glass factory, and a prefabricated-housing plant.

Ulan Bator has had rail connections with the Trans-Siberian trunk line since 1949 and with Peking since 1956. Roads connect the city with the U.S.S.R., China, and various towns in Mongolia. Ulan Bator also has an international airport. The city has an estimated population of 262,600 (1969).

U.S.S.R.

UNION OF SOVIET (sō'vǐ ĕt) **SOCIALIST RE-PUBLICS, EURASIA,** is the largest and one of the most powerful countries of the world. It has vast resources and enormous manpower. The Soviet economy is rich and diverse; its industrial and agricultural production are second only to the United States. The Union of Soviet Socialist Republics (U.S.S.R.) was the first country to have a communist government. It has been a leading communist force in world affairs in the 20th century. The United States and the U.S.S.R. have clashed many times over world issues during the years following World War II.

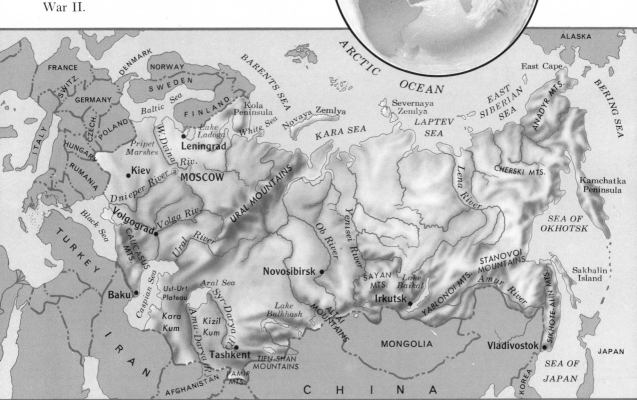

The U.S.S.R. has the largest area of any country of the world. It covers one-sixth of the land surface of the earth. This huge country sprawls over eastern Europe and northern Asia, extending almost 6,000 miles from the Polish border eastward to the Diomede Islands in the Bering Strait. The boundaries of the U.S.S.R. total more than 35,000 miles in length. One-third of this length is made up of land boundaries. The remainder is coastline. In Europe this vast area borders on Norway, Finland, the Baltic Sea, Poland, Czechoslovakia, Hungary, Rumania, and the Black Sea. In Asia it is bordered by Turkey, Iran, Afghanistan, China, Mongolia, and North Korea. Of all these countries, only Norway, Finland, Turkey, Iran, and Afghanistan are noncommunist countries. The Arctic Ocean forms the entire northern coast. Across the Arctic Ocean and the North Pole lies the North American continent. The eastern

State emblem of the U.S.S.R.

coast of the U.S.S.R. faces the Pacific Ocean. In the Bering Strait only about 2½ miles separate the Soviet Big Diomede (Ratmanov) Island from the U.S. Little Diomede Island.

The Soviet Union was formerly known as the Russian Empire, or simply Russia. In March 1917 the czar (emperor) was forced to abdicate in favor of a provisional government, which established a republic. By November 1917 Bolshevik (Communist) members of the European socialist movement took control of the principal soviets (councils) of workers' and soldiers' deputies, and then overthrew the provisional government. Shortly thereafter, separate soviet socialist republics were established in the Russian, Ukrainian, Belorussian, and Transcaucasian regions. On December 30, 1922, these four republics were united into the Union of Soviet Socialist Republics. By incorporating additional republics since 1922, the union has increased to its present total of 15 republics. Though the country often is still called Russia or Soviet Russia, the more correct short forms of its official name are the Soviet Union or the U.S.S.R.

The official state emblem of the Soviet Union has a crossed hammer and sickle against a globe that is illuminated by the rays of the sun and surrounded by stalks of grain. The Soviet motto "Workers of All Countries, Unite!" is repeated 15 times on the emblem in the various languages of the 15 union republics. Over the globe is a five-pointed red star. The state emblem symbolizes the Soviet policy of spreading communism throughout the world. The Russian bear is popular in the West as a symbol for the Soviet Union.

The Soviet Union is so big that it includes almost every type of landscape and climate. In the north there are arctic wastelands, where the frozen ground produces little vegetation. Great fields of grain grow on the country's vast fertile plains, called steppes. In the south are sandy desert wastelands that cover thousands of square miles. Near the Black Sea are subtropical regions that produce citrus fruits and grapes. The longest river of Europe, the Volga, flows through the Soviet Union. Among the country's many lakes is the Caspian Sea, the world's largest lake, and Lake Baikal, the world's deepest. The land is also broken by great mountain ranges such as the Urals, the Caucasus, and the Pamirs.

Since 1928 the Soviet Union has been transformed from a backward agricultural land into a powerful industrial country. Once known only for its grains and furs, the present-day Soviet Union has achieved prominence as the first country to launch an artificial satellite and the first country to put a man in space. The U.S.S.R. now works with great energy to increase its power and influence in the world.

I. Landscape

One of the most significant features of the U.S.S.R. is the sheer size of its land. Its area —almost 8,650,000 square miles—is more than two times that of the United States. In fact, the U.S.S.R. is nearly as large as the whole of North America. In an east-west direction the country spans over 170 degrees of longitude. There are 11 time zones within the country, compared with 7 in the continental United States, including 3 in Alaska. When it is 8 P.M. in Moscow it is 6 A.M. the next morning on the eastern tip of Siberia. The trip from the country's southernmost point at the Afghan border to its northernmost mainland point at Cape Chelyuskin covers more than 3,000 miles. This is nearly half the distance from the Equator to the North Pole. These vast distances have made communications a problem in the Soviet Union. On the other hand, the natural resources and variety of climates contained within the huge area give the country many advantages.

The Soviet landscape is rather flat and rimmed with mountains on the south and east. The Urals, a low north-south mountain chain, are centrally located. The country's highest point, Communism Peak in the Pamir Mountains, reaches an elevation of 24,590 feet. By contrast, elevations drop to 433 feet below sea level in the Karagiye Depression on the eastern shore of the Caspian Sea. According to its physical characteristics, the land can be divided into five major regions. These are the East European Plain, the West Siberian Plain, the Central Siberian Plateau, the Eastern Siberian Ranges, and the Southern Mountains.

The East European Plain forms almost all of the European U.S.S.R. It is a rolling lowland that rarely exceeds 1,000 feet in elevation. The southern part of the plain is quite flat except

FACTS ABOUT THE U.S.S.R.

CAPITAL: Moscow. NATIONAL ANTHEM: *"Gosudarstvenny Gimn Sovetskogo Soyusa"* ("National Anthem of the Soviet Union").

PHYSICAL

AREA: 8,649,489 square miles.

POPULATION (1970 census): 241,748,000; 28 persons per square mile; 56 per cent urban, 44 per cent rural.

MOUNTAIN RANGES: Altai, Caucasus, Cherski, Pamir, Tien Shan, Ural.

HIGHEST MOUNTAIN PEAKS (height in feet): Communism (24,590), Victory (Pobeda) (24,406), Lenin (23,405), Khan-Tengri (22,949), Revolution (22,880), Karl Marx (22,067), Elbrus (18,481).

LARGEST LAKES (area in square miles): Caspian Sea (152,239), Aral Sea (25,659), Baikal (12,162), Balkhash (7,115), Ladoga (7,100).

MOST IMPORTANT RIVERS: Amu-Darya, Amur, Dnieper, Dniester, Don, Donets, Lena, Northern Dvina, Ob, Pechora, Ural, Volga, Western Dvina, Yenisei.

PLACES OF INTEREST: Red Square; the Kremlin; Lenin's tomb; Moscow University; various museums and theaters in Moscow; the Winter Palace and other historical sites of Leningrad; Odessa, Yalta, and other resort cities along the coast of the Black Sea; Kiev; Volga-Don Canal; collective farms; ancient cities of Samarkand and Bokhara.

GOVERNMENT

FORM OF GOVERNMENT: Federal Soviet Republic.

HEAD OF GOVERNMENT: Chairman of Council of Ministers (Premier).

CHIEF OF STATE: Chairman of the Presidium of the Supreme Soviet.

LEGISLATURE: Consists of two houses: the Council of the Union and the Council of Nationalities.

VOTING QUALIFICATIONS: All citizens age 18 and over may vote.

POLITICAL DIVISIONS: Fifteen union republics.

NATIONAL HOLIDAYS: New Year's Day (January 1), International Labor days (May 1 and 2), Anniversary of the October Revolution (November 7 and 8), the U.S.S.R. Constitution Day (December 5).

FLAG: See FLAG, *Plate 9.*

TRANSPORTATION AND COMMUNICATION

RAILROADS: 83,015 miles.

ROADS (SURFACED): 283,593 miles.

TELEPHONES: 9,900,000.

RADIOS: 88,000,000.

TELEVISION SETS: 27,000,000

PEOPLE

CHIEF CITIES (1970 census—metropolitan population): Moscow (7,061,000); Leningrad (3,950,000); Kiev (1,632,000); Tashkent (1,385,000); Baku (1,261,000); Kharkov (1,223,000); Gorki (1,170,000); Novosibirsk (1,161,000); Kuibyshev (1,047,000); Sverdlovsk (1,026,000); Minsk (916,000).

CHURCH MEMBERSHIP: No official figures.

OFFICIAL LANGUAGE: Russian.

LEADING UNIVERSITIES: Moscow University, Leningrad State University, Tbilisi State University, Kharkov State University.

IMPORTANT MUSEUMS: In Moscow—Museum of the Revolution (history), Historical Museum, Tretyakov Gallery (Russian art), Armoury Museum in the Kremlin (royal treasures); in Leningrad—the Hermitage (art of all periods and cultures), Russian Museum (Russian art).

ECONOMY

MONETARY UNIT: Ruble; about .90 ruble equals 1 U.S. dollar.

LEADING INDUSTRIES: Agriculture, mining, and manufacturing.

CHIEF MANUFACTURED PRODUCTS: Iron and steel, machinery, chemicals, textiles.

CHIEF AGRICULTURAL PRODUCTS: Barley, corn, cotton, flax, oats, potatoes, rye, sugar beets, wheat.

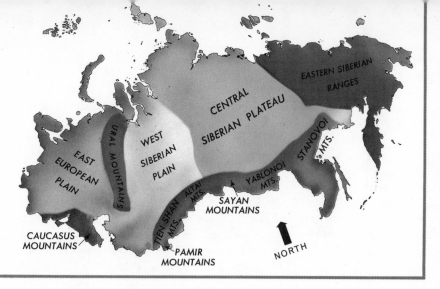

The vast land area of the Soviet Union includes a variety of land formations. The flat East European and West Siberian plains, separated by the Ural Mountains, are sometimes considered one great region. Farther east is the rugged Central Siberian Plateau, which borders the Eastern Siberian Ranges. High southern mountains form an almost continuous barrier between the U.S.S.R. and its neighbors to the south.

where streams have carved deep ravines into the surface. The Carpathian, Crimean, and Caucasus mountains rim this plain on the southwest and south. The long, low chain of the Ural Mountains separates the East European Plain from the West Siberian Plain to the east. The Siberian Plain is in Asia, so this range also separates Europe and Asia. For the most part the Urals are rounded and gently sloping. Unlike the southwestern and southern ranges, however, they form only a slight transportation barrier.

The West Siberian Plain stretches for more than 1,000 miles from the eastern slopes of the Ural Mountains to the Yenisei River. This lowland is probably the largest continuous flat area on earth. The central part is occupied by extensive bogs and marshes. A dry plain, crossed by the Trans-Siberian Railroad, makes up the southern part of the lowland. The plain is interrupted by a series of rolling hills in the Kazakh S.S.R. It then extends southward and merges with the desert areas of the southwestern Asiatic U.S.S.R.

The Central Siberian Plateau spreads out east of the West Siberian Plain and is bounded by the Yenisei and Lena rivers. The elevation of the plateau averages between 1,500 and 2,500 feet above sea level. Maximum elevations, however, rarely exceed 3,000 feet. The surface of the plateau is cut by valleys of rivers and streams.

The Eastern Siberian Ranges, in the north, stretch as much as 1,750 miles from the Lena River valley to the Bering Strait. This region is composed of mountain ranges averaging about 6,000 to 8,000 feet high, which are separated by plateaus and lowlands. The most extensive of the lowlands are found along the Indigirka and Kolyma rivers. Eastern Siberia is the least explored part of the mainland of the U.S.S.R., and available maps of the region are still being corrected. Volcanoes, many still active, are characteristic of the ranges on the Kamchatka Peninsula and on the Kurile Islands.

The Southern Mountains include ranges and plateaus that extend along the southern border of the Soviet Union from the western Ukraine to the Pacific Coast. There the region joins the Eastern Siberian Ranges. In the western Ukraine, the Carpathian Mountains reach heights of more than 6,000 feet but are rather easily crossed by roads. The Crimean Mountains also are comparatively low, the highest elevation being 5,069 feet. The northern slopes are gentle. The southern slopes, however, form an almost vertical wall that towers over the Black Sea. The Caucasus Mountains actually consist of two parallel chains that extend from the Black Sea to the Caspian Sea. The northern chain, the Greater Caucasus, reaches a height of more than 18,000 feet at the peak of Mount Elbrus, the highest point in Europe. This range is particularly rugged, but it is now crossed by several highways. The Lesser Caucasus Range, to the south, is much lower than the Greater Caucasus. (See CAUCASUS MOUNTAINS.)

East of the Caspian Sea, the Southern Mountains continue, with only minor interruptions, to the Pacific Ocean. Among the important ranges

are the Pamir, Tien Shan, Altai, Sayan, Yablo-
noi (Yablonovy), and Stanovoi. The greatest
heights are in the Pamir and Tien Shan systems,
where the two tallest Soviet peaks are located.
These are Communism Peak, 24,590 feet high,
in the Pamirs, and Pobeda (Victory) Peak, 24,-
406 feet high, in Tien Shan. Near Communism Peak is the Fedchenko Glacier, one of the
world's largest valley glaciers. This stream of
slowly moving ice is nearly 45 miles long.

II. Rivers, Lakes, and Seas

Throughout the history of the Soviet Union,
rivers and lakes have provided principal routes
for transportation and expansion. Even today,
water routes are important despite the availability of railroads, roads, and airplanes. Most
of the major rivers of the European U.S.S.R.
rise in the Valdai Hills, northwest of Moscow,
and radiate outward to various bordering seas.
From this upland the Western Dvina flows into
the Baltic Sea, the Dnieper into the Black Sea,
and the Volga, the longest river of Europe, into
the Caspian Sea. Another major river, the Don,
flows into the Sea of Azov. All of these rivers
are used extensively for transportation. A system of canals permits travel from Moscow to
any of the bordering seas. The Volga River system accounts for the greatest volume of freight.
It carries about half of the Soviet cargo that is
transported by rivercraft.

The river network of the Asiatic U.S.S.R. also
is extensive. It includes the Ob, Yenisei, and
Lena, all of which rank among the world's longest rivers. Unfortunately, for transportation
purposes, all three flow in the wrong direction.
That is, they flow northward into the seas of the
Arctic Ocean, where their mouths are blocked
by ice for most of the year. The Amur is the
only important river emptying into Pacific waters. For much of its course it marks the boundary between the Soviet Union and China. In
Soviet Central Asia, the Amu-Darya and the
Syr-Darya provide life-giving irrigation water
to the desert. Both rivers flow into the landlocked Aral Sea.

There are more than 250,000 lakes in the
Soviet Union. Two of the largest lakes, the
Caspian and the Aral, are called seas. Both of
them have salt water like the oceans. The Caspian Sea is surrounded by Soviet Union territory,
except for the southern end, which borders on
Iran. The Caspian is significant for fishing and
shipping. On the eastern Caspian shore, a large,
shallow gulf, the Kara-Bogaz-Gol, provides
various salts, including Glauber's salt. By the
mid-20th century, however, the Caspian's falling water level had considerably reduced its
commercial activities. The Caspian's surface in
the 1960's was more than 90 feet below sea
level. (See CASPIAN SEA.)

The Aral Sea, located in the desert land of
Soviet Central Asia, is also an important fish
supplier. Farther east is Lake Balkhash, which
has salt water on its eastern side, but is mainly
fresh in its western reaches. In the mountains
of southern Siberia is Lake Baikal, the deepest
lake in the world. It is 5,715 feet deep. The
northwestern part of the U.S.S.R. has many
freshwater lakes. Ladoga is Europe's largest
lake, and Onega, the next largest. These two
lakes form links in a canal system that connects
the Baltic and White seas. A number of artificial lakes, or reservoirs, also have been developed by damming, especially along the Volga.

The seas bordering the U.S.S.R. are of limited
importance because most of the extensive coastline is icebound for long periods each year.
Along the entire Arctic coastline only the western strip around Murmansk is open to shipping
the year around. The warming effect of the
Gulf Stream makes this possible. On the Pacific
Coast, only the Vladivostok area is kept open
throughout the winter. The chief seaports are
located along the Black and Baltic seas. All of
the seas are extensively used for fishing during
the ice-free periods of the year.

III. Plant and Animal Life

The Soviet Union has a great variety of plant
and animal life. This is because the country
covers such an enormous area that it includes
many types of climate and terrain. Plant and
animal life can be roughly classified according
to six zones, which vary in climate. From north
to south these zones are tundra, forest, steppes,
desert and semidesert, mountains, and subtropics.

During the tundra's short summer season, when the surface thaws and mosses and lichens grow, hunters search for fowl.

The Tundra is the narrow, treeless belt along the shore of the Arctic Ocean. It is characterized by long, severe winters and short summers of about two or three months. Precipitation is sparse, and because of low temperatures and low evaporation rates the ground remains snow-covered throughout the long winter. It is in this zone that the purga, a violent blizzard, occurs frequently. In summer many short-lived Arctic flowers bloom as the surface thaws. The subsoil, however, never thaws. Mosses and lichens abound in the zone, but it is generally too cold for tree growth. Only scattered dwarf willow and birch trees grow there. Soils are poor, marshy, and of no agricultural value. Typical wild animals include the lemming, arctic fox, arctic hare, ptarmigan, and snowy owl. In summer, flocks of geese and ducks visit the area and mosquitoes breed there in large swarms.

The Forest. Directly south of the tundra is a broad forest belt that extends to the East Siberian Ranges. This belt, which covers nearly half of the Soviet Union, provides a huge storehouse of valuable timber. Summers also are short there, but daytime temperatures become considerably higher than in the tundra. Precipitation is also more abundant, especially in the west. The trees are principally evergreens—including spruce, pine, and fir in the west, and larch, fir, and pine in the east. In the southern European forests, however, the evergreens are mixed with deciduous trees, such as birch, oak, ash, maple, and hornbeam. Moscow is located in this mixed forest belt. With the use of

fertilizers, soils in the southern part of the forest zone produce hardy crops, such as rye, oats, barley, wheat, flax, and potatoes. The belt also includes meadowland for cattle raising. Large areas of marshes and bogs within the forest zone remain largely unused because drainage operations are too costly. Animals of the forest include the bear, wolf, fox, elk, deer, lynx, hare, and the squirrel and other rodents. The Siberian forests are the chief source of Soviet furs.

The Steppes, or plains, run continuously from the Carpathian Mountains as far as the Altai and Sayan mountains. They then reappear to the east, even beyond Lake Baikal, in scattered patches. The steppes are warmer and drier than the forest zone. The small amount of annual precipitation—about 12 to 18 inches—is insufficient for tree growth. The winter snow cover is shallow and of short duration. Under the natural cover of grass is the famous chernozem (black soil), which resembles the soil of the North American prairies. This fertile land is ideal for agriculture. Today the Ukranian steppe is the principal granary of the U.S.S.R. It is sometimes called the "breadbasket of the Soviet Union."

Practically all of the steppes have been cultivated for years. However, some drier steppe soils east of the Urals were not used because of frequent droughts. In the mid-20th century the Soviet government began a program to cultivate these dry lands. In the first few years of the campaign, yields were good. Later yields, however, were rather poor. Natural animal life in the densely populated steppe zone is sparse. It consists for the most part of small rodents, such as ground squirrels, jerboas, voles, hamsters, and shrews.

The Desert and Semidesert occupies the area from about the bend of the Volga River at Volgograd to the foot of the mountains of Soviet Central Asia. Where precipitation falls below ten inches a year the steppe becomes semidesert. This becomes true desert where the precipitation is less than six inches a year. The greatest rainfall usually comes in the spring when a short-lived cover of grasses and flowers develops. It disappears as temperatures rise. Summers are hot and almost rainless. During most of the year, the ground has only a sparse cover of herbs and shrubs. In places it is completely bare, covered only by sand, clay, stones, or salt.

The semidesert soils are generally a light chestnut color. Desert soils, on the other hand, are gray and often have a high salt content. Irrigation has partially transformed desert areas along the major Central Asian rivers into fertile oases. There, excellent cotton and grapes and other fruits are produced. Desert wildlife includes ground squirrels, jerboas, snakes, tortoises, and lizards.

The Mountains. The southern mountain fringe is complex and distinctive because it has, to a large extent, plants, animals, and soils similar to the other zones. This is because of its extremes of altitude. It is possible, for example, to go from the desert at the base of a mountain to tundra at its summit.

The Subtropics are in a small zone. The zone is restricted to unconnected lowlands adjoining the Black and Caspian seas and south of the Caucasus Mountains in Transcaucasia. Because the Caucasus Mountains shelter these areas from cold, arctic air masses, the winters are moderate or even mild. Rainfall is heavy, sometimes measuring up to 120 inches a year on the Black Sea coast. Natural vegetation grows profusely and without interruption throughout the year. The trees are mainly deciduous types, such as oak and hornbeam, but also include a variety of evergreens. Tea and citrus fruits are distinctive crops of these subtropical areas. Animal life includes various types of deer and rodents.

IV. Climate

Most regions of the Soviet Union have a harsh climate. Exceptions include the subtropical areas along the Black and Caspian seas and some Pacific coastal areas. In most places winters are long and cold and summers are short and warm. Two major factors dominate climatic conditions. These are the land's northern location and its great distance from the moderating influence of the Atlantic Ocean. Most of the Soviet Union lies north of the United States (except Alaska). Moscow is about as far north as Kodiak, Alaska, and Odessa, on the Black Sea, is about the same distance north as Quebec, Quebec. Warm, moisture-bearing winds from the Atlantic Ocean must travel about 500 miles to reach the closest borders of the European U.S.S.R. To reach the interior of Siberia they must travel several thousand miles.

Great temperature ranges are characteristic of the country. January temperatures average from 23 degrees Fahrenheit in the border areas nearest the Atlantic to 58 degrees below zero in eastern Siberia. At Verkhoyansk and Oymyakon (Oimekon) in eastern Siberia, temperatures colder than 90 degrees below zero have been recorded. These are the coldest inhabited places in the world. In July, temperatures average between 60 and 70 degrees across most of the country. The average drops to about 40 degrees along the Arctic shores, and rises to about 86 degrees in Soviet Central Asia. A high of 122 degrees has been recorded in the desert region.

The wettest area is the Black Sea coast, where 80 to 120 inches of rain falls during the year. There are two dry areas where rainfall averages less than eight inches a year. These are the hot deserts of the southern U.S.S.R. in Asia and the cold desert of eastern Siberia. Precipitation over the greater part of the country averages between 12 and 24 inches, of which 25 to 30 per cent is snow. Along the shores of the Black and Caspian seas a snow cover is either completely absent or lasts up to about 20 days a year. But along the Arctic Coast, snow remains for more than 260 days each year. The depth of snow ranges from none in the south to an average of more than 36 inches along the Yenisei River.

The weather pattern at Moscow is typical of most of the settled areas of the European and Asiatic U.S.S.R. Snow begins to fall in October and covers the ground in November; then the rivers freeze over. During December, January, and February, the average daily temperature is about 14 to 18 degrees Fahrenheit. Northern and eastern winds may bring cold waves, however, during which temperatures drop as low as 20 to 30 degrees below zero. The snow is 15 to 20 inches deep by late January or early February.

Spring is a short season. It begins early in April and is accompanied by abruptly rising temperatures. As precipitation increases, the thawing surface of the ground becomes a mass of mud, and for a short period travel is difficult. Spring weather may be clear, warm, and dry one year, and cloudy, cold, and wet the next.

Summer lasts from early June to late August. July temperatures average about 65 degrees Fahrenheit, but during hot spells, temperatures may rise into the 90's. Fall, another short period, is alternately warm and cold. As temperatures drop, rainy and cloudy weather steadily increases. The first frost occurs in September. Throughout the year the duration of daylight varies from 7 hours in December to about 17 hours in June.

V. Origins of the People

According to early records, the Eastern Slavs probably developed as scattered tribes in the upper basins of such rivers as the Dniester, Dnieper, Western Dvina, and Volga. (See SLAVS.) During the European migrations from the 3rd to the 10th century, their homeland was probably what is today the Belorussian Republic and a few areas to the east and south. This was a land of woods and swamps, which protected them from wandering Germanic tribes and from the Asiatic hordes that invaded Europe. They probably spoke a common language, though it developed variations as the Slavs split into different groups. The early Slavs took their names from the regions in which they

lived. For example, the plains dwellers were known as Polyane, which means people of the field. The forest dwellers, on the other hand, were called Drevlyane, which means people of the trees. Their chief pursuits were farming, hunting, and fishing.

As the tribes grew, they expanded northward toward the lakes around the Gulf of Finland, and eastward into the region of the upper Volga and its tributaries. By the early 800's they had established two major centers—Kiev on the Dnieper, and Novgorod on Lake Ilmen.

The early Slavic culture was influenced by traders, immigrants, and conquerors from other lands. Venturesome merchants came mostly from Constantinople (Istanbul), the capital of the Byzantine Empire, and also from the Arab city of Baghdad. They traveled across the Black Sea and up the Dnieper. The merchants brought goods, taught crafts, and improved economic techniques. They were accompanied by Greek missionaries who preached Eastern Orthodox Christianity.

The 9th and 10th centuries were a period of emigrations from Scandinavian lands. One of the main groups from the north were the Rus. Their name is the source of the name Russia. Around 862 a Rus chieftain named Rurik established himself in Novgorod, about 100 miles south of present-day Leningrad. The Russians were ruled by Rurik's descendants, or those who claimed to be descendants, until the 13th century. From then until the end of the 15th century, the Mongols (Tatars) were overlords of the Slavs. Cut off from Western Europe by Lithuania and from the Black Sea by the Mongolian tribes, the Russian people expanded northward and eastward. When foreign rule came to an end, the Russians expanded even more rapidly. Finally, they controlled an area about 100 times larger than their original territory.

VI. Racial Groups

Over the centuries, Russia was invaded by foreign peoples, and Russians, in turn, conquered foreign lands adjoining their borders. In this way Russia became a land of many peoples. Today, the Soviet Union counts within its

The Soviet Union reaches from eastern Europe to the Pacific coast of Asia. No other country has such a variety of languages, clothing, customs, and types of people.

Sovfoto

Sovfoto

USSR Magazine from Sovfoto

USSR Magazine from Sovfoto

Sovfoto

The Slavs of the western U.S.S.R. are the largest nationality group. In the northwest are Latvians, Lithuanians, and the Finno-Ugric peoples. In the southwest are Armenian and Turkic peoples, typical of the Middle East. The eastern U.S.S.R. is peopled by Mongol types. In the far north are Laplanders and Eskimos.

Sovfoto

Sovfoto

borders at least 169 different peoples who speak more than 100 different languages or dialects and practice many religions.

The Slavs make up the largest single group. They comprise about three-fourths of the Soviet population. The Slavs themselves are divided into three main branches. The Great Russians form the largest branch, followed by the Ukrainians, and then the Belorussians, or White Russians. The Belorussians, often considered the purest Slavs, are generally of medium build, light skinned, and blue eyed. The Ukrainians include taller and somewhat darker people. The Great Russians, who are a mixture of Slav, Finno-Ugric, and Turkic groups, include both stocky and tall, dark and fair types.

Next to the Slavs, the Turkic people are most numerous. They comprise about one-tenth of the Soviet population. These rather oriental-looking people are descended chiefly from the Turkic and Mongol (Tatar) invaders of the 13th and 14th centuries. The Turkic people belong mainly to the Islamic faith. They make up leading groups of the population in four of the Soviet Union's five Central Asian republics. Kazakh is the only exception. Turkic people

also form the largest groups in Azerbaijan and in sections of the lower and middle Volga Valley. From three to four million people in the Soviet Union belong to Finno-Ugric groups, which include Finns, Karelians, Estonians, and Mordvins.

In the region of the Caucasus Mountains is a group composed mostly of Armenians and Georgians. They are akin to the Kurds, many of whom inhabit Transcaucasia, and to the Tadzhiks of Central Asia. This group is of mixed faith. Some are Eastern Orthodox, some are Muslim, and others have become atheist. Most Armenians belong to the Armenian Apostolic church.

In the Baltic region the Letts of Latvia and the Lithuanians form another distinct group of the Soviet Union. Their lands were annexed by the Soviet Union in 1940. Of the five million Jews who lived in the U.S.S.R. before the German invasion during World War II, only about two million were left after the war. The U.S.S.R. also includes a considerable number of Moldavians and Germans. In eastern Siberia are small tribes of Mongoloid stock, such as the Buryat and the Tungus.

The Cossacks of Russia are not a separate nationality. Originally they formed a class of farmer-soldier that received special privileges in return for military service under the czars. Although they are often associated with the Ukraine, Cossacks are of various areas and nationalities. They have traditionally lived in their own communities and have enjoyed considerable freedom.

VII. Religion

The official Soviet policy is to eliminate all religions within the country. Religious worship is permitted, but the spreading of any religion is strictly forbidden. Although the Soviet constitution guarantees religious freedom, Soviet law decrees that no one below the age of 18 be given formal religious training. On the other hand, the spread of antireligious (atheistic) propaganda is encouraged. In the past, organizations such as the League of Militant Atheists were the center of violent antireligious campaigns. Today the movement against religion is less violent.

The Eastern Orthodox church was the official church of the Russian Empire before the 1917 Revolution. It still retains its leading position, but government pressure has steadily decreased the number of members. Although the current number of followers is not known, in the mid-1950's there were about 22,000 congregations, 32,000 priests, and 100 bishops. The patriarch of Moscow is the head of the church.

The Muslims are the second largest religious group. They are mainly members of the Sunnite sect, except in Azerbaijan, where the Shiite sect is stronger. Both the Armenian and Georgian churches have large memberships in their respective areas. Estonia and Latvia are the main Protestant centers, and in Lithuania and the western Ukraine are the chief concentrations of Roman Catholics. There are a few Jewish congregations, mainly in the European U.S.S.R. and some Buddhists in Soviet Asia.

VIII. Employment and Recreation

In the Soviet Union about four-fifths of the workers are engaged in physical labor and about one-fifth in white-collar jobs. About 6 per cent

J. Allan Cash

St. Basil's Cathedral on Red Square in Moscow was built between 1554 and 1560. Today it is a popular museum and an outstanding example of Russian architecture.

of the employed population is engaged in service industries, such as stores and restaurants, and about 10 per cent in education, science, and public health. The proportions of men and women in various job classifications are nearly equal because women do much of the heavy labor in the Soviet Union. By the end of 1961 the Soviet Union had about 3,800,000 professional people (individuals with higher educations), and 5,600,000 semiprofessional people (individuals with secondary school educations).

Recreation, like almost all other Soviet activities, is largely government controlled. Since the Soviets took power, emphasis on physical culture and sports has steadily increased. This has become especially evident in the Olympic Games. In the past, athletes from the U.S.S.R. were seldom winners in these international contests. By the 1960's, however, Soviet athletes were prominent in most Olympic sports. The progress of women athletes in the Soviet Union has been especially notable.

Inexpensive activities such as hiking, camping, and swimming are favorites of individuals or small groups in summer. An extensive program of organized groups also permits participation in a wider range of sports, such as soccer, basketball, volleyball, gymnastics, and track. The activities of the leading soccer teams are followed with the same keen interest as is baseball in the United States. Reading and playing chess are common diversions. Chess tournaments receive wide publicity.

Cultural activities such as art, literature, and motion pictures are closely controlled to insure that they promote the doctrines of the Communist party. Ballet, a traditional Russian art form, continues to play a prominent role, especially in the major cities of Moscow and Leningrad. (See RUSSIAN LITERATURE.)

The domestic tourist industry is rather undeveloped in the Soviet Union, though it has grown rapidly under government control. Many resorts were established in the Crimea and Transcaucasia by the czarist nobility. Now these sites are used by workers who are awarded short vacations by the government.

Visits by foreign tourists to the Soviet Union have been closely regulated since the 1930's. A change in policy after 1953, however, has encouraged tours by foreigners, and the number of visitors has increased steadily. Intourist, the

Sovfoto

The subtropical climate of the U.S.S.R.'s Black Sea coast makes it a popular resort area.

government travel organization, arranges tours to developed areas in the European U.S.S.R., but it is difficult to gain access to other parts of the country. In 1960 an estimated 800,000 foreign visitors toured the U.S.S.R.

IX. Agriculture

The Soviet Union traditionally has been an agricultural country. But today, the largest percentage of Soviet workers by far are in industry. Agriculture remains the second largest Soviet occupation. Farm products represent only a

In recent years Soviet athletes have become prominent in world sports events. The U.S.S.R. hockey team eliminated Czechoslovakia from competition and went on to win the Olympic hockey championship during the IX Winter Games at Innsbruck, Austria.

A.F.P. from Pictorial Parade

The central section of the Svobodny state farm in Kazakhstan is typical of the hundreds of collective farm villages throughout the Soviet republics.

small percentage of the value of the country's total production.

Since 1928 the agricultural organization of the country has been divided into three basic units: (1) the *kolkhoz,* or collective farm; (2) machine-tractor stations (M.T.S.), which have been largely converted into repair-technical stations; and (3) the *sovkhoz,* or state farm.

The *kolkhoz* is a collective of individual farmers who pool their work and cultivate their land allotments jointly. Profits, in the form of money and produce, are distributed on the basis of each individual's contribution to the farm's operation. Each collective farmer also has a small personal plot of land for his family's use.

The number of collective farms reached over a quarter million in 1950, but the process of combining neighboring *kolkhozes* reduced the number to 41,300 by 1961. The collective farm system includes about 16,400,000 families. Each farm averages about 400 families and about 6,500 acres of cultivated land.

Until 1958 the *kolkhozes* were not equipped with heavy machinery such as tractors, plows, and combines. Supplying this machinery was the function of the M.T.S. Each M.T.S. maintained a pool of farm machinery that served from 10 to 30 or more *kolkhozes.* In return for the use of the machinery and machine operators,

the *kolkhoz* had to pay the M.T.S. a share of the crop. The M.T.S. system had been useful in the 1930's and 1940's when machinery was quite scarce, but it was basically inefficient. Much of its work was poorly done, and the plowing, planting, and harvesting operations were often badly timed. The 9,000 M.T.S. units finally were abolished in 1958, and most of their farm machinery was sold to the *kolkhozes.* They were then converted into repair-technical stations.

The *sovkhoz* is operated like a government factory. The government provides the necessary machinery, hires employees, and pays them wages. The *sovkhoz* usually cultivates larger areas than the *kolkhoz* and tends to specialize in one thing, such as wheat, cotton, or horse breeding. *Sovkhozes* played a relatively small role in Soviet agriculture until a 1954–1956 program to plow the virgin lands in the eastern areas of the Soviet Union. At that time several hundred new grain *sovkhozes* were established, mainly in northern Kazakhstan and western Siberia. These *sovkhozes* plowed up about 82 million acres of virgin land, which is used mostly for wheat growing. At first the yields from these lands were good, but by the 1960's they had fallen off and it began to appear that the program had failed. In 1961 there were about

Sovfoto

The 600-mile-long Kara Kum irrigation canal carries water to arid lands of Turkmen S.S.R.

8,300 *sovkhozes* in the Soviet Union. A *sovkhoz* now averages about 800 workers, who cultivate an area of about 24,000 acres.

After more than 45 years of Communist party rule, agriculture remains the least developed part of the Soviet economy. Collectivization is probably partly responsible for failures in agriculture. The system provides little personal incentive for the farmer. Bureaucratic handling of the farms has been inefficient. Quotas are often unrealistic, and, as a result, the discouraged farmer tries to spend more time on his personal plot of ground. Often, he gets better yields per acre than does the collective. Estimates indicate that Soviet farmers use from $2\frac{1}{2}$ to 16 times more labor than farmers in the United States to produce the same amount of crops per acre.

Another Soviet agricultural problem is the lack of arable land. The Soviet Union covers 15 per cent of the world's land surface, but only about 10 per cent of the country is suitable for farming. Much of the Soviet Union in Asia is too dry and too cold for agriculture. Most of the cultivated land forms a large, triangular area. The triangle is broadest in the west where it includes the area between Leningrad and Odessa and tapers off eastward as it extends to Lake Baikal. The only notable agricultural areas outside this triangle are the Caucasus and the places in Soviet Central Asia where irrigation water is available.

Grain crops occupy more farmland in the U.S.S.R. than any other. The chief grain is wheat, more of which is produced in the U.S.S.R. than in any other country. The largest quantities of winter wheat are harvested in the Ukraine and the northern Caucasus. Spring wheat is the dominant crop in the northern and eastern parts of the agricultural belt. Where climatic conditions are more severe, rye (from which traditional Russian black bread is made), oats, barley, and flax are grown. The Soviet Union is the world's leading producer of flax fiber. The potato, a hardy vegetable, is widely grown in the U.S.S.R. Other distinctive crops are sunflowers, grown for their seeds, and buckwheat. Sugar beets are grown mostly in the southern European U.S.S.R. The government has emphasized sugar-beet production, and the U.S.S.R. is now the leading country in producing beet sugar. Most of the Soviet cotton is produced in Soviet Central Asia and the Transcaucasus region.

By the use of modern equipment, such as these combines harvesting wheat, the U.S.S.R. is striving to increase its agricultural production. The Ukraine is the leading wheat-producing area of the country.

Sovfoto

Other products of the warm southern regions are tea, tobacco, and citrus and other fruits.

To increase the amount of feed for livestock, the Soviet government has encouraged corn growing. Formerly restricted to the Ukraine and to the northern Caucasus, corn is now grown in other areas. Climatic conditions do not permit the corn to ripen in these areas, but it develops enough to be used as fodder.

Livestock raising has been erratic during the years of Soviet administration. Collectivization and World War II caused tremendous declines in production. It was not until about 1955 that livestock production again reached the high levels of the pre-collectivization period.

Sheep are the most numerous form of livestock. They are widely raised, but most notably in the drier steppe and semidesert areas of the Caucasus and Soviet Central Asia. The famous Karakul sheep is raised in Soviet Central Asia. The Soviet Union is among the leading countries in breeding beef and dairy cattle and pigs. These livestock animals are most prominent among the Slavic groups who inhabit the country's moister regions. Horse production has declined because of the availability of trucks and tractors, but the Soviet Union still has one of the largest horse populations in the world. Goat production has also been reduced.

X. Forestry, Trapping, and Fishing

The Soviet Union is the greatest producer of timber in the world. The forest resources of the country cover almost two billion acres, about one-fifth of the world's reserves. Although the greater part of the forests are located in Siberia, most of the production comes from areas of the European U.S.S.R. that are more convenient to transportation. In the past, lumbering was a winter activity of the peasant. Now, organized timber crews equipped with power machinery operate on almost a year-round basis. One-third of the timber is still used for firewood. The rest goes to the construction, woodworking, and paper industries. Much of the timber is floated down rivers to the sawmills. The woodworking and paper mills are usually located close to the large cities of the European U.S.S.R. and of the eastern Urals region.

The vast forests of the Soviet Union are important for their abundance of furbearing animals as well as for their timber. The pelts of the sable, ermine, squirrel, and fox are highly valued. Furs have been a major Russian export since the 15th century, and today the Soviet Union is the largest fur producer in the world. In the forested areas of the Soviet Union, trapping and fur farming are major occupations of the population.

Millions of feet of timber, the "green gold" of Siberia, are floated annually down the Yenisei River to lumber mills.

"USSR Magazine" from Sovfoto

Sovfoto

One of the Soviet Union's richest petroleum fields is the Apsheron Peninsula on the Caspian Sea coast. The city of Baku, on the peninsula, is a busy center of oil operations.

Thousands of miles of ocean coastline and large inland lakes long have made fishing an important Soviet industry. Fishing is carried on in nearly every major water body that is ice-free for any part of the year. The Caspian is traditionally famous for such fish as herring and sturgeon. The sturgeon is a major source of the world-famous Russian caviar. The Caspian's production, however, has gradually dropped off since 1917, mainly because of the falling water level. The over-all fish catch, however, has increased. The Arctic Ocean now produces the largest volume of fish—including cod, herring, halibut, and bass. Also rapidly growing are the Pacific Coast catches, which provide salmon, herring, crab, and seal. The Soviet fishing fleet has been extending its operations to more distant seas, even as far as the Antarctic Ocean for whales.

XI. Minerals, Mining, and Manufacturing

One of the Soviet Union's greatest assets is its vast storehouse of coal and minerals. It provides the country with all the necessary raw materials for modern industry. Soviet estimates place the U.S.S.R. first in world reserves of coal, iron, manganese, copper, lead, zinc, nickel, bauxite, tungsten, mercury, mica, potash, and phosphates. The reserves of manganese, coal, and potash are estimated at more than half of the world total.

Coal has been the principal source of energy for Soviet industries. Most of the high-grade coal comes from four districts. These are the Donets Basin in the eastern Ukraine, the Kuznetsk Basin in western Siberia, the Karaganda Basin in the Kazakh S.S.R., and the Pechora Basin in the northeastern European U.S.S.R. The Donets district alone has been producing about three-fifths of all Soviet coking coal. Some lower-grade coal deposits also are located in the country. The Moscow area, for example, is noted for its deposits of brown coal.

The Soviet Union has placed great emphasis on petroleum exploration, and production has increased enormously since 1928. The vast de-

Belorussia does not produce oil, but huge refineries in the republic produce gasoline. They are supplied by a branch of the Friendship Trans-European oil pipeline.

Sovfoto

PRODUCTS OF THE U.S.S.R.

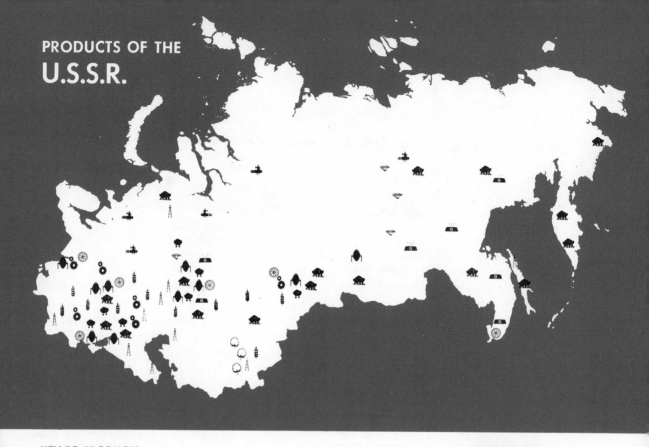

KEY TO PRODUCTS

- TIMBER
- COAL
- IRON ORE
- PETROLEUM
- STEEL
- MACHINERY EQUIPMENT
- TRANSPORT
- GOLD
- DIAMONDS
- WHEAT
- COTTON

LAND USE

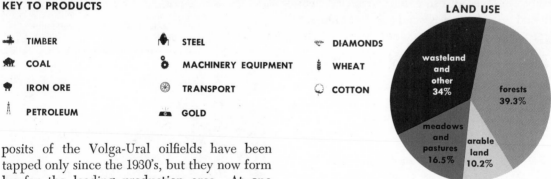

wasteland and other 34%

forests 39.3%

meadows and pastures 16.5%

arable land 10.2%

posits of the Volga-Ural oilfields have been tapped only since the 1930's, but they now form by far the leading production area. At one time the famous Baku area in the Azerbaijan S.S.R. produced about half the world's oil. Now, even though new oil discoveries have been made in the adjoining Caspian Sea, the area accounts for only a small percentage of Soviet oil. Soviet Central Asia is the third largest petroleum area. A small amount is also produced on Sakhalin Island in the Pacific. Natural gas is piped from gas fields in the western U.S.S.R. to larger cities, such as Moscow and Kiev.

Hydroelectric power also is developing rapidly in the Soviet Union. Between 1929 and 1957 hydroelectric power increased by more than 20 times. Huge hydroelectric plants have been constructed at such places as Kuibyshev and Volgograd on the Volga, and at Bratsk on the Angara in eastern Siberia. Many more electric-power stations were to be completed under the seven-year plan ending in 1965. Many of these new power stations are based on energy from coal, natural gas, and oil rather than from rivers.

The richest region for iron ore is the eastern Ukraine near the Donets Basin. The concentration of iron and steel plants at various Ukrainian industrial centers produce about half of the pig iron and two-fifths of the steel in the Soviet Union. The Urals region produces almost as much iron and steel as the Ukraine does. Some low-grade coal also is available in the Urals. The major iron and steel plants are located at Magnitogorsk, Chelyabinsk, and Nizhny Tagil. Large plants also have been established at Novokuznetsk in the Kuznetsk coal district and at Temir-Tau near the Karaganda coal deposits. Smaller iron and steel works are located in the Moscow, Leningrad, Caucasus, Volgograd, and Far Eastern areas.

The deposits and production of other minerals are concentrated mainly in the Urals, Kazakh S.S.R., and eastern Siberia. The Urals are well known as a treasure-house of minerals, including nickel, bauxite, copper, platinum, chromium, manganese, and asbestos. The Kazakh S.S.R. also is becoming important because of its rich deposits of copper, lead, zinc, nickel, manganese, molybdenum, and tungsten. From eastern Siberia come large quantities of gold, tin, diamonds, lead, and silver. The Kola Peninsula on the Barents Sea coast and the Caucasus Mountains of Central Asia also contain a variety of mineral reserves.

The vast variety of resources available in the U.S.S.R. has enabled the government to establish an extensive network of plants that manufacture many products. Light industry, which produces goods for the individual Soviet consumer, has been growing, but much slower than heavy industry, which produces huge machines for manufacturing and farming. Factories that produce railroad equipment, tractors, machinery, and mining and construction equipment are located near major steel plants in the Urals and the Donets Basin. Shipbuilding also is a major industry at leading ports.

Industries that require highly skilled labor—such as the manufacture of electrical and electronic equipment, precision instruments, or machine tools—are located mainly in the large cities of the European U.S.S.R. The textile industry is most extensively developed in the Moscow area, which is also the chief producer of textile machinery. Industries that do not require highly trained labor (linen, leather, or food processing)

The Kazakhstan Magnitka steel mill (above) is one of the huge plants the Soviets have built to increase their industrial production. The Uralelectroapparat plant in Sverdlovsk (below) produces power for heavy industry.

Photos, Sovfoto

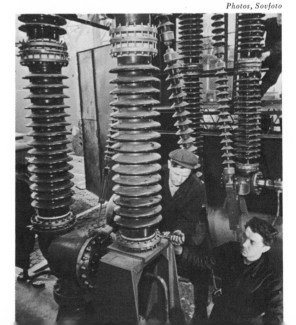

Sovfoto

In 1920 the U.S.S.R. began a new electrification program; since then many huge hydroelectric plants, such as the one at Kuibyshev (above) have been built. Today the U.S.S.R. is the world's second highest electrical producer.

tend to be located near market areas or near the sources of supply. The location of industry in the country follows much the same pattern as the distribution of population in the fertile triangle and in the heavily settled areas of the Caucasus and Soviet Central Asia.

XII. Transportation

In a country as large as the Soviet Union, the development of an efficient transportation system is an enormous undertaking. The peoples and resources are separated widely, and the unity of the country is dependent upon good communications. The railroads receive the heaviest usage. They carry about three-fourths of all freight and about two-thirds of all passengers.

The railroad network is dense in the European U.S.S.R. but quite sparse in Asia. The government, however, has been constructing new lines in the Asiatic sections. The most important Soviet railway is the Trans-Siberian, the world's longest railroad. It took from 1891 until 1915 to complete, and it is still the country's only rail link to the Pacific Coast. Altogether the Soviet Union has about 83,000 miles of track. This compares with about 216,000 miles of track in the United States, which is less than one-half as large in area as the Soviet Union.

Soviet railroads are used intensively and

have generally kept up with the transportation demands of rapid industrialization. Between 1928 and 1961, total rail freight increased by almost 17 times and passenger traffic increased by about 7 times.

Practically all of the Soviet rail network consists of wider-gauge tracks than those of other European countries. The small difference in track width was an important factor in both world wars. This is because enemy troops and supplies could not enter Soviet territory by rail without switching trains. In peacetime, however, this extra handling raises freight costs.

Before World War II the role of seaborne transportation was relatively small in the Soviet Union. Most of the long coastline was closed by ice for long periods each year. Except for the Murmansk area, the entire Arctic Coast is limited to a short navigation season. Leningrad, the chief Baltic port before World War II, faces a frozen harbor for several months each year.

Soviet oceangoing traffic grew rapidly after the wartime acquisition of the Baltic coastal territories and the northern East Prussian territory. The volume of seaborne cargo increased by almost seven times between 1940 and 1961. Most of the Soviet foreign trade moves through the seaports of the Baltic and Black seas. The Soviet Union is now able to make almost year-round use of the Baltic seaports of Tallinn, Riga,

Klaipeda (Memel), and Kaliningrad (Koenigsberg). The Black Sea coast has a number of excellent ports including Odessa, Kherson, Rostov, Novorossisk, and the petroleum ports of Batumi and Tuapse. The famous Black Sea naval base of Sevastopol is located on the western side of the Crimean Peninsula. Cargoes to or from Far Eastern areas usually use the Pacific Coast port of Vladivostok or the newer, neighboring port of Nakhodka.

In addition to foreign trade, Soviet merchant ships carry considerable cargo from one domestic port to another. The Caspian Sea, with its large shipments of petroleum from Baku, is by far the most heavily used for coastal traffic. It carries about a third of the freight transported by all seagoing Soviet ships. Astrakhan is an important Caspian port, along with Baku. The Black and Baltic seacoasts are important also for this type of domestic trade.

Inland waterways played an important role in the country's early history. They formed major trade, travel, and invasion routes. The government has increased the capacity of the water routes by improving the extensive system of canals in the European U.S.S.R. This has made it possible to travel by water from the Black and Caspian seas to the Baltic and White seas. The disadvantage to these waterways is that they are partially or completely frozen for three to seven months each year. Today the country uses more than 86,000 miles of its rivers for transportation. The Volga is the most important waterway in the European U.S.S.R. The major Asiatic rivers—including the Ob, Yenisei, Lena, and Amur—carry mostly timber.

The Soviet highway system has not received as much attention as some other forms of transportation. Most highways remain unpaved, and, in many places, road travel stops during the spring and fall muddy periods. As the number of motor vehicles increased, however, more emphasis was placed on the construction of all-weather roads. Since World War II the network of hard-surfaced roads has about tripled and now totals about 284,000 miles. The best highways radiate from Moscow, northwest to Leningrad, south and west to the Polish border at Brest, and southward to the Crimea. The country is also served by an expanding network of bus routes. Between 1950 and 1961 the number of routes increased from 1,900 to 8,400. The 517,000-mile bus network served 716 million persons in 1961.

Aviation is growing rapidly under Soviet administration. Fast air travel is important in helping overcome the great distances that separate areas of the Soviet Union. In 1961, passenger flights of the Soviet airline, Aeroflot, traveled about 10 billion miles and carried about 22 million persons. Most of the civil air traffic is domestic, but Aeroflot is also attempting to increase its international services. Air traffic is heaviest in the area between Leningrad and the Ukraine in the west, and between western Siberia and Soviet Central Asia in the east.

Pipelines are an old means of transporting petroleum in the Soviet Union. The first major oil pipeline, from Baku to Batumi on the Black Sea, was completed in the early 1900's. The network of pipelines remained relatively stable until the 1950's. Then, new oil discoveries caused more lines to be built. By the early 1960's the country had more than 12,500 miles of pipeline. A 3,000-mile pipeline to connect the Volga oil field to central and eastern Europe was completed in 1964.

The Volga River is the major transportation artery of the European U.S.S.R. It links the industrial centers with central and southern U.S.S.R. and the Urals.

"USSR Magazine" from Sovfoto

XIII. Communications

The Soviet Ministry of Communications operates all postal, telephone, and telegraph services. The number of telephones has been increasing, and by 1970 the country had about 9.9 million. Radio and especially television have developed more slowly. By 1970 there were about 88,000,000 radio sets, about 27,000,000 television sets, and more than 390 television stations.

In the Soviet Union there is no freedom of speech as it is known in the United States. Since the Revolution of 1917 the government has controlled the press of the country. It uses the press to spread the ideology of the Communist party. Nothing is printed without government approval, so there is little criticism of communist policies by Soviet newspapers. In the late 1950's and early 1960's, however, there appeared to be somewhat more freedom in publishing. According to Soviet sources, there are more than 10,000 newspapers being published in the country. They are printed in 67 national languages and 7 foreign languages. Among the most important national newspapers are *Pravda* and *Izvestia*. Handling international news is the Telegraph Agency of the Soviet Union (Tass).

XIV. Education

After the Communists came to power in 1917, they placed great emphasis on education. Illiteracy was to be wiped out, and the cultural level of the country was to be raised. The educational program was to be a key principle in making the Soviet Union one of the world's most powerful countries. Under the czars, education had been neglected for centuries. There were few schools and universities, and the masses remained illiterate. During the period around 1900, education under the czars first made notable progress, and by 1917 the country had about 100,000 primary and high schools and 10 universities.

At first the Communists tried to apply unique educational ideas. Students were allowed to make their own rules, plan their own studies, and lead a free classroom existence. The teacher had little authority. As in various other fields, the Communists had to abandon their original theories. The schools became instruments used to strengthen communist morality and ideology and Soviet patriotism. The authority of the teacher was restored, and an important part of the curriculum, at all levels, was teaching the principles of Marxism-Leninism, the basic communist philosophy. In four years of university study, students receive 600 hours of instruction in Marxism-Leninism. (See LENIN, NICOLAI; MARX, KARL HEINRICH.)

Schooling in the Soviet Union starts early. To enable mothers to work, nurseries are available for infants up to the age of three years, and kindergartens are available for children from three to seven. At seven, the child begins a basic ten-year educational plan. This involves four years of elementary school, three years of junior high school, and three years of senior high school. Part of the ten years may be spent in vocational school. After the ten-year program,

Schoolchildren in the Kazakh S.S.R. learn their lessons under trained supervision. The U.S.S.R. has greatly expanded educational facilities in all union republics.

Tass from Sovfoto

Sovfoto

In some special Soviet schools, children learn English as a second language. In the early grades they have one- or two-hour sessions daily. In the later ones some courses are taught in English.

students may go to work or begin higher education. Education also is extended to adults, and many factories are provided with schools to make workers more skilled at their trades. Through its school programs, the Soviet Union has almost eliminated illiteracy in the country.

The Soviet government has especially emphasized education in engineering and the sciences. These fields play vital roles in the Soviet industrial program. By the mid-1900's, Soviet schools were graduating more engineers than U.S. schools. Only about half as many secondary school graduates, however, go on to higher education as do in the United States. Instruction has been free since 1956, and at the higher levels, students who earn good grades receive scholarships that also cover living expenses.

The older universities of Moscow, Leningrad, and Kiev have been expanded, and new ones have been established. Altogether the country has more than 700 institutions of higher learning, including about 40 universities. More than 200,000 elementary and high schools in the Soviet Union are attended by more than 40,000,000 students.

XV. Government

In the Soviet Union the government is controlled by the Communist party. No other parties are allowed, so the country is, in effect, a dictatorship. Soviet citizens have little choice in the way they are to be governed because they do not have freedom of expression and cannot choose candidates for government office.

Membership in the party itself is not open to anyone who wishes to join. New members are chosen by party leaders on the basis of their loyalty to communism. The party is rigidly controlled by a body of leaders who form the Presidium, formerly called the Politburo. The number of members varies according to the desires of the group. In April 1962 it consisted of 16 members. These members make all the final decisions on matters of internal and external policy. The first secretary of the Presidium is usually its most powerful member. When a vacancy occurs in the Presidium, the new member is chosen on the basis of his devotion to the leaders of the party.

Throughout most of the history of the Soviet Union the single individual who dominated the Presidium ruled the country. First it was Nicolai Lenin, then Joseph V. Stalin, who was first secretary. Stalin was followed by Nikita S. Khrushchev, who became first secretary in 1953. These men have all exerted powers as great as those of the czars of Russia. The will of the party Presidium is enforced by the party organization and by secret police who arrest anyone disloyal to the government. In the past those arrested were executed or sent to concentration camps as forced labor. Recently there has been some relaxation of such police-state methods. After 40 years of Soviet methods, however, the average citizen knows that any opposition to the Communist party will bring reprisals.

In theory, the party is completely separate from the formal government structure. The Communist party is supposed to be a voluntary union of individuals dedicated to the principles of communism. In practice, the party controls all areas of Soviet life through its network of party cells. Groups of Communists form these cells within each government organization, military unit, factory, farm, and even in organiza-

The Communist party rules the Soviet Union. Delegates chosen at regional and territorial conferences represent their areas in sessions of the national congress, or Supreme Soviet, which meets in the Kremlin Palace of Congresses.

tions devoted to literature, art, and music. The membership of the party has been growing slowly, but as late as October 1961 it included only about 9,700,000 persons. This represents less than 5 per cent of the total population.

The first Soviet constitution was passed in 1918, revised a few times, and replaced in 1923. The present constitution was adopted in 1936. From the beginning, freedom of speech, assembly, and worship, as well as a free press and free elections, were all constitutionally guaranteed. These rights and freedoms never actually became realities. Elections were not free because opposition parties were not allowed. Nowhere was discussion of policies permitted, and the press obeyed the government. Except for a brief period during World War II, Orthodox, Catholic, Protestant, Jewish, and Islamic organizations continued to be suppressed. The Soviet Union has remained, in spite of its constitution, a totalitarian dictatorship.

The Soviet Union is a federation of 15 union republics. These republics are not independent as the name implies, but are really more like states. They have their own soviets, which are controlled by the national Supreme Soviet.

The national legislative body, or Congress, of the Soviet Union is called the Supreme Soviet. It consists of two houses. One, the Council of the Union, is elected by the people. One dele-

gate is elected for every 300,000 persons. The other, also an elected body, the Council of Nationalities, represents the different nationalities in the Soviet Union. It has a specified number of deputies for each nationality group.

Each union republic has 25 deputies; an autonomous republic has 11; an autonomous region, 5; and a national area, only 1. In the March 1962 election, 791 members were elected to the Council of the Union and 652 to the Council of Nationalities. Candidates for both houses are nominated by the Communist party, and there is only one candidate for each office. Both houses are elected for four-year terms by citizens 18 years of age and over.

The Supreme Soviet elects a Presidium, which carries on the functions of government between sessions of the Supreme Soviet. The Presidium's chairman, sometimes called the president, is the chief of state. Ministers for various government departments are appointed by the Presidium. The Council of Ministers is the chief executive and administrative unit of government. Its chairman is the country's premier. The historic meeting place of both the former czarist governments and today's Soviet governments is the Kremlin, which was once a medieval fortress. Within its walls are magnificent palaces and churches built by the imperial rulers of Russia. (See COMMUNISM; MOSCOW, U.S.S.R.)

XVI. Health and Welfare

The Soviet Union provides its citizens with free health and welfare benefits. To some degree, however, it is still possible for a patient to seek out a physician for private treatment. The number of physicians has increased steadily and now totals about 618,000. These are assisted in the rural areas by 515,000 feldshers (physicians' assistants). Medicine is a favorite occupation for women in the U.S.S.R., and in 1968 about 73 per cent of the physicians were women. Soviet advancements in medicine are reflected in the country's steadily declining death rate. Some diseases, such as malaria and smallpox, have been almost eliminated.

The principal health problem is the crowded living conditions in the cities. Construction of additional housing has eased the problem somewhat, but much more is needed. Social insurance for disability and old age is a government function that is administered by the trade unions.

XVII. Republics of the Soviet Union

Through the conquests of the Great Russians that began in about the 15th century, Russia became a country of many nationalities, differing in physical traits, culture, language, and religion. Many of these nationality groups sought to become independent after the revolution of March 1917. The Communists, however, prevented this after they came to power in November 1917. The Communist leaders promised equality to all nationalities. They discarded the name of Russia and in 1922 proclaimed the formation of the Union of Soviet Socialist Repub-

THE SOVIET SOCIALIST REPUBLICS

Republic	Capital	Area (square miles)	Population*	Republic	Capital	Area (square miles)	Population*
1. Armenian S.S.R.	Yerevan	11,506	2,493,000	9. Lithuanian S.S.R.	Vilnius	25,174	3,129,000
2. Azerbaijan S.S.R.	Baku	33,436	5,111,000	10. Moldavian S.S.R.	Kishinev	13,012	3,572,000
3. Belorussian S.S.R.	Minsk	80,154	9,003,000	11. Russian S.F.S.R.	Moscow	6,592,812	130,090,000
4. Estonian S.S.R.	Tallinn	17,413	1,357,000	12. Tadzhik S.S.R.	Dushanbe	55,251	2,900,000
5. Georgian S.S.R.	Tbilisi	26,911	4,688,000	13. Turkmen S.S.R.	Ashkhabad	188,455	2,158,000
6. Kazakh S.S.R.	Alma-Ata	1,048,339	12,850,000	14. Ukrainian S.S.R.	Kiev	232,046	47,136,000
7. Kirghiz S.S.R.	Frunze	76,641	2,933,000	15. Uzbek S.S.R.	Tashkent	174,170	11,963,000
8. Latvian S.S.R.	Riga	24,594	2,365,000	*1970 census.			

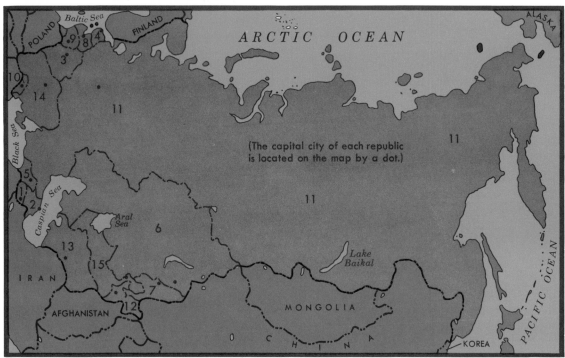

(The capital city of each republic is located on the map by a dot.)

lics. By then the Communists were in control of Russia (the lands inhabited by the Great Russians), Belorussia, the Ukraine, and Transcaucasia. These four territories became the first soviet socialist republics (S.S.R.'s), or union republics. Eventually, other territories were formed into union republics, until the present number of 15 was reached.

The Soviet Union also recognizes the cultural independence of smaller national groups. The more advanced of these are organized into autonomous (self-governing) soviet socialist republics (A.S.S.R.'s), which have about the same governmental setup as the S.S.R.'s. The less advanced groups form smaller units called autonomous regions and national areas.

The S.S.R.'s and the A.S.S.R.'s have their own constitutions, their own legislatures, and their own executives. Each has its own budget and its own courts. Although the constitution guarantees them the right to withdraw from the union, there is great doubt that secession is possible. The Communist party, which is under European Soviet control, dominates all the republics and territories. (See the separate articles on the soviet socialist republics.)

XVIII. History

The U.S.S.R. was formally constituted on December 30, 1922, but its history as a state actually began more than 1,100 years ago. According to the semilegendary version in the first Russian Chronicle, the Slavs of Novgorod invited a Scandinavian leader, Rurik, to rule and protect them. They feared attacks from their Finnish neighbors and possible invasion from Asiatic nomadic hordes. Rurik belonged to a group called the Rus. His rule, beginning in 862, established the first dynasty of Russian princes. Oleg succeeded Rurik and ruled from 879 till 912. He conquered areas farther south and made Kiev the center of his domain.

The Rus and other Scandinavians adopted some of the customs of the land and influenced the Slavic culture with their own customs. The spread of Christianity during the 11th century became a major force in the unification of the various tribes of Russia into a national people. Vladimir the Saint was the first ruler to accept Christianity, probably in 988. He adopted the Eastern Orthodox faith and kept continuous relations with the Byzantine Empire. Russian architecture, music, painting, and language reflects the Byzantine culture.

The Golden Horde

During the 11th and 12th centuries the grand dukes of Kiev held the main power of the land. In 1240 Kiev was destroyed by the Mongols (Tatars), and the Russian territory was split into numerous small states. The Mongols were called the Golden Horde, after the great gold-colored tent of their khan, Batu. Under the Mongols, three states emerged: Galicia in the west, Novgorod in the north, and Moscow in the east. Most early states, like Moscow, were governed by dukes with the help of councils composed of boyars (landed aristocracy) and church dignitaries. In other states, such as Novgorod, citizens formed a republican type of government.

The early dukes of Moscow acquired power and influence by acting as collectors of tribute for their Mongol overlords, who ruled from Sarai on the lower Volga. With the support of the Mongol rulers, the dukes were able to extend their own territories.

Soon the dukedom of Moscow gained precedence over all others in Russia. In the 15th century, Ivan III, the reigning Muscovite duke, acquired possession of the rival duchy of Tver and the republic of Novgorod. In 1480 he threw off the yoke of the Mongols. Constantinople had been occupied by the Turks, so Ivan III was also looked upon as the leader of Orthodox Christianity. He is often considered to be the founder of modern Russia.

When Ivan IV, or Ivan the Terrible, took the throne in 1533, Muscovy was a large and powerful state. He adopted the title of czar, a variation of the Latin *Caesar*. During his reign he made his power more absolute, crushing boyars and peasants alike. Having defeated the khans of Kazan and Astrakhan, he annexed all the valley of the Volga, and settlements were established as far as the White Sea and the Urals. In the latter part of his reign, Ivan IV became suspicious of all those around him. He reacted

862 The first dynasty of Russian princes is established by Rurik at Novgorod.

988 Vladimir the Saint becomes the first Russian ruler to accept Christianity.

1240 Mongolian invaders destroy Kiev and reign as overlords of Russia.

1480 Ivan III overthrows Mongolian rule.

1613 Michael Romanov is made czar, establishing the Romanov dynasty (1613-1917).

1689 Russia begins to develop as a world power under Peter the Great.

1762-1796 Under Catherine the Great, Russia gains territories from Poland and Turkey.

1812 Napoleon I invades Russia and occupies Moscow.

1813-1814 Napoleon I retreats and is defeated.

1856 Russia is defeated in the Crimean War.

1861 The serfs are freed by a law passed under Alexander II.

1904-1905 The Russo-Japanese War deals severe losses to Russia. The Revolution of 1905 breaks out.

1906 Russia's first representative government is assembled.

1914 Russia enters World War I.

1917 The czar abdicates, ending the Romanov dynasty. The Bolsheviks (Communists) gain power after the October Revolution.

1920 The Russian Civil War ends in victory for the Communists.

1922 The Union of Soviet Socialist Republics (U.S.S.R.) is formed.

1924 Nicolai Lenin dies, and Joseph V. Stalin begins his rise to power.

1928 The first of three five-year plans for speeding economic growth begins.

1941 The U.S.S.R. enters World War II after being invaded by Germany.

1943 The U.S.S.R. wins the Battle of Stalingrad.

1945 Germany surrenders.

1946-1948 The U.S.S.R. develops political control of Eastern Europe.

1953 Stalin dies, and Nikita S. Khrushchev begins his rise to power.

1957 The U.S.S.R. puts the first artificial satellite into orbit.

1960-1964 Hostility develops between China and the U.S.S.R. over their views of communism.

1961 The U.S.S.R. launches the first manned space flight.

1964 Khrushchev is retired. Leonid I. Brezhnev and Aleksei N. Kosygin take over Soviet leadership.

---

violently to any suspected disloyalty. On the basis of a suspected conspiracy at Novgorod, he destroyed that city. Near the end of his life he grew remorseful for his cruel deeds and became a monk. (See IVAN.)

The House of Romanov

After the death of Ivan IV in 1584 there followed 29 years of turmoil, caused mainly by conflicts over power between the boyars and the czars. Marauding Cossacks, Poles, and Swedes swept over Russia. In order to prevent the peasants from fleeing, they were forbidden—particularly under Boris Godunov—to leave the farms. This established serfdom in Russia. There was also considerable disagreement over the succession of czars. To end the chaos, the boyars chose Michael Romanov, a grandnephew of Ivan IV's first wife, as their ruler. By general agreement he was made czar in 1613. This began the Romanov dynasty, which reigned until 1917. (See ROMANOV, HOUSE OF.)

Under Michael and his successors, the Russian state was strengthened and new provinces

were added. The reign of Michael's grandson, Peter the Great, from 1689 to 1725, was one of the most significant in the country's history. It marked the rise of Russia as a world power. Peter was impressed with Western Europe and brought its culture to Russia. He was a ruthless, energetic leader who traveled widely to learn Western ways. By the defeat of Charles XII of Sweden, Peter extended Russian territory far to the west. Dissatisfied with Moscow, he built a new, modern capital, St. Petersburg (now Leningrad). Peter also introduced many social and governmental reforms. (See PETER I.)

Catherine the Great

Under the immediate successors of Peter the Great (Catherine I, Peter II, Anne, Ivan VI), Russia was weakly governed. The royal family had intermarried with Germans, which caused some resentment. A nationalist revolt put Elizabeth, the youngest daughter of Peter the Great, on the throne in 1741. Her nephew Peter III, a weak man, was deposed after half a year and was replaced by his German wife, Catherine, in

1762. Under Catherine II (called Catherine the Great), Russia once again had strong leadership. New territories were acquired, and contact with Western European culture continued.

Some of the new territory came from the partitioning of Poland in 1772, 1793, and 1795. Wars with Turkey brought the Crimea under Russian control and gave Russia an outlet to the Black Sea. Russia was now a European power, and all countries sent ambassadors to the court of Russia. Catherine wanted her court to be the most fashionable in Europe. An enlightened woman, she promoted art, literature, and education and was herself a notable writer. She introduced a legal system modeled along Western European lines. Catherine admired the French liberal writers and showed intentions of introducing domestic reforms. In actuality, however, she gave more power to the nobility and strengthened the bonds of serfdom. She died in 1796. (See CATHERINE THE GREAT.)

Liberation of the Serfs

Paul I, Catherine's son, was too weak to continue her policies. When his son Alexander I became czar in 1801, his first acts seemed those of a liberal and enlightened ruler. He encouraged public education, built several universities, and promoted industry and trade. While not daring to liberate the serfs entirely, he permitted the landowners to do so. Only about 47,000 serfs were freed, however.

During the reign of Alexander I, Napoleon

Two-thirds of the population of Russia were serfs at the beginning of the 20th century. They worked the land and performed much of the hard labor necessary in that nonindustrialized country. These peasant women, for example, towed barges on the Volga River.

Sovfoto

Bonaparte invaded Russia. Napoleon captured Moscow, but then was forced into disastrous retreat. (See NAPOLEON I.) His defeat gave Russia new territory and new status in world affairs. Russia exerted powerful influence over the Congress of Vienna (1814–1815), which followed the fall of Napoleon. After the Congress, Alexander I, fearing the revolutionary movements in Europe, became a more firm ruler. (See ALEXANDER [Emperors, Russian].)

The French Revolution introduced ideas of freedom that could not be entirely suppressed, even in Russia. Officers returning from military duty in France brought back with them ideas of political freedom and economic welfare almost unknown in Russia. Secret revolutionary societies sprang up, drawing their members chiefly from the educated nobility. After Alexander's death, a small revolutionary attempt in December 1825 was put down.

The vigorous measures of Alexander's brother and successor, Nicholas I, checked the attacks of the radicals. However, the defeat of Russia in the Crimean War (1854–1856) exposed the empire's weakness. (See NICHOLAS [Czars of Russia].)

When Alexander II, Nicholas' son, became czar in 1855, he made sweeping reforms in the hope of strengthening the country. His reign marked one of the great turning points of Russian history. He ordered the liberation of the serfs, introduced trial by jury, and permitted the provinces to be administered through their elected *zemstvos*, or councils. He favored industrial development. During his reign the railways were greatly extended, factory production was nearly tripled, and a modern banking system was introduced.

The emancipation of the serfs in 1861 failed to satisfy the peasants of Russia. They were interested in land ownership in addition to personal liberty. The greater freedom enjoyed by Russians under Alexander II had made possible an expansion of the opposition. Revolutionary activities developed among university students, the secret societies grew, and the peasant uprisings continued. Members of the nobility were also dissatisfied with the government. To these discontented elements was soon added another group, the proletariat, or city workers. They increased as industry grew. After the Polish uprising of 1863 was crushed, Alexander switched his support to the conservatives. By 1860 the Far Eastern area, north of Vladivostok, was seized from China. Russian troops subdued the Caucasus area and forcibly annexed most of the Central Asian region of Turkestan from the local khans. Alexander II sold Alaska to the United States in 1867. In 1881 he was assassinated by members of the People's Will, one of the many secret revolutionary societies in Russia. His son succeeded him.

The Revolutionary Setting

Alexander III announced himself in favor of autocratic rule. Repeated attempts were made to assassinate him as the revolutionary movement took on a decided socialist tendency. Thousands of political prisoners were shipped to Siberia. More thousands of opponents went abroad and carried on anticzarist activities from Germany, England, France, and Switzerland. Persecution of the Jews and other minority groups so increased under Alexander III that it brought protests from Western countries. Alexander died in 1894. His achievements included the beginning of the Trans-Siberian Railway, further industrialization, the extension of Russian power in Central Asia, and an alliance with France, but his harsh rule brought his country closer to revolution.

Nicholas II, last czar of Russia, inherited the complex situation left by Alexander III. Nicholas was a well-meaning but weak ruler at a time when great strength was required. The industrial growth of Russia continued, with the help of French capital and German technical assistance. Russia's ambitions in the Far East, however, involved her in a war with Japan during 1904 and 1905. Dissatisfaction with the czar's conduct of this war, the mistreatment of workers and minorities, and the czar's refusal to make concessions to liberal groups resulted in the Revolution of 1905. This started with a series of riots, strikes, and mob outbreaks. Eventually a general strike was called and actual revolutionary battles broke out.

In order to put an end to the revolt, the czar granted a constitution that limited his power and brought into existence the Duma, a national representative body. It met for the first time on May 10, 1906, but it was dissolved in July by the czar because the deputies were hostile to existing government policies. A second Duma elected in 1907 met the same fate when it proved to be even more hostile. A third Duma, elected soon afterwards, became established as a permanent part of the government and gradually extended its influence. Despite the almost constant domestic strife, the economy of the country had developed steadily up to the beginning of World War I in 1914.

During World War I the inefficiency of the

The October Revolution of 1917 swept the Bolsheviks (Communists) into power in Russia. Street fighting first began in Petrograd (now Leningrad) and quickly spread to Moscow.

U.P.I. Compix

Nicolai Lenin, leader of the communist revolution, spoke to a huge crowd in Red Square on May 1, 1919. The occasion was the unveiling of a monument to Stepan Razin, leader of the peasant revolt of the 17th century.

government of Nicholas II was clearly displayed. Russia entered the war on August 1, 1914. The Russians fought bravely for two and one-half years against superior German and Austrian armies. The troops suffered heavy losses, and many of the czar's advisers wanted to make peace with Germany. When strikes began in March 1917 in the capital, which had been renamed Petrograd, the government was too divided to act. After a few days, the strikes turned into revolution. The Duma formed a provisional government and asked the czar to abdicate. The czar abdicated in favor of the grand duke, who refused to rule. The royal family was later imprisoned and put to death, ending the Romanov dynasty.

The October (Bolshevik) Revolution

The provisional government, headed by Alexander Kerensky, had little real power. The soviets (councils) in various cities were largely in power. They were composed of Mensheviks, Social Revolutionaries, and Bolsheviks (Communists). The soviets were made up of soldiers, organized workers, and peasants. At first the Bolsheviks were the minority group. However, through strong leadership, they grew quickly

and gained power over the other groups. Originally established in 1903, the Bolsheviks were led by Nicolai Lenin and Leon Trotsky. The Bolsheviks demanded that the government be turned over to the soviets, that peace be made with Germany, and that the land be divided among the peasants. They organized an uprising in Petrograd in November 1917 and arrested all the members of the government except Kerensky, who fled. Because it was October according to the old Russian calendar, the event is often called the October Revolution. Soon after the revolt, the greater part of Russia was in the hands of the Bolsheviks.

Lenin called the new order a government of workers and peasants. In form it appeared to be democratic. Actually it was a dictatorship headed by a small group of Bolsheviks. The new government was confronted with many difficulties. The Germans were making new advances, and Russia was in no condition to continue fighting. In March 1918 Lenin accepted Germany's terms under the Treaty of Brest-Litovsk. The treaty forced Russia to give up Poland, Finland, the Baltic provinces (Estonia, Latvia, and Lithuania), the Ukraine, and Transcaucasia. Fearing that the Germans would seize the weapons and ammunition stored in Russia, the Allies (Great Britain, France, and the United States) landed a few thousand troops at Murmansk, Archangel, and Odessa in the spring of 1918. The Japanese landed troops at Vladivostok. The United States, mostly concerned with preventing Japanese expansion, also sent troops to Vladivostok.

The Russian Civil War

A civil war developed in Russia almost from the time the Bolsheviks took over in 1917. Lenin's main preoccupation was to crush his internal enemies. The Bolsheviks disbanded a legally elected constituent assembly that had passed a vote of no confidence in Lenin's government. Members of the assembly, who had been able to escape arrest (most of them anti-Communist Socialists), and their supporters formed provisional governments in many parts of Russia, Siberia, and Transcaucasia. Other provisional governments were formed by officers opposed to both communism and socialism. After World War I, the opponents of the Bolsheviks were divided, and the Allies withdrew all support from them, except in Poland. This enabled the Communists, led by Lenin and Trotsky, to destroy them one by one.

The civil war lasted until the end of 1920. It ended favorably for the Communists in Russia proper, Siberia, the Ukraine, Transcaucasia, and Central Asia. On the other hand the Bolsheviks were defeated in Finland, the Baltic provinces, and in Poland—all of which became independent.

During the civil war, a reign of terror was established by the Bolsheviks. Those who opposed them were deported or killed. Before the civil war was over, millions of people had died. In 1921 and 1922 drought and famine killed as many as 500,000 people. This figure would have been even higher had it not been for assistance from other countries, mainly the United States. Russia suffered terribly from the civil war. To bring economic recovery to the torn country, Lenin introduced the New Economic Policy (N.E.P.) in 1921. This policy restored a limited amount of private enterprise. All large-scale industrial installations, however, remained under the control of state trusts. By 1928 the N.E.P. had helped to restore the country's production to prewar levels.

Lenin died in January 1924. Immediately a struggle for power broke out among the other leaders. The chief contestants were Trotsky and Joseph Stalin, secretary-general of the Communist party. The conflict that broke out ended in a complete victory for Stalin. Trotsky was banished to Alma-Ata in 1928, and in the next year he left the country. He was murdered in Mexico in 1940. (See STALIN, JOSEPH VISSARIONOVICH; TROTSKY, LEON.)

The Five-Year Plans

As soon as he was sure of his political position, Stalin promoted an all-embracing five-year plan. It was drafted in 1927 and introduced in 1928. The plan aimed at generally transforming the economic life of the country by making it industrially powerful.

The first five-year plan also enforced collectivism in agriculture. It was met with considerable opposition. Officially, all land belonged to the state. The individual farmers, however, felt that they owned the land they had seized from the nobility in 1917. It was only by force that most of the 24,200,000 small peasant farms could be converted into 250,000 *kolkhozes* (collective farms). To subdue the most stubborn groups, and to intimidate the rest, the government drove the *kulaks* (prosper-

During the stormy civil war days from 1917 to 1920, millions of Russian people were killed and many towns were destroyed.

Sovfoto

ous farmers) from their homes and confiscated their property. The *kulaks* were wiped out as a class. They and other peasants were sent to forced labor camps in the northern sections of the U.S.S.R. There, many died from inadequate food, clothing, and sanitary conditions. Before being forced into collective farms, many peasants slaughtered their livestock. This action drastically reduced the supply of meat and dairy products and the draft (horse) power available for farm operations in succeeding years. It helped bring on a famine in 1932 and 1933. The number of peasants who were killed or who starved to death rose into the millions.

The Soviet government declared the first five-year plan to be complete nine months ahead of schedule. Although marked by considerable failure in agriculture, the plan was generally successful in speeding up industrialization in the Soviet Union. The development of a heavy industrial economy was continued by the next two five-year plans. The production of consumer goods for the average Soviet citizen, however, was ignored throughout this entire period.

The Stalin Purges and World War II

While the five-year plans were successful in modernizing Soviet industry, many flaws were apparent. Some of these were inefficiency among workers and managers, blunders in planning, and bureaucratic slowness. Stalin, perhaps afraid his power was threatened, began a reign of terror. From about 1936 to 1939 he conducted purges that swept the country. Old-line Bolsheviks, Army heads, and ordinary party workers were rounded up and accused of sabotage and conspiracy. Tens of thousands of people were executed, and millions were deported to remote areas of the Soviet Union.

Kiev (right) and many other Soviet cities were destroyed or heavily damaged by German bombing and artillery during World War II.

Photos, Sovfoto

The destruction caused by war and the rapidly increasing population after the war created great shortages of housing in the Soviet Union. To rebuild the cities and to provide housing for Soviet citizens, engineers used high-speed prefabricated construction methods (left). In many instances Soviet engineers built large new cities where no cities had existed before (below).

Sovfoto

On June 24, 1945, Soviet soldiers hurled captured Nazi military banners to the ground during Victory Parade ceremonies in Moscow to celebrate the end of World War II.

The purges virtually eliminated all opposition to Stalin.

The increasing power of Nazi Germany after 1933 alarmed the Soviet government and caused it to reverse its policy of hostility toward the Western powers. It sought to strengthen the Soviet Union through international agreements and by joining the League of Nations. European democratic states (chiefly Great Britain and France), however, were reluctant to enter into agreements with the U.S.S.R. Stalin then diverted German aggression by signing a friendship treaty with the Nazis in August 1939. In September of that year the Soviet Union and Germany divided Poland between them. In November the Soviet Army attacked and occupied part of Finland. In 1940 the Soviets invaded Estonia, Latvia, and Lithuania, and took Bessarabia from Rumania.

Germany broke its treaty agreement by invading the Soviet Union in June 1941. Hitler's armies overran the western part of the Soviet Union in the first 18 months of the war, but were stopped at Moscow, Leningrad, and Stalingrad (now Volgograd). The historic Battle of Stalingrad, in 1942 and 1943, especially, broke the German effort. Having reorganized their armies and with arms supplied by the United States, the Soviet government took the offensive in spite of its huge earlier losses. By the end of the war the Soviet Union had liberated all its territory; occupied Poland, Rumania, Bulgaria, Hungary, and parts of Czechoslovakia; and was in control of Eastern Germany. (See WORLD WAR II.)

The Iron Curtain

In 1945 the U.S.S.R. became one of the charter members of the United Nations. The Soviet Union demanded separate representation for each of the union republics. Through a compromise, however, individual representation was

U.S.S.R. Premier Nikita Khrushchev (second from right) presented the Soviet cosmonauts at an official welcome in Moscow in 1963. They are (left to right) Pavel Popovich; Gherman Titov; Andrian Nikolayev; Yuri Gagarin, the first man in space; Valentina V. Tereshkova, the first woman in space; and Valery F. Bykovsky, who orbited longest.

allowed only for the Ukraine, Belorussia, and for the rest of the U.S.S.R. as a unit. The Soviet leaders took advantage of confused postwar conditions in many parts of the world to extend communist rule. Communist-controlled governments were forced on the peoples of all the countries occupied by the Red Army. Poland, Rumania, Hungary, Czechoslovakia, East Germany, Bulgaria, and Albania became "satellite" states, virtually controlled by the Soviet Union. To be sure that these countries would stay communist, the Soviet Union cut off normal relations between its satellite empire and the West. Sir Winston S. Churchill, Britain's wartime prime minister, said that the U.S.S.R. had rung down an iron curtain across Eastern Europe. Ever since, the U.S.S.R. and its satellites have been called the iron curtain countries.

Postwar attempts to introduce Soviet-controlled regimes in Finland, Greece, and other countries failed. Yugoslavia became a communist state under Marshal Tito, but broke away from Soviet control. All the territories seized in 1940 from the Western border countries were reincorporated into the U.S.S.R., together with

the northern part of East Prussia (from Germany) and Ruthenia (from Czechoslovakia). In the Far East, the Soviet Union established a puppet government in Outer Mongolia, a large desertlike area. A few days before the Japanese surrender, Soviet troops invaded Manchuria and North Korea. Communist regimes were established in both areas. After the Japanese surrender, southern Sakhalin and the Kurile Islands were annexed by the Soviet Union.

Postwar Domestic Policy

The domestic policy of the Soviet government in the postwar years had two main objectives: the reconstruction of the severely damaged country, and the continued expansion of heavy industry. Stalin also maintained his drive to eliminate any real or potential disloyal elements. He especially suspected returning soldiers and Soviet civilians whom the Germans had forcibly moved to the West for war work.

After Stalin's death in March 1953, there was another Soviet scuffle for power. By 1956 it was clear that Nikita S. Khrushchev, the first secretary of the Communist party, was the winner. Like Stalin, he assumed dictatorial power.

In 1958 he also became chairman of the Council of Ministers (premier), the highest goverment post. Khrushchev's policies also stressed rapid industrialization. Industry, however, was well enough along so that more emphasis could be placed on agriculture and the production of consumer goods. Khrushchev also promoted a number of reforms in the educational and legal systems. Under Khrushchev, Stalin was denounced and eventually some police-state controls were relaxed. The Communists still held dictatorial powers, however.

Foreign Policy and the Cold War

After World War II a unique world political situation developed. The United States and the Soviet Union clearly emerged as the two greatest world powers. Hostility grew between the two, but both possessed atomic weapons, which kept open aggression in check. Instead, a war of ideologies developed. It pits the ideas of communism against those of democracy. The Soviet Union promotes communism wherever it can in the world, and the United States leads the fight to keep it from spreading. This conflict has become known as the cold war.

By the 1960's the Soviet Union was no longer the clear-cut leader of the communist world. China had been growing as a communist power, with Soviet support. The two countries were close allies until the Soviet Union began a policy of peaceful coexistence with the West. Some economic and cultural exchange began between East and West. China denounced this policy as a betrayal of Marxist-Leninist principles. By the mid-1960's it was evident that a major split had occurred in the communist world and Soviet leadership was threatened.

The new Soviet policy toward the West has been interpreted by some leaders as a thaw in the cold war. Certain Soviet actions, however, have tended to refute this. In particular, the discovery of Soviet missile bases in Cuba in 1962 was considered an act of hostility by the United States. U.S. President John F. Kennedy ordered the Soviet Union to remove its missiles. A few days later the U.S.S.R. agreed to the President's demand.

In the 1960's the Soviet Union gained considerable world prestige by putting the first man in space. A space race then developed between the United States and the Soviet Union. Though Soviet advances in science have been notable, agriculture continued to lag behind. The Soviet Union had to buy large quantities of wheat from the United States and other Western countries in 1963.

In October 1964 Khrushchev was forced to resign as the leader of the party and of the goverment. Leonid I. Brezhnev took over as first secretary of the party and Aleksei N. Kosygin became the new premier.

UNITARIAN (ū′nĭ tăr′ĭ ăn) **UNIVERSALIST** (ū nĭ vûr′săl ĭst) **ASSOCIATION** is a religious denomination created in 1961 by the merger of the Unitarian and Universalist churches. The Unitarian name came from a belief in the unity of God, as opposed to a belief in the Trinity of Father, Son, and Holy Spirit. The Universalist name came from a belief in salvation of all, as opposed to eternal punishment for some.

By the 17th century, certain religious groups in Poland, Hungary, and Transylvania held unitarian views; and John Biddle (1616?–1662) is known as the "father of English unitarianism." Both unitarianism and universalism came to America primarily from England, where there is still a strong Unitarian movement.

The most famous of the early New England clergymen who preached what was essentially unitarianism was Jonathan Mayhew (1720–1766). King's Chapel in Boston revised its prayer book in 1785 by removing all references to the Trinity. Joseph Priestley—a scientist noted as the discoverer of oxygen and a Unitarian minister at Leeds and Birmingham, England—moved to the United States in 1794 as a result of religious persecution. The church he established at Northumberland, Pennsylvania, in 1794 was probably the first church in America to bear the name Unitarian.

The origin of the Universalist church in the United States goes back to 1770, when the Reverend John Murray of London began preaching in America. Early Universalist churches were founded in Pennsylvania through the preaching of Benjamin Rush and George de

Benneville, both 18th-century physicians. In 1779 the first organized Universalist church was established at Gloucester, Massachusetts. Under the leadership of Hosea Ballou (1771–1852), Universalists largely became unitarian in thought.

William Ellery Channing, leader of the Federal Street Congregational church in Boston, became the leader of the Unitarian movement early in the 19th century and a large, liberal faction of that church embraced Unitarianism.

Unitarians and Universalists alike established preparatory and theological schools, as well as colleges, in various parts of the country. Unitarian Universalists differ considerably from other Protestant denominations in other respects than their historical views on the Trinity and universal salvation. They believe that Jesus was not divine, but rather a great teacher and leader among many other great religious leaders. They introduce the children in their church schools not only to the Christian Bible but to the Bibles of other world religions. They do not have an official creed, or statement of belief, to which all must agree. The Association includes individuals with widely differing ideas. They have done little missionary work, but both the Unitarian Service Committee and the Universalist Service Committee were known for their humanitarian work.

There are now some 1,200 churches and fellowships (groups not yet large enough to call a minister and thus become a church) in the United States. There are also Unitarian Universalist churches in Mexico and Canada.

A well-known work of the Association is carried on through the Beacon Press, which publishes works of scholars in the moral, religious, and educational fields who hold liberal views, whether or not they are members of the Association.

The Association is also a part of the International Association for Liberal Christianity and Religious Freedom. This organization has permanent headquarters in the Netherlands, and its purpose is "to open communication with those, who in all lands are striving to unite pure religion and perfect liberty, and to increase fellowship and co-operation among them."

UNITED ARAB REPUBLIC (U.A.R.), AFRICA, is the official name for Egypt. The name first applied to a union of Egypt and Syria formed on February 1, 1958. The union was considered a first step toward the unification of all Arab states. On March 8, 1958, Yemen joined the U.A.R. in a federation called the United Arab States. Yemen gave control of its foreign affairs to the U.A.R. Egypt's Gamal Abdel Nasser was elected president of the new republic.

The union was ended in September 1961, after Syrian Army officers revolted and established an independent Syrian government. Mahmoun al-Kuzbari, a lawyer, was named premier. Egypt continued to call itself the U.A.R.

The U.A.R. dissolved its federation with Yemen in December 1961. Differences between the royalist Yemenite government and the republican Egyptian government caused the separation. After a revolt in 1962, Yemen became a republic and the two countries resumed close relations.

Revolts by the armed forces in Iraq and Syria early in 1963 cleared the way for formation of a new U.A.R. Egypt, Syria, and Iraq signed an agreement that called for the three states to unite under a new constitution. For a short time it appeared as though the new republic would actually be formed. However, there was considerable hostility between Nasser and the political groups that controlled Syria and Iraq. The political groups were called the Baathists. As the hostility grew, hope for the republic dimmed. Another Iraqi revolt in November 1963 overthrew the Baathists in that country. The action revived the possibility of a new union. (See EGYPT.)

UNITED EMPIRE LOYALISTS were the colonists who remained loyal to King George and to Great Britain when the rest of the American colonists revolted. According to estimates, the Loyalists, or Tories as they were popularly called, made up about one-third of the colonial population. (See REVOLUTION, AMERICAN.)

Most Tories tried to stay out of the fighting, but many joined the British Army and fought against their countrymen. They were considered traitors, therefore, and after the war their lands were seized and many were persecuted or killed. As a result, many fled the young United States. Great Britain offered them land in Canada and food, money, and tools to help them start their new homes. About 60,000 Tories accepted Great Britain's offer; many of them became the first settlers of Ontario. They were given the right to call themselves United Empire Loyalists and to write the letters *U.E.L.* after their names.

Many other Loyalists joined them in Canada later. About 40,000 others moved to Florida, England, the Bahamas, and the West Indies.

UNITED KINGDOM, EUROPE, is an island

country off of the northwestern coast of the Continent, from which it is separated by the English Channel and the North Sea. The country has four main parts: England, Scotland, and Wales, which make up the large island of Great Britain, and a section of the northern part of the island of Ireland. Great Britain, Ireland, and a number of small nearby islands are often called the British Isles. (See ENGLAND; IRELAND, NORTHERN; SCOTLAND; WALES.)

From 1801 until 1927 the country was known as the United Kingdom of Great Britain and Ireland. In 1922, however, 26 Irish counties separated from the United Kingdom and formed a new country, the Irish Free State (now the Republic of Ireland). After that year, the title of the United Kingdom of Great Britain and Northern Ireland was often used, but it was not officially adopted until 1927.

The United Kingdom is a constitutional monarchy. That is, its government is headed by a king or queen whose powers are limited by a constitution. The actual head of the government is the prime minister. He is the leader of the party that has the largest number of candidates elected to Parliament, the lawmaking body. (See PARLIAMENT.)

The United Kingdom has a population of more than 52,000,000 persons (less than one-third the population of the United States). Its area, however, is only 94,211 square miles, or almost the size of the state of Oregon. London, the kingdom's capital, is one of the world's largest cities. (See LONDON.)

UNITED NATIONS (*nā'shŭnz*) is an international organization made up of almost all of the world's independent countries. It was formed to prevent war and to build a better world through international action. The United Nations (UN) constitution is known as the Charter. It was signed at San Francisco, California, on June 26, 1945, by representatives of the countries that participated in the United Nations Conference on International Organization.

In the Charter, the purposes of the UN are stated: (1) to maintain international peace and security by settling disputes peacefully or by taking steps to stop armed aggression; (2) to develop friendly relations among nations based on respect for equal rights and self-determination of peoples; (3) to achieve international co-operation in solving economic, social, cultural, and humanitarian problems; and (4) to serve as a center where the actions of nations can be combined in trying to attain these aims.

The Charter also defines the terms of membership. All "peace-loving" states that accept the obligations of the Charter, and that in the judgment of the UN are able and ready to carry out these obligations, may become members. The General Assembly, upon recommendation of the Security Council, admits new members by a two-thirds vote. A member may be suspended or expelled by vote of the General Assembly, if the Security Council so recommends.

The six principal organs of the UN are named in the Charter with their functions and powers. They are the General Assembly, the Security Council, the Economic and Social Council, the Trusteeship Council, the Secretariat, and the International Court of Justice.

General Assembly

UN activity is directed and supervised by the General Assembly. All members of the UN are members of the Assembly. It meets in regular session once a year, at which time it deals with questions of international concern. Each of the other UN organs submits reports to it, and the General Assembly may make specific

WE THE PEOPLES OF THE UNITED NATIONS DETERMINED

to save succeeding generations from the scourge of war, which twice in our lifetime has brought untold sorrow to mankind, and

to reaffirm faith in fundamental human rights, in the dignity and worth of the human person, in the equal rights of men and women and of nations large and small, and

to establish conditions under which justice and respect for the obligations arising from treaties and other sources of international law can be maintained, and

to promote social progress and better standards of life in larger freedom,

AND FOR THESE ENDS

to practice tolerance and live together in peace with one another as good neighbors, and

to unite our strength to maintain international peace and security, and

to ensure, by the acceptance of principles and the institution of methods, that armed force shall not be used, save in the common interest, and

to employ international machinery for the promotion of the economic and social advancement of all peoples,

HAVE RESOLVED TO COMBINE OUR EFFORTS TO ACCOMPLISH THESE AIMS.

Accordingly, our respective Governments, through representatives assembled in the city of San Francisco, who have exhibited their full powers found to be in good and due form, have agreed to the present Charter of the United Nations and do hereby establish an international organization to be known as the United Nations.

Preamble to the Charter of the United Nations.

recommendations to any organ. The Assembly also controls the budget, elects members to the various organs, and creates any organ it considers necessary to carry out UN work. For example, it established the Disarmament Commission, the UN Children's Fund (UNICEF), and a number of committees organized to do particular jobs. Important deliberations take place in plenary (full) session, but most of the General Assembly's work is done in these committees. The seven main committees deal with a variety of matters, such as legal, economic, or financial. There are also two procedural and two standing committees.

Each member nation may send a delegation of five representatives and five alternates to the General Assembly, but each nation has only one vote. (Individual countries decide the manner in which they elect their representatives. In the United States, the president appoints the delegates, with the approval of the Senate.) A two-thirds majority is required for a vote on important questions such as budgets, elections, and resolutions on political action. Other matters, classified as procedural questions, are decided by a simple majority.

The role of the General Assembly in keeping the peace is somewhat limited. It may consider the general problems of peace at any time, but it may make a recommendation on a particular dispute only when the Security Council is not dealing with it. If, however, the Security Council is deadlocked by a veto, it can request the General Assembly to meet in emergency session within 24 hours to consider the matter and make recommendations for action by the members. Such a request is made if a majority of seven members of the Security Council votes to do so. The General Assembly has had to meet in emergency session several times. In this way it has taken on more of the peacekeeping function because of the inability of the Security Council members to agree.

Security Council

The Security Council is entrusted with maintaining international peace and security. It is made up of 15 members and meets in continuous session. Five members are permanent—China (Nationalist), France, the U.S.S.R., the United Kingdom, and the United States. They are often referred to as the Big Five. The ten nonpermanent members are elected by the General Assembly for two-year terms.

Each of the members has one vote. Decisions on routine or procedural matters are made by a majority vote of nine. On all other matters the majority of nine must include the yes votes of all the permanent members who are voting. A no vote by a permanent member is a veto. In the peaceful settlement of a dispute, no member, not even a permanent one, may vote if it is a party to the dispute. Members of the UN who are not sitting on the Security Council, as well as nonmembers of the UN, may be invited by the Council to take part, without vote, if a matter of concern to them is being

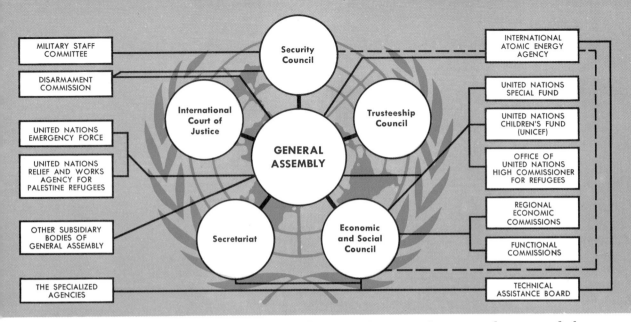

considered. Any member of the UN or the secretary-general may bring a matter that threatens the peace to the Council's attention.

The Charter provides that all parties to a dispute will settle their differences peacefully. They may do this by peaceful means of their own choice, or by referring the dispute to the Security Council. The Council may investigate the dispute and call upon the parties to settle peacefully. If the parties fail, the Council may recommend terms of settlement. It may recommend strong measures when the situation is a threat to the peace, a breach of the peace, or an act of aggression. In the case of the latter two, the Council may call for a cease-fire. It may call for diplomatic and economic penalties, and stoppage of all trade and communication. If these measures do not restore peace, the Council may recommend that the UN members form an armed force, as it did in the case of Korea.

If an armed attack occurs, the attacked nation may defend itself with its own armed forces or accept help from other UN nations acting jointly until the Council takes action to restore peace. Thus, regional arrangements such as the North Atlantic and the Southeast Asia treaty organizations, which provide for joint action in case of attack, are permissible under the Charter. (See NORTH ATLANTIC TREATY ORGANIZATION [NATO]; SOUTHEAST ASIA TREATY ORGANIZATION [SEATO].)

On the call of the Council, each member na-

tion has agreed to contribute armed forces, assistance, facilities, and the right of passage through its territory. A part of national air forces also is to be held available. The Military Staff Committee, composed of the chiefs of staff of the Big Five, advises and assists the Council in these military matters. By the terms of the Charter, the Council and this committee are to work out agreements with the UN members as to the size and nature of their contributions to the UN armed forces. To date, no such agreements have been made, because the cold war between the communist-dominated countries and the Western countries has prevented the permanent members of the Council from coming to terms.

This lack of agreement has threatened to prevent the Security Council from performing its major task—keeping the peace. In 1950, when South Korea was attacked by North Korea, the Council was able to agree to the use of an armed force only because the U.S.S.R. was not present to cast a veto. Because this would not always be the case, the General Assembly adopted in 1950 what are called the "Uniting for Peace" resolutions. These call on the Security Council to carry out its functions as stated in the Charter. They provide for action by the Assembly if the Security Council fails to take steps when the peace is threatened. They further recommend that the member nations keep armed forces available in case the As-

The UN Security Council (above) helps to maintain international peace. Ambassador Adlai E. Stevenson of the United States and Ambassador Carlos Sosa-Rodriguez of Venezuela (right) confer during the 1962 Cuban crisis.

sembly finds armed force necessary.

The Peace Observation Commission and the Collective Measures Committee were established by the resolutions. The former is composed of 14 members, including the permanent members of the Security Council. It makes on-the-spot investigations in areas where tension threatens international peace and security. The Collective Measures Committee, also with 14 members, investigates the possible measures that the Assembly might use to maintain international peace and security.

In 1952 another commission to deal with security questions was established by the General Assembly. This, the Disarmament Commission, is composed of all UN members. Its function is to study and prepare proposals for the regulation, limitation, and balanced reduction of all armed forces and all armaments; the elimination of weapons, such as the hydrogen bomb, that are capable of mass destruction; and the use of atomic energy for peaceful purposes. The Commission functions under the Security Council and also reports to the General Assembly.

Economic and Social Council

The Economic and Social Council is the organ that carries on the UN's economic, social,

and cultural activities. It is composed of 27 members, elected by the General Assembly to serve for three-year terms. Each member has one vote, and action is taken by majority decision. The Council meets in two regular sessions each year.

The aim of the Council is to promote higher standards of living, full employment, and economic and social progress and development; to find solutions to international economic, social, health, and related problems; to encourage international cultural and educational co-operation; and to bring about universal observance of human rights and fundamental freedoms without distinction as to race, sex, language, or religion. To carry out this work, the Council is assisted by numerous commissions and specialized agencies.

There are seven functional commissions and one subcommission under the Council. Their titles describe their activities: (1) Commission on International Commodity Trade; (2) Statistical Commission; (3) Population Commission; (4) Social Commission; (5) Commission on Narcotic Drugs; (6) Commission on Human Rights, under which is the Sub-Commission on Prevention of Discrimination and Protection of Minorities; and (7) Commission on the Status of Women.

The commissions conduct research and perform special services. They draft treaties for the Council to consider. When these are adopted by the UN, they become the basis of international law in the economic and social fields. The Commission on Human Rights prepared the Universal Declaration of Human Rights, adopted in 1948. This declaration was used in drafting constitutions for certain new nations, such as Israel and Indonesia. In a

MEMBERS OF THE UNITED NATIONS[1]

Afghanistan	1946	Greece		Niger	1960
Albania	1955	Guatemala		Nigeria	1960
Algeria	1962	Guinea	1958	Norway	
Argentina		Guyana	1966	Pakistan	1947
Australia		Haiti		Panama	
Austria	1955	Honduras		Paraguay	
Barbados	1966	Hungary	1955	Peru	
Belgium		Iceland	1946	Philippines	
Belorussian S.S.R.		India		Poland	
Bolivia		Indonesia	1950	Portugal	1955
Botswana	1966	Iran		Rumania	1955
Brazil		Iraq		Rwanda	1962
Bulgaria	1955	Ireland	1955	Saudi Arabia	
Burma	1948	Israel	1949	Senegal	1960
Burundi	1962	Italy	1955	Sierra Leone	1961
Cambodia	1955	Ivory Coast	1960	Singapore	1965
Cameroon	1960	Jamaica	1962	Somali Republic	1960
Canada		Japan	1956	South Africa	
Central African Republic	1960	Jordan	1955	Southern Yemen	1967
Ceylon	1955	Kenya	1963	Spain	1955
Chad	1960	Kuwait	1963	Sudan	1956
Chile		Laos	1955	Swaziland	1968
China (Nationalist)		Lebanon		Sweden	1946
Colombia		Lesotho	1966	Syria	
Congo, Democratic Republic of the	1960	Liberia		Tanzania[2]	1964
Congo, Republic of	1960	Libya	1955	Thailand	1946
Costa Rica		Luxembourg		Togo	1960
Cuba		Malagasy Republic	1960	Trinidad and Tobago	1962
Cyprus	1960	Malawi	1964	Tunisia	1956
Czechoslovakia		Malaysia[2]	1963	Turkey	
Dahomey	1960	Maldive Islands	1965	Uganda	1962
Denmark		Mali	1960	Ukrainian S.S.R.	
Dominican Republic		Malta	1964	Union Of Soviet Socialist Republics	
Ecuador		Mauritania	1961	United Arab Republic (Egypt)	
El Salvador		Mauritius	1968	United Kingdom	
Equatorial Guinea	1968	Mexico		United States	
Ethiopia		Mongolian People's Republic	1961	Upper Volta	1960
Finland	1955	Morocco	1956	Uruguay	
France		Nepal	1955	Venezuela	
Gabon	1960	Netherlands		Yemen	1947
Gambia, The	1965	New Zealand		Yugoslavia	
Ghana	1957	Nicaragua		Zambia	1964

1 Original members are listed in heavier type. Dates of admittance are given for others. List is complete as of May 1969.
2 Previously admitted as separate nations: Malaya in 1957, Tanganyika in 1961, Zanzibar in 1963.

number of countries it has been used by the courts to uphold civil rights.

In addition to the seven functional commissions, there are four regional economic commissions: the Economic Commission for Europe; the Economic Commission for Asia and the Far East; the Economic Commission for Latin America; and the Economic Commission for Africa. They perform a variety of tasks.

There also are 14 specialized agencies linked with the UN by special agreements. Some existed before the UN was founded, and some include, as members, nations that do not belong to the UN. These agencies are independent groups that work with the Economic and Social Council. They make reports to the Council, and the Council makes recommendations to them

and co-ordinates their policies and activities.

World Health Organization. The World Health Organization (WHO) was established in 1948. The goal of the agency is to promote the highest level of world health.

The various activities of WHO include research and advisory services. The organization's technical experts assist governments in expanding and strengthening their public-health programs. They help set up local health centers and train personnel.

WHO conducts worldwide campaigns against diseases, such as tuberculosis and malaria, which kill millions of people each year. These campaigns include mass vaccination and health education programs.

WHO acts as a clearinghouse for information.

Its daily radio broadcasts inform governments of the outbreak of disease and of the measures that should be taken to prevent epidemics. It recommends international standards and regulations for sanitation, medicines, quarantine restrictions, and reporting disease and causes of death. Through its publications, the organization informs governments of medical research being carried on throughout the world. It also publishes international disease statistics.

International Labor Organization. The International Labor Organization (ILO) was established in 1919 in association with the League of Nations. Its headquarters are at Geneva.

The goal of ILO is to help raise living standards throughout the world. To do so, it sets international labor and social standards; provides technical assistance; and collects and distributes information of social and economic interest. Representation in ILO is unique among international organizations. The delegations from the member nations are made up of four representatives—two representing government; one, labor; and one, management. Each representative has one vote.

Labor standards are set by ILO by international treaties known as conventions. When a member nation's government ratifies a convention, the convention becomes law in that nation. ILO has drafted more than 100 conventions. They deal with maximum hours of work, minimum wages for seamen, minimum age when children may begin work, workmen's compensation, and many other matters. Model codes of safety for factories, mines, and other places of work have been devised by the organization, and it has undertaken a program of assistance to governments for training workers and developing the skills necessary for economic advancement. ILO also assists governments to organize employment services and to work out social security and other modern labor legislation.

Food and Agriculture Organization. The UN organized the Food and Agriculture Organization (FAO) in 1945. Its headquarters are in Rome, Italy. The aims of the organization are to promote better nutrition, improve production and distribution of agricultural products, and better the condition of rural populations. Its many projects include helping to fight animal and plant diseases, introducing new seeds, promoting artificial insemination of cattle, fighting against soil erosion and land waste, and helping with reforestation. FAO has done much to improve the diets of the peoples of underdeveloped countries. It watches the world's food supplies so that recommendations for action to meet shortages or surpluses can be made.

The UN's Food and Agriculture Organization (FAO) aids such projects as this dam construction in Nepal.

Courtesy United Nations

United Nations Educational, Scientific and Cultural Organization. Established in 1946, the UN Educational, Scientific and Cultural Organization (UNESCO) attempts to contribute to world peace and security by promoting better understanding through education, science, and culture.

One of UNESCO's major objectives is to reduce illiteracy. Its several educational projects include aiding member nations in the reorganization of ineffective educational systems. In the scientific and cultural fields, as well, UNESCO carries on numerous activities, including research projects, technical assistance programs, exchange programs, and surveys. Its headquarters are in Paris, France.

International Bank for Reconstruction and Development. The International Bank for Reconstruction and Development (IBRD), or World Bank, came into being in 1945 to promote international investments that would aid in the postwar reconstruction and economic development of member nations.

The Bank encourages private foreign investments. However, when a member is unable to secure a loan from private interests, the Bank lends money from its resources or from funds borrowed by it. The Bank also has an advisory function. It sends missions of experts to member nations. The missions study the economies and then plan investment and development programs. The Bank's headquarters are in Washington, D.C.

International Finance Corporation; International Development Association. The International Finance Corporation (IFC) was established in 1956 and the International Development Association (IDA) in 1960. Both organizations are affiliated with the World Bank, and headquarters of both are in Washington, D.C.

IFC was established to aid economic development by encouraging private investment in the member nations. It invests directly, together with private investors, in business ventures in these areas.

IDA, like the World Bank, makes loans to member nations for their economic development. The terms of the loans, however, are more lenient than those of the Bank.

International Monetary Fund. The International Monetary Fund (IMF) came into being in 1945. Its task is to promote international monetary co-operation by helping to expand and balance international trade and by helping to stabilize currencies. The Fund works closely with the World Bank in performing this task.

Major changes in value of a member nation's currency cannot be made without the Fund's permission. The Fund enables a member to buy currencies of other countries to pay for imports. The Fund has a broad technical assistance program that provides experts to help members solve monetary problems. Headquarters of the Fund are in Washington, D.C.

International Telecommunication Union. The International Telecommunication Union (ITU), with headquarters at Geneva, Switzerland, was established in 1934. The organization's task is to establish international regulations for radio, telegraph, and telephone transmission across national boundaries. It helps in assigning frequencies for broadcasting stations, ships, planes, and all other types of radio communication. It works to reduce rates and improve communication services.

Universal Postal Union. The Universal Postal Union (UPU) was established in 1875 to regulate and improve international postal services. Its headquarters are in Bern, Switzerland. UPU fixes the rates, weight limits, and other regulations for regular foreign mail. It also regulates international parcel post, insured mail, subscriptions to periodicals, money orders, and C.O.D. articles.

World Meteorological Organization. The World Meteorological Organization (WMO), with headquarters in Geneva, Switzerland, was established in 1950. Its aim is to co-ordinate and improve meteorological activities throughout the world. To achieve this goal, it works toward the establishment of a worldwide network of meteorological stations. The organization also works to bring about the most rapid exchange of weather information. It promotes uniformity in observing and reporting weather conditions. Through its publications, WMO spreads this information so that it may be applied to farming, aviation, and shipping.

International Civil Aviation Organization. In 1947 the International Civil Aviation Organization (ICAO) was established to develop the principles and techniques of international air navigation. ICAO works to ensure the safe and orderly growth of civil aviation throughout the world. By means of treaties, it sets up traffic laws, air rights and duties, and standards that airplanes and pilots must meet to

UNICEF provides food, clothing, and medicine to children of devastated or poverty-stricken areas of the world.

assure safety in international air travel. At the same time, it promotes development of new airways and construction of new airports throughout the world. ICAO headquarters are in Montreal, Canada.

Inter-Governmental Maritime Consultative Organization. The UN established the Inter-Governmental Maritime Consultative Organization (IMCO) in 1958 to develop international co-operation in maritime navigation. The organization encourages high standards of safety and efficiency and works to eliminate unnecessary restrictions and unfair practices by both governments and shipping companies. The headquarters of IMCO are in London, England.

International Atomic Energy Agency. The International Atomic Energy Agency (IAEA) was established in 1957 with headquarters in Vienna, Austria. It had its origin in a proposal made before the General Assembly in 1953 by U.S. President Dwight D. Eisenhower.

The aim of IAEA is to further the peaceful use of atomic energy. To do this, it encourages its members to exchange services, materials, and equipment. It also promotes the exchange of scientific information, and it helps in the exchange and training of atomic scientists and in the development of safety standards for protection against atomic radiation.

Other Bodies. The General Assembly has created certain other bodies that are connected to the Economic and Social Council. While World War II was in progress, the UN Relief and Rehabilitation Administration (UNRRA) was set up to provide food, clothing, and medicines to war-devastated areas. It saw to the care of the many millions displaced by the war, finding shelter and food for them.

When UNRRA was dissolved in 1949, its functions were turned over to other UN bodies. Much of its work was carried on by the International Refugee Organization (IRO), a temporary specialized agency that was established in 1948 and dissolved in 1951. IRO helped more than a million refugees find new homes. Its work is now carried on mainly by the Office of the High Commissioner for Refugees (UNHCR) established in 1951. The UN Relief and Works Agency for Palestine Refugees in the Near East (UNRWA) also exists to assist with this work. The special care that UNRRA had given children was taken over by the UNICEF. It provides food, clothing, and medicines to children throughout the world. Its programs include helping underdeveloped countries organize feeding and health programs that will have long-range benefits for children of those areas. The UN Special Fund aids underdeveloped countries to finance large-scale economic projects.

Expanded Program of Technical Assistance

In 1949 the General Assembly approved a broad plan for aiding the development of member nations. This, the Expanded Program of Technical Assistance, is financed by voluntary contributions from UN members. The specialized agencies taking part in the Program and sharing its funds are IAEA, ILO, FAO, UNESCO, ICAO, WHO, ITU, WMO, and UPU. The Program brings their individual assistance projects into co-operation with one another and co-ordinates them so that they are better able to achieve their goals. The Bank and the Fund co-ordinate their activities with the Program, but do not share its funds.

The operations of the Program are coordinated and supervised by the Technical Assistance Board (TAB). It is made up of the secretary-general of the UN and the executive heads of the participating specialized agencies. TAB reports and makes recommendations to the Technical Assistance Committee (TAC) of the Economic and Social Council. TAC makes decisions on these recommendations and approves proposed assistance plans. TAC reports to the Economic and Social Council.

The Program provides technical aid by sending teams of experts to countries to advise the governments and to train local personnel; by providing fellowships or scholarships to citizens of underdeveloped countries; and by organizing regional training centers.

Many millions of dollars have been spent by the UN in this Program, and several thousand experts have gone all over the world to give technical assistance. They have helped to build penicillin factories, airports, and bridges; to modernize steel mills, mines, and shipbuilding; and to organize public-health and nursing programs, and soil-conservation and water-power projects. The many scholarships that have been awarded for study abroad enable men and women to learn valuable new skills that can help in their country's development. For example, they learn how to control malaria; how to improve farming, long-distance telephone systems, air transport services, and weather forecasting; and how to teach children to read and write.

Trusteeship Council

The UN trusteeship system is the method by which certain non-self-governing territories are administered. The Trusteeship Council is the UN organ that supervises the administration of the territories.

The Charter contains a "Declaration Regarding Non-Self-Governing Territories." It lists a series of obligations that members must accept for the administration of colonial peoples. They are: to recognize that the interests of the inhabitants come first; to promote to the utmost the well-being of the inhabitants, with due respect for native culture; to ensure their political, economic, social, and educational advancement; to develop self-government; and to report to the secretary-general on the conditions of the territories. The reports are considered by the General Assembly.

The Charter also defines the trusteeship system. This system has brought certain colonial territories under direct supervision by the UN. They include former League of Nations mandates that have not yet become self-governing. Mandates are colonial areas that were taken from Germany and Turkey after World War I and placed under the League of Nations. The League, in turn, mandated the areas to member nations for administration. Also under the UN trusteeship system are territories taken from the Axis powers in World War II. In addition, a colonial power may voluntarily place a colony in the system. This is done by a trusteeship agreement, which states the terms of administration and names the administering nation. One or more nations or the UN itself may ad-

Either the Security Council or the General Assembly can use armed forces to maintain peace—as was done in Korea, the Republic of the Congo (below), and Cyprus.

Courtesy United Nations

minister the territory.

The membership of the Council is equally divided between states that are administering trust territories and those that are not. All states that administer territories are automatically members, as are the permanent members of the Security Council that do not administer territories. The remaining members are elected by the General Assembly for terms of three years. Decisions of the Trusteeship Council are by simple majority. The Council meets in two regular sessions each year.

In placing a colonial area under trusteeship, part or all of the territory may be designated as a strategic area, that is, an area essential to the security or defense of the administering authority. The administering authority is then responsible to the Security Council rather than to the Trusteeship Council. The only areas that have been designated as strategic have been so designated by the United States. They are the former mandated Pacific Islands—the Mariana, Marshall, and Caroline islands—that the United States won from Japan in World War II.

To carry out its task of supervising the trusteeship agreements, the Trusteeship Council reviews the conditions in the trust territories each year. It may do this by sending an inspection mission to an area. The Council also receives and examines petitions from the inhabitants of a trust territory or from other interested persons. Sometimes a petitioner appears in person before the Council to express his grievances. The Council—from its visiting missions, from petitions, and from reports submitted by administering powers—is expected to gather the facts necessary to direct progress in the administration of the trust territories.

Of the original 11 UN trust territories, only two remain in the status of trusts. These are New Guinea, which is administered by Australia, and the Pacific Islands, administered by the United States. All of the others have joined with independent nations or have become independent states themselves. Togoland (United Kingdom) became part of Ghana in 1957. Togoland (France) became the Republic of Togo in 1960. Somalia (Italy) joined the former British Somaliland Protectorate in 1960 to form the Somali Republic. In 1961 the northern part of the Cameroons (United Kingdom) joined the Federation of Nigeria, and the southern part joined Cameroun (France) to become part of the Republic of Cameroon. Tanganyika (United Kingdom) became independent in 1961. Ruanda-Urundi (Belgium) be-

The General Assembly, which meets in regular session once a year, directs and supervises all UN activities. Each of the other UN organs submits reports to it. The Assembly's membership includes all UN member nations.

Courtesy United Nations

came two independent nations, Rwanda and Burundi, in 1962. Western Samoa became independent in 1962, and Nauru in 1968. The UN voted in 1966 to end the last League of Nations mandate, South West Africa, which had been administered by the Republic of South Africa.

International Court of Justice

The International Court of Justice is the judicial organ of the UN. It sits in permanent session at The Hague, Netherlands. The Statute, or governing law, of the Court is part of the Charter. All members of the UN are automatically parties to the Statute.

The Court has 15 judges. They are elected by the General Assembly and the Security Council for terms of nine years. They are selected for their qualifications, not their nationality. However, no two judges may be nationals of the same state. The Statute directs that the judges be selected so that the main forms of civilization and major legal systems of the world are represented.

Jurisdiction of the Court covers cases that parties submit to it and matters that are provided for in the Charter and in other treaties. States are not required to submit cases to the Court. They may settle their differences before other courts.

Only nations, not individuals, may bring cases before the court. The decisions of the Court are binding to the parties of a case and cannot be appealed. All decisions of the Court are made by a majority of the judges. If a party to a case fails to comply with the Court's decision, the other party may take the case before the Security Council, which may determine any action necessary to enforce the Court's judgment. The Court also gives advisory opinions upon request by the General Assembly and the Security Council. Other organs and agencies that have been authorized by the General Assembly may also call for advisory opinions.

Secretariat

The Secretariat is the organ that carries on the daily work of the UN. It is headed by the secretary-general, who is appointed by the General Assembly on the recommendation of the Security Council. He serves for a five-year term.

As chief administrative officer of the UN, the secretary-general is responsible for appointing and maintaining the Secretariat staff. He also has important political functions in that he is to bring to the UN's attention any threat or violation of the international peace and security. He also performs special tasks (such as political missions) assigned to him by other UN organs. He is required to submit an annual report to the General Assembly.

At its first session in 1946, the General Assembly appointed Trygve Lie of Norway as secretary-general. In 1950 his term was extended for three years, but he resigned after two. Dag Hammarskjold of Sweden was appointed in 1953 and again in 1957. When he was killed in an airplane crash in Africa in 1961, U Thant of Burma was made acting secretary-general. He was unanimously elected to a permanent term in 1962 and was re-elected in 1966.

The Secretariat is divided into several departments or offices. Each is headed by an under-secretary or an official of equal rank.

The Charter stresses the international character of the Secretariat. All members of the Secretariat take an oath of service not to accept instructions from any government or outside authority in their performance of UN work. They are international civil servants with allegiance to the UN. The staff members number approximately 5,200. They work in offices throughout the world, although the majority are at the UN's permanent headquarters in New York City.

Historical Development of the UN

During and after World War II, a series of events occurred that led to the founding of the United Nations. In August 1941 the Atlantic Charter was drawn up and signed by U.S. President Franklin D. Roosevelt and by British Prime Minister Winston Churchill. It proposed the establishment of a "permanent system of general security" and set forth basic principles of peace that later became part of the UN Charter.

On January 1, 1942, the 26 nations meeting at

The permanent headquarters of the UN, including the Secretariat Building, are located by the East River on Manhattan Island in New York City.

Washington, D.C., signed a declaration accepting the principles of the Atlantic Charter and pledging united effort to defeat the Axis powers. For the first time, the name United Nations was used, for this declaration was called the Declaration by United Nations.

In October 1943, China, the United Kingdom, the U.S.S.R., and the United States, meeting in Moscow, U.S.S.R., issued a Declaration of Four Nations on General Security, which is known as the Moscow Declaration. It recognized the need for setting up a general international organization to keep the peace. About a year later, in July 1944, an international monetary conference was held at Bretton Woods, New Hampshire. Forty-four nations attended and signed the agreement setting up the Bank and the Fund. Later that year the Dumbarton Oaks Conference met in Washington, D.C., with representatives from China, the U.S.S.R., the United Kingdom, and the United States. They drew up proposals for a world organization. These proposals, which were published for study and comment, became the basis of the UN Charter. The Yalta Conference attended by Franklin Roosevelt, Winston Churchill, and Joseph Stalin was held in the U.S.S.R. in February 1945. They agreed to call the San Francisco Conference. They also drew up a proposal for voting procedure in the Security Council.

The United Nations Conference on International Organization began in San Francisco in April 1945. Representatives from 50 nations were present. Poland was included as an original member of the United Nations, although its postwar government was not organized in time to send a representative to the conference. The number of original members who signed the Charter was, therefore, 51. On October 24, 1945, after the United States, the U.S.S.R., the United Kingdom, France, China, and a majority of the other nations ratified the Charter, the UN officially came into being.

At the same time that the Charter was signed, a Preparatory Commission was formed to set up a working organization. On January 10, 1946, in London, England, the General Assembly opened its first session, with representatives from the 51 participating countries. In August the property and assets of the League of Nations were transferred to the UN. In December 1946 the UN accepted from John D. Rockefeller, Jr., a gift of $8,500,000 to be used toward the purchase of a site of land in New York City for the organization's permanent headquarters. (See also LEAGUE OF NATIONS.)

U.S.A.

UNITED STATES, NORTH AMERICA, one of the world's greatest countries, extends across the North American continent from the Atlantic Ocean on the east to the Pacific Ocean on the west. Officially it is known as the United States of America, but often it is called simply America. It is made up of 50 states and the District of Columbia. Forty-eight of the states are in a compact group between Canada on the north and Mexico and the Gulf of Mexico on the south. The 49th state, Alaska, is on the Pacific Coast, west and northwest of Canada. The 50th state, Hawaii, is a group of islands in the North Pacific, about 2,400 miles southwest of California.

The United States ranks fourth in both area and population among the countries of the world. It is the world's wealthiest country, having excellent natural resources, which include fertile lands, huge forests, important rivers and lakes, and extensive mineral riches. With the aid of these resources, great cities and industries have been built, and vast farmlands have been developed.

The people of the United States are generally called Americans. They come from a variety of backgrounds and include peoples of every nationality, racial stock, and religion. Together, however, they form a highly unified nation. Americans live under a democratic form of government that gives them freedom and opportunity. They are well educated and have a productive economy. Employment is high, and workers generally earn more money and have more luxuries than workers in most other countries. As a result, Americans have attained one of the highest standards of living in the world.

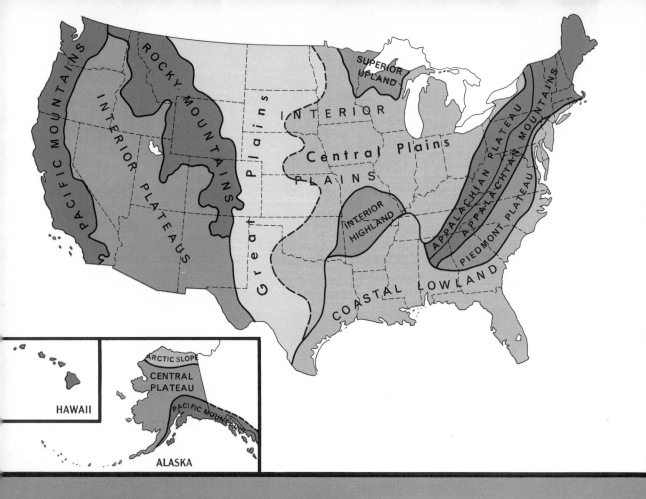

The United States has many different types of landscapes. It has North America's highest mountain peaks and lowest land surface, as well as the world's largest active and inactive volcanoes. In addition, there are hot sandy deserts, cold arctic wastelands, spectacular river canyons, broad flat lowlands, vast fertile plains, towering mountain ranges, warm tropic swamplands, thousands of miles of ocean coasts, great rivers, and thousands of freshwater lakes.

The country may be divided into many different regions. One way of dividing it is by land regions, or areas of similar landscapes and geographic features, as in the map above. These regions and their subregions are discussed in this article.

PLATE 1   UNITED STATES Almost every kind of climate and landscape can be found in the United States. Its varied scenery includes (1) rocky stretches of coast along the Pacific Ocean, (2) canyons formed from beautiful rock structures, and (3) shifting sand dunes in desert areas.

Courtesy Union Pacific Railroad

William E. Warne

PLATE 2 UNITED STATES The giant sequoia trees grow only in California. They are among the largest and oldest living things in the world. Some grow to heights of more than 300 feet, and some have been known to live more than 3,000 years.

1

2

PLATE 3 UNITED STATES (1) Hills, sculptured by wind and rain, rise above reclaimed desert land in the southwest. (2) "Old Faithful," the most famous of the many geysers in Yellowstone National Park, erupts hourly. (3) A natural bridge in Utah was formed from brightly colored sandstone.

Courtesy (1) U.S. Soil Conservation Service, photo by A. W. Jarrett; (2,3) Union Pacific Railroad

3

PLATE 4 UNITED STATES The seasons of the year produce varied effects in the colors of the land. (1) Evergreen growth and snow patches that remain in the peaks all year make these mountains in the northwest appear somewhat the same in all seasons. (2) Narcissus, sweet alyssum, and tulips mark the spring season all over the United States. (3) The rich gold of midsummer harvesting is a typical sight in farming areas.

Courtesy U.S. Soil Conservation Service, photos (1) by Herrin F. Culver, (2) Hermann Postlethwaite, (3) Robert Branstead

PLATE 5 UNITED STATES (1) During Indian summer in the Middle West the countryside turns to a hazy red and gold. The corn has been harvested and is standing in shocks. (2) A New England pond and dam turn to icy blue in winter. (3) Snow may come in the Rocky Mountain Region while the aspens are still in their yellow dress of fall.

PLATE 6 UNITED STATES One of the duties of the federal government is to protect and develop the natural resources of the country. (1) Buffalo herds are kept in wildlife refuges. Herds of buffalo once roamed over almost the entire country, but so many were killed by hunters that they nearly became extinct. (2) This contour-planted forest on steep land in a conservation district will prevent topsoil from washing off into the lake. The Department of Agriculture develops methods by which erosion is prevented. (3) A field day is being held so that farmers from surrounding farms can observe methods to improve their land. The engineering for the building of a one-acre pond to be used for drainage was done by the Department of Agriculture.

Courtesy U.S. Soil Conservation Service, photos by (1,3) Hermann Postlethwaite, (2) Herrin F. Culver

PLATE 7 UNITED STATES After the United States was settled, the appearance of the land was greatly changed. The people began to use the natural resources. The erection of buildings, dams, roads, and other structures, along with the clearing of swamp and forest sites, greatly altered the original look of the countryside. (1) The different crops cultivated on farms give the land various colors and patterns. (2) Contour farming adds to the design.

Courtesy (1) Union Pacific Railroad; (2) U.S. Soil Conservation Service, photo by W. H. Lathrop

PLATE 8   UNITED STATES Some natural resources must be industrialized in order to use them to best advantage. (1) Oil is kept in refinery storage tanks in Louisiana. Through various processes, products such as gasoline, waxed papers, T.N.T., alcohols, and many others are made wholly or partially from petroleum. (2) Steel foundries light up the sky in Pittsburgh, Pennsylvania, the "city of steel." Enormous amounts of coal and iron are used in these mills to make steel from which comes thousands of finished products.

Courtesy (1) Standard Oil Co. (N.J.); (2) Jones and Laughlin Steel Corp., photo by Scott d'Arazien

I. Landscape

The Coastal Lowland region extends along the country's Atlantic Coast from Cape Cod in Massachusetts southward into Mexico. That part of the region lying along the ocean is often called the Atlantic Coastal Plain, and the part along the Gulf of Mexico is known as the Gulf Coastal Plain. The region is mostly a flat belt with a surface that seldom rises higher than 500 feet above sea level. Low ridges and hills border the coast at places in Texas, Mississippi, and Alabama. There also are hilly sections in central Florida and in most of the states to the north. Swamps, marshes, and lagoons are found in many places along the coasts of Virginia, North Carolina, Florida, and Louisiana. Sand dunes and offshore islands are common.

Between Cape Cod and New York City the Coastal Lowland is quite narrow, and in some places it disappears entirely. The region includes the islands of Nantucket, Martha's Vineyard, and Long Island. The difference between the lowland and the higher Piedmont Plateau is marked by the fall line, so called because of the falls or rapids that result when the streams wear down the softer material of the coastal plain. (See FALL LINE.)

The Appalachian Mountain region is composed of a wide belt of rolling uplands, or plateaus, and low mountains that extend from central Alabama northeastward across the New England states into Canada. In the northeastern part of the region, east of the Hudson River Valley, are several areas of low, rounded mountain ranges that rise above the hilly New England upland. West of the Connecticut River Valley in Vermont and Massachusetts are the Green Mountains, from 3,000 to 4,000 feet high. They merge with the Berkshire Hills in Massachusetts, which join to the west with the Taconic Range. One of the highest peaks in the Appalachians is Mount Washington (6,288 feet), which lies in the White Mountains in northern New Hampshire. In the highlands of northern Maine, 5,268-foot Mount Katahdin is the highest point. (See GREEN MOUNTAINS; WHITE MOUNTAINS.)

It is believed that the northeast was once covered by a great, slowly moving ice sheet, or glacier. As the glacier melted, it left many of the features that are common in the northeast. Among them are rounded hills called drumlins, long low ridges called eskers, hundreds of lakes, and countless large boulders. (See GLACIAL PERIOD.)

Lying to the west of the narrow lowlands along Lake Champlain and the Hudson River are the Adirondack and Catskill mountains of New York. The two mountainous areas, separated by the Mohawk River Valley, have elevations ranging from 1,200 feet to Mount Marcy's 5,344 feet, the highest point in the state.

Farther to the southwest the Appalachian Mountain region has three major subdivisions. They are a central mountainous core, the Piedmont Plateau, and the Appalachian Plateau. The mountainous section is the part of the region usually called the Appalachians. It is made up of a number of separate mountain ridges and ranges, including the famous Blue Ridge Mountains, mainly in Virginia and North Carolina; the Great Smoky Mountains of Tennessee and North Carolina; the Cumberland Mountains, mainly in Tennessee and Kentucky; and the Allegheny Mountains, mainly in Pennsylvania and West Virginia. Mount Mitchell (6,684 feet) in the Blue Ridge chain is the highest peak in the eastern United States. Not all of the mountainous core, however, is rugged. In fact, there are many gently rolling river valleys that provide useful farmland. The beautiful Shenandoah Valley in northwestern Virginia is part of this region. (See APPALACHIAN MOUNTAINS.)

Bordering the mountains on the east is a belt of hilly upland, called the Piedmont Plateau. The belt is narrowest at the north where it crosses New Jersey and widest in the southern states of South Carolina and Georgia.

On the western side of the mountains, stretching from New York state to northern Alabama, is the Appalachian Plateau. In the northern states of New York, Pennsylvania, and West Virginia, it is usually called the Allegheny Plateau; in Kentucky, Tennessee, and Alabama, it is usually called the Cumberland Plateau. The land generally slopes away from the mountains toward the Interior Plains and the Gulf

Another way to divide the United States, with the exception of the separate states of Alaska and Hawaii, is by regions formed by groups of states. The six traditional geographic regions thus formed are the ones shown at right.

Coastal Plain. Within the Appalachian Plateau, heights vary from about 1,000 feet to more than 4,000 feet. The plateau is noted for its many underground passageways. Mammoth Cave is among the world's largest. (See CAVE.)

The Interior Plains region is the largest of the country's land regions. It includes most of the land between the Appalachian Mountains and the Rocky Mountains. There are two principal subdivisions: the Central Plains, which form the eastern part of the region, and the Great, or High, Plains, lying to the west. The Interior Plains region varies from 500 to 5,000 feet above sea level.

The easternmost part of the Central Plains, in Ohio, merges gradually with the hilly rim of the Appalachian Plateau. Farther south the boundary between the plain and the plateau is sharper. Much of the northern part of the Interior Plains was once covered by glaciers. These glaciers left behind fertile layers of soil after they melted. The glaciers also left other common surface features—such as moraines, drumlins, eskers, small lakes, and ponds. A large area in southwestern Wisconsin, however, was probably untouched by the glaciers. This section, known as the Driftless Area, is more rugged and has towerlike rock formations.

The Great Plains area is an extremely flat expanse of land between Canada on the north and southern Texas on the south. Along the base of the Rocky Mountains the plains reach elevations to 6,000 feet and slope gently eastward to the Central Plains. The boundary between the Great and Central plains is usually considered to be the 20-inch rainfall line. The Great Plains, west of the line, generally receive less than 20 inches of rain annually, and the Central Plains, east of the line, generally receive more. (See GREAT PLAINS.)

In contrast to the vast flat plains are such features as the Devils Tower in Wyoming, a column of rock 752 feet high; the Badlands in South Dakota, an area of interesting jagged rocks that have been carved by erosion; and the Black Hills in South Dakota and Wyoming.

The Interior Highland region is a small area of low mountains and hills mostly in southern Missouri, northwestern Arkansas, and eastern Oklahoma. Included in this region are the Ozark Mountains, the Boston Mountains, and the Ouachita Mountains; they are sometimes jointly called the Ozark Mountains or Ozark Plateau. Elevations range from less than 800 feet to more than 2,900 feet, with the highest point being Rich Mountain in the Ouachitas. (See OZARK MOUNTAINS.)

The Superior Upland region is a low, hilly plateau bordering Lake Superior in eastern Minnesota and northern Wisconsin and Michigan. Several short mountain ridges rise to heights of about 2,000 feet. Among them are the Misquah Hills and the famous iron-rich Mesabi Range of Minnesota, and the Porcupine and Huron Mountains of Michigan. This forest-covered region is dotted with hundreds of lakes. It is rich in iron and copper deposits. The Superior Upland is a part of a larger land region that includes most of northeastern Canada. It is the Laurentian Upland (Canadian Shield).

The Rocky Mountain region is along the eastern edge of the great highland area. In the United States the Rocky Mountains extend for more than 1,200 miles, from the Canadian border, through Montana, Idaho, Wyoming, Colorado, Utah and into northern New Mexico. The mountains continue in southern New Mexico and Texas, but these are not always considered part of the true Rockies. The Rockies are more than twice as high as the Appalachian Mountains. Many of the peaks are above 14,000 feet. (See ROCKY MOUNTAINS.)

The Rockies consist of many different ranges and basins (broad flat valleys). They may be divided into two major areas: the Northern and Southern Rockies, which are separated by the Wyoming Basin. The Rockies in and near Wyoming are often called the Middle Rockies.

The northern section is mostly in Idaho and western Montana. The highest peaks of the Northern Rockies are between 10,000 and 12,000 feet. Among the major mountain groups in the north are the Clearwater, Salmon River, Bitterroot, and Lewis ranges.

Included as parts of the Middle Rockies are Yellowstone National Park, Grand Teton National Park, the Absaroka Range, and the Big Horn Mountains, all of which are chiefly in Wyoming, and the Wasatch and Uinta mountains in Utah. Several mountain tops exceed 13,000 feet above sea level. The area is known for its spectacular scenery, such as Yellowstone Park's hot springs, waterfalls, and geysers. Between the Northern and Southern Rockies is a cluster of broad flat basins which together form the Wyoming Basin. Because of the lower elevation of this area it was used as a route by many pioneer wagon trains.

The Southern Rockies extend from southeastern Wyoming across central Colorado into northern New Mexico. Fifty-three named mountain peaks in Colorado are more than 14,000 feet high. About 300 more peaks rise to elevations above 13,000 feet. Because the mountain passes are all above 10,000 feet, early travelers usually avoided the Southern Rockies. Among the principal mountain groups are the Front,

Park, Sawatch, and Sangre de Cristo ranges and the San Juan Mountains. A wide mountain basin, the San Luis Valley, lies across the Colorado-New Mexico border. Among the well-known sights of the Southern Rockies are Rocky Mountain National Park, Pikes Peak, Mount Elbert, and the Garden of the Gods.

The Interior Plateaus, or Intermontane, region lies between the Rockies on the east and the Sierra Nevada and the Cascade Mountains on the west. *Intermontane* means "between the mountains." This region, mostly dry and covered with desert vegetation, may be divided into three large subdivisions: the Columbia Plateau, the Basin and Range area (or the Great Basin), and the Colorado Plateau.

The Columbia Plateau includes more than 100,000 square miles of land in eastern Washington and Oregon and southern Idaho. Much of the area is drained by the Columbia River and its tributaries. The rolling surface of the plateau consists of many layers of hardened lava, which flowed to the surface through volcanic cones and fissures thousands of years ago. In some places mountains rise above the general level of the plateau. The main rivers of the area have cut deep canyons through the lava and the mountain ranges. The canyon of the Snake River in places is more than 5,000 feet deep and in Hells Canyon reaches a depth of more than 8,000 feet.

The Basin and Range area borders the Columbia Plateau on the south and includes most of Nevada and areas in southern California, western Utah, southern Arizona, New Mexico, and Texas. Most of the landscape is desert flatland broken by short, widely separated, wooded mountain ranges. There are patches of irrigated land, which appear as rich oases in contrast with the desert. These include the Salt Lake City, Utah, area, the area along the Colorado River near Yuma, Arizona, and the Imperial Valley of southern California. Most of the streams that flow in this dry land never reach the sea but end in salt lakes in the basins. In the northern part of the region, basin elevations are more than a mile above sea level. Toward the Mexican border, however, elevations are much lower. In fact, Death Valley and

Imperial Valley in California are mostly below sea level.

The Colorado Plateau occupies much of central and eastern Utah, western Colorado, northern Arizona, and northwestern New Mexico. The Colorado River and its tributaries drain most of the region. The river flows generally southwestward from its source in the Rockies, cutting a deeper and deeper canyon. In northern Arizona it has carved the spectacular Grand Canyon. Throughout the plateau is a great variety of colorful and unusual natural features, such as the remarkable natural bridges of Utah and the petrified forest of Arizona. (See GRAND CANYON, THE.)

The United States is a land of great scenic beauty. Natural wonders—such as the Rocky Mountains, Grand Canyon, Niagara Falls, forests, lakelands, and seashores—attract millions of visitors each year.

Courtesy Rhode Island Development Council

Atlantic Coast, Rhode Island.

Courtesy State of Michigan Tourist Council

Keweenaw Bay, Michigan.

The Pacific Mountain region extends along the Pacific Coast from Canada to Mexico. It includes the high Sierra Nevada and the Cascade Mountains and the lower Coast Ranges and Klamath Mountains. The mountains are separated by several important lowland regions in Washington, Oregon, and California.

The Sierra Nevada is known for its jagged peaks, high altitude lakes, deep canyons, and spectacular waterfalls. The canyon cut by the

Cities add man-made variety to the U.S. landscape. New York City skyscrapers (below) form a gleaming skyline.

Courtesy The Bank of New York

Mount Philo, Vermont.

Mirror Lake, Yosemite National Park, California.

Kings River at one place is 8,000 feet deep. Popular sights in the Sierras are the beautiful Bridal Veil and Yosemite falls in Yosemite National Park. Mount Whitney, which reaches an altitude of 14,495 feet, is the highest point in the continental United States, excluding Alaska.

The Cascade Mountains are unusual in the United States because they include many volcanic peaks. There are hundreds of these cones from northern California, where Lassen Peak is the most recently active volcano on the U.S. mainland, to Glacier Peak in north central Washington. Mount Shasta and Mount Rainier are more than 14,000 feet in height. These cones have been quiet for many years. Lassen Peak first erupted in 1914 and displayed volcanic activity until 1921. Mount Mazama's six-mile-wide crater has filled with water and is called Crater Lake. (See CASCADE MOUNTAINS; SIERRA NEVADA.)

The Coast Ranges

are a low belt of mountains and hills that border the ocean in Washington, Oregon, and California. In southern Washington they are the Willapa Hills and farther north the Olympic Mountains. The Klamath Mountains are a low cluster extending from the coast eastward to join the Cascade Mountains. Elevations are commonly between 2,000 and 4,000 feet, although some peaks reach about 9,000 feet. Two

Monument Valley, Arizona, contains striking rock formations created by erosion.

of the best natural harbors in the United States —Puget Sound and San Francisco Bay—are formed by breaks in the Coast Range.

Alaska has three main land regions: the Arctic Slope, the Central Plateau, and the Pacific Mountains. The Arctic Slope is a flat to gently rolling plain that makes up the northernmost part of the state. The plain slopes northward from the Brooks Range, and, therefore, all of the region's rivers flow into the Arctic Ocean. Lying to the south is Alaska's largest land region, the Central Plateau. It is a rugged upland that reaches its greatest heights in the Brooks Range, where the highest peak is more than 9,200 feet. The Pacific Mountains form a rough arc that curves along or near Alaska's southern coast. They extend from the Alexander Archipelago northward to the Alaska Range and then southwestward to the Aleutian Islands. Mount McKinley, rising to 20,320 feet above sea level in the Alaska Range, is the highest point in North America. Katmai National Monument in Alaska is an area of volcanic activity and includes the Valley of Ten Thousand Smokes. (See ALASKA.)

Hawaii is composed of eight main islands and many smaller ones. The eight main islands are part of a volcanic mountain chain that is mostly submerged. The highest peaks of the chain are Mauna Kea (13,784 feet above sea level) and Mauna Loa (13,680 feet). Both are on the largest island, Hawaii. Mauna Loa has erupted a number of times in the 20th century. Kilauea, on the same island, has the largest active volcanic crater in the world. The crater has an area of more than four square miles. (See HAWAII.)

(For more detailed information on the land regions in each state, see the section on Landscape in each state article. Also see the six articles on the traditional geographic regions of the United States: MIDWESTERN REGION, NORTHEASTERN REGION, PACIFIC COASTAL REGION, ROCKY MOUNTAIN REGION, SOUTHERN REGION, and SOUTHWESTERN REGION.)

II. Climate

The climate of the United States is as varied as its landscape. The country may be divided into eight major climatic regions, or large areas in which the average weather conditions, such as temperature and rainfall, are somewhat alike. Within such a region, however, further variations may be caused by differences in elevation, large water bodies, mountains, and other reasons.

The Continental Moist climatic region is in the northeastern United States. In this region is all of the territory north of a line from northern Oklahoma to southern Virginia and east of a line through western North and South Dakota, Nebraska, and Kansas. Rainfall is heaviest in the eastern part of the area. The Atlantic coastal region receives an average of 40 to 60 inches (in.) of precipitation (rain and melted snow) annually. The states in the western part of the region receive about 20 to 40 in. annually. Most of the region receives its heaviest precipitation as rainfall during the spring and summer. In the New England states, however, the amount of precipitation is about the same in each season. Fortunately for the states in this region, most rainfall comes during the growing season. The growing season is that period between the last frost in the spring and the first frost in the fall. In most of this region the length of the growing season varies from about three months in the coldest areas to about seven months in the warmest. Places with a Continental Moist climate will usually have a wide range between the highest and lowest temperatures. January temperatures in much of the region average less than 32 degrees Fahrenheit (F.), and it is not unusual for temperatures to drop below zero. Summers are often hot and humid, with temperatures occasionally rising above 100 degrees F.

The Subtropical Moist climatic region lies to the south of the Continental Moist region and includes most of the southeastern part of the country. The coldest month in this region usually has an average temperature that is above freezing. Summers are long and warm. As in the region to the north, rainfall is heavier in the eastern part of the region. Eastern Texas averages about 20 to 40 in., and parts of Louisiana and Florida average up to 60 in. Snow is rare in this region, except in the mountainous

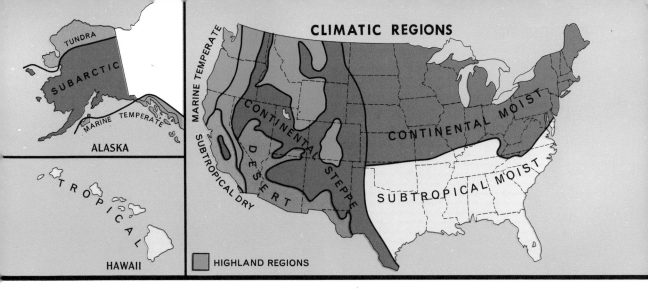

CLIMATIC REGIONS

areas. The growing season varies from about seven months in the north to almost the full year in Florida and southern Texas.

The Continental Steppe, or semiarid, climatic region covers most of the Great Plains, much of the Colorado and Columbia plateaus, and the Wyoming Basin. Rainfall in this area generally varies from about 10 to 20 in. yearly. In the north the Continental Steppe climate has even greater extremes in temperature than the Continental Moist. Winters are usually quite cold, and summer temperatures of more than 100 degrees F. are not unusual. The growing season is usually less than five months.

The Desert climatic region is located in the Basin and Range area. It includes southeastern California, parts of Nevada, Arizona, Utah, and New Mexico, and the western tip of Texas. The region usually receives less than 10 in. of rainfall a year. Summer temperatures are often extremely high. Winter days are generally warm, but winter nights are often quite cool. In the Imperial Valley the growing season lasts nearly the whole year.

The Marine Temperate climatic region extends along the Pacific Coast from northern California almost to the Alaska Peninsula. This area has cool summers and mild winters. It is unusual for temperatures to go much above 70 degrees F. or much below freezing. Frosts are rare. Rainfall is abundant and usually heavier in the winter months. The yearly average varies from about 30 in. to more than 150 in. Fogs are frequent in summer and fall, and the region

is noted for its many overcast days. The growing season ranges from about three months in the north to about eight in the south.

The Subtropical Dry climatic region lies south of the Marine Temperate region and west of the Sierra Nevada. It differs from the Marine Temperate region in that it has distinct dry and wet seasons. Almost no rain falls from the end of May through October. Most of the region has 15 to 25 in. of rainfall during the rest of the year. Snow is rare except in the mountains. In the Central Valley of California, summer temperatures are higher and winter temperatures are lower than along the coast. The average summer temperature on the coast is about 65 degrees F.; in the valley it is about 80 degrees F. The growing season ranges from about eight months to almost the entire year.

The Subarctic and Tundra climatic region covers most of Alaska. The tundra part of the region is a small area along the northern Alaska coast. The larger subarctic area has the widest range of temperatures of all climatic regions. Summers are short and warm, and winters are long and extremely cold. Temperatures may occasionally rise into the 90's during July, the warmest month. Throughout much of the region the average winter temperatures are below zero. Occasionally, extremes of more than 70 degrees F. below zero are recorded. Most of the region has about 20 in. of rainfall annually. The tundra climate has short, cool summers, with temperatures seldom rising above 50 degrees F. Temperatures average below freezing

Charlie Ott from National Audubon Society

Tundra region, Alaska.

The United States has a variety of climates. Most Americans, however, live in areas where the climate is moderate. Examples of intense extremes are the desert heat of Death Valley, California, and the severe cold of Alaska's tundra regions. Such places are sparsely populated. The Midwestern and Northeastern regions of the United States have four distinct seasons. They are the most heavily populated in the country.

Rain forest, Washington.

Alpha Photo Associates, Inc.

for up to ten months a year. The coldest months average about 10 to 20 degrees F. below zero. The tundra receives about 10 in. of precipitation annually, and fog is quite common.

The Tropical climatic region is found in Hawaii, which lies on the outer edge of the tropics. Not all of Hawaii is truly tropical, especially the areas at higher altitudes. The temperature averages about 75 degrees F. throughout the year in the lowlands, but it may drop to less than 20 degrees F. in the mountains. Honolulu, on Oahu, receives about 32 in. of rainfall yearly. However, rainfall varies vastly over the islands. On Kauai, for instance, the average annual rainfall ranges from 20 in. on the coast to 468 in. at the summit of the island. Snow falls at the highest elevations of Mauna Loa and Mauna Kea.

Weather Extremes. The hottest temperature recorded in the United States, 134 degrees F., was at Greenland Ranch in Death Valley, California, in July 1913. A number of other states have had temperatures of 120 degrees F. or higher. The country's coldest temperature, 76 degrees F. below zero, was recorded in Alaska in January 1886. Montana has recorded a temperature of 70 degrees F. below zero.

Greenland Ranch is probably, also, the country's driest place, averaging less than 2 in. of rainfall annually. Perhaps the country's snow-

Autumn countryside, Connecticut.

Courtesy State of Connecticut Development Commission

Cypress trees, Florida.   *Alpha Photo Associates, Inc.*

growing in each of these areas. Where the rainfall is heaviest, trees will usually grow. Where the rainfall is less than ten inches, deserts often occur. The areas that receive more than that but not enough for tree growth are the grasslands. Tundra vegetation grows at high altitudes and in the Subarctic and Tundra climatic region of Alaska. Certain kinds of animals live in each of these areas because they depend upon particular types of plants for food and are physically suited to the climate.

Woodland once stretched almost without break over most of the eastern third of the United States. Only small patches of the vast eastern woodland still remain. Three kinds of trees are mixed together in the eastern forests. Some, like the pine and hemlock, are ever-

iest place is Paradise Inn, Washington, which receives about 600 in. of snow annually.

The United States has an average of about 600 tornadoes each year. They most often occur in the spring in the states of Texas, Oklahoma, Kansas, Nebraska, and South Dakota. An average of 4 hurricanes strike the country's Atlantic Coast annually.

III. Plant and Animal Life

The United States may be divided into four general areas based on plant and animal life: woodland, grassland, desert, and tundra. Climate greatly determines the types of vegetation

Plant and animal life have changed somewhat since the early days of the United States. Much of the original forest was cleared for timber and farmland. Some animals and birds were hunted for food and became scarce. Today, national parks and game laws protect some of the country's plant and animal life.

Bighorn sheep, South Dakota.   Bull moose, Idaho.

Courtesy South Dakota Department of Highways   *Courtesy State of Idaho, Department of Commerce and Development*

Elk herd, Wyoming.   *Courtesy Wyoming Travel Commission*

Saguaro cactus in the southwest grow up to 50 feet high.

green, needle-bearing trees. Others, like the oak, hickory, birch, and maple, are broad-leaved deciduous trees that shed their leaves in winter. The third kind, which grow chiefly in the South, are broad-leaved trees that do not shed their leaves. These include varieties of oak, magnolia, and sweet bay.

Although the eastern woodland contains mixtures of trees, there are some pure stands, or forests, of pine. The white pine forests in Maine and in northern Michigan, Wisconsin, and Minnesota led to the early growth of the lumber industry of the northeastern United States.

Toward the eastern parts of the Interior Plains most of the trees have been cut to make room for farms and cities, but there are still scattered patches of trees.

Many kinds of animals live in the eastern woodland. Some of them—such as the black bear, beaver, otter, deer, skunk, and woodchuck—are found wherever large stands of trees grow. The moose, lynx, wolverine, and marten, however, are especially common in the northern parts of the eastern woodland. Farther south, the opossum, cottontail rabbit, fox, and raccoon are more numerous. Still farther south, in the swampy areas, are the alligator, crocodile, and manatee. Snakes also appear in the eastern woodland. Among the poisonous kinds are the rattlesnake, copperhead, water moccasin, and coral snake. These are found mostly in the South.

The woodland to the west includes Rocky Mountain areas and parts of California, Oregon, and Washington. It has a higher proportion of needle-leaved trees than the eastern forests. There are, however, patches of broadleaved aspens and birches in the mountains and some oaks and maples in the Willamette River Valley of Oregon. Toward the south, in California, needle-leaved trees become less common and oaks and other broad-leaved trees more common as the rainfall decreases. Lumber industries depend upon the great forests of the northwest.

Among the animals living in the western woodland are the black bear, grizzly bear, mink, raccoon, deer, elk, and muskrat. Along the Pacific Coast are many seals and sea lions.

The woodland in Alaska includes much of the southern coast east of Kodiak Island, and large parts of the Central Plateau. Trees common along the coast are the spruce, hemlock, and cedar. On the plateau are mixed stands of spruce, birch, and balsam poplar trees. There also are the aspen and cottonwood, especially in the west. Among the great variety of ani-

The American crocodile is one of the largest reptiles found in the United States. It inhabits swamps and rivers in warm states such as Florida and Georgia.

mals in Alaska's woodland are the caribou, moose, elk, bear, fox, sable, ermine, mink, lynx, otter, wolf, wolverine, muskrat, and beaver.

Hawaii's tropical woodland includes many species of trees, most of which do not shed their leaves. Among them are coconut, mango, avocado, mulberry, papaya, date, fig, and citrus fruit trees. In addition to domestic animals are the deer, mongoose, mouse, rat, bat, small lizard, and a variety of birds and insects.

The grasslands, before settlement, covered much of the inte-

Many Prairie dogs live on the western plains.

rior of the country. From central Illinois they fanned out as far as Canada and Mexico and west to the Rocky Mountains. There also were grasslands in the Central Valley of California, on parts of the Columbia and Colorado plateaus, and in marshy areas along the Atlantic Coast. These areas are still referred to as grasslands though crops have largely replaced the native grasses.

In the Central Plains, wild grasses once grew as tall as a man. Toward the west, where there is less rain, the grasses became gradually shorter. In early days the grasslands of Illinois and Iowa were called prairie. Today the former prairies provide excellent farmlands.

Farther west, on the Great Plains, the grasses were still shorter. These areas were the grazing lands of the great buffalo, or American bison, herds that once roamed over them. Today wide areas of the plains are used to grow wheat, barley, and other crops. Gradually the grasses thin out to the west.

East of the Rocky Mountains the grasslands are inhabited by the pocket gopher, pronghorn antelope, prairie dog, coyote, and jackrabbit. The buffalo has largely disappeared, except for small, carefully protected herds.

The deserts of the United States lie chiefly between the Sierra Nevada and the Colorado Plateau in the Basin and Range area. They include the cool sagebrush desert of Nevada and western Utah and the hot desert in southern Arizona and southeastern California. The difference between the two types of desert is caused mainly by elevation. In Nevada and western Utah, sagebrush grows thinly over the high basins. The sagebrush plains are broken in some places by small mountain ranges with a sparse cover of pine and juniper. Other dry climate plants, such as the yucca, are also in the sagebrush desert.

Farther south, in the desert of southern California and southern Arizona, the vegetation becomes more unusual. Sagebrush gives way to other bushy plants and to a great variety of cactus plants. One type of giant cactus, the saguaro, grows to a height of 50 feet. Among the animals of the desert are leathery-skinned reptiles, such as the iguana, horned toad, and Gila monster. Snakes also are common, including poisonous kinds, such as the rattlesnake. Desert mammals include the kangaroo rat, ringtailed cat, and peccary.

Plant life in the Tundra region of Alaska includes mosses, lichens, and grasslike plants called sedges. There are no trees, but the Tundra may include small shrubs. Tundra vegetation also grows at high altitudes in the mountains of the western United States. In Alaska the caribou, walrus, musk-ox, polar bear, and seal are common.

IV. Rivers and Lakes

The United States has some of the largest and most useful rivers and lakes in the world. Probably the best-known river system is the Mississippi-Missouri, which, with such branches as the Ohio, Illinois, Arkansas, and Platte, provides drainage for a large part of the Interior Plains. The Mississippi-Missouri, from the headwaters of the Missouri in the Rocky Mountains to the mouth of the Mississippi in the Gulf of Mexico, is 3,860 miles long.

Other important rivers in the United States include the Hudson and the Mohawk in New York, which provide a low-level passageway through the northern Appalachian Mountains; the Colorado in the Southwest, noted for the spectacular Grand Canyon it has cut; and the Columbia and Snake rivers in the Pacific Northwest. The dividing line between the eastward- and westward-flowing rivers of the United States runs through the Rocky Mountains and is called the Continental Divide.

The Great Lakes inland water system is one

The major U.S. rivers provide drainage, power, transportation, and recreation.

Courtesy Oregon State Highway Department

Crater Lake, Oregon.

Jack Zehrt—Publix Pictorial Service

Diesel-driven tugboats, which can transport many barges at once, have replaced Mississippi River steamboats.

of the most important in the world. It provides a water route for iron ore, wheat, coal, and other products from Lakes Superior and Michigan on the west, eastward through Lakes Huron, Erie, and Ontario, and through the St. Lawrence Seaway to the Atlantic Ocean. Passage between the Great Lakes has required construction of canals and locks, such as those at Sault Ste. Marie and the Welland Canal. (See GREAT LAKES and separate articles on individual lakes.)

Other large lakes in the United States include the Great Salt Lake in Utah, and Lake Champlain between New York and Vermont. There are many smaller lakes throughout the United States. In Minnesota and Wisconsin thousands of lakes dot the landscape.

V. The People

The United States is often called a melting pot because of the many racial and nationality groups that make up the population. It is a place where many traditions and ways of living have been mixed together. Most of the people who have come to the United States have been from countries of Europe.

The first immigrants to America found the land inhabited by North American Indians. The first Europeans to colonize the territory were the Spanish. They occupied areas in Florida, in the Southwest, and on the west coast. The next large group to arrive were the English. They formed the 13 original colonies on the east coast. Arriving with and after the English were such nationality groups as the Scottish, Irish, Dutch, French, and German.

Another early group to arrive in America were the Negroes, who were imported from Africa as slaves. Cultural traits of the Negroes also eventually influenced American culture. In the mid-1800's, immigration from Scandinavia and the Orient began increasing. After 1880 many immigrants came to the country from southern and eastern Europe, including Italians, Greeks, Jews, and Slavic peoples, such as the Poles.

In the United States there are still colonies of foreign peoples in large cities. Some neighborhoods are distinguished by certain foreign nationality traits. Some whole cities are even identified with a specific nationality group. With the passing of time and a slowdown of immigration, however, the foreign groups have become less distinct. An American nationality has become more and more clear. (See IMMIGRATION, UNITED STATES AND CANADIAN.)

Beginning in the year 1790, the U.S. government has counted the people living within its borders every ten years. The census of population taken in 1970 showed that the United States had 203,184,772 persons. The country had grown by nearly 24 million persons between 1960 and 1970. This is an average of almost 2.4 million persons each year. From 1950 to 1960 the average yearly increase in population was about three million. The 1970 U.S. population of almost 204 million was more than 51 times larger than the 1790 population of 3,929,-214. The center of population for 1790 was 23 miles east of Baltimore, Maryland. By 1970 it had moved more than 700 miles westward into Illinois. (See POPULATION; WESTWARD MOVEMENT.)

During the more than 180 years since the first census, the United States has become a country of many cities. By 1970 there were about 150 cities with 100,000 or more residents. New York City (7,867,760) was the country's largest metropolis. Within the greater New York City area there were more than 11 million people in 1970. Chicago, Illinois, and Los Angeles, California, with their suburbs, each had more than 6 million persons; Philadelphia, Pennsylvania, and Detroit, Michigan, both had more than 4 million persons.

Although the national trend has been toward larger city populations, a few states remain chiefly rural. In Vermont, for example, about 68 percent of the people live in rural areas. Other states that are largely rural include Mississippi, Alaska, West Virginia, South Dakota, North Dakota, and North Carolina. High urban percentages are more common in the northeast, but ur-

banization is not limited to that region. California, Hawaii, and Texas are all more than 79 percent urban. In many large U.S. cities there is a trend of movement from the central city to the suburbs. As a result, some are showing population losses. These include such cities as New York City; Chicago, Illinois; St. Louis, Missouri; and Boston, Massachusetts.

The percentage of older people in the United States has been increasing steadily. Today the average U.S. citizen can expect to live to about

A. L. Goldman from Rapho Guillumette

The U.S. population—which includes all racial stocks, many nationalities, and most religions—works and plays in such diverse areas as Manhattan's Central Park (above), rural Mennonite communities (below left), and the crowded streets of Harlem.

Jane Latta

Frank Dandridge—Pix from Publix

70 years of age. The average U.S. male marries when he is about 23, the female at about 20.

According to the 1970 census the United States had 177,612,309 inhabitants who identified themselves as white and 25,553,190 as nonwhite. People who identified themselves as Negro accounted for 22,672,570 of the nonwhite group, about 11.2 percent of the country's population. North American Indians, Japanese, Chinese, Filipinos, and people of other ethnic groups who identified themselves as neither white nor Negro accounted for about 1.4 percent of the population.

Today about 10 million foreign-born persons live in the United States. More than 600,000 of them came from each of the following countries: the United Kingdom, Ireland, Mexico, Italy, Germany, Canada, Poland, and the U.S.S.R.

VI. Religion

The U.S. Constitution guarantees freedom of religious worship to all Americans. The original colonists included many persons who came to America to escape religious persecution in other countries. Mostly these were people who belonged to some Christian faith. The Pilgrims who arrived on the *Mayflower* were looking for a place to worship freely.

Today most of the people of the United States belong to some type of church group. About 118 million Americans have declared mem-

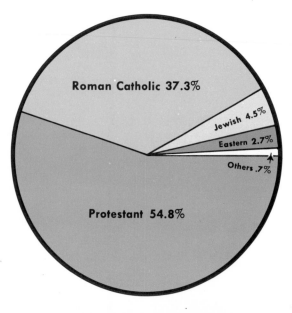

bership in the Protestant or Roman Catholic churches. The Protestants form the largest single religious grouping in the United States, though they are divided into many subgroups, such as Episcopalians, Baptists, Methodists, Lutherans, and Presbyterians. The second largest membership is in the Roman Catholic Church. More than 3.5 million belong to various Eastern Orthodox churches. About 5.8 million Americans are members of the Jewish faith. Other important religious groups in the United States include the Buddhists, Muslims, and Hindus. Thousands of persons worship in less well-known church groups.

VII. Language

The English, French, and Spanish all held territory during colonial times in what is now the United States. The English-speaking colonies grew more rapidly, however, and the United States was established by the English-speaking people. As a result, English became the only official language of the United States. Though it differs somewhat from the English spoken in England, it has the same grammar and basic structure. American English includes many words that came from immigrant groups, who usually had to learn English; these peoples often mixed it with their own native language. Their children sometimes learned the old language, but they went to American schools and learned English. The grandchildren of immigrants seldom learned the old language.

Within the United States, spoken English varies from region to region. These variants are called dialects; a person speaking a dialect is said to have an accent. There are few differences among the three main American dialects—usually called General, New England, and Southern—and they can usually be understood by all speakers of American English.

VIII. How the People Make a Living

The United States is the leading country of the world in the production of manufactured and agricultural products. Other countries are larger than the United States in both area and population, but the United States alone produces more than 40 percent of the total world output of goods and services. The might of

Stock exchanges are an important part of American business. There the stocks and bonds of large U.S. firms are bought and sold by stockbrokers.

Leonard Stern

U.S. industry was a leading factor in deciding the victories of World Wars I and II and is the basis for the country's great influence in the world today.

There are many reasons why the United States became the leading commercial country of the world. A few, however, are outstandingly important. The abundance of resources within the U.S. borders—fertile land, fuel, minerals, and hydroelectric power—made possible the rapid growth of U.S. industry. The development of excellent transportation, especially railroads, made it easy to bring raw materials together to make products. A free enterprise system of trade encouraged the growth of business and industry.

In colonial times most of the people earned a living in agriculture. Some people, however, were fur trappers, fishermen, lumbermen, traders, and shipbuilders. Others provided services or operated inns. Families made many of the everyday things that they needed, such as clothing and tools, and raised many of the foods that were needed. Tobacco and wheat flour were among the leading exports. Coal, iron, and copper mining provided work for a small number of colonists.

As the population grew and transportation improved, the fertile farmlands of the country's interior were settled. Corn became the chief crop of the plains, and cotton became the main crop of the southeast. Improvements in farm machinery meant that the farmers could do more work with fewer workers. They could also raise larger quantities. The expansion of railroads beginning in the mid-19th century sharply changed the course of the U.S. economy from agriculture to industry. By the end of the century, the value of all manufactured goods topped the value of all agricultural products for the first time.

The invention of the automobile had an important effect on the U.S. economy. Greatly increased production of automobiles beginning in the 1920's produced a great need for gasoline and other petroleum products. The U.S. oil industry grew to meet this demand. The chemical industries began to grow and create new kinds of useful materials. Synthetic fibers, such as nylon, rayon, and dacron, were developed for use in the making of clothing and in other industries. Factory output was greatly stimulated during World Wars I and II. The expansion of the aircraft industry was especially affected by

A worker scales loose rock on the Glen Canyon Dam project in Arizona. Such hydroelectric and irrigation projects provide many jobs, power for industry, and water for farming.

Courtesy Bureau of Indian Affairs, Department of the Interior

World War II. All of these events and many others led to an increase in the number of jobs available.

IX. Manufacturing

The U.S. manufacturing industries produce almost twice as much income as the next largest economic group. They employ more than 16 million persons. The North-eastern Region leads the country in manufacturing. It is followed closely by the Midwestern Region. These two regions combined contain more than half the manufacturing plants and workers. Within these regions are many of the world's leading industrial cities—including New York City; Chicago, Illinois; and Detroit, Michigan. The regions are served by an excellent transportation network, have good sources of power, and are near important raw materials. The largest of the many kinds of industries are those that produce processed foods, primary metals, machinery, transportation equipment, and clothing.

The Food-Processing Industry is the leading industry in the number of manufacturing plants and is among the leaders in the value of goods produced. One reason for

Steel mill blast furnace. *Courtesy Bethlehem Steel Corporation*

Manufacturing industries in the United States turn the country's raw materials into finished products. Metal ores are shipped to refining plants such as steel mills. There they are turned into finished metals, which are used by other industries to manufacture products.

Radar unit. *Charles E. Rotkin, P.F.I. from "Fortune" Magazine*

the growth of the food-processing industry is the movement of people from farms to cities. The demand for prepared food rose as fewer people grew the food they ate. City people living in apartments seldom have gardens or food-storage space. Also, there is an increasing demand for a greater variety of foods and more easily prepared foods.

Meat processing has become very important. For many years Chicago was the U.S. center of meat-processing activities. Today, however, processing is being done closer to the animal-raising areas, and Chicago is just one of several important locations, such as Kansas City, Kansas; St. Paul, Minnesota; Omaha, Nebraska; St. Louis, Missouri; and Fort Worth, Texas. Los Angeles

Huge petroleum refineries supply the country's oil needs. The United States is the world's largest oil producer.

and San Francisco, California, are major west coast centers.

Flour milling is among the oldest industries in the country. It makes wide use of machinery and employs a relatively small number of workers. Some milling companies have become important for such products as breakfast foods, cake mixes, packaged soups, and livestock feeds. Buffalo, New York, is the world's leading milling center.

About half of the U.S. sugar supply comes from sugar beets and sugarcane raised within the country. The rest is imported but is processed by U.S. refineries. Sugar-beet plants are mainly in the inland areas, from Michigan and Ohio westward to the Pacific coastal states. Sugarcane mills are located in the producing areas of Hawaii, Louisiana, Florida, and Puerto Rico. Cane refineries are chiefly in Louisiana and the Atlantic ports of Boston, Massachusetts; New York City; Philadelphia, Pennsylvania; Baltimore, Maryland; and Savannah, Georgia. San Francisco refineries process much of the output of Hawaii.

Canning and freezing plants are usually small and are mostly in rural areas or small cities near the sources of the product being packed. The making and bottling of soft drinks, beer, wine, and other alcoholic beverages provides about 200,000 jobs. Wine is made chiefly in the grape-growing regions of California, New York, Ohio, and Michigan. California is by far the leading state in wine production.

Chemistry is the basis of many important industries including those which make munitions, plastics, and soap.

The production of dairy products is another major U.S. industry. It employs about 274,000 workers. Wisconsin is by far the leading state for dairy products, although New York and Minnesota are also important. A large share of the country's butter comes from the creameries clustered in southeastern Minnesota, northeastern Iowa, and southwestern Wisconsin.

The Metal Industries. The primary metal industries are those that process the metallic ores that come from mines and those that roll, stretch, and shape the metals. The secondary metal industries turn the metals into finished products—such as automobiles, aircraft, appliances, and machinery. The most important metals are iron, aluminum, and copper.

Although the primary metal industry employs but a small percentage of the country's labor force, it is extremely important. Millions of workers in other industries earn a living by making goods of metal produced by the metal industry. Iron- and steelmaking employs the largest share of the primary metalworkers. Since the end of the 19th century the United States has been the world's leading manufacturer of steel. Production of crude steel in the 1960's has been about 100 million tons yearly. There are five major iron and steel areas in the United States: eastern, Pittsburgh-Youngstown, Chicago-Gary, Birmingham, and western.

The most important iron and steel area in the world is centered in the Pittsburgh-Youngstown area. The area has about half of the country's steel-producing capacity. The Chicago-Gary area on the southwestern shore of Lake Michigan accounts for about one-fifth of the country's steel-producing capacity. Ore supplies are transported to the Pittsburgh-Youngstown and Chicago-Gary areas by ship from Minnesota and northern Michigan. One-fifth of the country's iron ore and steel comes from the eastern area. (See IRON AND STEEL.)

The United States leads all countries in the production of refined copper. Copper processing employs a small number of people, but the annual output ranges between 1½ and 2 million tons. About one-fourth of the U.S. production comes from imported ores. Smelting plants are generally located near mines in leading copper states, such as Arizona, Utah, Montana, Nevada, Michigan, and New Mexico.

The aluminum industry is rather new among U.S. industries. Production of the metal began in the United States in the late 1880's. It was

Courtesy International Harvester "World"

Assembly line production revolutionized U.S. manufacturing. Specialized teams of workers synchronize their individual jobs to produce goods much faster than was possible with former methods. The spot welders at left swiftly complete their phase in the making of a truck body.

not until World War II, however, that there was much demand for the metal. To satisfy the great need for military aircraft, the aluminum industry expanded its production rapidly. The demand for the metal has been steadily rising, and the output exceeded two million tons annually through the early 1960's.

Industries that make products requiring metals include those that make fabricated metals, such as cans, bolts, wire, and hardware, and those that produce transportation equipment, and machinery. More than 5,500,000 workers, about one-third of all those working in manufacturing, make their living in these industries. There are about 1,600,000 workers making transportation equipment alone. About 740,000 work in the automobile industry, and more than 650,000 work in the aircraft industry. Southern Michigan is the center of the automobile industry. Aircraft manufacture is spread among many states, although the Pacific Coast states provide about half the output according to value. Most of the coastal states have important shipbuilding and ship-repair industries. Illinois and Pennsylvania are leaders in the manufacture of railroad equipment. Most of the other metal products industries are concentrated in the Northeastern and Midwestern regions.

Textiles and Apparel. The textile and apparel industries employ more than two million workers, who turn out a variety of products made of cotton, wool, and various synthetic fibers. Cotton is the most important of these in terms of both employment and value. The modern cotton textile industry in the United States started in New England in the late 18th century and flourished because of available waterpower and a damp climate favorable for spinning.

After the Civil War the South realized that it must turn to manufacturing to regain prosperity, and the cotton textile industry was the first modern industry to develop in the South. By the late 1920's North Carolina had replaced Massachusetts as the leader in cotton textile manufacturing. The industry developed from Virginia to Georgia because of a cheaper labor supply and the closeness to raw cotton. The South now dominates cotton textile production in the United States.

Woolen manufacturing also got its start in New England, and it remains an important industry there. The area around Boston is the leading district for woolen textiles, but Philadelphia and New York City are also important. The synthetic, or man-made, fibers, chiefly rayon and acetate, are growing in importance.

The apparel, or clothing, industries employ more people than the textile industries. About 1,300,000 of the more than 2 million textile workers are employed by clothing manufacturers. In contrast with the textile industries, which are frequently located in or near small towns, the apparel industries are concentrated chiefly in a few large cities, including New York City, Chicago, and Philadelphia. The cities provide both labor and markets. New York City in particular is noted for its garment district.

Printing and Publishing. The U.S. printing and publishing industry produces billions of copies of newspapers, magazines, books, pamphlets, cards, handbills, and other reading materials each year. Most of the large publishing companies have their headquarters in New York, Pennsylvania, New Jersey, or Illinois, but all other states also are involved in printing and publishing.

Other Industries. Several million Americans work for various other types of manufacturers, including those that produce furniture, glass, cement, paper, leather, rubber, tobacco products, chemicals, and many other products. Most of these industries are widely scattered throughout the United States. A few, however, are heavily concentrated in certain areas. For example, nearly all cigarettes are manufactured in three major tobacco-growing states—North Carolina, Virginia, and Kentucky. Pennsylvania and Florida make most of the cigars in the United States. Ohio is the leading center of the rubber industry, particularly tire and inner tube manufacturing. Massachusetts and Missouri lead in shoe manufacturing, and New York leads in most other leather goods industries.

Factories producing chemicals are located in

many areas of the United States, but especially in the Northeastern and Midwestern regions. Chemical factories are also important in Texas and Louisiana, where abundant raw materials are available, and in the southeastern United States, where hydroelectric power is plentiful.

X. Energy and Power

The United States uses tremendous amounts of power to run its industries and provide heat and light for homes. Most of the power used in U.S. manufacturing comes from such fuels as petroleum, natural gas, and coal. Until the 1950's, coal was the leading source of power. It has now been surpassed, however, by both petroleum and natural gas. In 1940, coal accounted for more than half the total energy produced. By 1963, coal and lignite supplied about one-fourth of the total; crude petroleum, about one-third; and natural gas, about one-third. Waterpower accounted for about 4 percent of the total energy produced in 1960. The construction of pipelines to transport fuel has played an important part in increasing the use of petroleum and natural gas.

Much of the power created by fuels and water is converted into electricity. Most of the electricity generated comes from steam plants, and about one-fifth comes from hydroelectric plants. Most of the electricity generated from steam plants is produced by burning coal. The electric utility industry is the largest single con-

Niagara Falls is a great scenic attraction, but it is useful as well as beautiful. The falls provide electrical power for both the United States and Canada.

Charles E. Rotkin, Photography for Industry

sumer of coal in the country. Grand Coulee Dam in Washington ranks as the largest single U.S. waterpower producer. The development of atomic energy has become increasingly important as a power source.

XI. Agriculture

United States farmers produce more food than the country can consume. Surplus agricultural products are exported to other countries or are stored by the government. Industry has surpassed agriculture in the value of production, but agricultural production has increased steadily. From 1940 to 1960 the value of agricultural production rose by about 55 percent. At the same time, the country's population rose by about 34 percent.

The increase in farm production has taken place at the same time that the number of farm workers and farms declined. This is because of the increased use of machinery and fertilizers and the merging of small farms into larger farms. On the modern farm, tractors, combines, corn and cotton pickers, hay balers, trucks, milking machines, field cutters, and other machines have replaced much of the hand labor and animal power of earlier days. Much of the land formerly required to produce feed for the work animals is now used to produce crops or meat animals. The development of chemicals for killing weeds and insect pests and for controlling plant and animal diseases has helped increase production. The use of fertilizers permits a higher yield on each acre of land.

The average size of the U.S. farm increased steadily during the mid-1900's. In 1960 the average farm was just over 300 acres. Of course, there are still some small farms, and the western states are noted for their large farms. The number of U.S. farms dropped from more than 6 million in 1940 to about 3,700,000 in 1959. The U.S. farmer is now able to feed himself and about 28 nonfarm persons. Some of his surplus production is exported.

The most important single crop grown in the country is corn. Farmers grow three to four billion bushels, valued at about four billion dollars, each year. Corn is produced in almost every state, but the leading ones are those of the Corn Belt—especially Iowa, Illinois, Indiana, Nebraska, Minnesota, Ohio, and Missouri. The United States produces about as much corn as the rest of the world combined. (See CORN.)

Wheat is the second most important grain crop, with an annual production of more than one billion bushels, valued at more than two billion dollars. Kansas is the leading wheat state. North Dakota, Montana, Oklahoma, Illinois, Washington, and Nebraska are other major wheat-producing states. (See WHEAT.)

The leading oat-growing states are Minnesota, Iowa, and Wisconsin; the leading barley states, North Dakota, California, and Montana; and the leading rice states, Texas, Arkansas, Louisiana, and California. North Dakota is the chief rye-producing state.

Some crops, such as cotton and tobacco, are called industrial crops because they are used by manufacturers to make products. Cotton ranks as the second most valuable crop next to corn. The country produces about $2,500 million worth of cotton each year. Texas is far ahead as the leading cotton-producing state. Mississippi, California, and Arkansas rank as the next largest producers.

Tobacco is another important industrial crop. The value of its annual production usually amounts to more than $1,300 million a year. North Carolina and Kentucky produce more than half the crop, but other southern states—such as South Carolina, Tennessee, Virginia, and Georgia—are also important growers. Peanuts are an important crop in several southern states, particularly Georgia, North Carolina, Alabama, Virginia, and Texas.

Large quantities of sugar are produced, but the country cannot produce nearly as much sugar as it consumes. About half the sugar used is imported. The United States grows both sugarcane and sugar beets, the two main sources of sugar. Sugarcane grows best in the warm, wet climates of Hawaii, Louisiana, and Florida. Sugar beets grow well in cooler, drier climates. California has become the leading sugar-beet-producing state. The value of the cane and beet crops is about equal. Soybeans—used for making vegetable oil, livestock feed,

Modern farming equipment (above) and improved irrigation (below) have helped increase U.S. agricultural production.

Courtesy (above) Allis-Chalmers; photo (below) Herb and Dorothy McLaughlin

From the pineapple of Hawaii (above) to the tobacco of the South (below), crops are abundant.

Photo (above) Herb Kane; courtesy (below) Kentucky Department of Public Information

paints and plastics, and for many other products—are another leading industrial crop. Illinois, Iowa, and Indiana lead the other states in soybean production.

Vegetable growing is widespread, but the major producing areas are usually near large cities and in warmer places, such as the Southern and Pacific Coastal regions, where the growing season is longer. The leading vegetables are white potatoes, tomatoes, lettuce, and beans.

Fruit-growing regions are also determined by markets and climates. The United States grows enormous amounts of citrus fruits, especially oranges. The country usually produces more than 100 million boxes of oranges yearly, much more than any other country. Oranges have the largest annual value among U.S. fruits. They are produced mainly in Florida and California. Following oranges in value are apples, grapes, peaches, pineapples, and strawberries. The United States also leads the world in the production of grapefruits and lemons. Farmers cultivate many other fruits, such as pears, prunes, cherries, and various kinds of melons. Tree nuts—such as walnuts, almonds, and pecans—bring considerable farm income.

Dairy farming is one of the leading types of agriculture in the United States. Although the number of dairy cows has decreased by about 30 percent since 1944, milk production in the early 1960's reached record high levels. About 125 billion pounds were produced in both 1964 and 1965—more than twice the amount produced by any other country. The increased production per cow in the United States has been possible through better breeding and feeding. Wisconsin, New York, and Minnesota are the leading milk-producing states. Dairy farmers earn money from the sale of cream and other dairy products, as well as milk. The United States is the world's largest producer of cheese.

Livestock raising, other than for dairying, is extremely important to U.S. agriculture. In 1964 the country had nearly 80 million cattle being raised chiefly for meat production. The leading beef-cattle-producing state is Texas, but Iowa, Nebraska, Kansas, California, Oklahoma, and Missouri are also important. The United States has about 53 million hogs and pigs. The livestock population also includes about 28 million sheep. The yearly value of cattle, hogs, and sheep amounts to about $17 billion. A specialized form of livestock raising is the production of about two billion broiler chickens each year.

XII. Mining

The history of employment in mining in the United States is similar to that of agriculture; that is, while production has increased greatly, the number of miners has steadily decreased. In 1920 the industry employed 1,230,000 workers, and the value of production was about $6 billion. In 1966, mining employed about 628,-000 workers, and the value of production had risen to $22,790 million.

Petroleum and Natural Gas. One reason for the reduced production of coal is that petroleum and natural gas have been replacing it for many uses. The petroleum industry began in the United States when Colonel E. L. Drake drilled a successful well near Titusville, Pennsylvania, in 1859. At first the desired product was kerosene for burning in lamps. The industry did not really boom until after the automobile created tremendous demands for gasoline and various lubricating oils and greases. In 1966 the industry employed about half the total of all mining workers.

Although Pennsylvania and other eastern states have some production and reserves, the center of the industry has shifted to the southwestern and western United States. The major areas of petroleum production are the midcontinent fields extending across northern Texas, Oklahoma, Kansas, and northern Louisiana; the Gulf Coast of Texas and southern Louisiana; California; and the Rocky Mountain Region. Texas is the leading state in production, followed by Louisiana, California, Oklahoma, and Wyoming.

The United States, with an output of 3 billion barrels in 1966, produces almost one-third of the world's petroleum. Estimates of the country's known reserves amount to about one-eighth of the world's supply. The consumption

Among the many ores mined in the United States, copper is one of the most important. Much of it comes from huge open-pit mines, such as this one in Nevada.

Charles E. Rotkin, P.F.I. for Kennecott Copper Co.

of petroleum products is so great, however, that additional large quantities are imported yearly.

Texas and Louisiana produce nearly three-fourths of the natural gas marketed in the United States. These two states also have more than two-thirds of the reserves. The United States is, so far, the only country in which natural gas has achieved major importance.

Coal. The coal industry has declined slightly since the 1920's, while petroleum and natural gas have been making great progress. In 1963 there were only 139,000 coal mining workers, less than half the number in petroleum and natural gas production. About 90 percent of the coal production is in the eastern half of the country, although more than half the reserves are in the western half. Though coal production has not been increasing in the United States, the country still ranks as one of the world's top producers. West Virginia leads in coal production, with nearly twice as much output as the next two highest states, Kentucky and Pennsylvania. Illinois, Ohio, and Virginia are other important producers.

Iron Ore is the most important metal mined in the United States. Iron and steel, made from iron ore, are used heavily by many of the country's most important industries. The U.S. mines usually produce more than 70 million tons of iron ore annually. About three-fourths of the total production comes from the Lake Superior area. The Mesabi Range in Minnesota alone accounts for about half of the total production. Minnesota is by far the country's

largest producer of iron ore, with Michigan following. Much of the iron ore production comes from gigantic open pits mined with huge mechanical shovels. Despite the high production of iron ore, it is also regularly imported, especially from Canada and Venezuela.

Other Metals. The United States mines a variety of other important metal ores, including copper, lead, zinc, bauxite, and uranium. Ferroalloy ores, such as molybdenum and manganese, are also significant. The copper mining industry supplies about one-fifth of the world's copper. Arizona produces about half the U.S. copper, and Utah about one-sixth. The remainder comes mainly from New Mexico, Nevada, Montana, and Michigan. The United States is also an important lead producer. Missouri, Idaho, and Utah have the most productive lead mines.

In the production of zinc, Tennessee leads over Idaho, New York, and Colorado. Arkansas mines most of the country's production of bauxite. Most of the uranium produced comes from the western states of New Mexico, Wyoming, Colorado, and Utah.

Nonmetallic Minerals produced in the United States are highly important to the chemical and construction industries. Among them are phosphate, potash, sulfur, salt, and sand, gravel, and stone. Florida produces more than 70 percent of all the phosphate in the United States, followed by Tennessee and Idaho. The country produces about 40 percent of the world's supply of phosphate and about 25 percent of the world's supply of potash.

Sulfur occurs in beds along the Gulf Coast of Texas and Louisiana. The beds, 25 to 300 feet thick, are 500 or more feet below the surface. Sulfur is important for its use in fertilizer manufacturing and also in petroleum refining, textile making, pulp and paper making, rubber manufacturing, and in the explosives, insecticides, and refrigeration industries. The United States produces about 50 percent of the world's sulfur. (See SULFUR.)

About 10 percent of the salt mined in the country is used for seasoning food, and the rest of it is used as an industrial raw material. The United States produces about 30 percent of the world's salt supply. Of this, about 60 percent is pumped from deep wells as brine. The rest is mined as rock salt or evaporated from sea water. Louisiana, Texas, New York, Ohio, and Michigan are the leading producers. (See SALT.)

From quarries in the United States come tremendous quantities of sand, gravel, and stone used in making cement and concrete and for other building uses. These building materials are produced in such large amounts that their value each year is greater than that of any metal ore. California and Michigan lead in sand and gravel production, and Pennsylvania leads in stone quarrying.

XIII. Lumbering

The forests of the United States are one of the country's most valuable resources. From them come lumber, wood products, pulp, paper, and many other important products. Most of the lumber produced comes from three areas —the Pacific Northwest, the Rocky Mountain states, and the South. More than 80 percent of the lumber produced is classified as softwood. It comes from such needle-leaf evergreens as the Douglas fir, white pine, and western yellow pine in the Pacific Northwest and Rocky Mountain states and the southern yellow pine in the South. The two western areas each produce

about 30 percent, and the South about 25 percent, of the softwood lumber cut in the United States. The New England states and the Great Lakes states were formerly important lumber producers. Their forests were so greatly cut, however, that they produce little timber today.

The forests yield valuable products besides sawn lumber. These include the cordwood or smaller pole timber used in making pulp and paper, naval stores, such as the turpentine and rosin produced chiefly from southern pines, and tannin used for tanning leather. Chips and other formerly wasted materials are now made into hardboard, insulation, and a number of other useful products. The United States needs more lumber and forest products than it can produce, and large quantities must be imported. This is especially true of newsprint (paper for newspapers), which comes from Canada. (See FORESTRY.)

XIV. Fishing

The fishing industry has been important since colonial times. Today it provides work for more than 225,000 people. About 85,000 U.S. boats or ships operate on rivers and lakes within the United States and in distant ocean fishing grounds. The total catch usually amounts to about two million tons each year, valued at about $400 million. Only about half the catch

A pondman at a lumber mill in Roseburg, Oregon, uses a pike pole to sort the logs being stored and to drive those to be sawed into the log chute.

Charles E. Rotkin, Photography for Industry

is used for food; the rest is used to make fish oils, fish meal, and fertilizer.

All the coastal regions of the United States have important fishing industries. Alaska, California, Massachusetts, Texas, and Louisiana are the leading states in value of catch. More menhaden is caught than any other kind of fish, but it is not used for food. The catch is used for making oil and fertilizer and for feeding livestock. Menhaden does not rank high in value. The shrimp, salmon, tuna, oyster, and crab all bring more money. Among the leading U.S. fishing ports are San Pedro and San Diego, California; Pascagoula, Mississippi; Empire and Cameron, Louisiana; Gloucester and Boston, Massachusetts; and Lewes, Delaware. (See FISHERY.)

XV. Transportation and Communication

Transportation in the United States has developed rapidly since the mid-1800's. At that time it took an overland stagecoach about 30 days to go from New York City to San Francisco, California. A hundred years later an airplane could cover the same distance in a few hours. Agriculture and industry expanded and prospered as transportation developed. Resources in remote areas could be developed, and fast, inexpensive transportation could bring

Charles E. Rotkin, Photography for Industry

Most of the tuna fish caught by U.S. fishermen are processed for canning. It is one of the most important commercial catches and one of the most popular of the food fish.

agricultural and industrial products to distant markets with little increase in costs. About 2,500,000 Americans work in the various branches of transportation—including railroads, bus lines, motortrucking, shipping, and others.

Railroads are the leading freight carriers in the United States. The amount of freight they carry, however, has dropped as other means of transportation developed. Railroads now move less than 45 percent of intercity (city to city) freight. Passenger transport by railroads has been reduced to a small part of total passenger movement. Private automobiles now carry about 90 percent of intercity passenger traffic, and airlines about 4½ percent. About 212,000 miles of railroad track (not counting sidings or duplicate tracks) cross the United States. The number of miles of track has been dropping steadily since the mid-1940's, but the United States is still one of the world's leading railroad countries. Much of the track mileage is concentrated in the Northeastern and Midwestern regions. Today, trains powered by oil-burning diesel engines have almost completely replaced the coal-burning locomotives.

The country has more motor vehicles and

Lumbering has always been Maine's chief industry. At Greenville, on the south end of Moosehead Lake, logs are floated to the mills enclosed in huge booms.

H. Armstrong Roberts

The Jones Falls Expressway in Baltimore, Maryland, is typical of the complex systems of highways now used in large U.S. cities. The country has more motor vehicles and more miles of road than any other country.

M. E. Warren

Inland waterways also carry about one-sixth of the intercity freight. Waterborne freight usually consists of bulky, rather low-value commodities, such as petroleum and petroleum products; coal and coke; sand, gravel, and stone; iron and steel; lumber; and grain. The major inland waterways include the Great Lakes system and the Mississippi-Missouri river system. The New York State Barge Canal provides a water route from the Atlantic

more miles of road than any other country, and airlines have made spectacular gains in passenger traffic. Air freight has more than doubled since 1955. In 1963, scheduled airlines operated almost 2,000 airplanes, about one-third of which were driven by jet or turboprop engines.

Pipelines now carry more than one-sixth of all intercity freight in the United States. Their cargo consists chiefly of natural gas, petroleum, and petroleum products. There are also some major water pipelines, such as those carrying water from Owens Valley in California and the Colorado River to Los Angeles, California, and from the Catskill Mountains to New York City. Most of the more than 155,000 miles of petroleum pipelines extend from the petroleum fields in the Southwest to the cities of the Atlantic Coast, the Midwest, and California.

Coast to the Great Lakes. (See TRANSPORTATION.)

Communications. One reason for the high levels of literacy and education in the United States is the widespread distribution of newspapers, magazines, and books. Newspaper circulation amounts to an average of slightly more than one newspaper per family per day. Magazine circulation averages more than two issues per person per year. More than 28,000 new books or new editions of older books are published each year, with total printings of about one billion copies.

More than 90 percent of all homes have radio sets, and about 90 percent have one or more television sets. Radio serves a variety of purposes besides providing entertainment and information for the general public. It is widely used by police and fire departments, airports, and by ships at sea.

More than half the world's telephones are in the United States. In 1963 about 84 million telephones in the country were used to make about 327 million calls a day. The United States also has extensive telegraph services and has radio and cable communications with more than 80 foreign countries.

Since colonial days a postal service has been recognized as a vital link in the communications network. In contrast with other means of communication, which are usually privately owned and regulated by the government, the U.S. postal service is a government enterprise. In 1963 it handled an average of about 360 pieces for each person. More than 33,000 post offices distribute mail. (See COMMUNICATIONS.)

XVI. Foreign Trade

The United States sells, or exports, many products to other countries and also buys, or imports, products from other countries. This exchange is called foreign trade.

The United States is the world's leading exporter and importer. The leading export is machinery of all types. Next come wheat and wheat flour, raw cotton, tobacco and tobacco products, and other agricultural goods. In addition, the United States exports such manufactured goods as chemicals; pulp, paper, and related products; rubber goods; many metal goods other than machines; medicines and drugs; textiles; and petroleum products. Coal and coke are also important U.S. exports. The country generally imports more than it exports of petroleum and metallic ores.

Leading imports include fuels, products of tropical agriculture, and raw or semimanufactured materials. Petroleum and petroleum products, coffee, newsprint, and cane sugar are among the leading imported products. Other imported items include iron ore and iron and steel products, meat, automobiles, fish, wool and wool products, and various ores. The United States must depend entirely upon other countries for certain products, including natural rubber, coffee, cocoa, and tea.

The United States carries on most foreign trade with neighboring countries in the western hemisphere. Canada, the most important trading partner, takes about 20 percent of the exports and supplies slightly more than 20 percent of the imports. Latin America also accounts for about 20 percent of both imports and exports. Western European countries take about one-third of the exports and supply about one-fourth of the imports. About 15 to 20 percent of foreign trade is with Asia, and about 4 percent is with Africa.

Most foreign trade is handled by ocean-going vessels. New York City, Philadelphia, Pennsylvania, and Baltimore, Maryland, on the Atlantic Coast receive a large part of the total imports, and Norfolk, Virginia, and New Orleans, Louisiana, are the leading ports for exports. West Coast ports, such as Los Angeles and San Francisco, California, and Seattle-Tacoma, Washington, handle smaller volumes of foreign commerce—along with many other ports on the Pacific, Gulf, and Atlantic coasts. Since the open-

Only 60 years after the first powered flight, aircraft carry freight and passengers at altitudes of more than 30,000 feet at speeds of nearly 600 miles per hour.

Courtesy United Air Lines

Photos (above) Rhodes Patterson; (below) Charles E. Rotkin, P.F.I. for Association of American Rail Roads

Inland waterways carry about one-sixth of all U.S. intercity freight. The major ones are the Great Lakes and the Mississippi-Missouri systems. Railroads are the leading freight carriers, however. There are about 215,000 miles of track throughout the country—concentrated primarily in the Northeastern and Midwestern regions.

ing of the St. Lawrence Seaway, Great Lakes ports, such as Chicago, Illinois, and Detroit, Michigan, have become more important in foreign trade. (See TRADE.)

XVII. Defense

The United States maintains an alert defense system to protect itself from attack by foreign powers. The Army, Navy, Air Force, and Marine Corps are all part of the defense system. In terms of its cost, defense could be called the biggest business in the country. Since the early 1950's more than 40 billion dollars—from 55 to 70 percent of the federal budget—has been allotted annually. In 1969 the money was spent in a variety of ways, including payment of salary and allowances to about 3,400,000 military officers and enlisted men and women. The Army was the largest branch of service, with about 1,000,000 persons, followed by the Air Force with 870,000, the Navy with about 760,-000, and the Marine Corps with about 300,000. In 1965 the country spent more than one billion dollars on its Military Assistance Program to help various foreign countries. The cost of developing, buying, and maintaining military equipment, however, accounts for the largest part of the defense budget. Since World War II the United States has worked hard on the development of atomic weapons. (See AIR FORCE; ARMY; NAVY.)

The military agreements and pacts that the United States has with various other countries are also important to defense. Through these pacts and agreements the country has extended its lines of defense all the way from its own shores through Western Europe, the Med-

A U.S. Saturn 1 (formerly C-1) carrier-vehicle rocket blasts off from Cape Kennedy with a thrust of 750 tons. Its second stage produces an additional 45 tons of thrust. It was designed to be used in Project Apollo, the manned moon-landing project. The rocket is 125 feet tall.

Courtesy NASA

iterranean, the Middle East, and Southeast Asia. The United States and Canada work especially close together to defend against attack from the north. Latin-American countries co-operate in the defense of the southern part of the western hemisphere. Since the defense of the countries of Western Europe is considered important to the defense of the United States, the country belongs to the North Atlantic Treaty Organization (NATO). The United States also belongs to the Southeast Asia Treaty Organization (SEATO) and is associated with the Central Treaty Organization (CENTO), which has headquarters in Turkey.

XVIII. Education

In the field of education the United States ranks among the world's most advanced countries. This is indicated by the country's high rate of literacy. In the early 1960's about 98 percent of the population 14 years of age and older could read and write. More than 28 percent of all Americans 25 years of age or older had completed high school, and about 8 percent had completed four or more years of college.

The administration of public schools is in the hands of state and city governments. They may, however, receive aid from the federal government. The U.S. Constitution provides for a separation of church and state. For this reason, religious education may not be taught in public schools. Public education is generally free through high school, and school attendance is compulsory. Specific requirements are set by local governments, but, generally, attendance is required between the ages of 7 and 16.

In 1964 and 1965 more than one-fourth of the total population of the United States was enrolled in schools or colleges. About 35,400,-000 children attended classes from kindergarten through the eighth grade, 12,700,000 were in high schools, and 4,800,000 went to colleges and universities. About six-sevenths of the elementary and high-school students were in public, tax-supported schools. Most of the remainder attended Roman Catholic institutions. About two-thirds of the college students were in public institutions, and about one-third were in private schools.

More federal and local tax money is spent on education than on any other single item except national defense. Yet in the 1960's the country suffered from a shortage of schools and teachers. To help local school districts combat these problems, the Congress in 1965 passed one of the most far-reaching aid-to-school bills in history. It provided for $1.3 billion in aid and was aimed specifically at the poorest school districts. (See EDUCATION.)

XIX. Government

The United States has a federal system of government. In such a system the power to govern is divided between a central authority (the national or federal government) and a number of local authorities (the 50 state governments). Matters that are believed to be of great importance to the country as a whole are handled by the national government. Agencies formed by the national government handle relations with other countries, national defense, mail, and the making and circulating of money. More local matters are handled by the state governments. These include control over public education, commerce, and roads and highways. (See UNITED STATES GOVERNMENT.)

FACTS ABOUT THE UNITED STATES

CAPITAL: Washington, D.C.
SYMBOLS: Uncle Sam; Bald Eagle.
MOTTO: "In God We Trust."
DATE OF INDEPENDENCE: July 4, 1776.
NATIONAL ANTHEM: "The Star-Spangled Banner."

The Great Seal of
the United States

★★★ The Stars and Stripes ★★★

The flag of the United States has 13
stripes, representing the 13
original states, and 50 stars, one
for each state in the Union.

PHYSICAL

AREA: 3,615,123 square miles, including 74,212 square miles
of inland water but excluding 60,960 square miles of the
Great Lakes; fourth largest country of the world; occupies
about 7 percent of the world's land area.

POPULATION (1970 census): 203,184,772; ranks fourth in the
world, with 6 percent of the world's population. Population
density, 56.2 persons per square mile. Urban population,
73.5 percent; rural, 26.5 percent.

CHIEF MOUNTAIN RANGES: Rocky Mountains, Appalachian
Mountains, Sierra Nevada, Cascade Mountains, Coast
Ranges, Ozark Mountains, Mesabi Range, Black Hills.

CHIEF MOUNTAIN PEAKS (height in feet): Mount McKinley,
Alaska (20,320); St. Elias, Alaska (18,008); Foraker, Alaska
(17,400); Whitney, California (14,495); Elbert, Colorado
(14,431).

LONGEST RIVERS (length in miles): Mississippi-Missouri (3,860);
Rio Grande (1,885); Arkansas (1,450); Colorado (1,440);
Yukon (1,265); Columbia (1,214), Snake (1,038), Red (1,018).

LARGEST LAKES (area in square miles): Superior (31,800, of
which 20,710 is in U.S.); Huron (23,000, of which 9,100 is in
U.S.); Michigan (22,400); Erie (9,930, of which 4,000 is in
U.S.); Ontario (7,600, of which 3,550 is in U.S.); Great
Salt (1,800); Iliamna (1,000); Okeechobee (700); Champlain
(490).

NATIONAL PARKS AND MONUMENTS: Total national parks
36, occupying 14,679,028 acres; national monuments, 85,
occupying 10,216,849 acres; other federal areas, such as
national seashores, national historic parks, national battlefields, national historic sites, and national recreation areas,
162, occupying 4,600,301 acres.

ECONOMY

AGRICULTURE: *Farmland,* 1,119,410,000 acres; *chief crops,*
corn, hay, soybeans, wheat, tobacco, cotton, sorghum, potatoes, oats, rice; *livestock,* cattle, milk cows, hogs and pigs,
sheep and lambs, horses and mules, chickens.

MANUFACTURING: Transportation equipment, nonelectrical
machinery, food and food products, electrical machinery,
chemicals and chemical products, primary metals, fabricated
metal products, printing and publishing.

MINING: Petroleum and natural gas, coal, copper ore, iron
ore, stone, sand, and gravel.

LUMBERING: *Commercial forest lands,* 510,000,000 acres; *production* (1968), 37,450 million board feet of lumber.

FISHING: *Number of fishing boats,* 84,200; *catch,* about 2
million tons.

MONETARY UNIT: Dollar; equal to 13.71 grains (1/35 ounce)
of gold.

Harris and Ewing

☆ **The Capitol** ☆

The Capitol building in Washington, D.C., is the meeting
place of the United States Congress.
The original design for the building
was submitted by architect William
Thornton. Construction began in
1793 and was completed in the
1830's. It was enlarged in the
1850's, and the dome was completed in the 1860's.

State	Total Area in sq. miles	Rank	Population 1970 Census	Rank	Density per sq. mi.	Electoral Votes	State	Total Area in sq. miles	Rank	Population 1970 Census	Rank	Density per sq. mi.	Electoral Votes
United States	3,615,123		203,184,772		56.2	538	Missouri	69,686	19	4,677,399	13	67.1	12
Alabama	51,609	29	3,444,165	21	66.7	9	Montana	147,138	4	694,409	43	4.7	4
Alaska	586,412	1	302,173	50	0.5	3	Nebraska	77,227	15	1,483,791	35	19.2	5
Arizona	113,909	6	1,772,482	33	15.6	6	Nevada	110,540	7	488,738	47	4.4	3
Arkansas	53,104	27	1,923,295	32	36.2	6	New Hampshire	9,304	44	737,681	41	79.3	4
California	158,693	3	19,953,134	1	125.7	45	New Jersey	7,836	46	7,168,164	8	914.8	17
Colorado	104,247	8	2,207,259	30	21.2	7	New Mexico	121,666	5	1,016,000	37	8.4	4
Connecticut	5,009	48	3,032,217	24	605.4	8	New York	49,576	30	18,190,740	2	366.9	41
Delaware	2,057	49	548,104	46	266.5	3	North Carolina	52,586	28	5,082,059	12	96.6	13
District of Columbia	67	51	756,510		11,291.2	3	North Dakota	70,665	17	617,761	45	8.7	3
Florida	58,560	22	6,789,443	9	115.9	17	Ohio	41,222	35	10,652,017	6	258.4	25
Georgia	58,876	21	4,589,575	15	78.0	12	Oklahoma	69,919	18	2,559,253	27	36.6	8
Hawaii	6,450	47	769,913	40	119.4	4	Oregon	96,981	10	2,091,385	31	21.6	6
Idaho	83,557	13	713,008	42	8.5	4	Pennsylvania	45,333	33	11,793,909	3	260.2	27
Illinois	56,400	24	11,113,976	5	197.1	26	Rhode Island	1,214	50	949,723	39	782.3	4
Indiana	36,291	38	5,193,669	11	143.1	13	South Carolina	31,055	40	2,590,516	26	83.4	8
Iowa	56,290	25	2,825,041	25	50.2	8	South Dakota	77,047	16	666,257	44	8.6	4
Kansas	82,264	14	2,249,071	28	27.3	7	Tennessee	42,244	34	3,924,164	17	92.9	10
Kentucky	40,395	37	3,219,311	23	79.7	9	Texas	267,339	2	11,196,730	4	41.9	26
Louisiana	48,523	31	3,643,180	20	75.1	10	Utah	84,916	11	1,059,273	36	12.5	4
Maine	33,215	39	993,663	38	29.9	4	Vermont	9,609	43	444,732	48	46.3	3
Maryland	10,577	42	3,922,399	18	370.8	10	Virginia	40,817	36	4,648,494	14	113.9	12
Massachusetts	8,257	45	5,689,170	10	689.0	14	Washington	68,192	20	3,409,169	22	50.0	9
Michigan	58,216	23	8,875,083	7	152.5	21	West Virginia	24,181	41	1,744,237	34	72.1	6
Minnesota	84,068	12	3,805,069	19	45.3	10	Wisconsin	56,154	26	4,417,933	16	78.7	11
Mississippi	47,716	32	2,216,912	29	46.5	7	Wyoming	97,914	9	332,416	49	3.4	3

TRANSPORTATION AND COMMUNICATION

RAILROADS: 212,000 miles of track.

ROADS: Total, 3,710,229 miles; municipal, 548,573; rural, 3,161,726, of which 2,391,325 miles are surfaced.

MOTOR VEHICLES: Total, 105,096,603; automobiles, 86,861,334; trucks and buses, 18,235,269.

CIVIL AVIATION: Federal airways, 142,000 miles; civil aircraft in operation, 133,316; general airports, 11,016 (excluding military).

NEWSPAPERS: 1,758 dailies, 7,612 weeklies, and 585 Sunday.

RADIO STATIONS: 4,167 AM, 1,888 FM.

TELEVISION STATIONS: 665 (excluding educational).

TELEPHONES: 115,200,700.

POST OFFICES: 32,002 (includes 117 in U.S. territories).

PEOPLE

LARGEST CITIES (pop. 1970): New York City (7,867,760); Chicago (3,366,757); Los Angeles (2,816,061); Philadelphia (1,948,609); Detroit (1,511,482); Houston (1,232,802); Baltimore (905,759); Dallas (844,401); Washington, D.C. (756,510).

NATIONAL BACKGROUNDS: Native born, 94.6 percent; foreign born, 5.4 percent.

CHURCH MEMBERSHIP: Of total population, about 63 percent are church members: Protestant, 54.8 percent; Roman Catholic, 37.3 percent; Jewish, 4.5 percent; others, 3.7 percent.

EDUCATION

ELEMENTARY SCHOOLS (1967–68): 85,779.

SECONDARY SCHOOLS (1967–68): 31,411.

COLLEGES AND UNIVERSITIES (1969): 2,525.

LITERACY: 97.6 percent.

GOVERNMENT

FORM OF GOVERNMENT: Federal Republic.

HEAD OF GOVERNMENT AND CHIEF OF STATE: President.

BRANCHES OF GOVERNMENT: Executive, legislative, judicial.

TYPE OF LEGISLATURE: Congress made up of two houses: Senate and House of Representatives.

NUMBER OF SENATORS: 100, with 2 from each state. Term of office, six years; one-third of total membership elected every two years.

NUMBER OF REPRESENTATIVES: 435, apportioned to states on basis of population; term of office, two years.

CONSTITUTION ADOPTED: 1789.

PRESIDENT'S TERM: Four years, may be reelected once.

POLITICAL DIVISIONS: 50 states and the District of Columbia.

VOTING QUALIFICATIONS: Minimum age is 18; residence requirements vary from six months to two years according to state; other requirements vary from state to state.

NATIONAL HOLIDAYS: New Year's Day, January 1; Washington's Birthday, February 22; Easter; Memorial Day, May 30 in most states; Independence Day, July 4; Labor Day, 1st Monday in September; Veteran's Day, November 11; Thanksgiving, 4th Thursday in November; Christmas, December 25.

XX. History

Less than 200 years ago—in 1776—the 13 American colonies declared their independence from English rule. At the close of the American Revolution in 1783, England recognized the independence of the colonies and the United States of America came into being. The young country was made up of only 13 states. Although the country's boundaries extended westward to the Mississippi River, few people had settled on the vast, flat plains that lay beyond the Appalachian Mountains.

The ancestors of most of the people who live in the United States today came from the British Isles, Europe, and Africa. For hundreds of years before the first settlers arrived, the region now called the continental United States was inhabited by natives. It was Christopher Columbus who first gave the name Indian to these people. He did so because he thought that he had arrived in the East Indies. (See INDIANS, NORTH AMERICAN.)

Throughout the long period that the Indians lived in North America before Columbus, the land must have presented a striking picture. Much of it was covered with dense forests in which wild ani-

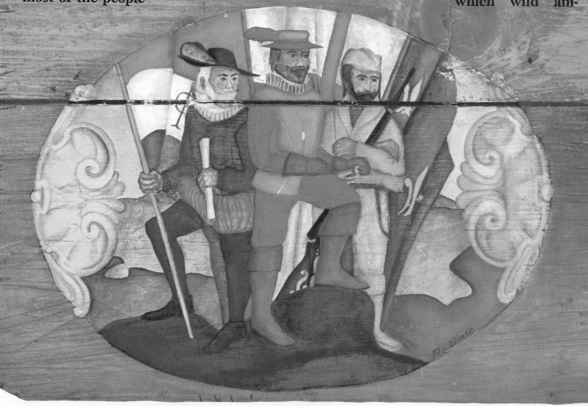

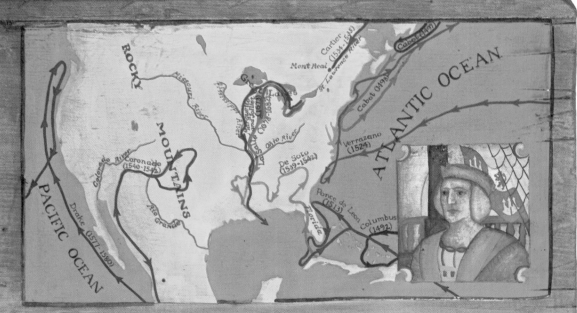

mals lived. The Indians had not developed a high state of civilization as had the Indians of Latin America. The dog was their only domesticated animal. They had only the most primitive tools. They lived a simple life, and their wants were few.

When the first Europeans arrived, the Indians were helpful to them. The newcomers learned from the Indians how to plant new and useful crops, how to live in the wilderness, and how to hunt and fish. It was not long, however, before the Indians found that their way of life was threatened by the white settlers. They saw their forest hunting grounds being cleared to make open fields and their forest trails becoming well-traveled roads. As settlers moved farther inland, conflicts arose with the Indians. Wars and treaties followed, and the Indians found themselves forced westward and confined more and more to limited lands. Their numbers decreased rapidly through disease brought by the Europeans.

When the king and queen of Spain learned that Columbus had actually discovered a new world in 1492, they lost little time in laying claim to it. They established colonies on the islands of the West Indies and in Mexico and Central America. They claimed all of South America except Brazil (claimed by Portugal).

In 1513 Juan Ponce de Leon, a Spanish explorer, landed on the east coast of what is now the state of Florida, where he hoped to find the Fountain of Youth. The explorer named the new land Florida and claimed it for Spain. In 1539 another Spanish explorer, Hernando de Soto, landed on the west coast of Florida with a large company of men. They explored the land to the north and west and were the first white men to see the Mississippi River. A year later another Spaniard, Francisco de Coronado, set out from Mexico and explored the southwestern part of what is now the United States. On the basis of these explorations Spain claimed nearly all the land that now forms the southern half of the United States. (See Ponce de Leon, Juan; De Soto, Hernando; Coronado, Francisco Vasquez de.)

Meanwhile, other countries were also becoming interested in the new land. In 1497 and 1498, John Cabot explored the northeast coast of North America. It was upon these voyages that England based her claim to America. (See Cabot, John Sebastian.)

In 1524 a French expedition commanded by Giovanni da Verrazano explored the coast of North America from the Carolinas northward. Ten years later another French expedition led by Jacques Cartier sailed up the St. Lawrence River. On a later voyage Cartier went up this river to a high point which he named *Mont Real*, meaning "mount royal." This is how the city of Montreal, Canada, got its name. (See Cartier, Jacques.)

Unlike Spain, England and France waited nearly 100 years before they established colonies in North America.

England made several unsuccessful attempts to establish settlements in North America near the close of the 16th century. The first perma-

Courtesy Trustees of the British Museum

Captain John Smith was one of the leaders of the English colonists who settled at Jamestown in 1607.

nent settlement by Englishmen was made at Jamestown, Virginia, in 1607. A group of English merchants, called the Virginia Company of London, had been given a charter by King James I that granted them the right to found a colony in the new land. The company provided the three ships in which the settlers crossed the Atlantic Ocean and also paid for the settlers' supplies. (See Jamestown, Virginia; Smith, Captain John.)

Jamestown was founded for commercial reasons. The land belonged to the company. The London merchants hoped that the settlers would find gold and send it and other valuable products back to England. No gold was found, however. Food supplies ran short. The settlement was on a low-lying, unhealthful site, and many colonists fell ill and died.

Within a few years the company decided to give each settler three acres of land that he could call his own. This was later increased to 50 acres. About this time another important event occurred. One of the settlers, John Rolfe, found a way of improving the quality of the tobacco that had been raised by the Indians of Virginia. This tobacco was soon in great demand in England and Europe, and the Jamestown colony began to prosper. (See Tobacco.)

The year 1619 was an eventful one for the Virginia colony. In that year the company introduced reforms and gave the colonists the right to share in making the laws for the colony. A representative assembly known as the House of Burgesses was formed—the first of its kind on American soil. Also in 1619 the first women settlers arrived, as did the first Negroes. The Negroes were not slaves but indentured servants who were bound to work for a master for a certain number of years.

In 1620 a group of Pilgrims established a settlement at Plymouth, Massachusetts. The Pilgrims were English Protestants who objected to some of the beliefs and practices of the Church of England. Some of them had gone first to live in the Netherlands.

The *Mayflower*, the ship in which the first Pilgrims sailed across the ocean, was to have landed in northern Virginia. It ran off course, however, and dropped anchor in the shelter of Cape Cod in Massachusetts. The leaders of the group decided to settle on the nearby shore. They first drew up a notable agreement called the Mayflower Compact. By signing this document they agreed to form a government of their own and to obey its rules and regula-

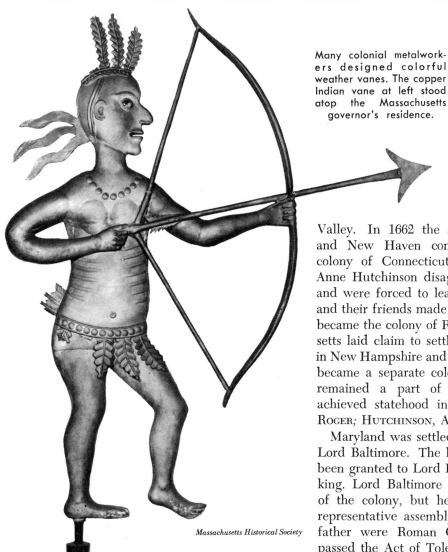

Many colonial metalworkers designed colorful weather vanes. The copper Indian vane at left stood atop the Massachusetts governor's residence.

Massachusetts Historical Society

called the "mother of colonies." Thomas Hooker led a group of settlers from Massachusetts to the upper Connecticut River Valley to form a new settlement. Other persons from Massachusetts settled in the lower Connecticut Valley. In 1662 the settlements of Hartford and New Haven combined to become the colony of Connecticut. Roger Williams and Anne Hutchinson disagreed with the Puritans and were forced to leave Massachusetts. They and their friends made settlements that in 1644 became the colony of Rhode Island. Massachusetts laid claim to settlements that were made in New Hampshire and Maine. New Hampshire became a separate colony in 1679, but Maine remained a part of Massachusetts until it achieved statehood in 1820. (See Williams, Roger; Hutchinson, Anne.)

Maryland was settled in 1634 by the Second Lord Baltimore. The land for this colony had been granted to Lord Baltimore's father by the king. Lord Baltimore was the sole proprietor of the colony, but he granted the settlers a representative assembly. Although he and his father were Roman Catholics, the assembly passed the Act of Toleration, which permitted any Christians to settle in Maryland. (See Baltimore, Lords.)

In 1609 Henry Hudson, in command of a Dutch ship, the *Half Moon*, sailed into New York Bay and up the river that later was to be named in his honor. (See Hudson, Henry.) The Dutch claimed this region, and in 1624 they sent a shipload of settlers. They called their colony New Netherland.

The English colonists in New England and Virginia looked upon the Dutch as intruders. After a long period of conflict an English fleet appeared in New York Bay in 1664 and seized the Dutch colony. The king of England gave the colony to the Duke of York and changed its name to New York. (See Colonial Beginnings in America.)

tions. (See Mayflower; Plymouth, Massachusetts.)

The Puritans, like the Pilgrims, were English Protestants who also objected to the practices of the Church of England. They did not want to separate from it, however, but thought that by remaining in the church they could reform, or purify, it. (See Puritans.) They decided to form a company and go to America where they could organize their church as they pleased. The Massachusetts Bay Company, which they formed, was granted land between the Charles and Merrimac rivers in Massachusetts. By 1630 nearly 1,000 Puritans had come to the new colony, and it soon prospered and grew strong.

The Massachusetts Bay Colony has been

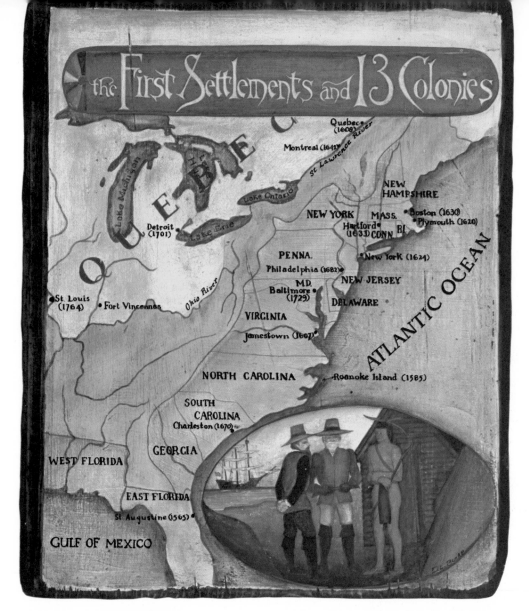

the First Settlements and 13 Colonies

Quebec (1608)
Montreal (1641)
St. Lawrence River
Lake Michigan
Lake Huron
Lake Ontario
Lake Erie
Detroit (1701)
NEW HAMPSHIRE
NEW YORK
MASS.
Boston (1630)
Plymouth (1620)
Hartford (1633) CONN. R.I.
PENNA.
Philadelphia (1682)
New York (1624)
NEW JERSEY
St. Louis (1764)
Fort Vincennes
Ohio River
M.D.
Baltimore (1729)
DELAWARE
ATLANTIC OCEAN
VIRGINIA
Jamestown (1607)
NORTH CAROLINA
Roanoke Island (1585)
SOUTH CAROLINA
Charleston (1670)
GEORGIA
WEST FLORIDA
EAST FLORIDA
St. Augustine (1565)
GULF OF MEXICO

Later Colonies

Pennsylvania was founded in 1681 by William Penn. The king granted Penn a large tract of land west of the Delaware River in settlement for a debt that he owed Penn's father. William Penn, who had become a Quaker, wished to found a colony where every man could worship God in his own way. (See PENN, WILLIAM; FRIENDS, SOCIETY OF.)

Penn believed that the Indians should be treated fairly and should be paid for their land. He drew up a plan of government for his colony and allowed the people to make their own laws. Philadelphia, known as the

"city of brotherly love," became the largest city in the colonies. Penn invited many people to come to his colony. Englishmen, many of whom were Quakers, settled in Philadelphia and along the Delaware River. Later, Germans came to the colony in large numbers and settled in the region extending westward to the Susquehanna River. Still later, Scotch-Irish settled in western Pennsylvania.

In 1702 the settlements of East and West Jersey were joined together to form New Jersey. The settlements made by the Swedes and the Dutch on the lower Delaware were controlled by Pennsylvania, but after 1704 Delaware was considered a separate colony.

In 1663 King Charles II of England granted a large tract of land along the Carolina coast to eight of his friends. Within a few years, two areas were settled—one in the north and another in the south. Later the colony was divided into North and South Carolina.

Georgia was the last of the English colonies to be founded in the land that was to become the United States. It was settled in 1732 by James Oglethorpe. (See OGLETHORPE, JAMES.) The founding of Georgia completed the chain of English colonies that extended along the Atlantic coast from Maine to the border of Spanish Florida.

(For further information about the colonies see the section on *History* in the individual state articles.)

Colonial Government and Economy

The government of each colony was patterned after the government of England. In the proprietary colonies, such as Maryland and Pennsylvania, the governor was appointed by the proprietor (the man to whom the king had given the colony). In some of the colonies the governor was appointed by the king. Only in Connecticut and Rhode Island was the governor elected by the people. Representative assemblies, resembling the English Parliament, were established in most of the colonies. Only citizens who owned property or paid taxes, however, were allowed to hold office or vote for members of the assembly.

In New England, where most of the people lived in villages and towns, local government was conducted by the town meeting. In the South, where most people lived on large farms and plantations, the county was the basis for local government.

The first settlers who came to live in the colonies were confronted with difficulties and hardships. They had brought only a few supplies with them. To exist they had to build homes, clear land, and plant crops. If friendly relations with the Indians were not established, the settlers had to protect their homes and families from attack.

Most of the early colonists were farmers because they had to produce their own food. In time, however, the living patterns of the colonists began to change. In New England, for example, where the soil generally was not suited to farming, the people turned to lumbering, shipbuilding, and fishing. The southern colonies found their soil and climate well suited to growing tobacco, rice, and indigo. Many southerners owned only small farms, but

U.S. Capitol Historical Society

On July 4, 1776, the Continental Congress adopted the Declaration of Independence. This painting, "The Signing of the Declaration of Independence," by John Trumbull shows the members of the Congress signing the document at Independence Hall in Philadelphia.

others established large plantations worked by slaves. They sent their crops to England in exchange for goods that were needed in their homes. The colonists of New York, New Jersey, and Pennsylvania found grain and stock farming profitable. They not only raised enough for themselves but produced wheat, flour, beef, and pork to sell to other colonies.

Trade was an important part of colonial life. The colonies traded with each other and also with England, Europe, and the West Indies. The colonial towns of Boston, New York, Philadelphia, and Charleston grew into busy commercial cities. Craftsmen such as cobblers, cabinetmakers, and metalsmiths began to ply their trades in their own homes. (See COLONIAL LIFE IN AMERICA.)

The colonists did not neglect learning. In 1647 a Massachusetts law required every town of 50 families or more to provide schooling for its children. Harvard College was founded in Massachusetts in 1636, the College of William and Mary in Virginia in 1693, and Yale College in Connecticut in 1701. The first printing press was set up in Massachusetts in 1638. By 1715 there were eight printing presses in the colonies. Postriders began carrying mail from one colony to another, and stagecoach lines were established between the colonial cities.

By 1750 the population of the colonies had reached 1,200,000. Some settlers had gone to live in the sheltered valleys of the Appalachian Mountains. The colonies became interested in the land that lay west of these mountains, but they were blocked by the French and the Indians.

In 1608—only one year after the settlement of Jamestown—the French had founded Que-

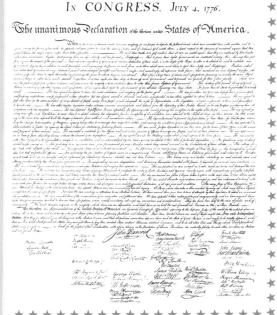

bec, the first permanent French settlement in North America. Frenchmen explored the upper St. Lawrence River, the Great Lakes region, and the Mississippi River Valley. One of them, Rene La Salle, planted a cross and the French flag at the mouth of the Mississippi River in 1682 and claimed all of the land drained by the river for France. (See CANADA; LA SALLE, RENE ROBERT CAVELIER, SIEUR DE.)

Both the French and the English built forts in western Pennsylvania to protect their claims to the upper Ohio Valley. In 1754 fighting began in this region between the French and English forces. The French and Indian War, as this conflict was called, ended in 1763 with the defeat of France and its Indian allies. The victory gave England control over all of French Canada and the territory between the Appalachian Mountains and the Mississippi River. (See FRENCH AND INDIAN WAR.)

A New Country

At the end of the French and Indian War, England faced new problems in America. The English government decided to exercise firmer control over colonial trade. The colonies were told that they should help pay for the cost of the war and for their future defense. The English Parliament passed laws to regulate colonial trade with England and other countries. A stamp tax was adopted, and taxes were levied on certain imports into the colonies. (See STAMP ACT; REVOLUTION, AMERICAN.)

Even though some of these laws were for the benefit of the colonies as well as for England, the colonists objected to them. They argued that since they were not represented in the English Parliament they should not be

Courtesy The New York Historical Society; photo by Paul Schutzer

"Pilgrims Going to Church" was painted by George H. Boughton, an Anglo-American artist. It is a scene of the early colonial days in New England. The men in the picture carry guns to protect the group from attack by hostile Indians.

Courtesy Philip S. Dalton and "Life" Magazine

"Boston Harbor: Long and Central Wharves" was painted by Robert W. Salmon, who arrived in the United States from England in 1829. The painting shows Boston in 1832 when it was the center of commerce of the United States.

PLATE 10 UNITED STATES

Courtesy of the Metropolitan Museum of Art

"Washington Crossing the Delaware" was painted by Emanuel Leutze during the middle 1800's.

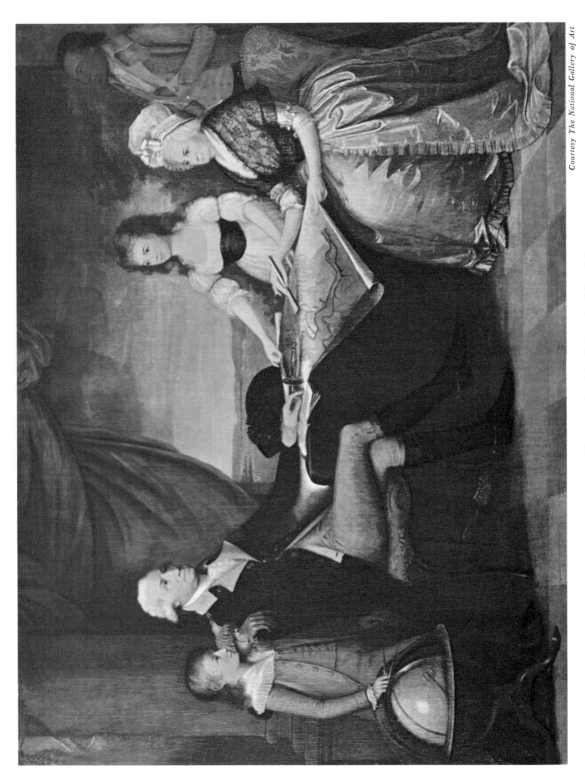

"The Washington Family" was painted by U.S. artist Edward Savage.

PLATE 12 UNITED STATES

Courtesy Washington University and "Life" Magazine

"Daniel Boone Escorting a Band of Pioneers into the Western Country" was painted by the U.S. artist George Caleb Bingham. It is of the trip that Daniel Boone made to Kentucky by way of the Cumberland Gap in 1775.

Courtesy Hall Park McCullough and "Life" Magazine

This detail of the painting "Emigrant Train" by U.S. artist Samuel Colman shows a covered-wagon train fording Medicine Bow Creek in the Rocky Mountains near Laramie, Wyoming.

taxed by it. More important was the fact that the colonists had come to feel self-sufficient by this time. They had had experience in governing themselves through their own assemblies and in fighting during the French and Indian War. Many of the people who lived in the colonies at that time had been born in America and considered it their home.

The First Continental Congress, made up of representatives from the 13 colonies, met in Philadelphia in 1774 to try to improve colonial relations with England. This effort failed and fighting broke out in Massachusetts between English troops and the colonial Minutemen. The battles of Lexington and Concord marked the opening of the American Revolution in April 1775. The Second Continental Congress then met and chose George Washington to command the colonial troops.

Many of the colonists opposed taking up arms against England, but others such as Samuel Adams in Massachusetts, Benjamin Franklin in Pennsylvania, and Thomas Jefferson and Patrick Henry in Virginia believed the colonies should assert their rights. Jefferson, with the aid of a committee, drafted a statement declaring that, "these United Colonies are, and of Right ought to be Free and Independent States." On July 4, 1776, this statement, called the Declaration of Independence, was adopted by the Second Continental Congress. (See DECLARATION OF INDEPENDENCE.)

The war for independence did not go well for the colonists at first. General Washington barely managed to keep his small army together because of defeats and lack of supplies. Finally the tide turned in the colonists' favor in 1777, when an English army under General John Burgoyne was defeated at the Battle of Saratoga. After that victory, France decided to help the colonies in their war against England. The fighting ended in 1781 with the surrender of the English forces at Yorktown, Virginia. By the Treaty of Paris in 1783, England recognized the independence of the United States. The new country extended from Maine to Florida and westward to the Mississippi River.

Before the war ended, the Second Continental Congress drafted the Articles of Confederation under which the new country was

New York was a bustling port city in the middle of the 18th century. Shown above is the old part built by the Dutch; below, the newer part built by the English.

The Bettmann Archive

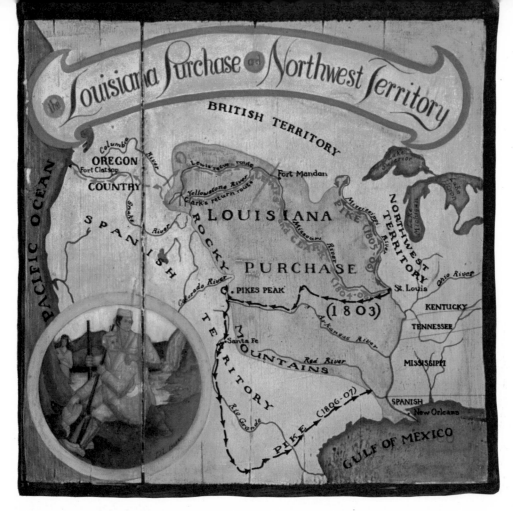

The Louisiana Purchase and Northwest Territory

to be governed. The Articles, adopted in 1781, provided for a loose union of states and reserved most of the powers of government for the states. Congress could not tax the people directly. It could not levy tariffs on imported goods or regulate trade among the states. The Articles made no provision for strong executive or law-enforcing branches of government. It soon became apparent that the states had not formed a strong union. (See ARTICLES OF CONFEDERATION.)

The Constitution

George Washington, Alexander Hamilton, James Madison, and other leaders became dissatisfied with the Articles of Confederation. A convention, therefore, was called to meet in Philadelphia in 1787 to amend the Articles. After the delegates assembled they decided to set the Articles aside and draft an entirely new

constitution. When the new constitution was ratified by the states, it became the supreme law of the land. The Constitution provided for a federal type of government—a union of states under a strong central government. It gave the federal government power to levy taxes and to regulate commerce. It stated clearly what powers the federal government had and what powers were reserved for the states.

The Constitution provided for three branches of government—legislative, executive, and judicial. The lawmaking body was to consist of a Senate, in which each state was to have two members, and a House of Representatives, in which each state was to have a number of representatives based on its population. (See CONSTITUTION OF THE UNITED STATES.)

Some people objected to the Constitution because it made no provision for the protection of individual liberties. Fortunately, provision had been made for amending the Constitution. When the first Congress assembled, a number of amendments guaranteeing individual rights and liberties were drawn up. After being ratified by the states, ten amendments were added to the Constitution. They are called the Bill of Rights. (See BILL OF RIGHTS.)

The new government under the Constitution was organized in New York City in 1789 with George Washington as the first president. Congress proceeded to exercise some of the powers that were granted to it by the Constitution. At the suggestion of Alexander Hamilton, secretary of the treasury, laws were passed that provided for the levying of a tax on whisky, the creation of a United States Bank, the payment by the national government of Revolutionary debts of the states, and the payment of all other government debts in full. (See HAMILTON, ALEXANDER; WASHINGTON, GEORGE.)

Hamilton and others among the merchant class believed that a strong central government should exercise the powers the Constitution gave it. These people came to be called Federalists. Thomas Jefferson and his followers, who included many laboring men and farmers, feared that the national government might exercise too much power. These people came to be called Anti-Federalists, or Republicans. It was in this way that political parties came into being. (See DEMOCRATIC PARTY; FEDERALIST PARTY; POLITICAL PARTIES; REPUBLICAN PARTY.)

Westward Expansion

The Constitution requires that a census of population be taken every ten years. The first census was taken in 1790. The population of the United States at that time was about four million. The states having the largest populations were Virginia, North Carolina, Pennsylvania, Massachusetts, and New York.

After the country became independent, it was expected that many people would move into the region between the Appalachian Mountains and the Mississippi River. In 1785 the Continental Congress had passed a law

providing for the survey of the land north of the Ohio River and for its sale to land companies and to individuals. Two years later the Ordinance of 1787 was passed. It organized this region as a territory and provided that in the future new states would be formed within the territory.

Settlers followed traders and explorers into the region west of the Appalachian Mountains. Some built flatboats at the forks of the Allegheny and Monongahela rivers in western Pennsylvania and floated down the Ohio River. Others passed through the Cumberland Gap in southwestern Virginia. In 1792 Kentucky was admitted to the Union as a state. In 1796 Tennessee became a state. Kentucky and Tennessee were the first states to be created west of the Appalachian Mountains.

Most of the people who settled in the West became farmers. They raised their own food and within a few years produced flour and salt pork for sale. They shipped these and other products on flatboats down the Ohio and Mississippi rivers to New Orleans, where they were transferred to oceangoing ships. (See PIONEER LIFE IN THE UNITED STATES.)

Difficulties soon arose over shipping at New Orleans. The land on both sides of the Mississippi River at that point belonged to Spain. Later, this region as well as the land along the west side of the Mississippi was transferred to France. Neither country was pleased to see U.S. citizens settle in the Mississippi Valley. (See WESTWARD MOVEMENT.)

In 1803 Thomas Jefferson, who had been elected U.S. president in 1800, decided that the United States should buy New Orleans and the land along the lower Mississippi from France. To everyone's surprise, France offered to sell to the United States all of her territory west of the Mississippi. The offer was accepted and with the payment of $15 million the United States received the entire territory of Louisiana. It almost doubled the size of the country. (See LOUISIANA PURCHASE.)

In 1804 Meriwether Lewis and William Clark set out from St. Louis to explore the Louisiana Territory. They and their men ascended the Missouri River, crossed the Rocky

Mountains, and followed the Columbia River to the Pacific Ocean. Two years later Zebulon Pike crossed the Louisiana Territory and followed the upper Arkansas River into the Rocky Mountains. The United States also expanded to the south. In 1819 Spain signed a treaty ceding Florida to the United States.

The New Country's Foreign Policies

In 1789, the year in which the new U.S. government was organized, a revolution began in France. The people rose against the king and set up a representative government. This civil war alarmed Austria, Prussia, and England. Within a short time, France was at war with her European neighbors and England—a war that was to drag on under the leadership of Napoleon for 15 years. (See FRENCH REVOLUTION; NAPOLEON I.)

At first many people of the United States felt that they should help the French in the war since France had helped them win their independence from England. Others were opposed to helping France because of the extreme measures taken by the leaders of the French Revolution. When England began interfering with U.S. overseas trade, Washington sent John Jay to England to try to improve relations with that country, but the resulting treaty was not popular. (See JAY, JOHN.)

During the Napoleonic Wars, when England and France were fighting, the United States tried to remain neutral. However, it could not carry on trade with either France or England without running into trouble with the other. To make matters worse, the English began stopping U.S. ships and searching them for English seamen who had deserted. Sometimes they forced U.S. sailors into their naval service. People who lived on the western frontier accused the English of supplying the Indians with arms. Finally, in 1812, the U.S. Congress declared war on England.

Several U.S. ships won battles at sea, but on land the war did not go well. A British force invaded and in 1814 set fire to several public buildings. The British were repelled in their attacks on Baltimore and New Orleans, but U.S. forces failed to drive them out of Canada. The war ended with the Treaty of Ghent. (See WAR OF 1812.)

During the early 1800's, Spain's colonies in Central and South America declared themselves independent. Later, Spain attempted to regain control over her colonies and it appeared that some European powers might help her do so. Under these circumstances, President James Monroe in 1823 issued a statement that has since become famous as the Monroe Doctrine. It stated that North and South America were no longer open to colonization and that any attempts by European countries to interfere with independent American governments would be regarded as unfriendly acts. (See MONROE DOCTRINE.)

Trade and Industrial Growth

In the 1790's the first textile mills for spinning yarn and weaving cloth were built in the United States. In 1793 Eli Whitney invented the cotton gin, which speeded up the separation of seeds from cotton fibers. The growing of cotton spread throughout the southern states, and the number of cotton mills in both the United States and England grew rapidly. The invention of the sewing machine by Elias Howe in 1846 completed the process by which cotton and wool could be made into finished

The industrial revolution brought great changes. Manufacturing was spurred by the invention of the cotton gin and the sewing machine, and farming was aided by the development of heavy farm machinery.

Photos, The Bettmann Archive

garments by the use of factory machines. (See COTTON; HOWE, ELIAS; WHITNEY, ELI.)

Other inventions helped the farmer. Cast-iron plows slowly replaced clumsy wooden ones. In 1831 Cyrus McCormick invented a horse-drawn reaper for harvesting grain. Horse-drawn harrows, drills, and mowers were invented, as well as a horse-powered threshing machine. These improvements helped grain farmers of the North as much as the cotton gin helped cotton farmers of the South. (See FARMING AND FARM LIFE; INVENTION.)

The making of factory machines and farm tools created a greater demand for iron. Blast furnaces fired by charcoal had been built in the colonies. The discovery of coal in Pennsylvania led to the use of coke in blast furnaces. Ironworks were set up for the manufacture of household utensils, farm implements, factory machines, and steam engines. (See INDUSTRIAL REVOLUTION, THE.)

The shipment of goods from factories to farms and from farms to towns and cities presented many problems. Goods were carried in packsaddles, carts, and wagons over rutted roads and on flatboats on the rivers.

The first hard-surfaced road was built from Philadelphia to Lancaster in Pennsylvania in the 1790's. It was built by the Lancaster Turnpike Road Company. People who used it were required to pay tolls. Many other companies were formed to build roads, and in 1803 the national government began to build the Old National Road that was to run westward from Cumberland, Maryland, through Ohio and Indiana to Illinois.

Meanwhile, men also became interested in building canals. The Erie Canal, completed in 1825, crossed New York, connecting Lake Erie with the Hudson River. Another canal, with railroad links that carried canal boats over the mountains, was built across Pennsylvania. Still other canals were built in the West, connecting the Great Lakes with the Ohio and Mississippi rivers. While canal boats traveled no faster than a man could walk, canals greatly reduced the cost of transporting goods and made travel easier. (See CANAL.)

The invention and improvement of the steam engine led to even greater developments in transportation and trade. The first successful steamboat, the *Clermont*, was built by Robert Fulton. It made its maiden voyage on the Hudson River in 1807. (See FULTON, ROBERT; SHIP.) The early 1830's saw the birth of U.S. railroads. In those years steam locomotives made successful runs on the Baltimore and Ohio Railroad in Maryland, the Charleston and Hamburg Railroad in South Carolina, and the Mohawk and Hudson Railroad in New York. Within the next 20 years these railroads were extended and others were built in the East, South, and West. By 1850 there were more than 9,000 miles of railroads in the United States. In another ten years some of these roads were joined together to form trunk lines. (See RAILROAD.)

Improvements in transportation encouraged the growth of mining, manufacturing, and trade. By 1840 the country's population had grown to more than 17 million. A third of the people lived in the West, and most of the western territories had been organized into states. Many persons had gone beyond the western borders in search of fortune and adventure. Fur traders penetrated the Rocky Mountains and the Pacific Northwest, and southern farmers moved into Texas.

Texas had declared itself independent of Mexico in 1836. In 1845 it was admitted into the United States. This led to a boundary dispute and a war between the United States and Mexico. When the war ended in 1848, the United States gained control of the entire Southwest except for the Gadsden Territory, which it purchased from Mexico in 1853. In 1846 the United States and England had agreed to divide the Oregon Country between them at the 49th parallel. By 1848 the United States had expanded to the Pacific Ocean. Thousands of pioneers followed the Oregon Trail to establish new homes in the Northwest. Other thousands of adventurers set out to find their fortunes in the goldfields of California.

Reform and Controversy

One of the purposes of the Constitution was to "promote the general welfare." During the period from 1820 to 1860 many persons proposed reforms of U.S. laws for the benefit of the people. There was much disagreement about the proposed reforms.

In 1787 only men who owned land and paid taxes were permitted to vote. By 1820 there were many men, such as traders and factory workers, who owned no land of their own but felt they should have the right to vote. State after state passed laws that extended the right to vote to all male citizens, regardless of property ownership.

Women began to demand the same rights. In many states women were granted the right to own property and to attend college, but they had to wait many years before gaining the right to vote and hold office. (See WOMAN SUFFRAGE.)

In earlier times schools were thought necessary only for those who were to become ministers, lawyers, and teachers. Now, people began to think that all children should receive an elementary education and that higher schools should be provided for those who wished to continue their education. Horace Mann of Massachusetts and De Witt Clinton of New York persuaded their states to support free public elementary and secondary schools.

Factory workers began to form trade unions. They demanded safer working conditions, shorter work days, higher wages, and free public schools for their children. In the 1840's national and state laws were passed limiting the working day to ten hours for certain kinds of work.

A notable political event of this era was the election of Andrew Jackson to the U.S. presidency in 1828. Jackson lived in Tennessee and was the first man from the West to be elected president. He believed that any man of average ability could hold a government job and that such jobs should be given to those who helped their party win the elections. This practice came to be called the "spoils system." While Jackson did not originate the spoils system, he was severely criticized for his use of it. (See CIVIL SERVICE; JACKSON, ANDREW.)

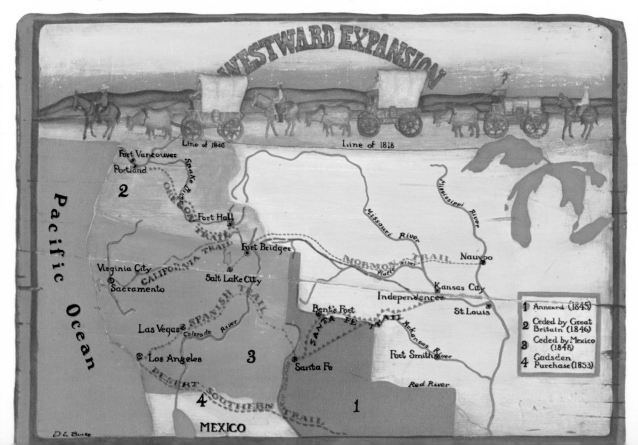

Dissension in the Union

Other problems were leading to heated and violent debates. These disagreements revealed a growing split between the East and West and especially between the North and the South.

One such debate occurred over the tariff question. In 1816 Congress passed the first protective tariff. It placed a tax on certain imported goods so that U.S. manufacturers and farmers would be able to sell their products at better prices. Few people objected to this tariff. But when another tariff was passed in 1828, with much higher duties on wool, hemp, and certain manufactured goods, South Carolina threatened to declare the act unconstitutional. In the Senate, Daniel Webster and Robert Hayne debated the right of a state to take such action. (See HAYNE, ROBERT YOUNG; TARIFF; WEBSTER, DANIEL.)

The greatest problem confronting the country at this time was slavery. When the first census was taken in 1790 there were more than 700,000 slaves in the United States. Most of them were in southern states where they worked in tobacco and cotton fields. Some people in both the North and in the South began to feel that slavery was evil and should be abolished. The Northwest Ordinance of 1787 had prohibited slavery in the region north of the Ohio River. By 1804 all of the northern states had abolished slavery, and in 1808 the importation of slaves into the country was prohibited. (See NEGROES, UNITED STATES.)

The invention of the cotton gin in 1793 and the expansion of cotton plantations had greatly increased the demand for slaves in the South. When Missouri applied for admission to the Union as a slave state, the northern states objected. A compromise was reached in 1820. It provided that Maine should come in as a free state and Missouri as a slave state, but that slavery should be prohibited in the rest of the Louisiana Territory north of parallel 36° 30'. (See MISSOURI COMPROMISE.)

During the 1830's and 1840's the debate over slavery continued. In 1848 a new crisis arose when the territory acquired from Mexico was to be organized. After heated debates in Congress another compromise was reached in 1850. California, where gold had been discovered in 1848, was admitted as a free state. The people who lived in the rest of this territory were to decide for themselves whether they should have slavery. The slave trade was abolished in the District of Columbia, and a stronger Fugitive Slave Law was passed. (See COMPROMISE OF 1850.)

Many people thought the Compromise of 1850 had settled the matter for good, but two years later the book *Uncle Tom's Cabin* by Harriet Beecher Stowe appeared. It aroused intense feeling in the North against slavery. In 1854 Congress passed the Kansas-Nebraska Act, which permitted people of these two territories—both north of the Missouri Compromise line—to decide whether they should have slavery. People from both the North and South rushed into Kansas to help decide the issue. Fighting raged in "Bleeding Kansas." Three years later the U.S. Supreme Court, in the Dred Scott case, declared the Missouri Compromise unconstitutional. (See DRED SCOTT DECISION; KANSAS-NEBRASKA ACT.)

The Bettmann Archive

An 1862 poster in Philadelphia, Pennsylvania, solicited Union Army recruits.

As the date for the 1860 presidential election approached, the debate over slavery became the main campaign issue. Two of the candidates—Abraham Lincoln and Stephen Douglas—both from Illinois, had debated the issues in 1858. Lincoln was chosen as the candidate of the Republican party, which had recently been formed in the North. The Democratic party split in two, the northern Democrats choosing Douglas and the southern Democrats choosing John C. Breckinridge. (See BRECKINRIDGE, JOHN CABELL; DOUGLAS, STEPHEN ARNOLD; LINCOLN, ABRAHAM.)

Ragged Union soldiers laid siege to Petersburg, Virginia, in 1864. A year later Confederate forces finally withdrew, thus opening the way to the capture of Richmond, the capital of the Confederacy.

The Country Divided

Shortly after the election of Abraham Lincoln as president in 1860, the southern states began to secede (withdraw) from the Union. They formed the Confederate States of America and elected Jefferson Davis of Mississippi as their president. (See CONFEDERATE STATES OF AMERICA; DAVIS, JEFFERSON.)

In his inaugural address Lincoln declared that he intended to preserve the Union and that he would hold and protect government property. When Confederate forces fired on Fort Sumter in Charleston Harbor, Lincoln called for 75,000 volunteers—and the Civil War, sometimes called the War Between the States, began. (See WAR BETWEEN THE STATES.)

. Neither side was prepared for war, but the North had more ships, railroads, men, and supplies, and was able to carry the war into the South. Northern ships blockaded southern ports and northern armies gained control over the border states. Fierce battles were fought in both the east and in the west. In 1863 Lincoln issued a proclamation that freed the slaves in the South. (See EMANCIPATION PROCLAMATION.) In that same year the Battle of Gettysburg was fought in Pennsylvania, where a large Confederate army had invaded the North. (See GETTYSBURG, BATTLE OF.) Although this battle marked the turning point of the war, fighting continued for another year and one-half. The war ended in April of 1865 at Appomattox Court House in Virginia when General Robert E. Lee surrendered the Confederate forces to General Ulysses S. Grant. (See GRANT, ULYSSES S.; LEE, ROBERT EDWARD.)

The Civil War settled two important points: that all people in the United States were to be free, and that no state could withdraw from the Union. In his second inaugural address, a few weeks before the end of the war, Lincoln said, "Let us strive . . . to bind up the nation's wounds . . . to do all which may achieve and cherish a just and lasting peace among ourselves and with all nations." Lincoln had drawn up a plan for the restoration of the Union. Then, only a few days after the close of the war, Lincoln was assassinated. The reins of the government fell into the hands of the vice-president, Andrew Johnson, and new plans for the restoration of the Union were drafted and put into effect by Congress.

The Country Reunited

At the close of the war the South lay in ruins. Most of the fighting had occurred there. Cities had been destroyed, bridges burned, and railroad lines torn up. Farms and plantations had been overrun by armies. Livestock had been killed and fields abandoned. In the last year of the war all of the slaves had been freed by the adoption of the Thirteenth Amendment to the Constitution. Many of the former slaves roamed about in search of work.

| Confederacy, 1861 | Union, 1861 | Confederate Battle Flag | Union, 1863 | Confederacy, 1865 |

Few were able to make a living. (See NEGROES, UNITED STATES.)

Radical Republicans, who were in control of Congress after the war, wished not only to keep the Republican party in power but also to punish the South for having started the war. The South was placed under military rule. New state constitutions were drawn up, and new state governments were formed. Men who had taken the side of the Confederacy were denied the right to vote and hold office. The new state governments were made to ratify the Fourteenth Amendment to the Constitution, which gave citizenship to all freedmen (former slaves). These years were known as the Reconstruction Period.

Freedmen and other people who knew little about government were elected to public offices in the new state governments of the South. Carpetbaggers from the North and scalawags from the South—politicians who were interested only in their own fortunes—wormed their way into public offices. Soberminded southerners and northerners tried hard to bring about good government in the South. In 1872 the radicals were turned out of Congress, and by 1877 the military rule of the South ended.

Within ten years after the Civil War ended, new economic systems developed in the South. Plantation farming by slaves was replaced by tenant farming and sharecropping. Railroads were rebuilt and extended. Lumbering flourished and textile mills were built. Birmingham, Alabama, became the center of a thriving steel and iron industry.

The discovery of gold in Colorado, Nevada, Idaho, Montana, and the Dakotas attracted fortune seekers from both the North and the South. The extension of the railroad to Kansas enabled Texas cattlemen to drive their herds to Kansas and then ship them by rail to eastern markets. The Homestead Act of 1862 offered free land to people who settled in the West. New western states were admitted to the Union when they had a large enough popula-

tion. Minnesota was admitted in 1858, Oregon in 1859, Kansas in 1861, Nevada in 1864, Nebraska in 1867, and Colorado in 1876.

New means of communication and transportation between the East and the Far West were established. In 1858 a stagecoach line, the Overland Mail, was opened between Missouri and California. In 1860 the pony express, operated by a chain of relay riders, began carrying mail between Missouri and California. A year later a telegraph line connected New York City and San Francisco, a distance of 3,500 miles. (See COMMUNICATION; PONY EXPRESS; POSTAL SYSTEM; TELEGRAPH.)

In 1862 Congress chartered two companies to build the first transcontinental railroad in the United States. The Union Pacific was to build its road westward from Omaha, Nebraska, and the Central Pacific was to build its road eastward from Sacramento, California. In 1869 the roads were joined at Promontory, Utah. (See RAILROAD; TRANSPORTATION.)

The year 1876 marked the 100th anniversary of the Declaration of Independence, and a Centennial Exposition was held in Philadelphia to celebrate the occasion. Hundreds of thousands of people came from all parts of the United States and from other countries to visit it. One of the exhibits they saw was the telephone, which had recently been patented by Alexander Graham Bell. The exposition showed the great progress the United States had made within its first 100 years.

Economic Growth

In 1864 the United States was the fourth most productive manufacturing country in the world. Thirty years later, in 1894, it ranked first. This came about through development of natural resources, rise of big business, improvements in transportation, and an increasing demand for manufactured goods.

The introduction of the Bessemer process for making steel and the discovery of rich iron-ore deposits in Alabama and in the Mesabi

"Held Up"
Newbolt H Trotter
about 1897

Courtesy
Smithsonian Institution

There were so many buffaloes on the Great Plains when the white settlers moved west that stampedes were dangerous to wagon trains. Frequently the herds even stopped the early railroad trains.

Range of Minnesota led to a rapid increase in the production of steel. (See IRON AND STEEL.) The discovery of oil in Pennsylvania in 1859 foreshadowed the coming of the gasoline engine, which led to the development of the automobile and of the airplane. In 1879 Thomas A. Edison invented the electric light. By the 1890's electric power was being used to operate streetcars and elevators. (See EDISON, THOMAS ALVA; ELECTRICITY.)

Within 40 years after the completion of the Union Pacific Railroad in 1869, railroads were built in most parts of the country. Four railroads were built through the West—the Northern Pacific, Great Northern, Southern Pacific, and the Atchison, Topeka and Santa Fe. At the same time, railroads began to use a standard-gauge track that made it possible to transfer loaded freight cars from one line to another.

By 1893 the Duryea brothers had made the first successful gasoline automobile in the United States. Within another ten years Henry Ford, Elwood Haynes, George Selden, and Ransom Olds developed other models and built factories to manufacture automobiles. (See AUTOMOBILE; FORD, HENRY.) In 1903 Orville and Wilbur Wright made the first successful flight in an airplane. The production of airplanes had just started when World War I began in 1914. (See AIRPLANE; WRIGHT, ORVILLE AND WILBUR.)

Andrew Carnegie and John D. Rockefeller were among the first men in the United States to organize business on a large scale. After establishing a steel mill in Pittsburgh, Pennsylvania, Carnegie leased iron-ore lands in the Lake Superior region and bought ships to carry the ore across the lakes. Then he bought a railroad that ran from Lake Erie to Pittsburgh and acquired his own coal mines in Pennsylvania. (See CARNEGIE, ANDREW.) When Rockefeller began the refining of petroleum, he leased oil lands and drilled oil wells. He gained control over certain railroads and pipelines for shipping at low rates. (See ROCKEFELLER FAMILY.)

Few men possessed enough money to build a railroad, oil refinery, or steel mill. The answer to this problem was found in forming a corporation. Shares, called stocks, were sold to people who were interested in investing their money in such industrial enterprises. In this way an almost unlimited supply of money could be obtained to establish a new industry. (See CORPORATION.)

The growth of big manufacturing corporations made necessary the hiring of a large force of workers. Each worker was trained to do only one step in the manufacturing process. The assembly-line method of making automobiles was introduced by Henry Ford in 1913. Large-scale industrial organization, division of labor, and the assembly line resulted in mass production.

New methods of distributing and selling goods were developed in the late 19th century. The Great Atlantic and Pacific Tea Company, founded in 1859, introduced the chain grocery store. By 1872 Montgomery Ward and Company had established the mail-order method of merchandising. Another mail-order business, Sears, Roebuck and Company, was founded in 1886. The establishment of rural free mail delivery in 1896 and the parcel-post service in 1913 made it easier for people on farms and in small towns and villages to purchase goods by mail.

By the beginning of the 20th century, factories were producing all sorts of goods—from locomotives and farm machinery to household utensils—in great quantities. Through developments in transportation and merchandising, a great variety of goods and services was becoming available to almost everyone.

Immigration

From 1840 to 1890 many immigrants came to the United States from Great Britain, Ireland, Germany, and the Scandinavian countries. Some of these people found jobs in eastern cities. Some helped build canals and railroads. Many of the German immigrants settled in midwestern cities, and the Scandinavian immigrants took up farmlands in the upper Mississippi Valley. Immigrants from China and other parts of Asia found jobs in California and other western states.

In the 1880's more and more immigrants came to the United States from the countries of southern and eastern Europe. In earlier years immigrants had come mainly from northern Europe. After 1900 more than one million immigrants of all nationalities arrived every year. Some of these people returned to their homelands after a few years, but the great majority remained in the United States. Most of them settled in big cities such as Boston, New York City, Philadelphia, and Chicago.

Toward the close of the 19th century some citizens felt that too many aliens were coming to the United States. In 1882 Congress passed a law prohibiting the immigration of insane persons, criminals, and paupers. This law also barred all laborers from China. In 1907 an agreement was reached with Japan whereby Japanese laborers were prohibited from migrating to the United States. In 1921 a new immigration law set up a quota system that allowed only a certain number of immigrants to come from each country. (See IMMIGRATION, UNITED STATES AND CANADIAN.)

Labor and Farm Movements

The growth of big business made it difficult for the individual worker to seek his own ad-

The Bettmann Archive

The discovery of oil and the development of petroleum refining were important in the invention of the automobile. Two of the earliest models were the Ford Quadracycle (1896) and the Ford Model A (1903).

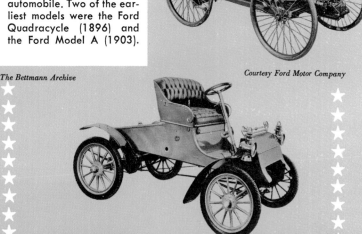

Courtesy Ford Motor Company

vancement. It was to deal with this situation that labor unions were organized. Unions for special types of workers, such as shoemakers and printers, had been formed in some cities before 1800. National unions, however, did not appear until after the Civil War. The National Labor Union, formed in 1866, and the Knights of Labor, formed three years later, were successful for a time but did not last long. The first national labor organization to achieve lasting success was the American Federation of Labor (A.F.L.), organized in 1886. It was a federation of craft and trade unions (such as the carpenters' union and plumbers' union) and therefore included mostly skilled workers. The A.F.L. advocated the eight-hour day, the six-day week, and the abolition of child labor. It was partly responsible for the formation in 1903 of a new government department, the U.S. Department of Commerce and Labor.

Some labor leaders believed that all workers in such basic industries as steelmaking, mining, and automobile manufacturing, rather than in specific trades, should have their own unions. In 1935 the Committee for Industrial Organization (C.I.O.) was formed and began the organization of such unions. By 1939 the C.I.O. (renamed Congress of Industrial Organizations) had organized a number of industrial unions and had a membership as large as that of the A.F.L. (See LABOR ORGANIZATION.)

United States farmers also came to see the need for an organization to promote their interests. In 1867 a group of farmers formed the National Grange of the Patrons of Husbandry. The Grangers advocated improvement of farm life, agricultural education, cooperative selling, and fair railroad rates. (See GRANGE.)

As a result of the farmers' complaints, Congress passed the Interstate Commerce Act in 1887. It created the Interstate Commerce Commission and made it responsible for regulating railroad rates. In 1906 the powers of the Commission were strengthened, and four years later its powers were extended to the regulation of cable, telegraph, and telephone companies.

In the late 19th century some large corporations gained monopolies in certain industries. This was done by obtaining control over competing firms or by driving them out of business. An industrial organization that controlled many or most of the companies within a single industry was called a trust. Such an organization was in a position to control production within an industry and to set high prices for its goods.

Many people, including small businessmen, farmers, workingmen, and merchants, protested against this practice. In 1890 Congress passed the Sherman Anti-Trust Act, which declared that certain monopolistic practices by trusts were illegal. Although no provision was made for the effective enforcement of the act, Theodore Roosevelt, upon becoming president in 1901, insisted upon its enforcement. In 1914 Congress created a Federal Trade Commission and gave it the power to prevent unfair methods of business competition.

Civil Service Reform

During this period a number of steps were taken to improve the government and to give people a more direct voice in it. The spoils system, which had been looked upon by many with approval in the time of Andrew Jackson, came to be considered the cause of graft and corruption in government. The assassination of President James Garfield by a disappointed office-seeker in 1881 created a demand for new laws to rid the government of the spoils system.

During the later 1800's and early 1900's, thousands of persons emigrated to the United States every year from Europe. Many, as the family at left, came from Italy.
The Granger Collection

Two years later Congress passed the Pendleton Act, which provided for the creation of a Civil Service Commission to give examinations to people who applied for certain positions in the national government. The number of positions filled by such civil service examinations has increased many times since 1883. (See CIVIL SERVICE.)

The Granger Collection

Fanfare has long been a part of U.S. presidential campaigns. This wood engraving from an 1876 newspaper shows a massive procession staged in New York City for Samuel J. Tilden.

During the early years of the country's history, voting was done in public and bystanders could tell how each person voted. Today the secret ballot, known as the Australian ballot, is in use throughout the United States. (See BALLOT.)

For many years candidates for political offices were chosen by party leaders at nominating conventions. The voters often were not pleased with the persons who were nominated. In 1903 Wisconsin passed a direct primary law which provided that an election, called a primary election, should be held so that the voters within each political party could choose a candidate for the U.S. Senate. Since that time the use of primary elections to choose candidates for local, state, and national offices has become widespread. In keeping with this development the Seventeenth Amendment, which provides that U.S. senators shall be elected by the people instead of by the state legislatures, was adopted and added to the Constitution in 1913. (See ELECTION.)

Two more amendments were added to the Constitution after World War I. The Eighteenth Amendment, adopted in 1919 (repealed in 1933), prohibited the manufacture and sale of intoxicating liquors. The Nineteenth Amendment, adopted the next year, gave women the right to vote.

The period between 1870 and 1920 was an age of growth and reform. It was a period of change in the relationship of government to business. Laws were passed to regulate industry, transportation, banking, and trade in order to protect the interests of workingmen, farmers, and the general public. People demanded an end of corruption in politics and business, greater safeguards for the country's health, better schools, and improved opportunities for people in all walks of life.

World Relations

Throughout its history the United States has carried on trade and maintained diplomatic relations with nearly every country in the world. It has tried to remain at peace and not become involved in wars, but it has not always been successful. In 1812, after years of effort to be a neutral, it became involved in a second war with England. In 1846 a dispute with Mexico led to the Mexican War.

As early as 1783 Russia had established fur-trading posts in Alaska. After fur trading became less profitable, Russia sold Alaska to the United States in 1867 for $7,200,000. (See ALASKA.)

Near the close of the 19th century the United States came into possession of territories that lay far beyond its borders. One of these was the Hawaiian Islands in the Pacific Ocean. For many years U.S. ships on their way to Asia had stopped at the islands to take on supplies and to trade. The U.S. government and U.S. businessmen had great influence in affairs of the islands. In 1898 Congress annexed the islands

Work on the Panama Canal was begun during the presidency of Theodore Roosevelt. In 1906 he posed while operating a steam shovel at the Culebra Cut.

and later organized them as a territory. (See HAWAII.)

In 1898 the United States and Spain went to war because of a dispute over Cuba. At that time Cuba and Puerto Rico were the only possessions that Spain held in the Western Hemisphere. In 1895 the Cubans revolted against their government. Three years later, while the revolt was still going on, a U.S. battleship, the *Maine*, was mysteriously blown up while visiting Havana Harbor. This event inflamed U.S. public opinion and helped bring on the Spanish-American War. Part of the U.S. fleet that was stationed in the Pacific Ocean captured Manila in the Philippine Islands, which belonged to Spain. United States forces invaded Cuba and destroyed the Spanish naval force in Cuban waters. At the close of the war the United States gained control over Puerto Rico, the Philippines, and the island of Guam. Spain was paid $20 million, and Cuba was granted independence. (See SPANISH-AMERICAN WAR.)

During the Spanish-American War it required two months for the battleship *Oregon* to sail from the Pacific Ocean to the Atlantic Ocean. It had to steam all the way around South America. The incident showed the need for a canal across the isthmus of Panama as a shortcut between the two oceans. A French company had tried to build such a canal but had failed. The United States then bought the company's rights to the canal.

At that time, Panama belonged to Colombia. When Colombia objected to the building of a canal by the United States, Panama declared its independence from Colombia. The United States at once recognized Panama as an independent country and bought a ten-mile-wide strip of land across Panama through which the canal was to be built. It also agreed to pay Panama a sum of money each year. In 1904, U.S. engineers began work on the canal. It took eight years to build and cost $300 million. In 1914 it was opened to the ships of the world. (See PANAMA CANAL.)

World War I

Just a few days before the first ship passed through the Panama Canal a war began in Europe. It resulted from a conflict of policies between two groups of European countries. Germany, Austria-Hungary, Turkey, and Bulgaria formed one group called the Central Powers. Great Britain, France, and Russia formed the other group called the Allied Powers. Although Italy had treaty agreements with the Central Powers, it joined the Allies.

The United States tried to remain neutral and succeeded in staying out of the war from 1914 to 1917. In 1916 President Woodrow Wilson was reelected, in part because "he kept us out of war." The U.S. position, however, became more and more difficult. The Allied Powers needed to buy U.S. goods, and the Central Powers were determined to stop this trade. German submarines destroyed Allied ships. United States citizens traveling on these ships lost their lives. The United States protested, but the war at sea went on. Most citizens felt that the Allies were fighting for democracy against countries whose governments were controlled by autocratic rulers, represented by the German kaiser. In April 1917 Congress declared war upon the Central Powers, and the United States entered a war that had already involved many countries.

United States factories increased their output of supplies needed for war. Ship-

In 1917, U.S. Marine Corps enlistment posters were used to attract volunteers.

yards operated around the clock producing destroyers, submarines, ships, and other types of craft. Men were drafted for military service. Liberty bonds were sold by the government to help meet the costs of the war.

United States troop and supply ships, convoyed by the Navy, crossed the Atlantic Ocean in great numbers. Two million men of the American Expeditionary Forces joined the soldiers of England, France, and the other Allied countries. They helped turn Allied defeats into victories on the battlefields of Europe. The U.S. Navy helped drive German submarines and destroyers from the Atlantic Ocean. In November 1918 Germany finally asked for peace. On November 11 an armistice was signed and the war was over. (See WORLD WAR I.)

Before the war ended, many Allied leaders had begun to draw up plans for the peace treaty. In 1919 these men met at Versailles, France, where treaties between the countries engaged in the war were drafted and signed. Among the many agreements was one that President Wilson insisted upon. It was the provision that a League of Nations be established to maintain peace among the countries of the world in the future. (See LEAGUE OF NATIONS.)

When the war ended, U.S. citizens quickly shifted their interests from world affairs to domestic problems. Factories and shipyards that had been producing war supplies were closed. Europe lay in ruins and was unable to carry on much trade with the United States. As a result, U.S. factories curtailed their production and laid off workers. Farmers who had expanded their production during the war were unable to sell their crops.

When the Treaty of Versailles, including the proposal to create a League of Nations, was put before the U.S. Senate, there was a heated debate. President Wilson set out on a speaking tour to persuade the people to support the treaty and the League of Nations. While he was in Colorado, he suffered a stroke that left him partly paralyzed. He lived to see the Senate reject the Treaty of Versailles and refuse to participate in the League of Nations. In 1920 the Republican party came into power again with the election of Warren G. Harding as president. (See WILSON, THOMAS WOODROW.)

Prosperity to Depression

Although the decade of the 1920's was to be one of the most prosperous periods in the history of the United States, it got off to a bad start. A minor depression occurred after the end of the war while the country was adjusting to a peacetime economy. During the presidency of Harding a number of scandals rocked the country.

One of these scandals came to be known as the Teapot Dome affair. Teapot Dome was one of three tracts of oil land that had been set aside for the use of the U.S. Navy. These tracts had been placed under the control of the Department of the Interior. The secretary of that department leased two of these tracts to private oil companies. Upon investigation it was dis-

The United States joined the war in Europe in 1917 and sent thousands of troops across the Atlantic Ocean.

The Bettmann Archive

covered that the secretary had accepted a bribe of $100,000 from one of the companies to which a lease was granted. The secretary was fined the amount of the bribe and sentenced to one year in prison.

Despite the postwar depression, political scandals, and a wave of industrial strikes, the economy improved in the early 1920's. High tariff laws were passed to protect U.S. industries and farmers from foreign competitors. Income and corporation taxes levied during the war were reduced. The government began reducing the national debt by redeeming the bonds that people had purchased during the war.

Factories boosted their output during the 1920's. The number of private automobiles increased from 8 million to 23 million. The new motion-picture industry grew so rapidly that by 1930 more than 20,000 theaters had been built. (See Motion Pictures.) The expansion of existing industries and the establishment of new ones—such as those producing rayon, airplanes, and radios—provided many jobs at good wages.

Consumers demanded an endless variety of goods—refrigerators, vacuum cleaners, radios, and other appliances for the home; better clothes to wear; automobiles for business and pleasure; and finer homes to live in. Buying on

Prosperity ended abruptly in 1929, and the country plunged into the Great Depression. Widespread poverty forced many people to join bread lines to get free food.

The Bettmann Archive

the installment plan became generally accepted. It enabled people to enjoy goods while paying for them, even though many bought beyond their means, and it created a demand for the production of more and more goods.

The 1920's were years of speculation. Everyone wanted to get rich quickly. Banks loaned money freely to farmers and businessmen to buy land and machinery. Many people bought land in California and Florida, intending either to sell it for a profit or to live on it after they retired. Millions of people began speculating in stocks and bonds. As security prices rose the investors borrowed money from banks and mortgaged their homes in order to buy more stocks and bonds. (See Coolidge, Calvin; Harding, Warren Gamaliel.)

Many persons began to think that prosperity had come to stay and that unemployment and depressions were things of the past. Others saw danger signals. Foreign trade began to fall off when other countries raised their tariffs in retaliation against high U.S. tariffs. There was excessive installment buying and borrowing of money for speculation. Banks became less willing to make loans to people for these purposes. By 1929 the building boom came to a halt. Unemployment increased. In October 1929 a financial panic occurred when prices on the New York Stock Exchange collapsed. The prices of stocks tumbled as thousands of stockholders tried to sell their stocks. The stock market crash marked the beginning of the Great Depression of the 1930's.

Herbert Hoover, who had been elected president in 1928, urged employers to maintain their wage rates and avoid laying off workers. Congress created the Reconstruction Finance Corporation (RFC) to make loans to industries, railroads, and banks. Other measures were taken to help businessmen, farmers, and workers. (See Hoover, Herbert.) When the presidential election year of 1932 arrived, millions of U.S. workers were still without jobs. Farmers were losing their farms through mortgage foreclosures. Banks, unable to collect the loans they had made, were closing their doors. State and local governments were complaining that they were no longer able to provide relief payments

to the unemployed. The Democratic candidate, Franklin D. Roosevelt, was elected president, promising a "New Deal" in the United States.

The New Deal

The New Deal began as soon as Roosevelt was inaugurated on March 4, 1933. The new president called Congress into special session and announced a four-day "bank holiday" during which all banks were closed. Congress started on a "hundred days" program of emergency legislation. New banking laws were quickly passed to help banks that were in distress and to reopen closed banks. Other laws were passed to create agencies to provide relief for the unemployed. The Civilian Conservation Corps (CCC) was set up to provide jobs for young men in conserving soil and forests. The Federal Emergency Relief Administration (FERA) granted money to state governments for unemployment relief. The Public Works Administration (PWA) provided funds for slum clearance, highway construction, harbor improvements, low-cost housing, and the building of hospitals and schools. The Works Progress Administration (WPA) provided funds for an even greater variety of projects to give jobs to the unemployed. (See ROOSEVELT, FRANKLIN DELANO.)

Other measures were passed to help business. The National Industrial Recovery Act (NIRA or NRA) required each industry to draft a set of rules by which its business was to be conducted. The act was challenged in the courts and was finally declared unconstitutional by the U.S. Supreme Court. Meanwhile the Federal Housing Administration (FHA) was created to encourage the construction industry, and the Reconstruction Finance Corporation continued to grant loans to railroads and industries.

The Agricultural Adjustment Act (AAA) was passed to control the production of livestock and farm crops and help increase farm income. Farmers who cooperated in the program were given cash payments as well. This act was also declared unconstitutional, but a substitute act that emphasized soil conservation was passed by Congress. The Tennessee Valley Authority (TVA) was set up to conserve the soil of the Tennessee Valley, prevent floods, and produce cheap hydroelectric power.

The National Labor Relations Act (Wagner Act) upheld the right of workers to organize unions and to bargain collectively with their employers. In 1938 another labor law, the Fair Labor Standards Act, was passed. It established minimum wages and maximum working hours for certain industries.

Another New Deal act that helped millions of people was the Social Security Act, passed in 1935. It provided assistance to people of retirement age, to the blind, and to mothers and dependent children. It also set up a system of unemployment insurance. The law has been amended many times so that farmers, domestic workers, self-employed workers, and others—in addition to industrial workers—are covered by it. (See SOCIAL SECURITY.)

By 1940 the country had made some progress toward recovering from the depression. Factory production had increased and more men were back at work. Farmers were enjoying better incomes. Yet at the very moment when people were feeling relief from the depression, another war broke out in Europe.

World War II

As early as the 1920's, disturbing reports were reaching the United States from abroad. In Italy the Fascist party gained control and its leader, Benito Mussolini, set himself up as dictator. The Fascists, dissatisfied with the outcome of World War I, set out to build a new Italian empire. (See FASCISM.) In Germany the Nazi party led by Adolf Hitler denounced the Treaty of Versailles and began to build a strong Germany. Hitler's dictatorial methods and his brutal persecution of the Jews turned U.S. opinion against him. (See HITLER, ADOLF; NATIONAL SOCIALISM.) In Asia the government of Japan fell into the hands of military forces preparing for war.

In 1931 Japanese forces attacked Manchuria, a province of China. Four years later Italy attacked Ethiopia in Africa. In 1937 Japan launched a full-scale attack on China. In 1938 German forces marched into Austria and united that country with Germany. A year later Germany invaded and occupied Czechoslovakia, a country with which the United States, Great Britain, and France had many close ties. In 1939 Hitler's forces launched a lightning attack on Poland. Soviet forces crossed Poland's eastern border at the same time and within a few days Poland was conquered and its territory divided between Germany and the U.S.S.R. When Germany invaded Poland, both England and France declared war on Germany, and World War II had begun.

During the winter of 1939–40 German military forces remained idle while the U.S.S.R. attacked Finland and took a slice of its territory. The German Army and Air Force went into action again in the spring and quickly conquered Denmark, Norway, the Netherlands, and Belgium. France came next. France fell within a few days after the attack began. Just before it ended, Germany and Italy formed an alliance called the Rome–Berlin Axis. Only England was left in the fight and through the long winter of 1940–41 it felt the full fury of attacks by German bombers.

The U.S. government tried to remain neutral, though the feelings of most of its people were on the side of England. By fall of 1940, the United States gradually began to extend military aid to England. At the same time the United States began to strengthen its Army and Navy for defense in case of attack.

In September 1940 Congress passed a law drafting young men for military service. Billions of dollars were appropriated for armaments. In 1940 Roosevelt was elected for a third term and thus became the first U.S. president to be elected more than twice.

The United States at War

In March 1941 Congress passed the Lend-Lease Act, which permitted the president to turn over military supplies to countries fighting against Fascism. In June, Hitler launched a surprise attack on the U.S.S.R. Then on Sunday, December 7, Japanese planes launched from air-

craft carriers attacked the U.S. naval base at Pearl Harbor, Hawaii. The attack came as a surprise and seriously crippled the U.S. fleet. The United States declared war on Japan the next day, and within a few days Germany and Italy declared war on the United States.

Efforts to strengthen the U.S. armed forces moved into high gear at once. Millions of men were taken from civilian life and trained to be soldiers. Industry was expanded to produce ships, tanks, planes, and other war supplies. By 1944, U.S. factories were producing twice as much as all the factories of Germany, Italy, and Japan combined. Through price control and the rationing of scarce consumer goods the country was put on a wartime economy.

After attacking Pearl Harbor, Japan took advantage of the fact that the United States was unprepared to carry the war immediately across the wide Pacific. Japan overran China and Southeast Asia. In the spring of 1942 the United States was forced to surrender the Philippines to Japan. Soon, however, U.S. and Allied naval forces were ready to take the offensive in the Pacific. In June 1942 they defeated the Japanese fleet in the Battle of Midway, the turning point of the war in the Pacific.

Meanwhile, in Europe, U.S. fliers had joined British pilots in air raids over Europe. They helped to destroy railroads, factories, oil refineries, and air and naval bases. The United States sent supplies to the U.S.S.R. to help the Soviets fight the invading German armies.

In the fall of 1942, U.S. and British troops landed in North Africa. With the aid of French troops stationed there, the German and Italian forces in North Africa were defeated. This opened the way for an Allied invasion of Europe by way of Sicily and Italy. Italy surrendered in September 1943, leaving Germany to fight alone in Europe. In June 1944 Rome fell to the Allies. Meanwhile, a powerful Allied force had gathered in England. On June 6, 1944, this

force, commanded by U.S. General Dwight D. Eisenhower, crossed the English Channel and invaded France. The final phase of the war in Europe·had begun. Also in 1944, forces led by U.S. General Douglas MacArthur recaptured the Philippine Islands and cut Japan off from her oil, rubber, and tin supplies.

From October 1944 to April 1945 Germany fought a losing battle against advancing Soviet armies on the east and Allied armies on the west. Mussolini was killed by his own countrymen, and Hitler died, probably by his own hand. On May 7, 1945, Germany surrendered and the war in Europe ended.

Early in 1945 U.S. Marines captured the islands of Iwo Jima and Okinawa, which were within striking distance of Japan. On August 6, 1945, a U.S. plane dropped a new kind of bomb on the Japanese city of Hiroshima. This one atomic bomb was so powerful that it destroyed nearly the whole city. Within a few days a second atomic bomb was dropped on Nagasaki, a Japanese shipbuilding center. On August 14, 1945, Japan surrendered.

World War II was the most destructive war in history. Over ten million Allied soldiers were killed in battle. Millions of civilians were killed or injured, mostly during bombing raids. People throughout the world were determined that it should be the last world war.

At the end of the war the United States quick-ly demobilized its armed forces. The GI Bill of Rights gave discharged veterans aid to continue their education. At the same time, industry stopped making war supplies and quickly returned to manufacturing civilian goods.

At the close of World War II the United States was the leading industrial power of the world. Its territory had not been ravaged by war. It was for this reason, in part, that other countries looked to the United States for leadership in the establishment of peace. At no time since then has the United States been able to ignore events in any part of the world.

Peace and Prosperity

Even before the war ended, leaders of the Allied powers had taken steps to insure the future peace of the world. In April 1945, delegates representing 50 countries met in San Francisco to plan the organization of the United Nations (UN). The purpose of the UN was to promote peaceful relations among the countries and to advance the social, economic, and political progress of all peoples of the world. (See UNITED NATIONS.)

When the war ended, most of the Allied governments expected to free the lands that had been occupied by foreign troops during the war. It soon developed, however, that the U.S.S.R., under the leadership of Premier Joseph Stalin, intended to maintain control over Eastern Eu-

During World War II the United States sent men and equipment to battle areas around the world. Shown here are U.S. troops landing at Iwo Jima in the Pacific in 1945.

The Bettmann Archive

No.	Name	Birthplace	Born		Inaugurated	Term of Office	Died	
1	George Washington	Va.	1732, Feb.	22	1789	8 years	1799, Dec.	14
2	John Adams	Mass.	1735, Oct.	30	1797	4 years	1826, July	4
3	Thomas Jefferson	Va.	1743, April	13	1801	8 years	1826, July	4
4	James Madison	Va.	1751, March	16	1809	8 years	1836, June	28
5	James Monroe	Va.	1758, April	28	1817	8 years	1831, July	4
6	John Quincy Adams	Mass.	1767, July	11	1825	4 years	1848, Feb.	23
7	Andrew Jackson	S.C.	1767, March	15	1829	8 years	1845, June	8
8	Martin Van Buren	N.Y.	1782, Dec.	5	1837	4 years	1862, July	24
9	William Harrison	Va.	1773, Feb.	9	1841	1 month—died in office	1841, April	4
10	John Tyler	Va.	1790, March	29	1841	3 years and 11 mos.	1862, Jan.	18
11	James Polk	N.C.	1795, Nov.	2	1845	4 years	1849, June	15
12	Zachary Taylor	Va.	1784, Nov.	24	1849	1 yr. and 4 mos.—died in office	1850, July	9
13	Millard Fillmore	N.Y.	1800, Jan.	7	1850	2 yrs. and 8 mos.	1874, March	8
14	Franklin Pierce	N.H.	1804, Nov.	23	1853	4 years	1869, Oct.	8
15	James Buchanan	Pa.	1791, April	23	1857	4 years	1868, June	1
16	Abraham Lincoln	Ky.	1809, Feb.	12	1861	4 years and 1 mo.—assassinated in office	1865, April	15
17	Andrew Johnson	N.C.	1808, Dec.	29	1865	3 years and 11 mos.	1875, July	31
18	Ulysses S. Grant	Ohio	1822, April	27	1869	8 years	1885, July	23
19	Rutherford B. Hayes	Ohio	1822, Oct.	4	1877	4 years	1893, Jan.	17
20	James A. Garfield	Ohio	1831, Nov.	19	1881	6 mos.—assassinated in office	1881, Sept.	19
21	Chester A. Arthur	Vt.	1830, Oct.	5	1881	3 years and 6 mos.	1886, Nov.	18
22	Grover Cleveland	N.J.	1837, March	18	1885	4 years	1908, June	24
23	Benjamin Harrison	Ohio	1833, Aug.	20	1889	4 years	1901, March	13
24*	Grover Cleveland	N.J.	1837, March	18	1893	4 years (2nd term)	1908, June	24
25	William McKinley	Ohio	1843, Jan.	29	1897	4 years and 6 mos.—assassinated in office	1901, Sept.	14
26	Theodore Roosevelt	N.Y.	1858, Oct.	27	1901	7 years and 6 mos.	1919, Jan.	6
27	William H. Taft	Ohio	1857, Sept.	15	1909	4 years	1930, March	8
28	Woodrow Wilson	Va.	1856, Dec.	28	1913	8 years	1924, Feb.	3
29	Warren G. Harding	Ohio	1865, Nov.	2	1921	2 years and 5 mos.—died in office	1923, Aug.	2
30	Calvin Coolidge	Vt.	1872, July	4	1923	5 years and 7 mos.	1933, Jan.	5
31	Herbert Hoover	Iowa	1874, Aug.	10	1929	4 years	1964, Oct.	20
32	Franklin D. Roosevelt	N.Y.	1882, Jan.	30	1933	12 years and 1 mo.—died in office	1945, April	12
33	Harry S. Truman	Mo.	1884, May	8	1945	7 years and 8 mos.		
34	Dwight D. Eisenhower	Texas	1890, Oct.	14	1953	8 years	1969, March	28
35	John F. Kennedy	Mass.	1917, May	29	1961	2 years and 10 mos.—assassinated in office	1963, Nov.	22
36	Lyndon B. Johnson	Texas	1908, Aug.	27	1963	5 years and 2 mos.		
37	Richard M. Nixon	Calif.	1913, Jan.	9	1969			

*Grover Cleveland is considered here to be both the 22nd and the 24th president, because his terms were not consecutive.

rope. Great Britain, France, and the United States conducted free elections in the sectors of Germany that they occupied, but Communist puppets ruled the Soviet zone of East Germany. Communists gained control over the government of China and the U.S.S.R. refused to agree to the unification of Korea when that question arose in the UN.

This division between the major powers of the world came to be called the cold war. One side included the Communist countries with the U.S.S.R. as their leader. The other side included many of the democratic countries with the United States as leader. Each side attempted to win the support of neutral countries.

In 1947 the United States formulated two new foreign policies. One was called the "Truman Doctrine," named for Harry S. Truman, who became U.S. president upon the death of Roosevelt in 1945. Its purpose was to provide economic and military aid to countries that were threatened by Communist aggression. The other was the "Marshall Plan," named for U.S. Secretary of State George C. Marshall. It offered economic help to the countries of Europe so that they might recover from the war and be able to resist the spread of Communism. In 1949 the United States joined Canada and ten European countries in forming the North Atlantic Treaty Organization (NATO) to defend themselves against possible attack by the U.S.S.R. In the same year, the U.S.S.R. conducted its first atomic-bomb test.

In 1950 war broke out in Asia. Communist forces of North Korea invaded South Korea in an attempt to unite all of Korea under their control. The UN Security Council immediately voted to send help to South Korea. President Truman ordered U.S. troops stationed in Japan to go to the aid of South Korea. They were

No.	Wives of the Presidents	Birthplace	Born	Died
1	Martha (Dandridge) Custis	Va.	1731	1802
2	Abigail Smith	Mass.	1744	1818
3	Martha (Wayles) Skelton	Va.	1748	1782
4	Dorothea (Dolly) (Payne) Todd	N.C.	1768	1849
5	Elizabeth Kortright	N.Y.	1768	1830
6	Louisa Catherine Johnson	England	1775	1852
7	Rachel (Donelson) Robards	Va.	1767	1828
8	Hannah Hoes	N.Y.	1783	1819
9	Anna Symmes	N.J.	1775	1864
10	Letitia Christian	Va.	1790	1842
10	Julia Gardiner	N.Y.	1820	1889
11	Sarah Childress	Tenn.	1803	1891
12	Margaret Smith	Md.	1788	1852
13	Abigail Powers	N.Y.	1798	1853
13	Caroline (Carmichael) McIntosh	N.J.	1813	1881
14	Jane Means Appleton	N.H.	1806	1863
15	(Unmarried)			
16	Mary Todd	Ky.	1818	1882
17	Eliza McCardle	Tenn.	1810	1876
18	Julia Dent	Mo.	1826	1902
19	Lucy Ware Webb	Ohio	1831	1889
20	Lucretia Rudolph	Ohio	1832	1918
21	Ellen Lewis Herndon	Va.	1837	1880
22	Frances Folsom	N.Y.	1864	1947
23	Caroline Lavinia Scott	Ohio	1832	1892
23	Mary Scott (Lord) Dimmick	Pa.	1858	1948
24	Frances Folsom	N.Y.	1864	1947
25	Ida Saxton	Ohio	1847	1907
26	Alice Hathaway Lee	Mass.	1861	1884
26	Edith Kermit Carow	Conn.	1861	1948
27	Helen Herron	Ohio	1861	1943
28	Ellen Louise Axson	Ga.	1860	1914
28	Edith (Bolling) Galt	Va.	1872	1961
29	Florence Kling	Ohio	1860	1924
30	Grace Anna Goodhue	Vt.	1879	1957
31	Lou Henry	Iowa	1875	1944
32	Anna Eleanor Roosevelt	N.Y.	1884	1962
33	Elizabeth (Bess) Wallace	Mo.	1885	
34	Mary (Mamie) Geneva Doud	Iowa	1896	
35	Jacqueline Lee Bouvier	N.Y.	1929	
36	Claudia Alta (Lady Bird) Taylor	Texas	1913	
37	Thelma Catherine Patricia Ryan	Nev.	1912	

soon joined by small contingents sent by other UN members. Chinese Communist troops, posing as volunteers, went to the aid of North Korea. A costly but limited war was fought. It ended in 1953 with the establishment of a neutral zone between North and South Korea. (See KOREAN WAR.)

The 1950's were prosperous years for the United States. The country's population continued to increase. The census of 1960 showed that the population was 179,323,175. The needs of this growing population created new markets for industry. Increased wages placed more money in the hands of consumers.

In 1952 Dwight D. Eisenhower was elected president, the first Republican to be elected to that office since 1928. He proved to be popular and in 1956 was reelected. He suffered two serious illnesses while in office.

One of Eisenhower's first official acts was to create a new cabinet post, the Department of Health, Education, and Welfare.

In 1954 the U.S. Supreme Court handed down an important decision about the Negroes in public schools. It said that white and Negro children should not be segregated, that is, required to go to different schools. Segregation was the rule in most southern states, and many southerners denounced the Court's decision. All during the 1950's and into the 1960's, Negroes in both the North and South protested against racial discrimination and demanded equal rights as U.S. citizens. (See NEGROES, UNITED STATES.)

Two important steps were taken by the U.S. government in the 1950's to improve transportation. One was the National Highway Program, passed by Congress in 1955, to build new and improved highways in all parts of the country. The other step was an agreement with Canada, signed in 1954, to build the St. Lawrence Seaway. When completed in 1959 the Seaway made it possible for oceangoing ships to travel up the St. Lawrence River and into the Great Lakes.

In foreign affairs, Eisenhower's first term brought a final settlement of the Korean War in 1953. In 1955 the president met at Geneva, Switzerland, with the government leaders of Great Britain, France, and the U.S.S.R. to discuss ways of promoting peace, but the cold war continued. Neither side was willing to accept the disarmament proposals made by the other.

The U.S.S.R. launched the world's first artificial earth satellite, Sputnik I, on October 4, 1957. It was followed on January 31, 1958, by the first U.S. satellite, Explorer I. These events were hailed as the beginning of a new Space Age. (See SPACE EXPLORATION.)

Alaska became the 49th state and Hawaii became the 50th state in 1959.

In 1960 John F. Kennedy was elected president. He was the first Roman Catholic president as well as the youngest man ever elected to the office. He called his program for change in the United States the "New Frontier."

In foreign affairs, Kennedy sought to develop a new image for the United States. He created the Peace Corps, an organization of volunteers to help people of underdeveloped countries; and the Alliance for Progress, a program involving

Vice-Presidents of the United States

	Name	Birthplace	Born	Entered Office	Died
1	John Adams	Quincy, Mass.	1735	1789	1826
2	Thomas Jefferson	Shadwell, Va.	1743	1797	1826
3	Aaron Burr	Newark, N.J.	1756	1801	1836
4	George Clinton	Ulster Co., N.Y.	1739	1805	1812
5	Elbridge Gerry	Marblehead, Mass.	1744	1813	1814
6	Daniel D. Tompkins	Scarsdale, N.Y.	1774	1817	1825
7	John C. Calhoun	Abbeville, S.C.	1782	1825	1850
8	Martin Van Buren	Kinderhook, N.Y.	1782	1833	1862
9	Richard M. Johnson	Louisville, Ky.	1780	1837	1850
10	John Tyler	Greenway, Va.	1790	1841	1862
11	George M. Dallas	Philadelphia, Pa.	1792	1845	1864
12	Millard Fillmore	Summerhill, N.Y.	1800	1849	1874
13	William R. King	Sampson Co., N.C.	1786	1853	1853
14	John C. Breckinridge	Lexington, Ky.	1821	1857	1875
15	Hannibal Hamlin	Paris, Me.	1809	1861	1891
16	Andrew Johnson	Raleigh, N.C.	1808	1865	1875
17	Schuyler Colfax	New York, N.Y.	1823	1869	1885
18	Henry Wilson	Farmington, N.H.	1812	1873	1875
19	William A. Wheeler	Malone, N.Y.	1819	1877	1887
20	Chester A. Arthur	Fairfield, Vt.	1830	1881	1886
21	Thomas A. Hendricks	Muskingum Co., Ohio	1819	1885	1885
22	Levi P. Morton	Shoreham, Vt.	1824	1889	1920
23	Adlai E. Stevenson	Christian Co., Ky.	1835	1893	1914
24	Garret A. Hobart	Long Branch, N.J.	1844	1897	1899
25	Theodore Roosevelt	New York, N.Y.	1858	1901	1919
26	Charles W. Fairbanks	Unionville Centre, Ohio	1852	1905	1918
27	James S. Sherman	Utica, N.Y.	1855	1909	1912
28	Thomas R. Marshall	No. Manchester, Ind.	1854	1913	1925
29	Calvin Coolidge	Plymouth, Vt.	1872	1921	1933
30	Charles G. Dawes	Marietta, Ohio	1865	1925	1951
31	Charles Curtis	Topeka, Kan.	1860	1929	1936
32	John Nance Garner	Red River Co., Tex.	1868	1933	1967
33	Henry A. Wallace	Adair Co., Ia.	1888	1941	1965
34	Harry S. Truman	Lamar, Mo.	1884	1945	
35	Alben W. Barkley	Graves Co., Ky.	1877	1949	1956
36	Richard M. Nixon	Yorba Linda, Calif.	1913	1953	
37	Lyndon B. Johnson	Gillespie Co., Tex.	1908	1961	
38	Hubert H. Humphrey	Wallace, S.D.	1911	1965	
39	Spiro T. Agnew	Baltimore, Md.	1918	1969	

United States–Latin American cooperation to solve Latin America's economic problems. Kennedy also achieved a step toward a disarmament treaty. In 1963 the United States, Great Britain, and the U.S.S.R. signed a treaty that banned all nuclear tests except those made under ground.

Little progress was made in settling other issues of the cold war. In 1962 U.S. relations with the U.S.S.R. worsened when Kennedy learned that Soviet missiles capable of attacking the United States had been installed in Cuba and demanded that the missiles be removed. The Soviet government complied, easing the threat of a nuclear confrontation between two world powers.

In domestic affairs, Kennedy made numerous proposals to Congress to relieve unemployment, provide medical care for the aged, and improve education. He urged Congress to reduce taxes to stimulate business. He supported legislation to protect the civil rights of Negroes.

On November 22, 1963, in Dallas, Texas, Kennedy was assassinated. Vice-president Lyndon B. Johnson became the 36th U.S. president.

Johnson successfully urged Congress to pass two Kennedy measures—a tax cut and a civil rights bill opening up all public accommodations to Negroes and guaranteeing equal job opportunities. He proposed a "war on poverty" to tackle the problems of the poor in the United States. Johnson also continued the policy of giving technical and financial assistance to the South Vietnamese government to aid it in its fight against the Viet Cong, a Communist-supported guerrilla force.

In 1964 Johnson was elected president in a landslide vote over his Republican opponent, Senator Barry Goldwater. During his full term, Johnson was successful in getting much of his legislative program passed by Congress. It included continuing the war on poverty, increasing federal aid to education, redeveloping urban

States With Dates of Admission to the Union and Their Capitals

For the original 13 states the date given is that of the ratification of the Constitution

State	Entered Union	Capital	State	Entered Union	Capital
Alabama	1819, Dec. 14	Montgomery	Montana	1889, Nov. 8	Helena
Alaska	1959, Jan. 3	Juneau	Nebraska	1867, Mar. 1	Lincoln
Arizona	1912, Feb. 14	Phoenix	Nevada	1864, Oct. 31	Carson City
Arkansas	1836, June 15	Little Rock	New Hampshire	1788, June 21	Concord
California	1850, Sept. 9	Sacramento	New Jersey	1787, Dec. 18	Trenton
Colorado	1876, Aug. 1	Denver	New Mexico	1912, Jan. 6	Santa Fe
Connecticut	1788, Jan. 9	Hartford	New York	1788, July 26	Albany
Delaware	1787, Dec. 7	Dover	North Carolina	1789, Nov. 21	Raleigh
Florida	1845, Mar. 3	Tallahassee	North Dakota	1889, Nov. 2	Bismarck
Georgia	1788, Jan. 2	Atlanta	Ohio	1803, Mar. 1	Columbus
Hawaii	1959, Aug. 21	Honolulu	Oklahoma	1907, Nov. 16	Oklahoma City
Idaho	1890, July 3	Boise	Oregon	1859, Feb. 14	Salem
Illinois	1818, Dec. 3	Springfield	Pennsylvania	1787, Dec. 12	Harrisburg
Indiana	1816, Dec. 11	Indianapolis	Rhode Island	1790, May 29	Providence
Iowa	1846, Dec. 28	Des Moines	South Carolina	1788, May 23	Columbia
Kansas	1861, Jan. 29	Topeka	South Dakota	1889, Nov. 2	Pierre
Kentucky	1792, June 1	Frankfort	Tennessee	1796, June 1	Nashville
Louisiana	1812, Apr. 30	Baton Rouge	Texas	1845, Dec. 29	Austin
Maine	1820, Mar. 15	Augusta	Utah	1896, Jan. 4	Salt Lake City
Maryland	1788, Apr. 28	Annapolis	Vermont	1791, Mar. 4	Montpelier
Massachusetts	1788, Feb. 6	Boston	Virginia	1788, June 25	Richmond
Michigan	1837, Jan. 26	Lansing	Washington	1889, Nov. 11	Olympia
Minnesota	1858, May 11	St. Paul	West Virginia	1863, June 20	Charleston
Mississippi	1817, Dec. 10	Jackson	Wisconsin	1848, May 29	Madison
Missouri	1821, Aug. 10	Jefferson City	Wyoming	1890, July 10	Cheyenne

areas, beautification of the country, a civil rights bill to ensure Negro voting rights, and Medicare, a health insurance plan for the aged.

The chief problem faced by Johnson during his administrations was the war in Vietnam. The U.S. role in Vietnam had gradually changed from one that was largely supportive and advisory to one of active combat. By the end of 1967 almost half a million U.S. troops were in South Vietnam. The costs and casualties of the war continued to mount. The escalation of the war caused great controversy among the American people. Pressure for ending the war increased. In 1968 peace talks began in Paris, France. While negotiations were under way, the fighting continued. (See VIETNAM WAR.)

In the mid-1960's domestic problems increased, particularly those of the city: unemployment, poor housing, inadequate transportation, the quality of public education. Riots erupted in many poverty-stricken Negro ghettos.

President Johnson declined to run for reelection in 1968. Richard M. Nixon, a Republican, became the 37th U.S. president, defeating Hubert H. Humphrey. The Vietnam war and rising inflation were serious problems for Nixon. In 1969 he began a plan for reducing U.S. involvement in Vietnam. In July 1969, U.S. astronauts became the first men to land on the moon.

In the early 1970's U.S. involvement in Vietnam and the expansion of the fighting into Cambodia and Laos were chief causes of growing discontent within the country. The first postal strike in U.S. history, campus disorders, continuing recession and inflation, the quality of the environment, and unemployment were among other problems that concerned the nation during 1970 and 1971.

UNITED STATES GOVERNMENT is a large organization of many parts that controls and directs the affairs of the country. It has more than two million men and women on its civilian payroll in addition to many thousands in the armed forces.

The U.S. Constitution divides the responsibility of governing into three branches: legislative, executive, and judicial.

Legislative

Congress—the government's legislative or lawmaking branch—has two chambers, or houses, the Senate and the House of Representatives. Two senators are elected from each state. The present membership, therefore, is

100. Senators serve a six-year term, and either 33 or 34 are elected every two years.

Unlike the senators, all members of the House of Representatives serve two-year terms. Their terms do not overlap because they all take office at the same time. The number of representatives was not fixed by the Constitution as was the number of senators. Instead, the number was allowed to increase as the population grew. Originally there was to be one representative for every 30,000 persons in each state, and every state was to have at least one representative. As the population grew, the membership of the House rose until 1912, when it reached 435 members. Since then the number has been held at 435, even though the population continues to grow. In fact, according to the 1970 census, the average seat in the House now represents about 468,972 persons.

To qualify for election to the Senate, a person must be at least 30 years of age, must live in the state from which he or she is chosen, and must have been a citizen of the United States for at least nine years. Candidates for the office of representative must be at least 25 years of age and have been a citizen for at least seven years. They also must (at the time of election) live in the state that they represent.

Congress convenes in January of every year and works until the two houses agree to close the session. Two such yearly sessions make up a term of Congress. A new term of Congress begins each odd-numbered year when the newly elected members of the House take office. Terms are numbered in order, beginning with the first Congress, which met in 1789. (See CONGRESS OF THE UNITED STATES; LAWMAKING.)

Executive

The executive branch of the national government is headed by the president of the United States, who is sometimes called the chief executive. This branch of government is charged with seeing that the laws passed by Congress are put into effect and enforced. The president may also recommend that Congress pass certain laws and may veto bills passed by Congress if he does not approve of them. In addition, the president plays an important role as the representative of the United States in foreign affairs.

The president is assisted by the vice-president and the cabinet, an advisory group made up of the department heads. In addition to his duties as presiding officer of the Senate, the vice-president often entertains visiting foreign officials and represents the United States at meetings in foreign countries.

To qualify as a candidate for the presidency or vice-presidency, a person must be at least 35 years of age, must have been born a citizen of the United States, and must have lived in the country for at least 14 years.

The executive branch includes 12 main departments, each headed by a secretary, and also many independent agencies that are not in the main departments. Through these departments and independent agencies the president directs the work of the government.

The departments and their years of establishment by Congress are: Department of State, 1789; Department of the Treasury, 1789; Department of Defense, 1949 (replaced War and Navy Departments established 1789, 1798, respectively); Department of Justice, 1870 (though attorney general had been a cabinet member since 1789); Post Office Department, 1872 (though postmaster general had been a cabinet member since 1829); Department of the Interior, 1849; Department of Agriculture, 1889 (replacing a department created in 1862); Department of Commerce, 1913; Department of Labor, 1913; Department of Health, Education, and Welfare, 1953; Department of Housing and Urban Development, 1965; and Department of Transportation, 1966.

The president appoints the secretaries of the departments, with Senate approval. Congress may pass laws to increase or reduce their duties. Congress may also impeach (charge with misconduct) and remove them from office. (See IMPEACHMENT.) The secretaries, however, are responsible to the president, who may dismiss them without the approval of Congress.

A law passed by Congress in 1886 provided that, if both the president and vice-president died, resigned, or were unable to serve, the secretaries would succeed to the presidency in

PLATE 1   UNITED STATES GOVERNMENT All federal laws are decided and passed upon in the Capitol Building in Washington, D.C., where the U.S. Congress meets. (1) The Ulysses S. Grant Monument is at the west entrance of the Capitol Building, facing the Mall. (2) At a joint meeting of the Senate and the House of Representatives in the House, or south wing of the Capitol Building, the two legislative bodies listen to a speech.

Photos, (1) William E. Warne; (2) "Post Dispatch" Pictures, photo by Paul Berg

PLATE 2 UNITED STATES GOVERNMENT

The buildings and monuments in Washington, D.C., the capital of the United States, reflect both historical significance and beauty of architecture and landscape. (1) The Executive Mansion, or White House, is the official residence of the president. It is a simple, dignified building surrounded by a broad lawn and gardens. (2) Abraham Lincoln's bedroom in the White House is now used for high-ranking male guests. (3) Cherry trees surround the Tidal Basin, and the Washington Monument, a marble obelisk, is one of Washington's most conspicuous and popular landmarks. (4) The huge statue of Lincoln inside the national memorial in Potomac Park faces the Washington Monument and Capitol Building.

Courtesy (2) U.S. Navy; Photos, (1) Hermann Postlethwaite; (3,4) William E. Warne

the order in which their offices were created. The 1947 law on presidential succession placed the speaker of the House first in line after the vice-president, followed by the presiding officer of the Senate, and then the members of the cabinet. The Twenty-fifth Amendment (1967) introduced a new system of succession. Under this amendment the vice-president's office no longer remains vacant if he becomes president. Instead, he nominates a new vice-president. This nomination must then be confirmed by Congress.

The Cabinet. The secretaries of the departments and the U.S. ambassador to the United Nations form the president's cabinet. (See CABINET.) They hold office as long as the president wishes. The president is responsible to the country for each member and his work. A new president may choose to keep some of the members of the previous cabinet but often appoints new ones.

State. The chief duties of the Department of State are to maintain friendly relations between the United States and other countries, to build up foreign trade and commerce, and to protect U.S. citizens and their property abroad. In carrying out these duties the Department of State performs many tasks. It supervises the entire Foreign Service. This includes the offices of ambassadors, ministers, and consuls in other countries. Through these representatives, the department works with foreign governments.

The Department of State also aids in making and enforcing treaties and other agreements with foreign countries. It issues passports to U.S. citizens who travel abroad. (See PASSPORT.)

Treasury. An operation as large as the United States government takes in and spends huge sums of money. The Department of the Treasury is responsible for handling most of this money. It collects taxes for the government and arranges to borrow money through the sale of government bonds. It takes care of paying the salaries of government workers and meeting other expenses. Branches of the department include the Bureau of Customs, the Bureau of Narcotics, and the United States Secret Service.

Defense. The Department of Defense unites the military services. Three secretaries heading the Army, Navy, and Air Force advise the sec-retary of defense, who is a member of the cabinet. The Constitution makes the president commander in chief of the Army and the Navy.

The Army was organized under the War Department, now the Department of the Army. It trains men for defending the country and directs its fighting forces in time of war. Its engineers helped build the Panama Canal, and it supervises the Canal Zone. (See ARMY.)

The Navy Department, like the War Department, was once a cabinet department but is now under the Department of Defense. The Navy must be ready at all times to protect distant possessions, foreign commerce, or the country's safety. It builds and equips war vessels, aircraft, navy yards, and naval bases. The Navy maintains a system of communications between ships at sea and shore stations. (See NAVY.)

The country's air forces were part of the Army until 1947. In that year they became independent, and the U.S. Air Force came into being. It must be ready to defend the country against air attack and to use bombing planes and long-range missiles to attack an enemy.

Justice. The Department of Justice is headed by the attorney general. He is the chief law officer of the U.S. government and is its legal adviser. His department is responsible for bringing into court people who violate federal laws.

The attorney general appears personally in the Supreme Court of the United States in very important cases. The services of his department are often used in writing new laws. The solicitor general aids the attorney general. He also represents the U.S. government before the Supreme Court. One of the most important branches of this department is the Federal Bureau of Investigation. This bureau investigates violations of federal laws and works to find and arrest the offenders. (See FEDERAL BUREAU OF INVESTIGATION.)

In maintaining law and order, the Department of Justice also does many other things. Among its most important officials are the U.S. district attorneys and marshals, who enforce federal laws. Lawsuits for or against the U.S. government are handled by lawyers in the Department of Justice. The department operates federal prisons and other federal penal institu-

THE GOVERNMENT OF THE UNITED STATES

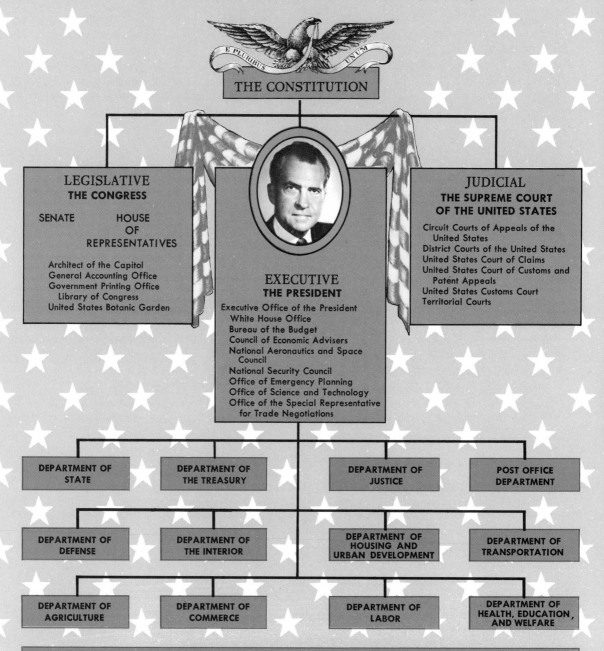

THE CONSTITUTION

LEGISLATIVE
THE CONGRESS

SENATE   HOUSE
OF
REPRESENTATIVES

Architect of the Capitol
General Accounting Office
Government Printing Office
Library of Congress
United States Botanic Garden

EXECUTIVE
THE PRESIDENT

Executive Office of the President
  White House Office
  Bureau of the Budget
  Council of Economic Advisers
  National Aeronautics and Space
    Council
  National Security Council
  Office of Emergency Planning
  Office of Science and Technology
  Office of the Special Representative
    for Trade Negotiations

JUDICIAL
THE SUPREME COURT
OF THE UNITED STATES

Circuit Courts of Appeals of the
  United States
District Courts of the United States
United States Court of Claims
United States Court of Customs and
  Patent Appeals
United States Customs Court
Territorial Courts

DEPARTMENT OF STATE	DEPARTMENT OF THE TREASURY	DEPARTMENT OF JUSTICE	POST OFFICE DEPARTMENT
DEPARTMENT OF DEFENSE	**DEPARTMENT OF THE INTERIOR**	**DEPARTMENT OF HOUSING AND URBAN DEVELOPMENT**	**DEPARTMENT OF TRANSPORTATION**
DEPARTMENT OF AGRICULTURE	**DEPARTMENT OF COMMERCE**	**DEPARTMENT OF LABOR**	**DEPARTMENT OF HEALTH, EDUCATION, AND WELFARE**

INDEPENDENT OFFICES AND ESTABLISHMENTS

Atomic Energy Commission
Civil Aeronautics Board
District of Columbia
Export-Import Bank of Washington
Farm Credit Administration
Federal Communications Commission
Federal Deposit Insurance
  Corporation
Federal Maritime Commission
Federal Mediation and
  Conciliation Service

Federal Power Commission
Federal Reserve System, Board of
  Governors of the
Federal Trade Commission
General Services Administration
Interstate Commerce Commission
National Aeronautics and Space
  Administration
National Labor Relations Board
National Mediation Board
National Science Foundation
Railroad Retirement Board

Securities and Exchange
  Commission
Selective Service System
Small Business Administration
Smithsonian Institution
Tax Court of the United States
Tennessee Valley Authority
United States Civil Service
  Commission
United States Information Agency
United States Tariff Commission
Veterans Administration

tions. It has the duty to protect citizens' rights under the Constitution. The Immigration and Naturalization Service is one of its branches.

Post Office. The postmaster general is the head of the Post Office Department. This department supervises the carrying of the mails by railways, steamships, airplanes, and other means of transportation. It operates the post offices throughout the country and provides such services as postal savings, registered mail, parcel post, and money orders.

Interior. The Department of the Interior protects and develops the natural resources of the country. The department looks after the public lands of the United States and studies the nature and location of national resources. It also has some control over the use of oil, coal, natural gas, water power, minerals, and other products of the earth. The department protects the country's fish, wild animals, and birds. The national parks and playgrounds of the country are under its supervision, as are the health, welfare, and education of Indian citizens. (See CONSERVATION.)

Agriculture. The Department of Agriculture helps farmers, ranchers, and others interested in agriculture. Many of its experts conduct experiments and study animal diseases, plant diseases, and insect pests. They help farmers with problems of soil conservation, buildings, machinery, and water supply. (See AGRICULTURE.)

Commerce. The main purpose of the Department of Commerce is to serve the businessmen of the country. The department promotes foreign and domestic commerce. It encourages such industries as mining, manufacturing, shipping, and fishing. It aids small business enterprises and develops uniform standards for business practices. The Department of Commerce takes a population census every ten years and gathers other statistics to aid business people.

The department's Weather Bureau forecasts and reports weather conditions. Its Patent Office records and protects inventions and the rights of inventors.

Labor. The Department of Labor serves the wage earners of the United States. It tries to improve their working conditions and to open opportunities for employment. The department also aids in settling disputes between workers and employers and helps prevent strikes. It includes the Bureau of Apprenticeship and Training, which sets the standards of apprenticeship for skilled workers in industry, and the Bureau of Labor Standards, which helps promote the health and safety of workers.

Health, Education, and Welfare. The Department of Health, Education, and Welfare protects the general public in many ways. It collects and pays out old-age and other insurance through the Social Security Administration. Federal pure food and drug laws are enforced through the Food and Drug Administration. The department includes the Public Health Service, which builds hospitals and operates research laboratories, and the Office of Education, which helps with educational research.

Housing and Urban Development. In 1965, Congress voted to create an eleventh cabinet department to deal with housing and the problems of cities. It combined the various government agencies dealing with urban problems.

Transportation. A twelfth department, the Department of Transportation, was created in 1966 to deal with the country's transportation problems. It operates the Coast Guard except in wartime, when it is operated by the Navy.

Independent Agencies. Congress has set up more than 40 government agencies that are not within any of the 12 cabinet departments. These agencies do not report to any cabinet officer. The United States Civil Service Commission, created in 1883, is one of them. It holds examinations and selects qualified persons for government work. (See CIVIL SERVICE.)

The Interstate Commerce Commission was started in 1887. The commission governs all transportation that is carried on between the states. This includes railroads, trucks, ships, and gas and oil pipelines. It sets the rates (charges) for passengers, freight, and express. (See INTERSTATE COMMERCE COMMISSION.)

The Federal Reserve System supervises the U.S. banking system. Through its 12 Federal Reserve districts it is able to see that enough money is in the banks to carry on the business of the country. (See FEDERAL RESERVE.)

The Veterans Administration looks after the

welfare of former servicemen. It manages the educational programs, hospitals, and other forms of aid to war veterans and their families.

The Tennessee Valley Authority (TVA) operates dams, locks, and power plants on the Tennessee River. These control floods, improve navigation, and produce electric power. (See TENNESSEE VALLEY AUTHORITY.)

The General Services Administration takes care of government buildings and property.

The Federal Trade Commission has the duty of investigating and stopping any unfair ways of doing business.

The National Labor Relations Board, which was formed in 1935, has two major tasks. First, it supervises elections that allow workers to vote on whether or not they want to be represented by a labor union. Second, it seeks to prevent employers from using unfair labor practices.

The Federal Communications Commission, set up in 1934, regulates all radio, telephone, telegraph, and cable services between states and to and from foreign countries. This seven-member agency has the power to set rates and to issue and revoke licenses. It also sets standards for radio and television programs.

The Atomic Energy Commission was created in 1946. It took charge of government plants and laboratories that had produced the first atomic bombs in World War II. It was given responsibility for directing government work with atomic material for war and peace.

Before and during World War II the president and Congress formed many special war agencies to help fight the war. These included the Selective Service System, the Office of Price Administration, and the War Production Board. In 1958 the National Aeronautics and Space Administration was formed. It was made responsible for directing all United States projects for the exploration of outer space.

Other Advisers to the President. In addition to the cabinet and the independent agencies, the president has many other official advisers.

The National Security Council was formed after World War II to aid the president in matters of defense. In addition to the president, it includes the vice-president, the secretary of state, the secretary of defense, and the director of the Office of Emergency Planning.

The Bureau of the Budget, with a staff of about 600 people, is the agency that advises the president on such matters as government reorganization and financial affairs.

Judicial

The judicial branch of the national government is the federal court system. It is responsible for interpreting laws made by Congress and seeing that they are correctly applied. The Supreme Court of the United States is the highest court in the country. It consists of a chief justice and eight associate justices, all of whom are nominated by the president of the United States and appointed after approval by the Senate. Generally, the court deals with cases in which laws are believed to disagree with the Constitution or when it is believed that an error of law has been made by a lower court.

Most cases tried in the federal court system are first heard in the District Courts. There are 87 District Courts in the 50 states, one in the District of Columbia, and one in Puerto Rico. Together they have more than 300 judges. There is one Court of Appeals in each of the 11 judicial circuits into which the United States and its territories are divided. From 3 to 9 judges work in each circuit. Congress has also created several special courts to deal with other kinds of cases.

UNIVERSE (*ū′nĭ věrs*) is not only the earth and the earth's solar system, but the Galaxy to which this solar system belongs (called the Milky Way) and all the other galaxies as well. It is at least 10,000 times older than man.

Primitive man thought that the earth was the center of the universe and that the stars moved about it. When he learned that the earth was one of the planets which circle around the sun, he believed that the sun was the center of the universe. But as he studied the heavenly bodies more, he learned that his own great solar system was only a small part of the Galaxy of the Milky Way; and that even this was only one among countless other galaxies.

It is almost impossible to imagine the size of the universe, but some idea of it can be

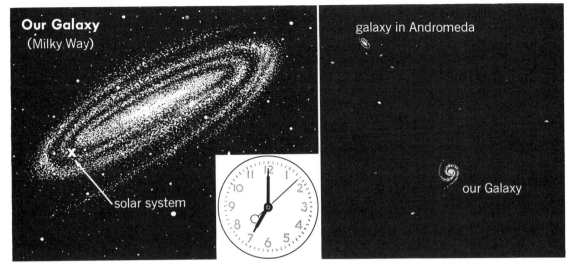

The universe contains many galaxies. Left: One of these is our Galaxy, with the solar system. The many stars appear as the Milky Way. Right: Our nearest neighbor galaxy is the one in the constellation Andromeda. In between lie trillions of miles of empty space. Inset: The universe is old. If one day equalled its age, man's time on earth would equal about eight seconds.

had from the way astronomers measure distances. They do this by measuring the distance light travels in one year. But even this is almost impossible to imagine, for light travels 186,282 miles, or 7½ times around the world, in one second. Yet astronomers measure distances in the universe by thousands of light-years.

What the Stars Are Made Of

The earth belongs to a family of nine (including Pluto) major planets and their moons. These planets and moons, together with the minor planets (asteroids) and comets, move around the sun and form our solar system. (See SOLAR SYSTEM.)

At the center of our system of planets is the sun, whose diameter is about 109 times that of the earth. The sun is like those stars which make up most of the universe. Unlike the earth, it is a boiling fire of gases with a surface temperature of about 10,800 degrees Fahrenheit. This is the main difference between the stars and the planets, for the planets and their moons are solid. They do not give off light of their own, but reflect the light shining on them from the sun.

Because of the very high temperatures inside the stars, the matter within them is always burning. This matter is almost entirely hydrogen atoms. Ordinary burning touches only the outside of the atoms, but when the temperature reaches billions of degrees, the nucleus also burns and the atoms break up. (See ATOM.)

This breaking up of atoms produces the energy which the sun pours out into space as light. If an ice bridge two miles thick and wide were built from the earth to the sun, solar energy would melt it in one second.

Each star is made up of billions times billions of glowing atoms. When very hot, each kind of atom shines with light of a different color. The color the atoms give off while they are burning describes the star itself. It is by studying these rainbows of color that astronomers learn the secrets of the stars.

Our Solar System and Galaxy

Perhaps the easiest way to tell the planets and moons from the stars in our Galaxy is to watch them. Over a few months a planet will move across the sky. The stars, however, keep their place in their constellations.

Most of the stars are like our sun, which may be called a common star. There are stars which are 10,000 times fainter than our sun, and there are stars which are just as many times brighter. There are stars which are not much larger than the earth in size, and there are stars which are a billion times larger than the sun. Most of the stars do not live alone. There are millions of double stars, which give the best information about the make-up of the stars. For example, the brightest star in the sky, Sirius, is actually two stars circling around each other like waltzing dancers. But because they are very far away, they are seen as only one tiny star.

Stars are arranged in large groups. As huge as the solar system seems, it is small compared with these groups of stars, which are called stellar systems or galaxies. There are 200,000,-000,000 stars in *the* Galaxy in which our solar system is found, the Milky Way.

Even the great galaxies have an order. The Milky Way has its own center, and groups of stars, pairs of stars, and individual stars all race around at unbelievable speeds in a certain pattern of traffic. From the center of the Galaxy, our own sun is 30,000 light-years away. It is 15,000 light-years from the edge. It takes about 200,000,000 years for it to go around the Galaxy in a huge orbit.

If it were possible to look down on the Galaxy from above, it would look something like a great pinwheel. A very bright central part occupies about one-fifth the whole body. This is the region where most stars are and where, therefore, the distances between them are the smallest. Their combined light looks like a large brilliant globe with a wide haze around it. Around the center are thick spirals of stars. From this center, dark and light patches spread out, making a spiraling web of stars.

Other Galaxies

Across an empty space of about 150,000 light-years is a double galaxy, the two Magellanic Clouds. But in relation to the total universe, this double galaxy seems just across the street.

Outward again several hundred thousands of light-years is one of the spiral galaxies. This is the Andromeda spiral with its four satellite stellar systems. A very brilliant galaxy, the one in Andromeda marks the limits of the space occupied by the *local group* of galaxies.

They include our own Galaxy, the Magellanic Clouds, the Andromeda spiral and its companions, and a half-dozen others. Beyond this family lies a great expanse of space in which there are millions of other galaxies.

The universe is constantly changing. Over great periods of time, its billions of parts are building up and dying. No one is sure how this actually happens, but the building blocks are space, time, matter, radiation, and chance. Perhaps it will give some picture of these great changes to think of trillions and trillions of the smallest particles of matter, hydrogen atoms, being hurled into space. The atoms are then swirled and tossed and finally pushed by great cosmic explosions to make an embryo, or center, of a future star. From all sides particles swoop on it until, growing rapidly, it begins to shine.

When full grown, a star remains as a burning ball of fire for a long time. But finally it will expand to an enormous size, shrink back into a huge chunk of hot rock and then break up into bits which are whirled and thrown throughout the universe, to be finally caught up again and formed into a new star. Our sun is a mature star that will change like all the others, but only very slowly.

UNIVERSITY (ū ni vēr′si tē) **AND COLLEGE** (kŏl′ĕj). The modern university began many centuries ago. In medieval times any corporation or society organized for a common interest was called a university. The earliest educational universities were merely societies of scholars or teachers formed for mutual protection. There were no permanent buildings. Instructors and students simply rented a hall or a large room.

These institutions grew. Buildings were bought for the housing and teaching of the scholars. Certain legal rights and privileges were obtained. Universities became permanent. The first medieval university was that of Salerno, Italy. As far back as the ninth century it was well known as a school of medicine. For many years it was Europe's most famous medical center. Some of its teachings came from Arabic sources. There were Jewish teachers and pupils at a time when Jews were given few privileges. Salerno was formally made a university in 1231.

Toward the end of the 12th century another well-known Italian university developed at Bologna. Salerno was only a school of medicine, but Bologna was a many-sided institution. It first earned a reputation as a law school. In the course of time faculties (departments of instruction) of medicine, arts, and theology were added. The teachers, following the example of the students, formed themselves into guilds or "colleges." The certificates or licenses to teach that were required for admission to the instructors' guilds became the earliest form of academic degree. Students, regardless of their future calling, finally came to seek the professor's license or degree as indication of a good education.

The University of Paris, most famous of the medieval schools of higher learning, was officially organized in the last half of the 12th century. Like many other early universities of northern Europe, it grew out of a school attached to a cathedral. It was attached to the Cathedral of Notre Dame and was famed far and wide as a center of theological learning. Three other faculties were added later in canon law, medicine, and the arts. The University of Paris became the model for all the later universities of Europe.

Among the colleges united under its head was the College of the Sorbonne, founded in the 13th century for the teaching of theology. The Sorbonne still survives.

Paris served as the model for the two great English universities, Oxford and Cambridge, both of which were legally recognized by the 13th century. As at Paris most emphasis was placed upon teaching theology. A noteworthy feature of these English institutions was the development of the college system in the university.

Of the universities that came into existence in the Middle Ages some, such as the University of Salerno, no longer exist. Among those that survived besides Bologna (Italy), Oxford, and Cambridge are the universities at Cracow, Poland; Vienna, Austria; Heidelberg, Jena, Berlin, Germany; Dublin, Ireland; and Edinburgh, Scotland.

Definition of a University

Much confusion exists in the United States concerning the nature of a university and the term is often misused. The chief difference between a college and a university is that the university usually includes a number of colleges. Many institutions pretend to be universities when they are not. On the other hand, some colleges are more like universities. There also are numerous institutions for technical training where much more than mere instruction in technical subjects is offered. Illustrations of this are the Carnegie Institute of Technology, Pittsburgh, Pennsylvania, with its tremendous research work, Massachusetts Institute of Technology in Cambridge; Virginia Polytechnic Institute in Blacksburg; and the Georgia School of Technology in Atlanta.

A university was defined by the National Education Association as "an institution of higher education, having as a nucleus a college in which the so-called liberal arts are taught in a course of three or four years for the degree A.B. (Bachelor of Arts), and in addition one or more departments for the learned professions, medicine, law, or divinity—or it may be for advanced or post-graduate work, along any lines of learning or investigation."

Officials of the ordinary university usually include a board of trustees or overseers. They manage the financial affairs of the institution and engage faculty members and a president. The president acts as the executive of the university. In most universities a dean is placed at the head of each college.

Definition of a College

The term *college* originally meant any society or union of persons engaged in common activity or granted certain powers and rights to carry on a common work. There is a college of cardinals which elects the pope at Rome. The United States has an electoral college which meets to choose the president and vice-president. The word college has come to mean one certain thing in the United States: an institution attended after graduation from high school and one that gives general rather than highly specialized or technical training.

In Great Britain the word college originally meant, in connection with education, a group organized to help its members get educational advantages. The early colleges were self-governing societies which taken together made a university. Some of these developed into independent schools. In general, they were concerned chiefly with student organization and discipline and became endowed schools for student residence. The great English universities of Oxford and Cambridge, for instance, are

A 1740 engraving by William Burgis depicts Harvard College at Cambridge, Massachusetts, as it was about 1725.

made up of a number of colleges. Each of these colleges provides lodging and instruction for its members, but the examinations and degrees are given by the university.

A good definition of the true modern college in the United States was given by the Carnegie Foundation for the Advancement of Teaching. It is: "An institution to be ranked as a college must have at least eight professors giving their entire time to college and university work, and a course of four full years in liberal arts and sciences, and should require for admission not less than the usual four years of academic or high school preparation, or its equivalent, in addition to the preacademic or grammar school studies."

The colleges of the United States do not always meet the high standard of this definition. Any institution of higher education having but one faculty and offering a single course of

studies is likely to be known as a college. The course of studies is usually confined to basic and somewhat advanced courses in the liberal arts. These courses include social studies (history, economics, sociology, and so on), the humanities (language, literature, philosophy, etc.), and the natural sciences (physics, mathematics, biology, chemistry, and so on).

A college and a university differ in the fact that the university in addition to a liberal arts college also includes other special colleges or schools. These special schools give instruction in professions such as law, medicine, forestry and the like. There usually is also a graduate college which provides advanced instruction and research in the liberal arts. Colleges are sometimes preparatory schools for universities in the sense that students go to college first and then take graduate work in a university.

Higher Education in the New World

Before the Revolutionary War the colonists had founded ten colleges. The number has steadily increased. In 1960 there were more than 1,800 so-called "institutions of higher learning" in the United States.

The first college in the United States was Harvard, founded at Cambridge, Massachusetts, in 1636. It was named after its first benefactor, John Harvard. Next followed William and Mary College in Williamsburg, Virginia (1693). Yale was founded at New Haven, Connecticut, in 1701. Princeton was founded in New Jersey in 1746 and was originally the College of New Jersey. Columbia in New York City was founded in 1754 and was originally known as King's College. With the exception of William and Mary

A 17th-century view of Cambridge University, England, is shown in an engraving from *Cantabrigia Illustrata*, 1670.

all these are universities today. They are *endowed* universities, meaning that they are maintained by invested funds, student fees, and the gifts of benefactors. Other noted endowed institutions in the United States are Cornell, Ithaca, New York; Leland Stanford, Stanford, California; Duke, Durham, North Carolina; Dartmouth, Hanover, New Hampshire; New York University; the University of Chicago, Illinois; and the University of Pennsylvania, Philadelphia. Johns Hopkins (Baltimore, Maryland) and Clark (Worcester, Massachusetts) universities were founded for graduate or advanced work only.

State Universities

Besides the endowed institutions in the United States there are many state universities such as the universities of Michigan in Ann Arbor; California in Berkeley; Wisconsin in Madison; and Illinois in Urbana. These are mostly supported by state taxes and are managed by trustees appointed by the governor or elected by voters. Almost every state in the union has its own university where the students of that state are given an education at very little cost to them. Municipal universities, such as the University of Cincinnati in Ohio, are patterned after the state institutions.

Numerous colleges and universities are endowed or were first endowed by religious groups. Harvard and Yale were started by the Congregationalists, Princeton by Presbyterians, Brown in Providence, Rhode Island, by Baptists, Wesleyan in Middletown, Connecticut, by the Methodists, and Rutgers, New Brunswick, New Jersey, by members of the Dutch Reformed church. The Roman Catholics support Notre Dame, Notre Dame, Indiana; Fordham, New York City; the Catholic University of America, Washington, D.C.; and others.

Among leading Canadian universities are McGill University, Montreal, Quebec; the University of Toronto in Ontario; Queen's University at Kingston, Ontario; Laval at Quebec, Quebec; and Acadia and Dalhousie in Wolfville and Halifax, Nova Scotia, respectively. There are also universities in the provinces of Alberta, New Brunswick, British Columbia, Manitoba,

Courtesy University of California

The University of California at Berkeley on San Francisco Bay maintains campuses in eight other cities.

and Saskatchewan.

The opportunities for women in university education have increased in the United States. State institutions are open to both men and women. These are called coeducational schools. Almost all endowed institutions admit women in their graduate and professional schools. Many of the endowed universities offer undergraduate courses only to men, but there are a number in which men and women can take the same studies. Some institutions provide separate colleges for women, such as Barnard College at Columbia University, New York City. In addition there are excellent colleges in the United States devoted to the education of women only. The oldest of these is Mount Holyoke at South Hadley, Massachusetts, founded in 1837.

The junior college is a modern development and usually consists of grades 13 and 14. In 1960 there were more than 500 such colleges in the United States. Frequently they form part of a city school system. The course of study is equal to two years at a regular college.

University extension courses originated in England and have proved very successful in the United States. This movement has for its main purpose the extension of opportunity for higher education to all the people. Many universities offer correspondence courses, lecture classes off the campus, and home study classes. The subjects offered in extension work include many regular university courses.

Entrance Requirements and Degrees

The entrance requirements vary in different universities and colleges. Completion of a four-year standard high school course usually forms the lowest basis for admission. The subjects required for entrance depend upon the particular university and the course of study to be followed. A course of work completed in a secondary school (high school) is termed a "unit." The entrance requirements are usually stated in terms of such units. From 14 to 16 units are ordinarily required for admission. All information regarding entrance into any university may be obtained from its registrar. From about 1930 there has been a tendency for many colleges and universities to require a smaller number of specified units of high school work for admission.

Until recently the usual course of undergraduate study in a university in the United States began with the 13th grade. The course included four college years and led to a bachelor's degree. It now is possible to secure this degree in less time in many institutions. This is particularly true for students who take up graduate work leading to a master's or doctor's degree. From 1942 to 1954 The University of Chicago had a special program so that a student could receive the bachelor's degree at the end of the 14th grade.

The Bachelor of Arts degree given by colleges in the United States is usually based on cultural courses. These are courses in the liberal arts. Students who wish to specialize in technical sciences often enter schools that specialize in them, such as the Massachusetts Institute of Technology. At the end of four years they receive the Bachelor of Science degree, which is also given in most other colleges and universities. Today most students who go to college for a general liberal education decide within two years what career they want to follow.

The years after World War I brought to universities in the United States a greatly increased enrollment. This was followed by criticism of "quantity production" educational methods. A practical result of this criticism was the establishment of several "experimental" colleges.

During World War II university education by extension or correspondence was made available to people in the armed services through the Armed Forces Institute. At the end of World War II college enrollment increased greatly. This increase was mainly the result of the federal government's financing of the education of qualified veterans through the G. I. Bill of Rights. (See EDUCATION.)

UPPER (ŭp'ēr) **VOLTA** (vōl'tä), **AFRICA,** is a country in western Africa. It has an area of 105,886 square miles bordered on all sides by land. On the northeast is Niger; on the southeast is Dahomey; on the south is Togo, Ghana, and Ivory Coast; and on the west and north is Mali.

Upper Volta is a vast, nearly level plateau ranging between 650 and 1,000 feet in elevation. The Black Volta, White Volta, and Red Volta rivers all begin in Upper Volta. Between November and March, Upper Volta is cool and dry. The rest of the year is hot, and the rainy season is short. Daily temperatures at Ouagadougou often are more than 100 degrees Fahrenheit in April and May. The rainfall is about 40 inches in the south, but decreases to less than 10 inches in the north. The soils are poor. The vegetation is chiefly grass with some wooded areas.

Almost all of the people of Upper Volta are Negroid. The largest group is the Mossi, who live mainly in the central part of the country. French is the official language, but most of the people speak African languages. There are large groups of Muslims and Christians. A great

Locator map of Upper Volta.

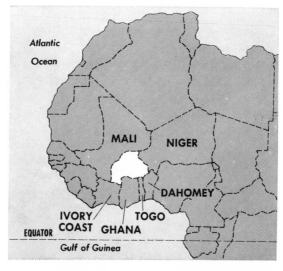

many of the people, however, worship according to tribal customs.

The population of Upper Volta is unevenly distributed. Few people live in some areas because of lack of water or the danger of floods or sleeping sickness. Most of the people live in rural areas in the central and southern parts of the country. The two largest towns are Ouagadougou, the capital, and Bobo-Dioulasso, a busy commercial center. A railroad about 700 miles long runs from Ouagadougou to Bobo-Dioulasso and on to the port of Abidjan in Ivory Coast.

Upper Volta is an agricultural country. Livestock is important and makes up a large part of the country's exports. The farmers raise cattle, horses, donkeys, sheep, and goats. Most of the crops are cultivated on small farms. Millet, sorghum, corn, peanuts, shea nuts (*karite*), yams, cotton, and rice are the major crops. There is little mineral production although deposits of gold, manganese, and bauxite have been found. Manufacturing is limited to rice, cotton, fats, and oils processing.

When the French reached the Upper Volta area in the late 19th century, they found a powerful Mossi empire. In 1896 the French established a protectorate over the area. In 1919 Upper Volta became a French colony and a part of French West Africa. It remained as such until 1932 when it was divided among the neighboring colonies. In 1947 Upper Volta was restored to its status of 1932. It became an independent republic in August 1960, and in September of the same year it was admitted to the United Nations.

According to the 1960 constitution, executive power is held by a president elected by the people. The president appoints and heads a council of ministers. The law-making body is the National Assembly. In 1960 Maurice Yameogo became the country's first president. He resigned in 1966 and a military junta seized power. Lieutenant Colonel Sangoule Lamizana took office as head of state. The population is 5,040,000 (1968 estimate).

URAL (*ū′räl*) **MOUNTAINS, U.S.S.R.,** are one of the most important physical features in the

Locator map of the Ural Mountains.

U.S.S.R. They stretch 1,250 miles from the Arctic Ocean in the north almost to the Caspian Sea in the south. These mountains divide European U.S.S.R. from Siberia, the Asian section of the U.S.S.R.

The Urals are important not so much for their height as for their position. The highest peak, Mount Narodnaya, is only 6,214 feet high and most of the peaks are much lower. The north-south direction of the Urals, however, has a great effect on the climate. Moist, mild Atlantic air cools and loses its moisture when it rises to cross the Urals. Siberia is much drier and colder than the European part of the U.S.S.R.

The Urals are one of the world's richest mineral areas. Large deposits of high-quality iron ore, manganese, nickel, copper, platinum, bauxite, gold, asbestos, precious stones, petroleum, and uranium are found there. Many of these deposits were not discovered until World War II and after. Because of these minerals, the central Urals have recently become an important manufacturing area. Three large and rapidly growing cities are located there: Sverdlovsk, Chelyabinsk, and Magnitogorsk (which is actually built on a mountain of iron ore). These cities had a great growth during World War II. During that time people and industry were moved eastward to the Urals, far from the fighting zone.

Since World War II the Ural area has continued to grow, both in population and industrial importance. (See UNION OF SOVIET SOCIALIST REPUBLICS, THE.)

URANIUM ($\bar{u}\,r\bar{a}'n\breve{\imath}\,\breve{u}m$) is a metal that is one of the heaviest elements. It is about two and one-half times as heavy as steel. Uranium is thought of as a rare metal, but in the earth's surface it is more common than many others, including mercury or silver.

Ore, rich in uranium, is found in a number of places such as the Republic of Congo (formerly Belgian Congo) in Africa; the Great Bear Lake, Bancroft, and Blind River districts in Canada; the southwestern part of the United States; Australia; and the Ural Mountains in the U.S.S.R. The most common ores are pitchblendes and carnotites.

Each ton of ore produces about five pounds of uranium oxide (U_3O_8), which when refined will yield about four and one-half pounds of uranium metal. The ore is mined and refined by methods similar to those for other ores.

Clean, pure uranium metal is as shiny as silver, but after only a few minutes exposure to air the surface of the uranium becomes dull and turns brown. The film is uranium and oxygen (oxide) and protects the metal underneath.

Uranium chips and dust will often burst into flame simply by being in contact with air. In fact, uranium oxidizes (combines with oxygen) so easily that it is difficult to make alloys containing uranium because the uranium quickly changes to uranium oxide.

The greatest difference between uranium and most other metals is the natural radioactivity of uranium. (See RADIATION.) The metal slowly changes by giving off alpha, beta, and gamma radiation. These come out of the uranium atom. (See ATOM; ATOMIC ENERGY.) By giving off radiation, the uranium atom changes, and becomes another radioactive element. This element is in turn changed by giving off more radiation. This changing process, known as the Radioactive Uranium Series, goes on as long as a radioactive element is left. Fourteen steps take place in this series. One of the steps produces radium, and the last step produces lead.

Courtesy Tracerlab, Inc.

A Geiger counter is an aid in uranium prospecting.

This ends the series, for lead is not radioactive. To change from uranium to lead in nature takes billions of years.

Discovery and Uses

Little had been known about uranium until recent years. In 1896 Henry Becquerel was using uranium ore in some of his experiments when he discovered natural radioactivity. Further research work was started the next year by Marie and Pierre Curie. They discovered that most of the radioactivity in the uranium ores they were using came from the radium in the ore. Radium was present for radium and uranium are found together in nature. (See CURIE, PIERRE AND MARIE; RADIUM.)

From then until 1940 uranium was used mostly in experiments by scientists. Some ordinary uses were found for it as a color in pottery glaze, in dyeing fabrics, and in some industrial processes. Physicists were interested in its radioactive properties, and chemists were interested in its chemical and physical properties. Uranium became a very important metal during World War II in the effort to make an atomic bomb and use atomic energy.

The products of uranium that have become best known are U-235 and plutonium. These two are the most important forms of material used in either atomic bombs or in reactors for atomic energy. U-235 is one of the natural forms of uranium in the uranium series. It is known as an *isotope* or form of uranium. Only very small amounts of it are found in uranium ore. It took a great deal of work and expense to get the pure U-235 used in the first atomic bomb. Plutonium is a man-made product of uranium and is heavier.

Other than being useful as a material for weapons, uranium is used as a fuel in nuclear reactors. In reactors uranium is used in many shapes (as strips, cylinders, and tubes). Under some conditions it is mixed or alloyed with other metals. It is also useful in its oxide form and is sometimes dissolved in solution.

URUGUAY (*ur'ŭ gwī'*), **SOUTH AMERICA,** is the smallest independent country in area on the continent. It is bounded by water on three sides—the Atlantic Ocean on the east, the Rio de la Plata on the south, and the Uruguay River on the west. Across the rivers is Argentina, and to the north lies its other large neighbor, Brazil. Most Uruguayans are primarily of Spanish and Italian descent. They make their living chiefly by livestock raising or in related fields of commerce and industry. Officially the country's name is Republica Oriental del Uruguay (Eastern Republic of the Uruguay).

Land and Climate

About 90 percent of Uruguay's territory is hilly. The rest is a fringe of coastal and riverbank lowland that extends along the wa-ter boundaries of the country from the Brazilian border to the city of Fray Bentos, near the mouth of the Uruguay River. Farther northward, along the river, the hills reach to the river's edge. About 70 miles inland from the Atlantic Coast is the drainage divide, a long narrow belt of hills. The divide stretches from the Brazilian border southward to Montevideo, the national capital. To the west of the divide, streams flow to the Uruguay or the Plata. To the east, they flow to Lake Mirim or the Atlantic Ocean. The summits of the hills of the divide are highest in the north, where, near the Brazilian border, they reach to 2,000 feet.

At the highest elevations, the land surface is uneven, and the stream valleys are steep sided and narrow. Lower down, the valleys broaden out into wide, flat plains near the mouths of the rivers. The principal river, other than those forming borders, is the Rio Negro, which flows to the Uruguay. Also important are the Queguay, the Santa Lucia, and the Cebollati rivers. The interior rivers of Uruguay are most useful as power sources, especially the Rio Negro, where modern hydropower plants supply much of the country's electric requirement.

The climate of Uruguay is mild, although

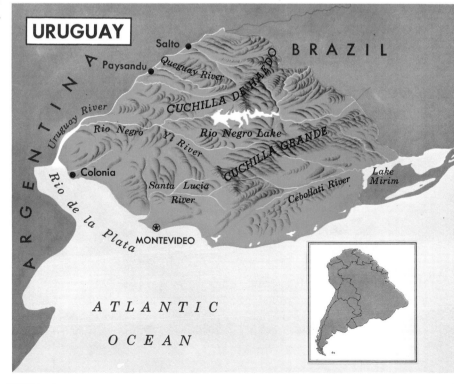

it is almost subtropical in the warm north-west. Temperature changes are often rapid, and strong winds from the southwest are common. In the north, summer days are hot, but nights are cool. The winter months—June, July, and August—are never continuously cold. Frosts are few, and snow is practically un-

Beautiful Montevideo is a bustling capital and popular resort city. The Obelisk (left), a noted landmark, honors the patriots of independence. In Plaza Independencia (below right) stands a statue of Jose Artigas, Uruguay's national hero. Sandy beaches (bottom) line the city's oceanfront.

(left) J. Allan Cash—Rapho Guillumette, (below right) Carl Frank—Photo Researchers, (bottom) Authenticated News International

known. The coldest month has an average temperature of about 50 degrees Fahrenheit, and the warmest, about 71 degrees. In the south, temperatures are about the same. At Montevideo the average annual temperature is 62 degrees Fahrenheit. Uruguay has no regular dry or rainy season. Rain usually falls in every

month of the year, although there are occasional prolonged dry spells.

Even though Uruguay's climate is mild, crop growing is not highly developed. The country suffers from many insect pests and plant diseases, and winter is never cold enough to check them. Climate is, however, favorable to grass growth and the livestock industry. Forests are limited, covering less than 3 percent of the total area of the country. In contrast, about 74 percent of the land is grassland, which is used for pasture. Only about 12 percent is used for crops. Pastures are concentrated on the hills, and crops on the lowlands.

Animal life has become somewhat sparse in Uruguay. The rhea (the American ostrich) is still sometimes seen, and the puma, jaguar, fox, deer, wildcat, water hog, and various rodents are among the other animals of Uruguay.

People

The first Uruguayans were of mixed origins, with Spanish fathers and Indian mothers. The males were Gauchos, the cowboys of the colonial period, who made their living by rounding up herds of half-wild cattle. During the colonial period more and more Spaniards entered the country. During the 19th century, and until World War I, Italian and French immigrants arrived in considerable numbers. Only a few World War II refugees arrived from Europe, and some Brazilians and Argentines migrated to Uruguay in more recent years. The Uruguayan population today is mostly white. Less than 10 percent is mestizo (mixed Indian and white), and less than 1 percent is Negro or mulatto. Pure-blooded Indians are extinct.

About one-half of all Uruguayans live in cities located in the lowlands of the Plata and the Uruguay. These include Montevideo, Paysandu, and Salto. Other towns, similarly located but with considerably smaller populations, are Fray Bentos, Colonia, and Mercedes. Montevideo is the largest city of the country and one of the largest in South America. (See MONTEVIDEO.) Spanish is the official language in Uruguay, and, although there is no established state religion, most of the population is Roman Catholic.

Futbol (soccer) ranks as the favorite sport of the Uruguayans. Teams from Uruguay have competed for the *futbol* world championship several times. Uruguayans sometimes spend months preparing for Carnival, the three-day holiday before Lent. It includes gay parties, colorful costumes, and spectacular parades.

Economy

Uruguay is chiefly a livestock-raising country, and most Uruguayans make their living by raising cattle or sheep, or by working in related industries. The country's few forests and mineral deposits cannot support sizable forestry or mining operations, and crop raising ranks far behind livestock raising. Most large-scale industry is based on the processing of animal products. Principal exports include wool, meat and meat products, and hides and skins.

In no other Latin-American country do the people depend upon livestock raising as in Uruguay. There are about 22,000,000 sheep and 8,900,000 cattle—that is, about ten times as many sheep and about three times as many cattle as there are people. About three-fourths of the land is used for pasture.

Livestock raising supports an important meat-processing industry. During colonial times the area along the Uruguay River was the center of a meat-drying industry that remained important even after *frigorificos* (meat-processing plants) appeared early in the 20th century. At first the *frigorificos* were not too successful. Today, however, meat-processing is one of the most important industries in the country. Montevideo, Paysandu, Salto, and Fray Bentos, all on the Plata or the Uruguay, are well known for their meat-freezing and -processing plants.

Crop raising is a minor occupation when compared with livestock raising. Largely as the result of governmental encouragement, however, it has increased through the mid-1900's. Since 1940 the amount of cropland has been doubled. Today more than 8,600 square miles are used as cropland. Principal crops are wheat and other grains, grapes for wine, other fruits, and sugarcane.

The transportation system in Uruguay is among the finest in Latin America. Domestic

airlines, highways, and railroads fan outward from Montevideo and penetrate to all parts of the interior. Montevideo is a major stop on international ocean and air routes. All-weather roads link the major towns. A modern highway connects Montevideo and Colonia, and a ferry links Colonia to Buenos Aires, Argentina, across

On Uruguay's plains, gauchos (cowboys) round up cattle for shipment to market (top). A sea lion colony on Lobos Island (center), off the Uruguayan coast, provides one of the country's interesting attractions. Huge sheep herds graze on extensive Uruguayan pastureland (bottom). Sheep form the basis for Uruguay's important wool industry.
(Top) Carl Frank—Photo Researchers, (bottom) Authenticated News International, (center) courtesy Pan American Union

the Rio de la Plata. The Pan-American Highway connects the capital with the small city of Acegua on the Brazilian border. Altogether, the country has more than 23,500 miles of roads.

The nationally owned Uruguayan railroad has a total length of about 1,900 miles and provides connections between Montevideo and other principal Uruguayan towns. Four main trunk lines branch out from the capital. The Plata is navigable for ocean vessels all along the southern border, and the Uruguay is navigable for smaller ships as far upstream as Salto. Including the internal rivers, such as the Negro and Cebollati, Uruguay has about 700 miles of water routes. Air transport is well developed, and scheduled national and international flights use the airport at Montevideo daily.

FACTS ABOUT URUGUAY

CAPITAL: Montevideo.

NATIONAL ANTHEM: *Himno Nacional de Uruguay* ("National Anthem of Uruguay").

AREA: 68,536 square miles (about the size of the state of Washington); about 8,695 square miles of the land area is cultivated.

POPULATION: 2,556,020 (1963), 2,682,000 (1964 estimate); 39 persons per square mile; 82 percent urban, 18 percent rural.

CHIEF LANGUAGE: Spanish.

CHIEF RELIGION: Roman Catholic.

LITERACY: About 80 percent 10 years of age and over can read and write.

HIGHEST POINT: About 2,000 feet.

LARGEST LAKE: Rio Negro Lake.

MOST IMPORTANT RIVERS: Cebollati, Negro, Plata, Queguay, Santa Lucia, Uruguay.

FORM OF GOVERNMENT: Republic.

HEAD OF GOVERNMENT AND CHIEF OF STATE: President.

LEGISLATURE: National Assembly (Senate and Chamber of Deputies).

VOTING QUALIFICATIONS: Compulsory; 18 years of age and over.

POLITICAL DIVISIONS: 19 departments.

CHIEF CITIES: (1963) Montevideo (1,202,890), Salto (57,714), Paysandu (51,645).

CHIEF MANUFACTURED AND MINED PRODUCTS: Beverages, chemicals, building materials, food, metal and mechanical products, textiles.

CHIEF AGRICULTURAL PRODUCTS: *Livestock*, cattle, sheep; *crops*, barley, corn, flaxseed, oats, rice, sugarcane, sunflower seeds, wheat.

MOST IMPORTANT HOLIDAYS: Constitution Day (July 18), Independence Day (August 25), Carnival (held for three days before Lent).

FLAG: Colors are blue, white and gold. (See FLAG.)

CURRENCY: Peso; about 200 pesos equal one U.S. dollar.

Education and Government

More than 80 percent of Uruguay's people can read and write, making the country one of the most literate in South America. According to the constitution, elementary education is free and compulsory. In general, six years of elementary school are followed by six years of secondary school. In the secondary school, students take a four-year general course and a two-year upper course. The University of the Republic, in Montevideo, is the largest in Uruguay. Tuition at the university is free for all students. The Technical University provides vocational training.

Uruguay is a republic. For the first time in 15 years, a president was inaugurated in 1967 for a five-year term. The offices of president and vice-president were abolished in 1952, and a National Council took over the executive powers of government. Under a new constitution approved by the people in 1966, the council was abolished. The legislature is known as the National Assembly and is composed of a Senate, elected at large, and a Chamber of Deputies. Members of the chamber are elected from the 19 Uruguayan departments in proportion to population. Uruguay has two political parties, the liberal Colorados and the conservative Blancos, or Nationalists.

History

The first European expedition to land on Uruguayan soil was led by Spanish explorer Juan Diaz de Solis in 1516. Juan de Solis was killed that same year by the Charrua Indians. Ferdinand Magellan and Sebastian Cabot also visited the Plata region in the early 16th century.

This small country has been known by several names. As a part of the Spanish Empire's Viceroyalty of the Rio de la Plata, it was called the Banda Oriental, or Eastern Bank, because of its location on the eastern bank of the Uruguay River. In the 1800's, as a part of Brazil, it was known as the Cisplatine Province. Only in 1830, with independence, did it assume its present name. Uruguayans today are sometimes referred to as *Orientales*, or Easterners.

Early settlement of the Rio de la Plata region was discouraged by the lack of precious metals thought to be in the area and the fierce resistance of the Indians. In the 17th century the Portuguese, coming from Brazil on the north, pushed all the way south to the banks of the Plata. In 1680 they established a fortress on the site of the present-day city of Colonia. The Spaniards themselves founded no permanent settlement until 1726, when Montevideo was established as a garrison town to serve as a stronghold against the rapidly growing Portuguese colony. The Banda Oriental then became a battleground on which the Portuguese and the Spanish, and later the Brazilians and Argentines, fought for supremacy. In 1777 the Spanish defeated the Portuguese at Colonia.

In the early 19th century, Uruguay was caught up in the spirit of revolt against Spain that swept South America. The leader of Uruguay's fight for independence was Jose Gervasio Artigas, who has been called the father of Uruguay. Artigas organized the freedom-loving Gauchos and Creoles (South American-born Spaniards) to fight for a free Uruguayan state. His forces not only fought the Spanish, but, because a struggle for colonial leadership developed, he also fought the Argentines and Portuguese Brazilians. Finally, in 1820, Artigas was defeated by the Portuguese and forced into exile. (See ARTIGAS, JOSE GERVASIO.)

In 1821 Uruguay was annexed by Portuguese Brazil and became the Cisplatine Province of that country. Four years later the Uruguayans revolted against Brazilian authority and declared their independence. At the same time, they declared that their allegiance belonged to the new country of Argentina. A war between Argentina and Brazil followed, and it was not until 1828 that peace was achieved. In that year the English persuaded both the Argentines and the Brazilians that Uruguay should become a separate country. In 1830 the Uruguayan constitution was ratified.

A great domestic struggle for power followed independence. For nearly 100 years the country was periodically torn by political rivalries that often resulted in armed conflict and open rebellion against the elected government. As early as 1836 fighting broke out between political groups, and two principal political parties emerged. The conservative Blancos, known for the white flag they carried, opposed the liberal Colorados, who carried a red flag. These names have been continued, with somewhat different meanings, down to the present time. In 1880 President Lorenzo Latorre resigned, declaring that the Uruguayans were ungovernable.

During the early 1900's the country developed much greater political stability and made considerable economic progress. Uruguayan products increased in value in the world markets, a large immigration of Europeans began, and educational progress was made.

During the last 50 years Uruguay has made much progress. In the fields of politics and social legislation, elections and constitutional changes were carried on in an atmosphere of general peace and order. Great improvements were made in the transport system, the quality of animals raised, and agricultural production. During the mid-20th century the Uruguayans enjoyed one of the highest standards of living in Latin America. In 1965, however, inflation became a serious problem. This situation was somewhat improved in 1966.

During World War II, Uruguay broke its diplomatic relations with the Axis powers and cooperated actively with the Allied war effort. Today it is a member of the Organization of American States, the Alliance for Progress, and the Latin American Free Trade Association.

UTAH (ū'tạ), **UNITED STATES,** is in the Rocky Mountain region of the western part of the nation. It is bordered on the north by Idaho and Wyoming, east by Colorado, south by Arizona, and west by Nevada. The name Utah comes from the Ute Indian word Eutau, meaning "high up." Utah's nickname is the "Beehive State."

The beautiful red rock canyons and mesas of the Colorado Plateau in the south hold rich deposits of uranium. In the north-central section is the world's largest open-pit copper mine, the nation's largest salt lake, and the state's largest cities. Salt Lake City, the capital; Ogden; Provo; and Logan are in this area. All are manufacturing cities. Salt Lake City is also the world headquarters for the Church of Jesus Christ of Latter-day Saints.

Landscape

Utah has three land regions: the Rocky Mountains, the Basin and Range, and the Colorado Plateau. The chief Rocky Mountain ranges in Utah are the Uinta and the Wasatch

Courtesy Utah Tourist and Publicity Council

These unusual rock features in Monument Valley were formed by wind erosion.

mountains. Running east and west below the Wyoming border is the Uinta Range. The state's highest point, Kings Peak (13,528 feet), is in this range. In north central Utah is the rugged, but lower, Wasatch Range, running north and south. Extending generally southward from this range is a belt of highlands which forms the western edge of the Colorado Plateau and the eastern border of the Basin and Range region.

In the Basin and Range region (or Great Basin) are many short mountain ranges separated by broad, flat valleys or basins. The region is rimmed by high mountains that long ago

enclosed huge Lake Bonneville. Today all that is left of the 19,-000 square mile lake is Great Salt Lake. (See GREAT SALT LAKE.)

The surface of the Plateau region drops in huge steps from the center of the state toward the Colorado River. Steep, richly colored cliffs ranging from several hundred to more than 2,000 feet in height separate the steps. Many of the streams that join the Colorado River have cut deep canyons across the plateau.

Three of the state's large rivers—the Bear, Weber, and Provo—begin in the Uinta Mountains and flow into the Great Basin. The Bear and Weber rivers empty into Great Salt Lake. The Provo River flows into Utah Lake, the state's largest body of fresh water. The Sevier is Utah's longest river. In the southeast the Colorado River cuts through colorful desert land.

Climate

Utah has a dry climate with warm summers and cold winters. The average annual temperature is about 48 degrees. In January, the coldest month, temperatures average about 12 degrees in the Uinta Mountains and 36 degrees in the southwest corner. The average for the warmest month, July, ranges from 60 degrees in the mountains to 84 degrees in southwestern Utah.

The annual rainfall is 13 inches. This ranges from less than 5 inches in the Great Salt Lake Desert to about 40 inches in the high north-central mountains. Much moisture comes in the form of snow, which in midwinter piles up 100 inches or more in the mountain valleys.

At places along the southern border the growing season is more than 200 days. In the Rocky Mountain region it is shorter than 60 days. Most agriculture in Utah is dependent upon irrigation because of the state's generally arid climate.

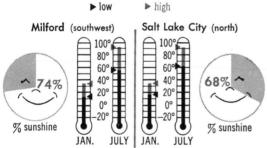

Average Daily Temperature
▶ low   ▶ high

Milford (southwest)   Salt Lake City (north)

74%   68%

% sunshine   % sunshine

JAN. JULY | JAN. JULY

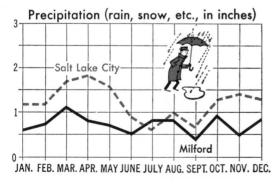

Precipitation (rain, snow, etc., in inches)

Salt Lake City

Milford

JAN. FEB. MAR. APR. MAY JUNE JULY AUG. SEPT. OCT. NOV. DEC.

Animal Life

Animal life is plentiful in Utah. Among the large animals in the highlands are mule deer, elk, cougars, bobcats, antelope, coyotes, and bighorn sheep. Small herds of buffalo (bison) still roam the Colorado Plateau.

Courtesy United States Steel Corporation

A steel works near Provo.

Among the many fur-bearing animals, rodents, and reptiles are beavers, minks, ringtailed cats, porcupines, prairie dogs, rattlesnakes, horned toads, and lizards.

Millions of migratory birds stop to rest and feed at Utah's bird refuges near Great Salt Lake. Two of the main bird flyways of North America cross Utah. (See MIGRATION, section on *Bird Migrations*.) Sea gulls, herons, pelicans, geese, swans, ducks, and teal are among the birds found around the lake. In the highlands are pheasant, partridge, wild turkeys, eagles, hawks, and vultures.

Resources

Utah has deposits of more than 200 minerals, some of which are very large. Among its most valuable minerals are petroleum, copper, coal, uranium, gold, iron ore, zinc, Gilsonite, vanadium, stone, sand, and gravel.

Water is another important resource in Utah. Large dams have been built on many rivers to hold back water for irrigation. They also supply hydroelectric power for industry.

Unusual Features of Interest

Broad mesas, colorful cliffs, and deep gorges are some of the interesting features of Bryce Canyon and Zion National parks. Both parks are in the plateau region. Eight national monuments also preserve the beauties of nature. At Arches National Monument, near Moab, are many natural bridges and tall, towerlike rocks. One of the world's largest natural bridges is in Rainbow Bridge National Monument near Utah's southern border. At Dinosaur National Monument the fossil remains of prehistoric animals are preserved in a scenic canyon setting.

The People

The cliff dwellings of southeastern Utah were once the homes of the state's earliest people, the Anasazi Indians. Their houses of fitted stone, and their canals, show that these cliff dwellers were skilled in architecture and irrigation. (See CLIFF DWELLERS.)

When the white man came, three main tribes of Indians were living in the Utah country. The Utes and Shoshones lived on the eastern and northern plains. The Paiutes lived on the plateau in the southwest.

In 1776 two young Spanish priests from New Mexico, Father Silvestre Escalante and Father Francisco Dominguez, traveled as far as Utah Lake. The first trappers entered the northern part in the early 1800's. They built forts in

Air view of the Bingham open-pit copper mine.

Courtesy Utah Department of Publicity and Industrial Development, Clyde Anderson photo

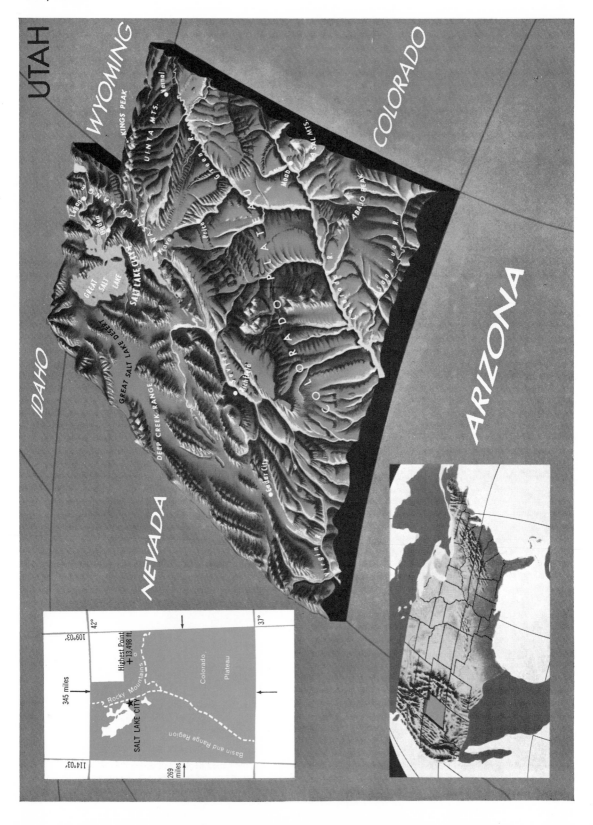

UTAH

WYOMING

COLORADO

IDAHO

NEVADA

ARIZONA

KINGS PEAK

Vernal

UINTA MTS.

LA SAL MTS.

ABAJO PEAK

GREAT SALT LAKE

SALT LAKE CITY

Logan

Ogden

Provo

GREAT SALT LAKE DESERT

DEEP CREEK RANGE

COLORADO PLATEAU

Price

Green R.

San Juan R.

Colorado R.

Dirty Devil R.

Virgin R.

Cedar City

109°03'

42°

37°

Highest Point
+ 13,498 ft.

345 miles

Rocky Mountains

SALT LAKE CITY

Basin and Range Region

Colorado Plateau

114°03'

269 miles

Nickname: "Beehive State"
Capital: Salt Lake City
Motto: "Industry"
Date admitted to the Union: January 4, 1896
Order of admission as state: 45th
Song: "Utah, We Love Thee"

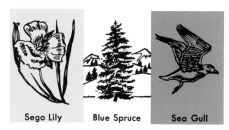

Sego Lily   Blue Spruce   Sea Gull

Physical

AREA: 84,916 square miles, including 2,535 square miles of water; 2.3 percent of total United States; 11th state in size.

POPULATION (1970): 1,059,273; 0.5 percent of total United States; 36th state in population; 12.5 persons per square mile; 80.4 percent urban, 19.6 percent rural.

MOUNTAIN RANGES: Wasatch, Uinta.

CHIEF MOUNTAIN PEAKS (height in feet): Kings Peak (13,528); Hayden Peak (12,473); Marsh Peak (12,219); Nebo (11,877).

LARGEST LAKES: Great Salt, Utah, Bear, Strawberry.

MOST IMPORTANT RIVERS: Colorado, Green, San Rafael, Virgin, Sevier, Bear, Provo, San Juan.

NATIONAL PARKS AND MONUMENTS: Parks: Bryce Canyon, 36,010 acres (established 1928); Canyonlands, 257,640 acres (1964); Zion, 147,035 acres (1919). Monuments: Arches, 82,953 acres (1929); Capitol Reef, 254,242 acres (1937); Cedar Breaks, 6,155 acres (1933); Dinosaur, 206,234 acres in Utah and Colorado (49,494 acres in Utah; 1915); Hovenweep, 505 acres in Utah and Colorado (160 acres in Utah; 1923); Natural Bridges, 7,600 acres (1908); Rainbow Bridge, 160 acres (1910); Timpanogos Cave, 250 acres (1922). Recreation Areas: Glen Canyon, 1,196,545 acres in Utah and Arizona (1,084,578 acres in Utah; 1958); Flaming Gorge, 108,400 acres in Utah and Wyoming (58,000 acres in Utah; 1968).

STATE PARKS: Total of 13, including Brigham Young Winter Home, Dead Horse Point, Dixie, Pioneer Monument (includes "This Is the Place").

INDIAN RESERVATIONS: Navajo, Skull Valley, Goshute, Shivwits, Uinta, and Ouray.

ADDITIONAL PLACES OF INTEREST: Bingham Canyon, Bear River Migratory Bird Refuge, Bonneville Salt Flats.

Transportation and Communication

RAILROADS: 1,725 miles of track; first railroad, California border to Promontory, 1869.

ROADS: Total, 39,439 miles; surfaced, 22,392 miles.

MOTOR VEHICLES: Total, 601,436; automobiles, 468,570; trucks and buses, 132,866.

AIRPORTS: Total, 82; private, 24.

NEWSPAPERS: 5 dailies; 50 weeklies; 4 Sunday; first newspaper, Deseret News, Salt Lake City, 1850.

RADIO STATIONS: 41; first station, KSL, Salt Lake City, 1922.

TELEVISION STATIONS: 8; first station, KTVT, Salt Lake City, 1948.

TELEPHONES: Total 563,700; residence 405,000; business 158,700.

POST OFFICES: 231.

People

CHIEF CITIES: Salt Lake City (175,885); Ogden (69,478); Provo (53,131); Bountiful (27,853); Orem (25,729); Logan (22,333).

NATIONAL BACKGROUNDS: 96.4 percent native-born; 3.6 percent foreign-born.

CHURCH MEMBERSHIP: Of the total state population, 73.5 percent are church members: 4.9 percent Protestant, 5.9 percent Catholic, 88.9 percent Mormon, and 0.3 percent Jewish.

LEADING UNIVERSITIES AND COLLEGES: Brigham Young University, Provo; University of Utah, Salt Lake City; Utah State University, Logan; Weber College, Ogden; Westminster College, Salt Lake City.

MUSEUMS: Daughters of Utah Pioneers Memorial Museum, Salt Lake City; Latter-day Saints Bureau of Information and Museum, Salt Lake City; Springville High School Art Museum, Springville; Field House of Natural History, Vernal, prehistoric exhibits.

SPECIAL SCHOOLS: Utah State Training School (for mentally handicapped children), American Fork; Utah Schools for the Deaf and the Blind, Ogden.

CORRECTIONAL AND PENAL INSTITUTIONS: Utah State Prison, Point of the Mountain; State Industrial School, Ogden.

Government

NUMBER OF U.S. SENATORS: 2.

NUMBER OF U.S. REPRESENTATIVES: 2.

NUMBER OF STATE SENATORS: 28. TERM: 4 years.

NUMBER OF STATE REPRESENTATIVES: 69. TERM: 2 years.

STATE LEGISLATURE CONVENES: January of each year.

SESSION: Regular, 60 days odd years, 20 days even years; special, 30 days.

CONSTITUTION ADOPTED: 1896.

GOVERNOR'S TERM: 4 years. He may succeed himself.

NUMBER OF COUNTIES: 29.

VOTING QUALIFICATIONS: Legal voting age; residence in state 1 year, in county 4 months, in precinct 60 days.

STATE HOLIDAYS: Lincoln's Birthday, February 12; Arbor Day, April 29; Memorial Day, May 30; Pioneer Day, July 24; Columbus Day, October 12.

ANNUAL STATE EVENTS: General Conference of the Latter-day Saints (Mormons), Salt Lake City, April; Days of '47 Celebration, Salt Lake City, July; Ute Indian Sun Dance, Uinta, July; Utah State Fair, Salt Lake City, September.

Historic Events

1776—Fathers Escalante and Dominguez explore Utah region.

1824—James Bridger discovers Great Salt Lake.

1826—Jedediah Smith leads expedition across Utah region.

1832—Antoine Robidoux begins first permanent white settlement in Uinta Basin.

1847—Brigham Young leads group of Mormons into Utah region.

1848—Treaty of Guadalupe Hidalgo ends Mexican War and gives Utah region to U.S.; sea gulls help destroy crop-eating crickets.

1850—Utah Territory is organized.

1863—George Ogilvie registers first mining claim in Utah.

1865–1868—Ute-Black Hawk War.

1867—Mormon Tabernacle is completed in Salt Lake City.

1896—Utah becomes 45th state.

1906—Open-pit copper mining begins at Bingham.

1952—Uranium deposits are discovered near Moab.

1958—Construction begins on Flaming Gorge Dam.

1965—Legislature reapportioned to improve representation.

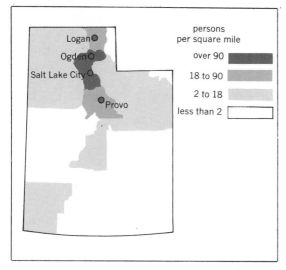

Where the people live.

the foothills of the Uintas.

The first white man known to have seen the Great Salt Lake was James Bridger. In 1824 he boated down the Bear River and part of the way around the Great Salt Lake. Later, Colonel John C. Fremont made two exploration trips into the area for the United States government. Maps and reports from his 1843 expedition helped the Mormons to reach the Great Basin.

The first Mormon pioneers arrived in 1847. Many were New Englanders who had a great interest in education and the arts. Every settlement was planned to include people skilled in every trade needed to build a good town. Mormon converts also came from many nations of northern Europe. This made the population a mixture of nationalities.

People came to Utah from Greece, Italy, Austria, and other southeast European countries to work in the mines and to herd sheep. Many settled near the coal mines in Carbon County. The mines at Park City, 30 miles southeast of Salt Lake City, attracted many Irishmen.

Three-fourths of Utah's people live within 90 miles of Salt Lake City, the largest city and capital. (See SALT LAKE CITY.) Ogden, the second largest city; Provo; and Logan are also northern cities. All have colleges or universities and are industrial centers. Eight other cities have more than 10,000 people: Bountiful, Brigham City, Clearfield, Layton, Murray, Orem, Roy, and Tooele, all in Utah's north-central area.

Smaller interesting cities are: St. George, gateway to the southwest, and Cedar City with its branch agricultural college. Vernal, an important eastern city, is in the Uinta Basin. On the Colorado River, in the far southeast, the little towns of Moab and Monticello are now uranium centers.

How the People Make a Living

Manufacturing. One of the leading occupations in Utah is manufacturing. Many of the manufacturing plants process the resources supplied by the state's farms and mines. About 20 percent of the people who work in manufacturing are employed in industries that process metals and minerals.

One of the nation's leading milling, smelting, and refining regions is in Salt Lake and Tooele counties. United States Steel Corporation's large steel plant at Geneva is among Utah's largest employers.

Copper is processed at a large mill and refinery near Magna. Petroleum is refined at Salt Lake City and North Salt Lake. Mills at Salt Lake City, Mexican Hat, and Moab process uranium.

Earth-moving equipment and other heavy machinery, chemicals, and electronic equipment are manufactured in Salt Lake City. Engines for jet aircraft are made near Ogden. Rocket engines for guided missiles are manufactured west of Brigham City.

The processing of foods is another leading industry. Meat packing is centered at Ogden.

Sources of income.

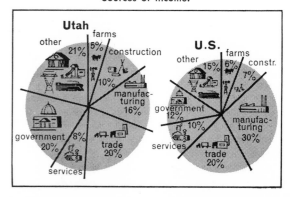

Fruits and vegetables are canned, preserved, and frozen at plants in Cache and Weber counties. In the same area are beet sugar refineries and flour mills.

Other important industries include printing and publishing; the manufacture of stone, clay, glass, wood, petroleum, and coal products; and the making of clothing.

Mining. Also of significance among the ways of earning a living is mining. The state produces about two percent of the value of the nation's mineral production. Metals make up about half of Utah's mineral value; petroleum accounts for nearly one-fifth. The state is among the leaders in production of asphalt, copper, gold, iron ore, lead, molybdenum, potassium, silver, uranium, and vanadium.

Little petroleum was produced in Utah before 1948; however, the presence of oil was known long before. Mormon pioneers used oil from seeps (natural pools on the surface) to grease the axles of their covered wagons.

Petroleum is now the state's leading mineral. The large Aneth field in San Juan County is the leading producer. About 85 percent of Utah's production comes from San Juan County.

Most of the copper produced in Utah comes from Kennecott Copper Corporation's huge open-pit mine in Bingham Canyon. This mine is the world's largest copper producer. More than one-fifth of the copper mined in the United States comes from there. The mine is also an important source of gold, silver, and molybdenum.

Coal lies under about one-fifth of Utah's land surface. Carbon and Emery counties are the leading producers. Much of the coal is used by the steel plant at Geneva. The steel mill also uses iron ore from Iron County and clay from Utah County.

Silver has been produced in about 80 mines. Before 1870 little silver was found. Then the great Silver Reef Mine near St. George started production. About $80,000,000 worth of silver has been taken from that mine. Today silver is worth less to the United States, so many silver mines are closed.

Uranium deposits produce about 733,000 tons of high-grade ore each year. Most of the ore comes from mines in San Juan County.

Utah's sand, gravel, and cement works provide material for roads and homes. Many beautiful buildings throughout the west are decorated with Utah marble and onyx.

Utah has the only known commercial deposit of Gilsonite, which is a variety of asphalt. It must be mined with care, or it will explode. The Gilsonite veins are near the Colorado-Utah border in the area of the Green River. The mineral is shipped as a water solution by pipeline to refineries in Colorado. There it is converted into coke and gasoline.

Agriculture. Most of Utah's farm land is used as pasture for livestock. Sales of livestock and livestock products make up about 80 percent of the yearly farm income. Livestock includes beef and dairy cattle, sheep, hogs, and poultry, especially turkeys.

Field crops are usually grown on irrigated land. Important grain crops are wheat, barley,

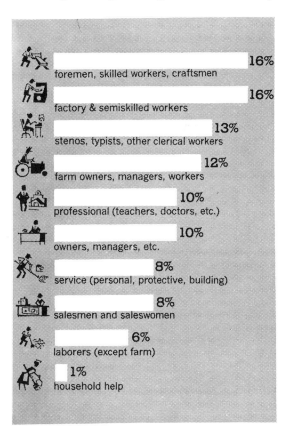

How the people make a living.

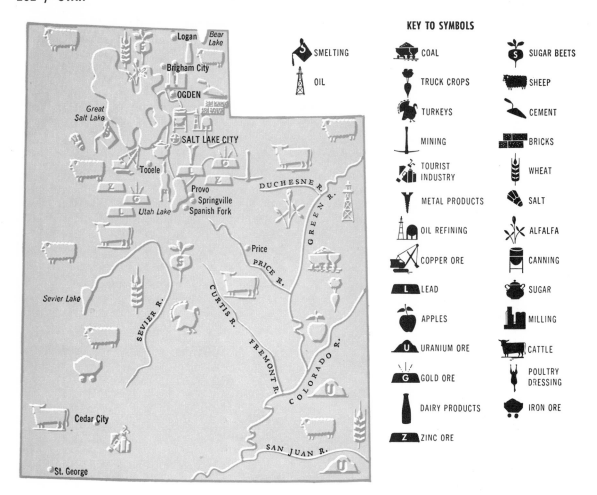

KEY TO SYMBOLS

SMELTING

OIL

COAL

TRUCK CROPS

TURKEYS

MINING

TOURIST INDUSTRY

METAL PRODUCTS

OIL REFINING

COPPER ORE

LEAD

APPLES

URANIUM ORE

GOLD ORE

DAIRY PRODUCTS

ZINC ORE

SUGAR BEETS

SHEEP

CEMENT

BRICKS

WHEAT

SALT

ALFALFA

CANNING

SUGAR

MILLING

CATTLE

POULTRY DRESSING

IRON ORE

Map labels: Logan, Bear Lake, Brigham City, OGDEN, Great Salt Lake, SALT LAKE CITY, Tooele, Provo, Springville, Spanish Fork, Utah Lake, DUCHESNE R., GREEN R., Price, PRICE R., CURTIS R., FREMONT R., COLORADO R., Sevier Lake, SEVIER R., Cedar City, San Juan R., St. George

VALUE OF PRODUCTS
(FIGURES IN $ MILLIONS)

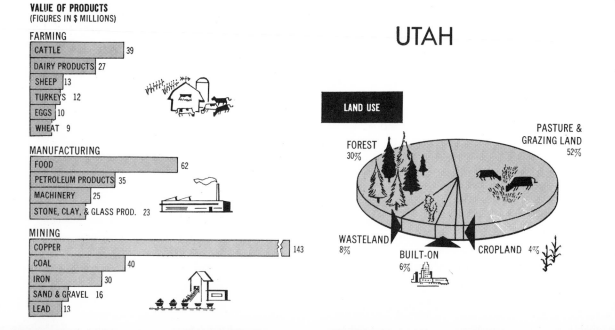

FARMING

CATTLE	39
DAIRY PRODUCTS	27
SHEEP	13
TURKEYS	12
EGGS	10
WHEAT	9

MANUFACTURING

FOOD	62
PETROLEUM PRODUCTS	35
MACHINERY	25
STONE, CLAY, & GLASS PROD.	23

MINING

COPPER	143
COAL	40
IRON	30
SAND & GRAVEL	16
LEAD	13

UTAH

LAND USE

FOREST 30%

PASTURE & GRAZING LAND 52%

WASTELAND 8%

BUILT-ON 6%

CROPLAND 4%

corn, and oats. Large crops of hay, sugar beets, and potatoes are harvested each year. Peas, corn, and tomatoes are raised chiefly for commercial canning.

Cherries, pears, apples, peaches, apricots, and melons are grown on irrigated land. The Uinta Basin produces excellent honey.

Government Employment. More Utah people work for federal, state, or local government than for any private industry. Of almost 60,000 government workers, about one-fifth have defense jobs. Within Utah the United States Department of Defense has an air force base, supply depots, a proving ground, and an air research center. Thousands of people work for the Reclamation Bureau, Forest Service, National Park Service, and many other agencies.

Transportation

Many different types of transportation have been used during Utah's short history. People have traveled on foot and on horseback, by canoe, wagon, prairie schooner, and stagecoach, by railway, automobile, and airplane—all within less than 100 years.

One of the great events of United States railroad history took place in Utah. On May 10, 1869, a golden spike was driven at Promontory, north of Salt Lake City, to complete the first transcontinental railroad. The Union Pacific and the Central Pacific met at that point. (See RAILROAD, *History.*)

The first commercial airplane flight in the western United States took place in 1925. The flight went from Salt Lake City to Los Angeles, California.

Government and Education

Mormon settlers started a government in 1849. They named the provisional state Deseret. In 1850 a territorial government was set up by the United States Congress, and the name was changed to Utah. This government continued until 1896, when Utah became the 45th state.

The government has three branches—executive, legislative, and judicial. The elected executive officers are the governor, secretary of state, treasurer, auditor, and attorney general. Each serves a term of four years.

The legislature is made up of two elected groups of members—the Senate and the House of Representatives. The voters also may take part in making laws by using the powers of initiative and referendum. (See INITIATIVE, REFERENDUM, AND RECALL.)

The state Supreme Court, district, county, and city courts make up the judicial branch.

The people of Utah have encouraged education from the time of settlement in 1847. Schoolhouses were among the first public buildings constructed by the Mormons. In 1860 the territorial government set up the public-school system. The first free school was started six years later at American Fork. School attendance is required of children from ages 6 to 18.

The state supports nine colleges and universities. Among these is the University of Utah (Salt Lake City), set up in 1850 by the territorial legislature. It was first called the University of Deseret. The Mormon church supports three institutions of higher learning—the largest is Brigham Young University at Provo. Among the many other private schools the largest is Westminster College at Salt Lake City. The Intermountain School for Indians at Brigham City is the largest of its kind in the United States.

Religion

About 75 percent of Utah's people are church members. Of these, about 89 per cent are members of the Church of Jesus Christ of Latter-day Saints (Mormons). Salt Lake City, world center of Mormonism, has many religious and historic buildings linked with this church. In Temple Square are the large and beautiful Mormon Temple, the Tabernacle with its world-famous organ, the Assembly Hall, and the Museum. (See MORMONISM.)

Health, Welfare, and Recreation

The state's Department of Public Health program for handicapped children is one of the finest in the country. The state supports a tuberculosis hospital in Ogden and a mental hospital at Provo. The Utah State Training School at American Fork is for the mentally handicapped.

Good crop yields are possible in Utah with irrigation.

Useful trades are taught at the Utah Schools for the Deaf and the Blind at Ogden, at the Vocational School and Commission for the Blind at Salt Lake City, and at the Central Utah Vocational School at Provo.

Utah's many kinds of recreation attract more than 4,000,000 vacationers each year. Many tourists enjoy the drive along the Alpine Scenic Loop, or visit the old Alta mining camp; Bingham Canyon with its huge copper mine; the Flaming Gorge Dam; and the motion-picture

Alta, in the Wasatch Range, provides excellent skiing.

locations at Kanab, Cedar City, and St. George, where "westerns" are filmed.

Racing is a spectacular sport at the Bonneville Salt Flats. World speed records for land travel of more than 600 miles per hour have been set at the Salt Flats.

History

The settlement of Utah was part of the great westward movement of pioneers. (See WESTWARD MOVEMENT.) The original pioneer company of about 150 people, under the leadership of Brigham Young, entered the Salt Lake Valley in July of 1847. They were members of the Church of Jesus Christ of Latter-day Saints.

The route of the Mormon migration followed the Oregon Trail as far as the eastern front of the Wasatch Mountains. The Mormons then turned southwest and struggled through the high passes to the Salt Lake Valley. (See TRAILS, U.S. HISTORIC.)

On their first day in the valley, the men turned the water from a canyon stream onto the land. The water ran in the first irrigation canals dug by white men in Utah. Within the first six weeks the pioneers built a fort for protection from the Indians. By October 2,000 Mormons had arrived in Utah.

More than once the early pioneers felt their lives depended upon God. For this reason, they have made much of the "miracle of the gulls." In 1848, the first spring after their arrival, the Mormons planted large crops. The lives of everyone depended on the success of these first crops. In late spring great hordes of crickets swarmed down from the foothills. They attacked the new crops, and the people could see that soon all of the wheat and corn would be eaten.

Men, women, and children beat the crickets with brush brooms; they made fires to burn and smoke them out; they swept them into long ditches and buried them—but still the crickets came. The people knelt in the fields and prayed for help. Suddenly the sky was filled with the bright, white wings of sea gulls soaring in from the Great Salt Lake. The birds devoured the crickets, and enough wheat was spared to save the people. In memory of this event the Mormons built the beautiful Sea Gull Monument in Temple Square, Salt Lake City.

In 1848 the colonizers planned the first civil government of the mountain area. The following year a constitution was drawn up for the provisional state of Deseret. Brigham Young was elected governor.

By 1850 there were about 27 settlements and more than 11,000 people in the region. In that year the provisional state became the Utah Territory of the United States. Young continued as governor until 1857.

In 1869 the transcontinental railroad was completed, and the famous Wells, Fargo and Company's horse-drawn coaches gave way to the engine-drawn coach. The mining industry grew rapidly during the next 20 years. Deposits of gold, silver, lead, zinc, iron ore, and copper had been found in the 1850's and 1860's, but few minerals were produced in large amounts before rail transportation arrived.

On January 4, 1896, Utah became the 45th state to join the Union.

During the early 1900's the building of smelters at Magna, Tooele, Garfield, and Murray made Utah one of the world's leading smelting regions.

In 1943 the Geneva steel plant was built as a part of the World War II expansion program. Since that time Utah has filled an important position in the defense plans of the nation. The United States Defense Department has seven large installations in Utah. Utah is also important to the nation's defense as a leading source of uranium. This mineral is used in the production of nuclear power.

Conservation of water and the reclamation of land have been a great part of the history of Utah. (See LAND RECLAMATION.) The Strawberry Valley Project, built during 1912–1916, supplies water for more than 42,000 acres. Other projects completed or under construction in the 1960's include the Upper Colorado River Storage Project, the Weber Basin Project, Glen Canyon Project, Flaming Gorge Project, Central Utah Project, and Emery County Project. These huge reservoirs and dams, which will enable the state to have more irrigated farmland, hydroelectric power, and recreation area, are the key to Utah's future economic growth.

Courtesy Salt Lake City Chamber of Commerce

Sea gulls saved the first crops of Mormon pioneers. The gulls are honored by this monument in Salt Lake City. The Mormon Temple is in the background.

UTOPIA (ū tō′pē ä) is an ideal, imaginary place or state of mind. A utopian society has perfect political, economic, and social conditions.

Sir Thomas More, an English writer, told of such a place in his book *Utopia* (1516), first published in Latin. In it, More described a perfect island country that he named *Utopia* from the Greek meaning "no place." As with most writings on utopias, the book was actually a criticism of the conditions of the time.

More borrowed his idea for *Utopia* from the *Republic*, written by the Greek philosopher Plato. (See PLATO.) Many other books have been written about utopias. The best known are Samuel Butler's *Erewhon* (an almost reverse spelling of *nowhere*) (1872); Edward Bellamy's *Looking Backward* (1888), about a socialistic utopia in Boston in A.D. 2000; and James Hilton's *Lost Horizon* (1933), about the mythical country of Shangri-La.

UZBEK (uz′běk) **SOVIET SOCIALIST REPUBLIC, U.S.S.R.,** is one of the largest and most important republics of Soviet Central Asia. The republic, which is also called Uzbekistan, is the principal cotton-producing area in the Soviet Union. It is bordered by the Kazakh Soviet Socialist Republic (S.S.R.) to the north and west, the Turkmen S.S.R. and Afghanistan to the south, and the Tadzhik S.S.R. and Kirghiz S.S.R. to the east. The republic has an area of 174,170 square miles.

Most of Uzbek S.S.R. is a sandy desert lowland. The part west of the Aral Sea rises to the Ust-Urt Plateau, and in the east it extends into the foothills and valleys of the Tien Shan and Alay mountains. The streams that flow from these mountains provide water for the irrigation of desert land. They include the Amu-Darya, Syr-Darya, and Zeravshan rivers and their tributaries.

Uzbek summers are extremely hot and dry. Winters are generally cold and cloudy. Precipitation averages between 4 and 8 inches a year, except in the mountains.

Irrigation agriculture is the most important activity in Uzbekistan. The long, hot summers are exceptionally favorable for growing cotton, rice, and the mulberry trees that are necessary for the production of silk. Uzbekistan also produces wheat, cattle, and Karakul sheep.

Industrial plants in various Uzbekistan cities process the locally produced cotton, silk, and other agricultural products and ship them to all parts of the Soviet Union. Tashkent, the capital and largest city, manufactures agricultural

Locator map of Uzbek S.S.R.

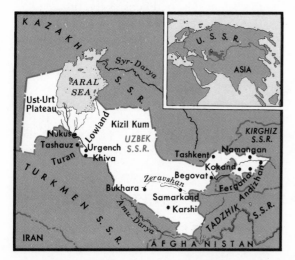

and other heavy machinery. It is also a major Soviet cultural, educational, and transportation center for Central Asia. (See TASHKENT.) Chirchik is the site of a hydroelectric station and a large plant that produces mineral fertilizers and other chemicals. Samarkand and Bukhara are educational and textile centers. Other major cities include Andizhan, Namangan, Kokand, and Fergana.

The Uzbek republic has a well developed railroad system that connects all the important inhabited areas. Tashkent is the principal air center of Soviet Central Asia. The Uzbek S.S.R. is relatively poor in mineral resources.

Uzbekistan has a history that dates back to the pre-Christian era. Samarkand was a thriving capital city when captured by Alexander the Great in the 4th century B.C. It was later invaded and ruled by various Asian groups, including the Arabs, Turks, and Mongols. It reached its height of glory as the capital of Tamerlane, or Timur, in the 14th century. (See TAMERLANE.) At that time the city became a world famous cultural center with schools, a college, and an astronomical observatory. Many of the beautifully decorated buildings that were built during the period are still preserved. Among the most famous are several Muslim mosques and the tomb of Tamerlane.

Bukhara early became a trading center for caravan routes from distant areas of Asia. Bukhara, Kokand, and Khiva became the capital cities of three separate Muslim states. These states were forcibly incorporated into the Russian Empire in the second half of the 19th century. In 1924, the Soviet government established the Uzbek area as one of the union republics of the U.S.S.R.

One-third of the population lives in cities. Three-fifths of the inhabitants are Uzbeks, a Muslim group of Turkic people, who have been long engaged in agriculture. Russians, with 14 percent of the total, are the second largest group. Most Russians live in the larger cities. Other important groups are the Tatars, Kazakhs, Tadzhiks, and Kara-Kalpaks.

In 1970, the population of the republic was 11,963,000, a 45 percent increase over the population of 1959.

VALENTINE'S (*văl'ĕn tīnz*) **DAY,** February 14, is a special day for honoring sweethearts. This custom is very old. It may go back to Roman times when a special festival, called the Lupercalia, was held on February 15. On that day all the young girls put their names in a box and each young man drew out a name to pick his sweetheart for the next year.

During the Middle Ages February 14 was the date when people believed birds found their mates. So the day was set aside to honor all lovers. The people found new ways of celebrating the day. For example, they used to kiss the "first-met," the first young woman whom a young man happened to meet on that day.

By chance this special festival for sweethearts came on St. Valentine's Day, a day that honors several Christian saints named Valentine. But the idea of honoring sweethearts has nothing to do with the saints for whom the day is named.

In the 19th century the custom began of sending valentines, pretty decorated cards or pieces of paper, to the boy or girl one liked best. Often these young couples exchanged gifts as well. Then the idea of sending comic valentines became popular. Today Valentine's Day is most important for children. They usually send valentines to many friends, not just to one.

VALPARAISO (*văl'pä rā'zō*), **CHILE,** is a large city on the Pacific Coast of central Chile. The city, on a small sheltered bay, is the most important seaport for the fertile Valley of Chile, where most of the country's people live. The name of Valparaiso means "Valley of Paradise."

Valparaiso is second in size and importance only to Santiago, the capital. It is one of the largest seaports on the west coast of South America and the second-largest industrial center of Chile, manufacturing such products as foodstuffs, clothing, furniture, cement, and boats.

The city is built on the steep slopes of the coastal range of the Andes Mountains. The business district is on the waterfront, and large homes are at a higher level. Most of the laborers live still farther up the hillsides. Elevators carry people up the slopes, and winding streets and paths have also been built. Important public institutions include the Naval Academy and the Santa Maria Technical University.

Founded in 1536, Valparaiso grew slowly. In 1906 the city was almost destroyed by an earthquake. It was rebuilt, however, and had a population of 252,865 in 1960.

VAN BUREN (*văn bū'rĕn*), **MARTIN** (1782–1862), was the eighth president of the United States. In a long political career he held many offices: New York State legislature, United States Senate, governorship of New York, secretary of state, vice-president of the United States, and finally the presidency from 1837 to 1841. So skilled was he in politics that he was called the "Little Magician." He helped to start and organize the modern Democratic party.

Martin Van Buren was born on December 5, 1782, in the village of Kinderhook in the Hudson Valley of New York. He was the third of five children of Abraham and Maria Van Buren. Martin's parents ran a tavern in Kinderhook. He received his earliest education helping his father run the tavern and listening to the customers' talk.

Young Van Buren attended the village schools. After graduation, at the age of 14, he became a clerk in the office of a local lawyer. He finished his training in a law office in New York City. In 1803 he returned to Kinderhook and began the practice of law. In 1807 he married his sweetheart Hannah Hoes. Four sons were born before her death in 1819.

Political Career

Like his father, young Martin became active in the Republican party of Thomas Jefferson. Van Buren started his long political career with his appointment as surrogate of Columbia County (1808). A surrogate was an important county official. In 1812 he was elected to the Senate of New York. Within ten years he had gained control of the New York Republican party. His success was due to his personality and to his skill at political organization.

After the War of 1812 the Federalist party began to disappear. Many former Federalists

Library of Congress

Martin Van Buren, U.S. President, 1837–1841.

joined the Republican party. Nationally the period 1817–1825 is called the "Era of Good Feeling" because there was only one political party ruling the nation. But in New York the Republican party was divided into several quarreling groups.

Van Buren became the leader of the Republican group opposed to DeWitt Clinton and his followers. He organized a political machine called the Albany Regency. In it were a group of able political leaders who controlled the party. Those who supported the Regency were given political jobs. Those who opposed them were removed. This use of the "spoils system" helped make a strong party in New York. In 1821 the New York legislature elected Van Buren to the United States Senate. (In those days the people did not vote for senators.)

The presidential election of 1824 was unusual. There were four leading candidates: John Quincy Adams, Henry Clay, William H. Crawford, and Andrew Jackson. Van Buren supported Crawford, but when the votes were

counted Jackson had the most electoral votes. However, since he did not have a majority, the House of Representatives had to choose from the three highest candidates: Jackson, Adams, and Crawford. According to the Constitution, in a House election each state has one vote. Van Buren tried to persuade the New York congressmen to vote for Crawford, but Adams received their vote. Adams won the election and became president.

Van Buren was re-elected senator in 1827. By this time he was turning to Jackson as his choice for the presidency in the next election. He may have thought that he could use the popular general to reorganize his political party and defeat Adams. Van Buren ran for governor of New York in 1828, the same year that Jackson defeated Adams for the presidency. When Jackson picked Van Buren as secretary of state, he resigned as governor. In 1831 Van Buren resigned as secretary of state and Jackson next appointed him minister to England. However, the Senate, which had to approve the appointment, refused to accept him.

When Jackson ran for re-election in 1832 Van Buren was his running mate. They won the election in a landslide. During his term as vice-president, Van Buren supported Jackson. In turn, Jackson made it clear that Van Buren was his choice for the next presidential nomination. A convention of the party (now called Democrats) nominated him for the presidency in May 1835.

Presidency

In the election of 1836 Van Buren was opposed by a number of candidates. The enemies of Jackson now formed a new party called the Whigs. (See WHIG PARTY.) They could not agree upon one candidate for the presidency and so ran a number of candidates, each of whom

Hannah Van Buren.

Culver Service

was strong in some part of the country. Although the popular vote was extremely close, Van Buren received a majority of the electoral votes.

The chief event of Van Buren's presidency was the disastrous Panic of 1837. At the time of the election, business was booming. Many people were buying and selling land in the hope of making a quick profit. Canals and railroads were being built. Much of this prosperity was based on loans from banks. Suddenly in 1837 the boom collapsed. Many banks and businesses failed. It was the most serious depression in the country's history. The idea that it was the government's job to help fight a depression did not exist at that time. Van Buren believed that the depression would have to work its way out.

The most important measure proposed by Van Buren was the "Independent Treasury" or "Subtreasury" system. While president, Jackson had destroyed the Bank of the United States, which was a corporation in which the government held stock. (See JACKSON, ANDREW.) Van Buren wanted to break the connection between the banks and the federal government. By his plan all government money would be placed in an independent treasury in Washington, D.C., and in certain subtreasuries throughout the country.

In the field of foreign affairs Van Buren was faced by troubles caused by a rebellion in Canada. Many supporters of the Canadian rebellion gathered on the United States side of the Niagara frontier. War with Great Britain threatened. Van Buren urged United States citizens to be neutral and sent General Winfield Scott to the border to preserve peace. Gradually the crisis passed. There was also a dispute over the location of the border between Canada and Maine. It was called the Aroostook War, although there was no fighting.

The Whigs blamed the Democrats for the Panic of 1837 and looked to the election of 1840 with confidence. They nominated General William Henry Harrison, who had defeated the Indians at the Battle of Tippecanoe in 1811. For vice-president their candidate was John Tyler of Virginia.

The campaign was something new in American politics. Few people talked about the issues. The parties held huge meetings and parades. Whigs chanted, "Tippecanoe and Tyler too," and, "Little Van's a used up man." Harrison was called the champion of the common people, while Van Buren was labeled an aristocrat. The election results were 234 electoral votes for Harrison and 60 for Van Buren.

After the Presidency

Van Buren returned to Lindenwald, his farm in Kinderhook, expecting to be the Democratic candidate for president in 1844. Henry Clay expected to be the choice of the Whigs. Many people favored joining, or annexing, Texas to the United States. Some were against annexation because of fear of war with Mexico and because Texas would mean more slave territory in the Union. Both Clay and Van Buren published letters opposing annexation without the consent of Mexico. The Democratic nominating convention favored expansion, and picked James K. Polk instead of Van Buren.

The "Little Magician" returned to New York where he became involved in a split in the New York State Democratic party. The slavery question was becoming important and in 1848 the

VAN BUREN'S LIFETIME

1782	Van Buren born.
1783	American Revolution ends.
1803	Louisiana Purchase.
1808	Van Buren a surrogate.
1812	War with England.
	Van Buren state senator.
1815	Van Buren attorney general of N.Y.
1820	Missouri Compromise.
1821	Van Buren U.S. senator.
1825	Erie Canal opened.
1829	Van Buren secretary of state.
1830	1st passenger railroad.
1831	Van Buren resigns.
1832	Nullification issue.
1833	Van Buren vice-president.
1836	Texas revolt.
PRESIDENT	
1846	Mexican War.
1848	Van Buren Free-Soil candidate.
1861	U.S. Civil War.
1862	Van Buren dies.

Van Buren's Term of Office (1837–1841)

1837	Business panic. Rebellion in Canada. Capture of Osceola. Murder of Elijah Lovejoy. Chicago becomes a city.
1838	Underground Railroad. Aroostook War in Maine.
1839	1st baseball game. Goodyear vulcanizes rubber. Teachers' training school in Massachusetts.
1840	Population passes 17,000,000. Independent Treasury Act. Liberty party formed. Van Buren defeated by Harrison.

antislavery Democrats nominated Van Buren for the presidency. Later, antislavery people from all parties organized the Free-Soil party and chose Van Buren to be their candidate. (See FREE-SOIL PARTY.) He did not win any electoral votes in the election.

As events of the 1850's led to war, Van Buren hoped that the Union could be saved. When war came he supported Lincoln. He died on July 24, 1862, at Lindenwald.

Van Buren's United States

The desire to expand was becoming a real force in the country during the time of Martin Van Buren. A few people had made the long trip to the Oregon country before he became president. Within two years after he left the White House, large wagon trains were moving along the Oregon Trail. To the southwest Texas was an independent country asking for admittance as a state. (See TEXAS.) In Florida the Seminole Indians were on the warpath, but in 1837 Osceola, their leader, was captured. (See OSCEOLA.)

The slavery question was exciting people. Those who believed in doing away with slavery (abolitionists) became more active. (See ABOLITIONISTS.) At times violence broke out. In Alton, Illinois, in 1837, a proslavery mob murdered abolitionist Elijah Lovejoy. In 1840 the Liberty party was formed as the first Abolitionist political party. The Underground Railroad was helping slaves escape to Canada.

In literature Washington Irving and James Fenimore Cooper were writing. Ralph Waldo Emerson was questioning many religious ideas. The first photograph in the United States was taken, and Charles Goodyear, an inventor, was experimenting with processes for vulcanizing rubber. Some workers were making progress in having only a ten-hour working day. In Massachusetts Horace Mann founded the first teachers' training school. Chicago became a city in 1837.

VANCOUVER (*văn ko͞o′vẽr*), **BRITISH CO-LUMBIA.** Vancouver is the largest city in British Columbia and the third largest in Canada. It covers an area of 45 square miles.

Courtesy National Film Board

British Columbia produces millions of board feet of lumber each year. Much of it goes to Vancouver for export.

Vancouver is on the Pacific Coast, about 18 miles north of the state of Washington. Westward, across the Gulf of Georgia, rise the mountains of Vancouver Island and to north and east the mountains of the Coast Range.

The city is a shipping and manufacturing center. Its people work in offices, shipyards, factories, grain elevators, fish and fruit canneries, oil refineries, sawmills, and wood veneer plants. It is the largest wheat shipping port on the Pacific Coast of North America.

The busy freight yards and port used by many steamship lines show how Vancouver lives up to its motto: "By sea and land we prosper." It is at the end of the Canadian Pacific, Canadian National, and Pacific Great Eastern railways. In addition, it has the busy international airport on Sea Island.

Most of Vancouver's people are of British descent, but there are large groups of Chinese, Japanese, Sikhs (from northern India), Scandinavians, Germans, Ukranians, and Poles.

In the heart of the city is Stanley Park, 1,000 acres of forests, playing fields, and beaches. The stadium, which was built in Exhibition Park for the British Empire Games held in 1954, is the largest in Canada. On the peninsula of Point Grey, in the western part of the city, is the University of British Columbia. It is the second largest university in Canada.

In 1792 Captain George Vancouver sailed into Burrard Inlet. The first settlers came about 70 years later. They were prospectors who had failed to find gold. By 1880 Vancouver was no more than a few wooden houses near a sawmill in the forest. In 1885 Vancouver became the western end of the Canadian Pacific Railway, and the city was created in 1886. The settlement, which had been called Gastown and later Granville, became known as Vancouver. In 1891 it became a world port with Canadian Pacific steamship service to the Orient. The gold rush of the 1890's speeded the city's growth.

The population is 410,375 in the city proper and 892,286 in the metropolitan area (1966).

VANCOUVER ISLAND, BRITISH COLUMBIA.

Vancouver Island is the largest island on the west coast of the Americas. It is 285 miles long with an area of 12,408 square miles. On its rugged west coast is the Pacific Ocean. On the south it is divided from the United States by Juan de Fuca Strait. Its eastern boundary is the Gulf of Georgia, and its northern is Queen Charlotte Sound.

Ages ago the island was part of a chain of mountains reaching as far north as Alaska. Volcanic action sank some of the mountains beneath the ocean, leaving many islands. The highest peaks on Vancouver Island, the Golden Hinde, Mount Elkhorn, and Victoria Peak, stand more than 7,000 feet above sea level. Because they rise sharply from the sea, they appear higher.

The climate of Vancouver Island is generally milder than that on the mainland of British Columbia. This is because of the warming effect of the ocean. Rainfall is very heavy along the west coast, where several points have from 100 to 160 inches yearly. The eastern and southeastern coasts receive less, Victoria having as little as 27 inches.

Coniferous (evergreen) trees grow very large in the mild, wet climate of Vancouver Island. This makes the lumber industry important to the island. When the trees have

Locator map of Vancouver Island.

been cut down, the logs are hauled to large sawmills at Port Alberni, Chemainus, Victoria, and other points along the coast. There are pulp and paper mills at Port Alberni, Nanaimo, Port Alice, and other centers. Plywood and shingles are also important products of the forests. Hydroelectric power for the forest industries and for cities and towns is developed near Campbell River and Jordan River. Some electricity is carried from the mainland across the Gulf of Georgia by submarine cables.

Farming is carried on in several fertile areas of Vancouver Island. There are many dairy farms in the Duncan and Courtenay districts. Most of the daffodils and other bulbs grown in Canada are raised in the Saanich Peninsula north of Victoria. This area is also noted for its small fruits, poultry, and fur farms.

Mining became an important industry in the Nanaimo district after the discovery of coal in 1852. But the only large coal mine in operation at present is at Tsable River, 60 miles north of Nanaimo. Salmon brought in by fishing vessels are canned in plants along the coast.

Victoria is the main city on the island and capital of the province. (See VICTORIA, BRITISH COLUMBIA.) Nanaimo, with a population of 15,188 (1966) is the point where buses, trucks, and trains meet vessels from Vancouver, 36 miles across the gulf. Port Alberni, on an inlet from the Pacific Ocean, has 13,755 people. Like

Courtesy Canadian Consulate General of Chicago; photo, R.C.A.F.

Victoria, showing the Parliament Buildings (lower left) facing the Inner Harbor.

Nanaimo it is a lumbering and pulp and paper milling center.

The island was discovered in 1774 by the Spaniard Juan Perez. Captain James Cook's visit in 1778 gave the British claim to the region. It was managed by the Hudson's Bay Company until 1849, when it was made a British crown colony. In 1866 it united with British Columbia. (See BRITISH COLUMBIA.)

The population of the island is 333,951 (1966).

VANDALS (văn′dŭlz) were one of the several groups of Teutonic tribes who helped to destroy the Roman Empire. They came originally from the basin of the Oder, where they spent their time fighting the Goths and the Lombards. In the time of Constantine I they were defeated by the Goths. The Vandals were allowed by the Romans to settle as a subject people in a region known as Pannonia which included the northeastern part of the present Austria and the western part of Hungary.

They remained in Pannonia for about 60 years. Then the nation emigrated to Gaul. The Franks defeated them and in A.D. 409 the Vandals, under the leadership of Gunderic, crossed the Pyrenees into Spain. The Silingian Vandals settled in Andalusia, and the Asdingians in Galicia. The Silingians were wiped out by the Goths and the armies of the empire. The Asdingians prospered. They finally marched across Spain and took the place of their kindred in Andalusia.

In 428 or 429 Bonifacius, the count of Africa, who was having a quarrel with his government at Rome, invited the Vandals to settle in his province. More than 80,000 of them went over to Africa under their king Genseric. Bonifacius soon found that his guests were more to be feared than the Romans, and asked them to return to Spain, but it was too late. The Vandals proceeded to conquer northern Africa for themselves. By 430 only the cities of Carthage, Hippo, and Cirta were holding out against them. In 435 they made a treaty with Rome under which Carthage and the surrounding province were to remain Roman. The Vandals were to occupy the other six provinces.

Genseric did not observe the treaty. In 439

he seized Carthage and reigned over all Roman Africa. He was more interested in robbery than he was in making conquests. He persecuted the Catholic Christians, looted and burned the churches, and tortured the priests until they revealed the hiding places of the church treasures. In 455 Eudoxia, widow of the Emperor Valentinian, made the same mistake as Bonifacius. She invited Genseric to give her his support at Rome. Genseric occupied the city, and looted it for 14 days. There was no resistance, so he did not burn the city or harm the buildings. He simply took back to Africa everything that was not nailed down, including Eudoxia and her daughters. This exploit had much to do with making the term "vandal" mean one who destroys precious things he is too rude to appreciate—even though the Vandals actually did not destroy in such fashion.

In 477 Genseric was succeeded by his son Hunneric. Hilderic, who became king in 523, was a Catholic, and restored the bishops to their churches. He was unpopular, and his warlike cousin Gelimer deposed and imprisoned him. This gave the Emperor Justinian a chance to intervene. Belisarius landed in Africa at the head of a Byzantine army in 533. One Vandal army was away in Sardinia, but he beat the other and entered Carthage. When the Sardinian army returned, the Vandals met him with their full strength at Tricameron. After a stubborn battle they were defeated, and Gelimer took to flight, surrendering in 534. Many of the Vandals were taken into the Byzantine army and the rest disappeared from history.

VANDERBILT (*văn′dẽr bĭlt*) **FAMILY.** Among the most prominent of United States families are the Vanderbilts, whose stupendous fortunes were made in steamboat and railroad transportation. The most important members of the family are described in this article.

CORNELIUS VANDERBILT (1794–1877). At the age of 16, Cornelius Vanderbilt borrowed $100 from his mother and bought a sailing boat. He used it as a ferry from Staten Island, New York, his birthplace, to New York City. With that as a start, he amassed a fortune of $100,000,000. He made $20,000,000 in his lines of steamboats, from which came his title of "Commodore." At the age of 50 he began to purchase the stock of the New York and Harlem Railway. His interests in railroads increased, and about 1864 he withdrew his capital from the steamship lines, and in 12 years made $80,000,000 in railroads. The "Vanderbilt system" of railroads included the New York Central and Hudson River Railroad, and the Lake Shore and Michigan Central. When the *Merrimac* threatened Federal shipping in the War Between the States he offered the government the use of his swiftest steamer. Later he gave $1,000,000 to endow Vanderbilt University at Nashville, Tennessee.

WILLIAM HENRY VANDERBILT (1821–1885). The son of Cornelius Vanderbilt, William Henry Vanderbilt began work as a bank clerk at a salary of $150 a year, which was rapidly raised to $1,000. When his health gave way, his father bought him a farm on Staten Island, from which he earned a comfortable living for 20 years. When he was made receiver for the Staten Island Railroad, he proved an able executive, speedily clearing off the debt. Vanderbilt established a ferry service to New York City. He succeeded his father as president of the New York Central, and added to the Vanderbilt system the West Shore and the Nickel Plate railroads, becoming one of the greatest authorities in the world on transportation. He inherited $85,000,000 and left $200,000,000.

CORNELIUS VANDERBILT II (1843–1899). The eldest son of William Henry Vanderbilt, from whom he inherited $50,000,000, Cornelius Vanderbilt II was educated by private tutors and began his business life as a bank clerk, but later took up railroading. He was a director in more than 30 railroads, and gave generously to many institutions. Rosa Bonheur's "Horse Fair" was his gift to the Metropolitan Museum, New York.

WILLIAM KISSAM VANDERBILT (1849–1920). The second son of William Henry Vanderbilt, from whom he inherited $50,000,000, William Kissam Vanderbilt was educated at Geneva, Switzerland, and began his career as a bookkeeper, but soon went into the family business. He was director of 14 railroads besides other industrial companies. William K. Vanderbilt, with his brothers, presented the $250,000 Kissam Hall to Vanderbilt University in memory of their mother.

GEORGE WASHINGTON VANDERBILT (1862–1914). The third son of William Henry Vanderbilt, George Washington Vanderbilt was noted for his many gifts to schools and colleges, and for his 120,000-acre estate Biltmore, at Asheville, North Carolina, where, in 1892, Gifford Pinchot conducted experiments in forestry and agriculture.

CORNELIUS VANDERBILT III (1873–1942). The son of Cornelius Vanderbilt II, Brigadier General Cornelius Vanderbilt III was graduated from Yale in 1895. He was a colonel of United States Army Engineers in 1917, and was director of many banks, railroads, and insurance companies.

VAN DYCK (*văn dīk'*), SIR ANTHONY (1599–1641). The Flemish artist, Sir Anthony Van Dyck, was one of the world's greatest masters of the art of portrait painting. Many people are familiar with Van Dyck's courtly ladies and

Portrait of Sir Thomas Hanmer, cupbearer to Charles I, painted by Anthony Van Dyck.
Courtesy the Cleveland Museum of Art, John L. Severance Collection

gentlemen, robed in silk and velvet, and bedecked with fine laces and gold chains. He also did some religious, historical, and mythological paintings.

Van Dyck was born in Antwerp, Belgium, the seventh of 12 children. His father was a well-to-do merchant of that city. When the boy was a little over ten he was apprenticed to a painter. Before he was 19 he was a full member of the Antwerp Guild of Painters. For a few years he worked in the studio of Peter Paul Rubens. Then he set out for Italy where he spent the greater part of the next five years studying especially the great Venetian masters. There, too, he painted many of the portraits of beautiful ladies and proud nobles which are found in all the great galleries of the world. Returning to Antwerp in 1628 he came under the influence of Rubens and painted many religious paintings, although as court painter he was still doing many portraits.

In 1632 at the invitation of King Charles I he went to England, where he became court painter, and was knighted. He painted numerous portraits of the king, the queen, their children, and the nobility of England. The portrait of "Charles I on Horseback" now in the Louvre, Paris, is an excellent example of Van Dyck's finest work. It is a splendid character painting of the King, with a spirited horse, figures, and detailed background. In Dresden is the widely known picture of the three children of Charles I, in which the artist shows their innocence and grace with a sure and delicate touch. "Christ Crucified Between the Two Thieves" is in the Antwerp gallery. It is his greatest religious painting, and one of the world's masterpieces. He is well represented in the galleries of the United States.

Charles granted Van Dyck a pension, besides paying him for the many portraits he painted. Van Dyck also made much money from other commissions. He lived very extravagantly and luxuriously, and contracted many debts. At the time of his death he was without means and broken in health.

In his use of color, his elegance, and the ease with which he painted, Van Dyck was a master. He ranks next to Titian (Tiziano Vecellio) as a portrait painter. As a painter of refinement, polish, and distinction, and as a master of dress, furniture, and other externals, he was unexcelled.

VAN GOGH (*vän gŏκ*), VINCENT (*vĭn sĕnt'*)

(1853–1890), was one of the great Dutch masters of painting. Although his painting career lasted only ten years, he made about 800 oil paintings and 700 drawings. Everything in Van Gogh's pictures seems to be moving and alive.

Van Gogh was born at Groot Zundert, in the Netherlands. His father was a Protestant minister and when Van Gogh was a young man he felt he too should enter the religious life. After studying theology he did missionary work among the miners at Wasmes, Belgium. But his free time he spent in drawing and he finally went to Brussels, Belgium, to study art. After this, he spent several years on his father's farm painting simple peasant scenes, the moorlands, and still life. "The Potato Eaters" is the chief work of this period. It is a study of a group of laborers seated at a table beneath a lamp. Under the lamplight their faces show all the misery and dullness of their lives.

Later in Paris he became interested in the Impressionist school of painting. He stopped painting with dull browns and umbers and began to use the clear, bright colors that are found in his later work. After two years in Paris he settled at Arles in Provence. There he painted the fruit trees all aglow with sunlight; the great sunflowers; the plain room in which he lived, and a portrait of himself with his strange, restless blue eyes.

He always looked for color and more color. He even tried to show shape, weight, and the feeling of a landscape through his use of color. In his last years he had periods of insanity, and finally killed himself. During his lifetime his brother Theo was the only one who believed in his art and helped him. (For an example of his work, see Plate 22 in the article PAINTING.)

VAN HORNE (*văn hôrn'*), SIR WILLIAM COR-NELIUS

(1843–1915), is given much of the credit for building the Canadian Pacific Railway. He did his work so well that the railway was opened five years ahead of schedule.

Van Horne was born near Joliet, Illinois. At the age of 14 he went to work as a telegraph operator. In the following years he worked for many railroads as ticket agent, dispatcher, and general manager. In 1880 he was made general superintendent of the Chicago, Milwaukee and St. Paul, then the largest system in the United States. A year later he became general manager of the Canadian Pacific. He shared with Lord Strathcona the job of building a transcontinental railway across the plains and through the Rocky Mountains.

Under his direction, 500 miles of line were built in 1882. In 1885, when a rebellion started among the half-breeds and Indians, troops were needed in western Canada. Van Horne said that he could move troops and supplies from Quebec to the Saskatchewan River in ten days' time by an all-Canadian route. The authorities laughed, but he went ahead with his plans. He laid rails on a roadbed that was in some places formed only of ice or snow. The soldiers rode in large sleighs where there were no rails. The trip took only four days.

It was for such services that he was made president of the railway company in 1888, and that in 1896 he was knighted by Queen Victoria. He retired as president of the railroad in 1899. In 1902 he completed a 350-mile railroad in Cuba, and in 1908 he finished a railroad in Guatemala.

VANILLA (*vä nĭl'ä*)

is a flavoring agent used in chocolate, ice cream, candy, and in cooking. It is sometimes used in perfume and soap, and once was used in medicine.

Vanilla flavoring or extract is made from vanilla beans. The vine which bears the long vanilla beans belongs to the orchid family. Its bell-shaped flowers are a greenish yellow; the leaves are broad. Its slender yellow pods or beans contain an oily black pulp full of tiny black seeds. The name means "little pod" in Spanish.

The vanilla vine grows in rich lowlands where the air is damp and hot, and the soil is loose. It is native to Mexico, but it is also grown in Madagascar, the West Indies, Java, and other tropical islands. The vines are grown from slips, and are allowed to climb up posts or trees to which they cling with their aerial roots. The vines are kept carefully pruned, and will often live for 50 years.

Just before the beans are ripe, they are cut from the vine. They are cured by heat in large oven rooms, then exposed to sun and air, and finally put in tightly closed places to sweat. This treatment shrinks the beans and changes the color from yellow to brown. They are graded according to size, aroma, and soundness, and packed in tins, or crates for shipping.

In making vanilla extract, the beans are chopped and mixed with alcohol which absorbs their flavor. Real vanilla is expensive. *Vanillin* is a cheaper substitute which is not quite so good. It is made either chemically or from the tonka bean, the seed of a South American tree.

Hernan Cortes, the Spanish conqueror of Mexico, dining with the Aztec chief Montezuma, was served a delicious drink called *chocolatl*, made of chocolate and vanilla. Cortes was so pleased with the drink that he introduced both vanilla and chocolate into Europe.

VAN LOON (*văn lōn'*), **HENDRIK** (*hĕn'drĭk*) **WILLEM** (*vĭl'ĕm*) (1882–1944), was a United States historian, journalist, and lecturer. Many of Van Loon's books were written especially for children. These books, often illustrated with his own sketches, were popular with adults also.

Van Loon was born in Rotterdam, the Netherlands, in 1882. He came to the United States to live when he was 21 years old. He studied at Harvard and Cornell universities. After graduating from Cornell in 1905, he was for a time a newspaper correspondent in Russia. After this, he continued his studies at the University of Munich in Germany, where he received a Ph.D. degree in 1911. His first book, *The Fall of the Dutch Republic,* was published in 1913. He returned to the United States in 1918 to become a history professor and journalist.

The Story of Mankind, Van Loon's sixth book, was an immediate success when it was published in 1921. This history of the world won the first Newbery Medal as the best book for children published in that year.

During the next 20 years he wrote 33 books, most of which explained difficult subjects. Five of these became best sellers. *The Story of the Bible* and *Van Loon's Geography* were other books of his that were popular with both young readers and adults.

VATICAN (*văt'ĭ kăn*) **CITY, ITALY.** Vatican City is the world's smallest independent state, with an area of 0.17 square miles. It lies in the midst of Rome. It is the place of government of the Catholic Church. (See ROMAN CATHOLIC CHURCH.) Within this area is little more than the Vatican Palace (the pope's residence), the gardens, and the large and well-known St. Peter's Basilica. Every year thousands of Christian pilgrims go to Vatican City to visit the basilica and receive the pope's blessing. The pope, the head of Vatican City, rules through a civil governor. Vatican City has its own flag, post office, railway station, and money. Its telephone system and radio broadcasting stations are the gifts of the people of the United States. Support for this tiny state comes chiefly from contributions made by Catholics throughout the world.

The Vatican Palace is next to St. Peter's Basilica, and is said to contain more than 1,000 rooms. Some of these rooms are art museums, and others are libraries. The Vatican Library, in a separate wing, is one of the greatest in the world. (See LIBRARY.) The Sistine Chapel has paintings on its walls and ceiling by the famous artist, Michelangelo Buonarroti.

Vatican City has diplomatic relations with other countries, and, in 1959, representatives from 47 nations were accredited to the Holy See (Vatican City). The United States had full diplomatic relations with the Vatican from 1848 to 1867. At times during 1939–1950, the presidents of the United States had personal representatives at Vatican City.

In the 4th century, when the church gained civil liberty under Constantine, it began to grow in temporal (political) as well as in spiritual power. Gradually the pope extended his political control over a large territory in central Italy. In 1859 the land under his con-

The Vatican Palace is the home of the government of the tiniest state in the world—Vatican City.

trol, called the Papal States, covered about 16,000 square miles.

During the 19th century, the many states of Italy were united. In 1870 Rome was made the national capital, and the Papal States were made part of the Kingdom of Italy. The Italian government offered to guarantee the pope's independence and to pay for the loss of his possessions. The offer was not accepted, and, in protest, the pope retired to his palace as a voluntary prisoner. There, for nearly 60 years, the popes lived in seclusion.

In 1929 an agreement ended the conflict between the pope and the Italian government over the occupation of the Papal States and the seizure of Rome. The Lateran Treaty was signed by representatives of the Italian government and Pope Pius XI and the Vatican City state was set up. The Vatican was also paid for the loss of the Papal States.

The population of Vatican City is 935 (1964).

VELAZQUEZ (*vā läth′kāth*) or **VELASQUEZ** (*vā läs′-*), **DIEGO** (*dyä′gō*) **RODRIGUEZ** (*rō-thrē′gäth*) **DE** (*thā*) **SILVA** (*sēl′vä*) **Y** (*ē*) (1599–1660), is generally considered to be one of the great painters of the world. Until 1500 Spanish painting was quite like Italian. Near the end of that century, three fine Spanish painters brought new fame to their country. Velazquez was one of these.

Velazquez was born in Seville, Spain. For five years he was the pupil of Francisco Pacheco and learned to paint figures with strong light and shade. The subjects were mainly scenes of simple life in the eating houses and kitchens of his time. He did not make them look better but painted them as they were.

At the age of 23 Velazquez was called to the royal court in Madrid by King Philip IV to become the court painter, a high honor for the young artist. From that time on his only duty was to paint portraits of the royal family. Because he no longer had to paint a large number of pictures for his living, he spent the rest of his life improving his skill as an artist. He searched for new problems to experiment with and to solve, and his work was far advanced for the age. His paintings show a wonderful skill in using the paint to show skin, satin, velvet, metal, and wood. Although the paintings are usually of people, everything in a

LINFANTE. MARGVERITE

Alinari

As court painter for Philip IV, Velazquez often painted portraits of the royal children. This portrait of the Infanta (Princess) Marguerite is in the Louvre, Paris.

picture was painted with care.

From his portraits of the king's family, one can learn much about the royalty of the time. Philip IV was a tall, nervous person with a difficult face to paint. His wife and daughters, the Infantas Maria Teresa and Marguerite, were not particularly beautiful. The handsome member was the king's son, Prince Baltasar Carlos, who was one of the artist's favorite models. Besides the nobility Velazquez is known for his paintings of the dwarfs and jesters who entertained the royal children, and for his portrait of Pope Innocent X.

VENEER (*vĕ nēr'*) **AND PLYWOOD** (*plī′wụd*). Veneer is a thin sheet of high-grade wood covering a surface of cheaper wood. It may be as thin as $\frac{1}{100}$ inch or as thick as $\frac{3}{8}$ inch. The ancient Egyptians cut thin sheets of rare, beautifully grained woods and glued them over the surface of common woods to make furniture for the wealthy. For centuries veneer was made by hand. It was slow, hard work. With the use of wood-working machines and better glues, veneer is made much more easily and quickly. This has led to wider use of veneers not only for decorative furniture, doors, and paneling, but for many ordinary uses. Veneers cut from common woods are made into boxes and berry and fruit baskets, or are glued together into plywood for homebuilding and other construction.

The modern methods of cutting veneer are by peeling, slicing, or sawing. In peeling, the log is turned on a huge lathe against a sharp knife which peels the veneer in long sheets, much as paper toweling is unrolled. About nine-tenths of all veneer is cut this way. In slicing, a machine with a sharp, sturdy knife slices veneer sheets of the desired thickness from a squared-up log. In sawing, just as in a lumber mill, the squared-up log is sawed into thin slices. The veneer is cut to proper size and thoroughly dried. It is glued under pressure to the article for which it is intended. Later the veneer is sanded to a satiny smoothness.

The most popular furniture veneers are black walnut, white oak, mahogany, Spanish cedar, and rosewood. Veneers used in construction are made into plywood. Most such veneers are Douglas fir. Veneers used for containers are gum, poplar, pine, and cottonwood.

Plywood

Probably the most important of all veneer uses is making plywood. Plywood is made by glueing together an odd number (three, five, seven or more) of veneer sheets (plies) placed crosswise to form a wood-and-glue sandwich. Under heavy pressure the layers of wood and glue become plywood. To speed the process, heat is often used. Each ply has its grain direction at right angles to the next ply. This construction gives plywood greater strength than a board of the same size.

Before plywood, boards could be no wider or no longer than the tree from which they were cut. Plywood panels, however, can be made almost any size. The most common size is 4 by 8 feet and $\frac{3}{8}$ inch thick. For special uses plywood may even be 3 or 4 inches thick. After about 1933 new waterproof glues made plywood useful for boatbuilding, house siding, and other outdoor products. Production of Douglas fir plywood increased rapidly. In 1942, 31 plants in Washington and Oregon made 1,782,000,000 square feet of Douglas fir plywood. In 1956, 122 plants in five Pacific Northwest states produced 5,420,000,000 square feet. Plywoods of mahogany, gum, walnut, birch, and oak are popular for decorative paneling and fine furniture. Gum, poplar, basswood, and other woods are used extensively in crating and industrial plywood. Ponderosa pine, southern yellow pine, and red gum are also important in plywood production.

VENEZUELA (*věn′ŭz wā′ lä*), **SOUTH AMERICA,** is a republic that lies between the Equator and the Caribbean Sea. Its neighboring countries are Guyana (formerly British Guiana) to the east, Brazil to the southeast, and Colombia to the southwest and west. Its chief source of income is petroleum. Venezuela has the largest petroleum-producing field in Latin America. Development of the petroleum industry in the 20th century has brought many improvements to the country and its people. The country's official name is the Republic of Venezuela.

Landscape

Venezuela may be divided into four major regions: the Venezuelan Highlands, the Maracaibo Lowlands, the Orinoco Llanos (Plains), and the Guiana Highlands.

The Venezuelan Highlands are a branch of the Andes Mountains, which cross the border from Colombia. They extend, rugged and high, toward the Caribbean Sea and then curve eastward along the coast. Except for the Maracaibo Lowlands, they leave only small, narrow, coastal lowlands wedged between the mountains and the sea. The highest mountains of the Venezuelan Highlands are in the Sierra Nevada de Merida Range. Some snowcapped peaks reach more than 16,000 feet.

The real heartland of Venezuela lies within this highland region. Most of the population and some of the chief cities are located in the region's valleys and basins. Caracas, the capital city, occupies one basin. There is also much agricultural and industrial activity in the Venezuelan Highlands.

The Maracaibo Lowlands, in the northwestern part of the country, are surrounded on three sides by high mountains. To the north, the lowlands open to the Caribbean Sea. Lake Maracaibo, a large body of fresh water, is in the center of these lowlands. Beneath the lake and along its shores lie some of the largest petroleum-producing fields in Latin America.

The Orinoco Llanos extend from the Venezuelan Highlands southward to the Orinoco River. *Llanos* is the Spanish word for plains. This large, flat area is covered with coarse, tall grass and patches of scrubby trees. Along the rivers are broad, flat floodplains, but back from the rivers the plains are slightly higher and gently rolling. During the rainy season much of the land is flooded, and only the higher areas stand as islands above the water. The land of this region is used for cattle grazing and some crop growing. Scattered through the northern and western parts of the region are important petroleum fields.

The Guiana Highlands, which are south of the Orinoco River, cover about half of Venezuela. The massive, rounded hills and the higher, flattopped plateaus and mesas are cut by narrow, deep river valleys. In a remote part of these highlands are the spectacular Angel Falls, the world's highest waterfall. This region is difficult to travel in, and few people live there. Activity is confined to the northern edge of the Guiana Highlands, where huge deposits of iron ore are being worked.

Climate and Plant Life

Venezuela lies in the tropics, but different parts of the country vary in climate, depending upon their altitude and their exposure to the rain-bearing winds. The lowlands are hot, and in humid places, such as the Maracaibo Lowlands, the climate is quite uncomfortable. On the other hand, some mountain peaks are so high and cold that they are always covered with snow. Temperatures in Venezuela change more from day to night than they do from season to season. Differences in rainfall distinguish the country's two seasons. The rainy season lasts from April through October, and the dry season lasts from November through March. In the Orinoco Llanos the land is flooded during the rainy season, but it becomes parched during the dry season.

Differences in climate are reflected in the vegetation of Venezuela. The dry coastal lowlands and the slopes and valleys that face away from the wind have a sparse cover of plants. Tropical rain forests grow on the windward slopes of the Venezuelan Highlands. Above the tree line the mountains are poorly covered with grasses or grasslike plants. In the Maracaibo Lowlands the vegetation changes gradually from tropical rain forest on the lower slopes of mountains, through forest in which some trees lose their leaves, to scrub woodlands near the coast. In the Orinoco Llanos are tropical grasslands, with scattered spots of scrubby trees and small areas of tropical rain forest in the wettest places. The Guiana Highlands are covered with tropical grasslands mixed with tropical forests.

Rivers and Lakes

Venezuela's largest and most important river is the Orinoco. With its tributaries, it drains four-fifths of the country. Oceangoing boats can navigate the lower part of the river, as far up as Puerto Ordaz. A large hydroelectric dam on the Caroni River, a tributary of the Orinoco, supplies power to industry in the region. Other rivers in Venezuela are short and, except for those in the Maracaibo Lowlands, are seldom used for navigation. Lake Maracaibo is the largest lake in Venezuela. A channel has been cut through the sandbar that separates the lake from the Gulf of Venezuela so that ocean ships can approach the petroleum fields on the shores of the lake.

Animal Life

Among the animals native to Venezuela are pumas, jaguars, ocelots, monkeys, sloths, and anteaters. There are also peccaries, deer, tapirs, and several kinds of rodents and reptiles. The birdlife includes many migrating species that

FACTS ABOUT VENEZUELA

CAPITAL: Caracas. **NATIONAL ANTHEM:** *Himno Nacional de Venezuela* ("National Anthem of Venezuela").

AREA: 352,143 square miles; more than twice the size of California.

POPULATION: 7,523,999 (1961); 9,030,030 (1966 estimate); 21.4 persons per square mile; 62.5 percent urban, 37.5 percent rural.

CHIEF LANGUAGE: Spanish. **CHIEF RELIGION:** Roman Catholic.

LITERACY: About 89 percent of the people can read and write.

MOUNTAIN RANGES: Venezuelan Highlands, Guiana Highlands.

HIGHEST PEAKS: La Columna (16,411 feet), Humboldt (16,214 feet), La Concha (16,148 feet).

LARGEST LAKES: Maracaibo, Valencia.

MOST IMPORTANT RIVERS: Orinoco, Apure, Paragua, and Ventuari.

FORM OF GOVERNMENT: Federal Republic.

HEAD OF GOVERNMENT AND CHIEF OF STATE: President.

LEGISLATURE: Senate and Chamber of Deputies.

VOTING QUALIFICATIONS: Compulsory for men and women over 18.

POLITICAL DIVISIONS: 20 states, 2 federal territories, a federal district, and federal dependencies.

CHIEF CITIES: (1965 estimate) Caracas (786,863), (1966 estimates) Maracaibo (558,953), Barquisimeto (244,793), Valencia (196,411).

CHIEF MANUFACTURED AND MINED PRODUCTS: Petroleum and petroleum products, beverages, cement, chemicals, coal, diamonds, gold, iron ore, natural gas, processed food, processed metals, and textiles.

CHIEF AGRICULTURAL PRODUCTS: *Crops*, bananas, beans, cocoa, coffee, cotton, corn, eggs, potatoes, rice, sesame, sugarcane, tobacco, wheat, and yucca; *Agriculture*, cattle, horses, pigs, and sheep.

FLAG: *Colors*, yellow, blue, red, white. (See FLAG, *Plate 7*.)

CURRENCY: Bolivar; 4.50 bolivars equal one U.S. dollar.

---

inhabit the shores of streams and lagoons for part of the year.

Natural Resources

Venezuela is rich in natural resources, especially petroleum and iron ore. Income from the sale of petroleum and iron ore largely has been responsible for Venezuela's development since World War II. Petroleum is the main support of the country's economy. The petroleum fields in the Maracaibo Lowlands are among the richest in the world. Other, smaller fields are in the Orinoco Llanos. Venezuela's iron ore deposits are also extremely large and rich. The country also has small deposits of a variety of other minerals, including gold, but few of them are mined in large quantities.

The People

The land that is now Venezuela was originally inhabited by Indians who belonged to a variety of small, scattered tribes. In northern Venezuela the majority were Caribs or Arawaks. Most of the Indians were killed, died, or intermarried with the Spanish conquerors. Today a large part of the Venezuelans are mestizos (people of mixed European and Indian ancestry). Only small numbers of pure Indians still live in scattered and remote parts of the country. Negroes were brought to Venezuela to work on coastal plantations. Today Negroes and mulattoes represent a small but important part

of the population, especially near the Caribbean coast. According to the 1961 census, about 20 percent of the population is white. This white population has increased since 1945 and has continued to increase through the 1960's because the country has attracted large numbers of European immigrants. Most of these immigrants live in large cities or in the petroleum and other mining centers.

The overwhelming majority of Venezuelans are Roman Catholics. The constitution, however, guarantees freedom of worship. Spanish is the language of the republic.

About 70 percent of the people live in the basins and valleys of the Venezuelan Highlands, especially in the central section. About half of the Venezuelans live in cities, which are growing fast. Increasing numbers of people are moving to urban industrial centers in an attempt to better their way of life.

Caracas, the capital and largest city, lies in a pleasant basin in the highlands. Because the city is more than 3,000 feet above sea level, the climate is mild and pleasant, while the coastal area, only a few miles away, is hot. (See CARACAS.) In the coastal area is the town of La Guaira, the seaport of Caracas. Maracaibo, Venezuela's second largest city, is an important trade and manufacturing center and the most important Venezuelan seaport. It ranks as one of the world's largest exporters of petroleum products.

KEY TO PRODUCTS

CATTLE		DIAMONDS	
HOGS		IRON ORE	
BANANAS		PETROLEUM	
COCOA		FOREST PRODUCTS	
COFFEE		PETROLEUM REFINERIES	
CORN		STEEL	
SUGARCANE		TEXTILES	
	GOLD		

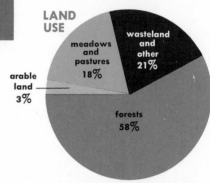

LAND USE

arable land 3%
meadows and pastures 18%
wasteland and other 21%
forests 58%

ANNUAL VALUE OF PRINCIPAL PRODUCTS

MANUFACTURING	$927,761,000
food	335,497,000
beverages	117,789,000
textiles	58,462,000
mineral products	55,456,000
metal products	51,222,000

MINING	$2,513,000,000
petroleum	2,383,090,000
iron ore	127,060,000
diamonds	1,774,000
gold	834,000

AGRICULTURE	
cattle, numbers of	6,605,000
hogs, numbers of	1,848,000
coffee	$57,466,000
corn	26,139,000
eggs	25,139,000
bananas	19,294,000

Economy

Since 1935 Venezuela has changed from an agricultural to a largely industrial country. This change was based chiefly on the development of petroleum and iron ore mining by foreign-owned companies. Since 1945, other industries have developed, cities have grown in population, much new construction has taken place, and agricultural modernization has begun.

Mining. Only a small part of the Venezuelan labor force works for the petroleum industry, but it provides more than half of the republic's income. Most of the petroleum is exported.

Iron is Venezuela's second most important mineral. In comparison with the petroleum industry, however, iron ore mining contributes a small amount to the economy. Most of the ore is exported to the United States, but the Venezuelan government opened a steel plant in 1962. Some coal, gold, and diamonds are also mined.

Agriculture. Little of Venezuela's land is suitable for raising crops. Nevertheless, about one-third of the country's workers still make their living by farming or raising livestock. Most of the farmers grow food for Venezuelans, but some coffee and cacao are grown for export. The best agricultural lands are in the Andes valleys, the Maracaibo Lowlands, and around Lake Valencia, which is near Caracas. Much of the land in the Orinoco Llanos is used for cattle grazing, though the region is handicapped by floods and by droughts. The only large areas of cropland in the llanos are in the few costly government-sponsored irrigated farm projects in the northern part of the region. Agricultural and stock-raising practices have been improved since 1945 as a result of government aid. Backward and inefficient methods, however, are still common. The country still must import some food.

Industry. Most of the industrial workers live in the central part of Venezuelan Highlands in the cities of Caracas, Maracay, or Valencia, which have most of the country's textile and food- and beverage-processing plants. Petroleum is refined in the Maracaibo Lowlands and on the Paraguana Peninsula. Chemical industries that use petroleum as raw material are being developed near Puerto Cabello. San Tome, in the Orinoco Llanos, is the site of a government-owned steel mill.

Foreign Trade. Venezuela imports goods and materials that it cannot sufficiently produce within the country. Besides food, these include raw materials for industry and agriculture, fuels, machinery, transportation equipment, and construction equipment. The United States is Venezuela's most important supplier and the chief customer for its petroleum.

Transportation and Communications

Venezuela's main cities and centers of economic activity are served by adequate transportation. The country needs to improve connections, however, with areas away from main routes. Railroads are of little importance in the overall transportation system, and only about 9,500 miles of Venezuela's 19,000 miles of road are paved. Modern superhighways connect Caracas with La Guaira and Valencia, and three main branches of the Pan American Highway pass through Venezuela. A five-mile-long bridge, completed in 1962, spans Lake Maracaibo. It connects the city of Maracaibo to the lake's eastern shore. Another bridge, spanning the Orinoco River at Ciudad Bolivar, is among the world's longest suspension bridges.

The Venezuelan government owns about

Courtesy Creole Petroleum Corporation from Pan American Union

Herds of cattle graze on the Llanos, Venezuela's plains region. Venezuelan cowboys, or llaneros, are comparable to the Argentine gauchos of the pampas.

3,000 miles of pipelines for carrying petroleum from the producing fields to refineries or ports and to carry natural gas to large cities. Venezuela is in a good location for shipping. It has many ports along the Caribbean coast. The entrance to Lake Maracaibo and the delta of the Orinoco River have been dredged for ocean-going vessels. Now tankers can approach the oil fields on the eastern shore of Lake Maracaibo, and large ore boats can reach the inland port of Puerto Ordaz on the Orinoco. Venezuela has a sizable merchant marine fleet, but foreign ships carry most of the international trade.

Air transportation was developed after 1945 to move cargo and passengers quickly and to serve remote areas. In early 1966 Venezuela

Derricks dot the surface of petroleum-rich Lake Maracaibo, one of Venezuela's greatest sources of wealth. Windswept palm trees reflect the lake's tropical setting.

Courtesy Standard Oil (N.J.) from Pan American Union

had 63 airports capable of handling large airplanes.

Education

The number of Venezuelans who can read and write has increased markedly since 1958, when the government launched an ambitious education program. In the mid-1960's it was reported that about 89 percent of the people were literate. Children are required to attend

History

Christopher Columbus discovered the land that is now Venezuela in 1498 on his third voyage to America. The following year Alonso de Ojeda returned and led an expedition along the Caribbean coast to Lake Maracaibo. There the explorers found Indian huts built on piles over the shallow water along the shores of the lake. This scene reminded them of Venice, and they named the region Venezuela, meaning

Courtesy (left) Pan American Union; photo, (below) Carl Frank—Photo Researchers

The Angostura Bridge (left), completed in 1967, is the first to span Venezuela's broad Orinoco River. The bridge, one of the world's longest, links the country's mineral wealth and growing industry south of the Orinoco with the more developed northern area. Tall, twin towers distinguish the Simon Bolivar Center (below) in Caracas, Venezuela's bustling capital.

primary school, and free education is available through college. More schools are needed, however, especially in rural areas. The largest of Venezuela's eight universities is the Central University in Caracas.

Government

Venezuela is divided into 20 states, 2 federal territories, and the federal district, which includes Caracas, the capital. The president is elected by popular vote for a term of five years. The Congress is made up of a Senate and a Chamber of Deputies. All citizens over 18 years of age may vote. The constitution guarantees the citizens broad social, political, and economic rights. The average income of the Venezuelans is high for Latin America. The cost of living in Venezuela, however, is high, and the wealth is unevenly distributed. Some people are quite wealthy, but many are poor and live in extreme poverty. Since 1958 the government has sponsored many programs designed to improve living conditions. Emphasis has been placed on plans to improve public health and housing.

Little Venice.

Other Spaniards made regular voyages along the coast of Venezuela. One of the first permanent European settlements on the South American continent was founded in the early 1520's at Cumana. The Spaniards took pearls, gold, and Indian slaves from Venezuela. They, however, did not find the great mineral wealth and culturally advanced Indians that they sought. Eventually, the Spaniards who did settle in Venezuela made their living from agriculture, either to supply themselves with food or to have goods for export. They slowly conquered the local Indian tribes and founded towns along the coast and in the Venezuelan Highlands.

Although Spain tried to maintain political and economic control over the colony, most of the power was in the hands of people of Spanish descent who were born in Venezuela. The Roman Catholic church also had political and economic power, but neither the church nor the landowners of the country could agree or unite. Each small region within Venezuela acted quite independently of all others. These conditions continued to hamper Venezuela into the 19th century.

Venezuela was one of the first regions to revolt against Spain. The people born in America resented Spain's attempts to control them. In 1810, after Napoleon's conquest of Spain, leaders from Caracas set up their own government. The struggle for independence, however, was long and destructive. Simon Bolivar, a native of Caracas, became the leader and liberator of all northwestern South America. After fighting for more than ten years, he defeated the Spanish forces and made Ecuador, Colombia, and Venezuela into the federation of Gran Colombia. Venezuela, however, declared its separate independence in 1830.

For more than 100 years after its independence, Venezuela had a series of dictatorships, new constitutions, and civil wars. Army generals and landowning aristocrats controlled the country. Although some of them maintained peace and tried to introduce economic and social improvements, many did not. There was much conflict among leaders of different parts of Venezuela, and many injustices existed.

In 1830 General Jose Antonio Paez became the first president of Venezuela, and for many years he dominated the government. His rule was honest, and under him the country's economy progressed. Another notable leader was General Antonio Guzman Blanco, who came to power in 1870. He began a program to improve public education, reorganized the financial system, and launched a program of public works. His rule, however, was dictatorial, and the people received few benefits.

Venezuela's petroleum industry was built up under Juan Vicente Gomez between 1909 and 1935, although he was president only part of that time. He encouraged U.S. and Dutch companies to develop Venezuela's petroleum resources. The income from petroleum brought wealth to the government and improved living conditions for many people. Other industries and agriculture, however, were neglected. Gomez eliminated opposition by force and sought personal wealth and power.

In 1945 a revolution supported by a majority of the Venezuelans overthrew the president, Isaias Medina Angarita. A new constitution was drawn up, and a new president, Romulo Gallegos, was elected. Many reforms were begun. The new government tried to move too fast, however, and it made powerful enemies. A group of army officers seized power in 1948. Major Marcos Perez Jimenez became dictator. His rule was cruel and corrupt. He permitted no political freedom and abandoned health and education programs in favor of spectacular construction projects that had little value.

Jimenez was overthrown in 1958, and Romulo Betancourt was elected president later that year. He reintroduced the reforms of the 1945 government. Betancourt hoped to develop a communications network, to improve education and health facilities, to reform agriculture, and to develop industry. Raul Leoni was elected president in 1963. He continued and expanded Betancourt's programs. His regime was troubled by guerrilla activity, much of it led by Cuban Communists. Both Leoni and Betancourt were members of the Democratic Action Party. In 1968 Rafael Caldera, a member of the opposition Social Christian Party, was elected president.

Italia Nostra Association

Venice, built on small islands off the coast of Italy, is separated from the open Adriatic Sea by narrow sandbanks. The site was chosen for its favorable defensive position.

VENICE (věn'ŭs), **ITALY,** is the most important city of northeastern Italy and was for a time during the Middle Ages the most powerful city in the world. Much of Venice's present importance stems from its rich history, during which the city's magnificent churches, palaces, bell towers, bridges, and canals were built. These sights have made Venice an important tourist center.

Venice occupies one of the world's most remarkable sites. The land on which it is built is a group of islands and mud flats in a lagoon off the Adriatic coast of Italy. All buildings have to be supported by pilings driven deep into the mud. In between the islands and flats are channels of the Adriatic Sea, straightened and controlled to form the canals of Venice. These canals serve as the broad, beautiful thoroughfares of the city.

A visitor to Venice can get an excellent view of the old city from the high bell tower of the Church of San Giorgio Maggiore located on an islet on the south side of the city. Parts of the structure date from the 16th century. To the northwest can be seen the Grand Canal, the city's major watery avenue, which winds through the main part of Venice in the shape of a backward "S." This canal divides the city into two roughly equal parts. Many of the other smaller canals serve as arteries that are connected to the Grand Canal. The city itself is attached to the mainland of Italy by a road and rail causeway about $2\frac{1}{2}$ miles long.

North of San Giorgio Maggiore, across the broad Canal Della Giudecca, is St. Mark's Square (Piazza San Marco), which is flanked by magnificent buildings erected in a variety of architectural styles. The St. Mark's Church is the most famous religious building in the city and is one of the world's great examples of Romanesque-Byzantine architecture. It is richly decorated with mosaics and is a virtual museum of sculpture of many periods. Much of the church's rich decor was acquired through an early law that required merchants to contribute materials from their travels for the adornment of St. Mark's.

Next to St. Mark's is the Ducal, or Doge's, Palace, a superb example of Venetian Gothic architecture. The building served as the home of the doges, or chief magistrates, of Venice during the city's independent period. The first building on the site was constructed in the 9th century, but it was destroyed by fire. The palace as it appears today dates largely from the 14th and 15th centuries. Among the palace's distinguishing features are its long, arched porticoes and upper facade of pink marble. Behind the palace is a narrow canal, spanned by the Bridge of Sighs, over which many persons were led to prison.

At opposite sides of St. Mark's Square are

two elaborate Renaissance buildings, the Old and the New Procuratie, once the residences of the procurators of St. Mark, who supervised the work of the citizens. Also in the square are the Old Library, famous statues, other historic monuments, shops, and cafes. A colorful feature of St. Mark's is the flock of pigeons that inhabit the square. They are cared for by the city.

A trip along the Grand Canal provides one of the most fascinating activities for a visitor to Venice. The canal is crossed by ornate bridges and flanked by majestic old buildings. The most famous and striking of the bridges is the Rialto Bridge, which was completed in the 16th century. Among the important buildings on the canal are the Ca' d'Oro, said to be the most beautiful palace on the canal; the Academy of Fine Arts, whose gallery contains the finest collection of Venetian master painters; the Palazzo (Palace) Pesaro, which is the seat of the Gallery of Modern Art and the Museum of Oriental Art; and the Church of Santa Maria della Salute, with its paintings by the Venetian artists Titian and Tintoretto.

Other important religious buildings of Venice include the Church of Saints Giovanni e Paolo, where many of the city's most noted doges are buried; the Church of Santa Maria Gloriosa

(Top left) Fritz Henle—Photo Researchers, (right) J. Allan Cash from Rapho-Guillumette

The unique gondolas of Venice (above) have long been one of the most colorful features of the city. They provide one of the city's chief forms of transportation. A 320-foot-high bell tower (right) overlooks St. Mark's Square, noted for its large flock of pigeons. St. Mark's Church stands nearby.

Authenticated News

The Grand Canal and the buildings that flank it appear much as they did during medieval times. The Rialto Bridge, a major attraction, has spanned the canal since the 1500's.

dei Frari, famous for its masterworks of art and the tomb of Titian; San Sebastiano, which is decorated with the works of the artist Paolo Veronese and also contains his tomb; and San Zaccaria, originally built in the 9th century and decorated with the works of some of the city's noted artists.

Important works of art are housed also by the Museo Civico Correr and Ca' Rezzonico, an 18th-century museum. Venice has produced many famous artists. (See BELLINI FAMILY; TINTORETTO; TITIAN; VERONESE, PAOLO.)

The city is protected from the open sea by a series of sandbank islands that stretch between Venice and the Adriatic. They are called *lidi*. The most famous of the *lidi* is the Lido, which is world renowned as a beach resort.

The chief means of travel within Venice is by boat. The narrow city streets cannot accommodate automobile traffic, and automobiles are not allowed within the city. The flat-bottomed gondola has been for centuries the traditional boat of the canals. It has a long, narrow structure, upturned at each end, with an open or curtained cabin in the center for passengers. Usually, only one man, called a gondolier, propels the boat. He stands at the back of the boat and rows and steers with a single long oar. Today many other kinds of boats use the canals, including large motor-driven launches.

The city is commercially important as a port and for its light industries. Venetian factories produce fine glassware, fabrics, and jewelry.

History

Venice owes much of its rise to power to the refugees who fled there from the mainland to escape attack from such invaders as the Goths, Franks, Huns, and Lombards. There is evidence, however, that by the mid-5th century the islands already had a small population dependent upon fishing for a living. The islands presented a particularly favorable defensive position, being protected from sea attack by the *lidi* and from land attack by the lagoons and marshy shoreline. The early settlers built dikes, cut channels, developed harbors, and established a profitable sea trade.

A considerable rivalry developed among the various island centers settled by the refugees, but Venice gradually became dominant. Venice remained relatively apart from the political struggles on the mainland. But in the late 8th and early 9th centuries the Franks attempted to conquer Venice, as well as the other island areas. In the ensuing struggle the Venetians defeated the Franks. A treaty was signed with Charlemagne, king of the Franks. It recognized Venice's trading rights. This marked the recognition of Venice as an independent state.

Venice continued to grow and prosper during the next several centuries. It expanded its trade and its position in the Adriatic and on the trade route to the eastern Mediterranean Sea. It became the chief point for the exchange of goods between Europe and Asia. Venice was selected to provide shipping for the men, animals, and materials of the Fourth Crusade. The city used the manpower from this undertaking to defeat local rivals. The fall of Constantinople to the Crusaders in 1204 is chiefly attributed to the Venetians. Despite several costly wars with Genoa, Venice increased its trade and wealth and in 1450 was the chief sea power of the world and a huge colonial empire. Its population at that time was about 200,000.

The decline of Venice began shortly thereafter. Constantinople fell to the Turks in 1453, and, despite treaties providing for friendly trade, numerous wars resulted. Wars with the Turks and a campaign against European powers were especially costly. Perhaps the greatest cause of decline, however, was the discovery of sea routes around Africa to India and the East Indies. These routes reduced the importance of Venice as a key port in trade between western Europe and the East.

Venice lost its colonial empire through the 16th, 17th, and 18th centuries, and in 1797 was captured by Napoleon. Control then passed between France and Austria until the Venetians voted to join the kingdom of Italy in 1866.

In the following 100 years, Venice regained some of its power. It now competes with Naples for second place among Italy's ports. Venice has retained its reputation as an artistic and cultural city. It is now noted as a tourist center and the site of prominent film, sculpture, and other festivals. The population of Venice is about 355,000 (1963 estimate).

VENTRILOQUISM (*věn tril′ō kwĭz′m*) is a special way of talking to make the voice seem to come from some place away from the speaker. People used to think that a ventriloquist spoke from his stomach. In fact, the word itself comes from the Latin words *venter*, "belly," and *loqui*, "to speak."

Actually, however, the ventriloquist forms his words in his larynx. But before he begins to talk, he takes a very deep breath. Then while he talks, he lets it out very slowly through his throat, which is almost closed. His tongue is pulled back into his mouth and only the very tip of it moves. He is careful to move lips and face as little as possible.

By long practice a ventriloquist can learn to make his voice seem to come from a dummy or from any object he wishes.

The art of ventriloquism is very old. It was known among the ancient Egyptians, Hebrews, Greeks, and Chinese.

Some people think that ventriloquism may explain the "speaking statues" of Egyptian history and the oracles of the Greeks. Perhaps these statues and oracles only seemed to speak because the priests who took care of them were really ventriloquists.

Ventriloquism is common among certain groups of people, such as the Zulus of southeastern Africa, the Maoris of New Zealand, and the Eskimos of North America. It is also a popular kind of entertainment. Edgar Bergen, with his dummy, Charlie McCarthy, made ventriloquism popular on radio and in the movies. Many other entertainers have used the same idea on television.

VENUS (*vēn′nŭs*) (APHRODITE) was the Roman goddess of love and beauty. Her Greek name was Aphrodite. Two different myths, or stories, tell about her birth. One says that she was the daughter of Jupiter (Zeus), the king of the gods, and Dione, a goddess.

Alinari

Ancient Greek statue of Venus, called the Venus of Capua.

The other tells that she was born from the foam of the sea. She rose out of the water, standing on a sea shell. Then the west winds blew her gently to the island of Cyprus. The Seasons dressed her and then led her forth to meet the gods.

Because of Venus' great beauty, all the gods fell in love with her and wanted to marry her. But Jupiter decided that she must marry Vulcan (Hephaestus). Vulcan was the heavenly smith who had made Jupiter's thunderbolts. But Venus loved Mars (Ares), the god of war.

Venus had an embroidered girdle, or wide belt, which made anyone who saw her wearing it fall in love with her. Sometimes she lent it to the other goddesses. Her chariot was usually pulled by sparrows, doves, swans, or swallows.

Venus' special month was April, the month of love. Myrtle and roses were her special flowers.

Once Venus, Minerva, and Juno each claimed a certain golden apple that was supposed to belong to the most beautiful goddess. A young shepherd, Paris, was chosen to judge their quarrel. Paris picked Venus as the winner. To thank Paris, Venus gave him Helen as his wife. Paris took Helen, who was Greek, to Troy. When all the great Grecian princes went to Troy to bring her back, the Trojan war began.

The second planet from the sun is named for Venus.

VERACRUZ (*vĕr'à krōōz*), **MEXICO.** On the hot and humid Gulf of Mexico, 264 miles east of Mexico City, is the most important seaport in Mexico. Veracruz was the first Spanish settlement in Mexico. It was founded by Hernan Cortes in 1519. The present port city, dating from 1599, has had an exciting history. In the 17th and 18th centuries pirates attacked and captured it. The French seized the city twice, in 1838 and 1861. It fell to the United States in the Mexican War, and again in 1914.

Today Veracruz is an interesting combination of old and new. Modern buildings and docking facilities contrast with Spanish colonial buildings. A great new lighthouse overlooks the breakwater which protects the docks from the storms. The city has modern sanitation and many fine homes set on wide avenues.

Railroads and highways connect Veracruz with Mexico City and the interior highlands.

The most important products shipped from Veracruz are vanilla, sugar, coffee, and chile. Machinery, chemicals, and wheat from other countries enter Mexico here. In addition to its shipping, Veracruz is important for the manufacture of cigars, shoes, rum, beer, and chocolate. Fishing is an important occupation.

The population of Veracruz is estimated to be 121,408.

VERB (*vĕrb*). The two most important parts of a sentence in English are the subject and the verb.

The subject names the person or thing that is being talked about. The verb expresses an action performed by the subject, or states a condition concerning the subject. When one says, "The dog walks," the action word *walks* tells what the dog does. When one says, "Tigers are in India," the verb *are* expresses the fact that tigers exist, while the phrase *in India* tells where.

Verbs are divided into two classes according to the way in which their past tense and past participle forms are made. Regular verbs form the past tense and past participle by adding *d*, *ed*, or *t* to the present tense form. Examples: *Move, moved, moved; walk, walked, walked; sleep, slept, slept.* Irregular verbs form the past tense and the past participle by changing the vowel, as in *sing, sang, sung; drive, drove, driven;* or by a complete change of word, as in *go, went, gone.* A few irregular verbs have the same form throughout, as in *set, set, set; cast, cast, cast.*

The changes made in a verb to indicate changes of time form what is called *tense.* Here are examples of tense forms in the first person for a regular and an irregular verb.

Tense	Regular	Irregular
Present	talk	sing
Past	talked	sang
Future	shall talk	shall sing
Present Perfect	have talked	have sung
Past Perfect	had talked	had sung
Future Perfect	shall have talked	shall have sung

In modern English, future time may be expressed in several ways. The usual manner of expressing future time is to use the future tense. It is formed by placing *shall* or *will* before the present tense form of the verb. It is customary to use *shall* as the auxiliary in the first person: I shall go, we shall go. *Will* is the auxiliary for the second and third persons: you will go, she will go, they will go. In expressing strong determination we may say I will go, we will go; or she shall go, they shall go.

Verbs are said to agree with the subject in number and person. For nearly all verbs this means only that *s* is added to the present tense form of the verb to form the third person singular of the present tense. One says, *he writes, she talks, it goes.* The verb *to be* is a special case. As this verb has many different forms, particular care must be taken to see that the form of the verb agrees with the subject in number and person. The following table shows this agreement:

Person	Present Tense Singular	Plural
1st	I am	we are
2nd	you are	you are
3rd	he, she, it is	they are

Person	Past Tense Singular	Plural
1st	I was	we were
2nd	you were	you were
3rd	he, she, it was	they were

Transitive and Intransitive Verbs

Some verbs express an action which is carried over to an object. For example, John threw the ball. In this statement the action *threw* carries over to the *ball* which is said to have received the action. When a verb expresses an action carried over to an object it is called a *transitive* verb (transitive means literally "going across.") Other verbs express an action which is performed by the subject but does not carry over to an object. When one says, "Mary entered and sang," the actions *entered* and *sang* refer to Mary only. Verbs so used are called *intransitive* verbs.

Another group of verbs is called *linking* or *copulative* verbs. The use of these verbs is to join the subject to some idea limiting or describing the subject. Examples are: The boys *were* happy; the grass *looks* green.

Verbs are described as being *active* or *passive.* In the sentence "The builder completed the house," the action, *completed,* is performed by the subject, *builder,* upon the object, *house.* For this reason the verb is said to be in the active voice. In the sentence "The house was completed yesterday," the subject, *house,* is acted upon by the verb, *was completed;* a verb of this type is said to be in the passive voice.

Verbs may state a fact, express a doubt or condition, or give a command. The distinction between these uses of the verb is called *mode* or *mood.* A verb which makes a statement of fact is said to be in the indicative mode. Example: Large oaks grew in the park. A verb expressing a condition contrary to fact or expressing a doubt is said to be in the subjunctive mode. Example: If only he *were* here. (He is not here.) I doubt whether he *be* strong enough for the task. This latter construction is still in good use in formal writing but has largely disappeared from speech. The use of the verb to express a command is called the imperative mode. Examples: Take me home. Stay there!

There are several words formed from verbs which have uses different from the usual function of the verb. These words are called verbals. The three verbals are the *participle,* the *gerund,* and the *infinitive.*

The present participle is formed by adding *ing* to the present tense form of the verb (verbs ending in *e* drop the *e* when adding the *ing*). Examples: walk, *walking;* build, *building;* ride, *riding;* telegraph, *telegraphing.* The past participle is formed by adding *ed* to the present tense form of regular verbs or by a special form in the case of the irregular verbs. Examples: wreck, *wrecked;* plan, *planned;* strike, *struck;* swing, *swung;* broke, *broken.* Participles may be used as adjectives; that is, they may describe or limit the meaning of a noun or pronoun. Thus, one may say: the *running* brook, the *driving* wind, the *broken* ice.

The gerund is formed exactly like the present participle; that is, by adding *ing* to the present tense form of the verb (dropping the *e* if the verb ends in one). Hence the gerund can not be distinguished from the present participle in form, but it is recognized by its use in the sentence. It is a verbal noun. In the sentence "Swimming is good exercise," the word *swimming* is the subject of the sentence since it is the thing you are talking about. It is also clearly a noun formed from the verb *swim* and is, therefore, a gerund.

The gerund, even though used as a noun, may take an object. In the sentence "Raising vegetables is his hobby," *raising* is the gerund, *vegetables* is its object, and the two words *raising vegetables* form a gerund phrase which is the subject of the verb *is.*

The infinitive is formed by placing the preposition *to* before the present tense form of the verb: to speak, to run, to go, to broadcast. The infinitive may be used as a noun: *To run* far is tiring. It may be used as an adjective: Furnished houses *to rent* are scarce. It may also be used as an adverb: John rose *to recite* his poem.

To conjugate a verb is to arrange all the parts of the verb in an orderly sequence of tenses and modes.

VERBENA (*vẽr bē′nä*). Because of their beautiful and often fragrant flowers, the garden verbena is popular as an annual garden plant.

The colors of the flowers range from pure white to rose-colored, carmine, violet, and purple. The flower clusters are commonly about two inches across and contain a dozen or more flowers each.

The genus *Verbena* has nearly 100 species that occur chiefly in tropical and subtropical America. About 20 are native to the United States, and a very few occur in Europe. The species grow somewhat like shrubs. The leaves grow opposite each other on the stems. While a number of the wild species of verbena are striking and attractive, others are inconspicuous weeds.

The lemon-scented verbena of gardens, prized for the fragrance of its leaves, is not a true verbena. The sand verbenas of western North America belong to the same family as the four-o'clocks and are not related to the true verbenas.

A few of the sand verbenas are used for borders and gardens with sunny exposures. The species are annual or perennial, with fragrant red, yellow, or white verbenalike flowers, from which their name comes. The plants often occur in large masses in the deserts of western North America. When in flower during winter and spring they add an almost indescribable beauty to the landscape.

How to Grow Verbenas

These plants are easily grown from seeds sown in flats or pans in February or March. As soon as the seedlings are up an inch they should be transferred to two-inch pots and kept in a cool, well-lighted room until May. They can then be transplanted to the garden where they should be spaced about a foot apart.

If verbena plants are obtained from a florist or from a dealer in plants they usually will be in flower, and one can obtain the colors desired. Seeds may also be planted directly in the garden as soon as the season becomes settled and warm. The flowers will usually begin to bloom in July and continue until frost.

Left: Verbena plants grow somewhat like shrubs. Right: The flower cluster of a verbena is about two inches across and has 12 or more flowers.

Photos, J. Horace McFarland Company

VERDI (*vär′dē* or *vär′dē*), **GIUSEPPE** (*jōō-zēp′pä*) (1813–1901), Italy's greatest composer of opera, was born at Le Roncole, near Busseto. He was a poor peasant. As a small child he sang in the church choir, and he played the organ and piano. When he was 19 the townspeople sent him to study music at the Milan Conservatory, but he was not accepted. He then studied counterpoint with Vincenzo Lavigna, the coach of the opera. His first opera *Oberto* was produced in 1839.

Brown Brothers

Giuseppe Verdi.

He married his childhood sweetheart, Margherita Barezzi, when he was 23. By the time he was 27, his wife and two small children had died, and he had written *Un Giorno di Regno*, an opera which was a failure. He was very unhappy and stopped writing opera.

The director of the opera persuaded him to write music again. The opera *Nabucco* (1842) marks his first success Verdi wrote 15 operas in 10 years. They included the popular *Rigoletto*, *Il Trovatore*, and *La Traviata*.

Verdi began his last period of composing with *Aida*. He was asked to write this opera about Egypt for the opening of the Suez Canal in 1869. In the last 15 years of his life, Verdi wrote his two greatest masterpieces, *Otello* and *Falstaff*. The librettos (stories) were taken from plays by William Shakespeare. He also wrote a *Requiem Mass*.

Although Verdi became wealthy and famous, he was happiest in his country home. He and his second wife, an opera singer, lived quietly there. His wife died in 1897, and Verdi died in 1901 at the age of 87.

VERMEER (*vēr mär′*), **JAN** (*jăn*) (JAN VAN DER MEER VAN DELFT) (1632–1675), was one of the Dutch School of painters of the 17th century.

For the next two centuries he was completely forgotten. But now his reputation is steadily growing as one of the important painters of his period.

Vermeer was born in Delft, the Netherlands, where he lived all his life. Not much is known of his life. He apparently was an art dealer as well as a painter. He was a member of the Delft painters' guild, and was probably a pupil of Carel Fabritius. Some students of Vermeer's work believe that he also studied with Rembrandt van Rijn. Vermeer painted mainly household scenes, city views, and portraits. His paintings are clear, simple, and charming. They glow with calm, radiant light, illuminating his favorite colors of blue in all shades, and lemon yellow. He dressed nearly all his figures in these colors. He used a rich, deep blue in many of his interiors to gain the effect of daylight.

His "Young Woman with a Water Jug" is in the Metropolitan Museum of Art, New York City. Among Vermeer's works in European galleries are "The Lace Maker" at the Louvre in Paris; "Woman and Soldiers," and "Woman Reading," Dresden, Germany; "The Geographer," Frankfurt, Germany; "The Milk Maid," Amsterdam, the Netherlands; and "Head of a Young Girl" and "View of Delft" in The Hague, the Netherlands.

VERMONT (*vēr mŏnt′*), **UNITED STATES,** the "Green Mountain State," forms the northwest corner of New England. Its boundaries are the Canadian Province of Quebec on the north, New Hampshire on the east, Massachusetts on the south, and New York and Lake Champlain on the west. From north to south Vermont is 157 miles long. Along the Canadian border it is 92 miles wide and along the Massachusetts boundary it is only 41 miles wide.

The name Vermont comes from the French words *monts verts* which mean "green mountains." The Green Mountains run down the center of the state from Canada to Massachusetts. These mountains are a part of the great Appalachian system. (See GREEN MOUNTAINS, NORTH AMERICA.)

Vermont is a rural state. Most of its people

Courtesy Vermont Development Commission

A Vermont dairy farm. Mount Mansfield is in the distance.

live in the country or in small towns and only 22 cities have a population of more than 5,000.

Manufacturing and agriculture are the chief occupations. Vermont also has a large income from its year around tourist trade.

Among Vermont's abundant mineral resources are granite, marble, asbestos, slate, and talc. Another important resource is its vast forests.

Vermont's many lakes, ponds, and streams contain many kinds of fish. Lake Champlain and Lake Memphremagog are Vermont's largest lakes, and Otter Creek is its longest river.

Landscape

Vermont has three major land regions: the Green Mountains, the Champlain Lowland, and the New England Upland. The Green Mountains separate the other two regions. To the west, and extending halfway down the state, is the Champlain Lowland. It is level land and good for raising crops. To the east of the mountains is a plateau region called the New England Upland or Vermont Piedmont.

The Green Mountain region includes a number of highlands and small mountain ranges. In the southwest are the Taconic Mountains, in the center are the Worcester Range, the Orange Hills, and the Northfield Mountains, and in the north are the Lowell Mountains.

The Green Mountain region averages about 2,000 feet above sea level. The state's highest peak is Mount Mansfield (4,393 feet).

There are a few peaks which are not a part of the Green Mountain region. These peaks are in the uplands in the eastern part of the state and are not grouped together as ranges, but are separate mountains called monadnocks. An example of a monadnock is Mount Ascutney which is 3,320 feet high.

Lake Champlain extends from Canada southward about 112 miles. It is 12 miles wide near Burlington, but narrows to only a few hundred feet across in its southern portion. Vermont's longest river, Otter Creek, empties into Lake Champlain.

The mountains are cut by swift streams and dotted by more than 400 lakes and ponds. Lake Memphremagog and Lake Champlain are popular with tourists, vacationers, and fishermen. The Connecticut River flows along the entire border between Vermont and New Hampshire.

Climate

Warm days and cool evenings are common

Average Daily Temperature

▶ low   ▶ high

Bennington (south)   Burlington (north)

50%   46%

% sunshine   % sunshine

JAN. JULY | JAN. JULY

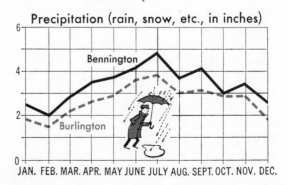

Precipitation (rain, snow, etc., in inches)

Bennington

Burlington

JAN. FEB. MAR. APR. MAY JUNE JULY AUG. SEPT. OCT. NOV. DEC.

during the summer months. Daytime temperatures in the summer are seldom over 90 degrees Fahrenheit, but are quite often in the 80's. Temperatures at night are usually between 60 and 70 degrees. Temperatures as low as 50 degrees below zero and as high as 107 degrees have been recorded in Vermont.

Snow falls in the highlands as early as October. In the lowlands snow falls in December and stays on the ground until March or April. The annual snowfall is about 70 to 80 inches in the Champlain Lowland and 100 to 110 inches in the mountains. This heavy snowfall and quite low humidity make Vermont an ideal winter sports area. Annual rainfall is about 32 inches in the lowlands and 50 inches in the mountains.

Animal Life

Large herds of deer roam Vermont's wooded areas. Other wild life includes bears, deer, raccoons, foxes, bobcats, squirrels, rabbits, partridges, quails, and ducks.

Trout, *ouananiche* or landlocked salmon, pickerel, pike, and other fish are found in the lakes and streams. Vermont's wildlife is protected by its Fish and Game Service, which enforces strict conservation laws.

Resources

Vermont is the United States' largest producer of asbestos and among the largest producers of marble, granite, and slate. Yet the total value of Vermont's mineral production is less than one per cent of the national total.

Marble is quarried along the western side of the Green Mountains, and high-quality granite is quarried on the eastern side. There are large asbestos deposits in the north central part of the state near Belvidere Mountain.

The states' vast forestlands are another important resource. Two-thirds of Vermont is covered with forests of white pine, fir, maple, spruce, yellow birch, and beech trees.

In addition to Lakes Champlain and Memphremagog, Vermont has more than 100 bodies of water larger than 75 acres in area. Best known are Lakes Bomoseen, Caspian, Willoughby, and St. Catherine. The reservoir

Courtesy American Forest Products Industries

These birch logs will be made into veneer.

at Jacksonville is the largest artificial lake in the state.

The People

The fertile lands around Lake Champlain and the large number of fish in its waters attracted Indians to settle there. Between A.D. 1100 and A.D. 1500 the Iroquois and the Algonkian fought over the area and the Algonkian were pushed out of the valley. Later, in 1609, Samuel de Champlain defeated the Iroquois. Soon the Mahican, Pocumtuc, Pennacook, and Abnaki (all tribes of the Algonkian family) returned to the lands around the lake.

For about 150 years after Champlain's visit the French were the principal European settlers in the Champlain Valley. The area was not opened for permanent settlement until after the French were finally driven from the Champlain Valley during the French and Indian War.

Beginning in 1761 settlers poured into the Vermont area from the New England colonies and New York. Most of these pioneers were of English, Scottish, or Irish descent. Many were veterans of the war. The census of 1790 shows that there were 83,000 English and 2,000 Scottish people in Vermont, most of whom came from Massachusetts, Connecticut, and New Hampshire.

Vermont's population is no longer as all Yan-

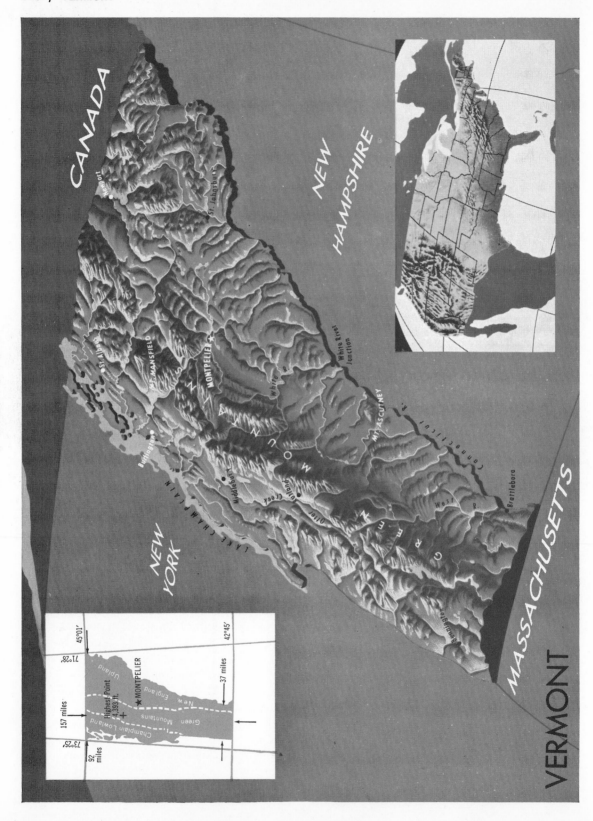

CANADA

NEW HAMPSHIRE

Newport

St. Johnsbury

White River Junction

St. Albans

MT. MANSFIELD

MONTPELIER ★

MT. ASCUTNEY

Connecticut R.

GREEN MOUNTAINS

Burlington

Middlebury

Otter Creek

White R.

West R.

Brattleboro

Bennington

LAKE CHAMPLAIN

NEW YORK

MASSACHUSETTS

VERMONT

45°01'

71°28'

73°25'

42°45'

157 miles

92 miles

37 miles

MONTPELIER ★

Highest Point 4,393 ft.

Champlain Lowland

Green Mountains

New England Upland

Nickname: "Green Mountain State"
Capital: Montpelier
Motto: "Freedom and Unity"
Date admitted to the Union: March 4, 1791
Order of admission as state: 14th
Song: "Hail, Vermont"

Red Clover   Sugar Maple   Hermit Thrush

Physical

AREA: 9,609 square miles, including 335 square miles of water; 0.27 percent of total United States; 43rd state in size.

POPULATION (1970): 444,732; 0.2 percent of total United States; 48th state in population; 46.3 persons per square mile; 32.2 percent urban, 67.8 percent rural.

MOUNTAIN RANGES: Appalachian, including Green.

CHIEF MOUNTAIN PEAKS (height in feet): Mansfield (4,393); Killington Peak (4,241); Ellen (4,135); Camel's Hump (4,083); Cutts Peak (4,080).

LARGEST LAKES: Champlain, Bomoseen, Memphremagog, Whitingham, Seymore.

MOST IMPORTANT RIVERS: Connecticut, Lamoille, Winooski, Otter Creek, White, West.

NATIONAL PARKS AND MONUMENTS: None.

STATE PARKS: Total of 34 including Branbury, St. Albans Bay, Sand Bar, Crystal Lake, Gifford Woods, Emerald Lake, Elmore, Silver Lake.

ADDITIONAL PLACES OF INTEREST: Queechee Gorge; Smuggler's Notch; Granite Quarries, Barre; Hyde Log Cabin; Calvin Coolidge Home; Battle Monument, Bennington; St. Anne's Shrine, Isle La Motte; Marble Exhibit, Proctor; Sand Bar Bridge; Scott Covered Bridge.

Transportation and Communication

RAILROADS: 811 miles of track; first railroad, White River Junction to Bethel, 1848.

ROADS: Total, 14,320 miles; surfaced, 12,356 miles.

MOTOR VEHICLES: Total, 214,539; automobiles, 178,652; trucks and buses, 35,887.

AIRPORTS: Total, 44; private, 31.

NEWSPAPERS: 9 dailies; 14 weeklies; first newspaper, *Vermont Gazette and Green Mountain Post-Boy* of Westminster, 1781.

RADIO STATIONS: 19; first commercial station, WDEV, Waterbury, 1931.

TELEVISION STATIONS: 6; first station, WCAX-TV, Burlington, 1954.

TELEPHONES: Total, 221,200; residence, 157,200; business, 64,000.

POST OFFICES: 296.

People

CHIEF CITIES: Burlington (38,633); Rutland (19,293); Barre (10,209); Brattleboro (9,055); Montpelier (8,609); St. Albans (8,082); Bennington (7,950).

NATIONAL BACKGROUNDS: 94.0 percent native-born; 6.0 percent foreign-born.

CHURCH MEMBERSHIP: Of the total state population, 52.7 percent are church members: 42.1 percent Protestant (including Congregational, 13.7 percent; Methodist, 11.8 percent; Episcopal, 6.0 percent; Baptist, 4.9 percent), 57.3 percent Catholic, and 0.6 percent Jewish.

LEADING UNIVERSITIES AND COLLEGES: University of Vermont and State Agricultural College, Burlington; Middlebury College, Middlebury; Norwich University, Northfield; St. Michael's College, Winooski Park.

MUSEUMS: Robert Hull Fleming Museum, Burlington, art; Shelburne Museum, Shelburne, historical buildings; State Historical Museum, Montpelier, state history; Bixby Library Museum, Vergennes, war relics; Thomas W. Wood Art Gallery, Montpelier, 19th- and 20th-century paintings.

SPECIAL SCHOOLS: Austine School for the Deaf, Brattleboro; Brandon Training School (for mentally handicapped), Brandon.

CORRECTIONAL AND PENAL INSTITUTIONS: State Prison, Windsor; Woman's Reformatory, Rutland; Weeks School, Vergennes.

Government

NUMBER OF U.S. SENATORS: 2.

NUMBER OF U.S. REPRESENTATIVES: 1.

NUMBER OF STATE SENATORS: 30. TERM: 2 years.

NUMBER OF STATE REPRESENTATIVES: 150. TERM: 2 years.

STATE LEGISLATURE CONVENES: January, odd-numbered years.

SESSION LIMIT: None.

CONSTITUTION ADOPTED: 1793.

GOVERNOR'S TERM: 2 years. He may succeed himself.

NUMBER OF COUNTIES: 14.

VOTING QUALIFICATIONS: Legal voting age; residence in state, 1 year; in township, 90 days.

STATE HOLIDAYS: Lincoln's Birthday, February 12; Town Meeting Day, first Tuesday in March; Bennington Battle Day, August 16; Columbus Day, October 12.

ANNUAL STATE EVENTS: County Dairy Festivals, statewide, June; Cracker Barrel Bazaar, Newbury, July; Craft Fair, Shelburne, August; Forest Festivals, statewide, October; Vail Grange Harvest, Pomfret, fall.

Historic Events

1609—Samuel de Champlain discovers lake later named for him.

1666—French build fort at Isle La Motte.

1690—English settle at Vernon.

1724—First permanent white settlement started by English at Fort Dummer near Brattleboro.

1754-1763—French and Indian War; British force French to leave Vermont region.

1764—King's Council of England fixes New York's eastern boundary to include all of Vermont region; New Hampshire also claims Vermont.

1771—Ethan Allen organizes "Green Mountain Boys" to oppose New York rule.

1775—Disputes between New York and New Hampshire lead to fighting at Westminster; Green Mountain Boys capture Fort Ticonderoga from British during American Revolution.

1777—Vermont declares independence from Great Britain; adopts first state constitution to forbid slavery and offer universal male suffrage.

1791—Vermont ratifies U.S. Constitution to become 14th state.

1805—Montpelier becomes capital of state.

1814—Battle of Plattsburg on Lake Champlain during War of 1812.

1864—Small band of Confederate soldiers raid St. Albans during the American Civil War.

1923—Calvin Coolidge of Vermont becomes U.S. president.

1927—Floods cause millions of dollars damage in Vermont.

1959—350th anniversary celebration of discovery of Lake Champlain.

1965—Legislature reapportioned according to population.

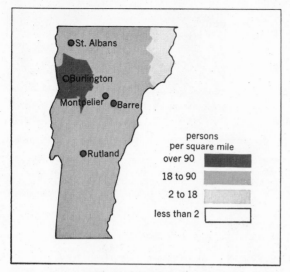

Where the people live.

Lumbering was the first large industry in Vermont. The settlers cut many trees as they cleared their land for crops. These were burned and the ash was shipped to Europe for sale as potash.

About 3,700,000 acres of Vermont are commercial forestland. More than 300 sawmills cut wood and as many factories make wood products. Among the many wood products are baskets, baseball bats, bowling pins, flooring, oars and paddles, snowshoes, trailers, and toothpicks. Almost every section of Vermont has furniture and woodworking shops. Lumbering and woodworking employ about 7 percent of those working in manufacturing.

Because of the large deposits of high quality minerals, quarrying and mining and related industries are important. These industries provide work for many people. The principal minerals are granite, marble, slate, limestone, asbestos, talc, mica, and clay.

kee as it was in 1790. About 8 percent are foreign-born, chiefly French and other Canadian, Scottish, Italian, Swedish, Polish, English, and Welsh. Except for the French Canadians, Vermont's foreign-born citizens are almost all to be found in its larger towns.

Only 32.2 percent of the people now live in urban areas, far below the 73.5 percent average for the United States. Many young people leave Vermont and a large number of retired persons come into the state; thus the average age of the people has been rising.

The largest city is Burlington, which borders Lake Champlain. It is the state's commercial, transportation, and educational center. Rutland, the second largest city, is in the center of an important marble quarrying area. Barre is in the center of the granite quarrying region, as is Montpelier, the capital of the state. St. Albans, raided by Confederates in 1864, claims the title of being the northernmost battlefield of the U.S. Civil War.

How the People Make a Living

Manufacturing and agriculture each provide jobs for about 34 percent of the working people. Most industries are small, and make a great variety of products. Among the larger industries are machine tools, textiles, stone cutting, dairy products, clothing, foods, furniture and wood products, paper, and publishing.

How the people make a living.

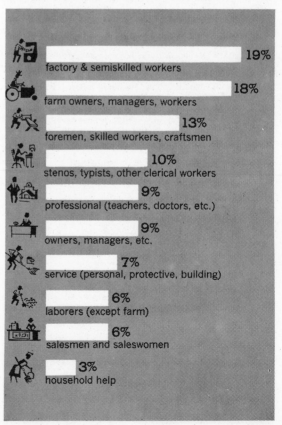

factory & semiskilled workers 19%

farm owners, managers, workers 18%

foremen, skilled workers, craftsmen 13%

stenos, typists, other clerical workers 10%

professional (teachers, doctors, etc.) 9%

owners, managers, etc. 9%

service (personal, protective, building) 7%

laborers (except farm) 6%

salesmen and saleswomen 6%

household help 3%

Machine tools are manufactured at Springfield and Windsor; organs and optical glass at Brattleboro; scales at Rutland and St. Johnsbury; and textiles and plastics in Bennington, Randolph, and Burlington. Other manufactured products include cereals, roofing, paper, cheese, butter, hosiery, dyestuffs, gelatin films, and woodware. Vermont leads all other states in the production of maple syrup, maple sugar, and maple products. Several large processing plants are in Lyndonville, St. Johnsbury, and Barre.

Dairying is the most important part of Vermont's agriculture. Nearly 10,000 dairy farms supply the creameries where butter and cheese are made. Most of the milk produced on the farms is shipped to Boston, Massachusetts, or New York City. About three-quarters of Boston's milk comes from Vermont. Milk also is shipped to condensed milk plants all over New England.

The most important crop is hay, used as feed for dairy cattle and horses. Other farm products are potatoes, oats, corn, soybeans, turkeys, chickens, eggs, sheep, apples, and honey.

Tourists add a great deal to the state's income. The many lakes, streams, mineral springs, and mountain resorts bring a large number of tourists to Vermont each year. The state is a year around resort area.

Vermont has many seasonal or part-time jobs. Part time help is hired in September and October to work in the orchards. February through April is maple sap processing season, and hay is harvested in spring and summer. Workers are also hired at potato harvest time.

Transportation and Communication

By far the greatest share of Vermont's goods and passengers move over its highways. Trucks and buses have taken over a large part of the freight and passenger trade from the railroads. Even the mail is being transported more and more by mobile highway post offices. More than one-fourth of the roads are paved.

Vermont is also served by railroads and airlines. Bus lines have been carrying passengers along the major highways since 1923.

In the late 1700's toll roads or turnpikes connected Vermont's most important towns. Free

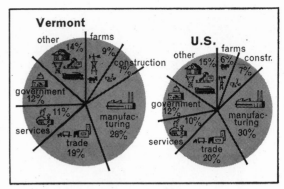

Sources of income.

public highways took the place of the turnpikes. The last of the old turnpikes gave up toll collections in 1917.

From 1760, most of the produce moving northward to Montreal went by way of Lake Champlain. In 1823 the Champlain canal was opened, connecting the lake with the Hudson river. After that, more and more Vermont goods went southward to Albany and New York. Today, fuel oil and gasoline are brought into Lake Champlain from the Hudson river in special barges.

Vermont's first commercial radio station began broadcasting in 1931. There are now many radio broadcasting stations in the state. Vermont's pioneer television station is in Burlington.

Government

Vermont's state constitution provides for a government with three divisions: the executive, the legislative, and the judicial. Each of the 14 counties is allowed at least one state senator. The number of senators a county may have depends upon its population. Each city and township has a representative in the state House of Representatives.

The legislators elect a chief justice and four associate justices to the Supreme Court every two years. Municipal judges are appointed by the governor.

The voters elect officers including the governor, the lieutenant governor, secretary of state, auditor of accounts, and a state treasurer. All of these officers serve two years.

Vermont was the first state in the Union to allow universal manhood suffrage, that is, to

VERMONT

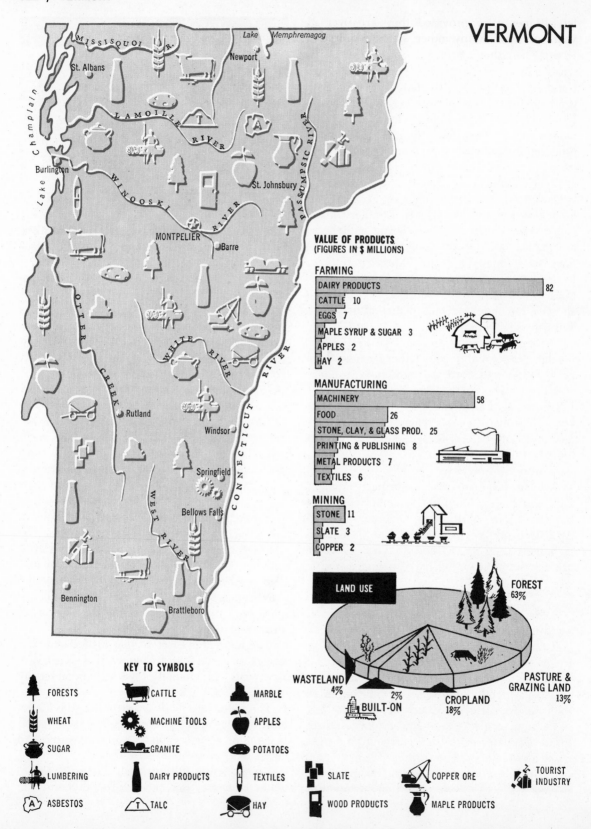

VALUE OF PRODUCTS
(FIGURES IN $ MILLIONS)

FARMING

DAIRY PRODUCTS	82
CATTLE	10
EGGS	7
MAPLE SYRUP & SUGAR	3
APPLES	2
HAY	2

MANUFACTURING

MACHINERY	58
FOOD	26
STONE, CLAY, & GLASS PROD.	25
PRINTING & PUBLISHING	8
METAL PRODUCTS	7
TEXTILES	6

MINING

STONE	11
SLATE	3
COPPER	2

LAND USE

FOREST 63%

PASTURE & GRAZING LAND 13%

CROPLAND 18%

BUILT-ON 2%

WASTELAND 4%

KEY TO SYMBOLS

- FORESTS
- WHEAT
- SUGAR
- LUMBERING
- ASBESTOS
- CATTLE
- MACHINE TOOLS
- GRANITE
- DAIRY PRODUCTS
- TALC
- MARBLE
- APPLES
- POTATOES
- TEXTILES
- HAY
- SLATE
- WOOD PRODUCTS
- COPPER ORE
- MAPLE PRODUCTS
- TOURIST INDUSTRY

let all men vote provided they are over 21 years of age. Many other states required a voter to be either a taxpayer or property holder.

Education

Vermont's Constitution of 1777 stated that "a school or schools shall be established in each town." Also it recommended "one grammar school in each county, and one university in the state."

Today Vermont's educational system has become very much like that forecast in its first constitution. One and two room schools are common in the mountainous areas. The state also has about a dozen schools offering higher education.

The University of Vermont, Middlebury College, Goddard College, and Marlboro College, all are coeducational. Norwich University is a military school; Bennington and Trinity Colleges are women's schools; and St. Michael's College is for men. Junior college courses are offered at Green Mountain Junior College, Vermont Junior College, and Champlain College. There are state teachers colleges at Castleton, Lyndon Center, and Johnson.

The University of Vermont in Burlington was chartered by the state in 1791. Its library of about 200,000 volumes is the largest collection of books in the state.

Apple blossom time. Vermont is chiefly a farming state.

Courtesy Vermont Development Commission

Courtesy Vermont Development Commission

The state capitol at Montpelier.

Religion

The Vermont Constitution of 1777 guaranteed that all men should have the right to worship at any church of their choice. But certain rights were not given to citizens who were not Protestants. Thus, in its early days, Vermont was almost entirely Protestant. Catholics, Quakers, and Jews lost some of their rights because of their religious beliefs. Over the years the Catholic Church has grown, however, and now is the largest religious group in Vermont.

In the early part of the 19th century several unusual religious movements had their beginnings in Vermont. Among these were the Perfectionists and Millerites.

Joseph Smith and Brigham Young, founders of the Church of Jesus Christ of Latter Day Saints (Mormonism), were both born in Vermont.

Health and Welfare

As early as 1886 Vermont had a Board of Public Health with power to check on sanitation and epidemics. From time to time it gained new powers, such as the regulation of schoolhouses and other public buildings, barber shops, slaughter houses, and the inspection of food and drugs. In 1949 the Board of Health was reorganized. It now controls public sanitation.

Medical and public health advantages include the State nursing service, school clinics, dental clinics, cancer, polio, X-ray, tuberculosis,

H. Armstrong Roberts

A typical New England church with its steeple.

and mental health service.

A Department of Public Welfare was created in 1923 to care for children and blind people, and to direct welfare work and rehabilitation. The care of the poor has been a responsibility of local towns since Vermont's first days as a state.

The school for delinquent boys and girls at Vergennes, the State Prison and House of Correction for men at Windsor, and the Women's Reformatory at Rutland are run by the Department of Institutions and Corrections.

Recreation

Vermont's summer activities include mountain climbing, hiking, swimming, camping, picnicking, and golfing. In the fall hunters are out after deer, bears, raccoons, foxes, rabbits, ducks, and woodcocks. In the winter, skiing fans may choose from more than 30 major skiing and winter sport areas. Fishing is good in all seasons, but spring and early summer are the best times for trout and landlocked salmon. Bass, pike, perch, and pickerel are caught in midsummer and fall.

The Long Trail, a footpath along the highest elevations of the Green Mountains, is enjoyed by many hikers. The trail extends from Massachusetts to Canada.

History

In 1609 Samuel de Champlain, Governor of "New France," came to Lake Champlain with a war party of Algonkian Indians. At that time the Iroquois controlled the lake, but Champlain's expedition defeated them in a battle near Ticonderoga. This was the first in a series of battles which continued for 150 years.

When the Dutch surrendered "New Netherlands" to England in 1664 they gave the eastern boundary as the Connecticut River. This made all of Vermont a part of New York. At that time Vermont was a wilderness, inhabited only by a few bands of Indians. The French, however, set up a fort at Isle La Motte in 1666 to protect Canada against the Iroquois Indians and English colonists.

The English settled Vernon, near Brattleboro, in 1690 and built a small fort at Chimney Point on Lake Champlain. In 1724 they built Fort Dummer, near Brattleboro. This was the first large English settlement on Vermont soil.

During the French and Indian War (1754–1763), the British, under the leadership of General Jeffrey Amherst, built a road across Vermont from Charlestown, New Hampshire, to the shore of Lake Champlain opposite Crown Point, New York. General Amherst used this road to bring soldiers and supplies for his "big push" in 1759 when he forced the French to retreat to Canada. In 1760 Montreal surren-

Vermont maple sugar is known throughout the country.

Courtesy Vermont Development Commission

dered. The power of the French and Indians was broken. Vermont was at last open for peaceful settlement. (See FRENCH AND INDIAN WAR.)

The colony of New Hampshire claimed almost all of Vermont and started to give pioneers charters or permits to settle. For several years, therefore, Vermont was known as the New Hampshire Grants. In 1764 the King's Council in England fixed New York's eastern boundary at the Connecticut River. The settlers did not like New York's form of government, so in 1771 they organized volunteer groups called The Green Mountain Boys who opposed the King's order. (See ALLEN, ETHAN.)

New York did not recognize New Hampshire's claims. By 1775, the disputes between the two states had become so bitter that fighting broke out at Westminster. The start of the American Revolution prevented a war between the two states.

In 1777 Vermont declared its independence, first calling itself New Connecticut. For 14 years Vermont was an independent republic. In 1790 the boundary problem with New York was settled. Then in January, 1791, Vermont adopted the United States Constitution and was admitted to the Union on March 4, 1791. Vermont was the first new state after the original 13. Montpelier was chosen as the capital in 1805.

Vermont grew rapidly. In 1823 the Champlain Canal was cut through to the Hudson River, greatly increasing Vermont's trade with New York. In 1848 the first railroad and the first telegraph line came to Vermont. Commerce and agriculture increased. But Vermont's growth was slowed down by the United States Civil War (1861–1865). The state sent nearly 35,-000 men, more than 5,000 of whom died in the service.

After the United States Civil War a great shift in population began. People had already started to move from rural areas into villages within the state, or even out of Vermont. Factories and quarries attracted more and more workers, while farming became less and less profitable.

The Spanish American War (1898) brought fame to Admiral George Dewey of Montpelier. Admiral Dewey was in command at the Battle of Manila Bay in the Philippine Islands.

In 1923 President Warren G. Harding died and Calvin Coolidge of Plymouth, Vermont, became the President of the United States. Several years before, another Vermonter, Chester A. Arthur, had succeeded to the presidency on the death of James A. Garfield.

In 1927 a flood did great damage to Vermont and in 1938 a hurricane caused more than $12,-000,000 damage.

World War II (1941–1945) brought prosperity to Vermont, but took more than 1,200 lives as service casualties. The period since World War II has been a prosperous one for Vermont. In addition to the growth in industry, the growth of the winter-sports business and tourist trade has been very important to Vermont's income. About 1,500,000 people now tour the state each year. From November to March, more than 35 ski areas are in operation. Other seasons bring tourists who fish, hunt, and hike in the mountains and around Vermont's many lakes.

VERNE (*vĕrn*), **JULES** (*jōolz*) (1828–1905), French writer and a founder of modern science fiction, prophesied submarines, dirigibles, television, and space travel long before any of these developments seemed even probable.

He was born at Nantes, France, where perhaps he got his love of adventure by talking to the sailors of the port. At the age of 12 he tried to go to sea as a cabin boy but was caught in time by his father and hauled ashore. He studied law, then tried to earn his living in the theater. He wrote a comedy in verse which was produced. After marrying at the age of 29 Verne settled down in Paris as a stockbroker. At the Scientific Press Club, to which he belonged, the members were fascinated by the possibilities of the balloon. In 1862 Verne tried his hand at writing a scientific adventure story, *Five Weeks in a Balloon*. This was something new in literature and the publisher to whom he took it was so pleased with it that he asked Verne to write two volumes a year for 20 years, promising him an income of $4,000 a year.

When he wrote *A Journey to the Center of the Earth* (1864) and *From the Earth to the Moon* (1865) Verne became one of the world's

Photo, Brown Brothers

The scene of *Michael Strogoff*, by Jules Verne, is laid in imperial Russia. Michael is a courier for the czar. In the thrilling climax he fights a duel with his enemy, Ivan Ogareff. Nadia, Michael's sweetheart, looks on.

most popular writers. So vivid and plausible did his stories seem that people offered to accompany him if he would try to reach the moon in actual fact. *Twenty Thousand Leagues Under the Sea* appeared in 1869, suggested by accounts of the ocean bottom which Verne, while on a voyage to North America, heard from the sailors of the ship *Great Eastern*. The ship had just laid the first transatlantic cable. *Around the World in Eighty Days* (then an achievement which seemed next to impossible) came out as a serial in the Paris newspaper *Le Temps* (*The Times*). It aroused such interest that bets were laid on whether Phileas Fogg, the hero of the book, would get back to London in the 80 days. The Paris correspondents of newspapers in the United States cabled home summaries of the chapters as they appeared.

Verne died at Amiens, France, at the beginning of the century which brought so many of his dreams to reality.

VERONESE (*vā rō nā′sā*), **PAOLO** (*pä′ō lō*) (1528–1588). Paolo Veronese was one of the last of the great Venetian painters of the Renaissance. He left behind him many evidences of the splendor, pomp, and magnificence of his time. This master, whose real name was Paolo Cagliari, was born in Verona, Italy, from which he took the name Veronese. After painting there and in Mantua, he established himself in Venice. There he did some of his finest painting in frescoes for the Palazzo Ducale and for various churches, particularly that of San Sebastiano. He shared his work in the latter with Titian and Tintoretto. In addition, Veronese painted many pictures for nobles and rich merchants. His fancy ran riot in decorating the palace of two Venetian patricians. This work remains today as one of the marvels of interior decorating.

Veronese loved the life he lived and reproduced it on his canvases. He liked rich food, beautiful clothing, music, dogs, birds, and all luxuries. His great skill, his splendid use of color, and his command of composition enabled him to paint true pictures of elaborate scenes. They had all the glitter and pomp of Venetian life. He crowded his canvases with men and women in rich costumes, with musicians, dwarfs, and animals against a luxurious background. His works are full of beauty and movement, but they lack the depth which characterizes the work of the greatest masters. Whatever his subject, Venetian architecture was always the setting he used. His best-known work is "The Marriage at Cana," which contains about 100 life-size characters. It represents a banqueting scene of the utmost magnificence. Other representative works are "The Rape of Europa," "Feast in the House of Simon the Pharisee," and "The Vision of St. Helena."

VERROCCHIO (*vär rôk′kyō*), **ANDREA** (*än-drä′ä*) **DEL** (1435–1488), was one of the great sculptors of the Italian Renaissance. Not much is known of his life. He was born in Florence, Italy, and became a goldsmith, sculptor, and painter. It is thought that he was a pupil of Donatello, the celebrated Italian sculptor.

Verrocchio kept a goldsmith's shop. Two of his pupils and assistants were Lorenzo di Credi and Leonardo da Vinci. Verrocchio taught the young men both sculpture and painting. Da Vinci soon became a much better painter than his master. Verrocchio, "enraged that a child should excel him," gave up painting in despair. The only painting which is definitely known to be his is called the "Baptism of Christ." It hangs in the Uffizi Gallery at Florence.

Verrocchio's chief fame rests on his works in bronze. Two of these, "David" and "Christ and St. Thomas," are in Florence. The statue of the Venetian general Bartolommeo Colleoni on horseback is in Venice, Italy. It is considered one of the most important statues of the Renaissance. (For a picture of the Colleoni statue see SCULPTURE.)

VERSAILLES (*vĕr si′*), **FRANCE,** is a suburb of Paris located on the southwestern outskirts of that capital city. The large and elegant Palace of Versailles, built chiefly by Louis XIV in the 17th century, has given the site its importance. Before then, only a small village existed. Garden crops are grown in the area, and a few factories distill liquor or make shoes. Versailles, however, is mainly a city of homes and a center for tourists.

The main palace, built between 1661 and 1708, was constructed around a chateau begun in 1624 by Louis XIII. It is an elaborately decorated building three stories high, with long wings that extend into the surrounding parks. More than 200 acres of gardens surround the palace. Nearby are two smaller palaces, known as the Trianons. The Grand Trianon was built in the 1680's by Jules H. Mansart, Louis XIV's architect, who was also one of the chief designers at the main palace. Louis XV had the Petit Trianon built in the 1760's. Not all French leaders have used or kept up the palaces. In 1830 they were made a museum. Some improvements were made from 1928 to 1932 and after World War II by the Rockefeller family. In 1963 the French government began a restoration of the rooms of the main palace in furnishings of historical periods of the past three centuries.

Several well-known historical events have taken place at the Versailles Palace. The agreement ending the American Revolution was signed there in 1783. At the beginning of the French Revolution, Louis XVI allowed the elective court of the people to meet at the palace, where they pledged on June 20, 1789, to draw up a new constitution for France. On October 5, however, the people of Paris, who resented paying taxes to support the royalty at Versailles, marched on the palace. The next day the royal family and court were taken to Paris. The Treaty of Versailles, ending World War I, was signed in the palace's Hall of Mirrors.

Versailles has a population of 84,860 (1962).

VERTEBRATE (*vĕrt′ ŭ brŭt*) is any animal belonging to the subphylum Vertebrata, animals with a backbone. This group is a subdivision of the phylum Chordata. The backbone of vertebrates is a flexible column made up of a number of connected sections of bone or cartilage. These sections are called vertebrae, from which the animals get their name. (See ZOOLOGY.)

The backbone, or vertebral column, forms the central part of the vertebrate skeleton. The skeleton is a supporting and protective arrangement of bone or cartilage. It includes ribs, a skull, and in many cases paired limbs. Vertebrates never have more than two pairs of limbs. In some forms, such as snakes, these limbs are missing. In others, they may be modified to form flippers, wings, or fins. In man, one pair has become arms and the other, legs.

Vertebrates have a central collection of nerves, the spinal cord, enclosed within the vertebral column. These nerves connect the animal's brain with every portion of its body.

Vertebrates are the most complex forms of animal life. In addition to having specialized skeletons, nervous systems, and blood circulation systems, they have digestive and muscular systems that are much more highly developed than those of other animals. Their bodies are enclosed in a protective covering such as fur, feathers, or scales.

There are seven major classes of living vertebrates. The most primitive of these, Agnatha, includes lampreys and hagfishes. Outwardly they resemble the much more highly developed eels, but members of this class have a soft skeleton of cartilage rather than bone. They lack biting jaws, having instead round, sucker-like mouths armed with sharp teeth. They have no paired fins. A slightly more advanced class of vertebrates is Chondrichthyes, or the non-bony fishes, such as sharks and rays. Members of this class also have skeletons of cartilage but generally have paired fins and biting jaws. The third class, Osteichthyes, includes such familiar fishes as tuna and goldfish. These fishes have bones hardened by calcium. The fourth class, Amphibia, includes frogs, salamanders, and their relatives. The fifth class, Reptilia, includes snakes, lizards, and their relatives. The sixth class, Aves, includes all the birds. The seventh and highest class of vertebrates, Mammalia, includes the animals with hair, such as man. An eighth class, Placodermi, or jawed fishes, is extinct. All major vertebrate classes have a variety of species that adapted to their environment and survived. Some form of mammals, for example, lives in every kind of climate.

The seven living classes of vertebrates all have backbones, or vertebrae.

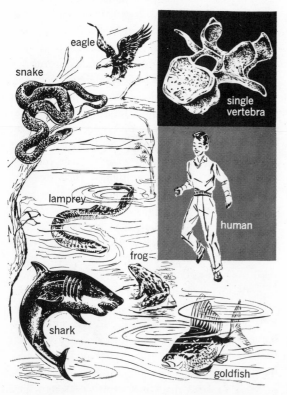

eagle

snake

single vertebra

human

lamprey

frog

shark

goldfish

VESPUCCI (*vĕ spoō′ chē*), **AMERIGO** (*äm ē rē′ gō*) (1454–1512), was an Italian merchant and adventurer for whom the continents of America were named. Vespucci was born in Florence, Italy. He worked for the Medici family and was sent by them to Spain in 1492. There he helped to outfit ships for Columbus' second trip to the New World in 1493.

The early voyages of Columbus had reached only the West Indian Islands. Vespucci claimed that he was the first European to reach the mainland of South America. This was on June 16, 1497, eight days before John Cabot reached Nova Scotia. Some authorities, however, think that Vespucci's voyage was not made until 1499. (See COLUMBUS, CHRISTOPHER.)

Amerigo Vespucci.

Vespucci made several other voyages. On a trip in 1501 he sailed along the coast of South America to what later became Argentina. Other explorers thought that they were near Asia, but Vespucci realized that he was near a new continent. He wrote this in letters that were later published. His information was used by a German map maker who drew one of the first maps of the New World and was the first to use the name America for the new continent.

Vespucci became a Spanish citizen in 1505, and in 1508 he was appointed chief pilot or navigator of Spain. He was in charge of preparing maps of the newly discovered territory and planning routes to the New World.

VESTA (*vĕs′ tŭ*) was the Roman goddess of fire and the sister of Jupiter, the king of the gods. In Greek mythology she was known as Hestia. Because fire was important in the home, Vesta was also the goddess of the hearth (fireplace) and of the home. In Roman times the fire for cooking and heating was built on the hearth, which was the most important part of the home. Vesta was honored in the home by the Romans, who prayed to the goddess before starting the hearth fire.

In Rome there was a temple where Vesta was worshiped. On its altar a sacred fire always burned. Tending the fire were six unmarried women known as vestal virgins in honor of Vesta, who never married. They wore white robes and lived in great splendor. Besides seeing that the fire did not go out, the vestal virgins brought water from a sacred spring, prepared sacrifices to Vesta, and looked after the holy objects in the temple. They were highly honored, but if they broke their vows they were stoned to death or buried alive. Each maiden served the goddess for 30 years. Vesta's festival, the Vestalia, was held on June 9.

VESUVIUS (*vŭ soo' vē ŭs*), **MOUNT, ITALY,** is a famous volcano, eight miles southeast of the city of Naples. It has erupted many times, causing enormous damage and loss of life. In the mid-1960s, Vesuvius' height was measured at 4,203 feet, but this has changed after each eruption. Its base measures about 30 miles around. The volcano has two summits—Monte Somma, the old and lower cone, and Vesuvius proper, the newer cone, which is partly encircled by Somma. An electric cable car takes sightseers nearly to the mouth of the crater.

The first recorded eruption of Vesuvius was in A.D. 79. Three Roman cities, including Pompeii, were buried under ashes and mudflow. Although strong earthquakes preceded the eruption, the people of these cities had believed the crater was inactive and were caught by surprise. An eyewitness account of the eruption was written by Pliny the Younger, in two letters to the Roman historian, Tacitus. (See POMPEII, ITALY.)

After this disaster, Vesuvius was only mildly active, with mostly minor eruptions, until the 11th century. It rested then for about 500 years. In 1631, earthquakes preceded another great explosion that poured lava over the villages on its slopes, killing several thousand people. Since then

Vesuvius has been in a fairly constant state of activity, and eruptions have occurred in regular cycles. Major eruptions were in 1779, 1794, 1822, 1872, 1906, and 1944. Part of the crater blew off in 1906, and Vesuvius' height was reduced to 3,668 feet. In 1944 lava poured down the mountain, burying several small towns. The lava build-up raised the height of Vesuvius more than 500 feet.

Since the mid-1800's, the Vesuvian Volcano Observatory has operated near the top of the mountain. It has sensitive instruments, such as seismographs, to measure earthquakes, and pyrometers, to record the temperature at the crater. These help to predict eruptions. A chair lift has been constructed for viewing the crater. (See VOLCANO.)

VETERANS (*vĕt' ē rŭnz*) **DAY** is a legal holiday set aside to honor all men and women who have served in the armed forces of the United States. It is observed on November 11, the date on which the peace treaty was signed in 1918 to end World War I.

Until 1954, when an act of the U.S. Congress changed the name, the holiday was known as Armistice Day. After World War II, it was recognized as a day of tribute to the dead of that war as well as those who died in World War I. After the Korean War, the day was dedicated to all who have served the United States in its armed forces and to the memory of those who died in battle.

Veterans Day is observed with speeches and parades, and floral tributes are placed on the graves of servicemen. Special ceremonies are conducted at the Tomb of the Unknowns, the national shrine in Arlington National Cemetery, Virginia, where unidentified U.S. servicemen from World Wars I and II and the Korean War are buried in three crypts.

Group naturalization ceremonies in which aliens become U.S. citizens have become a part of Veterans Day activities. (See CITIZENSHIP; NATURALIZATION.) In Canada and Great Britain, the day is known as Remembrance Day.

VETO (*vē' tō*) means to protest against, or to prevent, or to refuse to accept an action. The word comes from Latin for "I forbid." In the area of government, veto takes on a very special meaning.

Hundreds of years ago in England, a monarch might proclaim a law. If Parliament vetoed (voted against) the law, it would not be used. Occasionally, Parliament might pass a law and the monarch would veto it. Although the monarch still has this right, it has not been used since 1707. However, from these English uses, the idea was adopted by the early colonial governments of North America.

The Constitution of the United States includes the right to veto laws made by Congress. This right was given to the president. Congress might pass a bill which the president would sign in order to make it a law and to show his approval. If the president disapproved, he might veto the bill. (See LAWMAKING.)

The Supreme Court of the United States might hold the law to be unconstitutional. This would be a veto in fact although not called by that name. Another form of the veto is used in the Security Council of the United Nations. Each of the five permanent members of the Council has the veto power. (See UNITED NATIONS, THE.)

What has been said of the federal government would also apply to all state governments except North Carolina. The state legislature could pass a law and present it to the governor for signature. He might refuse to approve and to sign it. This would be using his veto right. Nevertheless, the power to veto legislation is limited.

The federal Constitution says that every bill passed by Congress must be presented to the president before it becomes a law. If he approves it, he signs it and it becomes a law. If he does not approve it, he returns it to the house where it originated and states his objections to it. That house may then reconsider it. If two-thirds still approve it, the other house then reconsiders it. If both houses still approve the bill by a two-thirds vote, it becomes law. This is called "overriding" the presidential veto. The president's veto causes reconsideration but his disapproval is without effect.

The Constitution also says that if any bill is not returned by the president within ten days (Sundays excepted), the bill becomes law as if he had signed it. But if Congress adjourns and the bill cannot be returned within ten days, it does not become law.

This last provision brings up an interesting part of the law-making process called the *pocket veto*. Suppose Congress has fixed its day for adjournment on the tenth day of the month. On the second day of the month a bill is passed and presented to the president for his signature. The president does not favor this bill but merely puts it in "his pocket" and does nothing about it. The bill will not become law because Congress will have adjourned before ten days have passed. This is a pocket veto.

The veto is one of the methods of carrying out the idea of "checks and balances" between the three branches of government. The president may veto bills, but Congress may override the veto. The Supreme Court may hold laws to be unconstitutional, but Congress may impeach the president or the Supreme Court justices. This idea of checks and balances was in the minds of the men who wrote the Constitution.

VIBURNUM (*vǐ bêr′nǔm*), shrubs or small trees of the honeysuckle family. About 150 species are known, found mostly in eastern Asia and North America. Many of these are grown as ornamental plants.

Japanese snowballs, with their round clusters of white flowers, are a variety of viburnum.

J. Horace McFarland Company

Flowers of most viburnums are small, and white or creamy in color. They grow in many-flowered, often showy clusters. In some species small fruit-producing flowers are surrounded by a circle of much larger flowers that do not produce fruit. In the viburnums known as snowballs, none of the flowers produces fruit.

The fruits are berrylike, with hard, one-seeded pits. When ripe, the fruits are blue, red, yellow, or black, according to species. Many are foods of birds.

Viburnums show interesting differences in leaf shapes. A few species are evergreen, but the leaves of most turn to beautiful shades of rosy-purple, red, or yellow in autumn.

VICE-PRESIDENT (*vīs prĕz' ŭd ŭnt*) is the second presiding officer of a club or business organization, and in some countries the second presiding officer of the government.

Under the United States Constitution the vice-president becomes president in case the president is removed from office by impeachment, or in case of his "death, resignation, or inability to discharge the powers and duties of the said office." According to the Constitution, the vice-president's duty is to preside over the Senate. He has no vote when matters are being decided by the Senate except in case of a tie. In recent years the vice-president has been given other duties by the president, and the task of presiding over the Senate has normally been performed by a senator. The vice-president attends meetings of the cabinet and visits other countries as a U.S. representative.

An important change in the Constitution was made when the Twenty-fifth Amendment (1967) was ratified. It provided that the vice-president would become "acting president" in case the president was unable to carry out his duties. It also provided that whenever the office of vice-president was vacant the president would appoint someone to fill the office, with the approval of both houses of Congress.

The vice-president is elected at the same time and in the same manner as the president, and he must have the same age, citizenship, and residence qualifications. Originally, the man who received the second highest vote in the presidential elections was made vice-president. This was changed, however, after a bitter dispute over the election in 1800, when Thomas Jefferson and Aaron Burr received equal votes. By the Twelfth Amendment (1804) the president and vice-president are elected on separate ballots. The vice-president receives a salary of $62,500 yearly, plus a $10,000 expense account. In 1966 Congress approved the building of an official home for him. (See PRESIDENT.)

VICTOR (*vĭk'tēr*) **EMMANUEL** (*ĕ măn'ū ĕl*). Three kings of the House of Savoy were named Victor Emmanuel. The first ruled Sardinia. The last two were kings of a united Italy.

VICTOR EMMANUEL I (1759–1824), the second son of Victor Amadeus, was born at Turin. The kingdom of Sardinia then included not only the island of Sardinia itself but parts of southeastern France and northern Italy as well. When the Sardinian army fought against the armies of France from 1792 to 1796 Victor Emmanuel assumed active command. In 1802 he became king of Sardinia. At that time all his kingdom, except Sardinia itself, was in the hands of the French, then under the rule of Napoleon. After the Napoleonic wars Piedmont, Savoy, Nice, and Genoa were restored to him. Victor Emmanuel I left the throne to his brother, Charles Felix, in 1821.

VICTOR EMMANUEL II (1820–1878), the first king of Italy, was born at Turin. His father, Charles Albert, had ruled Sardinia from 1831 to 1849. He had become the head of the movement to unite the separate Italian states. He had declared war on Austria. After having been badly beaten at Novara in 1849, he felt that his son might obtain better terms with Austria. Therefore he gave the crown to him on the battlefield. Victor Emmanuel II chose his ministers wisely. In the affairs of the state he practiced the most rigid economy, encouraging trade and industry.

He gained the good will of England and France by joining them in the Crimean War. In 1859, backed by France, he declared war on Austria. He had previously maneuvered Austria into declaring war on Sardinia, an act which lost to Austria the sympathy of Europe. Austria was defeated and Lombardy was added to Victor Emmanuel's dominions. Tuscany, Parma, and Modena won their liberty; Romagna revolted against the pope. In 1860 all four states by their own wishes accepted Victor Emmanuel as king. Garibaldi freed the two Sicilies, as Sicily and southern Italy were called, and the Sardinian army captured Umbria from the pope. The House of Savoy then ruled all Italy except Rome. In 1860 Victor Emmanuel was declared King of Italy by a national parliament gathered at Turin. After defeating Austria in 1866 Italy gained Venetia. The kingdom was finally completed when in 1870 the French garrisons were withdrawn from Rome and Victor Emmanuel took possession of the capital.

VICTOR EMMANUEL III (1869–1947) was the grandson of Victor Emmanuel II and was born at Naples. He came to the throne in 1900 after the assassination of his father, Humbert I. He was thoroughly trained as a soldier and made a study of German military methods. When Italy entered World War I in 1915, he immediately went to the front, where he remained throughout the war. When the Fascists marched on Rome in 1922 he refused to proclaim martial law lest it plunge Italy into civil war. Instead he called on Benito Mussolini to form a new ministry. Under Mussolini, Victor Emmanuel lost almost all his powers as king. After Mussolini lost all authority Victor Emmanuel remained king until 1946. On May 9 of that year he abdicated his throne in favor of Crown Prince Humbert and fled to Egypt.

VICTORIA (*vĭk tō'rĭ ä*) [QUEEN OF ENGLAND] (1819–1901). One of the most glorious periods of English history was that of the reign of Queen Victoria. It was then that the British Empire grew to its greatest size and importance. (See ENGLAND.)

Alexandrina Victoria was born at Kensington Palace, the granddaughter of George III and the only child of his fourth son, Edward, Duke of Kent. (See HANOVER, HOUSE OF.) Her father and his brothers, except King William IV and the Duke of Cumberland, died when she was still a girl. When William IV died in 1837, she became queen. She was crowned on June 28,

Culver Service

Queen Victoria.

1838, at the age of 19.

The Whigs and the Tories were the main political parties at this time (later the Whigs became the Liberals and the Tories the Conservatives). Like her family before her, Victoria favored the Whigs. The Whigs were in power during the early part of her reign. Her first minister was Lord Melbourne, whom she admired. He was a charming old gentleman who kissed the queen's hands and treated her with much respect. In 1839 the Whigs lost power, and Victoria caused a crisis by refusing to change her Whig ladies-in-waiting for Tory ladies, as was the custom. This greatly angered the people, and she was for a time very unpopular.

Prince Albert, her cousin and the son of the Duke of Saxe-Coburg-Gotha, taught the young queen that she must not play favorites. She and Prince Albert were married in 1840. They lived a model family life, setting a fashion of respectability. Even today, the Victorian Era reminds people of good manners and a highly moral way of life. The Queen and Prince Albert had nine children, four sons and five daughters. Their eldest daughter married the Crown Prince of Prussia and became the mother of the German emperor William II. Their eldest son became King Edward VII.

Albert succeeded in making peace between the Queen and Sir Robert Peel. She supported Peel when he repealed the Corn Laws in 1841. (See PEEL, SIR ROBERT.) She was greatly displeased with Benjamin Disraeli when he accused Peel of betraying his party. Peel's ministry was replaced in 1846. A Whig government took over, with Lord Palmerston as foreign minister.

Palmerston was not trusted by Victoria and Albert. They disliked the way he acted without the advice of other ministers. Moreover, he was causing other countries to distrust the policies of England. But in 1855, when Palmerston became prime minister, he was the most popular statesman in England. The people therefore began to turn away from the royal couple. During the Crimean War (1854–1856), Albert was even suspected of being a Russian spy. In the end his conduct won the respect of everybody. Parliament in 1857 gave to him the title of prince consort.

On December 14, 1861, Prince Albert died. The queen mourned for her husband the rest of her life. The people were naturally sympathetic at first. Later they complained that they never saw their queen, but with Disraeli's help she regained her popularity. Disraeli became leader of the House of Commons in 1852 and prime minister for the first time in 1868. (See DISRAELI, BENJAMIN.) At first the Queen disliked him, but soon she was won over by the personal attention he gave to her. She came to depend upon him in the same way as, long ago, she had depended upon Lord Melbourne.

When Gladstone followed Disraeli as prime minister in 1868, Victoria sympathized with the Tories. She never learned to like Gladstone or to approve of his reforms. Nevertheless she realized that the reforms were wanted by the people. For example, she opposed the army reforms, but she helped in getting them passed by the government.

As Queen she took her position as head of the army very seriously. During the Crimean War she founded the order of the Victoria Cross, the most highly prized English war decoration. During the Boer War (1899–1902) she recognized the courage of the Irish troops by giving the army permission to wear the shamrock on St. Patrick's Day. She also established the regiment of the Royal Irish Guards.

Disraeli came back to power in 1874, and two years later persuaded Parliament to bestow the title of Empress of India on Victoria. She strongly supported his policy of English control over other lands. With Gladstone back in power after 1880, she did her best to prevent him from undoing Disraeli's work.

In 1887 the 50th year of her reign was celebrated by a jubilee. Delegates from all parts of the world came to London. Her diamond jubilee ten years later was even more impressive. She was the grandmother of most of the crowned heads of Europe. At the time of her death, she had 31 grandchildren and 37 great-grandchildren, and all of them came to London to do her honor. There had never before been such a pageant of royalty in Europe.

When the Boer War broke out in October 1899, the old queen gradually broke under the strain. She died after a reign of $63\frac{1}{2}$ years, the longest in English history.

VICTORIA, BRITISH COLUMBIA. Victoria is the capital and second largest city of British Columbia. It is a well-known tourist center on Juan de Fuca Strait at the southern tip of Vancouver Island. Victoria enjoys more sunshine (over 2,000 hours yearly) than any other Canadian city except Lethbridge, Alberta. It also receives less rain (27 inches) than any other large center along the Pacific Coast of Canada.

The stone Parliament Buildings overlook the Inner Harbor, as does the Empress Hotel. Near the center of the city is Beacon Hill Park. There are rose gardens and flowering shrubs, a lake which is the home of many ducks and swans, and a tall totem pole. Butchart Gardens and Malahat Drive on the Island Highway near the city attract thousands of visitors each year.

In metropolitan Victoria, which includes Saanich and several other nearby communities, there are 173,455 people. This makes it the second largest metropolitan area in British Columbia. Although Victoria is noted as a residential and tourist center, it also has two large shipyards, lumber, shingle, and plywood mills, a paint factory, and fish processing plants. Steamers from Seattle and Port Angeles, Washington, and from Vancouver, British Columbia, use the docks in the land-locked Inner Harbor. Large ocean ships load cargoes of lumber and grain at the Outer Wharf.

Many students take part of their university course at Victoria College. Royal Roads is one of the three colleges in Canada for the training of officers for the Army, Navy, and Air Force. Esquimalt is the Pacific base for ships of the Royal Canadian Navy and has a large government dry dock and naval dockyard. It is also the center where many men are trained for the Canadian Navy.

Victoria, named after the British queen, was founded in 1843 by James Douglas. It was the headquarters of the Hudson's Bay Company on the Pacific Coast. In 1849 it became the capital of the crown colony of Vancouver Island. When the Canadian province of British Columbia was formed in 1871, Victoria was chosen as its capital. (See BRITISH COLUMBIA.)

The population of Victoria is 57,453 (1966).

VIENNA (*vē ĕn'ä*), **AUSTRIA.** The city of Vienna is on the right bank of the Danube River at a natural crossroads. It is there that the Danube route to eastern Europe meets the route from Poland and Czechoslovakia to the Mediterranean Sea. Before World War II Vienna was the fourth largest city in Europe. Confined for about 600 years by its fortified walls, Vienna started growing in all directions, building factories, parks, and model garden apartments for the poor, when the walls were taken down in the 19th century. On the old foundation of these walls was built the Ringstrasse, a beautiful boulevard bordered with trees and fine buildings. Another boulevard, the Gurtel, was built later on the outside ring of fortifications. It divides the city from its suburbs. In the center of the Ringstrasse is the core of Viennese life. There is the old palace, residence of the emperors until 1918. Also inside the Ringstrasse are the state opera,

the museums of art, arms, and natural history, and the university. There, too, is the fine old Cathedral of St. Stephen, the tower of which may be seen from every part of the city.

The cathedral as well as a number of other buildings were damaged during World War II. Through the center of the old town run the fashionable shopping streets. In the palatial houses of the old nobility lived the leaders of the republic, and the ambassadors from foreign countries.

Although Vienna has been the center of many arts, it has been particularly noted for its fine musical performances and its rich musical tradition. Many of the world's greatest artists were heard first in Vienna. The moderate price of concerts and operas made the best music available to all. The names of Mozart, Schubert, Beethoven, Haydn, and Richard Strauss are closely woven into the history of Vienna.

Learning, too, had an importance in Viennese life. The university was noted for its medical school, where students and doctors from all over the world came for instruction. Dr. Sigmund Freud made Vienna the seat of the modern school of psychology and psychoanalysis until the Nazis seized Austria in 1938.

Vienna has been notably a luxury-producing city, for it manufactures fine leather goods, millinery, toys, and beautiful jewels. The reopening of the annual industrial fairs gave a new life to all industry, and created a fresh demand for Vienna's products.

One of the well-known institutions of Vienna

The imperial palace, or Hofburg, in Vienna was the residence of the Hapsburg rulers of Austria.

Customs Tourist Information Office

A view of one of Vienna's blocks of modern apartments built for workingmen and their families.

Austrian Tourist Information Office

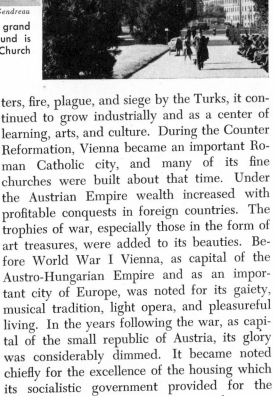

Photos (above), Fryer from Black Star; (right) Screen Traveler from Gendreau

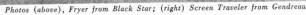

Above: The Austrian parliament building stands on Vienna's grand boulevard, the Ringstrasse. The tall spire in the background is the Vienna city hall called the Rathaus. **Right:** The Votive Church and a park in Vienna.

has been the coffeehouse, introduced in the 17th century and since then firmly established in Vienna. In these cafes during peacetime one found much of Vienna at some time during the day, enjoying the news and gossiping over a cup of coffee and special Viennese cakes.

The people of Vienna are a mixture of many races, Slav, Teutonic, and Magyar. Many years spent together, with the interests of the city in common, have made them a united people.

Situated on the blue Danube, in the very center of Europe, Vienna has long been a meeting place for the charm of the ancient East and the progress of the West. The city was first important as the capital of the duchy of Austria, controlling the important overland trade routes to the Holy Land. From Vienna set out adventurous knights on their holy, and often profitable, journeys, and to it returned the merchant followers of the Crusades with the rich merchandise of the East. With the rise in power of the Hapsburg family, Vienna became the capital of the Holy Roman Empire.

Although the city met with frequent disas-

ters, fire, plague, and siege by the Turks, it continued to grow industrially and as a center of learning, arts, and culture. During the Counter Reformation, Vienna became an important Roman Catholic city, and many of its fine churches were built about that time. Under the Austrian Empire wealth increased with profitable conquests in foreign countries. The trophies of war, especially those in the form of art treasures, were added to its beauties. Before World War I Vienna, as capital of the Austro-Hungarian Empire and as an important city of Europe, was noted for its gaiety, musical tradition, light opera, and pleasureful living. In the years following the war, as capital of the small republic of Austria, its glory was considerably dimmed. It became noted chiefly for the excellence of the housing which its socialistic government provided for the working population. In this respect, for many years, Vienna led the world.

An important goal of the Allied armies in their fight against the Axis, Vienna was the scene of heavy fighting in World War II,

After its liberation in 1945 it was occupied by U.S., French, British, and Soviet forces. The hardships of world wars stripped Vienna of much of its former glory, and the once gay city is now struggling to regain its importance. The population of Vienna is 1,616,125.

VIENTIANE (*vyăn tyän'*), **LAOS,** is the capital and largest city of the country. It lies along the broad Mekong River in the western part of Laos. Vientiane is the center of the country's political, industrial, and cultural life. Within the capital are the central government offices, foreign embassies, and the nation's only broadcasting station. International airlines land their jets at the nearby airport. Buses connect Vientiane with outlying farm villages.

The little industry of Laos is found in the vicinity of Vientiane. It includes charcoal plants; brick, match, soap, and cigarette factories; sawmills; and rice mills. Most of the shops are run by the Chinese. Vientiane's power facilities cannot provide electricity for all its homes, and water is often hauled by truck.

In the 16th century, when Vientiane was known as Vien Chang, it became the residence of the Laotian king. Today the royal residence is at Luang Prabang. Before World War II Vientiane was more a small, rural town than a city, but it has grown considerably since then. The population is 162,000 (1962 estimate).

VIETNAM (*vē ĕt'năm'*), **ASIA,** is the easternmost part of Indochina, the largest and most heavily populated part of the area that was known as French Indochina. (See INDOCHINA.) Vietnam is divided into two countries: North Vietnam (Democratic Republic of Vietnam) and South Vietnam (Republic of Vietnam). The two countries were formed in 1954. Since that time South Vietnam has been under almost constant attack by revolutionary forces supported by Communist North Vietnam. By the 1960's, the United States and other countries were involved in the conflict, and a serious world crisis had developed. Throughout the world the U.S. involvement was condemned by those who felt the United States was interfering in Vietnamese affairs and praised by those who felt the United States was defending freedom and confining Communism.

Vietnam is a long, narrow, and S-shaped region. It extends about 1,000 miles from north to south, but is less than 50 miles wide in some places. On the north is China; on the east and south, the South China Sea; and on the west, Laos and Cambodia. North Vietnam has an area of 60,156 square miles, and South Vietnam has an area of 66,897 square miles. Each is about the size of the state of Washington.

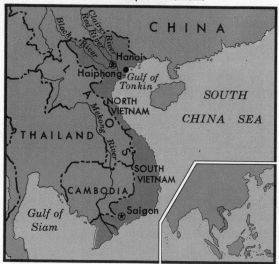

Locator map of Vietnam.

Under the French, Vietnam was composed of three provinces: Tonkin, Annam, and Cochin China. According to the Geneva Conference of 1954, Tonkin and the northern half of Annam are in North Vietnam, and Cochin China and the southern half of Annam are in South Vietnam. The dividing line is along the 17th parallel (17 degrees north latitude).

Land and Climate

Vietnam is mountainous. The rugged highland called the Chaine Annamitique runs the entire length of the country, from northwest to southeast. Most of the people live in two lowland deltas—one in the north, and one in the south. There, the soil is rich and the land is flat.

In Tonkin (the northern area), the delta is formed by the Red River and its branches, the Clear (Claire) and Black Rivers. This is one of the most crowded farm areas on earth, with an average of more than 1,500 persons living on each square mile. In the delta are Hanoi, capital of North Vietnam, and Haiphong, the chief seaport.

The Mekong delta, in the south, is much larger and is not as densely populated. It is the heart of South Vietnam and contains its major seaport and capital city, Saigon. (See SAIGON.)

Vietnam has a tropical monsoon climate. In the South Vietnam lowlands, the weather is hot all year, though the temperature drops somewhat during the rainy season. The climate in the north is slightly cooler, and the seasons are

losophies.

Vietnamese life centers around the farm village, of which there are thousands. Each village, with its bamboo and thatch houses, has from 500 to 1,000 people. The Vietnamese do not like to leave their homes. Nevertheless, almost 1,000,000 refugees left Communist North Vietnam to resettle in the south after the Geneva Conference of 1954 established a boundary line between the two states.

The Chinese, numbering about 850,000, are an important group in Vietnam. Most of them live in Saigon, where they control much of the banking and industry. There are also about

FACTS ABOUT SOUTH VIETNAM
(REPUBLIC OF VIETNAM)

CAPITAL: Saigon.
AREA: 66,897 square miles.
POPULATION: 15,715,000 (1964 estimate).
HIGHEST POINT: Over 8,000 feet.
FORM OF GOVERNMENT: Republic.
CHIEF OF STATE: President.
HEAD OF GOVERNMENT: Premier.
POLITICAL DIVISIONS: 3 regions divided into 41 provinces.
CHIEF PRODUCTS: *Manufactured, processed agricultural and forest products; Agricultural, cassava, corn, peanuts, rice, rubber, sugarcane, tea; Livestock, buffalo, pigs.*
CURRENCY: Piastre; about 118 piastres equal one U.S. dollar.

FACTS ABOUT NORTH VIETNAM
(DEMOCRATIC REPUBLIC OF VIETNAM)

CAPITAL: Hanoi.
AREA: 60,156 square miles.
POPULATION: 15,916,955 (1960 census); 17,700,000 (1965 estimate).
HIGHEST POINT: Over 10,000 feet.
FORM OF GOVERNMENT: People's Republic.
CHIEF OF STATE: President.
HEAD OF GOVERNMENT: Premier.
POLITICAL DIVISIONS: 28 provinces, 2 municipalities, and 1 special zone.
CHIEF PRODUCTS: Corn, cotton, rice, sugarcane, sweet potatoes.
CURRENCY: Dong; about 3.5 dongs equal one U.S. dollar.

more distinct. Most of Vietnam gets from 70 to 80 inches of rainfall a year. The central coastal area has as much as 120 inches of yearly rainfall, and severe typhoons often occur in late summer and fall. Heavy jungle foliage grows in parts of the lowland area.

People

The Vietnamese (formerly called Annamese) make up about 89 percent of Vietnam's population. A people of the Mongoloid race, they are short, fairly light in skin color, and have high cheekbones. In appearance, religion, and culture, the Vietnamese are much like the Chinese, whose ancestors were probably their ancestors. The Vietnamese religion is a mixture of Buddhism, Taoism, and Confucianism. There are also about 2,000,000 Roman Catholics and about 2,000,000 followers of Cao Dai, a religion that began in the 1920's in Vietnam and mixes Christianity with various Oriental religious phi-

1,000,000 primitive mountain tribesmen of mixed Mongoloid and Malay races.

Economy

Agriculture is the most important part of the economy in both North and South Vietnam. About three-fourths of all the Vietnamese people are farmers, and most of them grow rice. Rice takes up more land area than all other crops put together. South Vietnam usually exports some rice.

After rice, the next most important crop in South Vietnam is rubber. Much of it is produced on plantations, and it also is exported. Other important crops in South Vietnam include corn, copra, sugarcane, tobacco, cassava, peanuts, pepper, tea, and sweet potatoes. In North Vietnam, sugarcane, corn, cotton, tea, tobacco, oilseeds, and sweet potatoes are important in addition to rice. There is also some silkworm culture. The forests of Vietnam provide lumber, and fish caught in the coastal waters and rivers are an important source of food. Livestock, including buffalo and pigs, are raised in both the north and the south.

South Vietnam leads North Vietnam in agricultural production, but North Vietnam has richer mineral resources. These include coal, phosphates, salt, tin, chromite, iron, and zinc. The north also leads the south in manufacturing. North Vietnam, however, must import rice. South Vietnam has plenty of rice, but it must import most of its manufactured goods. The major industries in both states are largely those that process agricultural products—such as rice, rubber, sugarcane, and cotton.

was one of resisting Chinese invasion from the north and expanding to the south.

In the late 16th century, French missionaries came to Annam, which was then divided into northern and southern dynasties. In 1802 the French helped the leader of the southern dynasty become the emperor of a united Annam. Mistreatment of French missionaries and converts led to a French military expedition. This resulted in the establishment of Cochin China (the southern province) as a French colony in 1867. Between 1862 and the early 1900's, Tonkin, Annam, Cambodia, and Laos were annexed and the area was united as French Indochina.

Under French rule the emperor of Annam re-

Traffic clusters around the French-style city hall in downtown Saigon (left). Vietnamese farmers cultivate rice in flooded paddies (center). Farm village houses are often raised on stilts to protect against floods (right).

(Left) T. Kautsch-Pix from Publix, (center and right) John Bryson-Rapho Guillumette

A railway along the coast connects Saigon and Hanoi, and lines connect North Vietnam and China. Rivers are also used for transportation. Saigon is a major Asian port.

History

The history of Vietnam can be traced to a kingdom of Annam in what is now North Vietnam. As early as 207 B.C. the kingdom came under the control of the Chinese Viets who expanded to the south and called their new territory Nam Viet (Viets of the South). The Chinese dominated the country until A.D. 938 when independence was established. The country's history from that time until the 19th century

mained as head of state. The French controlled government, business, and trade.

In the early part of World War II Japan occupied the country. After Japan's defeat in 1945 the French tried to rule again in Indochina. They were faced with an organized state led by the Communist national leader Ho Chi Minh and his political party, the Vietminh. France refused to recognize the state. Instead, it backed Bao Dai in forming a new state of Vietnam allied to France. Civil war broke out in 1946 and lasted about seven years. During that time the Communists received aid from the Soviets and the Chinese. Non-Communist forces were supported by French troops and supplies and U.S. equipment.

Early in 1954 the Vietminh defeated the French at Dien Bien Phu, leaving the Communists largely in control in the north. Later that year an armistice was negotiated at Geneva, Switzerland. Control of the northern sector was given to the Vietminh forces and control of the southern sector to the Bao Dai forces. The purpose of the armistice was to give Vietnam a chance to hold elections that would establish a unified country. These elections were never held.

In the northern sector the Democratic Republic of Vietnam (North Vietnam) was established as a Communist-type state controlled by the Vietnamese Workers' Party. The Communist national leader Ho Chi Minh became president and held office until his death in 1969. The country receives aid from both the U.S.S.R. and China.

In the southern sector, the Republic of Vietnam (South Vietnam) was established. In the 1950's, the South Vietnamese government, led by President Ngo Dinh Diem, became increasingly unpopular. An anti-government movement called the National Liberation Front (NLF) developed. Vietcong, soldiers of the NLF, began engaging in guerrilla warfare in the South Vietnamese countryside.

In 1963, a military group managed to overthrow Diem. The government remained unstable for several months, as one group after another seized power. While political changes occurred in Saigon, the Vietcong continued revolutionary activities. The power of the NLF grew steadily within South Vietnam. In the early 1960's the NLF began receiving support from Communist North Vietnam. The South Vietnamese government, aided by the United States, fought to control the country.

In 1967 South Vietnam adopted a new national constitution. This provided for a president, a vice-president, and a two-house legislature, all to be elected by popular vote, and an independent judiciary. In the same year, two former generals—Nguyen Van Thieu and Nguyen Cao Ky—were elected president and vice-president of the country. Under their leadership, the war against the Vietcong continued. Finally, in 1968, negotiations to end the war began in Paris, France. The talks continued into 1970, but no major agreements were reached.

VIETNAM WAR is a military conflict that started in French Indochina in 1946. At the beginning, the war was a struggle for Vietnamese independence from French rule. Eventually it developed into a conflict of grave international concern. It increased friction between major world powers and heightened tension around the world. (See INDOCHINA, ASIA; VIETNAM, ASIA.)

Origins of the War. Throughout World War II, French Indochina was occupied by Japan. Until March 1945, the local French administrators, police, and soldiers were permitted to continue in office. Then the Japanese abruptly changed this policy. They proclaimed Vietnam (the Indochinese provinces of Tonkin, Annam, and Cochin China) an independent state and restored the former emperor, Bao Dai, as its head. When World War II ended, the Allies occupied Vietnam and assigned Great Britain and Nationalist China to disarm the Japanese. The country was divided at the 16th parallel, with China in command of the north and Great

Strategic points in the Vietnam War.

Britain of the south. In the south, the British helped the French back to power.

A different and more complex situation existed in the north. During the closing months of World War II, a Vietnamese nationalist movement had established itself in northern Indochina. This movement was led by Ho Chi Minh, founder of the Indochinese Communist Party. Under his leadership, several nationalist groups had joined to form the Vietnam League for Independence, or the Vietminh. Following the Japanese surrender in August 1945, the Vietminh formed a government with Ho Chi Minh as its head. This government established itself in Hanoi and proclaimed independence in the name of the Democratic Republic of Vietnam (DRV). Thus, when the Nationalist Chinese arrived, they found the DRV in control of the north.

In March 1946, France and the DRV entered into an agreement that recognized the territory of the DRV as a free state in the Indochinese Federation and the French Union. The agreement also provided that the question of unification of all Vietnam would be decided by referendum (popular vote). In exchange, the DRV agreed to permit the French Army to enter its territory. Both sides agreed to hold further discussions to settle their remaining differences.

Chief among these differences was the dispute over Cochin China, the southernmost province of Indochina. This dispute led to clashes between French and Vietminh troops. Unable to come to terms, the two sides continued to fight. In November 1946 the French attacked Haiphong. On December 19 the Vietminh retaliated by assaulting the French in Hanoi. This action marked the opening of the Vietnam War.

The First Phase: 1946–1954

When the fighting began, the French had an apparent military advantage. Well-armed French forces scored easy victories in capturing cities and holding major highways. But the countryside belonged to the Vietminh, who fought in small units, using guerrilla tactics. More important, the Vietminh had popular support, while the French did not. In 1949 the French sought to win this support by restoring Emperor Bao Dai and giving him political concessions they would not extend to the Vietminh. France, however, retained real power in administration, military affairs, and diplomacy.

The Communist takeover in China coincided with the widening of the war in Vietnam. Military victories by DRV forces in the area of the Chinese border permitted the Vietminh to have unrestricted access to its neighbor and to receive both equipment and training from the Chinese. By January 1950, both China and the U.S.S.R. recognized the DRV. A month later, the United States recognized the Bao Dai government. Thus, both Vietnamese governments gained international standing, making any real settlement of the war more difficult. The United States, which had begun to assist France in 1949, steadily increased its aid through the years. By 1954 it was paying 80 percent of the total cost of waging the war.

The Siege of Dien Bien Phu. From 1950 to 1954 the war increased its intensity and spread beyond Vietnam. A Vietminh thrust into Laos finally brought about the last major French–Vietminh battle. It took place at Dien Bien Phu in northwest Vietnam. There, in an isolated valley, the French established a fortress to control the Vietminh movements into Laos. Dependent upon aircraft for supplies, the French miscalculated the Vietminh ability to bring heavy artillery to the battle and to sustain an assault against a major fortified position. On May 7, 1954, the fortress fell, and fighting declined as the conflict shifted to the negotiating table.

The Geneva Conference, 1954. Under the sponsorship of Great Britain and the U.S.S.R., the French, the Vietnamese, and other interested parties met in Geneva, Switzerland, to negotiate a settlement of the war. The discussions produced a military agreement, which was signed by the French and the DRV. A final declaration was agreed to by all participants except the United States and the Bao Dai government. The military agreement called for: (1) the temporary division of Vietnam at the 17th parallel, with the French in the south and the Vietminh in the north, (2) the creation of a demilitarized zone (DMZ) at the dividing line,

(3) 300 days of free movement by troops and civilians between the two areas, (4) a ban on the increase of troops and military equipment, and (5) a ban on further military alliances for either side. A declaration of the conference called for elections by 1956 to unify Vietnam.

The Second Phase: 1956–1965

The Diem Government. As a result of political conditions within South Vietnam, war in that country resumed. In 1955 a change of government had taken place. Ngo Dinh Diem, premier of South Vietnam and a determined anti-Communist, had replaced Emperor Bao Dai as head of state. The actions of Diem's government displeased many segments of the population. In 1956 the government refused to carry out the election provisions of the Geneva Accords. Furthermore, Diem sought to establish his authority through the use of force. He discouraged any political dissent in South Vietnam.

Gradually, an active anti-government movement developed. Using guerrilla tactics, this movement attempted to overthrow the Diem regime. Eventually, the struggle grew into a full-scale civil war. The anti-government group, which was named the National Liberation Front (NLF), included former supporters of the Vietminh. Its goals were the withdrawal of foreign troops from Vietnam and the unification of north and south. In January 1961, Communist North Vietnam announced its approval of the NLF and began supplying aid in the form of training and equipment.

The Vietcong. Although the NLF was not originally a Communist organization, its members were referred to by the Saigon government as *Vietcong,* meaning Vietnamese Communists. The Vietcong fought the government in several ways. They made surprise attacks on government officials in Saigon. They raided farm villages, using terrorism to gain control of the people. In addition, they used propaganda—posters, radio broadcasts, meetings—to turn the South Vietnamese citizens against their government. During the early 1960's, much of South Vietnam came under Vietcong control.

The Military Coup, 1963. Meanwhile, within Saigon and the South Vietnamese government, several attempts were made to overthrow the

During the 1960's, fighting ranged throughout South Vietnam. The nature of guerrilla warfare made rapid movement of troops a necessity. Helicopters, right, were a key means of transport for U.S. and South Vietnamese troops. War became a constant feature of life for the South Vietnamese. Farmers, below, continued work as bombs exploded nearby. On occasion, Vietcong penetrated major southern cities. In February 1968, Saigon became a battlefield, below right.

(Right and below right) UPI Compix, (below) Camera Press—Pix from Publix

Diem regime. A popular protest headed by Buddhist monks and students led finally to a successful take-over by a military group in November, 1963. But Diem's military successors were also incapable of bringing the civil war to a halt. The new government was weak and could not retain power. Between 1963 and 1965, several changes in government occurred, but Vietcong strength and influence grew.

Growing U.S. Involvement. During the 1960's, the United States became deeply involved in the political and military affairs of South Vietnam. After the Geneva Conference in 1954, all French forces had been withdrawn from the country. In the same year, the United States had become South Vietnam's chief source of military and economic assistance. U.S. aid had increased steadily after 1954.

As Diem's control over the country weakened, he required increasing help. His army outnumbered the Vietcong but was unable to defeat them. Between 1961 and 1963, the number of U.S. military personnel in South Vietnam increased from 2,000 to 15,500. After the military coup, troop buildup continued, and U.S. advisers became active in fighting the Vietcong.

Gulf of Tonkin Incident. On August 4, 1964, two U.S. destroyers were reportedly attacked by North Vietnamese PT (patrol) boats in the Gulf of Tonkin. In retaliation, the United States attacked North Vietnamese military installations. This was the first U.S. attack on North Vietnamese territory. Congress approved, by resolution, the president's use of force to protect U.S. men and equipment and to assist nations of SEATO (Southeast Asia Treaty Organization). In the following months, other anti-U.S. attacks occurred. The United States continued to retaliate. In 1965 the U.S. policy shifted to direct participation in the war.

The Third Phase: 1965–1970

In the mid-1960's the war evolved into an international conflict. Troops of the South Vietnamese government were assisted by U.S., Korean, Australian, New Zealand, Thai, and Philippine units. The Vietcong drew support—primarily supplies—from the U.S.S.R. and China.

Between 1965 and 1967, the United States increased its forces in Vietnam to about 500,000 men, assuming a leading role in the war. Enjoying superiority in the air and at sea, U.S. aircraft bombed targets in North Vietnam to prevent the movement of troops and supplies.

Despite wide support within South Vietnam, the Vietcong were unable to win a military victory. They suffered heavy losses as the war progressed. Then in February 1968 the NLF launched a devastating attack on South Vietnamese cities and towns, including Saigon. This offensive made the U.S. and South Vietnamese governments realize that military victory could be farther away than had been thought.

Underlying Issues of the War. The political system in South Vietnam was a major point of friction between the two sides. The NLF had always challenged the legality of the Saigon government. They called for a new government in

In North Vietnam, Vietcong guerrillas prepare for an attack with a detailed military briefing, left. Women in the capital city of Hanoi, below, work on the reconstruction of a factory destroyed during U.S. bombing raids.

(Left) UPI Compix, (below) Gamma—Pix from Publix

which all social classes, nationalities, political parties, and religious groups would be represented. The military rulers in Saigon, however, wanted Communists and neutralists excluded.

The opposing sides were also divided on the issue of foreign involvement in Vietnam. The NLF called for the expulsion of U.S. and other non-Vietnamese forces. Saigon wanted an end to North Vietnamese intervention in the south. Another issue was land reform. The Vietcong promised to redistribute land—traditionally owned by feudal-like landholders—to the peasants. But in March 1970 the Saigon government passed a U.S.-backed land reform act that guaranteed land to each South Vietnamese peasant.

The United States, considering the NLF an aggressor, justified its intervention under the commitments of the SEATO treaty, in which it had agreed to defend South Vietnam against armed attack. The NLF charged the U.S. with "neo-colonialism" and called for the overthrow of the Saigon government. North Vietnam denied that its support of the NLF constituted aggression. It claimed only to be helping to liberate the south.

Negotiations Begin. For three years an unbridgeable political gap existed between the two sides. Finally, U.S. President Lyndon B. Johnson took the first step toward ending the deadlock. On March 31, 1968, the president ordered a partial halt in the bombing of North Vietnam, in order to get peace talks started. Not long afterward, on May 13, representatives of the United States and North Vietnam met in Paris, France, to begin preliminary talks. They were joined in December 1968 by representatives of the NLF and the Saigon government.

On April 30, 1970, U.S. and South Vietnamese combat forces entered Cambodia in an attempt to destroy Communist headquarters for South Vietnam. (See also CAMBODIA.) U.S. President Nixon called the action temporary. He linked it to the success of his Vietnamization program, through which U.S. troops were being replaced with South Vietnamese forces in an attempt to shift the combat burden of the war to South Vietnam. In an attempt to stop the supply flow from North Vietnam to the Vietcong, South Vietnamese troops, aided by U.S. planes, invaded the neutral kingdom of Laos in February 1971.

VILLA (*vē′ä*), **FRANCISCO** (*frän sēs′kō*) **(PANCHO)** (1877–1923), was a powerful military leader of the Mexican Revolution. He was born Doroteo Arango in San Juan del Rio, Durango. He changed his name to Francisco Villa, but became known as Pancho.

In 1910 he joined Francisco Madero's revolution against President Porfirio Diaz. While in the service of Madero, Villa was jailed for insubordination by Victoriano Huerta, Madero's chief military leader. Villa escaped and fled to Texas. After the assassination of Madero and Huerta's establishment of a new government, Villa returned and joined forces with the aspiring political leader, Venustiano Carranza.

Pancho Villa was a powerful leader of the Mexican Revolution who, at one time, controlled most of Mexico.

Culver Pictures, Inc.

Because of his military victories, Villa's importance and power grew. When the Huerta government fell, he and Carranza began fighting for control. Villa established an alliance with Emiliano Zapata, the powerful Indian leader in southern Mexico. Between them they managed to push Carranza out of Mexico City and to control most of the country.

Villa was inevitably defeated, however, because of his unwillingness to assume civilian control of the country and his inability to agree to orderly processes. From a crest of complete power in 1915, he was slowly forced into retreat and later into obscurity by the Carranza forces. In desperation he crossed the border to raid Columbus, New Mexico, in 1916, hoping that American intervention would follow and embarrass the Carranza government. A U.S. expedition under General John Pershing did pursue Villa but without success. Villa was finally bribed to retire in 1920, and was assassinated three years later.

VINCI (*vēn'chē*), **LEONARDO** (*lā'ō när'dō*) **DA** (*dä*) (1452–1519). In 1482 Leonardo da Vinci wrote to Ludovico Sforza, Duke of Milan, regarding a position. He spoke of himself as an inventor of engines of war, a builder of movable bridges and chariots, and an engineer skilled in the science of artillery and sieges. Then he added a postscript to his letter saying, "I will execute sculpture in marble, bronze, or terra cotta; also in painting I can do as much as any other, be he who he may." Since the writer was fully capable of proving his claims, this letter gives some idea of the almost universal character of the genius of Leonardo.

Leonardo was born at Vinci near Florence, Italy. His talent for drawing led his father to place him at the age of 18 with Andrea del Verrocchio. Verrocchio was a Florentine artist who was gifted in many different kinds of art. (See VERROCCHIO, ANDREA DEL.) While Leonardo was studying in Florence, his mechanical genius was discovered in his architectural designs and engineering schemes. This mechanical knowledge was valuable during the years he was in the service of the Duke of Milan (1483–1499). He invented new machinery for defense in the numerous wars that engaged the Italian people. He built canals and planned an extensive irrigation system. He made plans for the Cathedral of Milan and supervised the pageants and masques given at the castle. He also worked for 17 years on a huge statue of Francesco Sforza, the Duke's father, on a horse. The statue was never cast and the clay model was destroyed by French soldiers at the capture of Milan in 1500.

While in the employ of the Duke, Leonardo found time to organize the Milanese academy and there composed studies in optics, perspective, anatomy, and proportion. These studies were published first in Paris in 1551 under

Gramstorff Bros., Inc.

"Mona Lisa," by Leonardo da Vinci. This painting is sometimes called "La Gioconda" because it is a portrait of the wife of Zanobi del Giocondo.

the title *Treatise on Painting.* Although he was busily engaged in many different kinds of occupation, Leonardo painted his greatest work, the "Last Supper," in the refectory of the Dominican Convent, Santa Maria delle Grazie, in Milan.

In 1500 he returned to Florence and was again employed as architect and engineer. This time he was in the service of Cesare Borgia, Duke of Romagna. Then came a remarkable incident. He was commissioned to paint a battle scene on one wall of the council hall, and his rival, the young Michelangelo Buonarroti, was given another wall. Leonardo chose "The Battle of the Standard," a struggle for a flag on a bridge, and in two years completed his cartoon, or preliminary painting. According to all accounts, it was breathtaking in its expression of battle frenzy. Leonardo continued his experiments in making the actual painting. The colors ran, and he gave up the task, leaving final honors to his rival. During this period he also painted the portrait "Mona Lisa," which he himself never considered finished.

In 1512 Leonardo went to Rome, but friendship for Francis I drew him towards France. In the Castle of Cloux, near Amboise, France, he passed his remaining years.

Paintings and Drawings

Leonardo had a great thirst for knowledge and new achievements. These, together with his ideals of perfection, were responsible for his leaving few finished works, but such are of supreme beauty. Among them, the paintings which still survive and are known to be his work are the "Last Supper," in Milan, and the "Virgin of the Rocks," "The Virgin with St. Anne" and the "Mona Lisa," all in the Louvre, Paris. "The Adoration of the Magi" in the Uffizi Gallery, Florence, and the "St. Jerome" in the Vatican, Rome, are unfinished. Others which were thought to be painted by him have been much repainted or are the works of his pupils. Two of these are in the Louvre: "Portrait of Lucrezia Crivelli" and the "John the Baptist."

His drawings are masterpieces of the Renaissance, sufficient in themselves to have brought everlasting glory to the artist. Two of the most highly valued are "The Virgin with St. Anne" in the Royal Academy, London, and "The Adoration of the Magi" in the Louvre. In them his fine sense of composition, his chief contribution to art, is revealed, as well as his command over space, light, and line. Much of the excellence of design has been lost in his paintings because Leonardo was continually experimenting with the mixing of colors and many of his colors have faded. For this reason, too, the oil paints he used scaled and blackened and his pictures, particularly the "Last Supper," are in a state of half ruin. It is known, from the writings of people living in his time that his pictures came near to absolute perfection in their color effects. In his work with light and shadow he was the forerunner of Rembrandt van Rijn. (See REMBRANDT HARMENSZ VAN RIJN.)

The "Mona Lisa" is probably the best-known portrait, if not the best-known painting, in the world. In 1911 it was stolen from the Louvre and the whole world was aroused over the theft. It was found two years later in Florence and returned to its place in the Louvre. This painting is also known as "La Gioconda," after the lady who posed for it. The figure of a woman is seen against a landscape background of rich brown-red color which is repeated in the many large folds of the sleeves. It is said that the sweet, smiling expression on the woman's face was caused by the music and other diversions Leonardo furnished for her entertainment while he worked on her portrait. Critics now think that the face of Mona Lisa has a mysterious expression because of her strange smile which is difficult to describe. Walter Pater's essay on "Mona Lisa" is a favorite interpretation of this famous painting. Like the "Mona Lisa" the Madonnas of Leonardo are endowed with a half-mystical smile which distinguishes them from those of earlier artists. This sweetness became exaggerated and affected in some of his followers, notably Raphael Sanzio.

"Last Supper"

In his "Last Supper" Leonardo combined psychology and drama in a magnificent composition. This scene, which had been painted often, had been treated by artists since Giotto di Bondone and Giovanni Cimabue in much the same manner. Leonardo tried something different. He grouped Jesus and his disciples on one side of a long refectory table and presented a scene in the nature of a trial. In this way he showed the effect upon the disciples of Jesus' declaration, "One of you shall betray me." The expression on each face is an interesting character study. The attitudes and gestures flow in a rhythmic composition that is unsurpassed in art. The effect is heightened by the use of perspective which causes the lines in the architecture of the room to seem to meet just above the figure of Jesus.

As a scientist and inventor Leonardo was centuries ahead of his time. Because he wrote his notes with his left hand, backhanded and from right to left across the page, for many years they were not understood. One of his most famous scientific experiments was an oft-repeated attempt to build a practical airplane. It seems probable that he failed only because he lacked an engine to drive it.

Although he was a great man of science, Leonardo had the tenderest of feelings. He could dissect a dead animal with exactness and calm, but he was so soft-hearted toward living animals that he disliked to see a bird caged. He used to buy whole cages of them when he saw them on the streets of Florence and set them free.

VINEGAR (*vĭn'ĭ gŭr*) is a sour liquid made by the fermentation of slightly alcoholic liquids. Wine was probably the first liquid from which vinegar was made. The word *vinegar* comes from the French words *vin*, which means wine, and *aigre*, which means sour. Today, however, vinegar is made from any of many liquids.

Vinegar fermentation is caused by a tiny plant organism or bacterium popularly known as "mother of vinegar." It depends on direct contact with air for its growth. The action of this bacterium on alcohol forms acetic acid. This makes up from about 5 to 7 percent of the vinegar and gives it its sour taste. Any fermented liquor containing alcohol can be made into vinegar. In the United States vinegar made from apple cider is preferred. In Great Britain malt vinegar is popular. Wine which is tightly bottled does not turn into vinegar.

The way to make vinegar quickly, therefore, is to have as much of the liquid exposed to the air at one time as possible, without causing too much evaporation. For this reason a cask, or vat, which is divided into three compartments, one on top of the other, is often used. The middle compartment, which is the largest, is separated from the top one by a platform bored with tiny holes. From each of these hangs a short piece of string. When the liquor is poured into the top compartment, it begins leaking through the holes and falls, drop by drop, from the strings. The middle compartment is full of vinegar-soaked beechwood shavings through which the liquor trickles until it reaches the sieve bottom. From there it filters into the lowermost compartment. For a strong vinegar two or more filterings are required.

L. W. Brownell

Meadow violets have perfumed blossoms and heart-shaped green leaves.

VIOLET (*vī'ō lŭt*) is a large genus of flower that has about 400 species. Mythology says that it was Aphrodite's sacred flower. It has been known since earliest times and was the symbol of the ancient city of Athens. North America has the greatest number of species. It has been named the state flower of Wisconsin, Illinois, New Jersey, and Rhode Island.

Most kinds of violet are low-growing, compact bushes, but others are more upright and may be a foot tall. Some of the species have delicately perfumed blossoms borne amid heart-shaped, deep green leaves. In color violets range from white through light yellow and blue to purple. Examples are the bird's-foot violet and the violas and pansies commonly grown in gardens. The flower called dogtooth violet is not a true violet but belongs to the lily family.

Although perfume is made from violets with odor, most kinds of violet are odorless. Sometimes the blooms are crystallized into candies or used in salads.

In the wild state most violets grow on rich, moist soils in the shade of trees or bushes. An exception to this is the bird's-foot violet, commonly found in sunny spots on sandy soils or rocky ledges. Wild violets multiply by means of seeds or runners which spread out from the parent plants and take root. The cultivated types are usually grown from divisions of the old plants. The two most important rules in the care of violets are to give enough but not too much moisture and to supply plenty of shade. Early spring is the best time to plant them. If they grow slowly weeding is necessary. Often they grow vigorously and compete readily with other plants.

VIOLIN (*vī'ō lin'*) **FAMILY** is a group of instruments that belongs to a larger family called the stringed instruments. In the violin family the strings are set in motion by drawing a bow across them. The moving strings make the sound or tone. (See MUSICAL INSTRUMENTS.)

Violin

The most popular instrument in the violin family is the *violin*. It is the smallest in size and highest in pitch. With its high and pure tone it is the singer among musical instruments, important both as a soloist and as the backbone of the orchestra. It was brought into the orchestra by Claudio Monteverdi, one of the first operatic composers, around 1600. A symphony orchestra may have from 16 to 20 "first" violins and the same number of "second" violins.

The distant ancestor of the violin, the *rebec*, came from India into Persia and Arabia. It reached Europe through Spain when the Mohammedans invaded that country. The *crwth* of the Welsh bards, a stringed instrument played with a bow, was then combined with the rebec. It became the viol of the troubadours in the 13th century. From these instruments, called *viols, Geigen,* and *fidels,* came the violin. The violin reached perfection toward the end of the 17th century with the violinmaker Antonio Stradivari. (See STRADIVARI, ANTONIO.)

Among early great violinists were Arcangelo Corelli and his pupils Antonio Vivaldi and Giuseppe Tartini, who were also excellent composers. In the early 19th century Nicolo Paganini amazed the world by his spectacular playing. Other famous violinists of the 19th century were Ole Bull, Joseph Joachim, and Pablo Sarasate y Navascues.

Leopold Auer was the outstanding violin teacher at the beginning of the 20th century. He was born in Hungary and studied violin under Joseph Joachim. He taught leading violinists in St. Petersburg (Leningrad), Russia, and later in the United States, where he became a citizen in 1926. Among his pupils were Mischa Elman, Efrem Zimbalist, Jascha Heifetz, and Toscha Seidel. Another famous violinist-teacher was the Belgian Eugene Ysaye. The performer who enjoyed the greatest popularity in the early 20th century was Fritz Kreisler. (See KREISLER, FRITZ.) Well-known modern violinists are Zino Francescatti, Nathan Milstein, Isaac Stern, Yehudi Menuhin, Joseph Szigeti, and David Oistrakh.

How the Violin Is Played

The violin is made of fine wood and strung with four strings. The strings are stretched from one end of the body to the other and across a bridge. They are tuned in fifths (E, A, D, G), which means five steps apart on the musical scale. The violin is held under the chin and resting on the left shoulder or collarbone. It is played when the bow, which is strung with many fine horsehairs, is drawn across the strings with the right hand.

Different tones are made when the left hand presses the strings at various points on the finger board. A *sordine,* or mute, is a little device which deadens vibrations and gives a veiled sound. *Pizzicato* is the name of the effect given when the strings are plucked with the fingers of the right hand. *Harmonics* are tones made by touching the strings with the left hand so lightly that they do not touch the finger board as they ordinarily do. When the string is lightly touched in this way, the vibra-

VIOLIN
SCROLL
PEGBOX
PEGS
NUT
FINGER BOARD
PURFLING
SOUNDBOARD
UPPER BOUTS
MIDDLE BOUTS
VIBRATING CENTER
BRIDGE
SOUND HOLE
EDGE
LOWER BOUTS
STRING HOLDER

Photo, Courtesy Rudolph Wurlitzer Company

The parts of the violin and the violin family. Violin (upper left), viola (lower left), cello (right), and string bass (center).

tions of the fundamental tones are stopped and only the overtones can be clearly heard. It makes a flutelike tone.

The standard-sized violin used by adults is called full size. A three-quarter-sized instrument is for young persons about 11 years of age. A half-sized instrument is suited for a young person of about nine or ten. A half-sized instrument is several inches shorter in length and not actually half the size of the standard full-sized instrument. There are also sizes other than these. It is possible for a young child to learn to play the violin because of the smaller sizes that are made.

Viola

The viola is larger than the violin and sounds deeper and richer in quality of tone. It has the three lower strings of the violin—A, D, and G—and a fourth string, C. This string sounds a fifth (five steps) lower than the G. The alto or viola clef, with middle C on the third line,

is usually used in writing music for the viola. The method of playing the viola is about the same as that of playing the violin. The only new thing to learn is how to read the alto clef.

During the 17th century there were two ancestors of today's viola. The *viola da gamba* (*gamba* is the Italian word for "leg") rested on the floor and was held between the knees; it was played like the modern cello. The *viola da braccio* rested on the shoulder like the violin (*braccio* is the Italian word for "arm"). The history of viola making is similar to that of violin making.

The viola is a very important part of the string choir of an orchestra. It was not highly thought of for a long time, but during this century the viola has come into its own. Fine performers on the viola, such as Maurice Vieux, Lionel Tertis, and William Primrose, did much to bring about this change, and modern composers have become more and more interested in this instrument for solo work.

Violoncello

The name violoncello is often shortened to cello. *Cello* is Italian for "small"; thus a violoncello was at first a "small viol." The viol, the parent instrument of the whole violin family, was a large instrument and became the double bass, or string bass. The strings of the cello have the same letter names as those of the viola, but they sound one octave (eight steps) lower. The violin uses the treble clef, the viola the alto clef, and the cello the bass clef for its music. The violin and viola are held under the chin when played. The cello is too large, and so it stands on the floor and is held between the knees. Few instruments have the beauty and richness of tone of the cello when played by an expert. Like violins and violas, cellos are made in different sizes so that a child of ten, or even younger, can learn to play the instrument.

String Bass

The string bass is often called the double bass or contrabass. It has the same shape as the violin, viola, and cello, but it is the largest in size. Thus it sounds the lowest of the four. The bass clef is used for its music. In fact, the bass sounds so low that the notes must be written one octave higher than they actually sound; otherwise there would not be room on the music paper. On each of the other three instruments of the violin family the strings are tuned in fifths (five steps apart), but those of the bass are tuned in fourths (four steps apart)—G, D, A, and E. The strings of the bass, which are thick and heavy, are tuned with the help of metal cogwheels.

Two types of bows are used to play the string bass. The French bow looks much like a cello bow, while the German bow is wider and longer. The German bow is held with the fingers under the bow and the thumb above; the French bow is held with the fingers over the bow and the thumb under.

There are two types of basses, the flat-back and the swell-back. As their names show, the shape of the back of one is flat while that of the other is curved. Both are used by professional players. The flat-back type can be made much less expensively. Some basses are made of plywood (several thin sheets of wood glued together). Such instruments are less expensive to keep in condition for the material does not crack, but their tone is not the finest.

The commonest size bass used by adults is the three-quarter size, but many sizes have been made. In 1849 an "octobass" was built which was 13 feet in height. In 1889 an American instrument maker built a "grand bass" which was 15 feet high.

The bass is very large and looks as if it would be clumsy to play. But there are several advantages in playing the bass. First, the bass music in an orchestra or band is the foundation of the harmony. Second, one who has played the piano can learn to play the bass much more quickly than the other three instruments of the violin family.

VIPER (*vī′pēr*). The families of vipers and pit vipers include some of the most poisonous snakes in the world. The rattlesnake, the water moccasin, and the copperhead of North America, the deadly bushmaster and fer-de-lance of South America, the poisonous adder of Europe, the horned viper of Africa, and the chain viper of India, all belong to these families. All vipers have thick bodies and flat, triangular heads. Their poison fangs, located in their upper jaws, are really very long teeth, pierced by a channel which connects with the poison glands. This poison is more deadly in some kinds of snakes than in others.

In most species the young are born alive, but

All vipers have thick bodies and flat, triangular heads. Occasionally the African sand viper grows to be 30 inches long, but the average length is 25 inches.

in a few species they are hatched from eggs.

The vipers are divided into two families: the true vipers, found only in the Old World, and the pit vipers of the New World, and some parts of Asia. These can be distinguished by the hollow between the eye and the nostril. Among the pit vipers are the rattlesnake, copperhead, water moccasin, and bushmaster. The bushmaster, 12 feet long, is the largest venomous snake in the Americas. It lives in the jungles of Central and South America. It is the only pit viper known to lay eggs.

One of the best-known of the true vipers is the common adder, a small snake marked with jagged bands along its back. It is found from England eastward through northern Europe. Others are the asp of southern Europe, which has a flatter nose than the common adder, and the puff adder of northern Africa, which is a dull, sandy brown. The horned viper of northern Africa, which has a spike over each eye, is supposed to be the asp with which Cleopatra killed herself. The most deadly of the vipers is the chain or Russell's viper of India and southern Asia, which is often five feet long.

VIREO (vĭr′ē ō), a small (4 to 6½ inches), insect-eating bird that belongs to the large order of perching birds. Vireo comes from a Latin word meaning greenish, and these birds are sometimes called greenlets. Its plumage (feathers) is greenish or yellowish olive, olive-brown, or gray on the upper part of the body. The lower part may be white, whitish, yellow, or gray. The cap (head feathers) may be a contrasting color, sometimes black or reddish brown. Except for a little coloring on the wings in some species, there are usually no spots or streaks.

The wings may be long and pointed or short and rounded. The strong bill is slightly hooked. About 50 species of the family are found in South and Central America, north through Canada, and in the West Indies. About 12 species live in the United States.

Vireos live in the forests and forest edges, and in garden trees quite close to houses. Although insects are their main food, they sometimes eat fruit, such as berries. Most vireos

The red-eyed vireo is noted for its cheerful song, which continues from morning to night.

are migratory, that is, they winter in the warm south, then return to the north early in the spring. The song of the vireo is cheerful and, in some species, very musical.

The red-eyed vireo is probably the most common vireo in the United States. Its deep, cup-shaped nest is lined with grasses and often decorated with bark and paper. These small, well-built nests hang from the fork of a tree branch, usually close to a house. The vireo lays two to five white, lightly speckled eggs. Both parents help to feed and care for the young birds.

Other kinds of vireos may build their nests higher or lower in the trees than the red-eyed. The yellow-throated and warbling vireos like nesting spots more than 15 feet above the ground, but they too may build them in a back yard.

VIRGIL or **VERGIL** (vẽr′jĭl) (PUBLIUS [pŭb′-lĭ ŭs] VERGILIUS [vẽr jĭl′ĭ ŭs] MARO [mā′rō]) (70–19 B.C.). Virgil was the most famous poet of ancient Rome, and one of the great poets of all time. He grew up near Mantua, Italy, on a small farm. Although his family was not wealthy, he was given a good education and sent to Rome to finish his studies.

Virgil was very fond of the country and country life. Many of his poems were inspired by the beauty of the Italian countryside and its people. When he started to write poetry he imitated the Greek poet Theocritus, who wrote about shepherds, their lives in the country, and their rustic songs. This kind of poetry is usually called "pastoral," from *pastor,* meaning shepherd; but Virgil's poems were called *Eclogues,* meaning "selections."

When Virgil was about 30, his small farm near Mantua was seized by the government, along with other lands to be given as rewards to soldiers returning from the civil wars. The farm was returned to Virgil through the help of government men who were interested in the young poet. One of the *Eclogues* expresses his thanks to the young ruler Octavian (later called Augustus). The poem is written as a conversation between two shepherds; one of them is a "disguise" for Virgil himself; the other represents the peasants who lost their farms and had no friends to help them.

Another of the *Eclogues* describes a future time when the world would be peaceful and happy, with no more wars. This new "golden age" was to begin at the birth of a child in that very year (40 B.C.). The poem sounds so much like Old Testament prophecies of the birth of the Messiah that all through the Middle Ages Virgil was regarded as a prophet. It is probable, however, that he was speaking of the child of Octavian born about that time.

The *Eclogues* have served as models for many poems in English, Italian, and French. English pastoral poetry often combines details from Virgil and from the Psalms, which are the pastoral poetry of Hebrew literature.

Virgil's next important work was a long poem about farming. The *Georgics,* meaning "work on the land," is divided into four books, on tilling the soil, tree growing, animal raising, and beekeeping. In the *Georgics,* Virgil wrote his best descriptions of the country and the simple life he himself enjoyed. By this time he was the most admired of Roman poets, and the leader of a circle of literary men gathered by Maecenas, the minister of state under Augustus. Virgil and his poet friend Horace did more than any other writers to make this period the "Golden Age of Latin Poetry."

The *Aeneid* was Virgil's last and greatest work. It is an epic poem about the legendary founder of the Roman race. (See AENEID.) For his hero Aeneas, Virgil pictured his own ideal of a good ruler. The portrait may have been the emperor Augustus. It was certainly a model for Augustus and all future emperors to follow.

Virgil spent ten years writing the *Aeneid,* and even then he did not consider it finished. Just before he died, on his way to Greece in 19 B.C., he asked that the poem be destroyed. Fortunately Augustus refused to follow the poet's wishes, and the poem was published after Virgil's death.

VIRGINIA (*vẽr jĭn′yà* or *vẽr jĭn ĭ à*), **UNITED STATES,** is in the southeastern part of the country. It is a South Atlantic state, with Maryland and West Virginia to the north; West Virginia and Kentucky to the west; and Tennessee and North Carolina to the south.

The name Virginia honored Queen Elizabeth I of England who was known as the "virgin queen." The state is sometimes called the "mother of presidents" because eight United States presidents were born there.

Virginia is shaped like a triangle, with Chesapeake Bay in the east. Broad rivers divide the flat land of the coastal lowland into long peninsulas. Central Virginia is an area of rolling hills, farms, and forests. The Blue Ridge and Allegheny Mountains, which cut across the western part of the state, are separated by the beautiful Valley of Virginia.

The population centers are: the area around the harbor of Hampton Roads; the capital city of Richmond; northern Virginia near Washington, D.C.; and the railroad and industrial city of Roanoke. About one-half of the people live in and around these cities. Manufacturing, farming, and providing services to tourists are the main occupations.

Landscape

The state has three land regions: the Coastal Lowland, the Piedmont, and the Appalachian Highland. The Coastal Lowland, also called the Tidewater, extends from the Atlantic Ocean westward to the fall line of the major rivers. It is up to this line that the rivers are navigable. (See FALL LINE.) Most of the Lowland is from 80 to 120 miles wide. It is mainly flat, although it has some hills, none over 400 feet high. Across the Chesapeake Bay is another part of the Coastal Lowland known as the Eastern Shore. This narrow strip is a part of the Delmarva Peninsula that extends southward from Maryland.

Three major rivers divide the mainland portion of the Lowland into four parts: south of the James River is Southeast Virginia; between the James and the York rivers is The Peninsula; between the York and the Rappahannock rivers lies the Middle Peninsula; between the Rappahannock and the Potomac rivers is the Northern Neck.

The Piedmont lies between the Lowland and the Blue Ridge Mountains. The word piedmont comes from Latin and means "at the foot of the mountains." The width of the region ranges from about 40 miles in the north to more than 180 miles in the south. The James River flows across the Piedmont and divides it almost in half.

The southern part is known as Southside. Most of the Piedmont is higher than the Lowland and has many rolling hills. It includes the foothills of the Blue Ridge Mountains, some of which are as high as 1,200 feet.

The Appalachian Highland region is a part of the great Appalachian Mountain chain of

Scene in the Blue Ridge Mountains near Roanoke.

Courtesy Virginia State Chamber of Commerce

North America. It is made up of several mountain ranges. The largest and best known are the Blue Ridge and Allegheny mountains. The state's highest peak, Mount Rogers (over 5,700 feet), is in the area south and west of Roanoke known as Southwest Virginia.

Between the Blue Ridge and the Allegheny mountains lies the Valley of Virginia, which is a part of the Great Appalachian Valley. The Valley extends for more than 300 miles from the state border above Winchester, southwest to the Tennessee border. The Shenandoah Valley is the northern part of the Valley of Virginia.

The most fertile soil in the state is the limestone soil of the Valley of Virginia. It is good for farming and pasture. Much of the other soils of the state are mixed with clay.

Chesapeake Bay is Virginia's most important body of water. Ships from all over the world come into the bay to the harbor of Hampton Roads. The James, York, Rappahannock, and Potomac rivers flow into Chesapeake Bay. The huge Dismal Swamp is south of Portsmouth. Lake Drummond, in the center of the Swamp, is the largest natural body of fresh water in the state.

About three-fifths of the land of Virginia is covered by forests, chiefly pine and oak. There are large areas of rich blue grass in the Appalachian Highland.

Climate

Virginia has a mild climate, with warm summers and cool winters. The average annual temperature is about 58 degrees Fahrenheit. The warmest areas are the Lowland and the southern Piedmont. Winter temperatures there are mild and the summer temperatures often rise above 90 degrees. But in the western parts of the state the climate is colder, especially in the Appalachian Highland where winter temperatures often fall below freezing and sometimes drop to zero or below.

The annual rainfall averages from 40 to 45 inches. Every part of the state has enough rain for farming. Snow falls to depths of from five to ten inches in the Lowland to 25 or 30 inches in the northern part of the Appalachian Highland.

Except in the west, the snow does not usually remain on the ground for longer than a day or two. Hurricanes and gales from the Atlantic Ocean sometimes sweep the Lowland.

The frost-free growing season is from 150 days in the Southwest to as many as 240 days along the Lowland coast.

Animal Life and Resources

The state has a great variety of wildlife. There are deer, black bears, foxes, squirrels, opossum, polecats, and different kinds of snakes. The streams and lakes are well stocked with fish.

Virginia ranks high among the states in the production of coal, its chief mineral resource. Limestone is next in importance. Virginia is one of the few states that sells lime to other states. Granite, sandstone, greenstone, slate, marble, and soapstone are also important. Lead and zinc are the most valuable metallic minerals. Manganese is of some importance.

Unusual Features of Interest

Among the most interesting natural features in the state are the beautiful caverns of the Shenandoah Valley. The best known of these are Luray, Endless, Shenandoah, Grand, Massanutten, and Skyline. The Natural Bridge near Lexington is a huge bridge of rock carved by water. In Southwest Virginia, water also has carved the Natural Tunnel through a mountain ridge.

Other natural features include Mountain Lake atop a 4,000 ft. mountain, the hot mineral springs of the Alleghenies, and Breaks Interstate Park with its beautiful river gorge.

The People

In 1607 thousands of Indians lived in the Virginia area. Most of them lived east of the Blue Ridge Mountains. Although only about 2,000 Indians live in the state today, the Indian heritage remains. Many rivers and cities, such as Roanoke, bear Indian names.

The first white settlers came to the area from England in 1607. The Virginia Company of London governed the colony until 1624 when it came under the control of the King of England. During the next 150 years thousands of English

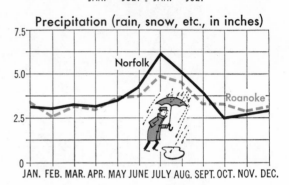

Average Daily Temperature

▶ low   ▶ high

Norfolk (coast)   Roanoke (west)

62%   58%

% sunshine   % sunshine

JAN. JULY | JAN. JULY

Precipitation (rain, snow, etc., in inches)

Norfolk

Roanoke

JAN. FEB. MAR. APR. MAY JUNE JULY AUG. SEPT. OCT. NOV. DEC.

settlers came to farm the land and to escape hardships at home. These people were most important in settling the Tidewater and Piedmont regions of Virginia. Large numbers of them were members of the Church of England. After the American Revolution, the church became the Episcopal Church in America. (See PROTESTANT EPISCOPAL CHURCH.)

The Blue Ridge Mountains were a barrier that slowed the westward movement of Virginia colonists. But German and Scotch-Irish settlers reached the Valley of Virginia from Pennsylvania. Thousands of these people came into the Valley between 1730 and 1775.

Today the white population of Virginia consists of descendants of the English, Scotch-Irish, German, and other western Europeans. About 19 per cent of the people are Negroes. Slightly more than one per cent of the state's residents are foreign-born.

About half of the people of Virginia live in the Tidewater and in the area near Washington, D.C. The rest are scattered throughout the state. At one time Virginia was a rural area, but today almost 65 per cent of the people live in cities and towns. Norfolk and Richmond are the two largest cities.

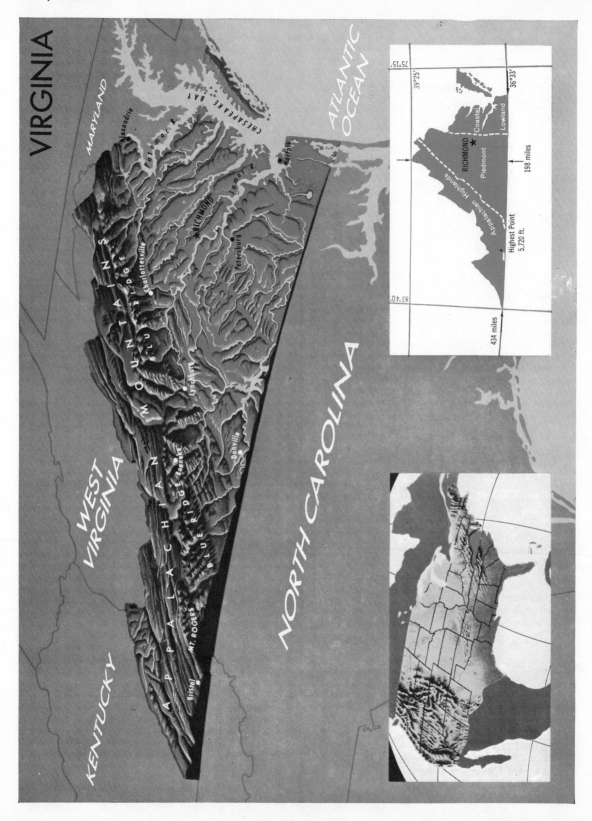

VIRGINIA

MARYLAND

ATLANTIC OCEAN

CHESAPEAKE BAY

Alexandria

Potomac R.

RICHMOND

James R.

Norfolk

Charlottesville

BLUE RIDGE

Petersburg

Lynchburg

APPALACHIAN MOUNTAINS

WEST VIRGINIA

Roanoke

BLUE RIDGE

Danville

NORTH CAROLINA

KENTUCKY

MT. ROGERS

Bristol

75°15'

39°25'

36°33'

Coastal

Lowland

RICHMOND

Piedmont

Appalachian Highlands

198 miles

83°40'

Highest Point
5,720 ft.

434 miles

Nicknames: "Old Dominion"; "Mother of Presidents"
Capital: Richmond
Motto: *Sic Semper Tyrannis* ("Thus Always to Tyrants")
Date admitted to the Union: One of original 13 states
Order of admission as state: 10th to ratify U.S. Constitution,
June 25, 1788
Song: "Carry Me Back to Old Virginia"

Dogwood   Flowering   Cardinal
           Dogwood

Physical

AREA: 40,817 square miles, including 976 square miles of water; 1.1 per cent of total United States; 36th state in size.

POPULATION (1970): 4,648,494; 2.3 per cent of total United States; 14th state in population; 113.9 persons per square mile; 63.1 per cent urban, 36.9 per cent rural.

MOUNTAIN RANGES: Appalachian, including Blue Ridge, Allegheny, Shenandoah.

CHIEF MOUNTAIN PEAKS (height in feet): Rogers (5,720); White Top (5,520); Hawksbill (4,049); Elliot Knob (4,458).

LARGEST LAKES: Drummond, Claytor, Buggs Island, Philpott.

MOST IMPORTANT RIVERS: Potomac, Rappahannock, York, James.

NATIONAL PARKS AND MONUMENTS: National Park: Shenandoah, 193,539 acres (established 1935). National Historical Parks: Appomattox Court House, 938 acres (1954); Cumberland Gap, 20,176 acres in Virginia, Kentucky, and Tennessee (7,478 acres in Virginia; 1940); Colonial, 9,430 acres (1936). National Monuments: Booker T. Washington, 218 acres (1956); George Washington Birthplace, 394 acres (1930). National Seashore: Assateague, 36,630 acres in Virginia and Maryland (5 acres in Virginia; 1965).

STATE PARKS: Total of 18 including Claytor Lake, Douthat, Fairy Stone, Hungry Mother, Pocahontas, Prince Edward, Staunton River, Westmoreland.

ADDITIONAL PLACES OF INTEREST: Arlington National Cemetery; Dismal Swamp; Jamestown Island; Monticello, near Charlottesville; Mount Vernon, near Washington, D.C.; Chesapeake Bay; Natural Bridge, near Lexington; Williamsburg; Skyline Drive.

Transportation and Communication

RAILROADS: 4,084 miles of track; first railroad, Weldon, North Carolina, to Petersburg, Virginia, 1833.

ROADS: Total, 60,705 miles; surfaced, 59,526 miles.

MOTOR VEHICLES: Total, 2,161,278; automobiles, 1,816,787; trucks and buses, 344,491.

AIRPORTS: Total, 161; private, 115.

NEWSPAPERS: 32 dailies; 97 weeklies; 13 Sunday; first newspaper, *Virginia Gazette*, Williamsburg, 1736.

RADIO STATIONS: 173; first station, WRVA, Richmond, 1925.

TELEVISION STATIONS: 18; first station, WTVR, Richmond, 1948.

TELEPHONES: Total, 2,336,300; residence, 1,668,400; business, 667,900.

POST OFFICES: 975.

People

CHIEF CITIES: Norfolk (307,951); Richmond (249,621); Virginia Beach (172,106); Newport News (138,177); Hampton (120,779).

NATIONAL BACKGROUNDS: 98.5 per cent native-born; 1.5 per cent foreign-born.

CHURCH MEMBERSHIP: Of total state population, 38.5 per cent are church members: 91.7 per cent Protestant (including Southern Baptist, 29.7 per cent; Methodist, 29.5 per cent; Presbyterian, 8.3 per cent; Episcopal, 6.9 per cent; Disciples of Christ, 4.7 per cent), 7.1 per cent Catholic, and 1.2 per cent Jewish.

LEADING UNIVERSITIES AND COLLEGES: University of Virginia, Charlottesville; College of William and Mary, Williamsburg; Virginia Polytechnic Institute, Blacksburg; Virginia Military Institute, Lexington; Virginia State College, Petersburg.

MUSEUMS: Museum of Arts and Sciences, Norfolk; Museum of Fine Arts, Richmond; Mariners Museum, Newport News; Valentine Museum, Richmond; War Memorial Museum, Newport News.

SPECIAL SCHOOLS: Lynchburg Training School (for mentally handicapped), Colony; Petersburg Training School (for mentally handicapped), Petersburg; Virginia Schools for the Deaf and Blind, Staunton and Hampton.

CORRECTIONAL AND PENAL INSTITUTIONS: Virginia Penitentiary, Richmond; Correctional Farms, White Gate, Capron, Goochland, State Farm; Schools for Girls, Bon Air and Peaks Turnout; Schools for Boys, Beaumont and Hanover.

Government

NUMBER OF U.S. SENATORS: 2.

NUMBER OF U.S. REPRESENTATIVES: 10.

NUMBER OF STATE SENATORS: 40. TERM: 4 years.

NUMBER OF STATE DELEGATES: 100. TERM: 2 years.

STATE LEGISLATURE CONVENES: January, even-numbered years.

SESSION LIMIT: Regular, 60 days; special, 30 days.

CONSTITUTION ADOPTED: 1970.

GOVERNOR'S TERM: 4 years. He may not succeed himself.

NUMBER OF COUNTIES: 96; independent cities, 38.

VOTING QUALIFICATIONS: Legal voting age; residence in state 1 year, in county 6 months, in precinct 30 days.

STATE HOLIDAYS: Lee-Jackson Day, January 19; Memorial Day, May 30.

ANNUAL STATE EVENTS: Shenandoah Apple Blossom Festival, Winchester, April; Azalea Festival, Norfolk, April; Pony Swim and Roundup, Chincoteague Island, July; Tobacco Festival, Richmond, September; Harvest Festival, Roanoke, October.

Historic Events

1607—Jamestown established; America's first permanent English settlement.

1619—House of Burgesses is established.

1624—Virginia becomes royal colony of England.

1676—Bacon's Rebellion.

1776—Virginia declares itself an independent state.

1788—Virginia ratifies U.S. Constitution.

1798—Virginia Resolutions protest Alien and Sedition Laws.

1831—Nat Turner's slave rebellion.

1861—Virginia secedes from Union.

1865—American Civil War ends at Appomattox.

1870—Virginia is readmitted to the Union.

1908—Staunton first U.S. city to adopt city-manager government.

1957—Virginia celebrates 350th anniversary of Jamestown.

1964—Legislature reapportioned according to population.

1969—Linwood Holton elected first Republican governor since Reconstruction.

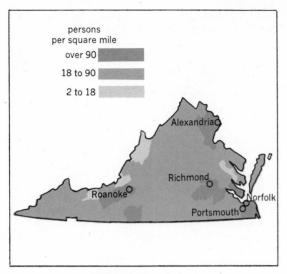

persons
per square mile

over 90

18 to 90

2 to 18

Alexandria

Richmond

Roanoke

Norfolk

Portsmouth

Where the people live.

Norfolk, on the south side of Hampton Roads, is the state's leading port and one of the country's major seaports. It is also an important railroad and industrial city. The Norfolk Naval Base is one of the U.S. Navy's chief training and supply centers. (See NORFOLK.)

Richmond, the capital of the state, is the center of Virginia's tobacco industry. Other industries such as chemicals, food, and textiles are important. Richmond is also an educational center with five institutions of higher learning within its boundaries. The city is noted for its historical sites, such as the capitol building which was designed by Thomas Jefferson. Patrick Henry made his "Give me liberty or give me death" speech in St. John's Episcopal Church. The "White House of the Confederacy" is now a Confederate museum. (See RICHMOND.)

Newport News, the fourth largest city, is on the north side of Hampton Roads. It ranks next to Norfolk as a port and has the state's greatest shipbuilding yards. Portsmouth and Hampton are other cities on Hampton Roads. The Norfolk Naval Shipyard at Portsmouth is the United States government's oldest shipyard.

Roanoke, a growing industrial center, is the only large city west of the Blue Ridge Mountains. It is a transportation center where railroad cars and locomotives are also manufactured.

Petersburg is noted for its tobacco industry and is also a leading trunk and bag manufacturing center. Alexandria is a business center for northern Virginia. The *Alexandria Gazette* is the oldest daily newspaper in the United States in continuous publication. Lynchburg, the largest city of the Piedmont, is a leading tobacco market. The manufacture of boots, shoes, and cast iron pipe are major industries.

How the People Make a Living

Manufacturing is the state's leading industry. About one-fifth of the working people earn a living in this way. Many also work in agriculture, the tourist industry, retail and wholesale trade, and federal government service.

Manufacturing. The many factories scattered throughout the state produce a wide variety of goods. These include man-made fibers and other chemical products, cigarettes and tobacco products, furniture, lumber and wood products, ships, textiles, food products, and railroad cars and equipment.

Virginia is one of the most important manufacturers of man-made fibers in the United States. The production of these fibers—nylon, orlon, and cellophane—brings more money to the state than any other manufacturing industry. Large plants are located in several places in-

One of the largest private shipbuilding yards in the world is at Newport News, Virginia.

Courtesy Newport News Shipbuilding and Dry Dock Company, Nixon photo

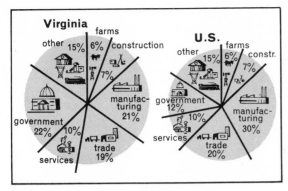

Sources of income.

canning and preserving fruits and vegetables are scattered throughout the state.

Agriculture. Although many different crops are raised, more than half of the state's farm income comes from poultry and livestock. Poultry includes chickens, eggs, and turkeys. Most of the chickens are raised in the Shenandoah Valley and Eastern Shore. Rockingham County is the turkey-raising center.

Virginia has excellent pasture lands. Large numbers of beef and dairy cattle are raised in nearly all counties of the Piedmont and the Appalachian Highland. Thousands of sheep are also raised in the Highland. Large numbers of pigs and hogs are raised in southeastern Virginia and in the Shenandoah Valley. The farmers in the southeast fatten their hogs on peanuts, a major crop of that area. Suffolk is one of the world's largest peanut markets.

Tobacco has been the leading cash crop of Virginia since colonial days. The state ranks

cluding Waynesboro, Front Royal, Narrows, and near Richmond. Fertilizer, explosives, drugs, and cleaning materials are some of the other chemical products. Virginia is also a major producer of tobacco products, especially cigarettes. Most of the tobacco factories are in Richmond and Petersburg.

The forests furnish the raw material for the lumber and lumber products industry. Furniture is manufactured at Martinsville. Paper and pulp mills are located at Covington and West Point. Other wood products include excelsior, barrels, and fruit and vegetable baskets.

The state ranks high in the nation in shipbuilding. This industry is centered at Hampton Roads in the cities of Newport News, Norfolk, and Portsmouth. Some of the largest commercial and military ships are built at Newport News.

More people are employed in the making of textiles than in any other manufacturing industry in the state. The Dan River Mills at Danville is one of the largest cotton cloth making plants in the world. There are also a number of woolen mills in the state and a rug making factory at Glasgow.

Many factories process the products of Virginia's farms and fisheries. Suffolk is noted for salted nuts and peanut candy. Richmond is a center for bakery products. Factories processing dairy products are found in cities throughout the state. The Shenandoah Valley has many poultry and apple packing plants. Meat packing is important in the Valley and in Richmond. Seafood plants are found in the Chesapeake Bay area. Flour and feed mills and plants for

How the people make a living.

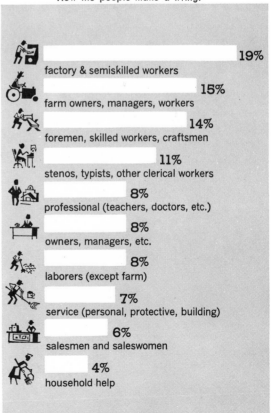

factory & semiskilled workers — 19%

farm owners, managers, workers — 15%

foremen, skilled workers, craftsmen — 14%

stenos, typists, other clerical workers — 11%

professional (teachers, doctors, etc.) — 8%

owners, managers, etc. — 8%

laborers (except farm) — 8%

service (personal, protective, building) — 7%

salesmen and saleswomen — 6%

household help — 4%

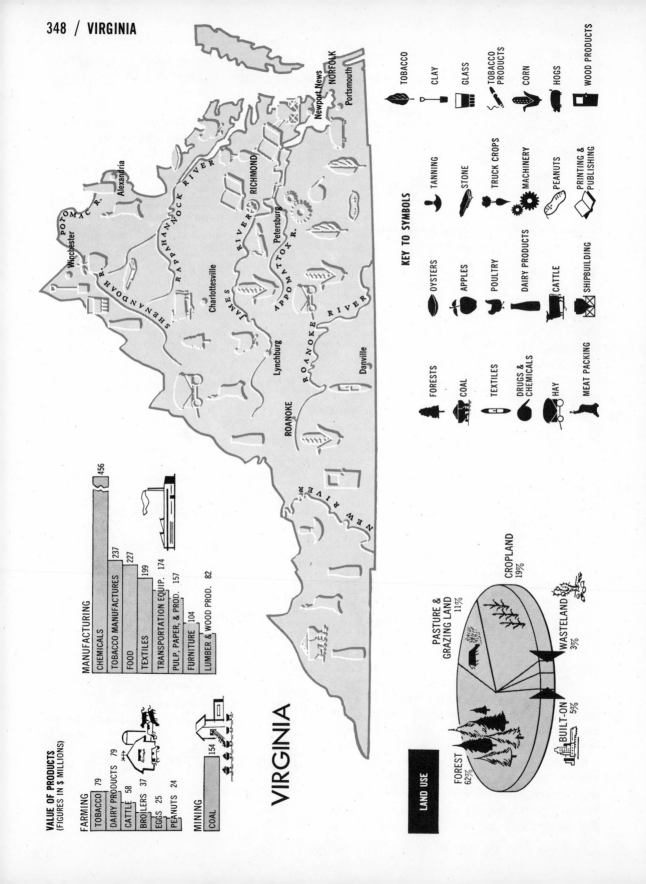

VIRGINIA

KEY TO SYMBOLS

TOBACCO
CLAY
GLASS
TOBACCO PRODUCTS
CORN
HOGS
WOOD PRODUCTS

TANNING
STONE
TRUCK CROPS
MACHINERY
PEANUTS
PRINTING & PUBLISHING

OYSTERS
APPLES
POULTRY
DAIRY PRODUCTS
CATTLE
SHIPBUILDING

FORESTS
COAL
TEXTILES
DRUGS & CHEMICALS
HAY
MEAT PACKING

VALUE OF PRODUCTS
(FIGURES IN $ MILLIONS)

FARMING
TOBACCO 79
DAIRY PRODUCTS 79
CATTLE 58
BROILERS 37
EGGS 25
PEANUTS 24

MINING
COAL 154

MANUFACTURING
CHEMICALS 456
TOBACCO MANUFACTURES 237
FOOD 227
TEXTILES 199
TRANSPORTATION EQUIP. 174
PULP, PAPER, & PROD. 157
FURNITURE 104
LUMBER & WOOD PROD. 82

LAND USE

FOREST 62%
PASTURE & GRAZING LAND 11%
CROPLAND 19%
WASTELAND 3%
BUILT-ON 5%

among the leaders in the nation in tobacco raising. Tobacco is grown chiefly in the south-side and in some counties of the southwest.

Other products of the farms include apples, peaches, pears, cherries, plums, potatoes, sweet potatoes, and vegetables. The Eastern Shore is the leading truck farming area because of its long growing season. Corn is raised in all parts of the state but much of it is used as an animal feed. Hay is also raised throughout Virginia. More acres are planted in hay than in any other crop. Wheat and other grains are raised in the Piedmont and the Valley.

Fishing. Chesapeake Bay, the center of the seafood industry, is rich in oysters and crabs. One of the most valuable Chesapeake Bay fish, the menhaden, is not used for food but instead is added to poultry feeds and used in fertilizer. Menhaden oil has more than 150 different uses. It goes into such products as soap, linoleum, and paint.

Mining. Virginia is rich in mineral resources. Most of the coal mines are located in the southwest. Lead, zinc, manganese, gypsum, and salt are also mined there.

Granite is found throughout the Piedmont, but the chief granite quarries are along the region's eastern edge. Most of the granite is sold as crushed rock for road building.

Limestone, found in the Valley, is used in making products such as cement, carbide, soda,

Treating cotton fabric in a large textile mill.

Courtesy National Cotton Council

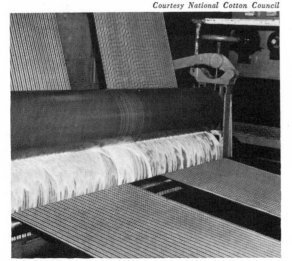

Courtesy Virginia State Chamber of Commerce

Tobacco auction. Tobacco is one of Virginia's main crops.

fertilizer, soap, glue, glass, paint, and road surfacing materials. Large lime manufacturing plants operate near Roanoke.

Tourist Industry. Each year the state receives thousands of visitors who come to enjoy the beautiful scenery, natural wonders, vacation resorts, and many places of historical interest. Millions of dollars have been spent to rebuild Williamsburg so that it will appear the same as when it was the capital of the Virginia colony. The city's attractions include the handsome capitol building, the magnificent "governor's palace," Raleigh Tavern, and Bruton Parish Church. (See WILLIAMSBURG.)

Near Williamsburg are the historic spots of Jamestown Island and Yorktown. Stratford Hall in the Northern Neck was the birthplace of Robert E. Lee. George Washington's home, Mount Vernon, is in the northern part of the state near Washington, D.C. Thomas Jefferson's beautiful house, Monticello, stands on a hilltop near Charlottesville. At Staunton in the Valley is the old Presbyterian manse where Woodrow Wilson was born. Other historic sites include battlefields of the War Between the States.

Transportation

Water transportation has always been important to Virginia. Hampton Roads, at the mouth of the James River, is a fine and busy harbor on

Courtesy Virginia State Chamber of Commerce

Virginia's Capitol, designed by Thomas Jefferson.

the east coast. Small ships travel the major rivers to ports such as Richmond, Petersburg, Fredericksburg, and Alexandria. The Dismal Swamp Canal connects the Chesapeake Bay and Albemarle Sound, North Carolina. This canal is a part of the Atlantic Intracoastal Waterway.

Roads and highways connect all parts of the state. In 1958 the state's first modern turnpike, the Richmond and Petersburg Turnpike, was opened.

Bridges have replaced most of the ferries that used to carry vehicles across the large Tidewater rivers. The James River bridge near Newport News is more than four miles long. In 1957 a bridge and tunnel was completed across Hampton Roads. But the state's greatest project is the bridge and tunnel system across the Chesapeake Bay connecting the Eastern Shore and the Tidewater mainland.

The state has many commercial, private, and government airports and airfields. The National Airport and Dulles International Airport serve nearby Washington, D.C. Other large airports are at Richmond, Norfolk, and Roanoke.

Government

Virginia is one of four states that call themselves commonwealths. The present constitution, adopted in 1970, provides for legislative, executive, and judicial branches.

In 1619 the first representative governing body in America met at Jamestown. It was known as the House of Burgesses. From this has developed the present lawmaking body of the state. It is called the General Assembly and is made up of a Senate and a House of Delegates.

The governor heads the executive branch. Other elected officials are the lieutenant governor and the attorney general. The governor chooses the treasurer, the secretary and the heads of the executive departments.

The Supreme Court of Appeals is Virginia's highest court. It has seven members, who are elected by the General Assembly. Every county has a circuit court whose judges are also chosen by the Assembly. The larger cities have circuit or corporation courts and police courts.

Each county of the state is governed by an elected Board of Supervisors which makes the county laws and sets the tax rates. The largest cities of the state are not under the control of the county, but instead have separate local governments. The independent cities, totaling 35 in the late 1960's, all have the city-manager form of government that originated in Staunton, Virginia, in 1908.

Education

The public school system is regulated by a State Board of Education made up of seven members appointed by the governor. The Superintendent of Public Instruction directs the educational program. All counties and cities have county and city school boards. There are more than ten state-supported colleges and universities. These include the University of Virginia, Virginia Military Institute, Virginia Polytechnic Institute, and the College of William and Mary, the second oldest college in the nation. There are more than 20 church-supported and private colleges.

Bookmobiles or traveling libraries are operated in some counties. The state library in Richmond is the largest of the state's public libraries.

Health and Welfare

Virginia has a strong public health program with a health department in every city and county. The Department of Health directs the program. Each city and county also has a Welfare Department or Board which is supervised by the State Department of Welfare and Institutions.

There are seven state-supported hospitals for the mentally ill. Eastern State Hospital at Williamsburg is the oldest state-supported hospital in the United States.

Recreation

Swimming, boating, and fishing are popular at such places as Virginia Beach, on the Atlantic Ocean, and at the beaches that line Chesapeake Bay and the Potomac River. Fish are plentiful in the streams and the many private fishing ponds. Northern Virginia, known for its fine horses, has several horse shows and fox hunts throughout the year.

More than 2,000,000 acres of state land are in national and state parks. Trout, bass, deer, and bear attract many fishermen and hunters to these areas.

History

Jamestown, the first permanent English settlement in America, was founded on May 14,

Dismal Swamp is a wild swampy forest near the coast of Virginia and North Carolina.

Courtesy Virginia State Chamber of Commerce

Courtesy Virginia State Chamber of Commerce

Oyster fishing in Chesapeake Bay.

1607. When King James I gave the Virginia Company of London the right to start a colony, about 100 colonists sailed to America in three small ships, the *Sarah* or *Susan Constant*, the *Goodspeed* or *Godspeed,* and the *Discovery*.

The early years at Jamestown were very difficult. Led by Captain John Smith, the colonists were able to survive. In addition to securing food for the settlers, Smith used his talents to explore the Tidewater rivers and the Chesapeake Bay, make a map of the area, and write the first history of Virginia. However, a little more than two years after the first landing, Smith was badly injured and had to return to England. The colonists, left without a capable leader, found it difficult to keep the colony going. (See JAMESTOWN; SMITH, CAPTAIN JOHN.)

Two important events helped save the settlement from ruin. In 1612 John Rolfe raised a crop of tobacco from seeds that he had received from the Spanish West Indies. The next year he sent some of the tobacco to England to be sold. Soon tobacco became the major crop and selling it brought prosperity to the colony. The second important event was the marriage of Rolfe to Pocahontas, the daughter of the Indian chief Powhatan. This marriage resulted in eight years of peace between the colonists and the Indians. (See POCAHONTAS.)

In 1619 the Virginia Company allowed the settlers to elect representatives to help make the colony's laws. This body, the House of Burgesses, continued to exist even after King James I took away the company's charter in 1624 and made Virginia a royal colony.

In the years that followed, the people were generally satisfied with the governing of Virginia as a royal colony. But about 1660, resentment against British rule began to grow. In 1676 Nathanial Bacon led a rebellion protesting the unfair rule of the king's representative, Governor William Berkeley. The rebellion was put down, however, and the unpopular administration continued. Bacon's Rebellion has been called the first revolt in the American colonies against English rule. (See BACON'S REBELLION.)

In the 18th century, settlers began moving into the Piedmont region. Large tobacco plantations developed in the area and Negro slaves became more important as plantation laborers than were white indentured servants. About this time a few German and Scotch-Irish settlers moved into the Valley of Virginia. Thousands more came after 1730, and they were joined by English settlers who crossed the mountains from eastern Virginia.

Throughout the colonies, more and more people were growing angry with British colonial rule. Virginia patriots, including Richard Henry Lee, Thomas Jefferson, and George Washington, were leaders in demanding that England respect the colonies' rights. Patrick Henry's protests against the Stamp Act aroused the colonists against "taxation without representation." (See individual biographies.)

As the situation grew worse, the colonists saw the need to join together and to act together. In September, 1774, the First Continental Congress met at Philadelphia with Peyton Randolph of Virginia as president. (See CONTINENTAL CONGRESS.)

On July 4, 1776, the Continental Congress adopted the Declaration of Independence written by Thomas Jefferson, one of Virginia's most famous citizens. (See JEFFERSON, THOMAS.) That same year, Virginia declared itself an independent state. Its constitution, drawn up by

George Mason, included the first bill of rights in the United States.

When the American Revolution broke out in 1775, Virginia became the scene of several battles. Norfolk was destroyed and many other towns were raided. Finally, at Yorktown on October 19, 1781, the fighting ended when the British general, Lord Cornwallis, surrendered to General Washington.

Several Virginians were among the American leaders who met in 1787 to draw up a new federal constitution. Washington served as president of the Constitutional Convention. James Madison, one of the Convention's most active delegates, is known as the "father" of the Constitution. In 1788 he was also one of the authors of *The Federalist*, a series of essays that recommended the adoption of the new Constitution. (See CONSTITUTION OF THE UNITED STATES; FEDERALIST, THE.)

Throughout its history Virginia has provided famous political leaders to the nation. The list of presidents includes George Washington, Thomas Jefferson, James Madison, James Monroe, William Harrison, John Tyler, Zachary Taylor, and Woodrow Wilson. John Marshall, the "great" Chief Justice of the United States, was also born in Virginia. (See individual biographies.)

During the 1700's and 1800's slavery became a problem in the state. Some Virginians, such as George Washington and George Mason, freed their slaves. After Nat Turner's slave rebellion in 1831, the General Assembly discussed abolishing slavery but failed to agree on a plan. By 1860 about one-third of the people living in the state were slaves. But only five per cent of the population owned slaves and almost three-fourths of those owned less than ten slaves each.

When South Carolina and the states of the lower South seceded during the winter of 1860–1861, Virginia remained in the Union. Most Virginians hoped that a way could be found to save the nation and prevent war. But Virginia seceded on April 17, 1861, two days after the federal government called upon the states to provide armed troops to put down the rebellion of the lower southern states. Although most

Virginians did not want to secede, they would not fight against other Southern states.

Richmond was made the capital of the Confederacy during the United States Civil War. Robert E. Lee, Thomas "Stonewall" Jackson, and James "Jeb" Stuart were among the many Virginians who served in the Confederate Army. The state was one of the major battle-grounds of the war. Lee was finally forced to surrender to General U. S. Grant at Appomattox in 1865. (See CONFEDERATE STATES OF AMERICA; JACKSON, THOMAS JONATHAN; LEE, ROBERT EDWARD; WAR BETWEEN THE STATES, THE.)

During the war the counties west of the Allegheny Mountains separated from the state and became West Virginia. During the Reconstruction period the remaining part of the state was organized into Military District Number One with the Federal army controlling the state's government. Although the state did not suffer corrupt "carpetbag rule" as did many of the other Southern states, the period was nevertheless a difficult one. (See RECONSTRUCTION.)

The state was readmitted to the Union in January 1870 and gradually began to recover from the destruction of the war. Short railroad lines were joined to longer ones and new railroads were built. Plantations were divided into smaller farms and a greater variety of crops were raised. Industry began to grow.

A public school system was established in 1870. William Henry Ruffner was the "father" of this school system and the state's first superintendent of public instruction. Colleges for Negroes, such as Hampton Institute, were founded. Booker T. Washington, born a slave, graduated from this school to become an outstanding Negro leader. (See WASHINGTON, BOOKER TALIAFERRO.)

Carter Glass of Lynchburg was the "father" of the Federal Reserve System. Admiral Richard E. Byrd of Winchester was the first man to fly across the North and South Poles. His brother, Harry F. Byrd, was a leading United States senator for thirty years.

In recent years progress has continued in Virginia. Since the end of World War II many new factories have been established and agriculture has improved. Millions of dollars have been

J. Horace McFarland

In the fall the five-pointed leaves of the Virginia creeper turn to scarlet. Poison ivy leaflets are similar but are only three instead of five.

spent in meeting the needs of the people in the areas of education, transportation, and health.

VIRGINIA CREEPER (*krēp'ēr*) is a graceful vine, also called American woodbine and five-leaved ivy. It grows wild from Quebec to Mexico, and is sometimes grown as an ornamental climber. In autumn the Virginia creeper is especially beautiful when its clusters of dark blue berries on red stems are ripe, and its leaves have turned scarlet and deep crimson.

The whole leaf has three to seven (usually five) pointed, coarsely toothed leaflets. Poison ivy has similar leaflets, but never more than three. The berries provide food for birds.

Growing wild, Virginia creeper scrambles over the ground or climbs high in trees. It clings firmly by adhesive disks at the tips of tendrils. When cultivated, it covers walls, fences, or buildings, or serves as a ground cover. Virginia creeper is hardy, grows in almost any soil, and is difficult to destroy when it is not wanted. New plants are grown from seeds, cuttings, or layers. A similar woodbine, without adhesive disks on its tendrils, grows over much the same area. Both belong to the vine family, Vitaceae, as does the common grape.

VIRGIN (*vēr'jin*) **ISLANDS, WEST INDIES,** lie between the Atlantic Ocean and the Caribbean Sea. They are 40 to 50 miles east of Puerto Rico. The western islands are owned by the United States and the eastern islands by the

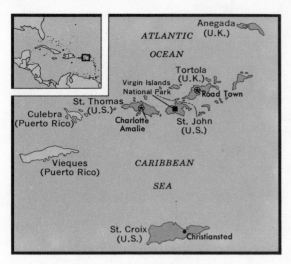

Locator map of the Virgin Islands.

British. Although there are nearly 1,600 in all, only about 100 are large enough to be called "islands." The rest are called cays, or islets. The Virgin Islands were discovered in 1493 by Christopher Columbus on his second voyage. Because there were so many he named them for St. Ursula and her 11,000 virgins.

These tropical islands lie at about 18 degrees north latitude. They are in one of the main paths of hurricanes which usually strike in late summer. Most of the year the temperature is in the 70's.

The people are about 80 percent Negro, mostly descendants of the slaves brought over from Africa to work on the sugar plantations. They are United States citizens. The United States larger islands include St. Croix, St. John, and St. Thomas. The U.S. also owns nearly 50 cays. They are all hilly, forested, and rugged, with jagged coastlines and many bays and harbors. All have beautiful scenery and attract many tourists.

St. Thomas, which includes the capital city Charlotte Amalie, has almost half the people of the Virgin Islands. The one large industry, rum production, is centered on St. Thomas. The largest island is St. Croix, used mostly for farming. St. John, the smallest of the three, has the fewest people. On it is the Virgin Islands National Park.

The president of the United States appoints the governor but the people of the territory elect their own legislature. They cannot send any representatives to Congress.

The British Virgin Islands are a colony ruled by an administrator appointed by the British monarch. They are about one-half as large in area as the United States territory, and have only about one-quarter as many people. Road Town, the capital, is on Tortola, the only large island. The main occupations in the British islands are stock raising and fishing.

The islands have had an interesting history. French, Dutch, Spanish, English, and Danes all fought for them. Finally, in the 17th century colonies were established by the British and the Danes. In 1917 the United States bought the Danish Virgin Islands to protect the entrance to the Panama Canal.

The Virgin Islands have 63,200 inhabitants (1970); 52,700 of these live on islands owned by the United States.

VIRUS (*vī'rŭs*) AND VIRUS INFECTION

(*ĭn fĕk'shŭn*). Viruses are very small particles which may cause disease in man, animals, and plants. In 1848 Louis Pasteur learned that small plants called bacteria can cause diseases. Bacteria can be grown in sugar solutions; they can be colored with certain dyes and seen under the microscope. But bacteria will not pass through very fine filters. (See BACTERIA.)

Like bacteria, viruses cause many infectious diseases. However, viruses are much smaller than bacteria, and will pass through the finest filters. They cannot be grown in sugar solutions but will grow and multiply in the presence of living tissue. Viruses are too small to be seen in ordinary light microscopes—they have to be photographed through electron microscopes. Because they are so small and need so many things to make them grow, scientists think viruses are not living matter at all. Viruses are something between the living and nonliving matter. They are parasites, and they depend completely upon their host. (See PARASITE AND SAPROPHYTE.)

Viruses cause many diseases. In attacking organs of the body, each group of viruses causes a different group of diseases. Some of the diseases caused by viruses that attack the skin are chickenpox, smallpox, measles, German measles, and fever blisters. Other viruses cause diseases of nerve tissue, such as rabies (hydrophobia), brain fever, and poliomyelitis (infantile paralysis). A third group of viruses cause diseases of internal organs. Yellow fever, influenza, the common cold, and viral liver inflammation are examples of this group. Virus infections may also attack plants and cause great damage. (See PLANT DISEASE.)

Control of Virus Infections

Great discoveries have been made in controlling virus infections. Long before the cause of infections was known, Edward Jenner discovered a way to protect people from getting infections. In the 1790's this English country doctor noticed that a mild case of cowpox (a disease like smallpox) would give protection against an attack of dangerous smallpox. The cowpox virus is a *vaccinia*, and the method of protection which Jenner used is called *vaccination*. (See JENNER, EDWARD.)

The bite of a sick dog was always very serious. In 1885, Pasteur used the idea of vaccination to save the life of a boy bitten by a dog with rabies. Since that time, Pasteur's treatment for rabies has been used in hospitals throughout the whole world.

The control of yellow fever is an important chapter in the history of virus diseases. Until about 1900, many people died of this virus infection every year. In that year Major Walter Reed, a United States army doctor, was sent to Cuba to study the disease. He discovered that the yellow fever virus was carried from the sick people to healthy people by a mosquito. By cleaning out swamps and other breeding places of mosquitoes, yellow fever was stamped out. Vaccination against yellow fever was developed about 1937. (See REED, WALTER.)

During the 1950's Jonas Salk, a young United States doctor, worked on a vaccine against poliomyelitis. He and others first separated the viruses that cause the disease. Then these virus particles were grown in parts of monkey kidneys. After a great deal of work, a vaccine was prepared. This vaccine will protect most people against the paralyzing infections of poliomyelitis.

The least harmful virus infection, but the greatest nuisance, is the common cold. In the United States more people have colds than any other disease. Colds cause children to miss school; they keep workers away from their jobs. Colds leave the patient tired, and a more serious illness may follow a simple cold. Because immunity (or resistance) after a cold is very short, many people get more than one cold during a year. Methods of vaccination are being studied to find a way to prevent colds.

The antibiotics that are helpful in bacterial diseases are not always useful in virus diseases. However, they are important in preventing the bacterial infections that may follow virus infections. (See ANTIBIOTICS.)

If a person has a virus infection, he should get plenty of rest, eat the right foods, and drink lots of fluids. It is important to keep the disease from spreading to others. (See HEALTH.)

VISION (*vĭzh'ŭn*), or sight, is the most informative and far-reaching of the senses. The sense of touch can explore only objects within reach. Strong odors are carried by the wind but the fragrance of a flower can be smelled little more than a few inches away. Even loud noises can be heard for only a few miles. Taste is limited to things put in the mouth.

But vision is sensitive to the light of stars millions of miles away. At night the glow of a firefly, less than a thousandth as bright as a candle flame, can be seen. Through vision a whole landscape or a speck of dust can be seen.

More than nine-tenths of all information about the world is gathered by seeing. Without sight it would take a long time to learn the shape of a room, the arrangement of furniture, and the kinds of objects that are on tables and shelves. A single glance tells much more than can be learned through the other senses.

Reflected Light

Without light, no one can see. By day the light comes from the sun. Light waves are reflected from the surface of objects. Reflected light passes through the *pupil* of the eye, forming an image on the *retina*, a carpetlike screen of cells at the back of the hollow eyeball.

Each of the retina's 130,000,000 cells is sensitive to light. When light strikes a cell a chemical change takes place. This starts an impulse in a nerve fiber, which travels through the optic nerve to the seeing portion of the brain. (See EYE.)

The sun's light is white, made up of all the colors of the spectrum, from red to violet. When a beam of white light is passed through a prism, it spreads it out to form a color spectrum on a white screen. The same division of light takes place in the sky when the sun's white light is spread by raindrops to form a rainbow. (See SPECTRUM AND SPECTROSCOPE.)

When white light falls on an object, only part of it is reflected. The rest is absorbed. If only the red part is reflected, the object looks red, and if only blue light is reflected, the object looks blue. Some of the cells of the retina, called the *cones*, are sensitive to color. The impulses they send over the fibers of the optic nerve are color messages. The rod cells are not sensitive to color, but they respond to very little light. In near darkness, only the rod cells respond. Then no colors are seen, only shades of gray. (See COLOR.)

The rod cells are sensitive because of a substance called *rhodopsin*, or visual purple. In bright light, this substance turns colorless. In the dark, it gradually turns again into visual purple. This is why it takes a person's eyes a few minutes to adjust to the darkness of a motion-picture theater. If he has been in a bright light, it takes about five minutes for enough visual purple to build up so that he can see well enough to find a seat. Half an hour later there is still more, and he can see still better.

Binocular Vision

Binocular vision is sight with two eyes. Each eye sees a slightly different picture. You can test this by looking at a can with a printed label, placed on the table a foot or two from your nose. Look at it first with one eye, then with the other. The right eye sees a little more of the right side of the can; the left eye sees more of the left. Each eye sends its message to the brain, where the two are put together.

The brain "sees" only one picture.

Hold a pencil at arm's length. Look at it while you move it closer and closer to your nose. Your eyes must turn toward each other to keep it in view. When it is very close, a person watching you would say you are cross-eyed.

Now hold two pencils, one at arm's length, the other halfway between it and your nose. Look first at the far pencil—and you see two of the closer one. Look at the closer one, and the far one seems to be two.

Binocular vision helps in judging distances. Hold a stick between the thumb and forefinger of each hand, with your arms wide apart. Now, quickly, bring the sticks together and try to make their tips touch. Try it first with one eye shut and then with both eyes open. With one eye shut, you will often miss by a few inches.

A man with one eye can drive a car, but he must be very careful of distances. He cannot be quite sure how rapidly another car is approaching. Other visual information gives him clues to distance, of course. The image on the retina becomes larger as the other car approaches; and he sees the car in relation to the roadway and trees beside the road.

People see most objects in relation to each other. They relate distance to *perspective*, the effect which makes railroad tracks or overhead wires appear to meet in the distance. (See PERSPECTIVE.)

What you see depends in part on what you are trying to see. For example, select a small object across the room, such as a doorknob. Close one eye, and hold up a finger so that it blocks the view of the doorknob from the open eye. Now, without moving your finger, open the closed eye. The finger almost disappears.

Now close one eye and cup your hand over the other, blocking the entire view. When you open the closed eye, the brain responds to the messages it sends. It almost ignores the messages from the covered eye. Part of the field of vision is always blocked. Look toward your left as far as you can and close your left eye. Part of the scene is blocked by your nose. But with both eyes open you are not bothered by this obstacle. The brain takes two partial pictures and fits them together in one whole one.

NORMAL EYE

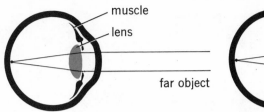

image of object
focused on retina

muscle
lens

far object

near object

in a normal eye, the lens changes shape to focus pictures of far and near objects on the retina at the back of the eye. Far objects are focused farther forward than near objects, but the normal eye adjusts itself to these differences.

FAR-SIGHTED
eyeball too short

NEAR-SIGHTED
eyeball too long

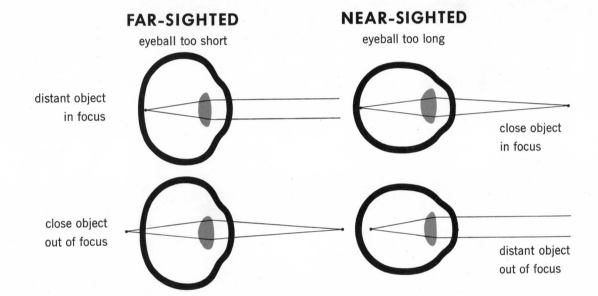

distant object
in focus

close object
in focus

close object
out of focus

distant object
out of focus

When the eyeball is too short, objects more than a few feet away can be seen clearly, but near objects focus too far back to be seen clearly. Because persons with such eyes can see only far-away things clearly, they are called far-sighted. When a person's eyeball is longer than normal, only near objects focus properly on the retina. Such a person is near-sighted. Near-sightedness and far-sightedness can be corrected by placing artificial glass lenses (spectacles or contact lenses) in front of the natural lenses of the eyes. These change the focus from too far back, or too far forward, to the correct position.

CORRECTED BY GLASSES

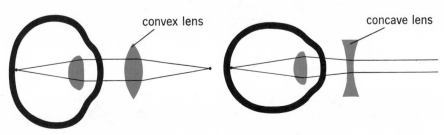

lenses of glasses
bend light rays
so that they are
focused on retina

convex lens

concave lens

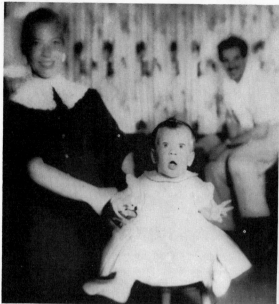

Photos, Ben and Sid Ross

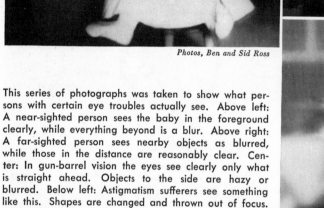

This series of photographs was taken to show what persons with certain eye troubles actually see. Above left: A near-sighted person sees the baby in the foreground clearly, while everything beyond is a blur. Above right: A far-sighted person sees nearby objects as blurred, while those in the distance are reasonably clear. Center: In gun-barrel vision the eyes see clearly only what is straight ahead. Objects to the side are hazy or blurred. Below left: Astigmatism sufferers see something like this. Shapes are changed and thrown out of focus. Below right: Cataracts cause clouding or fogging of the eye lens in some spots, with clearer vision in other spots.

A baby must learn to use his vision. He learns to turn his eyes to follow a moving object. He learns to focus, so that near or far objects are seen clearly. Before long his visual mechanics work well. But his vision is still poor, because he understands little of what he sees.

What is seeing? The explanation sounds simple: the *lens* focuses an image on the retina, and this picture is transmitted to the brain. But this is not all that happens. What the brain sees is very different from the pictures formed on the retina.

Suppose you were holding a motion-picture camera, filming an outdoor scene. Instead of holding the camera steady, you jerked it wildly, pointing it for a second at the grass, then at a treetop, then a cloud, a bird flying, and a squirrel leaping from branch to branch. When the film was developed and shown, confusion would appear on the screen. No one in the audience could make sense of the pictures. Yet your eyes do this kind of thing all the time. Seldom are they at rest. If you stand outdoors, looking at the scene around you, your eyes stop for only a second to glance at the grass, treetop, cloud, bird, or squirrel.

The brain does not see a series of quick snapshots. The seeing part of the brain records each picture and remembers it. It adds them together and gives them meaning, so that the whole picture is seen, not the parts. In a second, it draws upon the store of memories in the brain. A tree, a cloud, a squirrel—these have been seen before. It takes only a glance to recognize them.

"Dog" suggests a picture, but not a very special one, because there are many kinds of dogs, all sizes and shapes. "Cocker spaniel" sharpens the picture. "Black cocker spaniel" sharpens it still more.

The writer paints a picture with words. He may have the black cocker spaniel playing in bright sunshine with a blue ball, tossing it in the air and chasing it. As each visual idea is added, the mental picture becomes clearer.

Visual memories can be called upon in other ways. If a photograph is shown to a person who has never before seen one, he may be unable to see its meaning. If he were to see a number of photographs of familiar things, he would soon learn to understand this kind of picture. Then photographs of unfamiliar places would have meaning to him.

Just as writers suggest pictures with words, artists also call on visual memories. With a few quick strokes of a pencil a person can draw an outline that means "chair." With only a few more strokes a caricaturist can draw a few simple curves which seem to be like the face of a noted person.

Defects of Vision

Seeing includes the use of many parts of the eye, the optic nerve, and the parts of the brain that see and interpret the eye's messages. Damage to any of these parts may cause blindness or poor vision.

If the eyeball is a little too short from front to back, it may be difficult to see nearby objects clearly. This defect, *farsightedness,* is easily corrected by glasses. So is *nearsightedness,* a difficulty in seeing distant objects clearly.

Astigmatism is a distortion (out of shape) of vision, caused by a *cornea* that is not quite spherical. Glasses can correct for this.

Cataract is a disease of the lens, a cloudy film blocking vision over all or parts of the transparent window. It can often be corrected by surgery.

Some people are color blind. A person who is partly color blind can see differences in colors, but not the full range. He may not be able to tell the difference between red and green. A few people are completely color blind. They cannot see any one color as different from another, though they see all of the shadings from light to dark. Color blindness is usually not curable, but it is not a great handicap.

Because the eye has many delicate working parts, it is easily damaged. Permanent blindness can be caused by a carelessly thrown stone or dart. In many factories, workmen must wear safety glasses to protect their eyes from flying bits of metal.

Some diseases of the eye and optic nerve can cause blindness; others may cause some loss of vision. As in almost all diseases, the chances of cure are far better if a doctor is consulted as soon as any signs appear. Some diseases cause no pain. The first signs may be "tired" eyes, or blurring somewhere in the field of vision.

Care of the eyes will help insure good sight through a person's whole lifetime.

VISUAL (*vĭzh'ū ăl*) **EDUCATION** is teaching and learning by seeing. When a person opens his eyes to look at an object or to watch something happening, and tries to understand what he sees, he is learning *visually.* In this way people learn from their experiences, both in school and in other activities.

Visual education is different from teaching and learning through the use of words. Words are symbols for real things. They stand for the thing, but they are not the thing itself. To learn from words a person first must know what the words mean, that is, what it is that each word represents. (See LANGUAGE.) In visual education a person either looks at the thing itself, or sees a fairly accurate picture of it.

Visual education uses lifelike materials or experiences for teaching. Students learn by observation when the subject to be studied is brought into the classroom. At other times, students go out to see things happening in the world around them. Students also get visual learning experiences from looking at pictures.

Classroom experiments are part of visual education.

Hays from Monkmeyer

Post Dispatch from Black Star

This girl learns how the Colonists carded wool by carding some fibers herself.

The many kinds of visual aids include field trips, telecasts and motion pictures, filmstrips and slide pictures, models, pictures, posters, charts, graphs, and maps. Museum exhibits that include dioramas, models, specimens, and pictures are also visual materials.

Different types of visual materials give students different kinds of experiences. When an experience affects all or most of the five senses, it is called *multisensory.* If it requires only the use of hearing and sight it is called *audiovisual.* The names *visual education* and *visual teaching aids* are usually given to any teaching material that does not just use the written or spoken word.

Many subjects are learned best by firsthand observation. In a classroom laboratory experiment, or on a field trip, students learn by watching and listening to things. They may be studying the way a plant grows or the way an animal behaves or the ways of earning a living in a community. Students may learn through experiences that require seeing, hearing, touching, smelling, and even tasting. When all of the senses are used, the student can get a real knowledge of the subject. This increases his understanding of later discussion and reading.

With subjects that cannot be observed firsthand, other visual materials help the student.

Sound motion pictures or telecasts make use of both sight and hearing. Moving images with sound come closer to the real thing than still pictures, or any other teaching material. However, still pictures are useful in giving a more complete understanding of objects and events than is given by words alone.

The same is true with other types of visual materials, such as maps, charts, and graphs. However, unlike still pictures, these are not the images of real things. They present information in a special visual language. To use maps, charts, and graphs, students have to know symbols. For example, on a map a small dot may stand for 10,000 people. It would not be possible to show a picture of 10,000 people on one small spot on the map. But to understand this map the student must know that the dot stands for 10,000 people. He must also know enough to understand how large a community of 10,000 people would be. (See GRAPH; MAPS AND MAP MAKING.)

To understand words, students must have some knowledge of the real things that words represent. This helps them to see the image of the thing in their mind when they see or hear the word that represents it.

Visual materials are used in schools for this purpose. If to the reader the word "train" is merely a five-letter word that rhymes with

Motion pictures bring the outside world to the classroom.

Post Dispatch from Black Star

"rain," he will not get much meaning from the word. But if he knows that a train is something with wheels that rolls down a track, making a great deal of noise, and that it carries people or freight, he can keep on reading to find out who is riding on the train or where it is going. If he does not know all these things about trains, the student may learn them from a field trip to a railroad station, a motion picture of a train, or a model of a train. Each type of visual aid can help make the meaning of the word clear. Words and pictures are both part of education to help the student learn.

VITAMIN (*vī'tä mĭn*). Vitamins are a group of substances found in foods. In addition to proteins, fats, carbohydrates, and minerals, the body needs vitamins for life and health. The exact chemical make-up of these substances was not known when they were first discovered. They were called vitamins, and as different ones were studied they were named by letters, as A, B, C, etc.

Vitamin A, a colorless substance in itself, is made in the body from the substances which give the yellow color to carrots, sweet potatoes, and other fruits and vegetables. Cows form vitamin A from these same substances in grasses, and it becomes part of the cream in milk.

Vitamin A is important to the health of the eyes, skin, teeth, and bones. It helps to keep in a healthy condition the mucous membrane which lines the breathing passages. When this membrane is healthy, infection is less likely to occur. The foods that supply vitamin A are the deep-green, leafy vegetables, the yellow vegetables, and fruits, eggs, liver, butter, and fortified margarine.

Early investigators thought there was only one vitamin B. Later it was found that there were several, and so they are called the *vitamin-B complex*. Numbers are added to the letter B to name them.

Vitamin B was first found by doctors who were trying to cure beriberi. Beriberi is a disease that once was common among oriental people whose diet was chiefly white rice. When the people ate brown, or unpolished rice, beri-beri was prevented or cured. The substance that caused this cure was found by soaking rice bran (the outer coating of the rice grain) in water. What was at first believed to be one vitamin in the rice bran has since been separated into ten or more vitamins.

Thiamine (vitamin B_1), *riboflavin* (B_2), and *niacin* are three members of the B complex which keep many parts of the body healthy and working well. The nervous system, the digestive system, and the skin all show disturbances when there are not enough of these vitamins in the diet. Because it does so much to help a person feel well, thiamine has been called the "morale vitamin." Riboflavin helps to keep the eyes and skin healthy, particularly the skin at the base of the nose, the corners of the mouth, and the surface of the tongue. Niacin, probably along with other B vitamins, prevents or cures pellagra. This is a serious and disabling disease, in which the skin of the forearms and hands, or legs and feet, becomes red and rough; there are also digestive disturbances and sometimes nervous symptoms. Since the late 1930's, when the people of the South began to add more milk and fresh vegetables to their diets, pellagra is seldom seen in the United States.

Foods which provide thiamine include: pork, legumes (peas and beans), liver, whole grain or enriched bread, and cereals. Riboflavin is found in milk, eggs, liver, heart, greens, and lean meat. Niacin is found in chicken, turkey, liver, fish, lean meats, and the legumes.

Pyridoxine (vitamin B_6) works as part of an enzyme that helps the body to use protein. There is seldom a lack of pyridoxine in human diet. Foods which provide pyridoxine include fish, lean meats, liver, kidney, heart, and grains.

Pantothenic acid is another member of the B complex. Its work is to help the body make use of the energy in foods. Many foods provide this vitamin: eggs, milk, meat, fish, oatmeal, broccoli, cabbage, tomatoes, potatoes, and others.

Folic acid and *vitamin B_{12}* each play a part in building red blood cells. They are both B complex vitamins. Lack of either or both will cause anemia, a condition in which red blood cells in the body are not normal, or there are not enough of them. Vitamin B_{12} has been used in the treatment of certain types of anemia. Kidney, liver, eggs, milk, and meats provide B_{12}. Fresh green vegetables, whole grains, kidney, and liver supply folic acid.

There are still other members of the B complex, but those listed above have been studied most by nutritionists and other scientists.

Ascorbic acid (*vitamin C*) helps to keep connective tissues, bones, teeth, and the walls of the blood vessels firm and strong. It is the vitamin which prevents scurvy. Scurvy is a serious disease which was common among the crews of ships until late in the 19th century. Eating certain fresh foods prevents or cures scurvy. Ascorbic acid is found in greatest quantities in the young, actively growing parts of plants. Oranges, grapefruit, tangerines, tomatoes, and raw cabbage give a good supply of this vitamin. Canned and frozen juices of citrus fruits and tomatoes are also rich sources of vitamin C.

Vitamin D makes it possible for the body to use the minerals calcium and phosphorus in building strong, straight bones. Growing boys and girls need to increase the length and size of their bones rapidly. Not many foods contain vitamin D. Because of this, it is a good idea to take a vitamin D capsule or liquid, or to use milk fortified with vitamin D, regularly as long as the body is growing. The body can make a substance which can become vitamin D through action of the sun's rays. This happens at or near the surface of the skin. This may provide enough vitamin D for the person who has finished growing.

Vitamin K must be present in the body so that the blood will clot normally at any point of injury. Vitamin K is found in many foods. Lack of this vitamin in man's diet is not common.

Very small amounts of each vitamin are enough for the needs of the body. A person eating a good variety of foods gets all the vitamins now known to be needed, with the possible exception of vitamin D. A good guide to follow when choosing foods is the "basic

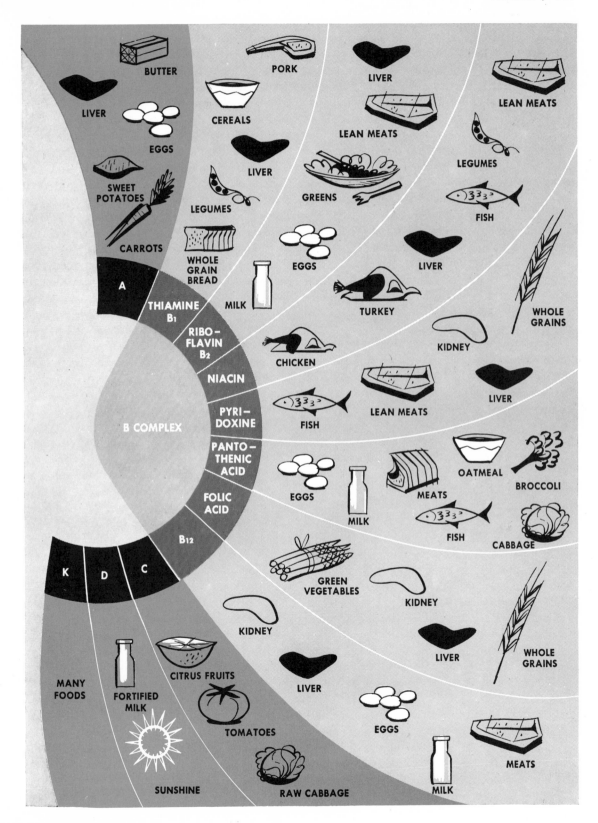

seven." (See NUTRITION.) Special vitamin-rich foods and capsules are not needed. In fact, many of the vitamins can not very well be stored in the body. When they are taken in amounts greater than can be used, they are discharged from the body. Thus nothing is gained from taking vitamins that are not needed.

It is harmful to put too much of certain vitamins into the body. This has been found to be true of vitamins A and D, when large amounts have been taken in capsules or liquids. Fortunately, when a good variety of foods is the source of the vitamins, there is no danger of harm from too much of any of them.

VLADIVOSTOK (*vlăd ĭ' vŏs tŏk'*), **U.S.S.R.,** is a Pacific Ocean port, naval base, and railway city at the Asiatic end of the Trans-Siberian Railway and the North Polar sea route.

The warm Tsushima Current in the Sea of Japan keeps the temperature from becoming very cold in winter. The harbor in the Bay of the Golden Horn can be kept open for trade all year. However, the Arctic Sea route to European Russia is open for only a few weeks in summer. Goods that are shipped from Vladivostok's port to European U.S.S.R. include coal and oil, lumber, soybeans, vegetable oils, furs, fish, and grain. The chief Soviet Pacific fishing and whaling fleet is based there.

The city grew in importance as an industrial center after World War II, when the U.S.S.R. began to develop Siberia's resources. Industries include airplane manufacturing, shipbuilding, lumber milling, and food preparation.

Vladivostok is the capital of the Primorski region of the Russian Soviet Federated Socialist Republic. The city has a technical institute, a maritime academy, a teacher's college, and an institute of fisheries and oceanography. In 1970 the population of Vladivostok was 442,000.

VOLCANO (*vŏl kā' nō*) is an opening in the Earth's crust through which hot gases and molten or solid rock are erupted, or blown out. The erupted material piles up around the opening and forms a cone-shaped mound. A single, central crater may be the only outlet, but often smaller openings, or vents, may occur on the slopes of the cone.

The word "volcano" comes from Vulcano, the name of an active volcano on one of the Lipari Islands, near Italy. According to Roman mythology, Vulcano was where Vulcan, the god of fire, had his forge. (See VULCAN.)

Volcanic eruptions are perhaps the most spectacular natural phenomenon to be seen on Earth. They have caused great loss of life and have done enormous damage to property. During the past 400 years nearly 200,000 lives have been lost as the result of some 430 volcanoes erupting.

The rock that is erupted from a volcano may be produced in a variety of forms. It may be in the form of lava, which is molten rock. This material may be a thin, rapidly flowing substance or thick and slowly moving. It may be erupted in the form of cinders that resemble clinkers from a coal fire. Rock may be erupted in the form of black smoke, which is really ash, or finely powdered rock. Pumice may also be produced. This is rock that is so full of tiny bubbles that it is sometimes light enough to float. (See LAVA.)

Volcanoes that have erupted within historic times are considered either active or dormant. There are also many thousands of extinct volcanoes. The way in which a volcano erupts depends on the pressure of the gases and the kind of lava.

In general, there are three types of volcanoes: explosive, quiet, and intermediate. In the explosive type, the material discharged is largely gas, ash, and pumice, with little lava. The quiet type produces mainly lava that flows with only minor explosions. The intermediate type is a combination of the explosive and the quiet types.

Explosive volcanoes tend to produce stiff lava. This type of rock usually contains a high proportion of silica in which case it is known as rhyolite. The lava is squeezed out under high pressure somewhat as toothpaste is pressed from a tube. Steep-sided cones are formed.

The quiet type of volcano tends to produce lava with a low proportion of silica. This lava, known as basalt, is more fluid than rhyolitic lava and melts at lower temperatures. Much less gas pressure is necessary to create an eruption. Vol-

Courtesy (center right)
Gernsheim Collection, The
University of Texas At Austin,
(above and bottom right)
Ewing Galloway,
(left) UPI Compix

The island of Surtsey off the coast of Iceland, left, was formed by volcanic eruptions from the sea floor that began on November 14, 1963. Botak, Bromo, and Semeru in Java, above right, are volcanoes of the explosive type. Mount Vesuvius in the Bay of Naples in Italy is the most famous volcano of the intermediate type. Among its recent eruptions was one in 1872, center right. Kilauea in Hawaii, bottom right, is a volcano of the quiet type.

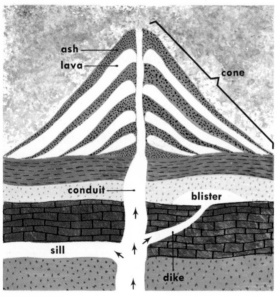

canoes of this type have gently sloping sides. Their eruptions last longer than those of the explosive type. (See BASALT.)

The most spectacular example of an explosive volcano is Krakatoa, located in Sunda Strait, Indonesia. Until 1883 Krakatoa had been inactive for two centuries. In a great eruption that year, four-and-a-half cubic miles of ash were blown out at one time, leaving a hole five miles wide. The whole top of a mountain that had been 2,600 feet high was disintegrated, leaving a hole 1,000 feet below sea level. A 120-foot tidal wave was created, killing some 36,000 people in Java. The sound of the eruption was heard as far away as Australia.

Mount Pelee, in the West Indies, is also an explosive volcano. When it erupted in 1902 it completely destroyed the city of Saint Pierre on the island of Martinique; 30,000 lives were lost.

The great basins produced by the explosion and collapse of volcanic mountains are calderas, from the Spanish word for "cauldron." Crater Lake, Oregon, which is six miles across and 4,000 feet deep, was formed in this way during prehistoric times. One of the largest calderas known, with an average diameter of 16 miles, is in northwestern New Mexico. Mt. Katmai, in Alaska, is another volcano of the explosive type. It last erupted in 1953. (For illustration, see NATIONAL PARKS AND MONUMENTS.)

The volcanoes of Hawaii are examples of the quiet type, which produces basaltic lava. The islands themselves are the tops of great volcanic mountains built up from the ocean floor. Mauna Loa and Kilauea are the only active volcanoes in Hawaii today. Every few years they erupt great streams of fluid lava. In 1959 Kilauea erupted, forming a lava lake in its crater more than 400 feet deep. Before it could harden, the lava drained back into the volcano. In January 1960 another lava eruption from Kilauea destroyed the village of Kapoho and flowed down into the ocean. (See HAWAII, UNITED STATES, *Hawaii.*)

Mount Vesuvius, in Italy, is the most famous example of an intermediate-type volcano. Until A.D. 79 Vesuvius was thought to be extinct. In that year, however, it erupted, destroying the city of Pompeii at its base. The volcano has erupted occasionally since then. In March 1944 an eruption destroyed the village of San Sebastiano on the slope of Vesuvius. (See POMPEII; VESUVIUS, MOUNT.)

The rare and spectacular formation of a new volcano could be seen in Paricutin, Mexico, in 1943. In a farmer's field about 200 miles west of Mexico City a fissure suddenly appeared. Smoke and gas issued from the hole, followed by red-hot rocks and ash. The next morning a cone 120 feet high had risen. Eight months later the cone had grown to 1,500 feet. Two villages were destroyed, including Paricutin, after which the volcano was named. Since 1952 the volcano has been dormant.

Many of the Earth's active volcanoes are found around the periphery, or border, of the Pacific Ocean. This region is also an area of earthquake activity. Volcanoes are common in regions where there are arc-shaped chains of "young" mountains, such as in the Aleutian Islands, near Alaska, or the Andes Mountains of South America. In these areas earthquakes are also common. Not all young mountain ranges where earthquakes occur, however, have volcanoes. There are no volcanoes, for example, in the Alps or the Hima-

layas. These are mountains formed by the compression and buckling of the Earth's crust. In order for magma, which is unerupted lava, to form deep in the Earth, special conditions are necessary. These include unusually high temperatures and changes in pressure which lower the melting temperatures of rocks. Magma is lighter than solid rock and so is forced upward by the weight of the rock above. This can occur following the buckling and lifting that create a mountain range. The weight of the mountain mass may cause fractures deep into the Earth. Volcanic lava comes from the magma in such low pressure zones. Fractures may also open onto the ocean floor, creating underwater volcanoes. A volcano is always connected to a nearby pool of melted rock in the crust and does not receive its lava from the deepest parts of the Earth. (For map, see EARTHQUAKE.)

VOLGA (*vŏl'gȧ*) **RIVER, U.S.S.R.,** known in Russian legend and song as "The Mother Volga," is the longest river in European Russia. It is a busy river; steamers and barges carry cargo between different points on its long course. The Volga is navigable to within 75 miles of its source. Canals connect the river with most of the other waterways of European Russia.

The Volga rises in the Valdai Hills northwest of Moscow, and reaches the Caspian Sea

Locator map of the Volga River.

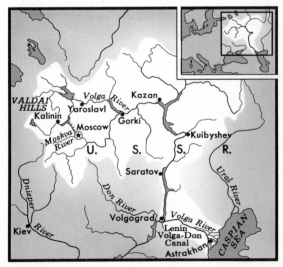

after a twisting 2,293-mile course. It flows first generally eastward and then southward. The river has a drainage basin of 532,818 square miles. In the Caspian Sea the Volga has built an enormous delta, through which it divides into many mouths.

The Volga descends very slowly throughout its course with an average drop of about four inches per mile. The river is wide and shallow. At Kalinin it is 710 feet wide, and from Kazan to its mouth almost two miles wide. But its shallow depth means that sandbars often make navigation difficult. It is frozen for three to five months in the winter.

Important cities along the Volga's banks are Kalinin, Gorki, Kazan, Kuibyshev, Volgograd (formerly Stalingrad), and Astrakhan. Most of these cities grew up at points where north-south river trade met east-west trade. Volgograd was built where the Volga bends westward to within 45 miles of the Don River. At Volgograd much of the Volga River trade moves by canal westward to the Don River and into the Black Sea. Little freight is carried downstream beyond Volgograd.

Cargoes carried downstream on the Volga include timber and manufactured goods from the forests and industrial areas of the upper river basin. Grain and flour, products of the steppe, and petroleum from the Caspian area, are the chief cargoes shipped upstream.

VOLLEYBALL (*vŏl'ĭ bạl'*). The game of volleyball was invented in 1895 by William G. Morgan, physical director of the Young Men's Christian Association in Holyoke, Massachusetts. Morgan wanted a game for businessmen that was less strenuous than basketball. He stretched a tennis net across the gymnasium at a height of 6 feet 6 inches and took the rubber bladder from a basketball for a ball. Two teams then batted this ball back and forth across the net.

Volleyball has since become a game with official rules, and is played by using skill and strategy. The United States Volleyball Association (U.S.V.B.A.) formed in 1928 sets the official rules and standards for equipment and play.

Modern volleyball is played both indoors and outdoors. The game can be played at any speed, depending on the age and skill of the players.

A volleyball court is 30 feet wide and 60 feet long, with a net stretched tightly across the middle of the court at a height of 8 feet for men and 7 feet 6 inches for women. The net is lowered a few inches for younger girls and boys. The rules for the men's and women's games are the same.

The volleyball itself is a leather-covered rubber bladder not less than 26 inches or more than 27 inches in circumference, and weighs not less than nine ounces or more than ten ounces when properly inflated with air.

Under U.S.V.B.A. rules, there are six players on each team. They stand in two lines of three players facing the net. One player of the serving team stands behind the end line of his side and serves the ball by striking it with the hand or fist so that it goes over the net into the court of the receiving team.

The receiving team players may send the ball back to the opponents' court by striking it with the hands or any part of the body. The ball may be struck three times before it recrosses the net to the serving team, but the same player may not strike it twice in a row. The ball must be clearly batted. If it is caught and thrown, it is counted against the team catching it. Girls' rules at one time allowed a player to strike the ball twice in succession. A new rule allows only one strike.

A game is usually 15 points, and the winning team must have an *advantage* or lead of 2 points to win a game. A point is scored whenever the serving team wins a *rally*—that is, whenever the receiving team fails to return the ball legally to the serving team. A team wins a match when it wins two of a three-game series. Points can be scored only by the serving team.

If the serving team loses a rally, the serve passes to the other team. Each time a team wins the serve, the players *rotate* or move in a clockwise direction to the next position. The server then serves as long as his team wins the rallies.

If the serving team violates one of the rules, it is a *fault,* and the serve goes to the other team. The serving team wins a point if the opponents commit a fault. Some faults are: stepping on the court line while serving; stepping over the center line beneath the net; touching the net while the ball is in play; reaching over the net; allowing the ball to touch the floor; catching and throwing the ball instead of clearly batting it; batting the ball out of court; and hitting the net with the serve, even though the ball may fall over the net.

A good volleyball player should be able to serve both underhand and overhand. The overhand service is harder to do, but the other side finds it hard to return. Players should also be able to pass the ball by batting it with both hands so that it floats gently up to a teammate who is called a *set passer* or *setter.* The job of the set passer is to *set up* the ball high in the air near the net so that the *spiker* can leap into the air and drive the ball, or *spike* it, down into the opponents' court to win the rally. A good spiker can strike the ball with tremendous force. A spiked volley-ball may travel at a speed of 162 feet per second.

Volleyball is played in more than 60 countries by more than 50,000,000 people every year. In some countries it is also a great spectator sport. Volleyball was introduced as an Olympic sport in 1964 at Tokyo, Japan. The U.S.S.R. won the men's championship, and Japan won the women's championship.

VOLTAIRE (*vŏl tār′, vŏl′tār,* or *vŏl târ′*) (pen name of FRANCOIS MARIE AROUET) (1694–1778). Voltaire was the most important of the writers and thinkers who lived in France in the 18th century, just before the French Revolution. He lived a long life, and he never stopped writing about people's right to be free and to think for themselves. He attacked the government, which oppressed their lives, and the church, which, he felt, did not allow them liberty of faith. He pointed out all the weaknesses of the society in which he lived. Although Voltaire can not be said to have started the French Revolution, he helped prepare men's minds and hearts for it when it did come. (See FRENCH REVOLUTION.)

Francois Marie Arouet was born in Paris. In 1718 he took the name Voltaire. From the very first, Voltaire was in trouble with the powerful people about whom he wrote. By the time he was 24 he had been exiled from France and imprisoned. In 1726 he felt it wise to go to England, where he stayed for three years. His experiences there turned out to be very important. He saw in England a society where there was far more freedom than he had known in France, and

Volleyball is a team game which may be played either indoors or outdoors.

Courtesy Chicago Board of Education

far greater tolerance of others' opinions and beliefs.

After returning to France he continued to write and continued to be in trouble. For many years Frederick the Great of Prussia had been inviting Voltaire to visit his court. By 1750 it seemed wise for Voltaire to leave the country again, and he spent the next three

Culver Service

Voltaire.

years in Berlin. He quarreled often with Frederick and finally left Prussia. He bought an estate on the border between France and the Republic of Geneva. There he was safe and free from censorship.

In February 1778 he returned to Paris. Society welcomed him. His new play opened. But the excitement of Paris life was too much for him at 84. He became very ill and died on May 30.

Much of what Voltaire wrote in his lifetime is not of interest today. He wrote over 50 plays, but they are little read or remembered. What is important now are the long poems and prose works of social criticism. In these he made fun of the government and the church of his day.

The poems were all witty, making fun of people and customs. *La Henriade,* one of the most important, was published in England. Its subject is religious freedom. After returning from England, Voltaire published a series of letters to the English, praising English freedom and tolerance.

The *Philosophic Dictionary* is a collection of short essays, some only one paragraph in length, on a wide variety of subjects, such as "Law," "Marriage," and "Faith." In every one Voltaire made attacks on the church and state.

Perhaps the most useful single book of Voltaire's for our day is the short novel *Candide,* published in 1759. Voltaire was annoyed by the statement of the German philosopher G.

W. von Leibnitz that this was "the best of possible worlds." Candide, the young hero of the novel, has many adventures with his friend, Dr. Pangloss. By the time the book is ended, Voltaire has pointed out how many evils there are in the world—earthquakes and wars, religious intolerance, cruelty, greed, disease, and injustice. Voltaire never felt that the world he lived in was the best of all possible worlds, and he did his best to improve it.

VULCAN (*vŭl'kăn*) (HEPHAESTUS). Vulcan was the name the Romans gave to Hephaestus, the Greek god of fire. Hephaestus was the son of Zeus and Hera. Of all the gods, only he was not handsome. In fact, he was born crippled, and his mother, angered by his lameness, threw him down from Mount Olympus. Two sea goddesses rescued him and took care of him. Hephaestus learned to be a smith and returned to Olympus. To get revenge on his mother he sent her a golden throne in which invisible chains held her imprisoned. Dionysus finally persuaded Hephaestus to free Hera after making him drunk.

Hephaestus was also a jeweler, architect, and armorer for the gods. He built their palaces and made chairs and tables that moved about the halls of Olympus under their own power. Apollo's chariot was built by Hephaestus. At his flaming forge under Mount Etna he made suits of armor for Achilles and Aeneas, and thunderbolts for Zeus, who gave him the beautiful goddess Aphrodite (Venus) for his wife. To help him in his work, Hephaestus forged two handmaidens of gold who could move about and speak.

The word volcano comes from his Latin name, and the process of treating rubber with sulfur and heat is called vulcanization.

VULTURE (*vŭl'ţūr*). Vultures are large birds of prey. They belong to the same order of birds as the falcons, hawks, and eagles. There are five vultures in the New World, all belonging to the same family. They are the turkey vulture, the black vulture, the king vulture, the California condor, and the South American or Andean condor. The Old World vultures of

Europe, Asia, and Africa belong to the same order as, but to a different family from, the vultures of North and South America. All vultures feed on carrion (dead animals).

Vultures are sometimes called buzzards. This is an incorrect term. Buzzards are really European hawks. Probably the name was given to the vultures by early settlers who thought they looked like hawks in flight.

The *turkey vulture* is the most graceful of the American vultures. It is often described as the master glider. It glides in circles high in the air, with its wings slightly uptilted. Once in a while it interrupts its gliding with a few slow flaps. Turkey vultures are far from graceful, however, when they come down to earth. Their heads are small, naked, and warty, their bills are hooked and their claws blunt.

They look humpbacked when they perch on the ground. They walk slowly and clumsily, hissing and grunting at each other.

The turkey vulture is about 2½ feet long and its wingspread about 6 feet. Its feathers are black. The naked head and neck are red. In the air it looks different from the other vultures because of its long, slender tail. In summer it may be found as far north as Connecticut and Minnesota. It winters southward from New Jersey and Ohio.

A hollow log, a stump, or even a cavity in the ground serves as a nest for the two dull white eggs with chocolate or lavender markings. When the young birds hatch they are covered with soft white down. By the end of the summer they have a full coat of black feathers, but their naked heads are black instead of red.

Upper left, the king vulture, with a wingspread of about 8 feet. Upper right, the turkey vulture, about 2½ feet long with a wingspread of about 6 feet. Center, the Andean condor, around 4 feet long with a wingspread of more than 10 feet.

They are fed food that has been partially digested in the parent's stomach and spit up.

The *black vulture* is much like the turkey vulture in looks and habits. However, its naked head is always black. It has a white area on the underside of the wings near the tips. Its wings are broader than those of the turkey vulture, and its tail is short. When it flies the wings are held almost horizontally. It flaps them more frequently and more rapidly than the turkey vulture does. It is about 2 feet long and has a wingspread up to $4\frac{1}{2}$ feet. Maryland, Ohio and Missouri represent its northern limits.

Both the turkey vulture and the black vulture roost in flocks at night. In the daytime they soar about searching for food. When one vulture discovers food, others quickly join it. They gather around the dead animal and tear it apart with their hooked beaks.

The *California condor* has a wingspread of about ten feet. Its body is around four feet long, and it weighs as much as 25 pounds. Its naked head is orange. There is a loose ruff of black feathers at the base of the neck. The black feathers of its back are edged in brown. There is a line of white feathers on the wing tips.

These giant birds are beautiful in flight. There are very few of them living today because many of them died when they ate poisoned bait put out by cattlemen to kill coyotes, wolves, and bears. Today efforts are being made to keep this bird from becoming entirely extinct. Like the turkey vulture and the black vulture, it is very useful in cleaning up dead animal bodies.

The *South American* or *Andean condor* is a little over four feet long. Its wingspread exceeds ten feet. The male has a ruff of soft white feathers around its neck. Both male and female have a broad white bar of white feathers across the upper surface of the wings. The rest of their feathers are glossy black.

This is the only member of the vulture family that sometimes kills animals for food. It eats eggs, young sea birds, and young mammals. It also eats any dead animals that it can find. It is not protected as the North American vultures are. It is one of the largest living birds that can fly.

The most brightly colored South American vulture is the *king vulture*. It has shiny white body feathers and black wings and tail. Its head is yellow, red, blue, and black.

For a long time people have wondered how vultures discover the dead animals they eat. Charles Darwin said they had unusual eyesight and could see the animal while they were soaring. Others thought that they must smell the dead animal. Many experiments have been performed since Darwin wrote about the vultures. It is known that vultures have much better eyesight than human beings have. They can see small things from great distances. But they have hardly any sense of smell.

The North American vultures are not destroyed around farms or in small towns and seem to know that they are safe. At stock-killing time on western ranches they gather in numbers and save the rancher the labor and expense of getting rid of the unused parts of the animals killed. It is even told of their waiting for death. Let an animal fall from exhaustion, or become caught in a swamp, and soon these watchers gather and look on with greedy eyes.

VYSHINSKY (*vŭ shin' skē*), **ANDREI YANUAR-IEVICH** (*yä noō är yĕ' vich*) (1883–1954), was a Soviet Russian politician and jurist. He served his country as foreign minister and as delegate to the United Nations.

Vyshinsky was born in Odessa. He studied law at the University of Kiev. Early a revolutionary, he joined the Communist Party in 1920. He taught criminal law and later headed Moscow University, 1925–1928.

As chief public prosecutor, 1935–1939, Vyshinsky conducted the trials of dictator Joseph Stalin's rivals. They were executed or jailed.

He served as first deputy foreign minister, 1940–1949, and held the top ministerial post after that until 1953. As a deputy, he was active in bringing Rumania under Communist control. Vyshinsky represented the U.S.S.R. at the United Nations from 1945 to 1949 and from 1953 until his death.